# CAREER
# OPPORTUNITIES
# IN RADIO

Sʜᴇʟʟʏ Fɪᴇʟᴅ

Foreword by
Cʜʀɪss Sᴄʜᴇʀᴇʀ
Editor of *Radio* Magazine

## Ferguson
*An imprint of* ☑® Facts On File

*This book is dedicated to the loving memory*
*of my mother, Selma Field,*
*who helped me achieve all my dreams . . .*
*and never let me give up.*
*You're always with me in my heart.*

**Career Opportunities in Radio**

Copyright © 2004 by Shelly Field

Ferguson
An imprint of Facts On File, Inc.
132 West 31st Street
New York NY 10001

**Library of Congress Cataloging-in-Publication Data**

Field, Shelly.
    Career opportunities in radio/Shelly Field; foreword by Chriss Scherer.
        p. cm.
    Includes bibliographical references and index.
    ISBN 0-8160-5088-0
    1. Radio broadcasting—Vocational guidance. 2. Radio—Vocational guidance. I. Title.
HE8689.4.F54 2004
384.54′023′73—dc21                                                          2003055219

Ferguson books are available at special discounts when purchased in bulk quantities for businesses, associations, institutions, or sales promotions. Please call our Special Sales Department in New York at (212) 967-8800 or (800) 322-8755.

You can find Ferguson on the World Wide Web at http://www.fergpubco.com

Cover design by Nora Wertz

Printed in the United States of America

VB Hermitage 10  9  8  7  6  5  4  3  2  1

This book is printed on acid-free paper.

# CONTENTS

# FOREWORD

Radio broadcasting is the oldest form of electronic media. With roots in electronics, telephony, communications, and entertainment, radio has evolved from a method of wireless message distribution to a source of information and entertainment. Radio has grown to be a medium that makes daily contact with almost everyone's life.

The first broadcast stations appeared in the early 1920s. Many early station licensees were hobbyists attracted to the newness of radio. Radio held a certain mystique as an emerging medium. Since then small improvements have been made to the broadcast systems, but for the most part the underlying radio transmission technology we know today is the same basic technology developed in the late 19th and early 20th centuries.

Radio has since given rise to other forms of media. One familiar example is television. Traditional radio broadcasting—often referred to as terrestrial radio—has seen two recent additions to the radio space: Internet radio and satellite radio. While these newer forms rely on transmission methods different from their terrestrial predecessor, they all offer audio services that are widely used.

In 2003 there were more than 12,000 radio stations in the United States. These stations cover the largest metropolitan areas and the smallest rural communities. They all serve their listeners' need for relevant information and entertainment. About one-fourth of all stations are licensed to large group owners. Nearly one-half share a common licensee with at least one other station. The remainder operate under single owners. Because of the varying size and reach each licensee offers, a wide range of opportunities to learn and grow within the radio industry exist.

While terrestrial radio has thrived on the transmission technology developed many years ago, it too is about to undergo a significant change. The digital technology used to create, store, and manipulate audio has been used in radio for several years. Radio transmission is on the verge of taking its next major step by converting to digital transmission. With this evolution comes enhanced services, including data and video. Radio is ready to mature to the next level, and the change is bound to bring new opportunities and spark a renewed interest in the industry.

Careers in radio broadcasting cover a wide range of possibilities that can draw on sales, management, technical, and creative skills. I started my career in radio as an announcer, then added some production duties and shortly moved to the technical side as an engineer. While not everyone can or wants to transition between departments, the opportunities exist. You may seek advancement through more traditional means, from salesperson to sales manager to general manager and perhaps even station owner.

Regardless of the path you choose, you will work in an exciting industry with close ties to other media, entertainment, sports, and news. However, the strongest tie for a radio station is in its local community. When someone you meet learns that you work for a radio station, an obvious spark of interest will likely come to his or her eye. That is the power of radio.

Many individuals working in radio do so because it is a passion and not simply a job. Once bitten by the radio bug, many people find it hard to leave. Although I work in the publishing industry today, I still serve the radio industry and deal with it every day. Having an interesting job that touches so many lives can be rewarding in itself, but to have fun and truly enjoy what you do is an unrivaled experience.

— Chriss Scherer, CSRE CBNT
editor, *Radio* magazine
chairman, Society of Broadcast Engineers
National Certification Committee

*Radio* magazine is a Primedia Business Magazines and Media publication. It was first published in 1994 as a spin-off to *Broadcast Engineering* magazine. It currently reaches more than 30,000 radio broadcast professionals in the United States and Canada.

Chriss Scherer has been the editor of *Radio* magazine since 1997. He began his radio career in 1983 as an announcer, later adding producer duties and becoming the chief engineer at several stations, including WEBE-FM, Westport, Conn.; WYCL-FM, Reading, Pa.; WZJM-FM, WJMO-AM, WZAK-FM, WMMS-FM, and WHK-AM, Cleveland, Ohio.

# ACKNOWLEDGMENTS

I would like to thank every individual, radio station, company, union, and association that provided me information, assistance, and encouragement for this book.

I acknowledge with appreciation my editor, James Chambers, for his continuous help and encouragement. I gratefully acknowledge the assistance of Ed Field for his ongoing support in this and every other project.

Others whose help was invaluable include Ellen Ackerman; Advertising Club of New York; Advertising Council; Advertising Research Foundation; Advertising Women of New York, Inc.; American Association of Advertising Agencies; Dan Barrett; Lloyd Barriger, Barriger and Barriger; Allan Barrish; Cindy Bennedum-Cashin; Eugene Blabey, WVOS; Joyce Blackman; Steve Blackman; Theresa Bull; Earl "Speedo" Carroll; Eileen Casey, Superintendent, Monticello Central Schools; Catskill Development; Anthony Cellini, Town of Thompson Supervisor; Dr. Jessica L. Cohen; Lorraine Cohen; Norman Cohen; Crawford Library staff; Daniel Dayton; W. Lynne Dayton; Carrie Dean; Charlie Devine; Direct Mail/Marketing Association, Inc.; Direct Marketing Educational Foundation, Inc.; Michelle Edwards; Scott Edwards; Ernest Evans; Sara Feldberg; Field Associates; Deborah K. Field, Esq.; Greg Field; Lillian (Cookie) Field; Mike Field; Robert Field; Finkelstein Memorial Library staff; David Garthe, CEO, Graveyware.com; John Gatto; Sheila Gatto; Morris Gerber; Larry Goldsmith; Sam Goldych; Alex Goldman; Hermann Memorial Library staff; Joan Howard; International Brotherhood of Electrical Workers; Jimmy "Handyman" Jones; K-LITE Radio; Karen Leever; Liberty Central School; Liberty Public Library Staff; Helena Manzione; Phillip Mestman; Rima Mestman; Beverly Michaels, Esq.; Martin Michaels, Esq.; Mix 97.1 FM; Monticello Central School High School Library Staff; Monticello Central School Middle School Library Staff; National Music Publishers Association; National Retail Federation; Earl Nesmith; Newburgh Free Library; New York State Employment Service; Nikkodo, U.S.A., Inc.; Ellis Norman, UNLV; Ivy Pass; Ed Pearson, Nikkodo; Public Relations Society of America; Doug Puppel; QVC; Harvey Rachlin; Ramapo Catskill Library System; Bill Reynolds, WSUL; Doug Richards; Joy Shaffer; Mark Sieczek; Raun Smith; Smith Employment Agency; Laura Solomon; Debbie Springfield; Matthew E. Strong; Sullivan County Community College; The Teenagers; United States Department of Labor; Brian Vargas; Kaytee Warren; Carol Williams; John Williams; John Wolfe; WSUL Radio; WVOS Radio; and WTZA.

My thanks also to the many people, associations, companies, and organizations who provided material for this book who wish to remain anonymous.

# HOW TO USE THIS BOOK

## Purpose

Many people dream of bantering with callers, hosting radio shows, and playing their favorite music on the air. Others dream of discovering the hot new song of the century and being the one to "break" it on their station. Some dream of owning their own radio station (or at least managing one). Others desire to work behind the scenes.

Like other broadcast and entertainment industries, radio remains a glamour field that attracts many who aspire to work in the industry.

One of the pluses of this industry is that there are widespread employment opportunities throughout the country, in small, medium, and major markets. Employment is expected to increase and the glamour of the industry will undoubtedly continue to attract people who want to be part of it.

While radio still broadcasts in traditional ways on AM and FM frequencies to home, office, and car radios, signals now also broadcast to personal computers via the Internet and new satellite radio services. This creates additional job prospects.

For those interested in a career in radio, the opportunities vary widely. Of course, the highest-profile jobs are those of popular on-air personalities. The industry also employs producers, writers, engineers, administrators, managers, support personnel, sales people, and many others. The popularity of radio station websites has created opportunities for Web designers and technicians, content producers, graphic artists, copywriters, and editors. Almost any skill you have may be parlayed into a career in some facet of the radio industry.

This book was written for everyone who aspires to work in radio but is not sure how to break into the field. The 73 jobs discussed in this book encompass careers in all facets of the radio industry.

If you are considering a job in radio, this is the book for you. It will help you determine what you might want to do in the broadcast industry and how you want to be involved. It offers career opportunities, describes where to locate them, how to train for each position, and most important, how to be successful in your quest.

The trick to locating a job is getting the right training, developing your skills, and using them to get your foot in the door. Once that happens, hard work and perseverance will help you climb the career ladder to other positions.

Read through the book and determine what you are qualified for, or how you can obtain training in your area of interest. You can then work toward getting into an exciting and rewarding career in radio.

## Sources of Information

Information for this book was obtained through interviews, questionnaires, and a wide variety of books, magazines, newsletters, television and radio programs, college catalogs, etc. Some information came from experience working in the industry. Other data was obtained through business associates in the various areas of the radio broadcast industry.

Among the people interviewed were men and women in all aspects of radio broadcasting. These include on-air talent; producers; engineers; sales executives; copywriters; news reporters and writers; sportscasters; marketing, public relations, promotion, community relations, and public affairs personnel; station owners; and individuals working in the management and administration end of radio stations. They also include individuals from unions, associations, schools, colleges, placement companies, human resources, and departments.

## Organization of Material

*Career Opportunities in Radio* is divided into 12 general employment sections. These sections are On-Air Careers; Careers in Radio News; Careers in Radio Sports; Sales and Support; Station Management and Administration; Marketing, Public Relations, Community Relations, and Special Events; Traffic; Engineering; Production and Programming; Promotion; Public Radio; and Radio Station Websites. Within each of these sections are descriptions of individual careers.

There are two parts to each job classification. The first part offers job information in a chart form. The second part presents information in a narrative text. In addition to the basic career description there is additional information on unions and associations, as well as tips for entry.

Appendixes are offered to help locate information you might want or need to get started looking for a job in the field. Names, addresses, phone numbers, fax numbers, websites, and e-mail addresses have been included to help you obtain information you might find useful. These will assist you in sending résumés for job possibilities or checking the availability of internships.

The appendixes include educational programs in broadcasting, public relations, and advertising; a directory of selected radio stations located throughout the country; listings of network and media job banks and radio-career websites; listings of state associations of the National Association of Broadcasters; a directory of trade associations and unions; a bibliography of books, media directories, and periodicals related to the radio industry; and a glossary.

Whether you choose to be an on-air personality or work in any other area of radio, your job will be exciting, fulfilling, and rewarding. Your career in radio is out there waiting. You just have to go after it!

—Shelly Field
www.shellyfield.com

# INTRODUCTION

History was made in Pittsburgh in 1920 when KDKA signed on the air as the first commercial radio station. Since that time, radio has emerged as a popular form of entertainment and information for millions of people.

In the early years, families would congregate in the room where the big radio stood and listen to popular shows just as we enjoy television today. Those who wanted "instantaneous" news tuned into radio broadcasts to hear the events in the world. Radio made it possible for historic events such as the Hindenburg zeppelin crash, the attack on Pearl Harbor, and the tragedy of 9/11 to be heard by many.

While radio was and still is an important vehicle for news coverage, it has become an even greater force in show business and the music industry.

Over the years radio became the vehicle for recording artists to showcase their music. A radio station playing a tune could make or break an artist and a song. From popular music to rock and roll, country, R&B, and rap, the music industry has depended on radio to cultivate music sales. Radio continues to be an important part of the success of recording artists.

As radio grew, new formats emerged. In addition to an array of music formats, other programming has become popular, such as talk, news, sports, and entertainment. Radio is now far reaching, with signals being broadcast over the Internet. The ability to tune into a station via the World Wide Web means stations can reach an audience around the corner or across the world.

The radio industry is a multibillion-dollar business. Thousands of people work in this industry. Whether you choose to have an on-air career or work behind the scenes, you can be one of them!

As you read the various sections in this book, searching to find the job you have always dreamed about, keep in mind that there are many ways to get into radio. I have provided you with the guidelines. The next step is yours to take.

Within each section of this book you will find all the information necessary to acquaint you with the important jobs in both industries. A key to the organization of each entry follows:

## Alternate Titles

Many jobs in radio, as in all industries, are known by alternate titles. These may vary from station to station. The duties of these jobs are the same—only the names are different.

## Career Ladder

The career ladder illustrates a normal job progression. Remember that in radio there are no hard-and-fast rules. Job progression may occur in almost any manner.

## Position Description

Every effort has been made to give well-rounded job descriptions. Keep in mind that no two stations are structured in exactly the same way. Therefore, no two jobs will be precisely the same. At some stations, individuals may report to others in management. Other stations may eliminate some positions or add others.

## Salary Range

Salary ranges for the job titles in the book are as accurate as possible. Salaries for a job will depend on the size, market, location, and prestige of the station, as well as the experience and responsibilities of the individual. In certain situations, such as those of on-air talent, an individual's popularity and drawing power are also major factors in earnings.

## Employment Prospects

If you choose a job that has an *excellent, good,* or *fair* rating, you are fortunate. You will have an easier time finding a job. If, however, you would like to work at a job that has a *poor* rating, don't despair. The rating only means that it is difficult to obtain a job—not impossible.

## Advancement Prospects

Try to be as cooperative and helpful as possible in the workplace. Don't try to see how little work you can do. Be enthusiastic, energetic, and outgoing. Do that little extra that no one asked you to. Learn as much as you can. When a job advancement possibility opens up, make sure that you're prepared for it.

## Education and Training

Although the book only gives the *minimum* training and educational requirements, this does not mean that it is all you should have. Try to get the best training and education possible. A college degree does not guarantee a job in radio, but it will help prepare you for life in the workplace.

## Experience, Skills, and Personality Traits

Requisite experience, skills, and personality traits differ from job to job. Whichever job you want to pursue, you need a lot of perseverance and energy. You also have to be articulate. An outgoing personality helps. Contacts are important in all facets of business; make as many as you can. These people will be helpful in advancing your career and helping you network.

## Best Geographic Location

Radio stations are located throughout the country. Smaller stations and those in less-populated areas will often have more opportunities for entry-level jobs or positions for those with less experience. Major-market stations are located in large metropolitan areas such as New York City, Los Angeles, Atlanta, and Chicago.

## Unions and Associations

Unions and trade associations offer valuable help in getting into radio, obtaining jobs, and making contacts. They may also offer scholarships, fellowships, seminars, and other helpful programs.

## Tips for Entry

Use this section for ideas on how to get a job and gain entry into the areas in which you are interested. When applying for any job, always be as professional as possible. Dress neatly and conservatively for interviews. Don't wear sneakers. Don't chew gum. Don't smoke in the reception area before an interview or during an interview. Don't wear heavy perfume or cologne. Always have a few copies of your résumé with you. These should look neat and professional. Have résumés typed and well presented. Make sure you check and recheck for errors in grammar, spelling, and content. Don't just rely on a spell and grammar checker.

If you are applying for a creative job, such as copywriter or graphic artist, put together a portfolio of your best work. Make it neat and imaginative. This will help illustrate your potential. Bring this with you to all interviews.

If you are interested in a job as on-air talent, make sure you put together a number of "air-checks" to send out to stations. These are short tapes highlighting your voice and style.

Use every contact you have. Don't get hung up on the idea that you want to get a job by yourself. If you are lucky enough to know someone who can help you obtain the job you want, take him or her up on the offer. It will be up to you to prove yourself at the interview and on the job; nobody can do that for you.

Use the Internet to help. Research companies, look for jobs, get ideas, and keep up with trends. If you don't have Internet access at home, most schools, colleges, and libraries offer free on-site access.

Be on time for everything. This includes job interviews, phone calls, work, meetings, sending letters, answering e-mails, etc. People will remember when you're habitually late, and it will work against you in advancing your career.

Learn something positive from every experience. Don't burn bridges. Don't talk badly about prior bosses, stations, or jobs. The world of radio is a small one. The colleague you talk about in Fort Wayne might be your new boss in Cleveland. The last piece of advice in this section is to do your best at all times. A good professional reputation will follow you throughout your career.

Have fun reading this book. Use it. It will help you find a career you will truly love. The world of radio can be both glamorous and exciting.

Don't get discouraged. Not everyone gets the first job he or she applies for. You may have to knock on a lot of doors, send out many résumés, and apply for a lot of jobs, but you will eventually find the job of your dreams. When you do get the job you have been dreaming about, share your knowledge and help others get into radio too.

We love to hear success stories. If this book helped you in your quest for a job and you would like to share your story, go to www.shellyfield.com and let us know.

Good luck!

# ON-AIR CAREERS

# ON-AIR PERSONALITY/DISC JOCKEY

## CAREER PROFILE

**Duties:** Introduces music, commercials, and news on radio; ad-libs; helps shape the personality of the station

**Alternate Title(s):** DJ; Announcer

**Salary Range:** $20,000 to $1 million+

**Employment Prospects:** Fair

**Advancement Prospects:** Fair

**Best Geographical Location(s):** Opportunities may be located throughout the country; smaller local communities offer opportunities for small-market stations; New York City, Los Angeles, Chicago, Atlanta, etc., for major market stations

**Prerequisites:**

**Education or Training**—College background, degree, or vocational training in broadcasting may be preferred

**Experience**—Experience in college radio helpful

**Special Skills and Personality Traits**—Pleasant speaking voice; comfortable with microphone; communications skills; ability to ad-lib; enjoyment of music; ability to project personality over the air

## CAREER LADDER

```
┌─────────────────────────────────┐
│      On-Air Personality/        │
│     Disc Jockey at Larger,      │
│   More Prestigious Station or   │
│        Program Director         │
└─────────────────────────────────┘

┌─────────────────────────────────┐
│   On-Air Personality/Disc Jockey │
└─────────────────────────────────┘

┌─────────────────────────────────┐
│        Student or Intern        │
└─────────────────────────────────┘
```

## Position Description

On-Air Personalities/Disc Jockeys have the most visible careers in the radio industry—they are the voice of the radio station.

It must be noted that the job titles of the on-air talent often depend, to a great extent, on who you ask in the broadcasting industry. While the term "Disc Jockey" was used exclusively in the past, today "On-Air Personality" is often used as well when referring to the on-air talent. Whatever the name, the On-Air Personality/Disc Jockey is a sought after career for many aspiring to work in the radio industry.

The main responsibility of the On-Air Personality/Disc Jockey is to introduce the music, commercials, news, and public announcements aired on a radio station. In order to be successful in radio, On-Air Personalities/DJs need to have some sort of style and personality that they project over the air. Those who do so develop a following of listeners, making them valuable to the station.

Most stations have at least one, if not more, On-Air Personality/Disc Jockey whose voice and style shines above the rest, making listeners feel that they are a part of the show. These individuals make their show an anticipated part of listeners' daily routines.

For example, people in New York City may turn on the radio daily to hear Howard Stern. Those in Los Angeles might tune in for Rick Dees. Those in Chicago, Atlanta, Las Vegas, and even the suburbs and rural areas may tune in to stations to hear the shows of their favorite On-Air Personality/Disk Jockey.

The more listeners a station has, the better their Arbitron ratings will be. Arbitron ratings are a television and radio rating service that indicates what percentage of people are listening to or viewing a particular show. Commercial rates are then based on these ratings. As commercial radio derives its income from selling advertisements, the more listeners, the more income a station can generate.

Stations with music formats may specialize in an array of styles of music. These include country, pop, easy listening, top 40, rock, R&B, and oldies. In addition to introducing the records, many On-Air Personalities/DJs offer facts to the listeners about the recording artists, their music, tours, etc. This makes listening more interesting. Most individuals ad-lib frequently during their shift about the music, events, traffic, or weather. This banter helps listeners become involved.

Depending on the size of the station and its structure, the On-Air Personality/DJ may have some leeway in the music played on his or her show. At some stations, he or she may choose the music from an approved playlist put together by the station's program or music director. At other stations, the music or program director is responsible for selecting the exact music to be played during each show.

In addition to introducing the music, the On-Air Personality/Disc Jockey is responsible for announcing commercials, giving weather and traffic reports and updates, and either introducing or reporting the news.

The On-Air Personality/Disc Jockey is expected to log or initial each song he or she plays as well as commercials, public service announcements (PSAs), news and weather reports, etc. This information is given to the traffic department for the log of daily station activities the FCC (Federal Communications Commission) requires.

On-Air Personalities/DJs may invite listeners to call in to give their opinions on music or events or to call in for on-air contests and promotions. Sometimes the station will schedule shows where two Disc Jockeys work together bantering back and forth. This often occurs during the morning or afternoon drive-time shifts.

One of the interesting things that happens to On-Air Personalities/Disc Jockeys, even in small-market radio, is they often become celebrities of sorts. As a result, they are asked to make public appearances for store promotions, station promotions, and charity events. In addition, many Disc Jockeys act as live DJs at clubs or events.

It's important to note that all radio is not live. There are stations that utilize the services of companies which prerecord the music for shows. On-Air Personalities/DJs then may prerecord introductions to the music, giving listeners the illusion that the show is live.

At most stations, On Air Personalities/Disc Jockeys are assigned time shifts in which to work. Shifts vary from station to station but usually range from three to five hours in length. The more popular the On-Air Talent/Disc Jockey is, the better the shift he or she is usually assigned. Depending on the station, the most-listened-to shifts may be the morning drive time, afternoon drive time, or early evening slots.

Many listeners identify so closely with the On-Air Personality/Disc Jockey that they consider him or her a friend. One of the challenges that stations have with On-Air Personalities/Disc Jockeys is that when they leave, their audiences often follows them to the new station.

In some situations, two On-Air Personalities/Disc Jockeys work together, feeding off each other. This is common in morning and late-afternoon drive-time shows.

At most stations, the On-Air Personality/Disc Jockey is responsible to the program director, music director, or station manager.

Additional duties of On-Air Personalities/Disc Jockeys may include:

- Doing voice-overs for commercials for the radio station
- Making special public appearances on behalf of the station
- Appearing at remotes
- Acting as the music or program director

## Salaries

Earnings for On-Air Personalities/Disc Jockeys can vary tremendously. There are some individuals who earn $20,000 a year. Others may earn $1 million plus. Variables include the size, location, prestige, and popularity of the station as well as the experience, popularity, and drawing power of the On-Air Personality/Disc Jockey.

In some stations, minimum earnings are negotiated and set by a union. It should be noted, however, that these are minimums. An On-Air Personality/Disc Jockey with a large following can usually negotiate higher earnings.

## Employment Prospects

Employment prospects for On-Air Personalities/Disc Jockeys are fair for those willing to work on a local or regional level. Job prospects become more difficult as individuals seek work in larger markets.

Openings may be located throughout the country. On-Air Personalities/Disc Jockeys may find work in small local or regional stations, larger stations, national stations, or public radio.

## Advancement Prospects

Career advancement for On-Air Personalities/Disc Jockeys is based on the type of following individuals build. Individuals may advance their career in a number of manners. Some build a following and then are able to ask for and obtain higher earnings Others move on to similar careers in larger or more prestigious stations. Many climb the career ladder by landing positions as music or program directors.

## Education and Training

Educational requirements vary for On-Air Personalities/Disc Jockeys. Many stations either prefer individuals to have a college background or degree or vocational training in broadcasting. Some stations may wave educational requirements if the individual has a great voice and has a following of listeners.

## Experience, Skills, and Personality Traits

Experience requirements vary from station to station. Many individuals obtain experience working at their college radio station, school radio club, or as an intern. Others start at a small station, get some experience, and begin moving up the career ladder. Stations may wave experience requirements if an individual meets other criteria and is an expert in the specific field in which the station wants a show.

An On-Air Personality/Disc Jockey needs a pleasant speaking voice and the ability to speak comfortably into a microphone. The ability to project personality over the air is essential. Liking music is a plus.

## Unions and Associations

On-Air Personalities/Disc Jockeys may belong to various bargaining unions and associations depending on the specific position they hold and the station for which they are working. These include the National Association of Broadcast Employees and Technicians (NABET) or the American Federation of Television and Radio Artists (AFTRA). Individuals or their stations might also be members of the National Association of Broadcasters (NAB).

## Tips for Entry

1. Get as much experience as possible working in broadcasting. Volunteer to work with your college radio station, join radio clubs, etc.

2. Many radio stations and associations offer internships or training programs. Internships give you both on-the-job training experience and the opportunity to make important contacts.

3. If you worked at your college radio station, make sure you put together a demo tape. If you haven't worked at all, consider putting together a mock tape to send to stations.

4. Many local stations advertise openings on the air as well as on their website. Check them out.

5. Job openings are also often advertised in the newspaper classified section under headings such as "Disc Jockey," "Radio," "DJ," "On-Air Personality," "On-Air Talent," and "Broadcasting."

6. Don't forget to read trade publications. *Billboard, Broadcasting,* and *Radio and Records* often have advertisements for stations with openings.

7. It is usually fairly easy to find a position in a small market because the turnover is so great. Find a job, get some experience, and climb the career ladder.

# ANNOUNCER

## CAREER PROFILE

**Duties:** Presents a variety of radio programming; introduces music, commercials, and news on radio; does station identifications; announces commercials; announces station liner notes

**Alternate Title(s):** Broadcaster; Radio Announcer; Disc Jockey

**Salary Range:** $20,000 to $55,000+

**Employment Prospects:** Fair

**Advancement Prospects:** Fair

**Best Geographical Location(s):** Opportunities may be located throughout the country; smaller local communities offer opportunities for small-market stations; New York City, Los Angeles, Chicago, Atlanta, etc., for major-market stations

**Prerequisites:**

**Education or Training**—College background, degree or vocational training in broadcasting may be preferred

**Experience**—Experience in college radio helpful

**Special Skills and Personality Traits**—Pleasant speaking voice; comfortable with microphone; communications skills; ability to project personality over the air

## CAREER LADDER

```
┌──────────────────────────────────────┐
│          Announcer at Larger,        │
│      More Prestigious Station or      │
│   On-Air Personality/Disc Jockey or   │
│  Announcer in Television Broadcasting  │
└──────────────────────────────────────┘

┌──────────────────────────────────────┐
│              Announcer               │
└──────────────────────────────────────┘

┌──────────────────────────────────────┐
│           Student or Intern           │
└──────────────────────────────────────┘
```

## Position Description

Anyone who has listened to radio has heard the voice of Announcers. They are the individuals who introduce the programming on radio. They may introduce recorded music or the news, sports, weather, or traffic reports. These functions may be done live or may be taped for broadcast at a later time.

In some stations the Announcer is called a disc jockey. Generally, however, the Announcer in a radio station does not develop the type of following a disc jockey or other on-air personality does.

Announcers introduce commercials during radio programming. They may also read the prepared commercial copy live on air. In many situations the Announcer records commercials. Once these commercials are produced and recorded, they may be used at any time. The Announcer may just read straight copy or may record a number of different voices to add interest to the commercial. Sometimes the Announcer is just one of the voices on a commercial. Commercial voices

may also include others at the station, including disk jockeys, advertising sales reps, or professional voice-over artists.

In many stations civic and not-for-profit groups send the station notices about their organization or their activities. Announcers may be expected to record an array of public service announcements that are then often inserted into the programming on a regular basis.

Announcers are often expected to do station IDs. These are the announcements where a station is identified. The station identification may be the call letters, the frequency on the radio dial, or a phrase that the station is identified with. For example, a station ID might be ABC, 92.1, or Mix 101. Station IDs may be recorded so that they can be aired throughout the broadcast day. In that way, when listeners hear it, they know what they are listening to.

If the Announcer is working live, he or she will be expected to log or initial each song that is played as well as every commercial, public service announcement, (PSA) and news and weather report. This information is given to the traffic department for the log of daily station activities the FCC (Federal Communications Commission) requires.

It's important to note that all radio is not live. Some stations are automated. Stations may utilize the services of companies that provide blocks of prerecorded music for shows. Announcers then may prerecord introductions to the music, giving listeners the illusion that the show is both live and local. In these situations, the Announcer also may prerecord station IDs, introductions to the news, and advertisements.

Depending on the structure of the station, the Announcer may be responsible to the station owner, station manager, program director, or music director.

Additional duties of Announcers may include:

- Doing voice-overs for commercials for the radio station
- Acting as newscaster
- Logging information into the traffic log

## Salaries

There is a large salary range for Announcers working in radio. Factors affecting earnings include the size, location, prestige, and popularity of the station, as well as the experience and popularity of the Announcer.

Some Announcers may make just $20,000, while others may earn $65,000 or more. Announcers who are the voice of syndicated shows may earn even more. These opportunities, however, are rare. Many Announcers also earn extra income by doing voice-overs for commercials. This brings in additional income.

In some stations, minimum earnings are negotiated and set by a union. It should be noted, however, that these are minimums. Announcers who are in demand usually can negotiate higher earnings.

It should also be noted that Announcers who are on-air personalities with a large drawing power can earn $200,000 or more.

## Employment Prospects

Employment prospects for Announcers who just handle on-air announcing duties are poor. Most stations use on-air personalities/disc jockeys to handle most of the on-air announcing responsibilities.

Opportunities may be available for Announcers to work at automated stations. Openings may be located throughout the country, in small local or regional stations, larger stations, national stations, or public radio.

## Advancement Prospects

Career advancement for Announcers is based to a great extent on career aspirations. Some Announcers find similar positions in larger, more prestigious stations, resulting in increased earnings. Others want to climb the career ladder

by becoming well-known disc jockeys or on-air personalities. Some Announcers also move into similar positions in television broadcasting.

## Education and Training

Educational requirements vary for Announcers working in radio. Many stations prefer individuals to have a college background or degree or vocational training in broadcasting. Smaller, more regional stations may just require a high school diploma. Some stations may wave educational requirements if the Announcer has a great voice.

## Experience, Skills, and Personality Traits

Many Announcers obtain experience working at their college radio station, school radio club, or as an intern. Others start at a small station, get some experience, and begin moving up the career ladder.

Two of the most important traits of Announcers are a pleasant speaking voice and the ability to speak comfortably into a microphone. The ability to read copy is also necessary.

## Unions and Associations

Announcers may belong to various bargaining unions and associations, depending on the specific position they hold and the station they work for. These include the National Association of Broadcast Employees and Technicians (NABET) and the American Federation of Television and Radio Artists (AFTRA). Individuals or their stations might also be members of the National Association of Broadcasters (NAB).

## Tips for Entry

1. Get as much experience as possible working in broadcasting. Volunteer to work with your college radio station, join radio clubs, etc.
2. If you work on your college radio station, make sure you put together a demo tape. If you haven't worked at all, consider putting together a mock tape to send to stations.
3. Internships give you on-the-job training, real work experiences, and the opportunity to make important contacts. Many radio stations and associations offer both formal and informal internships or training programs.
4. Many local stations advertise openings on the air as well as on their website. Check them out.
5. Job openings are also often advertised in the newspaper, so check the classified section under headings such as "Announcer," "Radio," "Disc Jockey," "On-Air Personality," and "Broadcasting."
6. Don't forget to read trade publications. *Billboard, Broadcasting,* and *Radio and Records* often have advertisements for stations with openings.

# TALK SHOW HOST

## CAREER PROFILE

**Duties:** Discusses subjects of general or specialized interest with guests and/or call-ins during radio show

**Alternate Title(s):** Host; Radio Personality

**Salary Range:** $20,000 to $1 million+

**Employment Prospects:** Fair

**Advancement Prospects:** Fair

**Best Geographical Location (s):** Smaller local communities offer opportunities for small-market stations; New York City, Los Angeles, Chicago, Atlanta, etc., for major-market stations

**Prerequisites:**

**Education or Training**—College background or degree required or preferred by most stations

**Experience**—Experience in broadcasting helpful, but not always required

**Special Skills and Personality Traits**—Understanding and knowledge of one or more subject areas; good speaking voice; comfortable with microphone; communications skills

## CAREER LADDER

```
┌─────────────────────────────────────┐
│   Talk Show Host with Larger,        │
│  More Prestigious Radio Station or   │
│     Syndicated Talk Show Host        │
└─────────────────────────────────────┘

┌─────────────────────────────────────┐
│          Talk Show Host              │
└─────────────────────────────────────┘

┌─────────────────────────────────────┐
│   Disc Jockey, News Reporter, or     │
│     Expert in a Particular Field     │
└─────────────────────────────────────┘
```

## Position Description

Many radio stations throughout the country have added talk shows to their programming. Other stations have changed to an all-talk format in an effort to attract new audiences.

Talk shows can center on a variety of subject areas or be more general in nature. Specific talk shows might focus on business, money and financial planning, cooking and food; or news and politics.

A Talk Show Host may be a known broadcasting personality or an expert in a specific field. Depending on the talk show subject, the Talk Show Host might be an attorney, a physician, stockbroker, veterinarian, or psychologist.

The Talk Show Host generally introduces the subject matter and guests who will appear during the show. He or she may do this by asking provocative questions of the guests or invite people to call in to give their opinions. Incorporating phone calls from the listening audience helps give the show a special flavor. Callers may comment on the subject, ask questions, and give their own opinions.

Successful Talk Show Hosts are experts at keeping shows interesting by bantering back and forth with guests and callers. Individuals must have the ability to think quickly in order to make this happen effectively. They must keep the program moving and help make it interesting.

Radio Talk Show Hosts may be responsible for developing ideas for shows and finding guests to appear. Depending on the size and structure of the station, this responsibility might be shared or given to a show producer or guest coordinator.

Talk Show Hosts may host daily shows or may only be responsible for hosting shows on specific days of the week. Shows may run from 30 minutes to full four- or five-hour shifts. Shows may be live or taped.

The Talk Show Host may be expected to read books or articles or view a television show or movie about a show subject. He or she may also be responsible for conducting pre-show interviews.

Additional duties of Talk Show Hosts may include:

- Introducing or reading newscasts, weathercasts, commercials, and/or public service announcements
- Making special public appearances on behalf of the station
- Acting as a disc jockey

## Salaries

Earnings for radio Talk Show Hosts can vary tremendously. There are some individuals who earn $20,000 a year. Others may earn $1 million plus. Variables include the size, location, prestige, and popularity of the station, as well as the experience, expertise, and responsibilities of the individual. Earnings are also dependent to a great extent on the popularity and drawing power of the individual and his or her show.

In some stations, minimum earnings are negotiated and set by a union. It should be noted, however, that these are minimums. A Talk Show Host with a following can usually negotiate higher earnings.

In some cases, Talk Show Hosts syndicate a show. In these situations, earnings will depend on the number of stations that buy the show.

## Employment Prospects

Employment prospects for Talk Show Hosts are fair for those willing to work on a local or regional level. Job prospects become more difficult as individuals seek work in larger markets. The great thing about this type of work is that a Talk Show Host and his or her show may become very popular at any time. There are many individuals who start off with a new show that hits it big and then the sky is the limit.

Openings may be located throughout the country. Talk Show Hosts might work in small local or regional stations, larger stations, national stations, public radio, or as noted previously, have syndicated shows.

## Advancement Prospects

Advancement prospects for Talk Show Hosts are based on the type of following individuals build. Those who increase their popularity will be in greater demand and able to ask for and receive increased earnings. Individuals often start off at a small station and after obtaining experience move on to a similar position at a larger or more prestigious station. Many Talk Show Hosts climb the career ladder by building a following for their show and having it syndicated.

## Education and Training

Educational requirements vary for Talk Show Hosts. Today most stations either require or prefer individuals to have a college background or degree. Formal education and expertise in a specific field also add credibility to the Talk Show Host.

## Experience, Skills, and Personality Traits

Experience requirements vary from station to station for Talk Show Hosts. Experience requirements will often be waived if an individual meets other criteria and is an expert in the specific field in which the station wants a show.

Experience working in broadcasting is useful, whether obtained in a college radio station, school radio club, local radio station, or as an intern.

A Talk Show Host should have a pleasant speaking voice and a good use of the English language. The ability to think quickly is essential. Expertise in one or more areas gives an individual an edge over other applicants.

## Unions and Associations

Radio Talk Show Hosts may belong to various bargaining unions and associations, depending on the specific position they hold and the station for which they are working. These include the National Association of Broadcast Employees and Technicians (NABET), the American Federation of Television and Radio Artists (AFTRA), and the Writers Guild of America (WGA). Individuals or their stations might also be members of the National Association of Broadcasters (NAB).

## Tips for Entry

1. Get as much experience as possible working in broadcasting. Volunteer to work with your college radio station, join radio clubs, etc.
2. Many radio stations and associations offer internships or training programs. Internships give you on-the-job training experience and the opportunity to make important contacts.
3. Host a mock show and make a demo tape and send it with your résumé and a cover letter to radio station owners, managers, and human resources directors. The yellow pages of the phone book will help get you started on some addresses.
4. Many local stations advertise openings on the air as well as on their website. Check them out.
5. Job openings are also often advertised in the newspaper classified section under headings such as "Talk Show Host," "Radio," "Radio Talk Show Host," and "Broadcasting."
6. Don't forget to read trade publications. *Billboard, Broadcasting,* and *Radio and Records* often have advertisements for stations with openings.
7. Become an expert in one or more fields. Then parlay your expertise to send your career in the direction you want.
8. It is usually fairly easy to find a position in a small market because the turnover is so great. You might want to contact your local radio station and offer to host a show on a subject in which you are an expert. Often, if you offer to find advertisers and are successful, a station will use your show.

# CAREERS IN RADIO NEWS

# NEWS DIRECTOR

## CAREER PROFILE

**Duties:** Determines which stories should be covered; assigns reporters to stories; develops news programming; directs activities in radio station's news department

**Alternate Title(s):** News and Public Affairs Director

**Salary Range:** $25,000 to $150,000+

**Employment Prospects:** Fair

**Advancement Prospects:** Fair

**Best Geographical Location(s):** Smaller local communities offer opportunities for small-market stations; New York City, Los Angeles, Chicago, Atlanta, etc., for major-market stations

**Prerequisites:**

**Education or Training**—Four-year college degree required or preferred by most stations; others may accept broadcasting-school certificate

**Experience**—Experience in broadcast or print news

**Special Skills and Personality Traits**—Objectivity; good judgment; communications skills; ability to write well; administrative and management skills

## CAREER LADDER

```
┌─────────────────────────────────┐
│      News Director for Larger,   │
│    More Prestigious Radio Station│
└─────────────────────────────────┘

┌─────────────────────────────────┐
│          News Director           │
└─────────────────────────────────┘

┌─────────────────────────────────┐
│ Newscaster or Assistant News Director │
└─────────────────────────────────┘
```

## Position Description

The News Director at a radio station is responsible for directing the activities of the station's news department. In large stations, the department may comprise a number of employees, including an assistant news director, sports director, assistant sports director, reporters, writers, newscasters, announcers, weather reporters, and meteorologists. In smaller stations, the News Director may be the sole news department employee. In those situations the individual has much more generalized duties than his or her counterpart in a large station.

Whatever the size of the station, the News Director plays an important role. He or she is responsible for determining the direction of the station's news and what news stories will be covered on-air. The News Director must determine the type of news programming that will be most effective for the station and its demographics. For example, how long will local news reports be? When will reports be aired? What about national or worldwide news and events? When and how will they be covered? What about sports news? All

these questions must be answered by the News Director. The individual often works with the station manager and/or owner in these tasks.

The News Director is expected to supervise and coordinate the other members of the news department, assigning shifts and stories to reporters. In many stations, the news staff covers local governmental meetings and other events in the community. The News Director is responsible for making sure that all important meetings and events are covered by the station. Sometimes, especially in smaller stations, the News Director is also a news reporter and expected to cover stories and events him or herself.

One of the major responsibilities of the News Director is deciding what stories will be covered and how much coverage they will receive. For example, will the station cover an election on-site, giving out results and reporting from the headquarters of various candidates? Or will they just report results at the end of the evening?

The News Director is responsible for making sure that the reporters seek out interesting and newsworthy stories and cover events. In order to decide what news stories to cover, the News Director must take a number of things into account. These include the demographics of the station. For example, who does the station reach and who do they want to reach? Is government important in the area? What about sports, schools, and civic groups? What is happening in the nation? The News Director always tries to find a local tie if possible to national stories.

After considering these issues, the News Director determines where he or she should send reporters, which reporters should go where, and what stories will be reported.

Often national news heard on a radio station comes from the various wire services, such as UPI (United Press International), AP (Associated Press), or Reuters. These organizations have large news staffs as well as freelancers who report all the up-to-the-minute developments. These reports go over a wire, or Teletype, and are printed out in thousands of newsrooms and television and radio stations throughout the world. Most newspapers, magazines, and television and radio stations pay for this service, which they use daily to report the news, weather, and sports. The News Director often reviews these news bits and determines which ones to air during a news broadcast. He or she may also assign this task to an assistant news director or reporter.

Many stations also utilize the services of such news syndicates as CNN, ABC, CBS, and NBC to handle the coverage of national and international news.

Another responsibility of the News Director at a radio station is developing news programming. This is often done in conjunction with the station manager. The objective is to develop programming that serves the needs of the community and attracts more listeners. The News Director may develop specific news- or public-service-related shows that are call-ins, opinion oriented, and/or have guests. The News Director will decide how often these should air, what the format will be, and choose a host. In some cases, the News Director may also be the host of the program him- or herself.

News Directors may work at stations with an array of formats ranging from music to news to all-talk to just sports. They may work at local, radio, network, or public radio stations.

In smaller stations News Directors also generally work as newscasters. That means that they usually write their own copy as well as report the news. Writing copy for radio newscasts is different than print news stories because the copy must not only be interesting but also tell the story in the allotted amount of time.

Additional duties of News Directors working in radio may include:

• Reviewing news bites and tapes before copy is aired
• Attending press conferences
• Resolving any production or technical problems
• Coordinating the activities of the news department with the traffic department

## Salaries

Earnings for News Directors working in radio vary greatly depending on the size of the station, its location and popularity as well as the experience and responsibilities of the individual. Annual earnings may range from $25,000 to $150,000 or more.

Earnings at the lower end of the scale will go to those just starting out or with limited experience in smaller stations. Compensation goes up for those with more experience, working in major-market stations, or stations with news-only formats.

## Employment Prospects

Employment prospects for News Directors are fair for those willing to work on a local or regional level. Prospects become more limited as individuals seek to work in larger markets. Individuals may also be required to relocate for some positions.

While openings may be located throughout the country, it is easier to break into the industry on a small, local level and work up from there. Many smaller stations hire individuals with little or no experience. While the salaries are low in these situations, the experience is worth the opportunity.

## Advancement Prospects

Advancement prospects for News Directors working in radio are fair. Individuals often start off at a small station and after obtaining experience move on to a similar position at a larger or more prestigious station. This results in increased responsibilities and earnings.

As individuals move up the career ladder from small-market radio to mid-market and major-market radio, advancement prospects become more difficult.

## Education and Training

Educational requirements vary for News Directors working in radio. Generally, most stations require or prefer individuals to have a four-year college degree. Good majors to consider for this type of job include communications, journalism, liberal arts, broadcasting, English or sports administration. It should be noted that smaller stations may not have the educational requirement. However, a college background may be useful in climbing the career ladder.

## Experience, Skills, and Personality Traits

News Directors working in radio generally have some sort of experience in broadcasting and/or news industry. Some individuals begin their career in radio news and are then promoted to the position of News Director. Smaller stations may hire an individual to be the news reporter/News Director if they have had experience working on their college radio station.

News Directors must understand the demographics of their station and of the community. Management and administrative skills are necessary. Good judgment is essential in this field. Communication skills are needed as well.

## Unions and Associations

News Directors working in radio may belong to various bargaining unions and associations, depending on the specific position they hold and the station for which they are working. These include the National Association of Broadcast Employees and Technicians (NABET), the American Federation of Television and Radio Artists (AFTRA), the Writers Guild of America (WGA), and the Radio and Television News Directors Associations (RTNDA). Individuals or their stations might also be members of the National Association of Broadcasters (NAB).

## Tips for Entry

1. Many radio stations and associations offer internships or training programs. Internships give you on-the-job training experience and the opportunity to make important contacts.

2. Get as much experience as possible working in broadcasting. Volunteer to work with your college radio station, even if you can't get work in the news department.

3. Local radio stations advertise openings on their own station as well as on their website. Check them out.

4. Smaller stations may only have a one- or two-person department. If you can find a job at one of these, while the pay is usually not great, you can obtain some experience as a News Director and then move on.

5. Job openings may be advertised in the newspaper classified section under headings such as "News Director," "Radio," and "Broadcasting."

6. Don't forget to read trade publications. *Billboard, Broadcasting,* and *Radio and Records* often have advertisements for stations with openings.

# ASSISTANT NEWS DIRECTOR

## CAREER PROFILE

**Duties:** Assists news director in directing the news room; helps determine which news stories should be covered; assigns reporters to stories; assists with the development of news programming

**Alternate Title(s):** Assistant Director of News and Public Affairs

**Salary Range:** $22,000 to $40,000+

**Employment Prospects:** Fair

**Advancement Prospects:** Fair

**Best Geographical Location(s):** Smaller local communities offer opportunities for small-market stations; New York City, Los Angeles, Chicago, Atlanta, etc., for major-market stations

**Prerequisites:**

**Education or Training**—Four-year college degree required or preferred by most stations; others may accept broadcasting-school certificate

**Experience**—Experience in broadcast or print news

**Special Skills and Personality Traits**—Objectivity; good judgment; communications skills; ability to write well; administrative and management skills

## CAREER LADDER

```
┌─────────────────────────────────┐
│         News Director           │
└─────────────────────────────────┘

┌─────────────────────────────────┐
│     Assistant News Director     │
└─────────────────────────────────┘

┌─────────────────────────────────┐
│  Newscaster, News Reporter, or  │
│       Assignment Editor         │
└─────────────────────────────────┘
```

## Position Description

The Assistant News Director at a radio station is second in command of the newsroom. He or she assists the news director in managing the activities of those working in the station's news department. Responsibilities will depend, to a great extent, on the size and structure of the station and its news department.

Large radio stations may have news departments complete with a news director, Assistant News Director, reporters, writers, researchers, newscasters, anchor people, sports directors, assistant sports directors, announcers, weather reporters, meteorologists, public affairs people, and more. Smaller stations may just employ a news director, perhaps an Assistant News Director, and a reporter. Very small stations may not have an Assistant News Director. Assistant News Directors working in bigger stations with larger news staffs will have more specific duties than their counterparts working at smaller stations.

No matter what the location of a radio station, on any given day, there are usually news stories of interest to listeners. The challenge, for both the news director and the Assistant News Director, is determining what stories to cover.

The Assistant News Director helps the director in determining what stories should be covered every day. Should a town meeting be covered by the station? What about a press conference at the mayor's office? Or a human interest story where a child is reunited with a parent?

Radio station news departments also generally receive many press releases and calendar notices of events that will be occurring in the community. These releases may come from public relations or marketing directors and publicists working in various businesses in and out of the listening community. They may also come from civic, community, and not-for-profit groups. The goal of publicists and marketing and public relations professionals sending releases to radio (and other media) is to get publicity. The Assistant

News Director along with the news director must determine what is newsworthy and of interest to their listeners.

In larger stations, where there are a number of reporters, individuals can't just decide who should cover what story on their own. The Assistant News Director must help the director assign stories to reporters. The two also must determine whether news reporters should "go out in the field" to cover the stories or just work on them from the studio.

In some stations, the news director will work one shift and the Assistant News Director work another. In this way, the greater part of the day is covered as it relates to the news department. In smaller stations, the Assistant News Director may also be a news reporter or newscaster.

An important function of the Assistant News Director is working with the director in determining the direction of the news at the specific station. To do this, the two must determine what type of programming will be most effective for the station and their demographics. In many situations both individuals will meet with the program director, station manager, and/or owner to determine how long local news reports should be and when they should be aired.

The Assistant News Director may be responsible for supervising the employees of the news department during his or her shift. If someone doesn't come in to work, he or she is often expected to fill in for them.

While it appears that news is always happening, sometimes it can seem like a "slow news day." On such occasions the Assistant News Director may be expected to seek out interesting stories him- or herself or assign reporters to the task.

In some stations, it is the responsibility of the Assistant News Director to review wire service stories to determine what might be interesting to the station's listeners. He or she might then either re-write the story for inclusion during the news report or assign a reporter or writer to this task.

Wire services such as UPI (United Press International), AP (Associated Press), or Reuters are organizations that have large news staffs as well as freelancers who report up-to-the-minute developments. These reports go over a wire or Teletype and are printed out in thousands of newsrooms and television and radio stations throughout the world. Most newspapers, magazines, and television and radio stations pay for this service which they use daily to report the news, weather, and sports.

In addition to regularly scheduled newscasts, the Assistant News Director is often expected to help develop news programming for the station. The objective is to develop programming that serves the needs of the community and attracts more listeners. This programming may be news or public service oriented and include editorials, call-in shows, opinion-oriented shows, talk shows, and those with guest interviews. The Assistant News Director, along with the news director, must not only develop the programming but also find hosts. In some cases the Assistant News Director may be asked to host shows as well.

Additional duties of Assistant News Directors working in radio may include:

- Reviewing news bites and tapes before copy is aired
- Writing news copy
- Resolving any production or technical problems
- Going out in the field to cover news stories

## Salaries

Earnings for Assistant News Directors working in radio vary greatly depending on the size of the station, its location and popularity, as well as the experience and responsibilities of the individual. Annual earnings may range from $22,000 to $40,000 or more.

Earnings at the lower end of the scale will go to those just starting out or with limited experience in smaller stations. Earnings increase for those with more experience, those working in major-market stations, and those working in stations with news-only formats.

## Employment Prospects

Employment prospects are fair for Assistant News Directors seeking to work in radio, despite the fact that not every station has someone in this position. Smaller stations may have someone in this position who is also handling the duties of a news reporter/newscaster.

As individuals seek employment in larger markets, prospects become more limited. It should be noted that individuals may also be required to relocate for positions.

## Advancement Prospects

Advancement prospects for Assistant News Directors working in radio are fair. Individuals often start off at a small station and after obtaining experience move on to a similar position at a larger or more prestigious station. This results in increased responsibilities and earnings.

## Education and Training

Educational requirements vary for Assistant News Directors working in radio. Most stations generally require or prefer individuals to have a four-year college degree. Good majors to consider for this type of job include communications, journalism, liberal arts, broadcasting, English, and sports administration.

## Experience, Skills, and Personality Traits

Assistant News Directors working in radio usually have experience working in the newsroom. Most were news reporters or newscasters before their appointment.

Assistant News Directors need a good command of the English language. Communications skills, both written and verbal, are also necessary. Good judgment is essential in this job. Management and administrative skills are also mandatory.

## Unions and Associations

Assistant News Directors working in radio may belong to various bargaining unions and associations, depending on the specific position they hold and the station for which they are working. These include the National Association of Broadcast Employees and Technicians (NABET), the American Federation of Television and Radio Artists (AFTRA), the Writers Guild of America (WGA), and the Radio and Television News Directors Associations (RTNDA). Individuals or their stations might also be members of the National Association of Broadcasters (NAB).

## Tips for Entry

1. Get as much experience as possible working in broadcasting. Volunteer to work with your college radio station, even if you can't get work in the news department.

2. Experience in print journalism may also be helpful. Consider a summer or part-time job working for a local newspaper.

3. Many radio stations and associations offer internships or training programs. Internships give you both on-the-job training experience and the opportunity to make important contacts.

4. Local radio stations advertise openings on the air as well as on their website. Check them out.

5. Smaller stations may only have a one- or two-person department. While the pay is usually not great, you can get experience as an Assistant News Director and move up the career ladder.

6. Job openings may be advertised in the newspaper classified section under headings such as "Assistant News Director," "Radio," and "Broadcasting."

# ASSIGNMENT EDITOR

## CAREER PROFILE

**Duties:** Determines which reporters should cover which news stories

**Alternate Title(s):** Assistant News Director

**Salary Range:** $22,000 to $40,000+

**Employment Prospects:** Poor

**Advancement Prospects:** Fair

**Best Geographical Location(s):** Areas such as Atlanta, New York City, Los Angeles, Chicago, etc., and other large cities hosting major-market stations or all-news radio will offer the most opportunities

**Prerequisites:**

**Education or Training**—Four-year college degree

**Experience**—Experience in broadcast newsroom

**Special Skills and Personality Traits**—Objectivity; good judgment; communications skills; people skills; organization; administrative and management skills; understanding and knowledge of broadcasting news room

## CAREER LADDER

```
┌─────────────────────────────────┐
│   Assignment Editor at Larger,  │
│   More Prestigious Station,     │
│   Assistant News Director, or   │
│        News Director            │
└─────────────────────────────────┘

┌─────────────────────────────────┐
│        Assignment Editor        │
└─────────────────────────────────┘

┌─────────────────────────────────┐
│   Newscaster or News Reporter   │
└─────────────────────────────────┘
```

## Position Description

In any given moment in most cities, news is happening. It might be a huge fire at one end of the city, a major announcement from the headquarters of a large company at another, striking teachers, a visit from a high-ranking government official, or any one of hundreds of other events or happenings. Sometimes the news events of the day are big, impacting many. Other times, news might mean a human interest story that is interesting to just a few.

The radio station news director is responsible for determining which stories are newsworthy for the station to cover and which are not. He or she may be assisted in this process by an assistant news director and often an Assignment Editor.

The Assignment Editor in the radio newsroom has a number of responsibilities. In addition to helping to decide what stories are going to be covered by the station news department, he or she decides who will cover them.

In many stations, the news department holds meetings to go over news events that will be occurring over the course of the day. While there is always the possibility of breaking news, the news department often knows about many of the news events well in advance. Publicists or organizations often send press releases or calendar notes to the news department informing them about stories, upcoming events, press conferences, meetings, etc.

The news department also may monitor the wire services, other news media, including television news, newspapers, or even other radio stations, to learn about newsworthy happenings. During these meetings the news director, assistant news director, and Assignment Editor will determine what news will be covered and how.

For example, will news reporters just rewrite parts of a press release to use in the news report, or should a reporter be sent out to cover a story? Who will cover the story? In some stations, there may be general news reporters, political reporters, education reporters, health reporters, etc. The Assignment Editor is in charge of assigning specific reporters to each story. He or she will additionally tell reporters whether they are going out in the field or handling the story from the newsroom.

The amount of coverage must be decided as well. Will a press release give enough information, or will the Assignment Editor need to assign a reporter to call one of the parties involved to get a statement? There are many decisions to be made in this position. The end result should be the best newscast possible.

Assignment Editors in radio newsrooms often monitor police and fire scanners. By doing this, the Assignment Editor can learn of late breaking news. Did someone report a fire at a school? Has a prisoner escaped? Was there just a big accident on the interstate? Is there a big fire at a local chemical plant? If these or any other news stories break, the Assignment Editor jumps into action.

If a breaking story is important, the Assignment Editor will pull reporters off stories they are working on to cover the new story immediately. He or she may assign reporters to interview law enforcement officials, people on the scene, and those who might have witnessed an event.

Sometimes the Assignment Editor will have reporters phoning in stories for news reports or news bulletins. In other situations, he or she assigns reporters to get taped pieces that must then be edited for the news.

It should be noted, that not all stations have an Assignment Editor. In smaller stations, the assistant news director will handle the responsibilities and functions of the Assignment Editor. Generally, Assignment Editors are found in major-market stations with large news departments or in stations hosting an all-news format.

Assignment Editors are often responsible for checking out stories themselves. They may find a story and bring it to the attention of the news director or assistant director. Getting a "scoop" or being the first station to cover something important is always a coup. At times when it appears to be a "slow news" day, the Assignment Editor may send out reporters to get interesting stories.

Additional duties of Assignment Editors working in radio may include:

- Supervising radio station newsroom activities
- Reviewing and editing news bites and tapes
- Directing special news bulletins

## Salaries

Earnings for Assignment Editors working in radio can range from $23,000 to $39,000 or more. Factors affecting earnings include the size of the station, its location and popularity, as well as the experience and responsibilities of the individual. Earnings increase for those with more experience, those working in major-market stations, and those working in stations with news-only formats.

## Employment Prospects

Employment prospects are poor for Assignment Editors seeking work in radio. As noted, not every radio station employs an Assignment Editor. Smaller stations generally have the assistant news director or news director handling the responsibilities of the Assignment Editor. These positions are more plentiful in major-market radio, those with large news departments, or all-news formats.

## Advancement Prospects

Once on the job, advancement prospects are fair. An Assignment Editor may climb the career ladder by locating a similar position at a larger, more prestigious station or by becoming an assistant news director or even a news director. Some individuals also move into similar jobs in television news.

## Education and Training

Assignment Editors generally are required to have a four-year college degree. Good majors to consider for this type of job include communications, journalism, liberal arts, broadcasting, and English.

## Experience, Skills, and Personality Traits

Assignment Editors working in radio usually have experience working in the newsroom. Most were news reporters or newscasters before their appointment. Organizational skills are imperative for this position. Communications skills, both written and verbal are also needed. Management and administrative skills and good judgment are essential. The ability to work on a multitude of projects without getting flustered is helpful.

## Unions and Associations

Assignment Editors working in radio may belong to various bargaining unions and associations, depending on the specific position they hold and the station for which they are working. These include the National Association of Broadcast Employees and Technicians (NABET), the American Federation of Television and Radio Artists (AFTRA), the Writers Guild of America (WGA), and the Radio and Television News Directors Associations (RTNDA). Individuals or their stations might also be members of the National Association of Broadcasters (NAB).

## Tips for Entry

1. Many stations offer both formal and informal internship programs. While an internship in any department at the station is helpful, if you can, seek out an internship in the newsroom.
2. Get as much experience as possible working in broadcasting. Volunteer to work with your college radio station, even if you can't get work in the news department.
3. Experience in print journalism may also be helpful. Consider a summer or part-time job working for a local newspaper.
4. Stations may advertise their openings on the air as well as on their website. Check them out.
5. Job openings may be advertised in the newspaper classified section under headings such as "Assignment Editor," "Assignment Editor-Radio," "Radio," "Assignment Editor/Assistant News Director," and "Broadcasting."

# NEWS REPORTER

## CAREER PROFILE

**Duties:** Develops news reports to be read on air; writes copy; checks facts

**Alternate Title(s):** Reporter; Newscaster

**Salary Range:** $20,000 to $75,000+

**Employment Prospects:** Good

**Advancement Prospects:** Fair

**Best Geographical Location(s):** Smaller local communities offer opportunities for small-market stations; New York City, Los Angeles, Chicago, Atlanta, etc., for major-market stations

**Prerequisites:**

**Education or Training**—Four-year college degree required or preferred by most stations; others may accept broadcasting-school certificate

**Experience**—Experience in college radio helpful but may not always be required; experience in print journalism helpful

**Special Skills and Personality Traits**—Pleasant speaking voice; good verbal and written communications skills; comfortable with a microphone

## CAREER LADDER

```
┌─────────────────────────────────┐
│     News Reporter for Larger,   │
│  More Prestigious Radio Station or │
│         News Director           │
└─────────────────────────────────┘

┌─────────────────────────────────┐
│         News Reporter           │
└─────────────────────────────────┘

┌─────────────────────────────────┐
│   News Writer or Entry-Level    │
└─────────────────────────────────┘
```

## Position Description

Most radio stations report local, regional, national, and international news in some manner. Many people tune into their local radio station just to hear the news. The News Reporter at a radio station is the individual responsible for developing the news format that is then reported on air.

The News Reporter holds an integral position in putting together newscasts. News reports may vary in length, depending on the station. Some stations have one- to six-minute reports or longer hourly. Many have full news reports, often lasting 30 minutes or more during the morning, midday, or evening drive time. No matter how long or short an actual newscast is, the preparation and development for it is a time-consuming project.

Depending on the size and structure of the station, the News Reporter may have a multitude of duties, ranging from developing news stories to writing news reports and reading them on air. Generally, individuals working in larger stations will have more specific duties. Those working in smaller stations may have more generalized duties.

News Reporters seek out news stories. In order to develop the news reports, he or she may interview and get statements from people relevant to the story. The News Reporter may get sound bites from people to make the news story more interesting and add depth. Sound bites are recorded bits of tape. To do this, the Newscaster tape-records comments from people, either in person or over the phone.

In some cases, the News Reporter asks questions of a person he or she is interviewing. In others, the News Reporter may record a certain piece of a meeting or an event for a sound bite. Once recorded, the tape generally goes back to the studio for editing before being aired. Sometimes a few pieces of a recorded interview are edited for use. Then a different piece of the interview is used for different newscasts and time schedules.

News Reporters often work in the field. They may attend meetings or events or seek out news stories for the news report. Reporters also may spend a great deal of the time on the phone obtaining information.

In some stations, the News Reporter must "find" the news on his or her own. He or she may receive tips, read press releases sent in to the station, read the newspaper, or use a variety of other sources. In some stations, an assignment editor or news director may select newsworthy items and events and assign specific News Reporters to cover them. However news is covered, it is essential that the News Reporter check the facts and make sure everything is 100% accurate.

When working in the field, a News Reporter may call in his or her news report. The report may then be recorded via phone and played during the newscast. In some instances, the News Reporter reports a news story "live" on air during a news report. There is nothing worse than being on air and being unclear about the subject you are covering. It is therefore important in these situations for the individual to write his or her report fully or at least have some notes so there will be no fumbling on air.

News Reporters must write each story in a manner that makes it interesting to the listening audience. News stories must also be written in a clear and concise manner that fits into the allotted time slot.

Depending on the size and structure of the station, the News Reporter may also be the newscaster or news anchor. This means that he or she will be responsible for doing the regularly scheduled news reports. News reports may be done live or may be prerecorded for broadcast.

News Reporters may be responsible for reporting local, regional, and national news as well as reporting sports, weather, and traffic conditions. While individuals may be expected to report news in a variety of areas, sometimes News Reporters specialize in a specific area of news reporting. For example, individuals may specialize in politics, finance, government, entertainment, sports, education, etc.

News Reporters obtain information for their reports in a number of ways. Some is gained firsthand. Other information is obtained through the wire services. Organizations such as UPI (United Press International), AP (Associated Press), and Reuters have large news and sports staffs as well as freelancers who report all the up-to-the-minute developments. These reports go over a wire or Teletype and are printed out in thousands of news rooms and television and radio stations throughout the world. Most newspapers, magazines, and television and radio stations pay for this service, which they use daily to report the news, weather, and sports.

News Reporters working in radio usually work shifts. These may vary by the station. Individuals can be assigned, for example, to the early-morning, midday, drive-time, evening, or night shift. Hours vary. In some stations shifts are three hours long. In others they are eight hours.

Additional duties of a radio News Reporter may include:

• Developing feature pieces on news-related subjects and events
• Performing research news reports
• Acting as news director and/or newscaster
• Rewriting wire service reports

## Salaries

Earnings for News Reporters working in radio vary greatly, depending on the size of the station, its location, and popularity. Earnings also are dependent on the experience, responsibilities, and popularity of the individual.

Those just starting out at a small station may only earn $20,000. Others who have more experience and are working at larger, more prestigious stations may earn $75,000 or more.

## Employment Prospects

Most radio stations employ at least one News Reporter. Many have more than one. Employment prospects for News Reporters aspiring to work in radio are good for those willing to work on a local or regional level. Opportunities may be available in larger stations for those with experience. Individuals may need to relocate for positions.

## Advancement Prospects

Advancement prospects for News Reporters are fair. Many individuals break into the industry on a small, local level, get experience, and work up from there. The most common method of advancement is locating a similar position at a larger, more prestigious station. This results in increased responsibilities and earnings.

Some individuals also climb the career ladder by being promoted to news director positions.

## Education and Training

Educational requirements vary for News Reporters working in radio. Today most stations require or prefer individuals to have a four-year college degree. Good majors to consider for this type of job include communications, journalism, liberal arts, broadcasting, and English.

## Experience, Skills, and Personality Traits

In many smaller stations, this is an entry-level job. Experience working on a college radio station or in print journalism is helpful. Larger stations generally require more experience.

In order to be successful at this job, individuals need a good command of the English language. Communication skills are necessary. The ability to write well is essential, as is a pleasant speaking voice. Individuals must also be comfortable speaking into a microphone. An inquisitive mind and sound judgment are also helpful in this position.

## Unions and Associations

News Reporters may belong to various bargaining unions and associations depending on the specific position they hold and the station for which they are working. These include the National Association of Broadcast Employees and Technicians (NABET), the American Federation of Television and Radio Artists (AFTRA), the Radio Television News Directors Association (RTNDA), and the Writers Guild of America (WGA). Individuals or their stations might also be members of the National Association of Broadcasters (NAB).

## Tips for Entry

1. Get as much experience as possible working in broadcasting. Volunteer to work with your college radio station on any level available.

2. Many radio stations and associations offer internships or training programs. Internships give you on-the-job training experience and the opportunity to make important contacts.

3. Obtain experience writing news stories by getting a part-time or summer job with a local newspaper.

4. Many local stations advertise openings on the air as well as on their website. Check them out.

5. Job openings are also often advertised in the newspaper classified section under headings such as "News Reporter," "Radio," "Writer-Radio News," "Writer," and "Broadcasting."

# NEWS WRITER

## CAREER PROFILE

**Duties:** Develops and writes copy for radio newscasts; gathers information for stories

**Alternate Title(s):** Broadcast Journalist

**Salary Range:** $18,000 to $45,000+

**Employment Prospects:** Fair

**Advancement Prospects:** Fair

**Best Geographical Location(s):** Opportunities may be located throughout the country in areas hosting radio stations

**Prerequisites:**

**Education or Training**—Four-year college degree required or preferred by most stations

**Experience**—Experience in college radio may be helpful; writing experience

**Special Skills and Personality Traits**—Writing skills; research skills; good command of the English language

## CAREER LADDER

```
┌─────────────────────────────────┐
│       News Writer for Larger,   │
│      More Prestigious Radio or  │
│  Television Station or Newscaster│
└─────────────────────────────────┘

┌─────────────────────────────────┐
│            News Writer          │
└─────────────────────────────────┘

┌─────────────────────────────────┐
│    Print Journalist or Entry-Level │
└─────────────────────────────────┘
```

## Position Description

No matter what format a radio station uses, most have some sort of news programming during the day. Depending on the size and structure of the station, the news department may encompass a news director, one or more assistant news directors, News Writers, newscasters, news anchors, researchers, copy editors, and more.

Sometimes the station uses the services of a news syndicate such as CNN, CBS, ABC, or NBC as the station's sole news source. At other times, the station may augment local news with national news reports from one of these syndicates. It should be noted that while News Writers may work for a specific station, an individual may also be a News Writer for a news syndicate.

Some stations may have just one person on staff who writes the news. Others may have more. The responsibilities of the News Writer will be dependent to a great extent on the size and structure of the station. In larger stations, the individual will generally have more specific duties. In smaller stations, the News Writer is often also the newscaster.

The function of the News Writer working in radio is to develop and write news stories and/or scripts. These are then read on air by either a radio news anchor, an in-studio reporter or the News Writer him or herself.

In order to write the news, the News Writer must first gather information. He or she may obtain information through a variety of sources, including press releases, interviews, or performing research. News Writers also gather a great deal of information through the wire services. UPI (United Press International), AP (Associated Press), and Reuters are all examples of wire services.

Wire services are organizations that have large news and sports staffs and freelancers who report all the up-to-the-minute news, developments, weather, etc. These reports go over a wire or Teletype and are printed out in thousands of newsrooms and television and radio stations throughout the world. Most radio stations, as well as newspapers, magazines, and television pay for this service, which they use daily to obtain sports news in addition to general news and weather.

News Writers take the information off the wires and then rewrite it to fit into the specific reports needed. In some instances, the wire service information will be used as a basis for an in-depth story. The News Writer may then do additional research to obtain even more information.

News Writers must be sure all information used in their news reports is accurate. Therefore, an important function of the Writer is checking information for accuracy before allowing it to be aired.

Successful News Writers turn out interesting and understandable reports. One of the challenges that the radio News Writer has is tailoring news stories to fit into the allotted time period.

In addition to writing the copy for regularly aired newscasts, News Writers may also be expected to read news briefs, special reports, or even the short "teases" used to attract interest in an upcoming news report.

News Writers working in radio may work from the office or out in the field to gather news and obtain information. They may attend press conferences, meetings, functions, and other events in an effort to get fresh information.

Copy for news reports may vary in length depending on the station, from approximately one minute to six minutes. Longer news spots may be expected during the morning, midday, or nightly news reports.

Many News Writers working in radio today are also expected to develop and write news stories or news bullets for the station's website. It should be noted that many stations today employ News Writers whose sole job is writing news copy for the website.

News Writers working in radio may work various shifts, depending on the size and structure of the station.

Additional duties of a News Writer working in radio may include:

- Writing feature pieces on news related subjects and events
- Performing research for special news reports
- Acting as newscaster

## Salaries

Earnings for News Writers working in radio vary greatly depending on the size of the station, its location, and popularity. Earnings also are dependent on the experience and responsibilities of the individual. Annual earnings might range from $18,000 to $45,000 or more.

Those just starting out will have earnings at the lower end of the scale. Those with more experience who are working at larger, more prestigious stations will have earnings at the higher end of the scale.

In unionized stations, minimum earnings for News Writers will be negotiated by the union.

## Employment Prospects

Employment prospects for radio News Writers are fair. Smaller stations generally have their news reporters write their own reports.

Positions may be located in stations throughout the country in small, midsize, and major markets. Individuals may find positions in stations utilizing a variety of formats, including music, sports, talk, and/or all news. Some News Writers working in radio also may work for news syndicates, such as CNN, CBS, ABC, or NBC.

## Advancement Prospects

Advancement prospects for News Writers working in radio are fair. The most common method of career advancement is locating similar positions in larger, more prestigious stations. This results in increased responsibilities and earnings.

Depending on career aspirations, some News Writers advance by becoming newscasters. Others may become television-news writers or print journalists.

## Education and Training

Educational requirements vary for News Writers working in radio. Today most stations require or prefer individuals to have a four-year college degree. Good majors to consider for this type of job include communications, journalism, liberal arts, broadcasting, English, or sports administration. There are some stations that will waive the educational requirement in lieu of experience.

## Experience, Skills, and Personality Traits

Experience requirements vary. In some stations, the position of News Writer may be an entry-level job. In others, experience writing in the broadcast industry is necessary. Some stations will consider applicants who were involved in this type of position in their school or college radio station.

The ability to write well is essential. A good command of the English language is necessary.

## Unions and Associations

News Writers working in radio may belong to various bargaining unions and associations, depending on the specific position they hold and the station for which they are working. These include the National Association of Broadcast Employees and Technicians (NABET), the American Federation of Television and Radio Artists (AFTRA), and the Writers Guild of America (WGA). Individuals or their stations might also be members of the National Association of Broadcasters (NAB) and/or the Radio Television News Directors Association (RTNDA).

## Tips for Entry

1. If you are still in school, volunteer to work with your college radio station.
2. Get as much experience writing as possible. If you can't get experience in broadcast writing, make sure you get some in print.
3. Many radio stations and associations offer internships or training programs. Internships give you on-the-job training experience and the opportunity to make important contacts.
4. Many local stations advertise openings on the air as well as on their website. Check them out.
5. Job openings are also often advertised in the newspaper classified section under headings such as "News Writer," "Radio," and "Broadcasting."

# NEWS PRODUCER

## CAREER PROFILE

**Duties:** Coordinates various aspects of radio news broadcasts; coordinates production elements; writes scripts; brings story ideas to table

**Alternate Title(s):** Executive News Producer

**Salary Range:** $20,000 to $65,000+

**Employment Prospects:** Poor

**Advancement Prospects:** Fair

**Best Geographical Location(s):** Opportunities may be located throughout the country; the most opportunities will be located in areas hosting all-talk or news formats

**Prerequisites:**

**Education or Training**—College degree required by most stations

**Experience**—Experience in radio broadcasting news required

**Special Skills and Personality Traits**—Understanding and knowledge of broadcast industry; communications skills; writing skills; ability to multitask; production skills

## CAREER LADDER

```
┌─────────────────────────────────┐
│   News Producer for Larger,     │
│ More Prestigious Station or Show, or │
│      Executive Producer         │
└─────────────────────────────────┘

┌─────────────────────────────────┐
│        News Producer            │
└─────────────────────────────────┘

┌─────────────────────────────────┐
│    Associate News Producer,     │
│       Guest Coordinator         │
└─────────────────────────────────┘
```

## Position Description

No matter where people are in the country, or the world for that matter, one thing they can count on is that news will be happening. Most radio stations report the news in some manner. Some stations may report just local news. Others may report regional, national, or international news as well. Radio-station news departments may be large or small, depending on the size and structure of the station. The news department may include, among others, news directors, assistant news directors, newscasters, reporters, writers, researchers, sportscasters, weather and traffic reporters, and News Producers.

The News Producer is the individual responsible for producing the on-air newscasts. Within the scope of the job, the Producer has a number of duties. The News Producer is expected to coordinate the various aspects of the radio news broadcast as well as the production elements. The individual is responsible for making sure that newscasts are the right length and done on time and within budget.

The News Producer may have a number of writing responsibilities. He or she may write scripts, introductions to the news, weather, or traffic reports, or even the actual newscasts.

When producing newscasts, there are a number of questions the Producer must think about. Will the newscasts be live or taped? Will there be live interviews with people in the news? Will the newscasts include interviews between newscasters and others outside the studio via telephone hookups? Will comments and quotes need to be edited from taped sources? Will the reporters be live on the scene or in the newsroom? The answers to these questions must be determined so that the Producer knows some of the technical areas he or she must address.

The News Producer decides what stories are covered during the newscast. He or she must determine the length of each news story in the newscast and where, during the newscast, each story will be placed. In some situations, this may be handled by the news director. The News Producer will also be in charge of choosing guests or others to be interviewed during newscasts.

The Producer is expected to determine how news will be presented. It's often interesting to see how different radio stations in the same area cover the same news stories in a totally different manner. Some may just report the facts. Others may include a unique or local angle. Sometimes one radio station will be live on the scene, while others report directly from the studio.

Often part of the job of News Producers is bringing good, exciting, or intriguing stories to the table. This responsibility is often handled with the help of the news director and assistant director and associate news producer. While news occurs continuously, finding a great story or an interesting way of presenting news is a talent that many good News Producers have.

The News Producer may be expected to develop a variety of news and public affairs programming for the station. The Producer, along with the news director and news reporters, will often hold brainstorming sessions to come up with new and innovative ideas for interesting programming.

The Producer is responsible for directing and supervising everyone involved in the production of the newscast or news programming. He or she may have one or more assistants helping with various tasks. It is the responsibility of the News Producer to make sure everything goes smoothly during the newscast. He or she must make sure the studio is set up correctly, seats are set up for the newscaster and any guests, headphones are available, and everything is in working order.

The News Producer may either do background research in the development of the news programming or supervise the research done by others in the newsroom. He or she may interview people, read articles or books, talk to experts, or browse the Internet to get information.

In addition to producing newscasts, the individual may also be expected to produce other types of news shows and public service programming.

Additional duties of radio News Producers may include:

• Producing additional types of programming
• Making sure any contracts or clearances are signed
• Overseeing assistant producers and other employees

It should be noted that in some stations, the News Producer may also be either the news reporter, newscaster, news director, news writer, or a combination. In situations where there is a dedicated person handling this position, it is a behind-the-scenes job.

## Salaries

Earnings for radio News Producers can vary tremendously, ranging from $20,000 to $65,000 or more. Variables include the size, location, prestige, and popularity of the station, as well as the experience, expertise, and responsibilities of the individual.

In some stations, minimum earnings are negotiated and set by a union. It should be noted, however, that these are minimums. Higher earnings are often negotiated. The highest earnings for News Producers generally go to individuals with a great deal of experience working in major markets or in large all-news or talk format stations.

## Employment Prospects

Employment prospects for News Producers seeking to work in radio are poor. As noted, in many stations the responsibilities of the News Producer are handled by others in the news department. While positions may be located throughout the country, the largest number of opportunities will exist in major markets and areas hosting radio stations with all-talk or news formats.

## Advancement Prospects

Advancement prospects for News Producers in radio are fair once they get the initial position. The most common form of career advancement for News Producers is finding similar positions in larger, more prestigious stations. This results in increased responsibilities and earnings. Individuals may also climb the career ladder by producing popular talk or radio shows. Some News Producers find positions as executive producers.

## Education and Training

Most radio stations require their News Producers to hold a four-year college degree. Good choices for majors include communications, broadcasting, journalism, English, public relations, marketing, and liberal arts.

## Experience, Skills, and Personality Traits

Experience requirements for News Producers vary from station to station. Generally, the larger the station, the more experience required. Some individuals obtain their experience as interns or working in the news room in various capacities. Some were on-air newscasters or news reporters who wanted the responsibility of producing the news shows. Other News Producers worked as desk assistants, guest coordinators, or assistant or associate producers before their current position.

Radio News Producers should be creative individuals with a full understanding of broadcasting and the news industry. The ability to set priorities is essential, as is the ability to think quickly. News Producers must be able to multitask without getting flustered. Organizational skills are mandatory. Breaking news may mean an entire newscast must be changed.

## Unions and Associations

Radio News Producers may belong to various bargaining unions and associations, depending on the specific position they hold and the station for which they are working. These include the National Association of Broadcast Employees and Technicians (NABET), the American Federation of Television and Radio Artists (AFTRA), and the Writers Guild of America (WGA). Individuals or their stations might also be members of the National Association of Broadcasters (NAB).

**Tips for Entry**

1. Get as much experience as possible working in broadcasting. Volunteer to work with your college radio station, join radio clubs, etc.

2. Many radio stations and associations offer internships or training programs. Internships give you on-the-job training experience and the opportunity to make important contacts.

3. If you can't find a formal internship program, see if you can create your own.

4. Keep in mind that your first goal is to get your foot in the door and then move up the ladder to success. Consider every job opportunity. If you find a job in radio in any area, offer to help people in other areas when you are done with your work. These experiences will give you a broad understanding of the industry.

5. Try to find a mentor in the station. He or she can help you reach your goals.

6. Many local stations advertise openings on the air as well as on their website. Check them out.

7. Job openings are also often advertised in the newspaper classified section under headings such as "News Producer," "Radio," "Radio News Producer," and "Broadcasting."

# BUSINESS REPORTER

## CAREER PROFILE

**Duties:** Develops business reports; reports business news on-air; writes copy; checks facts

**Alternate Title(s):** Business Editor

**Salary Range:** $20,000 to $75,000+

**Employment Prospects:** Fair

**Advancement Prospects:** Fair

**Best Geographical Location(s):** Smaller local communities offer opportunities for small-market stations; New York City, Los Angeles, Chicago, Atlanta, etc., for major-market stations

**Prerequisites:**

**Education or Training**—Minimum of four-year college degree required or preferred by most stations

**Experience**—Experience in business, economics, finance, etc., helpful

**Special Skills and Personality Traits**—Understanding of business, finance, and economics; pleasant speaking voice; good verbal and written communications skills; comfortable with microphone

## CAREER LADDER

```
┌─────────────────────────────────────┐
│   Business Reporter for Larger,      │
│  More Prestigious Radio Station or   │
│    Syndicated Business-Show Host     │
└─────────────────────────────────────┘

┌─────────────────────────────────────┐
│         Business Reporter            │
└─────────────────────────────────────┘

┌─────────────────────────────────────┐
│  News Reporter or Business Journalist │
└─────────────────────────────────────┘
```

## Position Description

Radio newscasts may include a variety of segments, including local, national and international news, weather, and often business news. The Business Reporter is the individual responsible for developing and putting together business reports for the radio news.

Today more than ever, people are interested in what is happening around them and how it relates to their wallet. The Business Reporter is the one responsible for telling the listeners what is happening in the business world.

Business Reporters may report on an array of business issues. These might include financial news stories, financial forecasts, business stories, and stock market reports among others.

In some cases, the Business Reporter may discuss national or international business issues. In others he or she may report on local business stories. In many situations, Business Reporters find a way to relate the news to their listening audience.

For example, the Business Reporter may be reporting on a national trend of high unemployment. He or she might then report on what businesses closed in the area and how many jobs were lost. The individual might then go on to report on work-force retraining that is being planned in the area.

Business Reporters, as all other reporters, have a multitude of duties, ranging from developing business stories to writing the business news reports and reading them on air. They may get business news in a number of ways.

A great deal of business news is often obtained from paid news services, such as UPI (United Press International), AP (Associated Press), and Reuters. These organizations have large staffs as well as freelancers who report all the up-to-the-minute developments in business, as well as all facets of news. These reports go over a wire or Teletype and are printed out in thousands of newsrooms and television and radio stations throughout the world. Once the news comes "off the wire," the Business Reporter must review it and determine what he or she wants to use for the business report. At that point, the Business Reporter often rewrites the piece so it fits into the format of the on-air business report.

In some stations, the news director, assistant news director, or assignment editor may assign newsworthy items and events for the Business Reporters to cover. Business Reporters may also obtain business news firsthand. He or she may seek out stories or may receive news releases or calls from people in the local business community who have a story to tell.

Business Reporters often interview and get statements from people relevant to the story. They may get sound bites from people to add depth to the story. Sound bites are recorded bits of tape. To do this, the individual will tape-record comments from people either in person or via a phone connection. The Business Reporter may go "out in the field" to get information for business reports or may spend time on the phone obtaining information.

Business Reporters must write each story in a manner that makes it interesting to the listening audience. News stories must also be written in a clear and concise manner that fits into the allotted time slot. Business reports may be done live or may be prerecorded for broadcast.

In addition to regularly reporting business and financial news, the Business Reporter may be expected to host business or financially oriented news shows or segments. This is one of the areas where Business Reporters can shine. Some develop a following and may have the opportunity to syndicate shows.

Additional duties of a Business Reporter working in radio may include:

- Developing feature pieces on business or finance related subjects and/or events
- Handling regular news reporting duties
- Developing business and/or financial articles for the station website

## Salaries

Earnings for Business Reporters working in radio vary greatly depending on the size of the station and its location and popularity. Earnings also are dependent on the experience, responsibilities, and following of the individual.

Those just starting out at a small station may only earn $20,000. Others who have more experience and are working at larger, more prestigious stations may earn $45,000 or more. Those with a great deal of experience and a following, either working for a very large station in a major market with an all-news format or hosting business or financial shows, may earn $75,000 or more. Earnings may skyrocket for individuals who have syndicated business reports.

## Employment Prospects

Employment prospects for Business Reporters are fair. It must be noted that while every radio station usually reports

business news, many stations do not have a special Business Reporter. Instead, general news reporters may report any business news that is important. Some stations also hire freelancers to handle special business reports.

However, with that said, many stations may have their news reporters specialize in specific fields. Those who want to break into this area, therefore, may work as a general news reporter in a smaller local or regional station and specialize in business. After obtaining some experience, the individual may have an easier time locating a position at a larger station as a full-time Business Reporter.

Opportunities in larger stations may be more readily available for those with experience. Individuals may need to relocate for this position.

## Advancement Prospects

Advancement prospects for Business Reporters are fair. As noted, many individuals break into the industry on a smaller local or regional level, get experience, and then find similar positions in larger, more prestigious stations. This results in increased responsibilities and earnings.

Some individuals develop a following and create a business-oriented radio show that is then syndicated.

## Education and Training

Most stations generally require their Business Reporters to hold a minimum of a bachelor's degree. Good majors to consider for this type of career include business, economics, communications, journalism, liberal arts, broadcasting, or English. Classes, seminars, and workshops in business areas, finance, and economics will also be helpful.

## Experience, Skills, and Personality Traits

Experience requirements vary from station to station for this position. Some Business Reporters were news reporters before their current position. Others may have worked in business or finance print journalism. The ability to understand and explain the stock market and business and financial news stories is essential.

Business Reporters need at least a basic knowledge and understanding of business and finance. A command of the English language, communication skills, and the ability to write well are also essential. As in other on-air radio positions, a pleasant speaking voice is necessary. Individuals should be comfortable speaking into a microphone and have an inquisitive mind and sound judgment.

## Unions and Associations

Business Reporters may belong to various bargaining unions and associations, depending on the specific position they hold and the station for which they are working. These include the National Association of Broadcast Employees and Technicians (NABET), the American Federation of Television and Radio Artists (AFTRA), and the Writers Guild of America (WGA). Individuals and their stations might also be members of the National Association of Broadcasters (NAB).

## Tips for Entry

1. If your local station does not have a regular business report, consider doing a demo tape where you put together two- to five-minute spots on some business or financial subject.
2. Many smaller stations hire freelancers to do business reports or stories. Consider sending a letter with your résumé to local stations to inquire about such a possibility.
3. If you are still in school, volunteer to work with your college radio station. Broadcast experience is always helpful.
4. Many radio stations and associations offer internships or training programs. Internships give you on-the-job training experience and the opportunity to make important contacts.
5. Obtain experience writing business stories by getting a part-time or summer job with a local newspaper.
6. Many local stations advertise openings on the air as well as on their website. Check them out.
7. Job openings are often advertised in the newspaper classified section under headings such as "Business Reporter," "Radio," "Business/Finance-Radio News," and "Broadcasting."

# WEATHER REPORTER

## CAREER PROFILE

**Duties:** Reports weather conditions and forecasts during newscasts and special weather reports; gathers information; writes copy

**Alternate Title(s):** Weather Forecaster

**Salary Range:** $19,000 to $55,000+

**Employment Prospects:** Fair

**Advancement Prospects:** Fair

**Best Geographical Location(s):** Smaller local communities offer opportunities for small-market stations; New York City, Los Angeles, Chicago, Atlanta, etc., for major-market stations

**Prerequisites:**

**Education or Training**—College degree required or preferred by most stations; others may accept broadcasting-school certificate

**Experience**—Experience in college radio helpful but not always required

**Special Skills and Personality Traits**—Pleasant speaking voice; good verbal and written communications skills; comfortable with microphone

## CAREER LADDER

```
┌──────────────────────────────────┐
│   Weather Reporter for Larger,    │
│ More Prestigious Radio Station or │
│        Television Station         │
└──────────────────────────────────┘

┌──────────────────────────────────┐
│         Weather Reporter          │
└──────────────────────────────────┘

┌──────────────────────────────────┐
│  News Writer, News Assistant, or  │
│            Entry-Level            │
└──────────────────────────────────┘
```

## Position Description

Many people turn on the radio first thing in the morning to hear what the weather will be for the day. The radio Weather Reporter is responsible for reporting the day's weather and forecasts during the station's newscasts. He or she may also be responsible for doing special reports.

Responsibilities of the Weather Reporter vary depending on the size and structure of the radio station, as well as the qualifications of the individual.

When reporting weather conditions, the Weather Reporter may include things such as barometric pressure, temperatures, wind velocity, and meteorological changes. Some Weather Reporters also give information such as smog alerts, pollen counts, temperature extremes, or other weather issues that may affect the health and/or lifestyle of listeners.

Weather Reporters on radio don't have the luxury of visual aids to help illustrate weather conditions as do their counterparts reporting the weather on television news.

There can be no map or other graphics showing temperatures, clouds, rain, snow, wind, or other weather conditions.

Radio Weather Reporters try to make their portion of the news as interesting as possible. Some Weather Reporters write their reports and then read them verbatim. Others may make notes and ad-lib as they go. In some cases, the Weather Reporter may also ad-lib with the news reporter and/or the on-air personalities.

Weather Reporters may compile their weather reports using a variety of methods. Some stations have people out in the field who gather information on the weather. Other stations use information provided by satellite weather services or wire services. Some stations may compile information from local, regional, state, or national governmental agencies. There are also stations that have their own equipment set up to monitor and gauge weather conditions.

It should be noted that Weather Reporters may just report the news or may be actual meteorologists who have a great deal of knowledge in this field. Weather reports may be live or taped for broadcast during newscasts.

Weather Reporters working in radio usually work shifts. These may vary by the station. Individuals can be assigned, for example, to the early-morning, midday, drive-time, evening, or night shift. Hours vary.

Additional duties of a Weather Reporter working in radio may include:

- Handling duties of news reporter or newscaster
- Rewriting wire service weather stories
- Doing special weather reports

## Salaries

Earnings for Weather Reporters working in radio vary greatly depending on the size, location, and prestige of the station as well as the experience, responsibilities, and popularity of the individual.

Those just starting out at a small station may only earn $19,000. Others who have more experience or work at larger, more prestigious stations may earn $55,000 or more.

In unionized situations, minimum earnings may be set by the local bargaining union.

## Employment Prospects

Employment prospects are fair for Weather Reporters seeking to work in radio. Individuals may find employment in small or midsize markets or major-market stations. Other opportunities might be located in public radio, affiliates, or on syndicated stations. Individuals may need to relocate for positions.

## Advancement Prospects

Advancement prospects for Weather Reporters are fair. Many individuals break into the industry on a small local level, get experience, and work up from there. The most common method of advancement is locating a similar position at a larger, more prestigious station. This results in increased responsibilities and earnings.

Depending on career aspirations, some individuals move into positions as newscasters, news reporters, or Weather Reporters on television.

## Education and Training

Educational requirements vary for Weather Reporters working in radio. Smaller stations may not require a college degree or background. However, a college degree is usually required for career advancement. Good majors to consider for this type of job include communications, journalism, liberal arts, broadcasting, mass communications, or English. Courses or seminars in meteorology will also be useful.

## Experience, Skills, and Personality Traits

In many smaller stations, this may be an entry-level job. Experience working at a college radio station or in print journalism is helpful. Larger stations generally require more experience. Some individuals may have been working in the newsroom as news assistants or news writers before becoming a Weather Reporter.

Individuals should have a pleasant speaking voice and a good command of the English language. Communication skills are necessary. The ability to write well is essential. Individuals must also be comfortable speaking into a microphone. The ability to develop a rapport with the listening audience is often what sets one Weather Reporter apart from another.

## Unions and Associations

Weather Reporters may belong to various bargaining unions and associations, depending on the specific position they hold and the station for which they are working. These include the National Association of Broadcast Employees and Technicians (NABET), the American Federation of Television and Radio Artists (AFTRA), the Writers Guild of America (WGA), and/or the American Meteorological Society (AMS). Individuals or their stations might also be members of the National Association of Broadcasters (NAB).

## Tips for Entry

1. Get as much experience as possible working in broadcasting. Volunteer to work with your college radio station on any level available.
2. Many radio stations and associations offer internships or training programs. Internships give you on-the-job training experience and the opportunity to make important contacts.
3. Many local stations advertise openings on the air as well as on their website. Check them out.
4. Job openings are also often advertised in the newspaper classified section under headings such as "Weather Reporter," "Weather Forecaster," "Radio," and "Broadcasting."

# METEOROLOGIST

## CAREER PROFILE

**Duties:** Forecasts weather conditions for radio newscasts and special weather reports; gathers data on atmospheric conditions

**Alternate Title(s):** Weather Forecaster

**Salary Range:** $25,000 to $65,000+

**Employment Prospects:** Poor

**Advancement Prospects:** Fair

**Best Geographical Location(s):** Smaller local communities offer opportunities for small-market stations; New York City, Los Angeles, Chicago, Atlanta, etc., for major-market stations

**Prerequisites:**

**Education or Training**—Bachelor's degree a minimum
**Experience**—Experience in college radio helpful but not always required
**Special Skills and Personality Traits**—Scientific aptitude; pleasant speaking voice; good communications skills; computer skills

## CAREER LADDER

```
┌─────────────────────────────────────┐
│   Meteorologist for Larger, More     │
│ Prestigious Radio or Television Station │
└─────────────────────────────────────┘

┌─────────────────────────────────────┐
│           Meteorologist              │
└─────────────────────────────────────┘

┌─────────────────────────────────────┐
│  College Student or Weather Reporter │
└─────────────────────────────────────┘
```

## Position Description

Meteorology is the study of the atmosphere. Meteorologists study the atmosphere's physical characteristics, motions, processes, and the manner in which it affects the environment.

Will we need to wear a sweater the next day? Will a long-sleeve shirt be too warm? Do we need an umbrella? Will it be cold or icy or snowy? We have all become accustomed to planning our day, to some extent, around the weather.

We all want to know what the weather is going to be in advance. Many of us tune in to a local television or radio station to hear the weather forecasts.

When it is sunny and pleasant outside, most people don't think of who has reported the weather. When it rains, snows, or the weather is poor in any manner, we often look to the weather reporter. However, in some cases, the weather reporter is just that. He or she is just the one to *report* the weather news that is forecasted by someone else.

The individual responsible for the actual forecasting of the weather is a Meteorologist. These individuals are trained in the science of forecasting and understanding the weather conditions. As part of their job, Meteorologists study information on air pressure, temperature, humidity, and wind velocity. They then take this information and apply physical and mathematical relationships to make both short- and long-range weather forecasts.

Meteorologists working in radio may have varied responsibilities. Some may be responsible for just the actual forecasting of the weather. Others may not only forecast the weather but also be responsible for reporting it on-air as well.

Some Meteorologists use weather balloons to measure the wind, temperature, and humidity in the upper atmosphere. Today many Meteorologists utilize more sophisticated weather equipment such as Doppler radar. This type of equipment has the ability to detect air-flow patterns in storm systems. This is especially important in areas prone to flash floods, tornadoes, and major storms.

Once the Meteorologist gets this information, he or she can develop the weather forecast. In some instances, the Meteorologist may be responsible for writing weather forecasts, weather reports, or weather bulletins. In others, he or she will give the information to a writer who will handle this task. Meteorologists who report the weather on-air will be responsible for a certain number of weathercasts each day. Weather reports may be live or taped for broadcast during newscasts.

Additional duties of a Meteorologist working in radio may include:

- Rewriting wire-service weather stories
- Getting information for smog alerts and pollen counts
- Handling duties of news reporter or newscaster
- Acting as a Meteorologist for an affiliated television station

## Salaries

Earnings for Meteorologists working in radio vary greatly, depending on the size, location, and prestige of the station, as well as the experience and responsibilities of the individual. Earnings may range from $25,000 to $65,000 or more annually.

In unionized situations, minimum earnings may be set by the local bargaining union.

## Employment Prospects

Employment prospects for Meteorologists seeking to work in radio are poor. Not every station employs a Meteorologist. Many stations utilize weather services instead. That does not mean it is impossible to break into the field. In the event that a station is looking to fill a position of a weather reporter, a Meteorologist may have an edge over others who might not have the training. Once in the door, individuals can obtain experience and locate a similar job in a station seeking someone with specialized training.

Individuals may find employment opportunities in small or midsize markets or major-market stations. Other opportunities might be located in public radio, affiliates, or on syndicated stations. Individuals may need to relocate for positions.

## Advancement Prospects

Advancement prospects for Meteorologists are fair. Many individuals break into the industry on a small local level, get experience, and work up from there. The most common method of advancement is locating a similar position at a larger, more prestigious station. This results in increased responsibilities and earnings. Depending on career aspirations, some individuals move into positions in television broadcasting.

Another option for a Meteorologist is to start a consulting service.

## Education and Training

The minimum educational requirement for Meteorologists is a bachelor's degree. Individuals may have a major in meteorology or may take a specific number of course hours in the

area. There are Meteorologists who have degrees in physics, earth science, geophysics, and atmospheric sciences.

Many Meteorologists obtain a master's or Ph.D. in meteorology.

## Experience, Skills, and Personality Traits

Experience requirements vary from station to station. In small stations where the Meteorologist is also the weather reporter, this may be an entry-level job. Generally, the larger the station, the more experience an individual needs.

Those working as weather reporters as well may need experience on-air.

Meteorologists should have a scientific aptitude with an inquisitive mind. Math skills are needed. Communication skills are mandatory. Those working as on-air weather reporters should have a pleasant speaking voice and a good command of the English language. The ability to write well is essential. Individuals must also be comfortable speaking in front of a microphone. Much of the work is done with computers, so computer skills are necessary.

## Unions and Associations

Meteorologists working in radio may belong to various bargaining unions and associations, depending on the specific position they hold and the station for which they work. These include the National Association of Broadcast Employees and Technicians (NABET), the American Federation of Television and Radio Artists (AFTRA), the Writers Guild of America (WGA), and/or the American Meteorological Society (AMS). Individuals or their stations might also be members of the National Association of Broadcasters (NAB).

## Tips for Entry

1. Look for an internship or apprenticeship in this field. Both will provide valuable on-the-job training. Many radio stations and associations offer internships or training programs.
2. If you plan to be an on-air weather reporter as well as a Meteorologist, get as much experience as possible working in broadcasting. Volunteer to work with your college radio station on any level available.
3. If you are still in school and getting a degree in meteorology, talk to the placement office. Many have placement services for their graduates.
4. Many local stations advertise openings on the air as well as on their website. Check them out.
5. Job openings are also often advertised in the newspaper classified section under headings such as "Meteorologist," "Weather Forecaster," "Radio," and "Broadcasting."

# ENTERTAINMENT REPORTER

## CAREER PROFILE

**Duties:** Reports entertainment news on-air; develops entertainment reports; writes copy; checks facts

**Alternate Title(s):** Entertainment Editor

**Salary Range:** $20,000 to $75,000+

**Employment Prospects:** Poor

**Advancement Prospects:** Fair

**Best Geographical Location(s):** Most opportunities will be located in major markets such as New York City, Los Angeles, Chicago, and Atlanta

**Prerequisites:**

**Education or Training**—Minimum of four-year college degree required or preferred by most stations

**Experience**—Broadcast or journalism experience preferred

**Special Skills and Personality Traits**—Understanding of entertainment industry; pleasant speaking voice; good verbal and written communications skills; comfortable with microphone; persuasive

## CAREER LADDER

```
┌─────────────────────────────────────┐
│  Entertainment Reporter for Larger,  │
│   More Prestigious Radio or          │
│      Television Station or           │
│  Syndicated Entertainment Reporter   │
└─────────────────────────────────────┘

┌─────────────────────────────────────┐
│       Entertainment Reporter         │
└─────────────────────────────────────┘

┌─────────────────────────────────────┐
│         News Reporter or             │
│   Print Entertainment Journalist     │
└─────────────────────────────────────┘
```

## Position Description

Many people are interested in hearing about the glitz and glamour of the entertainment industry. They want to hear about the comings and goings of television movie stars, sports personalities, recording groups, singers, and so on. They want to know what's happening in the entertainment industry, whether it be local, national, or international.

While some radio stations just have entertainment news as an addendum to their news reports, there are others who employ full-time Entertainment Reporters to provide entertainment reports. Many of these stations are in larger markets where entertainment news often breaks. New York, Los Angeles, and Chicago are some examples of major markets. Mid-market and smaller-market stations may also employ Entertainment Reporters. However, individuals in these positions may also be expected to report on other types of news.

Radio Entertainment Reporters may report on an array of entertainment events, performances, happenings, and people. Their reports may focus on local, national, or international entertainment news.

Specific responsibilities of Entertainment Reporters vary, depending on the size and structure of the radio station. In very large stations, Entertainment Reporters may be assigned to report on a particular area of entertainment, such as theater, music, film, or television. In other stations, individuals will be expected to cover all facets of entertainment.

Some Entertainment Reporters are assigned stories to report on. Others may receive tips. Entertainment Reporters often develop story ideas for their reports on their own, adding a unique angle. For example, a major recording star may have come into town to do a concert. That's news. However, focusing the report on how the singer went to visit the local school system to give tips to aspiring singers gives it a unique angle.

No matter what the report will be on, the Entertainment Reporter must get factual information. He or she may interview people to get leads and tips. All information must be checked. Accuracy is important in all fields of reporting, and the entertainment industry is no exception.

If nothing is happening locally, the radio Entertainment Reporter may report on national entertainment news. Was a new film released? How about a brand-new CD from a major artist? What's happening for the new television season? Were nominations announced for the Oscars?

Within the scope of their job, some radio Entertainment Reporters attend such entertainment events as concerts, ballets, movies, and plays. After seeing them, the Entertainment Reporter is expected to develop reviews for on-air reports.

Some Entertainment Reporters feature upcoming entertainment events in their on-air reports. To get information for these reports, they may review press releases and press kits sent by the promoters or organizers of the entertainment events.

Entertainment Reporters often call or visit people involved in the event to get comments or tape interviews to be included in on-air reports. The taped interviews may then be edited into sound bites to add depth to the story. Individuals may interview entertainers, celebrities, their managers, promoters, publicists, press agents, or even fans who are looking forward to attending an event.

A great deal of the entertainment news may be obtained from paid news services such as UPI (United Press International), AP (Associated Press), and Reuters. These organizations have large and knowledgeable staffs as well as freelancers who report the up-to-the-minute developments in entertainment as well as all facets of news. These reports go over a wire or Teletype and are printed out in thousands of newsrooms and television and radio stations throughout the world. Once the news comes "off the wire," the Entertainment Reporter must review it and determine what he or she wants to use for the entertainment report. He or she may then rewrite the piece, fitting it into the format of the on-air report.

Entertainment Reporters must write each story in a manner that makes it interesting to the listening audience. Each report must be written in a clear and concise manner that fits into the allotted time slot. Entertainment reports may be done live or may be prerecorded for broadcast.

To those who enjoy entertainment, the job of a radio Entertainment Reporter might be the perfect career. As part of the job, individuals get paid by the station to attend a variety of entertainment events, meet celebrities, and give their opinion on movies, concerts, films, and more.

One of the bonuses of being an Entertainment Reporter in radio is that the individual can live almost anywhere in the country and still report on the entertainment industry. Good Entertainment Reporters know how to research and often have a lot of contacts. Those who know how to relate entertainment news to the local area in an interesting manner will be successful.

Additional duties of Entertainment Reporters working in radio may include:

• Hosting entertainment oriented shows
• Handling regular news reporting duties
• Developing entertainment-oriented articles for the station's website

## Salaries

Earnings for radio Entertainment Reporters vary greatly, depending on the size of the station, its location, and popularity. Earnings also are dependent on the experience, responsibilities, and following of the individual.

Those just starting out at a small station may earn only $20,000. Others who have more experience and are working at larger, more prestigious stations may earn $45,000 or more. Those with a great deal of experience and a following working for very large stations with talk or news formats may earn $75,000 or more. Earnings may skyrocket for individuals who have syndicated entertainment reports.

## Employment Prospects

Employment prospects for Entertainment Reporters are poor. As noted, many stations do not have a reporter dedicated solely to the entertainment industry. Instead, general news reporters may report interesting entertainment news. Some stations also hire freelancers to handle special entertainment reports.

One way individuals break into the field is by beginning as a general news reporter and asking for entertainment-oriented assignments when possible. After obtaining some experience, the general reporter often has an easier time locating a position at a larger station as a full-time Entertainment Reporter.

The largest number of opportunities in this area will be located in major markets.

## Advancement Prospects

Once on the job, advancement prospects for Entertainment Reporters are fair. The most common method of career advancement is to locate similar positions at larger, more prestigious stations. Some individuals move into entertainment broadcasting in television. Still others are lucky enough to land positions as syndicated Entertainment Reporters or host well-received, entertainment-oriented shows.

## Education and Training

Most stations generally require their Entertainment Reporters to hold a minimum of a bachelor's degree. Good majors to consider for this type of career include communications, journalism, liberal arts, broadcasting, and English.

## Experience, Skills, and Personality Traits

Experience requirements vary from station to station for Entertainment Reporters. Some individuals were news reporters before their current position. Others may have worked as print entertainment journalists or as publicists in the entertainment industry.

An understanding of the entertainment industry is needed. It helps if the Entertainment Reporter enjoys attending an array of entertainment events. Contacts in the entertainment industry are very helpful.

A command of the English language, communication skills, and the ability to write well are also essential. As in other on-air radio positions, a pleasant speaking voice is necessary. Individuals need to be comfortable speaking into a microphone. Due to the nature of the job, the Entertainment Reporter should be personable and enjoy being with people.

## Unions and Associations

Entertainment Reporters working in radio may belong to various bargaining unions and associations, depending on the specific position they hold and the station for which they work. These include the National Association of Broadcast Employees and Technicians (NABET), the American Federation of Television and Radio Artists (AFTRA), National Entertainment Journalists (NEJ), and the Writers Guild of America (WGA). Individuals or their stations might also be members of the National Association of Broadcasters (NAB). Individuals might also be members of various entertainment associations.

## Tips for Entry

1. If your local station does not have a regular entertainment report, consider doing a demo tape where you put together two- to five-minute spots on entertainment subjects. Call the owner or station manager and ask if you can send a mock tape for review.

2. Many stations hire freelancers to do entertainment reports or stories. Consider sending a letter with your résumé to local stations to inquire about the possibility.

3. If you are still in school, volunteer to work with your college radio station. Broadcast experience is always helpful. Consider movie or theater reviews or try to interview celebrities who are in your area.

4. Many radio stations and associations offer internships or training programs. Internships give you on-the-job training experience and the opportunity to make important contacts.

5. If you are working as a reporter, remember to ask for entertainment-oriented assignments. Offer to cover entertainment stories, even if it isn't your shift.

6. Job openings are also often advertised in the newspaper classified section under headings such as "Entertainment Reporter," "Radio," and "Broadcasting."

7. Consider going to an entertainment-oriented conference. It is a good way to make contacts.

8. Industry organizations and associations usually hold annual conventions and conferences. Many of these host career fairs for the industry.

# TRAFFIC REPORTER

## CAREER PROFILE

**Duties:** Reports traffic conditions on-air; monitors, gathers, writes, and disseminates traffic information

**Alternate Title(s):** Mobile Reporter; Eye-in-the-Sky Reporter

**Salary Range:** $18,000 to $55,000+

**Employment Prospects:** Poor

**Advancement Prospects:** Fair

**Best Geographical Location(s):** More opportunities located in metropolitan areas hosting radio stations

**Prerequisites:**

**Education or Training**—College degree required or preferred by most stations; others may accept broadcasting-school certificate

**Experience**—Experience in college radio helpful but not always required

**Special Skills and Personality Traits**—Pleasant speaking voice; good communications skills; comfortable with microphone; ability to ad-lib

## CAREER LADDER

```
┌─────────────────────────────────────┐
│     Traffic Reporter for Larger,     │
│  More Prestigious Radio Station or   │
│       Other On-Air Position          │
└─────────────────────────────────────┘

┌─────────────────────────────────────┐
│          Traffic Reporter            │
└─────────────────────────────────────┘

┌─────────────────────────────────────┐
│           News Reporter              │
└─────────────────────────────────────┘
```

## Position Description

For those who need to drive to work and live in a metropolitan area or any area where traffic is a problem, the Traffic Reporter can often be a lifesaver. Whether an individual needs to know what route is best to get to work, current road conditions, or where an auto accident has closed a road, the Traffic Reporter can help.

The general function of radio Traffic Reporters is to check out the road conditions in an area and then report them to the listening audience. Within the scope of the job, the Traffic Reporter—or mobile reporter, as he or she may be called—may have varied responsibilities.

Traffic Reporters obtain information about traffic conditions in a number of ways, depending on the size and structure of the station. Some drive company vehicles around the main roads during the morning, midday, or evening rush hours, observing the traffic firsthand. They then transmit the information to listeners. This may be done via two-way radios, cell phones, or other transmission methods.

Some Traffic Reporters view the traffic firsthand by flying high above the roads in helicopters. Traffic Reporters in helicopters have the opportunity to see roads in various parts of the city from a unique angle. While Traffic Reporters on the road can be stuck in traffic themselves, the individual in the air doesn't have to face that challenge.

Traffic Reporters in the air often give live broadcasts telling listeners about what is happening down below. It might be a jackknifed truck, an overturned car, or traffic at a standstill.

It should be noted that not all stations have a Traffic Reporter. Some stations use private companies that monitor traffic and road conditions and then disseminate this information to various stations. Stations can also use helicopter companies whose pilots report information on road and traffic conditions. Other stations may utilize the services of a helicopter company to transport their Traffic Reporters. Many larger radio stations have their own helicopters.

The purpose of the Traffic Reporter's reports is to help listeners choose the best route based on the conditions. In addition to reporting traffic, the Reporter also gives listeners information on weather-related road conditions, including flooding, ice, snow, and wet roads. This helps listening drivers know when to exercise caution on the roads.

Traffic and road condition reports give listeners a reason to turn on the radio. Many people choose a favorite station to keep on during their drive to or from work, based on the helpfulness of the traffic reports.

Successful Traffic Reporters often ad-lib and banter back and forth with the disc jockey or other on-air personality currently on air. They may joke around or talk about other subjects to make the on-air broadcast interesting.

Traffic Reporters must be familiar with the area in which they are reporting. They must know the names of the streets, roads, highways, freeways, interstates, etc., on which they report.

While hours vary, Traffic Reporters are usually assigned shifts when the traffic is heaviest, usually during morning, midday, or afternoon rush hours. In some situations, the Traffic Reporter may be a part-time employee.

Additional duties of a radio Traffic Reporter may include:

- Handling duties of news reporter or newscaster
- Reporting the weather
- Disseminating the traffic and road conditions to various other sources, including television stations or the station's website

## Salaries

Earnings for Traffic Reporters working in radio can vary greatly, ranging from $20,000 to $55,000 or more. Variables affecting earnings include size, location, and prestige of the station, as well as the experience, responsibilities, and popularity of the Traffic Reporter.

In unionized situations, minimum earnings may be set by the local bargaining union.

## Employment Prospects

Employment prospects are poor for Traffic Reporters seeking to work in radio. An noted previously, not all stations employ Traffic Reporters. This does not mean that it is impossible to find a position in this area, it is just more difficult.

Those who aspire to this type of position should look to midsize and larger stations in cities and metropolitan areas that have more traffic. Opportunities might also be located in public radio, affiliates, and/or syndicated stations. Other possibilities include working for a company that reports and disseminates traffic information to radio stations. Individuals may need to relocate for positions.

## Advancement Prospects

Once on the job, advancement prospects for Traffic Reporters are fair. The most common method of advancement is locating a similar position at a larger, more prestigious station. This results in increased responsibilities and earnings. Depending on career aspirations, some Traffic Reporters move on to other areas of broadcasting, including becoming on-air personalities or disc jockeys.

## Education and Training

Educational requirements vary for radio Traffic Reporters. Most stations prefer or require their on-air talent to have a college background. While educational requirements may be waived, a college degree is usually helpful for career advancement. Good majors to consider for this type of job include communications, journalism, liberal arts, broadcasting, mass communications, and English. Courses or seminars in meteorology are also useful. Some Traffic Reporters may also have gone through broadcasting school.

## Experience, Skills, and Personality Traits

Traffic Reporters working in radio should have good communications skills with an excellent command of the English language. Individuals must have a pleasant speaking voice and be comfortable speaking into a microphone.

Traffic Reporters who drive around to monitor road conditions and traffic will need a clean driver's license. Those who report in the air from helicopters should be comfortable flying.

The ability to develop a rapport with the listening audience and ad-lib with others on the air is often what sets one Traffic Reporter apart from another.

## Unions and Associations

Traffic Reporters may belong to various bargaining unions and associations, depending on the specific position they hold and the station for which they are working. These include the National Association of Broadcast Employees and Technicians (NABET) and the American Federation of Television and Radio Artists (AFTRA). Individuals or their stations might also be members of the National Association of Broadcasters (NAB).

## Tips for Entry

1. Get as much experience as possible working in broadcasting. Volunteer to work with your college radio station on any level available.
2. Many radio stations and associations offer internships or training programs. Internships give you on-the-job training experience and the opportunity to make important contacts. If you can find an internship working with a Traffic Reporter, great. If not, any area will be helpful.
3. Many local stations advertise openings on the air as well as on their website. Check them out.
4. Job openings are also often advertised in the newspaper classified section under headings such as "Traffic Reporter," "Mobile Reporter," "Radio," and "Broadcasting."

# CAREERS IN RADIO SPORTS

# SPORTS DIRECTOR

## CAREER PROFILE

**Duties:** Determines stories that should be covered; assigns reporters to stories; develops sports programming

**Alternate Title(s):** Director of Sports Department

**Salary Range:** $27,000 to $150,000+

**Employment Prospects:** Fair

**Advancement Prospects:** Fair

**Best Geographical Location(s):** Smaller local communities offer opportunities for small-market stations; New York City, Los Angeles, Chicago, Atlanta, etc., for major-market stations

**Prerequisites:**

**Education or Training**—Four-year college degree required or preferred by most stations; others may accept broadcasting-school certificate

**Experience**—Experience in college radio helpful but not always required

**Special Skills and Personality Traits**—Understanding and knowledge of sports; communications skills; ability to write well; managerial skills

## CAREER LADDER

```
┌─────────────────────────────────┐
│     Sports Director for Larger,  │
│   More Prestigious Radio Station │
└─────────────────────────────────┘

┌─────────────────────────────────┐
│         Sports Director          │
└─────────────────────────────────┘

┌─────────────────────────────────┐
│        Sportscaster or           │
│     Assistant Sports Director    │
└─────────────────────────────────┘
```

## Position Description

In any given geographical area, there are a variety of sports stories. Some may be local or regional. Others may be national or even international. A Sports Director determines what sports stories a radio station covers.

The Sports Director is responsible for the station's sports department. In smaller stations, the Sports Director may also be the sports reporter or sportscaster. He or she may be expected to seek out sports stories, cover sports events, write sports stories, and be the on-air sportscaster. In larger stations, the Sports Director may be responsible for directing the activities of sports writers, reporters, sportscasters, etc.

In order to decide what sports stories to cover, the Sports Director must take a number of things into account. These include the demographics of the station. For example, who does the station reach and who does it want to reach? Are school sports important in the area? What about college sports? Does the area host a local sports team? What is happening in the national sports world?

After considering these issues, the Sports Director determines where he or she should send reporters, which reporters should go where, and what stories will be reported.

Often national sports news heard on a radio station comes from the various wire services, such as UPI (United Press International), AP (Associated Press), or Reuters. These organizations have large news and sports staffs as well as freelancers who report up-to-the-minute developments. These reports go over a wire or Teletype and are printed out in thousands of newsrooms and television and radio stations throughout the world. Most newspapers, magazines, and television and radio stations pay for this service, which they use daily to report the news, weather, and sports. The Sports Director often reviews these news bits and determines which ones to air during a sports broadcast.

The Sports Director develops sports programming for the radio station, often in conjunction with the news director and/or station manager. For example, in addition to regular sportscasts, the Sports Director may develop specific sports-related shows. Depending on the station, shows may be call-ins, opinion-oriented, and/or have guests. The Sports Director will decide how often these should air, what the format will be, and choose the host(s). In some cases, the Sports Director may also be the host of the program(s) him- or herself.

Sports Directors may work at stations with an array of formats ranging from music to news to all talk to just sports. They may work at local, network, or public radio stations.

Many music-oriented radio stations have only a small sports department. Individuals working there may be expected to perform more varied functions. These Sports Directors are usually expected to report current sports news, developments, and scores. In most cases, Sports Directors are responsible for putting together reports on national sports news as well as local developments. Individuals working in smaller local stations also report school, college, and amateur sports news.

In smaller stations where Sports Directors are also working as sportcasters, they must usually write their own copy for the sports report. They must be able to write interesting copy that tells the story in the allotted amount of time.

Individuals in this profession generally enjoy sports and know a great deal about them. They get to attend games and other sporting events as part of their job. They might be out on the field commenting on a game or in the locker room before or after a game doing interviews. In many cases, especially in smaller stations, the Sports Director handles many of the duties of sportscasters as well.

The Sports Director may obtain information for reports in a number of ways. Some information is gained firsthand. Other information is obtained through the wire services. Organizations such as UPI (United Press International), AP (Associated Press), and Reuters have large news and sports staffs as well as freelancers who report all the up-to-the-minute developments. These reports go over a wire or Tele-type and are printed out in thousands of newsrooms and television and radio stations throughout the world. Most newspapers, magazines, and television and radio stations pay for this service which they use daily to report the news, weather, and sports.

Additional duties of a Sports Director working in radio may include:

- Hosting sports programming
- Attending press conferences
- Performing color commentary at sporting events
- Doing newscasts

## Salaries

Earnings for radio Sports Directors vary greatly, depending on the size of the station, its location, and popularity, and the experience and responsibilities of the individual. Annual earnings may range from $27,000 to $150,000 or more.

Earnings at the lower end of the scale will go to those just starting out or with limited experience in smaller sta-

tions. Compensation goes up for those with more experience, those working in major-market stations, and those working in stations with sports-only formats. Earnings at the upper end of the scale are limited in radio.

Some Sports Directors working in radio also generate extra income by writing sports columns for newspapers or magazines.

## Employment Prospects

Employment prospects for Sports Directors are fair for those willing to work on a local or regional level. Prospects become more limited as individuals seek to work in larger markets. Individuals may also be required to relocate for some positions.

While openings may be located throughout the country, it is easier to break into the industry on a small local level and work up from there. Many smaller stations hire individuals with little or no experience. While the salaries are low in these situations, the experience is worth the opportunity.

## Advancement Prospects

Advancement prospects for Sports Directors working in radio are fair. Individuals often start off at a small station and after obtaining experience move on to a similar position at a larger or more prestigious station. This results in increased responsibilities and earnings.

As individuals move up the career ladder from small-market radio to mid-market and major-market radio, advancement prospects become more difficult.

## Education and Training

Educational requirements vary for radio Sports Directors. Generally, most stations either require or prefer individuals to have a four-year college degree. Good majors to consider for this type of job include communications, journalism, liberal arts, broadcasting, English, and sports administration. It should be noted that smaller stations may not have an educational requirement. However, a college background is useful in climbing the career ladder.

## Experience, Skills, and Personality Traits

Sports Directors working in radio generally have some sort of experience in broadcasting and/or the sports industry. Some individuals begin their career in radio news or radio sports and are then promoted to the position of Sports Director. Smaller stations may hire an individual to be the sports reporter/Sports Director if they have had experience working at their college radio station, or were sports writers for a college or local newspaper.

Successful Sports Directors understand the demographics of their station. Managerial skills are necessary. While not required, most Sports Directors have a genuine love of at least one sport and at least a basic understanding of the sports industry. Communication skills are needed as well.

## Unions and Associations

Sports Directors working in radio may belong to various bargaining unions and associations depending on the specific position they hold and the station for which they are working. These include the National Association of Broadcast Employees and Technicians (NABET), the American Federation of Television and Radio Artists (AFTRA), and the Writers Guild of America (WGA). Individuals or their stations might also be members of the National Association of Broadcasters (NAB), the National Sportscasters and Sportswriters Association (NSSA), and the Radio Television News Directors Association (RTNDA).

## Tips for Entry

1. Get as much experience as possible working in broadcasting. Volunteer to work with your college radio station, even if you can't get into the sports department.

2. Many radio stations and associations offer internships or training programs. Internships give you on-the-job training experience and the opportunity to make important contacts.

3. Local radio stations may advertise openings on the air or on their websites. Check them out.

4. Smaller stations may have a one-person sports department. If you can find a job at one of these, while the pay is usually not great, you can obtain some experience as a Sports Director and then move on.

5. Job openings may be advertised in the newspaper classified section under headings such as "Director of Sports-Radio," "Radio," "Sports Director," and "Broadcasting."

6. Don't forget to read trade publications. *Billboard, Broadcasting,* and *Radio and Records* often have advertisements for stations with openings.

# ASSISTANT SPORTS DIRECTOR

## CAREER PROFILE

**Duties:** Assists sports director in running of station sports department; helps determine which stories should be covered; assigns reporters to stories; develops sports programming

**Alternate Title(s):** Assistant Director of Sports

**Salary Range:** $23,000 to $45,000+

**Employment Prospects:** Fair

**Advancement Prospects:** Fair

**Best Geographical Location(s):** Smaller local communities offer opportunities for small-market stations; New York City, Los Angeles, Chicago, Atlanta, etc., for major-market stations

**Prerequisites:**

**Education or Training**—Four-year college degree required or preferred by most stations; others may accept broadcasting-school certificate

**Experience**—Experience in college radio helpful but not always required

**Special Skills and Personality Traits**—Understanding and knowledge of sports; communications skills; ability to write well; managerial skills

## CAREER LADDER

```
┌─────────────────────────────────┐
│         Sports Director         │
└─────────────────────────────────┘

┌─────────────────────────────────┐
│    Assistant Sports Director    │
└─────────────────────────────────┘

┌─────────────────────────────────┐
│          Sportscaster           │
└─────────────────────────────────┘
```

## Position Description

The Assistant Sports Director works with a radio station's sports director. The actual responsibilities of the Assistant Sports Director depend to a great extent on the size and structure of the station. Those working in larger stations often handle more specialized functions than their counterparts working in smaller stations.

Assistant Sports Directors work with the station's sports director in determining what sports stories are important and noteworthy. In smaller stations the Assistant Sports Director may also work as a sports reporter or sportscaster. In many situations the sports director works the day shift and the Assistant Sports Director works the evening shift.

The Assistant Sports Director works with the sports director by performing research to determine the demographics of the station—which general groups of people listen to the station. This information can often help the sports department develop more effective programming. For example, is the listening audience made up primarily of teenagers? If so, perhaps sports stories should cover school sports as well as national stories. Is the station located in a college town where college sports are important? If so, college sports stories must also be covered. Perhaps games should be covered live with color commentary.

The Assistant Sports Director may help develop surveys, questionnaires, etc., to help find out what the listening audience wants to hear in regard to sports. Armed with this information, the individual works with the Sports Director, programming director, and/or the station's general manager to develop appropriate programming. This often leads to the attraction of new listeners.

The Assistant Sports Director may be expected to seek out stories, cover sporting events, and write sports stories. Many Assistant Sports Directors are also on-air sportscasters.

The Assistant Sports Director helps direct the activities of the department's sports writers, reporters, and sportscasters.

He or she will work with the department director in determining where to send reporters, which reporters should go where, and what stories will be reported.

The Assistant Sports Director will help decide what national stories from the wire services, such as UPI (United Press International), AP (Associated Press), and Reuters, should be used. If an interesting sports news item comes across the wire, the individual may direct sports reporters to make calls or see if they can get additional information.

In many instances the radio station receives press releases from a variety of sources relating to the sports world. The Assistant Sports Director is often the one who reviews this information. He or she may then give the release to sports reporters for the broadcast, assign a reporter to get more information, or suggest that a reporter tries to get an interview.

Many music-oriented radio stations may have only a small sports department, made up of a sports director and perhaps an Assistant Sports Director. Individuals in these situations may perform varied functions in addition to their administrative and management duties.

In smaller stations where Assistant Sports Directors also work as sportscasters, they must usually write their own copy for the sports report. They must be able to write interesting copy that tells the story in the allotted amount of time.

Additional duties of radio Assistant Sports Directors may include:

• Handling duties of sports director in his or her absence
• Hosting sports programming
• Attending press conferences
• Performing color commentary at sporting events
• Doing newscasts
• Assisting Sports Director in developing budgets

## Salaries

Earnings for radio Assistant Sports Directors vary greatly, depending on the size of the station, its location, and popularity, and the experience and responsibilities of the individual. Annual earnings may range from approximately $23,000 to $45,000 or more.

Earnings at the lower end of the scale will go to those just starting out or with limited experience in smaller stations. Compensation goes up for those with more experience, those working in major-market stations, and those working in stations with sports-only formats.

Many Assistant Sports Directors working in radio also generate extra income by writing sports columns for newspapers or magazines.

## Employment Prospects

Employment prospects for Assistant Sports Directors are fair for those willing to work on a local or regional level.

Prospects become more limited as individuals seek to work in larger markets.

While openings may be located throughout the country, it is easier to break into the industry on the local level and work up from there. Many smaller stations hire individuals with little or no experience. While the salaries are low in these situations, the experience is worth the opportunity.

## Advancement Prospects

Advancement prospects for radio Assistant Sports Directors are good. There is a fair amount of turnover in smaller stations as individuals move on to positions at larger stations. The result of this is that the Assistant Sports Director may often be promoted to the position of sports director at the same station fairly quickly.

Another method of career advancement is for the individual to move on to a similar position at a larger or more prestigious station, resulting in increased responsibilities and earnings.

## Education and Training

Educational requirements vary for Assistant Sports Directors working in radio. Today many stations require or prefer individuals to have a four-year college degree. Good majors to consider for this type of job include communications, journalism, liberal arts, broadcasting, English, and sports administration. It should be noted that smaller stations may not have an educational requirement. However, a college background may be useful in climbing the career ladder.

## Experience, Skills, and Personality Traits

Assistant Sports Directors working in radio usually have some sort of experience in broadcasting and/or the sports industry. Some individuals begin their career in radio news or radio sports and are then promoted to the position when someone else leaves. Smaller stations may hire an individual to be the sports reporter/Assistant Sports Director if they have had experience working at their college radio station.

Management and administrative skills are necessary in this position. Communication skills are needed as well. Assistant Sports Directors usually have a genuine love of at least one sport and at least a basic understanding of the sports industry.

## Unions and Associations

Assistant Sports Directors working in radio may belong to various bargaining unions and associations, depending on the specific position they hold and the station for which they work. These include the National Association of Broadcast Employees and Technicians (NABET), the American Federation of Television and Radio Artists (AFTRA), and the Writers Guild of America (WGA). Individuals or their stations might also be members of the National Association of Broadcasters (NAB), the National Sportscasters and Sportswriters Association (NSSA), and the Radio Television News Directors Association (RTNDA).

## Tips for Entry

1. If you are interested in this type of position, get your foot in the door with any job in radio. Learn what you can and move up the ladder.
2. Get as much experience as possible working in broadcasting. Volunteer to work with your college radio station, even if you can't get into the sports department.
3. Many radio stations and associations offer internships or training programs. Internships give you on-the-job training experience and the opportunity to make important contacts.
4. Local radio stations may advertise openings on the air and on their websites. Check them out.
5. Job openings may be advertised in the newspaper classified section under headings such as "Assistant Director of Sports-Radio," "Radio," "Assistant Sports Director," and "Broadcasting."
6. Don't forget to read trade publications. *Billboard, Broadcasting,* and *Radio and Records* often have advertisements for stations with openings.

# SPORTSCASTER

## CAREER PROFILE

**Duties:** Reports sports news, events, scores, etc., on the air; interviews sports figures; gives color commentary

**Alternate Title(s):** Sports Announcer; Sports Reporter

**Salary Range:** $20,000 to $750,000+

**Employment Prospects:** Good

**Advancement Prospects:** Fair

**Best Geographical Location(s):** Smaller local communities offer opportunities for small-market stations; New York City, Los Angeles, Chicago, Atlanta, etc., for major-market stations

**Prerequisites:**

**Education or Training**—Four-year college degree required or preferred by most stations; others may accept a broadcasting-school certificate

**Experience**—Experience in college radio helpful but not always required

**Special Skills and Personality Traits**—Understanding and knowledge of sports; good speaking voice; comfortable with microphone; communications skills; ability to write well

## CAREER LADDER

```
┌─────────────────────────────────┐
│     Sportscaster for Larger,    │
│  More Prestigious Radio Station │
└─────────────────────────────────┘

┌─────────────────────────────────┐
│          Sportscaster           │
└─────────────────────────────────┘

┌─────────────────────────────────┐
│  Sports Writer, Radio Announcer, │
│          or Entry Level          │
└─────────────────────────────────┘
```

## Position Description

For those who enjoy sports, the job of a radio Sportscaster can be a dream job. Individuals in this profession generally enjoy sports and know a great deal about them. They get to attend games and other sporting events as part of their job. They might be out on the field commenting on a game or doing interviews in the locker room before or after a game.

Radio Sportscasters are the individuals responsible for reporting the sports news on-air at a radio station. Sportscasters may work for local, network, or public radio stations.

Radio stations vary by their formats, including those that are music-oriented, all talk, news, or all sports. Sportscasters' responsibilities vary depending on the type of station for which they work. Those working at all-sports radio stations generally have more specific duties than Sportscasters working at music, general talk, or news-oriented stations.

Many music-oriented radio stations may have only a small sports department. Individuals working there may be expected to perform more varied functions. These Sports-

casters are usually expected to report current sports news, developments, and scores. In most cases, radio Sportscasters are responsible for reporting national sports news as well as local developments. Individuals working in smaller local stations also report school, college, and amateur sports news.

Radio Sportscasters working at sports talk stations may have different duties and responsibilities. Depending on their job description, individuals may host a sports-oriented talk show, perform as the color commentator for sporting events, serve as a sports reporter, or interview sports personalities.

Radio Sportscasters who do "color" commentary have an interesting job. It is their responsibility to report the action they see to the listening audience and help listeners follow the action. Good "color" commentators can make an event exciting and help listeners feel as if they are watching the game themselves.

Most radio Sportscasters working at smaller stations do not specialize in just one sport. Instead they are expected to report on all sporting events. There are, however, some individuals who specialize in reporting one sport, such as basketball, baseball, or boxing. This generally occurs as the individual gains a following.

Radio Sportscasters are often expected to anchor sports reports during all newscasts in their shift. Sports reports may vary in length, depending on the station, from approximately one minute to six minutes. Longer sports spots may be expected during the morning, midday, or nightly news reports.

Individuals must usually write their own copy for the sports report. They must be able to write interesting copy that tells a story in an allotted amount of time. Some radio Sportscasters may, however, just read copy prepared by another writer. This usually depends on the size of the sports department, the specific station, and the writing talent of the Sportscaster.

Sportscasters often have their own scheduled shows one or more times a week. During these shows, they may discuss all aspects of sports, receive call-ins, or have special in-studio guests.

Many radio Sportscasters go into the field to cover sports action. They attend games, tournaments, matches, and bouts in a variety of sports. Individuals may just perform the color commentary at these events or may interview athletes, managers, officials, and fans about the events.

Sportscasters obtain information for their reports in a number of ways. Some information is gained firsthand. Other information is obtained through wire services such as UPI (United Press International), AP (Associated Press), and Reuters, each of which has a large news and sports staff as well as freelancers who report up-to-the-minute developments. These reports go over a wire or Teletype and are printed out in thousands of newsrooms and television and radio stations throughout the world. Most newspapers, magazines, and television and radio stations pay for this service, which they use daily to report the news, weather, and sports.

Sportscasters usually work shifts. These vary by radio station. Individuals can be assigned to the early-morning, midday, drive-time, evening, or night shift. Hours vary. In some stations shifts are three hours long. In others they are eight hours. A great deal of a Sportscaster's time is spent preparing for sportscasts, not necessarily on the air.

Additional duties of a radio Sportscaster may include:

• Developing feature pieces on sports-related subjects and events
• Performing research for sports reports
• Acting as sports director
• Attending press conferences

## Salaries

Earnings for radio Sportscasters vary greatly, depending on the size of the station, its location, and popularity. Earnings also are dependent on the experience, responsibilities, and popularity of the individual.

Those just starting out at a small station may only earn $20,000. Others who have more experience and are working at larger, more prestigious stations may earn between $40,000 and $100,000 or more. There are some popular radio Sportscasters who garner earnings of $750,000 or more, but these are few and far between.

It should be noted that many radio Sportscasters also generate extra income by writing sports columns for newspapers or magazines.

## Employment Prospects

Employment prospects for radio Sportscasters are good for those willing to work on a local or regional level. Job prospects become more limited as individuals seek work in larger markets.

While openings may be located throughout the country, it is easier to break into the industry on the local level and work up from there. Many smaller stations hire individuals with little or no experience. While the salaries are low in these situations, the experience is worth the opportunity.

## Advancement Prospects

Advancement prospects for radio Sportscasters are fair. Individuals often start off at a small station and after obtaining experience move on to a similar position at a larger or more prestigious station. This results in increased responsibilities and earnings.

Another way for Radio Sportscasters to climb the career ladder is by becoming the sports director at either the same or a larger station.

## Education and Training

Educational requirements vary for Sportscasters. Today most stations require or prefer individuals to have a four-year college degree. Good majors to consider for this type of job include communications, journalism, liberal arts, broadcasting, English, and sports administration.

## Experience, Skills, and Personality Traits

In some smaller stations, the job of Sportscaster is an entry-level position. In others, the individual must have experience working in radio. Many Sportscasters obtained experience in radio working at college radio stations or as sports writers for college or local newspapers.

In order to be successful at this job, individuals should have a clear speaking voice. A good command of the English language is necessary. The ability to write well is essential. Radio Sportscasters should be articulate and comfortable behind a microphone. While not required, the love of at least one sport and a basic understanding of the industry is helpful.

## Unions and Associations

Radio Sportscasters may belong to various bargaining unions and associations, depending on the specific position they hold and the station for which they work. These include the National Association of Broadcast Employees and Technicians (NABET), the American Federation of Television and Radio Artists (AFTRA), and the Writers Guild of America (WGA). Individuals or their stations might also be members of the National Association of Broadcasters (NAB), the National Sportscasters and Sportswriters Association (NSSA), and the Radio Television News Directors Association (RTNDA).

## Tips for Entry

1. Get as much experience as possible working in broadcasting. Volunteer to work with your college radio station, even if you can't get into the sports department.
2. Many radio stations and associations offer internships or training programs. Internships give you both the on-the-job training experience and the opportunity to make important contacts.
3. Make a demo tape and send it with your résumé and a cover letter to radio station owners, managers, and human resources directors. The yellow pages of the phone book will help get you started on some addresses.
4. Many local stations advertise openings on the air and on their websites. Check them out.
5. Job openings are also often advertised in the newspaper classified section under headings such as "Sportscaster," "Radio," "Sports Writer," and "Broadcasting."
6. Don't forget to read trade publications. *Billboard, Broadcasting,* and *Radio and Records* often have advertisements for stations with openings.

# SPORTS TALK SHOW HOST

## CAREER PROFILE

**Duties:** Discusses sports and sports-oriented subject on air; talks with guests and/or call-ins during radio show

**Alternate Title(s):** Sports Radio Personality; Host

**Salary Range:** $20,000 to $1 million+

**Employment Prospects:** Fair

**Advancement Prospects:** Fair

**Best Geographical Location(s):** Smaller local communities offer opportunities for small-market stations; New York City, Los Angeles, Chicago, Atlanta, etc., for major-market stations

**Prerequisites:**

**Education or Training**—College background or degree preferred or required by most stations

**Experience**—Experience in broadcasting helpful but not always required

**Special Skills and Personality Traits**—Full understanding and knowledge of sports; good speaking voice; comfortable with microphone; communications skills

## CAREER LADDER

```
┌─────────────────────────────────────┐
│   Sports Talk Show Host with         │
│   Large Following or for             │
│   More Prestigious Radio Station, or │
│   Syndicated Sports Talk Show        │
└─────────────────────────────────────┘

┌─────────────────────────────────────┐
│   Sports Talk Show Host              │
└─────────────────────────────────────┘

┌─────────────────────────────────────┐
│   Sportscaster                       │
└─────────────────────────────────────┘
```

## Position Description

For those who love sports and wish they could talk sports all the time, the job of a Sports Talk Show Host might be their dream job. In this position, the individual's main responsibility is to host a radio sports talk show. He or she also has the opportunity to share his or her opinions on sports news, events, and happenings on-air.

Sports Talk Show Hosts may host daily shows or may only host shows on specific days of the week. Shows may run from 30 minutes to full four- or five-hour shifts. Broadcasts may be live or taped.

Most talk shows are formatted in some way and sports talk shows are no exception. For example, the Host may be an expert in a certain sport and have the show center on that subject. Or the show producer or guest coordinator may invite different guests to discuss various sports-oriented subject matter. Depending on the Host and the show, the guests may include local or well-known athletes, coaches, and other sports personalities. Other guests may include print or broadcast sports reporters, sports authorities, or authors who have written sports-oriented books.

Whatever the format, it is the responsibility of the Sports Talk Show Host to keep the program moving and help make it interesting.

The Host generally introduces the subject matter and/or the guests who will appear during the show. He or she may also ask provocative questions of the guests or invite people to call in to give their opinions. Incorporating phone calls from the listening audience help give the show a special flavor. Callers may comment on the subject, ask questions, and give their own opinions. This type of format often makes people look forward to listening to programs.

Successful Hosts are experts at keeping shows interesting by bantering back and forth with guests and callers. Individuals must be able to think quickly to make this happen.

The Sports Talk Show Host on radio is often responsible for developing ideas for shows and finding guests to appear. Depending on the size and structure of the station, this responsibility might be shared or given to a show producer or guest coordinator.

The Sports Talk Show Host may be expected to read books and articles, attend sports-oriented events, and view television shows or movies about sports subjects. He or she may also be responsible for conducting preshow interviews.

Additional duties of Sports Talk Show Hosts may include:

- Introducing or reading newscasts, weathercasts, commercials, and/or public service announcements
- Making special public appearances on behalf of the station
- Handling the duties of the station's sportscaster, sports director, or sportswriter

## Salaries

Earnings for Sports Talk Show Hosts can vary tremendously. Some earn $20,000 a year, while the most successful may earn $1 million plus. Variables include the size, location, prestige, and popularity of the station, as well as the experience, expertise, and responsibilities of the individual. Earnings also are dependent to a great extent on the popularity and drawing power of the individual and his or her show.

In some stations, minimum earnings are negotiated and set by a union. It should be noted, however, that these are minimums. A Sports Talk Show Host with a following can usually negotiate higher earnings.

In some cases Sports Talk Show Hosts syndicate a show. In these situations earnings will be dependent on the number of stations that buy the show.

## Employment Prospects

Employment prospects for Sports Talk Show Hosts in radio are fair for those willing to work on a local or regional level. Job prospects become more difficult as individuals seek work in larger markets. That does not mean it is impossible. The great thing about being a Sports Talk Show Host or any other talk-show host is that shows may become very popular at any time. There are many individuals who start off with a new show that hits it big, and then the sky's the limit.

Openings may be located throughout the country. Sports Talk Show Hosts might work in small local or regional stations, larger stations, national stations, public radio, syndicated stations, or have syndicated shows.

## Advancement Prospects

Advancement prospects for Sports Talk Show Hosts are based on the type of following individuals build. Those who increase their popularity will be in greater demand and able to ask for and receive increased earnings. Individuals often start off at a small station and after obtaining experience move on to a similar position at larger or more prestigious stations. Many Sports Talk Show Hosts climb the career ladder by building a following for their show and having it syndicated. Depending on career aspirations some Sports Talk Show Hosts move into television.

## Education and Training

Educational requirements vary for Sports Talk Show Hosts. Today most stations require or prefer individuals to have a college background or degree. However, educational requirements may be waived for individuals with a great deal of expertise in the sports field.

## Experience, Skills, and Personality Traits

Experience requirements vary from station to station for Sports Talk Show Hosts. As with education requirements, experience requirements will often be waived if an individual meets other criteria and has much expertise in sports.

Experience working in broadcasting is useful, whether obtained at a college radio station, school radio club, local radio station, or as an intern.

A Sports Talk Show Host should have a pleasant speaking voice and make good use of the English language. The ability to think quickly is essential.

## Unions and Associations

Sports Talk Show Hosts may belong to various bargaining unions and associations, depending on the specific position they hold and the station for which they are working. These include the National Association of Broadcast Employees and Technicians (NABET), the American Federation of Television and Radio Artists (AFTRA), the Writers Guild of America (WGA), the National Sportscasters and Sportswriters Association (NSSA), and the Radio Television News Directors Association (RTNDA). Individuals or their stations might also be members of the National Association of Broadcasters (NAB).

## Tips for Entry

1. Get as much experience as possible working in broadcasting. Volunteer to work at your college radio station, join radio clubs, etc.
2. Many radio stations and associations offer internships or training programs. Internships give you on-the-job training experience and the opportunity to make important contacts.
3. Make a demo tape hosting a mock sports show and send it with your résumé and a cover letter to radio station owners, managers, and human resources directors. The yellow pages of the phone book will help get you started on some station addresses.
4. Many stations advertise openings on the air and on their websites. Check them out.
5. Job openings are also often advertised in the newspaper classified section under headings such as "Sports Talk Show Host," "Radio," "Radio Talk Show Host," "Broadcasting," and "Sports Broadcasting."

6. Don't forget to read trade publications. *Billboard, Broadcasting,* and *Radio and Records* often have advertisements for stations with openings.

7. Become an expert in one or more fields. Then parlay your expertise to send your career in the direction you want.

8. It is usually fairly easy to find a position in a small market because the turnover is so great. Find a job, get some experience, and climb the career ladder.

9. Consider breaking into the field on a small scale. You might want to contact your local radio station and offer to host a show on a subject in which you are an expert. Often, if you offer to find advertisers and are successful, a station will use your show.

# COLOR COMMENTATOR

## CAREER PROFILE

**Duties:** Describes the action at sporting events on-air; interjects facts and other information

**Alternate Title(s):** Play-by-Play Announcer

**Salary Range:** $20,000 to $750,000+

**Employment Prospects:** Poor

**Advancement Prospects:** Fair

**Best Geographical Location(s):** Largest number of opportunities found in areas with stations airing live sports coverage

**Prerequisites:**

**Education or Training**—College degree or background may be required or preferred

**Experience**—Experience in sports or college radio helpful but not always required

**Special Skills and Personality Traits**—Total understanding and knowledge of sport being covered; pleasant speaking voice; comfortable with microphone; communications skills; quick thinking

## CAREER LADDER

```
┌─────────────────────────────────┐
│    Color Commentator or         │
│   Sportscasters for Larger,     │
│ More Prestigious Radio Station or│
│     Sports Talk Show Host       │
└─────────────────────────────────┘

┌─────────────────────────────────┐
│      Color Commentator          │
└─────────────────────────────────┘

┌─────────────────────────────────┐
│  Sportswriter, Radio Announcer, or│
│           Athlete               │
└─────────────────────────────────┘
```

## Position Description

Color Commentators, also known as play-by-play announcers, are the eyes of the listeners during a sporting event. They watch sporting events and report the actions they see to the listening audience on-air as the action is happening. Those who are successful colorfully describe the plays of a game so that listeners can actually visualize what is occurring minute by minute. During games, Color Commentators interject interesting facts and statistics to grab the attention of the listeners. They also may compare the play on the field or the court with other games that were similar.

While announcing a sporting event, the Color Commentator often tells listeners what the situation is with the game and then explains what he or she expects players to do.

Individuals may have varied responsibilities, depending on the size and structure of the radio station and the sports department. Color Commentators may report on a variety of sports, including basketball, baseball, football, hockey, soccer, and boxing. They may provide color commentary on professional sports, college or high school sports, or a combination.

Some Color Commentators specialize in one sport. Others may handle the commentary for all the sports the station airs. It is important to note that some sports are seasonal. If the individual specializes, he or she may also work only seasonally. In these situations, the Color Commentator may handle other sports-reporting responsibilities.

In order to be effective in this type of position, the Color Commentator must know the history of the team, the players, the coaches, and the sport he or she is discussing, inside and out. He or she may give interesting facts about the players, the coaches, or the team in general to make the game even more interesting to listeners.

It's essential for Color Commentators to remain neutral while announcing on-air. As a Color Commentator, an individual can't root for his or her team. The Color Commentator must be an independent analyst.

Individuals in this profession generally enjoy sports and know a great deal about them. They get to attend games and other sporting events on the front line, as part of their job. Before or after the sporting event, they may go into the locker room to do interviews.

Additional duties of a Color Commentator may include:

- Doing regular sportscasts for station
- Performing research
- Attending press conferences
- Doing color commentary for television sports coverage

## Salaries

Earnings for radio Color Commentators vary greatly, depending on the size of the station, its location, and popularity. Earnings are also dependent on the experience, responsibilities, and popularity of the individual.

Those just starting out at a small station may earn only $20,000. Others who have more experience and are working at larger, more prestigious stations may earn $100,000 or more. Those who do the color commentary for professional basketball, football, or baseball games will earn more than their counterparts performing similar functions for college sports.

There are some popular Color Commentators who garner $750,000 or more annually, but these are few and far between.

It should be noted that many Color Commentators also generate extra income by writing sports columns for newspapers or magazines, hosting radio or television shows, etc.

## Employment Prospects

Employment prospects for radio Color Commentators are poor. The largest number of opportunities will be in areas hosting professional sports teams. Other opportunities may exist in locations where college sports are presented on radio.

## Advancement Prospects

Advancement prospects for Color Commentators are fair. They depend to some extent on career aspirations. Some individuals find similar positions at larger, more prestigious radio stations. Others find similar positions in television broadcasting.

Some Color Commentators climb the career ladder by becoming radio sportscasters at larger stations or sports directors. Still others use this career as an entry into hosting sports programs and writing sports columns.

## Education and Training

Educational requirements vary for Color Commentators working in radio. Most stations require or prefer individuals to have a four-year college degree or at least a college background. Good majors to consider for this type of job include communications, journalism, liberal arts, broadcasting, English, and sports administration. Educational requirements may be waived for individuals who have a great voice and colorful way of announcing games, or for former athletes who may be a draw for listeners.

## Experience, Skills, and Personality Traits

Experience requirements vary for this position. Some Color Commentators are former sports stars who want to get into broadcasting. In other situations, individuals may have experience in radio or print sports. Generally, the larger the station, the more experience will be required.

In order to be successful at this job, individuals should have a clear speaking voice. A total understanding of the sport being announced is essential. A good command of the English language is mandatory, as is the ability to think quickly. Radio Color Commentators should be articulate and comfortable behind a microphone.

## Unions and Associations

Color Commentators working in radio may belong to various bargaining unions and associations, depending on the specific position they hold and the station for which they work. These include the National Association of Broadcast Employees and Technicians (NABET), the American Federation of Television and Radio Artists (AFTRA), and the Writers Guild of America (WGA). Individuals or their stations might also be members of the National Association of Broadcasters (NAB), the National Sportscasters and Sportswriters Association (NSSA), and the Radio Television News Directors Association (RTNDA).

## Tips for Entry

1. Get as much experience as possible working in broadcasting. Volunteer to work with your college radio station, even if you can't get into the sports department.
2. If your school has a sports team, offer to do color commentary for the school or local radio station.
3. Many radio stations and associations offer internships or training programs. Internships give you on-the-job training experience and the opportunity to make important contacts.
4. Make a demo tape of color commentary on a sporting event and send it along with your résumé and a cover letter to radio station owners, managers, and human resources directors. The yellow pages of the phone book will help get you started on some addresses.
5. Many local stations advertise openings on the air and on their websites. Check them out.
6. Job openings are also often advertised in the newspaper classified section under headings such as "Color Commentator," "Play-by-Play Announcer," "Sportscaster," "Radio," and "Broadcasting."
7. Sometimes stations use freelancers as Color Commentators. This is a great way to get experience.
8. Look for radio stations that air live school or college sports These may consider someone with less experience.

# SPORTS PRODUCER

## CAREER PROFILE

**Duties:** Coordinates various aspects of radio sports programming; coordinates production elements; writes scripts; develops sports programming story ideas

**Alternate Title(s):** Executive Producer

**Salary Range:** $20,000 to $65,000+

**Employment Prospects:** Poor

**Advancement Prospects:** Fair

**Best Geographical Location(s):** Greatest number of opportunities will be found in areas with radio stations that air live sporting events or have sports formats

**Prerequisites:**

**Education or Training**—College degree required by most stations

**Experience**—Experience in radio broadcasting news required

**Special Skills and Personality Traits**—Understanding and knowledge of broadcasting and sports industry; communications skills; writing skills; ability to multitask and prioritize; production skills

## CAREER LADDER

```
┌──────────────────────────────────────┐
│      Sports Producer for Larger,      │
│  More Prestigious Station or Show or   │
│          Executive Producer           │
└──────────────────────────────────────┘

┌──────────────────────────────────────┐
│           Sports Producer             │
└──────────────────────────────────────┘

┌──────────────────────────────────────┐
│   Associate Sports Producer or        │
│     Assistant News Producer           │
└──────────────────────────────────────┘
```

## Position Description

Radio station sports departments vary in size depending on the specific station and its size and structure. Some sports departments may just include a sportscaster or a newscaster reporting sports news. Others are large. They may include a sports director, assistant sports director, sportscasters, sports reporters, sports researchers, sports talk-show hosts, directors, and Producers.

Generally, radio stations offering a large amount of sports programming, such as sportscasts, sports-oriented talk shows, and the airing of live sporting events, will have larger sports departments. While certain stations may utilize general producers to handle the production duties of sports programming, many stations employ Sports Producers.

The responsibilities of Sports Producers can vary depending on the situation and the type of programming the station airs. He or she may be responsible for producing station sportscasts, sports talk shows, or live sporting events. Within the scope of the job, the Sports Producer has a num-

ber of duties. It should be noted that in some stations, the Sports Producer may also be the sports reporter, sportscaster, sports director, or sports writer, or a combination of these. In situations where there is a dedicated person handling this position, it is a behind-the-scenes job.

The Sports Producer is expected to coordinate the various aspects of the sports-oriented broadcast as well as the production elements. The individual is responsible for making sure that scheduled sportscasts are the right length, done on time, and within budget.

Sports Producers responsible for the production of sports-oriented talk shows have other responsibilities. Producing this type of show takes some preparation, from determining the direction of the specific show and the intended audience to addressing technical issues. Will the show be live or taped? Will the host ask for calls from the listening audience? Will the show use guests? Will guests be in the studio with the host or will they need to use a telephone hook-up?

The Sports Producer of a sports-oriented talk show is expected to handle all show preparation. He or she must develop show ideas, concepts and themes. It is common for the Producer, sports director, and show host to hold brainstorming sessions to come up with new and innovative ideas for interesting shows.

The Producer is responsible for booking guests and setting up interviews with sports personalities, athletes, coaches, etc. The individual who has a rolodex full of phone numbers of potential guests and interview possibilities is a true asset to the show.

The Producer must make sure the studio is set up correctly and that chairs, microphones, and headphones are available for the sports-show host and all guests. He or she is responsible for directing and supervising everyone involved in the production of the programming. Depending on the specific show structure, he or she may have one or more assistants working on projects.

The Producer may be required to do research by interviewing people, reading articles and books, talking to athletes and others involved in sports, and browsing the Internet. The Sports Producer, like all other producers, may additionally have a number of writing responsibilities. He or she may write scripts, introductions for the show, possible questions for the host to ask guests, bios, etc.

If the sports talk show has call-ins, the Producer is often the individual answering the phones and screening calls while the show is on air. He or she may obtain the caller's name and question and/or comments before putting the call through to the host. Information may be fed to the host by means of computer technology or in writing. In some stations other employees handle this task.

Production duties become more of a challenge for the Sports Producer when he or she is responsible for producing the airing of live sporting events. The individual is expected to travel to the games to tape the sound for the show. He or she must make sure microphones are set up, the color commentator is there, and everything runs smoothly. As they are not physically in a typical studio, the Producer must always be on the lookout for complications and correct them quickly.

Additional duties of Sports Producers may include:

- Producing additional types of programming
- Making sure any contracts or clearances are signed by guests
- Overseeing assistant producers and other employees

## Salaries

Earnings for radio Sports Producers can vary tremendously, ranging from $20,000 and $65,000 or more. Variables include the size, location, prestige, and popularity of the station, as well as the experience, expertise, and responsibilities of the individual.

In unionized stations, minimum earnings will be negotiated for Sports Producers. It should be noted that these are only minimums and individuals may negotiate higher earnings. The highest earnings for Sports Producers generally go to individuals with a great deal of experience working in major markets or in large, sports-format stations.

## Employment Prospects

Employment prospects for Sports Producers seeking to work in radio are poor. As noted, in many stations, the responsibilities of the Sports Producer are handled by others in the news or sports department. This does not mean it is impossible to get a job in this area, just difficult.

The greatest number of employment opportunities will be located in areas hosting radio stations with a large amount of sports programming, as well as those that air live sporting events.

## Advancement Prospects

Advancement prospects for radio Sports Producers are fair once the initial position is obtained. The most common form of career advancement for Sports Producers is transferring to similar positions in larger, more prestigious stations. This results in increased responsibilities and earnings. Individuals may also climb the career ladder by producing popular talk or radio shows in sports or in another area. Other Sports Producers may find positions as executive producers in another area of radio broadcasting.

## Education and Training

Most radio stations require their Sports Producers to hold a four-year college degree. Good choices for majors include communications, broadcasting, journalism, English, public relations, marketing, sports administration, and liberal arts.

## Experience, Skills, and Personality Traits

Experience requirements for Sports Producers vary from station to station. Generally, the larger the station is, the more experience will be required.

Some individuals break into the career by working as interns or in the news or sports room in various capacities. Some Sports Producers were on-air sportscasters or newscasters who moved into producing. Other Sports Producers worked as guest coordinators or assistant or associate producers before their current position.

It is essential for radio Sports Producers to have a full understanding of broadcasting as well as the sports industry. They should be creative individuals with the ability to set priorities and multitask without getting flustered. Organizational skills are mandatory.

## Unions and Associations

Sports Producers may belong to various bargaining unions and associations, depending on the specific position they hold and the station for which they are working. These include the National Association of Broadcast Employees and Technicians (NABET), the American Federation of Television and Radio Artists (AFTRA), the Writers Guild of America (WGA), and the National Sportscasters and Sportswriters Association (NSSA). Individuals or their stations might also be members of the National Association of Broadcasters (NAB).

## Tips for Entry

1. Make sure you work at your school and/or college radio station, even if you don't work in the sports or news areas. It is important to obtain as much experience as possible working in broadcasting.

2. Many radio stations and associations offer internships or training programs. Internships give you on-the-job training experience and the opportunity to make important contacts.

3. If you attend a school with live sporting events that are aired on radio, talk to the station or your college adviser to see if they can set up an internship.

4. If you can't find a formal internship program, see if you can create your own.

5. Keep in mind that the goal in starting your career is to get your foot in the door and then move up the ladder to success. Consider every job opportunity. If you find a job in radio in any area, offer to help people in other areas when you are done with your work. These experiences will give you a broad understanding of the industry.

6. Many local stations advertise openings on the air and on their websites. Check them out.

7. Job openings are also often advertised in the newspaper classified section under headings such as "Sports Producer," "Radio," "Radio Sports Producer," "College Sports Radio Producer," and "Broadcasting."

# SPORTSWRITER

## CAREER PROFILE

**Duties:** Develops and writes copy for radio sportscasts; gathers information for stories.

**Alternate Title(s):** Broadcast Sportswriter; Copywriter

**Salary Range:** $18,000 to $45,000+

**Employment Prospects:** Poor

**Advancement Prospects:** Fair

**Best Geographical Location(s):** Opportunities may be located throughout the country in areas hosting radio stations

**Prerequisites:**

**Education or Training**—Four-year college degree required or preferred by most stations

**Experience**—Experience in college radio helpful; writing experience

**Special Skills and Personality Traits**—Understanding and knowledge of sports and sports terminology; writing skills; research skills; good command of the English language

## CAREER LADDER

```
┌─────────────────────────────────┐
│    Sportswriter for Larger,     │
│   More Prestigious Radio or     │
│ Television Station or Sportscaster │
└─────────────────────────────────┘

┌─────────────────────────────────┐
│          Sportswriter           │
└─────────────────────────────────┘

┌─────────────────────────────────┐
│  Sportswriter in Other Industry or │
│          Entry-Level            │
└─────────────────────────────────┘
```

## Position Description

A Sportswriter working in radio is responsible for developing and writing the sports news, stories, and/or scripts. These stories may be read by news anchors, in-studio reporters, or perhaps even sports reporters.

In smaller stations, the Sportswriter may also be the sportscaster or sports reporter. Depending on the size and structure of the station and the sports department, he or she may additionally be the sports director.

The Sportswriter working in radio is responsible for gathering information to be used in newscasts. He or she may obtain information through a variety of sources, including press releases, interviews, talking to people firsthand, or performing research. Some information is obtained through the wire services.

Organizations such as UPI (United Press International), AP (Associated Press), and Reuters have large news and sports staffs as well as freelance individuals who report all the up-to-the-minute developments. These reports go over a wire or Teletype and are printed out in thousands of newsrooms and television and radio stations throughout the

world. Most radio stations, as well as newspapers, magazines and television, pay for this service, which they use daily to obtain sports news in addition to general news and weather. The Sportswriter takes the information off the wires and then rewrites it to fit into the specific sports reports and format needed.

An important function of the Sportswriter is checking information for accuracy before allowing it to be aired.

In addition to writing the copy for regularly aired sportscasts, radio Sportswriters may also be expected to write sports briefs, special reports, or even the short "teases" used to attract interest in an upcoming sports report.

The Sportswriter must develop copy which is interesting, accurate, and credible, and fits into the time slot allotted for the sports. The radio Sportswriter must use punchy sentences and descriptive terms to get the point across quickly.

It is also important that the Sportswriter put together copy that is understandable by the majority of the listening audience. Unless the individual is working for a station geared exclusively toward sports, the writer must take into account that every person who listens to the sports report may not be a sports expert and therefore may not understand sports lingo.

Sportswriters working in radio often have the opportunity to attend games and other sporting events. They also may attend press conferences or go out into the field to get information.

Many Sportswriters working in radio today are also expected to write sports news and sports stories for the station's website. Depending on the station and its structure, the individual may be responsible for updating the website's sports section throughout the day. He or she may, for example, write stories about national sports news as well as local developments, school sports news, or scores for inclusion in the station website. It should be noted that in some stations, there might be a Sportswriter whose sole job is writing sports copy for the website.

Copy for sports reports may vary in length (depending on the station) from approximately one to six minutes. Longer sports spots may be expected during the morning, midday, or nightly news reports.

Sportswriters working in radio may work various shifts, depending on the size and structure of the station.

Additional duties of a radio Sports Writer may include:

- Writing feature pieces on sports-related subjects and events
- Performing research for sports reports
- Acting as sportscaster

## Salaries
Earnings for radio Sportswriters vary greatly, depending on the size of the station, its location, and popularity. Earnings are also dependent on the experience and responsibilities of the individual. Annual earnings might range from $18,000 to $45,000 or more.

Those just starting out will have earnings at the lower end of the scale. Those with more experience and who are working at larger, more prestigious stations will have earnings at the higher end of the scale.

At unionized stations, minimum earnings for Sportswriters will be negotiated by the union.

## Employment Prospects
Employment prospects for Sportswriters working in radio are poor. Smaller stations generally have their sports reporters write their own reports.

Positions may be located in larger stations or in stations geared specifically toward sports, talk, or news.

Many get into the industry by also doing sports reporting.

## Advancement Prospects
Advancement prospects for Sportswriters working in radio are fair. Individuals may advance by locating similar posi-

tions in larger, more prestigious stations. This results in increased responsibilities and earnings.

Depending on career aspirations, some Sportswriters advance by becoming sportscasters. Some individuals also go into sports writing for either television or the print industry.

## Education and Training
Educational requirements vary for radio Sportswriters. Today most stations require or prefer individuals to have a four-year college degree. Good majors to consider for this type of job include communications, journalism, liberal arts, broadcasting, English, and sports administration. Some stations will waive the educational requirement or preference in exchange for experience or a really great writing style.

## Experience, Skills, and Personality Traits
This may be an entry-level job for those who can find a position as a Sports Writer in a smaller station. Some stations will consider applicants who were involved in this type of position at their school or college radio station.

Generally, writing experience is necessary in some capacity, whether broadcast or print. The ability to write well is essential. A good command of the English language is necessary, as is an understanding of the sports industry.

## Unions and Associations
Sports Writers working in radio may belong to various bargaining unions and associations, depending on the specific position they hold and the station for which they are working. These include the National Association of Broadcast Employees and Technicians (NABET), the American Federation of Television and Radio Artists (AFTRA), and the Writers Guild of America (WGA). Individuals or their stations might also be members of the National Association of Broadcasters (NAB), the National Sportscasters and Sportswriters Association (NSSA), and the Radio Television News Directors Association (RTNDA).

## Tips for Entry
1. Get as much writing experience as possible. If you can't get experience in broadcast writing, make sure you get some in print.
2. If you are still in school, volunteer to work with your college radio station, even if you can't get into the sports department.
3. Many radio stations and associations offer internships or training programs. Internships give you on-the-job training experience and the opportunity to make important contacts.
4. Many local stations advertise openings on the air as well as on their website. Check them out.
5. Job openings are also often advertised in the newspaper classified section under headings such as "Sports Writer," "Radio," and "Broadcasting."

# SALES AND SUPPORT

# ADVERTISING SALES MANAGER

## CAREER PROFILE

**Duties:** Manages sales activities at radio station; assists salespeople, reps and account executives; recruits and hires sales staff; trains account executives; motivates department employees

**Alternate Title(s):** Sales Manager

**Salary Range:** $24,000 to $150,000+

**Employment Prospects:** Fair

**Advancement Prospects:** Fair

**Best Geographical Location(s):** Positions may be located throughout the country in small, midsize, and large radio stations

**Prerequisites:**

**Education or Training**—College background or degree required or preferred by most stations

**Experience**—Experience in broadcasting sales usually required

**Special Skills and Personality Traits**—Sales ability; organization; communications skills; ability to motivate others; articulate; understanding of broadcasting industry

## CAREER LADDER

```
┌─────────────────────────────────────┐
│ National Advertising Sales Manager at │
│ Larger, More Prestigious Station or   │
│     Advertising Sales Director        │
└─────────────────────────────────────┘

┌─────────────────────────────────────┐
│     Advertising Sales Manager         │
└─────────────────────────────────────┘

┌─────────────────────────────────────┐
│       Account Executive,              │
│ Assistant Advertising Sales Manager,  │
│     or Account Supervisor             │
└─────────────────────────────────────┘
```

## Position Description

Radio stations generate income by selling advertising space. In order to sell the commercial space, stations employ sales reps and account executives. The individual who oversees the sales staff is called the Advertising Sales Manager.

Within the scope of the job, Advertising Sales Managers have many responsibilities. One of the most important assets to a radio station is a good sales department. At some stations, the Advertising Sales Manager is responsible for recruiting and hiring the sales staff. At others, the human resources department handles the recruiting function. The Sales Manager often still does final interviews.

An important function of a Sales Manager is training the sales staff. In order to be able to sell effectively, the Sales Manager must make sure each rep knows as much about the station as possible. He or she must explain the demographics to reps and make sure that they understand all the rates and packages the station offers. The Sales Manager may hold regular meetings to inform the sales staff about any new packages and promotions the station is offering.

The individual may also teach the sales staff about selling techniques utilizing station policies. The Sales Manager may provide training for the sales staff on a one-on-one basis or may be expected to develop formal group training programs. In some cases the Sales Manager may be expected to seek out formal training programs offered by outside vendors.

Successful Sales Managers help their sales staff develop a strong sales pitch. This is often accomplished by giving salespeople information on the station as well as on the competition. This is essential so that the sales reps are knowledgeable about the strengths and weaknesses of the station and competing media in the marketplace.

The Advertising Sales Manager at a radio station is responsible for assigning accounts to each sales rep. In many instances, he or she will be expected to determine territories as well. Assignment of territories varies depending on the station structure and size. Territories may be divided by geographic location, such as towns or counties in the listening area. Territories may also be divided by types of business. Some stations also have salespeople who deal exclusively with national clients.

On occasion, potential customers will call a station to obtain information about the station, its rates, and demographics. These calls are given to the Sales Manager, who in turn refers them to the appropriate advertising account representatives.

The Sales Manager is expected to develop various promotional packages for advertisers in order to induce customers to purchase more commercial spots. Within the scope of this project, the individual must determine discount and package rates for customers while trying to increase monies coming in from advertising. These packages may include specials designed to induce new customers to try the station and test its effectiveness for their business. He or she may work with the station manager, promotion manager, and/or marketing manager on this project.

The Sales Manager is responsible for developing rate cards, information sheets on the station and its demographics, and other important fact sheets that may help the sales staff better sell commercial space. He or she may actively seek out testimonials from customers who are pleased with results from advertising on the station.

The Sales Manager at a radio station is expected to help account representatives bring in new business. He or she may direct the sales staff in methods to attract new business as well as motivating them to make cold calls to potential customers.

The Sales Manager is expected to assist the sales staff in their job. He or she is in place to help them succeed. While some individuals who are hired are natural born salespeople, others may need some help in picking up the basics. The Sales Manager may accompany new reps on sales calls to current station clients as well as prospective buyers to show them the ropes. The Manager may also go with the rep to visit clients in their places of work or set up sales meetings in other locations when the rep needs some assistance clinching sales.

The Sales Manager is expected to set goals for the sales staff. He or she must be aware of how salespeople are performing and meeting quotas. An important function of the Sales Manager is motivating the sales staff. Selling commercial space is not always easy. Every meeting does not always culminate in a sale. It is essential for the sales staff to remain upbeat and motivated. The Sales Manager needs to be effective in this task or risk losing his or her sales staff.

Additional duties of radio Advertising Sales Managers may include:

• Handling paperwork
• Writing copy for clients' commercials
• Developing sales materials, letters, and brochures
• Representing the station at events
• Handling national clients
• Acting as sales reps or account executives

## Salaries

Annual earnings for Advertising Sales Managers vary greatly, ranging from $24,000 to $150,000 or more, depending on a number of variables. These include the size, location, prestige, and popularity of the radio station. Other factors affecting earnings include the experience and responsibilities of the individual.

It should be noted that some Sales Managers in radio also act as salespeople. In these cases, they may also earn commissions on sales. While percentages can vary from station to station, they might range from 10% to 20%, with the average commission about 15%.

## Employment Prospects

Employment prospects for Advertising Sales Managers seeking to work in radio are fair. Those who are interested in entering this field can usually start by finding opportunities in small- or medium-market radio, get some experience, and move up the ladder.

There are many radio stations located throughout the country. Individuals may need to relocate to take a position.

## Advancement Prospects

Advancement prospects are fair for radio Advertising Sales Managers. There are several ways to climb the career ladder. The most common is to find a similar position in a larger or more prestigious station. Another option is to find a position as a sales director.

## Education and Training

Most stations prefer or require their Advertising Sales Managers to hold a college degree. Courses that might prove useful in selling include advertising, sales, business, English, psychology, sociology, writing, and communications. Seminars and workshops offered through private groups or trade associations may also be useful to the individual in honing sales skills.

Educational requirements may be waved by the station if the applicant has a proven track record in the field.

## Experience, Skills, and Personality Traits

Advertising Sales Managers working in radio need the ability to motivate others. They should be articulate, personable, and outgoing. Individuals should enjoy being around and dealing with people. An understanding of the broadcast industry is essential.

## Unions and Associations

Advertising Sales Managers or their stations may be members of their specific state's broadcasting association, the American Advertising Federation (AAF), the National Association of Broadcasters (NAB), the National Association of

Broadcast Employees and Technicians (NABET), and/or the Radio and Advertising Bureau (RAB).

## Tips for Entry

1. Many radio stations and associations offer internships or training programs. Internships give you on-the-job training experience and the opportunity to make important contacts.
2. Get experience selling. You might, for example, want to volunteer to sell ads for a local not-for-profit or civic group's journal. This is great for hands-on experience and to add to your résumé.
3. Many local stations advertise openings on the air and on their websites. Check them out.
4. Job openings are also often advertised in the newspaper classified section under headings such as "Advertising Sales Manager," "Advertising," "Radio," "Broadcasting," "Radio Sales," and "Broadcasting Sales."
5. Don't forget to read trade publications. *Billboard, Broadcasting,* and *Radio and Records* often have advertisements for stations with openings.
6. Send your résumé and a short cover letter to radio stations you are interested in working for. You can never tell when an opening exists.

# REGIONAL SALES MANAGER

## CAREER PROFILE

**Duties:** Manages regional sales activities for group of radio stations; assists salespeople, reps, and account executives; recruits and hires sales staff; trains and motivates sales staff

**Alternate Title(s):** Regional Advertising Sales Manager

**Salary Range:** $24,000 to $150,000+

**Employment Prospects:** Fair

**Advancement Prospects:** Fair

**Best Geographical Location(s):** Positions may be located throughout the country

**Prerequisites:**

**Education or Training**—College background or degree required or preferred by most stations

**Experience**—Experience in broadcasting sales required

**Special Skills and Personality Traits**—Sales ability; organization; communications skills; ability to motivate others; articulate; understanding of broadcasting industry

## CAREER LADDER

```
┌─────────────────────────────────────┐
│   Regional Sales Manager at Larger,  │
│      More Prestigious Station,       │
│    General Sales Manager, or         │
│     Advertising Sales Director       │
└─────────────────────────────────────┘

┌─────────────────────────────────────┐
│                                     │
│      Regional Sales Manager         │
│                                     │
└─────────────────────────────────────┘

┌─────────────────────────────────────┐
│        Account Executive,           │
│  Assistant Advertising Sales Manager,│
│      or Account Supervisor          │
└─────────────────────────────────────┘
```

## Position Description

Today many radio stations are owned by media or broadcasting conglomerates. These groups may own anywhere from two to 20 stations or more. In some cases the group owns a number of stations in close proximity to each other. This often affects the way advertising sales are handled. To begin with, if stations are relatively close to each other, the sales staff may be combined. A positive ramification for advertising sales may be that potential advertisers might want to advertise on more than one station.

In situations such as this, media groups may employ a Regional Sales Manager. This individual is responsible for managing the regional sales activities for a group of stations. Within the scope of the job, the Regional Sales Manager has a number of responsibilities.

The Regional Sales Manager and regional sales staff often work out of a main office location. The sales staff may also have offices in the various radio stations the media group owns.

The Regional Sales Manager assigns each member of the sales staff to a different territory. In some situations, territories may be assigned on the basis of geographic break-

downs. In others, territories may be assigned by the type of business. For example, one territory might cover retail, another restaurants and the hospitality industry, and still another business accounts. Territories might also be assigned by areas where each specific station is located.

When a media group owns a number of stations in an area, they often put together attractive packages to induce advertisers to buy spots on more than one station. What this means is that an advertiser might take 100 spots on one station, 60 on another, and 45 on yet another.

The Regional Sales Manager often works with station management, the general sales manager, marketing department, and/or the promotion department developing advertising packages. Packages might include specials designed to induce new customers to try one or more of the stations. Packages might also help advertisers determine which station might be more effective.

Radio stations generate most of their income by selling advertising space. As the income of stations is directly related to advertising sales, a good sales staff is essential. An important part of the job of the Regional Sales Manager is recruiting the best sales staff possible. To do this, the

Regional Sales Manager may place ads, review résumés, and interview potential salespeople. Even if the stations have human resources departments to handle these functions, the Regional Sales Manager will often sit in on final interviews and help in choosing just the right candidates.

Once members of the sales staff are hired, the Regional Sales Manager is expected to make sure that they are trained. In order for the sales staff to sell effectively, the Sales Manager is responsible for making sure they know as much as possible about all the promotions, rates, and packages being offered.

The Regional Sales Manager is expected to develop a variety of formal and informal training programs for the sales staff. Some training may be done on a one-on-one basis. Others may be done in groups. Sometimes, the Regional Sales Manager seeks out formal training programs offered by outside vendors.

The Regional Sales Manager is responsible for coordinating the sales activities of the sales staff to make sure everyone is doing an effective job. If he or she sees a problem, the individual will talk to the specific sales rep to determine how it can be solved. The Sales Manager keeps in close contact with all sales staff through meetings, phone, fax, and e-mail.

The Regional Sales Manager may be required to travel to areas where the various stations are located.

Regional Sales Managers must direct the sales staff in ways to attract new business, as well as motivate the staff to handle current customers. Individuals are expected not only to set goals for the sales staff but also to make sure they meet them as well.

Additional duties of radio Regional Sales Managers may include:

- Handling paperwork
- Developing sales materials, letters, and brochures
- Acting as sales reps or account executives

## Salaries

Annual earnings for Regional Sales Managers working in radio vary greatly. There are some Regional Sales Managers earning $24,000 and others earning $150,000 or more. Variables affecting earnings include the size, location, prestige, and popularity of the group of radio stations the individual works for as well as the experience and responsibilities of the individual.

It should be noted that some Regional Sales Managers in radio also act as salespeople. In these cases they may also earn commissions on sales. While percentages can vary from station to station, they might range from 10% to 20%, with the average commission about 15%.

## Employment Prospects

Employment prospects for Regional Sales Managers seeking to work in radio are fair, although individuals may need to relocate for a position. Opportunities may be located throughout the country. Media groups may own small-, medium-, or major-market stations or a combination.

## Advancement Prospects

Advancement prospects are fair for Regional Sales Managers. One of the most common methods for career advancement is for the individual to locate a similar position at a larger, more prestigious group of stations. Some individuals become advertising sales directors. Others may move into similar positions in television broadcasting.

## Education and Training

Most media conglomerates require their Regional Sales Managers to hold a college degree. Educational requirements may be waived if an applicant has a proven track record in the field.

Helpful courses in this field include advertising, sales, business, English, psychology, sociology, writing, and communications. Seminars and workshops offered through private groups or trade associations may also be useful to the individual in honing sales skills.

## Experience, Skills, and Personality Traits

In order to become a radio Regional Sales Manager individuals must have extensive experience in radio sales. Many have worked their way up the career ladder, starting as sales reps and account executives and then moving into account supervisor or assistant sales manager positions.

Regional Sales Managers must have a total understanding of the broadcast industry. The ability to motivate others and keep them in a positive frame of mind is essential. Individuals in this position must like dealing with people on a variety of levels. They need to be personable and outgoing with sales skills. As in all other sales management positions, the ability to multitask and work under pressure without getting flustered is mandatory.

## Unions and Associations

Regional Sales Managers or their stations may be members of their specific state's broadcasting association, the American Advertising Federation (AAF), the National Association of Broadcasters (NAB), the National Association of Broadcast Employees and Technicians (NABET), and/or the Radio and Advertising Bureau (RAB).

## Tips for Entry

1. Contact radio stations and media groups to find out about internship opportunities. If there are none available, ask about the possibility of creating one. Internships give you on-the-job training experience and the opportunity to make important contacts.

2. If you have sales ability you can sell anything. Get as much experience selling as possible. If you're still in school, get additional experience by volunteering to sell ads for a local not-for-profit or civic group's journal. This is great for hands-on experience and to add to your résumé.

3. Check out radio-station and media-group websites. Many advertise openings.

4. Job openings may also be advertised in the newspaper classified section under headings such as "Advertising Sales Manager," "Regional Sales Manager," "Regional Advertising Manager," "Regional Sales Manager-Radio," "Advertising," "Radio," "Broadcasting," "Radio Sales," and "Broadcasting Sales."

5. Don't forget to read trade publications. *Billboard, Broadcasting,* and *Radio and Records* often have advertisements for stations with openings.

6. Send your résumé and a short cover letter to media groups you are interested in working for. You can never tell when an opening exists.

7. If you're interested in this area, get your foot in the door by selling advertising for a radio station, learn as much as you can, and move up the ladder!

# NATIONAL SALES MANAGER

## CAREER PROFILE

**Duties:** Manages national sales activities for radio station; assists national salespeople, reps, and account executives; recruits and hires national sales staff; trains national account executives; motivates sales staff

**Alternate Title(s):** National Advertising Sales Manager

**Salary Range:** $24,000 to $150,000+

**Employment Prospects:** Fair

**Advancement Prospects:** Fair

**Best Geographical Location(s):** Positions may be located throughout the country in small, midsize, and large radio stations

**Prerequisites:**

**Education or Training**—College background or degree required or preferred by most stations

**Experience**—Experience in broadcasting sales usually required

**Special Skills and Personality Traits**—Sales ability; organization; communications skills; ability to motivate others; articulate; understanding of broadcasting industry

## CAREER LADDER

```
┌─────────────────────────────────────┐
│  National Sales Manager at Larger,   │
│    More Prestigious Station or       │
│      Advertising Sales Director      │
└─────────────────────────────────────┘

┌─────────────────────────────────────┐
│       National Sales Manager         │
└─────────────────────────────────────┘

┌─────────────────────────────────────┐
│         Account Executive,           │
│  Assistant Advertising Sales Manager,│
│        or Account Supervisor         │
└─────────────────────────────────────┘
```

## Position Description

Radio stations generate income by selling advertising space. Sometimes the commercial space is sold to local accounts such as banks, retail stores, restaurants, or businesses in the area. Many radio stations also sell commercial space to national accounts. Examples of national accounts might be Pepsi, Coke, American Airlines, Burger King, and Budweiser. The individual in charge of overseeing the national advertising sales staff is the National Sales Manager. This individual, who might also be referred to as the national advertising sales manager, has varied duties, depending on the size and structure of the station.

The National Sales Manager is expected to work with the national sales representatives. He or she may recruit and hire the national staff or may leave this function to the human resources department. One way or the other, the National Sales Manager will often sit in on final interviews and help in choosing just the right candidates.

Some stations also work directly with national sales-rep firms. Reps in these companies are used to sell the national

advertising space. The National Sales Manager in these cases may interview reps from the firm or the firm itself to make sure it is right for the station.

No matter the situation, the National Sales Manager is expected to make sure that reps solicit and sell commercial spots on the station to national accounts. In many instances this may involve also working with the advertising agencies which represent large corporations.

Sales reps or rep firms may have regional sales offices in cities throughout the country. The National Sales Manager is expected to visit these offices on a regular basis to coordinate sales activities and ensure that everyone is doing an effective job. He or she may be required to travel extensively, depending on the areas where sales offices are located. The National Sales Manager may also keep in close contact with sales reps by phone, fax, and/or e-mail.

An important function of the National Sales Manager is training his or her sales staff. In order to be able to sell effectively, the National Sales Manager must make sure each rep knows as much about the station as possible. He or she must explain the demographics to reps and make sure they understand all the rates and packages the station offers.

The National Sales Manager may hold regular meetings to inform the sales reps about any new packages and promotions the station is offering. During these meetings, the National Sales Manager may also go over format changes or other pertinent information that reps may use to make the station more appealing to advertisers.

The National Sales Manager may provide training for the national sales staff on a one-on-one basis or may be expected to develop formal group training programs. In some cases, he or she may be expected to seek out formal training programs offered by outside vendors.

It is essential to success for the National Sales Manager to help the national sales reps develop a strong sales pitch. This is especially important when dealing with national accounts. When a sales executive or rep is attempting to sell ad space to a local advertiser, generally they at least know of the station. Those selling to national accounts may not have that luxury. Advertising agencies for national advertisers may be hundreds or thousands of miles away.

The National Sales Manager is responsible for assigning accounts to each sales rep. In many instances, he or she will be expected to determine territories as well. Assignment of territories varies, depending on the station structure and size. Territories may be divided by geographic location or types of business.

In many stations, the National Sales Manager must develop various promotional packages for national advertisers in order to induce them to purchase an advertising package. Within the scope of this project, the individual must determine discount and package rates for customers while trying to increase monies coming in for advertising. These packages may include specials designed to induce new customers to try the station and test its effectiveness for their business. He or she may work with the advertising sales director, station manager, promotion manager, and/or marketing manager on this project. As noted, in order to sell commercial space to national accounts, sales must often go through advertising agencies, so packages must be attractive to the ad agencies as well.

The National Sales Manager works with the sales director in developing national rate cards, information sheets on the station and its demographics, and other important fact sheets that may help the sales reps better sell commercial space.

National advertising rates for commercial space are often higher than local rates. This is because advertising agencies buy the advertising space for clients at the higher rate and then charge the advertiser a commission. This is common business practice with advertising agencies.

The National Sales Manager is responsible for helping account and sales representatives bring in new business. He or she may direct the sales staff in methods to attract new business as well as motivating them to make cold calls to potential customers.

The National Sales Manager, like every other sales manager, is expected to assist the sales staff in their job. He or she is in place to help them succeed. At times, the individual may accompany reps on sales calls or attend meetings to help close a sale with a big advertiser.

National Sales Managers set goals for the national sales staff. It is up to the individual to keep abreast of how each sales rep is performing and ensuring that they are meeting sales goals. Within the scope of this function, he or she must constantly motivate the sales staff.

In smaller stations, the advertising sales manager may be responsible for handling the duties of a National Sales Manager. He or she may also be expected to bring in new national accounts.

Additional duties of radio National Sales Managers may include:

- Handling paperwork
- Dealing with advertising agencies
- Developing sales materials, letters, and brochures
- Representing the station at events
- Traveling to visit sales offices in various locations
- Acting as sales reps or account executives

## Salaries

Annual earnings for National Sales Managers vary greatly. There are some National Sales Managers earning $24,000 and others earning $150,000 or more. Variables affecting earnings include the size, location, prestige, and popularity of the radio station, as well as the experience and responsibilities of the individual.

It should be noted that some radio National Sales Managers also act as salespeople. In these cases they may also earn commissions on sales. While percentages vary from station to station, they can range from 10% to 20%, with the average commission about 15%.

## Employment Prospects

Employment prospects for National Sales Managers seeking to work in radio are poor. While there are many radio stations located throughout the country, some don't have a National Sales Manager but rather give stations these responsibilities to the general sales manager or sales director.

Opportunities may be more plentiful in mid-market and larger stations. Those seeking this type of career may need to relocate to find a position.

## Advancement Prospects

Advancement prospects are fair for National Sales Managers. One of the most common methods for career advancement is for the individual to locate a similar position at a larger, more prestigious station. Another option is to find a position as a sales director.

## Education and Training

Educational requirements vary from station to station. Most stations prefer or require the National Sales Managers to hold a college degree. Smaller stations may accept a college background. Educational requirements also may be waived by a station if an applicant has a proven track record in the field.

Helpful courses in this field include advertising, sales, business, English, psychology, sociology, writing, and communications. Seminars and workshops offered through private groups or trade associations also may be useful to the individual in honing sales skills.

## Experience, Skills, and Personality Traits

National Sales Managers working in radio generally have worked in radio sales. Those who are interested in entering this field often begin in a position where they may be handling national sales as well as local ones. Once they have some experience under their belt, they move to positions where they are just handling national sales.

Individuals need the ability to motivate others and keep them in a positive frame of mind. They should enjoy being around others and like dealing with people on a variety of levels.

National Sales Managers working in radio should be articulate, personable, and outgoing. An understanding of the broadcast industry is essential. The ability to multitask and work under pressure is mandatory in this field.

## Unions and Associations

National Sales Managers or their stations may be members of their specific state's broadcasting association, the Ameri-can Advertising Federation (AAF), the National Association of Broadcasters (NAB), the National Association of Broadcast Employees and Technicians (NABET), and/or the Radio and Advertising Bureau (RAB).

## Tips for Entry

1. Get as much experience selling as possible. You might, for example, want to volunteer to sell ads for a local not-for-profit or civic group's journal. This is great for hands-on experience and to add to your résumé.
2. Internships give you on-the-job training experience and the opportunity to make important contacts. Many radio stations and associations offer internships or training programs. Contact stations and inquire about opportunities.
3. Many local stations advertise openings on the air and on their websites. Check them out.
4. Job openings are also often advertised in the newspaper classified section under headings such as "Advertising Sales Manager," "National Sales Manager," "Advertising," "Radio," "Broadcasting," "Radio Sales," and "Broadcasting Sales."
5. Don't forget to read the trade publications. *Billboard, Broadcasting,* and *Radio and Records* often have advertisements for stations with openings.
6. Send your résumé and a short cover letter to radio stations you are interested in working for. You can never tell when an opening exists.
7. If you're interested in this area, get your foot in the door selling advertising for a radio station, learn as much as you can, and move up the ladder.

# ADVERTISING ACCOUNT REPRESENTATIVE

## CAREER PROFILE

**Duties:** Sells commercial air time to advertisers; services current accounts; brings in new accounts

**Alternate Title(s):** Sales Representative; Salesman; Saleswoman; Salesperson; Sales Rep; Account Rep; Sales Executive

**Salary Range:** $18,000 to $95,000+

**Employment Prospects:** Excellent

**Advancement Prospects:** Excellent

**Best Geographical Location(s):** Positions may be located throughout the country in small, midsize, and large radio stations

**Prerequisites:**

**Education or Training**—College background or degree required or preferred by most stations

**Experience**—Experience in sales helpful but not always required

**Special Skills and Personality Traits**—Sales skills; persuasive; articulate; understanding of broadcasting industry; self-motivated; aggressive; personable; outgoing nature

## CAREER LADDER

```
┌─────────────────────────────────┐
│  Account Executive at Larger, More │
│  Prestigious Station or Sales Manager │
└─────────────────────────────────┘

┌─────────────────────────────────┐
│  Advertising Account Executive   │
└─────────────────────────────────┘

┌─────────────────────────────────┐
│  Entry-Level or                  │
│  Sales Position in Other Industry │
└─────────────────────────────────┘
```

## Position Description

Radio stations make their money through revenue generated by selling advertising. Those responsible for selling commercial space to clients who want to advertise on the radio station are called Advertising Account Representatives. Depending on the station, individuals might also be referred to as sales representatives, salespeople, sales reps, account reps, or sales executives.

Advertising Account Representatives work with the station's sales manager, who assigns accounts to each rep. The individual is then responsible for servicing those accounts. The individual may call or visit the advertisers on a regular basis to determine when they want to advertise. Account Representatives must find out how many "spots," or commercials, the advertiser wants to run, as well as the length and the duration of the campaign. If the advertiser is running a specific commercial, the Advertising Account Representative must find out if the same commercial will be used for all spots or if the client wants to change their commercials.

The Advertising Account Representative is expected to tell clients about new promotions the station is running, as well as available discounts and package rates. Many Advertising Account Representative also offer suggestions for copy or content of commercials.

Potential customers often call the station to get more information about the station, its rates, and demographics. When these calls come in regarding possible advertising, the sales manager refers them to the appropriate Advertising Account Representative.

He or she must then either call them or send out advertising kits with rate cards, informational sheets on the station and its demographics, testimonials from other advertisers, etc. In some cases, the Advertising Account Representative will schedule an appointment with the potential client to discuss their advertising needs. In many situations, the Advertising Account Representative offers special discounts to new advertisers in order to get them to try advertising on the station and see if it is effective.

One of the major responsibilities of Advertising Account Representatives is to bring in new business. The individual may make what is known as "cold" calls to potential advertisers. These calls are made to people who have not expressed an interest in advertising on the station. After identifying himself or herself and the station affiliation, the Account Rep attempts to set up an appointment to tell the potential advertiser more about the station and advertising opportunities.

Every call will not result in an appointment. The Advertising Account Representative must have the ability to accept rejection without taking it personally. While these are difficult calls for some people, talented Advertising Account Representatives often love the challenge of obtaining new clients.

Another way Advertising Account Representatives increase business is by increasing the number of spots a current advertiser buys. This often occurs when a client is running special promotions, contests, sales, or events. Conversely, the client might increase their purchase of advertising spots if the station is running specials, discounts, promotions, or packages. It is up to the Advertising Account Representative to constantly update customers so they are aware of every advertising possibility.

The sales manager determines how territories will be set up for the sales staff. At some stations Advertising Account Representatives are free to sell commercial space to any advertiser. At other stations territories might be set up by types of clients, such as restaurants and food establishments, retail shops and stores, and entertainment. Still other stations set up territories by geographical locations.

Many radio stations provide training sessions for the sales staff. These may be in-house or may be offered by an outside training force. Advertising Account Representatives are expected to attend these training sessions and seminars as well as weekly staff meetings. During these meetings the sales manager may make suggestions regarding selling, offer helpful sales techniques, and discuss advertising specials and promotions the station is offering.

The Advertising Account Representative must stay up-to-date on various rates, discounts, and packages the station offers. He or she should also be able to explain them to advertisers in an easy-to-understand manner.

Many successful Advertising Account Representatives help develop marketing and advertising ideas for current or potential customers. Individuals also often brainstorm with clients in order to come up with effective advertising ideas. The more effective the ads and commercials are, the more customers will purchase.

A major responsibility of Advertising Account Representatives is keeping accurate records of advertisements sold, billings, etc. Individuals must write orders and make sure they get to the appropriate people and department at the radio station. In many situations, the Advertising Account Representatives are responsible for obtaining client approval of copy and commercials before they are aired.

In order to be successful, Advertising Account Representatives continually check with clients to make sure they are happy with their commercials and are being billed properly, as well as whether they want additional ads.

As no one is continually looking over the shoulder of Advertising Account Representatives, individuals must know how to set priorities and organize the work day. Advertising Account Representatives may work in the field or from their desk, making calls to current and potential clients. While individuals may work normal business hours, they may arrange sales calls after hours, in the evening or on weekends. Those who are most successful in this job are always trying to sell, even in social situations.

Additional duties of radio Advertising Account Representatives may include:

- Collecting success stories and testimonials from customers, illustrating how advertising on the station increased their business
- Writing copy for clients' commercials
- Representing the station at events

## Salaries

Annual earnings for Advertising Account Representatives can range from $18,000 to $95,000 or more, depending on a number of variables. These include the size and location of the radio station and the sales ability of the Advertising Account Representative. Individuals who sell more, earn more.

The reason many people love this job so much is that the sky's the limit on earnings. Most Advertising Account Representatives are paid on a commission basis. This means that for every dollar of advertising space an individual sells, he or she receives a percentage as part of his or her salary. Percentages can vary from station to station and might range from 10% to 20%, with the average commission about 15%.

It should be noted that many stations offer a weekly or monthly draw against salary to Advertising Account Representatives. They do this for a number of reasons; the first of which is to help beginning Advertising Account Representatives get into the swing of selling. The second is to adjust the take home pay of individuals in case they have had a "bad" week or month.

Radio stations also generally offer their Advertising Account Representatives fringe-benefit packages.

## Employment Prospects

Employment prospects for Advertising Account Representatives seeking to work in radio are excellent. Individuals who are sales oriented, aggressive, and hardworking will always be in demand.

There are many radio stations located throughout the country. Each of these stations hire at least one or two Advertising Account Representatives. Most hire more.

Those who are interested in entering this field can usually start by finding opportunities in small- or medium-market radio stations. As there is a high turnover in these positions because of advancement, there are usually openings.

## Advancement Prospects

Advancement prospects are excellent for Advertising Account Representatives. There are a number of ways to climb the career ladder. The most common is to sell more commercial space, which will increase earnings.

Advertising Account Representatives may also advance by finding similar jobs at larger, more prestigious stations, which charge more for their commercials, or by getting better selling "territories." Both of these will result in increased earnings for the Advertising Account Representative.

A third method of career advancement for Advertising Account Representatives is to become a sales manager at a radio station.

## Education and Training

Most stations prefer or require their Advertising Account Representatives to hold a college degree. Courses that might prove useful in selling include advertising, sales, business, English, psychology, sociology, writing, and communications. Seminars and workshops offered through private groups or trade associations also may be useful to the individual in honing sales skills.

Educational requirements may be waived by the station if the applicant is eager, aggressive, and shows potential for selling.

## Experience, Skills, and Personality Traits

Advertising Account Representatives working in radio should be articulate, personable, and outgoing. They should enjoy being around and dealing with people. Sales skills are essential.

This is not a position for the timid. Advertising Account Representatives must be confident people who believe in themselves and their station and can be pleasantly aggressive.

Self-motivation and the ability to work without constant supervision are mandatory. Individuals must be able to plan out their work day, make appointments, make calls, and go to appointments without someone looking over their shoulder.

An ability to work with numbers is helpful in figuring out costs and rates of ads and packages.

## Unions and Associations

Advertising Account Representatives or their stations may be members of their specific state's broadcasting association, the American Advertising Federation (AAF), the National Association of Broadcasters (NAB), the National Association of Broadcast Employees and Technicians (NABET), and/or the Radio and Advertising Bureau (RAB).

## Tips for Entry

1. Get as much selling experience as possible. You might, for example, want to volunteer to sell ads for a local not-for-profit or civic group's journal. This is great for hands-on experience and to add to your résumé.
2. Many radio stations and associations offer internships or training programs. Internships give you on-the-job training experience and the opportunity to make important contacts.
3. Many local stations advertise openings on the air and on their websites. Check them out.
4. Job openings are also often advertised in the newspaper classified section under headings such as "Advertising Account Representatives," "Advertising," "Radio," "Broadcasting," "Radio Sales," and "Broadcasting Sales."
5. Don't forget to read trade publications. *Billboard, Broadcasting,* and *Radio and Records* often have advertisements for stations with openings.
6. Send your résumé and a short cover letter to radio stations you are interested in working for. You can never tell when an opening exists.

# ADVERTISING COPYWRITER

## CAREER PROFILE

**Duties:** Develops and writes copy and scripts for client and company advertisements and commercials aired on radio station

**Alternate Title(s):** Copywriter

**Salary Range:** $21,000 to $48,000+

**Employment Prospects:** Good

**Advancement Prospects:** Good

**Best Geographical Location(s):** All locations offer employment possibilities; smaller local communities offer opportunities for small-market stations; New York City, Los Angeles, Chicago, Atlanta, etc., for major-market stations

**Prerequisites:**

**Education or Training**—College background or degree required or preferred by most stations

**Experience**—Experience requirements vary; writing experience necessary

**Special Skills and Personality Traits**—Creativity; good writing skills; command of the English language; persuasiveness; understanding of advertising

## CAREER LADDER

```
┌──────────────────────────────────────┐
│  Copywriter in Larger, More Prestigious │
│  Station, Senior Station Copywriter, or │
│       Copywriter in Agency              │
└──────────────────────────────────────┘

┌──────────────────────────────────────┐
│       Advertising Copywriter            │
└──────────────────────────────────────┘

┌──────────────────────────────────────┐
│          Entry-Level or                 │
│     Writer in Other Industry            │
└──────────────────────────────────────┘
```

## Position Description

Radio stations make their money by selling advertising. The individual responsible for writing the ads heard on the air is the Advertising Copywriter.

While most major companies advertising on national radio use the services of an advertising agency to write the copy for their commercials, there are many local, cable, and syndicated advertisements for which copy must be developed. These are generally prepared by the advertising department of the station.

The Copywriter works in the advertising department of the radio station. He or she has varied responsibilities and duties that depend on the size and structure of the station and its advertising department. No matter what the responsibilities, the main function of the Advertising Copywriter in a radio station is to develop creative, effective, unique, and stimulating copy for commercials.

Individuals must write copy that fits into the time allotted for commercial spots, so the Copywriter must be able to

condense his or her words into the required time frame of the commercial. Depending on the station, these spots might range from 30 seconds to two minutes. The Copywriter must also be adept at writing copy for longer ads.

Copywriters working for smaller stations are often responsible for everything from conceiving ad ideas to producing ads and getting them on the air. Those working for larger stations often have more specific duties. These individuals generally are just responsible for writing the commercial copy.

One of the more difficult aspects of the job of an Advertising Copywriter is that clients often have their own ideas of how commercials should sound and information they want included. It is up to the Copywriter to develop effective commercials that include what the client wants.

Copywriters often have to write a number of different drafts of copy for commercials. The copy must then be approved by the advertiser. Even if the advertiser approves the copy, the ad might run a couple of times and then the advertiser might decide it should be changed. At that point, the Copywriter will have to start all over.

Radio commercials may have different styles. The Copywriter must have the ability to write all styles, from straight copy to dialogue. The dialogue must be crisp, clear, and believable. In many cases, the Copywriter adds instructions for sound effects or voice-overs that will make the ad more effective.

Copywriters who are successful have the talent to write commercial copy in a way that stimulates enough interest in a product or service to make a consumer buy a product or call for the service.

Copywriters often work on multiple projects at the same time, many with tight deadlines. Individuals in this position are usually responsible to either a senior copywriter or the advertising manager.

Additional duties of radio Advertising Copywriters may include:

- Selling commercial space
- Producing commercials
- Acting as the "talent" for reading commercial dialogue that is taped

## Salaries

Earnings for radio Advertising Copywriters can range from approximately $21,000 to $48,000 and up. Variables include the size, location, and prestige of the station, as well as the experience and responsibilities of the individual.

## Employment Prospects

Employment prospects for Advertising Copywriters at radio stations are good. Those with little or no experience might find positions at smaller local or regional stations. Those who have experience and have proved themselves can often find openings in larger stations throughout the country.

## Advancement Prospects

Advancement prospects are good for creative, aggressive Copywriters working in radio advertising departments. Some find similar positions at larger, more prestigious stations. Many Copywriters climb the career ladder by becoming senior copywriters at the same or another station. Others move into the copywriting field in advertising agencies.

## Education and Training

Educational requirements among Advertising Copywriters in radio stations vary. Most stations require or prefer individuals to have a college background or degree. Good choices for majors include journalism, communications, English, public relations, marketing, advertising, and liberal arts.

There are many seminars, workshops, and courses in copywriting and advertising offered throughout the country. These are helpful for both the educational benefits and the opportunity to make important contacts.

## Experience, Skills, and Personality Traits

Experience requirements vary from station to station. Some smaller stations have no experience requirements for individuals who can demonstrate good copywriting skills. Larger stations often prefer some professional experience.

An understanding of the advertising and broadcast industries is essential. Advertising Copywriters working in broadcasting should have a good command of the English language, a sense of style, and a flair for writing. Creativity in both thinking and writing is essential.

## Unions and Associations

Adverting Copywriters working in radio may belong to various bargaining unions and associations. These include the Writers Guild of America (WGA), the American Marketing Association (AMA), the American Advertising Federation (AAF), and the National Association of Broadcasters (NAB).

## Tips for Entry

1. Get as much writing experience as possible. Volunteer to write press releases and promotional copy for not-for-profit or civic groups for hands-on experience.
2. Many radio stations and associations offer internships or training programs. Internships give you on-the-job training experience and the opportunity to make important contacts.
3. Many local stations advertise openings on the air as well as on their website. Check them out.
4. Job openings are also often advertised in the newspaper classified section under headings such as "Advertising," "Radio," "Copywriter," "Broadcasting," and "Advertising Copywriter."
5. Don't forget to read trade publications. *Billboard, Broadcasting,* and *Radio and Records* often have advertisements for stations with openings.

# ADVERTISING SALES ASSISTANT

## CAREER PROFILE

**Duties:** Coordinates day-to-day activities in advertising sales office; assists in the creation of promotional packages for advertisers; writes contracts and sales orders; assists sales manager and/or sales executives

**Alternate Title(s):** Sales Assistant; Advertising Sales Coordinator; Advertising Office Coordinator

**Salary Range:** $17,000 to $29,000+

**Employment Prospects:** Good

**Advancement Prospects:** Good

**Best Geographical Location(s):** Positions may be located throughout the country

**Prerequisites:**

**Education or Training**—High school diploma required; college background or degree helpful in career advancement

**Experience**—Experience in advertising or sales helpful but not required

**Special Skills and Personality Traits**—Organization; office skills; detail oriented; computer literate; math skills; ability to work under pressure

## CAREER LADDER

```
┌─────────────────────────────────┐
│      Advertising Account        │
│  Executive/Sales Representative │
└─────────────────────────────────┘

┌─────────────────────────────────┐
│   Advertising Sales Assistant   │
└─────────────────────────────────┘

┌─────────────────────────────────┐
│        Entry-Level or           │
│  Sales Position in Other Industry │
└─────────────────────────────────┘
```

## Position Description

The advertising department is very important to a radio station—it generates revenue for the station by selling commercial space to advertisers. Depending on the size and structure of the radio station, the advertising department may be large or just have a sales manager, perhaps an account representative/sales rep, and an Advertising Sales Assistant.

The Advertising Sales Assistant, or sales coordinator, as he or she may be called, is responsible for coordinating the various day-to-day activities in the advertising sales office. In order to be effective in this job the Sales Assistant must be very organized.

Sales Assistants are expected to work with many different people in the radio station. These include the sales manager, assistant sales manager, and advertising account representatives/sales reps, as well as people in the programming, traffic, marketing, promotion, public relations, and community relations departments.

All advertisers want to feel that they are getting the most "bang for their buck." The Sales Assistant often works directly with the advertising sales manager to create promotional packages for potential advertisers, as well as attractive packaging options for current advertisers. These packages often entice customers to add more commercials or advertise when they hadn't planned on advertising before.

The Sales Assistant is responsible for checking to see which commercial time slots have been sold and which are still available. He or she must make sure all contracts, sales orders, and other pertinent information regarding the sale of advertising space is updated and on file. The individual may also be expected to handle inter-office correspondence, such as memos, letters, and informational sheets for account representatives/sales reps regarding rates, packages, and station advertising promotions.

When potential advertisers call the advertising sales office, the Sales Assistant is expected to direct the call to the correct sales representative. He or she may also send out rate cards and other advertising information to both potential advertisers who call and customers who have spoken to sales reps.

When sales representatives are not available, the Sales Assistant may sell advertising space. He or she must therefore know how to read rate sheets and keep abreast of all advertising packages and promotions. When selling space, the Sales Assistant may write advertising contracts and orders. It's important to note, however, that the Sales Assistant is a salaried employee and most often does not receive commissions on sales.

Additional duties of radio Advertising Sales Assistants may include:

- Billing advertisers for commercial time
- Scheduling daily logs showing when commercials will be aired
- Sending conformation information to advertisers and/or advertising agencies stating when ads were aired

## Salaries

Annual earnings for Advertising Sales Assistants can range from $19,000 to $29,000 or more, depending on a number of variables. These include the size and location of the radio station and experience and responsibilities of the individual.

## Employment Prospects

Employment prospects for Advertising Sales Assistants seeking to work in radio are good. While smaller stations may have only one or two Sales Assistants, larger stations often hire more than one person for this position.

## Advancement Prospects

Advancement prospects are good for Advertising Sales Assistants. The most common method of career advancement is to become an advertising account executive/sales rep. Another option for climbing the career ladder is to find a similar position in a larger, more prestigious station, resulting in increased responsibilities and earnings.

## Education and Training

The minimum educational requirement for Advertising Sales Assistants in most stations is a high school diploma. A college background or degree will be helpful in career advancement.

## Experience, Skills, and Personality Traits

Advertising Sales Assistants should be highly organized individuals who can multitask effectively. The ability to work with numbers is helpful in figuring out costs and rates of ads and packages. Good phone skills are essential.

Advertising Sales Assistants should have a variety of office skills. The ability to work comfortably on a computer is usually needed. Communication skills are also necessary.

## Unions and Associations

Advertising Sales Assistants or their stations may be members of their specific state's broadcasting association, the American Advertising Federation (AAF), the National Association of Broadcasters (NAB), and/or the Radio and Advertising Bureau (RAB).

## Tips for Entry

1. Openings may be easier to locate in smaller markets. Get some experience and move up the ladder.
2. There is a great deal of turnover in these positions as a result of career advancement. Consider sending your résumé and a short cover letter to the station's owner, general manager, or human resources director.
3. Any experience in advertising or sales will be useful. When writing your résumé, make sure to include any advertising or sales-related jobs, part-time work, and summer jobs.
4. Many radio stations and associations offer internships or training programs. Internships give you on-the-job training experience and the opportunity to make important contacts.
5. Many radio stations advertise openings on the air and on their websites. Check them out.
6. Job openings are also often advertised in the newspaper classified section under headings such as "Advertising Sales Assistant," "Advertising," "Radio," "Broadcasting," "Radio Sales," and "Broadcasting Sales."

# STATION MANAGEMENT AND ADMINISTRATION

# GENERAL MANAGER

## CAREER PROFILE

**Duties:** Develops and articulates a vision of the station's future; keeps station sounding professional; manages personnel, budget, facilities, and other station resources; formulates and implements plans for the station's growth; develops station policies

**Alternate Title(s):** GM; Station Manager

**Salary Range:** $25,000 to $200,000+

**Employment Prospects:** Poor

**Advancement Prospects:** Fair

**Best Geographical Location(s):** Jobs may be located throughout the country in areas hosting radio stations

**Prerequisites:**

**Education or Training**—Four-year college degree

**Experience**—Extensive broadcasting experience

**Special Skills and Personality Traits**—Management and administrative skills; interpersonal skills; excellent verbal and written communication skills; Internet savvy; working knowledge of broadcasting; understanding of radio industry

## CAREER LADDER

```
┌─────────────────────────────────┐
│    General Manager at Larger,    │
│     More Prestigious Station     │
└─────────────────────────────────┘

┌─────────────────────────────────┐
│         General Manager          │
└─────────────────────────────────┘

┌─────────────────────────────────┐
│  Assistant Station Manager, Business │
│    Manager, or Program Director  │
└─────────────────────────────────┘
```

## Position Description

The General Manager at a radio station is the individual with the ultimate responsibility of overseeing everyone and everything that occurs. Within the scope of the job, the General Manager or GM has many duties.

The General Manager is expected to develop the vision of the station's future. He or she must communicate that vision to employees at the station so that they can bring the vision to fruition.

Duties of the General Manager will depend, to a great extent, on the size and structure of the station. At larger stations, the GM will have more specific duties than his or her counterpart in smaller stations. No matter the size of the station, the General Manager is expected to provide leadership to station employees.

It is essential to the success of the station that the General Manager maintain a positive and productive atmosphere. One of the main functions of the General Manager is to keep the station sounding professional. The GM will oversee the performance of disc jockeys, newscasters, sportscasters, weather reporters, announcers, and other on-air talent. The individual might offer suggestions to make shows better or to ensure that station policy is adhered to. The General Manager may meet with the program and/or music director to discuss format changes, policies, etc.

The General Manager also oversees the work of all other departments within the station. He or she often works closely with those in the operations end of the station, as well as advertising sales, promotion, marketing, community, and public affairs, etc.

The General Manager constantly tries to make the station better. He or she is responsible for finding ways for the station to grow. For example, the GM may work with the program director in creating new or innovative programming to increase the market share by attracting more listeners.

Depending on the size and structure of the station, the General Manager may be responsible for hiring new employees, reviewing the work of current workers, and terminating those who are not performing satisfactorily. In some cases this may be done by a human resources director.

As so much of the income of radio stations is dependent on the sale of commercial space, the General Manager is expected to find ways to increase sales. He or she may help motivate the sales staff, develop or approve new advertising sales packages and promotions designed to attract more advertisers, or sit in on sales meetings with reps, sales managers, and/or major clients.

The General Manager is responsible for developing station policies and procedures. This might entail anything from the way the playlist is chosen to the way news is presented. It is essential that the Federal Communications Commission's (FCC) policies be followed as well.

The General Manager of a radio station must cultivate relationships with local not-for-profit organizations and civic and business groups. He or she will often represent the station at community events or professional meetings. At times, the individual will be asked to speak in front of groups on behalf of the station.

It should be noted that in some situations, the General Manager is in charge of overseeing more than one station. In these cases each station may also have a station manager. It should also be noted that in smaller stations, the station owner may also fulfill the duties of the General Manager.

The General Manager oversees the station's finances and management. He or she is generally expected to develop budgets. While this may be done in conjunction with the business manager or department heads within the station, the GM is responsible for reviewing budget reports and keeping expenses within the budget.

The job of the General Manager can be stressful as well as rewarding. Overseeing a station means that the individual will be responsible for handling all problems. It also means that when the station is successful, the individual can see the fruits of his or her hard work paying off.

Additional duties of the radio General Manager might include:

- Overseeing the management of the station facility
- Handling the marketing, public relations, and advertising duties
- Serving as liaison between station employees and station owners

## Salaries

Annual earnings for General Managers working in radio can range from $25,000 to $200,000 or more. Variables affecting earnings include the geographical location, size, sales volume, and prestige of the station, as well as the experience and responsibilities of the individual. Those having earnings at the higher end of the scale will usually be in charge of more than one station.

## Employment Prospects

Employment prospects are poor for this position. This doesn't mean that it is impossible to obtain a job, but it is difficult.

## Advancement Prospects

The most common method of career advancement in this career is locating a similar position at a larger or more prestigious station. Advancement prospects for General Managers are based to a great extent on the size and the prestige of the station at which the individual currently works. The larger the station, the more difficult advancement prospects become.

## Education and Training

A minimum of a four-year college degree is generally required for this position. Good choices for majors include communications, broadcasting, public relations, advertising, business, journalism, marketing, liberal arts, English, and business.

Courses and seminars in all facets of the broadcasting industry, as well as marketing, public relations, and publicity, are helpful in honing skills and making contacts.

## Experience, Skills, and Personality Traits

A vast amount of experience in radio broadcasting is necessary to become a General Manager. Individuals must have a full working knowledge of station management. Leadership and team building skills are needed.

Both written and oral communication skills are essential. Excellent interpersonal skills are also mandatory. General Managers need the ability to handle many details and projects at one time without getting flustered and stressed.

A knowledge of publicity, promotion, public relations, and advertising is also necessary.

## Unions and Associations

General Managers working in radio may belong to various associations depending on the specific position they hold and the station for which they are working. The most prominent of these associations is the National Association of Broadcasters (NAB).

## Tips for Entry

1. Many radio stations and associations offer internships or training programs. Internships give you on-the-job training experience and the opportunity to make important contacts.
2. Get as much experience as possible working in broadcasting. Volunteer to work with your college radio station, join radio clubs, etc.

3. Many stations advertise openings on the air and on their websites. Check them out.
4. Job openings are also often advertised in the newspaper classified section under headings such as "General Manager," "Station Manager," "Radio" and "Broadcasting."

5. Don't forget to read trade publications. *Billboard, Broadcasting,* and *Radio and Records* often have advertisements for stations with openings.
6. It is usually easier to find a position in a smaller market. Find a job, get some experience, and climb the career ladder.

# OFFICE MANAGER

## CAREER PROFILE

**Duties:** Manages the radio station office; answers telephones; bookkeeping; returns phone calls; oversees office employees; solves problems

**Alternate Title(s):** None

**Salary Range:** $7 to $25+ per hour

**Employment Prospects:** Fair

**Advancement Prospects:** Fair

**Best Geographical Location(s):** Jobs may be located in areas hosting radio stations throughout the country

**Prerequisites:**

**Education or Training**—High School diploma or equivalent; on-the-job training; additional training may be required; see text

**Experience**—Office experience necessary

**Special Skills and Personality Traits**—Management skills; administrative skills; organization; computer skills; communications skills; good judgment; people skills

## CAREER LADDER

```
┌─────────────────────────────────────┐
│      Office Manager in Larger,       │
│     More Prestigious Station,        │
│   Business Manager, or Bookkeeper    │
└─────────────────────────────────────┘

┌─────────────────────────────────────┐
│          Office Manager              │
└─────────────────────────────────────┘

┌─────────────────────────────────────┐
│     Receptionist, Secretary, or      │
│      Administrative Assistant        │
└─────────────────────────────────────┘
```

## Position Description

Radio stations may employ an array of office staff members, including secretaries, administrative assistants, and receptionists. Many often employ an Office Manager as well.

Responsibilities of the Office Manager are dependent to a great extent on the size and structure of the station. Generally, the smaller the station, the more general the duties. The main function of the individual is to ensure the smooth operation of daily activities within the radio station.

The Office Manager is expected to coordinate the functions and activities of others in the office as well as in various departments in the station. Within the scope of the job, the individual may handle a variety of responsibilities. The Office Manager may be in charge of supervising and overseeing station office employees. He or she may be expected to coordinate schedules, monitor employee activities, and give out work assignments. The Office Manager is often responsible for reviewing work done by others in the office and making sure it is completed in a timely fashion.

If there are problems with employees or their work, the Office Manager may note the problem on their personnel file or discuss it with their supervisor. In stations where there is not a human resources department, the Office Manager may also assist in employee evaluations.

The Office Manager is expected to intervene in situations where there may be conflicts between employees. He or she may have discussions with employees and recommend possible solutions. In many instances, the Office Manager will also act as a liaison between the staff and management of the station.

Office Managers working in stations without a human resources department may also be in charge of writing and/or placing advertisements for employees, as well as reviewing applications and résumés. In these cases, he or she might additionally review applications and résumés, as well as handle initial interviews of potential employees.

The Office Manager is responsible for training new office employees. He or she also usually explains policies and procedures and gives instruction on how office equipment works.

The Office Manager is generally the individual people call when office or station equipment is not working properly. The Office Manager is then responsible for calling repair people or getting bids for the repair of the equipment.

In some stations, the Office Manager is also in charge of payroll. The individual may be expected to keep track of employee hours, sick days, vacation days, etc. He or she may send time cards to a payroll service or may be responsible for calculating and printing checks to be signed by the station owner.

It is the responsibility of the Office Manager at a radio station to troubleshoot problems as they occur. These may be problems within the office, customer related, or an array of other situations. Once the Office Manager hears of a problem, he or she must find a way to solve it effectively. The Office Manager may deal with others in the station to assist in the resolution.

For example, a listener may call the station regarding a prize that he or she won and never received. The Office Manager may call the promotion department to help find a solution. An employee may feel that his or her payroll check does not reflect the correct amount of hours worked. The Office Manager will either deal with it directly or, if there is a payroll manager, try to get to the bottom of the situation with the individual.

In some stations, the Office Manager will handle secretarial duties, including typing correspondence, envelopes, and reports. Individuals may need to use various software programs to accomplish different tasks. These might include more common programs such as Microsoft Word, Excel, or WordPerfect. Many radio stations also utilize specific software programs to keep track of programming.

If the station does not have a receptionist, the Office Manager may be responsible for greeting people in a courteous manner who visit the station. Visitors might include advertisers, potential advertisers, record company reps, and listeners.

He or she must answer the station's phones or calls in a professional and polite manner. The individual may also be responsible for screening calls or scheduling meetings and appointments for station staff.

Other duties of the radio station Office Manager may include:

- Ordering and inventorying office supplies
- Obtaining bids of supplies
- Handling accounts payable and receivable
- Screening visitors

## Salaries

Earning for Office Managers working in radio stations can range from $7 to $25 or more per hour. Variables affecting earnings include the geographic location, size, and prestige of the station, as well as the experience and responsibilities of the individual.

One of the perks for Office Managers working in radio stations is often free promotional tickets to concerts and events sponsored by the station.

## Employment Prospects

Employment prospects are fair for individuals seeking this position. Jobs can be located in radio stations throughout the country. It should be noted that in many stations the Office Manager job is twofold. For example, he or she may be hired not only to manage the office but also to handle the bookkeeping, human resources, or payroll.

## Advancement Prospects

Depending on career aspirations, Office Managers working in radio stations may advance their career in a number of ways. After obtaining experience, some individuals find similar positions in larger, more prestigious stations. Others may climb the career ladder by becoming station bookkeepers. Some may move on to similar work in other industries.

## Education and Training

Education and training requirements vary station to station. Generally, most stations prefer their Office Managers to hold a minimum of a high school diploma or the equivalent. Some prefer a college background or degree. This may be especially important in career advancement.

## Experience, Skills, and Personality Traits

Generally, individuals have some type of office experience before moving into this position. Sometimes this is secretarial. Other times the individual may have been an administrative assistant or worked as an assistant in another department.

Office Managers need to have excellent organizational, managerial, and communications skills. The ability to multitask and work under pressure is also essential. People skills are important to success in this position. Computer skills are also needed, and bookkeeping skills are a plus.

## Unions and Associations

There are no major associations specific to Office Managers working in radio stations.

## Tips for Entry

1. Job openings may be advertised in the classified sections of newspapers. Look under classifications such as "Office Manager," "Radio Station," "Broadcasting," and "Office Management."
2. Community colleges, secretarial schools, and vocational and technical schools may offer courses in various aspects of office work, computers, software, etc. These courses give you the working knowledge that may be useful in giving you the edge over other applicants.
3. Stop by radio stations to see if you can fill out an application. Remember to ask that your application be kept on file if there are no current openings.
4. You might also send your résumé with a cover letter asking about openings. Once again, remember to ask that your application be kept on file.
5. Many stations advertise openings on-air as well as on their websites.

# ADMINISTRATIVE ASSISTANT

## CAREER PROFILE

**Duties:** Provides administrative support to station management; schedules meetings; receives visitors; performs research; supervises clerical employees

**Alternate Title(s):** Executive Assistant

**Salary Range:** $7 to $25+ per hour

**Employment Prospects:** Fair

**Advancement Prospects:** Fair

**Best Geographical Location(s):** Jobs may be located throughout the country in areas hosting radio stations

**Prerequisites:**

**Education or Training**—Minimum of a high school diploma; college background helpful

**Experience**—Secretarial or office experience preferred but not always required

**Special Skills and Personality Traits**—Good judgment; computer skills; office skills; phone skills; typing skills; communications skills; organizational skills; people skills

## CAREER LADDER

```
┌─────────────────────────────────────────┐
│   Administrative Assistant in Larger,    │
│      More Prestigious Station, or        │
│  Coordinator or Department Employee      │
│        in Other Station Department       │
└─────────────────────────────────────────┘

┌─────────────────────────────────────────┐
│        Administrative Assistant          │
└─────────────────────────────────────────┘

┌─────────────────────────────────────────┐
│               Secretary                  │
└─────────────────────────────────────────┘
```

## Position Description

In order to help radio stations run smoothly and efficiently, many employ an array of support personnel. Depending on the size and structure of the station, these might include secretaries, receptionists, and Administrative Assistants.

The main function of the Administrative Assistant at a radio station is to provide secretarial and administrative support to the station management. Specific duties may vary.

In stations where there is a large clerical staff, the Administrative Assistant may often be the individual in charge of their supervision. He or she may be responsible for assigning work to their individuals as well. In some situations, the Administrative Assistant will be expected to train new clerical or support employees, explaining station policies and procedures.

Large stations often employ more than one Administrative Assistant. Small stations may or may not employ someone in this position.

Successful Administrative Assistants are organized and can multitask. They often are responsible for helping more than one individual in the station hierarchy. At one station the Administrative Assistant may be responsible for handling duties for the station manager, program director, and music director. At another, he or she may be responsible for

handling duties for the general manager, personnel manager, and business manager. It all depends on these specific station. It is easy to see, therefore, that Administrative Assistants must not only be able to handle multiple projects at one time but do so without getting flustered.

One of the differences between Administrative Assistants and secretaries on a lower professional level is that Administrative Assistants are often required to handle more administrative functions. While they may be asked to type correspondence, reports, letters, etc., individuals may also be asked to help develop simple letters or reports.

Administrative Assistants may need to know how to use various software programs to accomplish different tasks necessary to the station. These might include more common programs, such as Microsoft Word, Excel, or WordPerfect, as well as specific software to keep track of programming or advertising billing.

Administrative Assistants are often responsible for scheduling and coordinating meetings within the station. He or she may also be asked to schedule meetings with advertisers, sponsors, community leaders, or others at the request of station management. During meetings, the Administrative Assistant may be asked to take notes regarding discussions. He or she will then be responsible for typing them for review.

The individual may also place calls, return calls, or coordinate conference calls for those in station management. He or she is expected to take messages, give messages, and get names and phone numbers correctly. The Administrative Assistant is often also expected to screen calls for station management. In many cases, he or she will try to help callers, directing them to the correct people.

As part of the job, the Administrative Assistant is often in the loop on confidential matters. He or she may, for example, learn that the station manager is planning on terminating the program director or an on-air personality. It is essential that the Administrative Assistant understand that this information is confidential and cannot be passed on or discussed.

At times, the Administrative Assistant will be asked to receive visitors who have come to the station for meetings. He or she may be asked to give short tours of the station or introduce visitors to management or on-air personalities. Visitors might include advertisers, potential advertisers, record company reps, listeners, and sponsors. As the Administrative Assistant represents the station, it is essential that he or she be courteous and professional at all times.

Other duties of radio station Administrative Assistants may include:

- Answering letters and other correspondence
- Maintaining files of confidential and nonconfidential information
- Developing reports
- Sorting mail

## Salaries

Earnings for Administrative Assistants working in radio stations can range from $7 to $25 or more per hour. Variables affecting earnings include the geographical location, size, and prestige of the station as well as the experience and responsibilities of the individual.

One of the perks for Administrative Assistants working at radio stations is often free promotional tickets to concerts and events sponsored by the station.

## Employment Prospects

Employment prospects are fair for Administrative Assistants seeking to work in radio. Jobs may be located in radio stations throughout the country. While some station don't employ any Administrative Assistants, others employ more than one. Individuals may also find employment as Assistants in various areas of the radio station.

## Advancement Prospects

Depending on career aspirations, Administrative Assistants working in radio stations may advance their career in a number of ways. After obtaining experience, some individuals find similar positions in larger, more prestigious stations. This results in increased responsibilities and earnings. Others may find a department in the station in which they are interested in pursuing a career and move up the career ladder. For example, after obtaining experience, Administrative Assistants may move into the traffic, sales, or promotion departments.

One of the great things about being an Administrative Assistant is that individuals have an opportunity to get their foot in the door at a radio station, get some experience, and move into a position in which they are interested.

## Education and Training

Education requirements vary station to station. Most stations prefer Administrative Assistants to hold a minimum of a high school diploma. Some prefer a college background or degree. For those interested in climbing the career ladder in other areas of radio, a college background or degree will be especially useful.

Courses in computers and various software packages, as well as secretary courses may be helpful in honing skills.

## Experience, Skills, and Personality Traits

Stations often prefer their Administrative Assistants to have some type of office experience. Some, however, will hire individuals out of college who are interested in pursuing a career in radio and seeking experience.

Administrative Assistants need to have word processing and computer skills. The ability to type fairly quickly and accurately is also needed. Some positions may require the ability to take dictation.

Administrative Assistants need excellent communication skills, both verbal and written. They should be pleasant to be around and have good people skills. The ability to multitask, handle projects, and be organized is essential.

## Unions and Associations

There is no major professional association specific to Administrative Assistants working in radio.

## Tips for Entry

1. A position as an Administrative Assistant is a good opportunity to learn the workings of a radio station. Consider a job in this area if you are interested in getting your foot in the door. Learn what you can and move up the career ladder.
2. If you don't have basic office skills, you might want to take some courses at a local community college or vocational technical school in computers, various software, etc. These courses give you the working

knowledge that may be useful in giving you the edge over other applicants.

3. Jobs may be advertised in the classified sections of newspapers. Look under classifications such as "Assistant-Radio," "Administrative Assistant," "Executive Assistant," "Radio Station," and "Broadcasting."

4. Stop by radio stations to see if you can fill out an application. Remember to ask that your application be kept on file if there are no current openings.

5. Radio stations often advertise openings on the air as well as on their websites. Check them out.

# HUMAN RESOURCES MANAGER

---

## CAREER PROFILE

**Duties:** Manages operations of human resources department; supervises and monitors department employees; develops and administers policies; recruitment; oversees employee relations; develops and writes advertisements seeking employees; interviews potential station employees

**Alternate Title(s):** H.R. Manager; Director of Human Resources; H.R. Director

**Salary Range:** $25,000 to $50,000+

**Employment Prospects:** Poor

**Advancement Prospects:** Fair

**Best Geographical Location(s):** Jobs may be located throughout the country in areas hosting midsize and larger radio stations

**Prerequisites:**

**Education or Training**—Bachelors degree required or preferred

**Experience**—Experience in human resources preferred but not always required

**Special Skills and Personality Traits**—Interpersonal skills; communications skills; management skills; knowledge of federal and state employment laws; detail oriented; organized

## CAREER LADDER

```
┌─────────────────────────────────────┐
│  Human Resources Manager in Larger,  │
│   More Prestigious Radio Station or  │
│        Other Industry, or Director of│
│     Human Resources in Radio or      │
│           in Other Industry          │
└─────────────────────────────────────┘

┌─────────────────────────────────────┐
│      Human Resources Manager         │
└─────────────────────────────────────┘

┌─────────────────────────────────────┐
│ Assistant Director of Human Resources│
│      in Radio or Other Industry      │
└─────────────────────────────────────┘
```

---

## Position Description

Radio stations employ an array of personnel running the gamut from on-air talent to promotion and support and office workers. Attracting, training, and retaining the best employees available is essential to the success of every station.

Many midsize and larger radio stations have a human resources department. The individual in charge of overseeing the department is called the Human Resources Manager. In smaller stations, human resources responsibilities may be handled by the station's owner or general manager.

The Human Resources Manager directs the operation of the department. He or she is responsible for planning, organizing, and controlling everything that happens within the human resources department.

At very large stations, the H.R. Manager may oversee several areas. Each of these is headed by a manager specializing in a specific human resource activity. These might include employment, compensation, benefits, employee relations, and training and development. In smaller stations, the H.R. Manager may be responsible for handling the functions on his or her own or with the help of one or more assistants.

In some situations, the Human Resources Manager may develop, write, and administer policies. In others, these policies may be written by the station owner or general manager. These policies have a direct impact on the employees who are hired and the manner in which they are expected to work. They also have a great impact on the station atmosphere and the way the station functions.

The Human Resources Manager working in a radio station is responsible for strategic planning as it relates to human resources. The individual may be expected to develop programs designed to enhance training and retention.

Many radio stations throughout the country offer internship programs for individuals interested in learning more about radio as a career. The H.R. Manager is often expected to develop and implement these internship opportunities.

The Human Resources Manager is responsible for developing, writing, and placing advertisements for employees for the station. These may be placed in local media, national media, or in trade publications, depending on the situation.

Depending on the size and structure of the station and the human resources department, the H.R. Manager may screen potential applicants as well as interviewing them. The individual often works with others within the station in selecting employees. For example, the general manager or program director often select disc jockeys or other on-air personalities.

Other duties of the radio station Human Resources Manager may include:

- Developing employee relations programs
- Working with negotiators during contract negotiations
- Overseeing special projects and promotional events such as job fairs to stimulate recruitment of potential employees
- Developing and coordinating personnel programs

## Salaries

The radio station Human Resources Manager may earn between $25,000 and $65,000 or more annually. Factors affecting earnings include the geographic location, size, and prestige of the specific station, as well as the education, experience, and responsibilities of the individual. Those working for larger radio stations or media conglomerates usually earn more than their counterparts in smaller stations.

## Employment Prospects

As every station does not employ an individual in this position, employment prospects are poor for Human Resources Managers aspiring to work in radio. Those seeking jobs in this area may have to relocate to areas hosting great numbers of large stations.

## Advancement Prospects

Once an individual gets a foot in the door working in human resources in radio, advancement prospects are fair. Human Resources Managers might climb the career ladder by locating similar positions in larger or more prestigious stations.

Some find similar jobs in other industries or become directors of human resources.

## Education and Training

Most, but not all, radio stations usually require or prefer their Human Resources Managers to hold a minimum of a bachelor's degree. The best major is one earned in human resources. However, majors in other areas are often acceptable with work experience.

Additional courses, workshops, and seminars in human resources, labor relations, personnel, compensation, employee relations, and the retailing industry are very helpful.

A graduate degree may give one applicant an edge over another.

## Experience, Skills, and Personality Traits

Experience working in human resources and related areas is usually necessary for this type of position. There are, however, some individuals who just seem to move into this position after assuming the duties along with their regular job at a smaller station. Many have worked in human resources in other industries prior to their position in radio

Human Resources Managers should have supervisory and administrative skills. Writing and communications skills are also necessary. Individuals must have a working knowledge of federal and state employment laws.

## Unions and Associations

Those interested in learning more about careers in this field should contact the Society for Human Resources Management (SHRM). This organization provides professional guidance and support to its members.

## Tips for Entry

1. Jobs may be advertised in the newspaper classified section under headings such as "Human Resources," "Human Resources Manager," "Human Resources Director," "H.R. Director," and "Radio/Human Resources."
2. Send your résumé and a short cover letter to radio stations. Ask that they be kept on file if there are no current positions.
3. Many radio stations have job listings on their websites, and some even advertise their openings on the air.
4. Get experience working in the H.R. department in other industries. This may give you an advantage over another applicant.

# COMPENSATION AND BENEFITS MANAGER

## CAREER PROFILE

**Duties:** Oversees and coordinate employee wage, salary, and benefit programs in station; supervises payroll and benefits for office employees

**Alternate Title(s):** Payroll Manager; Benefits Manager; Compensation Manager

**Salary Range:** $24,000 to $53,000+

**Employment Prospects:** Poor

**Advancement Prospects:** Fair

**Best Geographical Location(s):** Jobs may be located throughout the country in areas hosting radio stations

**Prerequisites:**

**Education or Training**—Educational requirements vary; see text

**Experience**—Experience requirements vary from station to station

**Special Skills and Personality Traits**—Communications skills; people skills; interpersonal skills; computer skills; patience; familiarity with and understanding of compensation and benefits programs

## CAREER LADDER

```
┌─────────────────────────────────────┐
│  Compensation and Benefits Manager at│
│    Larger, More Prestigious Station, │
│  Director of Compensation and Benefits,│
│     or Human Resources Manager       │
└─────────────────────────────────────┘

┌─────────────────────────────────────┐
│  Compensation and Benefits Manager   │
└─────────────────────────────────────┘

┌─────────────────────────────────────┐
│   Payroll Clerk or Benefits Coordinator│
└─────────────────────────────────────┘
```

## Position Description

Some radio stations may have just a few employees. Larger stations often employ many people. No matter the number of employees, each needs to be paid correctly. Depending on the type of work, experience, and responsibilities, station employees may also receive various compensation packages.

The Compensation and Benefits Manager at a radio station is the individual responsible for making sure all employees at the station are paid correctly and receive the benefits promised to them.

The Compensation and Benefits Manager may have a variety of responsibilities. The individual is expected to oversee the employees in the compensation and benefits or payroll office, which may include benefits coordinators, payroll clerks, and benefit clerks. In some stations, the Compensation and Benefits Manager may be in charge of administering the health insurance and other benefit plans personally. In others, this task may be handled by a benefits coordinator.

Generally, station employees meet with the Compensation and Benefits Manager during the hiring process. The

individual is in charge of discussing the type of compensation the employee will receive for the job. Some employees are paid on an hourly basis. Others are compensated with a set salary. Some, such as those working in sales, may be paid on a commission basis.

The Compensation and Benefits Manager is also expected to explain the benefits that are offered as part of the job to each employee. Depending on the station, benefits may include health insurance, life insurance, pension plans, profit sharing, child care, educational reimbursement, paid holidays, sick days, and vacations.

In many cases, employees may have questions regarding compensation or benefits. The Compensation and Benefits Manager may answer these questions him- or herself or may refer employees to other employees working in the department for answers and assistance.

In certain stations, the Compensation and Benefits Manager is expected to track employee evaluations, promotions, length of time employees are in service, additional education and training information, etc. These factors are often used to determine employee raises. Raises are usually within the policy previously set by the station management.

Additional duties of the Compensation and Benefits Manager may include:

- Gathering information regarding salaries, wages, and benefits offered within the industry as well as the geographic area in which the station is located
- Analyzing the station's compensation and benefit programs and making recommendations for new ones
- Ensuring that employees meet the proper employment requirements
- Maintaining accurate files on employees and the compensation and benefits they receive

## Salaries

Earnings for Compensation and Benefits Managers working in radio stations can range from approximately $24,000 to $53,000 or more annually. Factors affecting earnings include the size, structure, prestige, and geographic location of the specific station, as well as the education, experience, and responsibilities of the individual.

## Employment Prospects

Employment prospects for Compensation and Benefits Managers aspiring to work in radio stations are poor. Smaller stations often have someone else at the station assume the responsibilities for this position. The best prospects for someone interested in a position in this field are in midsize and large stations. Media conglomerates hosting a group of radio stations will offer additional opportunities.

## Advancement Prospects

Compensation and Benefits Managers may climb the career ladder in a number of ways. Individuals may land a similar position at a larger, more prestigious station, resulting in increased responsibilities and earnings. Individuals may also be promoted to director of compensation and benefits at a larger station or in a different industry. Those who have the education and experience may even become assistant directors or directors of human resources.

## Education and Training

Educational requirements vary from station to station for Compensation and Benefits Managers. Many stations require or prefer that individuals hold a degree in human resources, personnel management, labor relations, compensation and benefits, business management, or economics.

In other stations, experience is accepted in lieu of education. This is often the case when an individual has moved up the ranks in the compensation and benefits area.

## Experience, Skills, and Personality Traits

Compensation and Benefits Managers should have experience in various areas of human resources, personnel administration, insurance administration, labor relations, benefits, and compensation. Individuals should have an understanding of insurance programs, retirement plans, labor relations, and wage and benefit trends.

Individuals should have excellent communications skills. Interpersonal skills are essential as well. Management, administrative, and supervisory skills are also needed. The ability to handle multiple projects at one time without becoming flustered is necessary.

## Unions and Associations

Those interested in learning more about careers in this field should contact the International Foundation of Employee Benefit Plans (IFEBP) and the American Compensation Association (ACA).

## Tips for Entry

1. Jobs may be advertised in the classified sections of newspapers. Look under classifications such as "Compensation Manager," "Payroll Manager," "Radio Stations," "Broadcasting," "Benefits and Compensation," and "Benefits and Compensation Manager."
2. Many radio stations advertise openings on the air or on their websites. Check it out.
3. Stop by radio stations and ask to fill out an application. Remember to ask that your résumé be kept on file if there are no current openings.
4. Contact the corporate offices of large media conglomerates.
5. Get experience working in payroll in any industry.

# PAYROLL CLERK

## CAREER PROFILE

**Duties:** Ensures that radio-station employee paychecks are correct; calculates earnings and deductions; computes pay; maintains backup files; researches payroll records

**Alternate Title(s):** Payroll Specialist; Payroll Technician; Compensation Clerk

**Salary Range:** $6 to $15 or more per hour

**Employment Prospects:** Fair

**Advancement Prospects:** Fair

**Best Geographical Location(s):** Jobs may be located throughout the country in areas hosting radio stations

**Prerequisites:**

**Education or Training**—Educational requirements vary; see text

**Experience**—Accounting or payroll background preferred but not always required

**Special Skills and Personality Traits**—Detail oriented; organized; ability to work accurately with numbers; data entry skills

## CAREER LADDER

```
┌─────────────────────────────────┐
│  Payroll Manager or Compensation │
│       and Benefits Manager       │
└─────────────────────────────────┘

┌─────────────────────────────────┐
│          Payroll Clerk           │
└─────────────────────────────────┘

┌─────────────────────────────────┐
│   Payroll Clerk in Other Industry,│
│   Payroll Trainee, or Entry-Level │
└─────────────────────────────────┘
```

## Position Description

No matter how many employees a radio station has, each expects that his or her paycheck is correct. Payroll Clerks, who may also be referred to as payroll specialists, payroll technicians, or compensation clerks, are the individuals who help ensure that this happens.

Specific responsibilities of Payroll Clerks depend on the radio station for which they work and the manner in which payroll is handled. Generally, Payroll Clerks are responsible for inputting data regarding employees' pay as well as maintaining and researching these records.

Payroll Clerks are responsible for calculating the earnings of the employee. This includes regular and overtime hours. Individuals must also calculate deductions such as income tax withholding, social security, credit union payments, insurance, pension plan deductions, etc. This task may be accomplished using computers.

At some stations, hourly employees punch time cards. At the end of the pay period, Payroll Clerks are responsible for screening the time cards to make sure there are no calculating, coding, or other types of errors. Pay is then computed by subtracting allotments such as retirement, federal and state taxes, insurance, etc., from the employee's gross earnings.

When a computer is used to perform these calculations, it will alert the payroll clerk to problems or errors in data. The individual can then adjust the errors.

In some situations, the station may retain the services of a payroll service. In these circumstances the Clerk is expected to obtain the information and give it to the service in a timely manner.

Payroll Clerks may be expected to enter the correct data on checks, check stubs, and master payroll sheets, or more commonly on forms for computer preparation of checks. Individuals are also expected to prepare and distribute pay envelopes.

Payroll Clerks may be called on by employees to correct problems in their checks or to explain calculations. These may include adjusting monetary errors or incorrect amounts of vacation time.

Other responsibilities of Payroll Clerks working in radio stations may include:

- Performing additional clerical tasks
- Maintaining records of employee sick-leave pay and non-taxable wages
- Typing, checking, and filing wage information forms
- Keeping wage and fringe benefit information on employees

## Salaries

Earnings for radio station Payroll Clerks can range from approximately $6 to $15 per hour or more. Factors affecting earnings include the experience, level of training, and responsibilities of the individual, as well as the geographic location, size, and prestige of the specific station.

## Employment Prospects

Employment prospects for Payroll Clerks are fair. Large stations may employ one or more people in this position. While even stations utilizing payroll services usually have at least one individual working in payroll, some stations include handling payroll in another position's responsibilities.

## Advancement Prospects

Advancement prospects for Payroll Clerks are fair. After obtaining additional experience and/or training, individuals may climb the career ladder by becoming payroll supervisors, payroll managers, or compensation managers in either radio or another industry.

## Education and Training

Educational requirements for Payroll Clerks varies from employer to employer. While some employers prefer a college or business school background, many employers will hire those with a high school diploma. While no specific training may be necessary, Payroll Clerks must be able to use adding machines, calculators, computers, and word processors. Knowledge or the ability to use office machinery may be self-taught or learned in high school or business courses at vocational or technical schools, community colleges, or adult education programs.

## Experience, Skills, and Personality Traits

Experience requirements, like education, vary from employer to employer. In many situations this is an entry-level position. Some employers, however, prefer or require experience in payroll.

Clerks should be be detail oriented and organized. The most successful Payroll Clerks enjoy working with numbers. The ability to work accurately and find and correct math errors is essential. Data entry skills are mandatory. Communications skills are helpful as well.

## Unions and Associations

There are no associations specific to this position.

## Tips for Entry

1. Jobs may be advertised in the newspaper classified section under such headings as "Payroll," "Payroll Specialist," "Payroll Clerk," "Payroll Technician," "Broadcasting Office," and "Radio."
2. Send your résumé and a short cover letter to radio stations or the main office of a radio conglomerate.
3. Many stations list openings on their websites as well as on the air.

# BILLING MANAGER

## CAREER PROFILE

**Duties:** Oversees billing department; supervises billing clerks; looks into errors and discrepancies on customer bills; handles customer service

**Alternate Title(s):** Billing Supervisor

**Salary Range:** $24,000 to $45,000+

**Employment Prospects:** Poor

**Advancement Prospects:** Fair

**Best Geographical Location(s):** Jobs may be located throughout the country in areas hosting midsize and larger radio stations

**Prerequisites:**

**Education or Training**—Training requirements vary; see text

**Experience**—Experience working in retail billing office necessary

**Special Skills and Personality Traits**—Aptitude for numbers; orderly; detail oriented; office skills; computer skills; communications skills; good judgment; customer relations skills

## CAREER LADDER

```
┌─────────────────────────────────────┐
│    Billing Manager in Larger         │
│  or More Prestigious Station or      │
│  Billing Manager in Other Industry   │
└─────────────────────────────────────┘

┌─────────────────────────────────────┐
│          Billing Manager             │
└─────────────────────────────────────┘

┌─────────────────────────────────────┐
│   Entry-Level or Bookkeeping or      │
│         Accounting Clerk             │
└─────────────────────────────────────┘
```

## Position Description

Many midsize and larger radio stations employ Billing Managers to keep track of monies owed to a radio station by advertisers.

The Billing Manager has a number of different responsibilities, depending on the size and structure of the station and the setup of the billing department. His or her main function is to oversee the billing department.

As part of the job, the Billing Manager is expected to coordinate and supervise the activities of the other employees in the department. These may include an assistant billing manager or supervisor, bookkeepers, and billing clerks.

The Billing Manager trains each employee so he or she can accomplish the assigned tasks. Today most billing statements are computer generated. Some stations utilize billing machines or special billing software to help prepare monthly statements for advertisers. The Billing Manager may show employees how to run computer or billing machines as well as explain how to use the software effectively.

The Billing Manager must make sure billing clerks fully understand everything about monthly statements. This includes rates, late charges, and unpaid balances. It also includes package discounts and credits of payments previously made. At some stations there are special codes for each charge. The Manager must also be sure the staff knows what each of these codes represents. This is essential when advertisers call up to complain about errors on the bill. Sometimes there truly is an error. Other times, the advertiser may not understand how to read the monthly statement.

The Billing Manager is expected to assist billing clerks when they cannot fully explain statements to advertisers. He or she is also called in when dealing with angry or irate customers. The Billing Manager often has the leeway to take off a late charge on an advertiser's bill. In many instances, he or she will work with the advertising sales department to make sure advertisers are satisfied.

The Billing Manager is responsible for setting the tone for customer service in the billing department. It is essential to a station's success to make the advertiser feel appreciated. This is especially important in the billing department, where advertisers call when there is a problem. The Manager tries to teach the staff how to maintain a good relationship with each advertiser.

In some stations, the Billing Manager may be expected to supervise the monitoring of advertisers' payments to make sure they are updated. In other stations, this may be turned over to collection.

Other duties of the Billing Manager in a radio station may include:

• Writing letters and other correspondence regarding advertisers' bills
• Answering advertisers' questions regarding billing
• Developing policies for the billing department

## Salaries

Annual earnings for radio station Billing Managers can range from $24,000 to $45,000 or more. Variables affecting earnings include the geographic location, size, and prestige of the specific station, as well as the experience, education, and responsibilities of the individual.

## Employment Prospects

Since every radio station does not employ Billing Managers, employment prospects are poor. In many situations, the duties of the Billing Manager are assumed by another individual in the station. The best possibilities for employment are with midsize and larger stations.

## Advancement Prospects

Billing Managers working for radio stations can climb the career ladder by landing similar jobs in larger or more prestigious stations. This results in increased responsibilities and earnings. Often Billing Managers working in radio advance their career by handling similar responsibilities in another industry.

## Education and Training

Educational requirements vary from job to job. Some stations require or prefer their Billing Managers to hold a college degree or at least have some college background. Others may hire individuals with a minimum of a high school diploma if they have experience and demonstrate that they can effectively handle the job. Courses in bookkeeping, accounting, computers, and accounting software are helpful.

## Experience, Skills, and Personality Traits

Billing Managers should like working with numbers. The ability to solve problems is needed. Individuals should be organized and detail oriented. Customer service skills and the ability to calm irate customers is necessary. Supervisory and leadership skills are also needed. An understanding of broadcast billing is also helpful.

## Unions and Associations

There is no major association specific to Billing Managers working in radio.

## Tips for Entry

1. Jobs may be advertised in the classified sections of newspapers. Look under headings such as "Billing Manager," "Billing Department," "Billing Supervisor," and "Broadcast Office Opportunities."
2. Stations often advertise openings on-air as well as on their websites. Check out possibilities.
3. Stop into local radio stations and ask to fill out an application. Remember to request that your application be kept on file if there are no current openings.
4. Radio stations often promote from within. Get your foot in the door as a billing clerk or other position. Learn what you can and climb the career ladder.

# RECEPTIONIST

**Duties:** Greets visitors at radio station; answers telephones; routes mail; files

**Alternate Title(s):** None

**Salary Range:** $6 to $20+ per hour

**Employment Prospects:** Fair

**Advancement Prospects:** Fair

**Best Geographical Location(s):** Jobs may be located in areas hosting radio stations throughout the country

**Prerequisites:**

**Education or Training**—High school diploma or equivalent; some stations may prefer a college background

**Experience**—Office experience preferred but not always required

**Special Skills and Personality Traits**—Pleasant personality; good judgment; people skills; communications skills; office skills; computer skills; phone skills; typing skills

```
┌─────────────────────────────────────┐
│        Receptionist in Larger,       │
│   More Prestigious Radio Station,    │
│    Administrative Assistant, or      │
│    Secretary in Other Industry       │
└─────────────────────────────────────┘

┌─────────────────────────────────────┐
│            Receptionist              │
└─────────────────────────────────────┘

┌─────────────────────────────────────┐
│   Entry-Level or Receptionist or     │
│   Secretary in Another Industry      │
└─────────────────────────────────────┘
```

## Position Description

The Receptionist at a radio station is the first person visitors see. He or she is also the last person a visitor is in contact with when leaving the station. With this in mind, it's easy to see that the impression created by the Receptionist at a radio station is very important.

The specific duties of the Receptionist will depend to a great extent on the size and structure of the station. In some stations, the Receptionist may also handle secretarial, clerical, or administrative duties.

One of the major functions of the Receptionist at a radio station is to greet visitors in a pleasant manner, welcoming them into the station.

Successful Receptionists greet visitors cheerfully and enthusiastically. It is their responsibility to make visitors feel good about the station from the moment they walk in the door.

A variety of guests may visit radio stations, including businesspeople, advertisers, listeners, representatives from record labels, radio show guests, and even celebrities promoting their new CDs or books. It is the responsibility of the Receptionist to make them feel welcome and comfortable.

When guests visit the station, the Receptionist must get their name and determine the reason for the visit. For exam-

ple, station listeners might come in to pick up a prize they have won from a station promotion. Advertisers may come in to meet with their sales executive. Community leaders or representatives from local not-for-profit and civic groups may visit to work on sponsorship programs. Once the Receptionist knows the reason for the visit, he or she can make sure the guest is directed to the correct person. The Receptionist generally calls or buzzes the person that the guest is coming to visit to find out if the guest should be sent in or seated. In some instances, the Receptionist will physically lead the guest to the correct office.

If the individual the guest is meeting is not ready, the Receptionist will ask the guest to be seated. He or she may offer them coffee, tea, or other refreshments. In an effort to make visitors comfortable, the Receptionist often talks to them while they are waiting.

As the Receptionist is often the individual who answers calls, the more information he or she has about the station and its programming and events, the better. The individual may route phone calls to the correct party or answer questions him- or herself. Questions on the phone or in person must always be handled in a courteous and cordial manner. It is essential for the Receptionist to understand that every call and visit is a potential station listener or advertiser.

Depending on the size and structure of the station, the Receptionist may also handle secretarial and clerical duties. These might include typing correspondence, envelopes, reports, etc., photocopying documents, maintaining files, sorting mail, and sending faxes.

Other duties of Receptionists working in radio stations may include:

• Handling secretarial and clerical duties
• Answering letters and other correspondence
• Handling accounts payable and receivable
• Getting information regarding traffic reports or weather-related closings or delays.

## Salaries

Earnings for radio station Receptionists can range from minimum wage to $20 or more per hour. Variables affecting earnings include the geographic location, size, and prestige of the station, as well as the experience and responsibilities of the individual.

One of the perks for Receptionists working at radio stations is often free promotional tickets to concerts and events sponsored by the station.

## Employment Prospects

Employment prospects are fair for individuals seeking this position. Jobs can be located throughout the country in radio stations of all sizes.

## Advancement Prospects

Receptionists working at radio stations may advance their career in a number of ways. After obtaining experience, some individuals find similar positions with larger, more prestigious stations. Others may climb the career ladder by becoming executive secretaries or administrative assistants. Some may move on to similar work in other industries.

Still others get their foot in the door at a radio station and move into a position that is open in another area in which they are interested.

## Education and Training

Education and training requirements vary station to station. Generally, most stations prefer that their Receptionists hold a minimum of a high school diploma or the equivalent. Some may prefer a college background.

## Experience, Skills, and Personality Traits

Experience requirements vary from station to station. While preference may be given to applicants with experience, this is often an entry-level position.

Receptionists need people skills and should truly enjoy being around others. They should also be pleasant to be around. Interpersonal and customer relations skills are essential. Communications skills are mandatory.

A pleasant speaking voice and phone skills are also needed for this type of position. Computer skills and familiarity with various software programs are a plus.

## Unions and Associations

There is no association specific to Receptionists working in radio.

## Tips for Entry

1. Jobs may be advertised in the classified sections of newspapers. Look under classifications such as "Receptionist," "Radio Station," or "Broadcasting."
2. Stop by radio stations and ask if you can fill in an application. Remember to ask that your application be kept on file if there are no current openings.
3. Local radio stations may advertise openings on the air and on their websites. Check them out.
4. With your résumé, send a letter asking about openings to the station manager, owner, or human resources director.

# SECRETARY

## CAREER PROFILE

**Duties:** Answers telephones; returns phone calls; files; types; routes mail; greets people

**Alternate Title(s):** Guy/Girl Friday

**Salary Range:** $6 to $20+ per hour

**Employment Prospects:** Fair

**Advancement Prospects:** Fair

**Best Geographical Location(s):** Jobs may be located in areas hosting radio stations throughout the country

**Prerequisites:**

**Education or Training**—High School diploma or equivalent; on-the-job training; additional training may be required; see text

**Experience**—Secretarial or office experience preferred but not always required

**Special Skills and Personality Traits**—Office skills; computer skills; phone skills; typing skills; communications skills; good judgment; people skills

## CAREER LADDER

```
┌─────────────────────────────────┐
│      Secretary at Larger,        │
│ More Prestigious Radio Station,  │
│  Administrative Assistant, or    │
│   Secretary in Other Industry    │
└─────────────────────────────────┘

┌─────────────────────────────────┐
│           Secretary             │
└─────────────────────────────────┘

┌─────────────────────────────────┐
│  Entry-Level, Receptionist, or  │
│   Secretary in Other Industry   │
└─────────────────────────────────┘
```

## Position Description

Many radio stations utilize the services of various support personnel, including Secretaries, executive secretaries, administrative assistants, receptionists, and more. These individuals help the station run smoothly.

Depending on the size and structure of the station, there may be one or more Secretaries employed. Secretaries handle a wide array of clerical duties. They are expected to type a variety of correspondence, envelopes, reports, etc. Typing may be done on a typewriter, word processor, or computer.

Individuals might additionally be required to use various software programs to accomplish different tasks. These might include more common programs such as Microsoft Word, Excel, or WordPerfect. Many radio stations also utilize specific software programs to keep track of programming.

The Secretary in a radio station might be asked to take and transcribe dictation or take shorthand. Depending on the situation, he or she may be expected to assist the station manager or any of the various departments with their clerical work. These might include management, programming, production, accounting, public relations, advertising, marketing, and traffic.

The Secretary may photocopy documents such as contest rules, programming notes, flyers, contracts, letters, and reports. He or she will also be responsible for filing, maintaining files, collating reports, sorting mail, and sending faxes.

If the station does not have a receptionist, the Secretary will be responsible for greeting visitors in a courteous manner. Visitors might include advertisers, potential advertisers, record company reps, and listeners.

The Secretary must answer the phones and return phone calls in a professional and polite manner. The Secretary may, for example, answer calls regarding station promotions. The individual may also be responsible for screening calls and scheduling meetings and appointments.

Other duties of the radio station Secretary may include:

- Answering letters and other correspondence
- Handling accounts payable and receivable
- Screening visitors
- Answering listeners' questions regarding the station, on-air personalities, or promotions
- Getting information regarding traffic reports or weather-related closings or delays

## Salaries

Earnings for Secretaries working at radio stations can range from $6 to $20 or more per hour. Variables affecting earnings include the geographic location, size, and prestige of the station, as well as the experience and responsibilities of the individual.

One of the perks for Secretaries is the availability of free promotional tickets to concerts and events sponsored by the station.

## Employment Prospects

Employment prospects are fair for individuals seeking this position. Jobs can be located in radio stations throughout the country. Larger stations often employ more than one Secretary.

## Advancement Prospects

Secretaries working for radio stations may advance their career in a number of ways. After obtaining experience, some individuals find similar positions in larger, more prestigious stations. Others may climb the career ladder by becoming executive secretaries or administrative assistants. Some Secretaries may move on to similar work in other industries.

Still others in this job, get their foot in the door at a radio station and move into a different position that opens up.

## Education and Training

Education and training requirements vary from station to station. Most stations prefer their Secretaries to hold a minimum of a high school diploma or the equivalent. Some prefer some college or secretarial school. Secretarial courses as well as those in computers and various software packages are helpful.

## Experience, Skills, and Personality Traits

Entry-level positions may be open in many stations. Experience working in an office environment may be required or preferred.

Secretaries should have excellent typing skills, with the ability to type between 55 and 65 words per minute accurately. Word processing and computer skills are usually necessary. The ability to take dictation is often required or preferred.

Successful Secretaries are also pleasant to be around. Interpersonal and customer relations skills are essential. Communications skills are mandatory.

## Unions and Associations

Individuals may obtain information about a career in this field by contacting Professional Secretaries International (PSI).

## Tips for Entry

1. There are community colleges, secretarial schools, and vocational and technical schools offering courses in various aspects of office work, computers, software, etc. These courses give you the working knowledge that may be useful in providing you with an edge over other applicants.

2. Jobs may be advertised in the classified sections of newspapers. Look under classifications such as "Secretary," "Radio Station," "Broadcasting," "Executive Secretary," "Administrative Assistant," and "Girl/Guy Friday."

3. Stop by radio stations to see if you can fill out an application. Remember to ask that your application be kept on file if there are no current openings.

4. Local radio stations may advertise openings on the air or on their websites. Check them out.

# BOOKKEEPER

## CAREER PROFILE

**Duties:** Recording accounts receivable and accounts payable

**Alternate Title(s):** Accounting Clerk; Bookkeeping Clerk

**Salary Range:** $7 to $25+ per hour

**Employment Prospects:** Fair

**Advancement Prospects:** Fair

**Best Geographical Location(s):** Jobs may be located in radio stations throughout the country

**Prerequisites:**

**Education or Training**—High school diploma or equivalent; on-the-job training; additional training may be required; see text

**Experience**—Bookkeeping or accounting experience preferred but not always required

**Special Skills and Personality Traits**—Aptitude for numbers; orderly; detail oriented; office skills; computer skills; communications skills; good judgment

## CAREER LADDER

```
┌─────────────────────────────────┐
│   Bookkeeper in Larger,         │
│ More Prestigious Radio Station or│
│          Accountant             │
└─────────────────────────────────┘

┌─────────────────────────────────┐
│          Bookkeeper             │
└─────────────────────────────────┘

┌─────────────────────────────────┐
│  Entry-Level Bookkeeping or     │
│      Accounting Clerk           │
└─────────────────────────────────┘
```

## Position Description

The Bookkeeper in a radio station is responsible for accurately recording all money received and spent. A great deal of money is involved in the running of radio stations. The station earns money by selling commercial space. Other monies are paid out to run the station.

Depending on the size and structure of the radio stations, there may be one or more Bookkeepers. In those stations where there is only one Bookkeeper, the individual will be responsible for all of the accounting duties. Stations with more than one individual in the department may have more specialized duties.

For example, at some stations the Bookkeeper may be responsible solely for accounts receivable or accounts payable. In others, one Bookkeeper may handle everything. Large radio stations may also have head Bookkeepers as well as entry-level clerks.

A major function of the station Bookkeeper is recording advertisers' billings. These often include the dates and times various commercials were run. The Bookkeeper is expected to prepare and send out these bills on a regular basis.

The individual may also be expected to monitor payments to ensure they are up to date. In some stations, the Bookkeeper may be required to call advertisers when bills are not paid on time. In others the advertising sales executive or rep may handle these functions.

Running a radio station can be expensive. There are a wide array of expenses, such as rents, payroll, consultants, advertising, taxes, loans, equipment, and supplies. It is the responsibility of the station Bookkeeper to handle these account payables. He or she is expected to review invoices and statements for accuracy and completeness, cut checks, have them signed by the correct party and send them out. Bills must be paid in a timely basis in order to avoid the station being charged late fees.

Bookkeepers at radio stations must post the details of each financial transaction. This may be done manually on paper, with adding machines, or with the help of a computer. Special accounting or bookkeeping software programs may be used, depending on the specific station.

The radio station may have one or more bank accounts. Individuals are responsible for totaling, balancing, and reconciling each account to ensure accuracy.

Many stations utilize codes for various categories of incomes and expenses. The Bookkeeper must code each invoice properly. This makes it easier to prepare reports detailing transactions and for annual budgeting purposes.

The individual may also be responsible for printing out and reviewing monthly management reports detailing accounts receivable, expenses, budget comparisons, etc.

Depending on the specific station and its structure, the Bookkeeper may also be responsible for handling payroll functions. In these cases individuals may collect time cards, tabulate hours worked and the pay due each employee.

Other duties of the radio station Bookkeeper may include:

- Performing secretarial functions
- Writing letters and other correspondence regarding accounts payable and/or receivable
- Answering advertisers' questions regarding billings
- Preparing reports for auditors

## Salaries

Earnings for radio station Bookkeepers can range from $7 to $25 or more per hour. Variables affecting earnings include the geographic location, size, prestige, and popularity of the station, as well as the experience and responsibilities of the individual.

Bookkeepers who handle the bookkeeping responsibilities of more than one station will also generally earn more than those handling just one station.

## Employment Prospects

Employment prospects are fair for individuals seeking to work as Bookkeepers in radio stations. Jobs can be found at radio stations throughout the country.

There are also many radio station conglomerates that hire Bookkeepers to handle the bookkeeping responsibilities for an entire group of stations.

## Advancement Prospects

Bookkeepers in radio stations may advance their career in a number of ways. After obtaining experience, individuals may take on additional duties or find similar positions in larger and more prestigious or popular stations. Some find employment for larger media groups handling more than one station. This results in increased responsibilities and earnings. Still others may climb the career ladder by taking additional training and becoming an accountant.

Some Bookkeepers find accounting positions in other industries.

## Education and Training

Education and training requirements vary from station to station. Most stations require their Bookkeepers to hold a minimum of a high school diploma or the equivalent. Many prefer a college background or some business courses. Classes in bookkeeping, accounting, computers, and accounting software are helpful.

## Experience, Skills, and Personality Traits

Bookkeepers should have a strong aptitude for numbers. Individuals need to be careful, orderly, and detail oriented. Bookkeepers should be comfortable using computers and able to use accounting software packages. Communications skills are essential to success in this field.

## Unions and Associations

There is no association specific to Bookkeepers working in radio stations. Individuals working toward becoming an accountant, might get additional information from the National Society of Public Accountants (NSPA) or the American Institute of Certified Public Accountants (AICPA).

## Tips for Entry

1. Courses and workshops in accounting and book-keeping techniques as well as bookkeeping and accounting software are helpful in making you more marketable.
2. Jobs may be advertised in the classified sections of newspapers. Look under classifications such as "Book-keeper," "Accounting Clerk," "Bookkeeping Clerk," "Broadcasting," and "Radio Station."
3. Stop by radio stations to see if you can fill out an application. Remember to ask that your application be kept on file if there are no current openings.
4. Many stations advertise openings on-air or on their websites.

# BILLING SPECIALIST

## CAREER PROFILE

**Duties:** Produces bills and statements for advertiser accounts; sends bills to advertisers; corrects errors on advertisers' bills

**Alternate Title(s):** Billing Representative

**Salary Range:** $7 to $25+ per hour

**Employment Prospects:** Fair

**Advancement Prospects:** Fair

**Best Geographical Location(s):** Jobs may be located throughout the country in areas hosting radio stations

**Prerequisites:**

**Education or Training**—High school diploma or equivalent; on-the-job training; additional training may be required; see text

**Experience**—Billing or bookkeeping experience preferred but not always required

**Special Skills and Personality Traits**—Aptitude for numbers; orderly; detail oriented; office skills; computer skills; communications skills; good judgment; customer relations skills

## CAREER LADDER

```
┌─────────────────────────────────┐
│  Billing Supervisor or Manager  │
└─────────────────────────────────┘

┌─────────────────────────────────┐
│       Billing Specialist        │
└─────────────────────────────────┘

┌─────────────────────────────────┐
│  Entry-Level or Bookkeeping or  │
│        Accounting Clerk         │
└─────────────────────────────────┘
```

## Position Description

The manner in which radio stations earn money is by selling commercial space on the air. Depending on the size and structure of the station, there may be a number of employees who take care of billing functions. Many stations utilize Billing Specialists to handle the billings and accounts of customers.

The Billing Specialist works in the billing department of the radio station. His or her main function is to produce the bills that are used for advertisers' accounts. Billing Specialists are responsible for taking information regarding advertisers' commercial buys and inputting it into a computer system. They do this by reviewing the rate each customer pays for commercials, the number of commercials taken, and any special packages and then calculating the total amount due from a customer.

Billing Specialists must input information into the computer based on each client's commercial buys. The individual must be sure the client's name, address, and account number are correct. In addition to charges for commercial space, the Billing Specialist may also include the dates and times commercials were aired, package rate information, unpaid balances, late charges, discounts, and credits.

Once bills are prepared, they are printed out. At this point, the Billing Specialist verifies them for accuracy and sends them to clients.

Even if bills are computer generated and checked for errors, there may be mistakes. When clients get bills they feel are wrong they often become angry or irate and call the station to complain. The Billing Specialist is then responsible for checking the bill, trying to find the errors, and preparing a corrected bill.

Often the mistake is not a mistake at all. Instead, the client may be upset about a bill carrying a late charge he or she does not feel should be included. Perhaps the bill was held up in the mail or the client forgot to make a payment. Whatever the situation, the individual tries to maintain a good relationship with the client. He or she may, for example, take off a late charge from a customer's bill or may refer the individual to the billing manager.

In some stations the Billing Specialist may be expected to monitor clients' payments to make sure they are up to date. If they aren't, the individual may be required to call the client and issue a friendly reminder.

Oftentimes clients call the billing department because they don't understand their bill. Billing Specialists must be able to explain the bills to customers in an easy-to-understand manner.

Other duties of the radio station Billing Specialist may include:

- Printing out monthly billing and payment reports
- Writing letters and other correspondence regarding clients' bills
- Answering clients' questions regarding billings

## Salaries

Earnings for radio station Billing Specialists can range from $7 to $25 or more per hour. Variables affecting earnings include the geographic location, size, and prestige of the specific station, as well as the experience and responsibilities of the individual.

## Employment Prospects

Employment prospects are fair for individuals seeking this position. Jobs may be located in both larger and smaller stations throughout the country. Depending on the size and structure of the station, there may be one or more Billing Specialists on staff. Individuals may work full- or part-time.

## Advancement Prospects

Billing Specialists working in radio may advance their career in a number of ways. After obtaining experience, individuals may take on additional duties or find similar positions in larger, more prestigious stations. Others may be promoted to billing managers.

## Education and Training

Billing Specialists generally must hold a minimum of a high school diploma or the equivalent. Many larger stations may prefer a college background or some business courses but don't require it. Classes in bookkeeping, accounting, computers, and accounting software are helpful.

## Experience, Skills, and Personality Traits

Billing Specialists should have a strong aptitude for numbers. Individuals need to be careful, orderly, and detail oriented. They should be comfortable using computers. There is often a lot of customer contact in this job. The ability to deal well with people is essential. Customer service skills are mandatory.

## Unions and Associations

There are no unions specific to Billing Specialists working in radio.

## Tips for Entry

1. Courses and workshops in billing, accounting, and bookkeeping techniques as well as billing software are helpful in making you more marketable.
2. Jobs may be advertised in the classified sections of newspapers. Look under classifications such as "Billing Specialist," "Billing Clerk," "Radio," and "Billing Office."
3. Stop by radio stations and ask to fill out an application. Remember to ask that your application be kept on file if there are no current openings.
4. Many stations advertise openings on the air or on their websites. Be sure to check it out.

# INTERN

## CAREER PROFILE

**Duties:** Performs tasks in specific departments of radio station while learning the broadcasting business

**Alternate Title(s):** Trainee

**Salary Range:** $0 to $7.50 per hour +

**Employment Prospects:** Good

**Advancement Prospects:** Good

**Best Geographical Location(s):** Jobs may be located in areas hosting radio stations throughout the country

**Prerequisites:**

**Education or Training**—High school diploma or equivalent minimum

**Experience**—No experience required

**Special Skills and Personality Traits**—Eagerness to learn; desire to enter radio broadcast industry; communications skills

## CAREER LADDER

```
┌─────────────────────────────────────┐
│  Staffer in Radio Station Department │
└─────────────────────────────────────┘

┌─────────────────────────────────────┐
│               Intern                 │
└─────────────────────────────────────┘

┌─────────────────────────────────────┐
│   Clerical Position or Student       │
└─────────────────────────────────────┘
```

## Position Description

One of the best ways to learn about a career in any industry is to become an Intern. Interns working at radio stations have the opportunity to work under the supervision of a manager or director and learn the business. Interns may be assigned to a specific department or may work in various departments throughout their internship. No matter what department an Intern works in, he or she gets hands-on experience and the opportunity to make important contacts.

Duties will vary depending on the department in which they are working. In many cases the Intern begins by handling a lot of the tedious work that no one else wants to do. As he or she becomes more experienced, the Intern learns to perform more difficult tasks. It should be noted that only the simplest of projects is performed without direct supervision.

Within the scope of the job, Interns might be asked to make phone calls, input data into a computer, or do special projects. They may address or stuff envelopes, help make arrangements, work on research, tabulate data, etc.

Interns working in specific departments may be assigned more specific duties, giving them the opportunity to learn an array of new skills. In this way, individuals can see if they would like a career in a specific area.

For example, Interns working in the advertising department may be taught how to help locate new advertisers as well as how to service current clients. They may make phone calls, visit clients with experienced sales executives, and learn how to write contracts.

Interns working in marketing, public relations, or public affairs may learn how to write press releases, handle publicity, and coordinate events. Those working in promotions will learn how to develop and implement promotions and special events. Those in the news department may learn how to write news reports, who to call to check facts, and how to perform effective interviews.

Whether or not an Intern is getting paid a salary, the individual is expected to function like a paid employee. The Intern must be at work when expected and arrive at work on time. Interns must remember that it is to their advantage to learn as much as possible at this time. Those who do more than asked, and excel, will often find themselves being asked to stay to fill a paid position.

Some stations host a formal internship program. In these cases, the Intern is responsible to the director of the program. In situations where there is no formal program, the Intern may be responsible to the supervisor or director of the department in which he or she is working or the station manager or owner.

Depending on the station and the situation, internships may last a summer, a college semester, or a few months.

Other duties of a radio station Intern may include:

- Handling clerical work
- Helping on remotes
- Greeting visitors
- Writing a paper on the internship experience for college credit

## Salaries

Many Interns do not earn a penny … and still feel the experience is worth a million dollars. Even when Interns do earn a salary, it is usually quite small. Some Interns use the program as part of their college experience, obtaining college credit for their work. Those who do earn a salary may receive a flat fee or be paid an hourly wage, ranging from minimum wage up to $7.50 or more an hour.

## Employment Prospects

Employment prospects are good for individuals seeking internships in radio stations. Internships can be found at radio stations throughout the country. There are many stations hosting formal internship programs. In some cases, individuals may need to "create" their own internship by talking to a station owner or manager.

## Advancement Prospects

As noted, individuals who are hard working, as well as eager learners who do more than is expected of them, are often offered positions within the station. When a position is not available at the same station, a letter of recommendation from a supervisor or general manager at one station will often give an applicant an edge over others vying for a job at another station.

Career advancement is dependent on specific career aspirations and the size of the station in which they want to work. Many individuals become staffers or coordinators in the department in which they had interned. For example, an Intern in the news department might become a news reporter or researcher after an internship. An individual who interned in the programming department might find a position in that department.

## Education and Training

Education and training requirements vary from station to station. Most stations prefer that their Interns have a minimum of a high school diploma or the equivalent. Many stations may want the individual to be in college.

## Experience, Skills, and Personality Traits

Interns generally do not need any experience. What they do need is the desire to learn about the radio and broadcasting industry. Interns should be bright individuals with good communications skills. Interns who are pleasant to be around and eager to do more than is expected of them will do well.

## Unions and Associations

There are no associations specific to Interns working in radio stations.

## Tips for Entry

1. Contact radio stations to see if they have formal internship programs. Find out what the qualifications are and apply.
2. If a radio station does not have an internship program, feel free to contact the station owner or manager to see if you can create an internship for yourself.
3. If you are still in college, the school may either know of an internship or have the ability to create one at a radio station.

# MARKETING, PUBLIC RELATIONS, COMMUNITY RELATIONS, AND SPECIAL EVENTS

# MARKETING DIRECTOR

---

## CAREER PROFILE

**Duties:** Develops and implements marketing plans and campaigns for radio station; handles station's day-to-day marketing functions; plans and implements special events; oversees advertising and public relations program

**Alternate Title(s):** Director of Marketing

**Salary Range:** $24,000 to $75,000+

**Employment Prospects:** Poor

**Advancement Prospects:** Fair

**Best Geographical Location(s):** Jobs may be located throughout the country in areas hosting radio stations

**Prerequisites:**

    **Education or Training**—Four-year college degree

    **Experience**—Marketing, public relations, and/or advertising experience required

    **Special Skills and Personality Traits**—Creativity; good verbal and written communications skills; marketing skills; ability to conceptualize; sales skills; understanding of radio industry

## CAREER LADDER

```
┌─────────────────────────────────────┐
│  Marketing Director for Larger,      │
│  More Prestigious Radio Station or   │
│  Marketing Director in Other Industry│
└─────────────────────────────────────┘

┌─────────────────────────────────────┐
│       Marketing Director            │
└─────────────────────────────────────┘

┌─────────────────────────────────────┐
│  Assistant Marketing Director or     │
│  Website Marketing Manager           │
└─────────────────────────────────────┘
```

---

## Position Description

In order to increase their market share, radio stations must find ways to market their station to the public. The Marketing Director at a radio station is in charge of planning, developing, and coordinating the station's marketing goals and objectives. Within the scope of the job, he or she must find ways to implement the station's marketing plan.

The Marketing Director is expected to develop programs designed to attract listeners, bring in new advertisers, and bring back those who have previously advertised on the station. The individual works to attain these goals in conjunction with various departments in the station, including promotion, public relations, advertising, public affairs, community relations, and programming. It should be noted that while every station needs marketing, not every radio station has a Marketing Director. The duties of the Marketing Director may be picked up by the station owner or manager or those in the public relations, advertising, or promotions departments.

As part of the job, the Marketing Director must be able to conceptualize, plan, and implement innovative programs, promotions, and special events. These might include a variety of promotions, sponsorships, special events, and programs. The Marketing Director is responsible for taking these projects from inception to fruition.

The Marketing Director is responsible for developing the concepts and campaigns that detail how the station will let potential listeners and advertisers know about the station. He or she is expected to determine how much and what type of advertising, promotion, public relations, and selling will be most effective. Within the scope of the job, the Marketing Director must decide the most effective techniques to market the station. He or she may perform research to determine the segments of the population listening to the station. This must then be compared to the segments of the population that the station is trying to attract. Once this is determined, the individual may direct marketing efforts to that segment.

The Marketing Director often works on marketing programs involving special events, programs, promotions, or sponsorships. The hope is that this will attract new listeners and, in turn, new advertisers.

At some stations, the Marketing Director may also be responsible for marketing the station's website. At others, this task may be handled by a website marketing manager.

Depending on the size and structure of the station, the Marketing Director may oversee the public relations, community relations, public affairs, promotions, and advertising departments. In some situations, the Marketing Director may also be responsible for handling the public relations and advertising functions of the website.

Additional duties of the radio Marketing Directors might include:

- Handling the public relations, community relations, and advertising duties for the station itself
- Representing the station at events
- Developing marketing budgets
- Designing and developing marketing materials
- Developing and providing advertising content

## Salaries

Annual earnings for radio Marketing Directors can range from $24,000 to $65,000 or more. Variables affecting earnings include the geographic location, size, and prestige of the specific station as well as the experience and responsibilities of the individual. Individuals working for a group of stations may earn $75,000 or more annually.

## Employment Prospects

Employment prospects are poor for Marketing Directors seeking to work in radio. While every station needs marketing, some stations utilize the services of other employees or even the station owner to handle the responsibilities of the job.

Positions are more likely to be located in midsize market and larger stations than small ones. Other employment possibilities include media conglomerates that own more than one station.

Some stations may retain a marketing consultant instead of having a Marketing Director on staff.

## Advancement Prospects

Marketing Directors working in radio may advance their career in a number of ways. Many individuals climb the career ladder by locating similar positions at larger, more prestigious stations. Others may become the VP of Marketing for either a single large station or a media conglomerate. Some Marketing Directors climb the career ladder by moving into positions as Marketing Directors in other industries. Still other individuals start their own marketing firms.

## Education and Training

Most radio stations require their Marketing Directors to hold a minimum of a four-year college degree. Good choices for majors include public relations, advertising, business, journalism, marketing, liberal arts, English, and communications. While smaller stations may prefer a college degree, it might not be a requirement.

Courses and seminars in marketing, public relations, publicity, promotion, the broadcast industry and web marketing are also helpful.

## Experience, Skills, and Personality Traits

Successful Marketing Directors are creative, innovative individuals with an ability to conceptualize ideas. Individuals should have great written and verbal communications skills and be highly articulate. The ability to handle many details and projects at one time without getting flustered and stressed is essential.

A working knowledge of publicity, promotion, public relations, advertising, and research techniques is also necessary.

## Unions and Associations

Marketing Directors working in radio may belong to a number of trade associations providing support and guidance. These might include the American Marketing Association (AMA), the Marketing Research Association (MRA), and the Public Relations Society of America (PRSA).

## Tips for Entry

1. If you are interested in pursuing a career in this area, look for internships in radio station marketing or promotions departments.
2. Positions may be advertised in the classified ad section of newspapers. Look under such headings as "Marketing," "Marketing Director," "Radio Station Marketing," and "Broadcast Marketing Opportunities."
3. Get experience handling marketing responsibilities at a smaller station, even if that is not your job title. Then use this experience to help you land a job in a larger station.
4. Send your résumé and a cover letter to radio stations you are interested in working for. Ask that your résumé be kept on file.
5. Look for jobs on-line. Check out sites such as www.hotjobs.com and www.monster.com to get started. Go from there.
6. Many radio stations advertise their openings on-air as well as on their websites. Check it out.
7. Take seminars and courses in marketing, promotion, public relations, publicity, and web marketing. These will give you an edge over other applicants, as well as help you hone your skills and make valuable contacts.

# MARKETING ASSISTANT

## CAREER PROFILE

**Duties:** Assists the marketing department in the implementation of marketing projects for radio station; assists in the day-to-day marketing functions

**Alternate Title(s):** Marketing Trainee

**Salary Range:** $15,000 to $24,000

**Employment Prospects:** Fair

**Advancement Prospects:** Good

**Best Geographical Location(s):** Jobs may be located throughout the country in areas hosting radio stations

**Prerequisites:**

**Education or Training**—Four-year college degree

**Experience**—Marketing, public relations, and/or advertising experience helpful but not usually required

**Special Skills and Personality Traits**—Computer skills; people skills; good written and verbal communications skills; organizational skills; creativity; understanding of radio industry

## CAREER LADDER

```
┌─────────────────────────────────────┐
│  Marketing Coordinator, Assistant    │
│  Marketing Director, Public Relations│
│  Coordinator, Assistant Public Relations│
│  Director, Promotions Coordinator,   │
│  Assistant Promotions Director, or   │
│  Advertising Coordinator             │
└─────────────────────────────────────┘

┌─────────────────────────────────────┐
│         Marketing Assistant          │
└─────────────────────────────────────┘

┌─────────────────────────────────────┐
│         Intern or Student            │
└─────────────────────────────────────┘
```

## Position Description

The marketing department at a radio station plans, develops, and coordinates the station's marketing goals and objectives. Their main goal is to increase the market share of the station in an effort to obtain more listeners and advertisers.

Depending on the station, the department may be large or just have one or two employees. Very large stations may have a director, assistant director, coordinator, assistant or trainee, and other staff members. Midsize or smaller stations will generally have a much smaller marketing staff.

The Marketing Assistant working in a radio station is responsible for helping the marketing director and his or her department market the station. Within the scope of the job, the individual may have varied responsibilities. The Marketing Assistant, in some instances, may feel like a glorified secretary. The individual may be expected to fulfill secretarial duties for the department. These might include typing letters and other correspondence, making and returning phone calls, filing, and inputting data into the computer. Marketing Assistants may be asked to keep records of the cost of programs, promotions, events, etc., as well.

The marketing department of radio stations holds regular meetings to discuss marketing strategies. Their goal is to come up with programs designed to attract listeners, bring in new advertisers, and bring back those who have previously advertised on the station. The Marketing Assistant will often sit in on these meetings, learning how new programs are developed and implemented. In the beginning, the individual may just listen. As he or she gains experience, the individual may offer suggestions for new ideas or their implementation.

It should be noted that while every station needs marketing, not every radio station has a marketing director. The duties of the marketing director may be picked up by the station owner or manager or those in the public relations, advertising, or promotions departments. In these cases, the Marketing Assistant will be expected to work with those individuals.

The marketing department often does a great deal of research in an effort to find the most effective techniques to market the station. As part of this function, the Marketing Assistant often helps perform research to determine the segments of the population listening to the station and to its competition. The Marketing Assistant may call people to ask their opinions about the station, mail or hand out questionnaires, do surveys, etc. Once the information is in, the Marketing Assistant may be asked to input it into a computer or to tabulate it. In this manner, collected research can be evaluated.

The Marketing Assistant with little or no experience may be responsible for collating reports, addressing and stuffing envelopes, and putting together press kits and marketing materials. As he or she gains more experience, the Marketing Assistant may begin writing reports, assisting in the development of press releases, marketing materials and announcements, letters, or copy for print ads to advertise events, etc.

The individual may be asked to place and deliver ads and commercials to the media. In some stations, these tasks may be handled by the advertising or public relations department.

The Marketing Assistant, as all other assistants, often does a lot of the "grunt" work, running around and doing tasks to free up the time of the director or assistant director of the department. He or she may be responsible for handling an array of details involved in the implementation and execution of events and projects handled within the department. This may involve making calls, handling correspondence, sending out bills, checking invoices, checking details, or picking up things.

The Marketing Assistant is often busiest when the marketing department is working on specific projects and big marketing events. During these times, the Assistant often attends to many of the little details necessary to make the project a success.

He or she may help coordinate marketing projects with the other departments within the station, including advertising, public relations, community affairs, community relations, programming, promotion, and management. The individual may be asked to hand deliver correspondence to each department to assure everyone is on the same page.

Marketing a radio station can be costly. The marketing department generally must develop and prepare an annual budget to be approved by station management. During the budget's development, the Marketing Assistant may handle clerical tasks such as gathering information and inputting it into the computer.

While this is generally a nine-to-five position, Marketing Assistants working in radio may need to work nights or weekends when an event is taking place. For those interested in a career in radio marketing, public relations, or promotion, this can be the ideal position to learn the ropes and get experience.

Additional duties of radio Marketing Assistants include:

- Assisting with public relations, community relations, and advertising duties
- Tracking tear sheets, clippings, visual cuts, and audiotapes of advertisements and commercials for events
- Tracking tear sheets, clippings, visual cuts, and audiotapes of publicity from events and projects

- Making sure contracts and agreements are signed before a promotion or events

## Salaries
Annual earnings for radio Marketing Assistants can range from approximately $15,000 to $24,000 or more. Variables affecting earnings include the geographic location, size, and prestige of the specific station, as well as the experience and responsibilities of the individual.

## Employment Prospects
Employment prospects are fair for Marketing Assistants seeking to work in radio. As noted, while every station does not have a marketing director, many have Marketing Assistants who work under the direction of other departments.

## Advancement Prospects
Advancement prospects are good for Marketing Assistants working in radio. Specific advancement is based, to a great degree, on the size of the station an individual is going to and his or her career aspirations. Individuals may climb the career ladder to become marketing coordinators, assistant marketing directors, public relations coordinators, assistant public relations directors, promotion coordinators, assistant promotion directors, or advertising coordinators.

## Education and Training
Radio stations generally require their Marketing Assistants to hold a four-year college degree. Good choices for majors include public relations, advertising, business, journalism, marketing, liberal arts, English, communications, and business. While smaller stations may prefer a college degree, it might not be a requirement.

Courses and seminars in marketing, public relations, publicity, promotion, the broadcast industry, and web marketing are also helpful.

## Experience, Skills, and Personality Traits
Experience requirements vary from station to station for this position. Generally, there is no experience requirement. Marketing Assistants working in radio need a variety of skills, including the ability to be comfortable working on a computer. Good written and verbal communications skills are also necessary. Organization and the ability to multitask are imperative.

Those who want to move up the career ladder should be creative with an ability to conceptualize ideas. A knowledge of publicity, promotion, public relations, and advertising as well as research techniques is helpful.

## Unions and Associations
Marketing Assistants working in radio may belong to a number of trade associations providing support and guidance.

These might include the American Marketing Association (AMA), the Marketing Research Association (MRA), and the Public Relations Society of America (PRSA).

## Tips for Entry

1. Internships are one of the best ways to get hands-on experience. Look for internships in radio station marketing or promotions departments.
2. Positions may be advertised in the classified ad section of newspapers. Look under such headings as "Marketing Assistant," "Marketing-Radio," "Radio Station Marketing," and "Broadcast Marketing Opportunities."
3. Get experience handling marketing responsibilities at a smaller station, even if that is not your job title. Then use this experience to help you land a job in a larger station.
4. Send your résumé and a cover letter to radio stations you are interested in working for. Ask that your résumé be kept on file.
5. Many radio stations advertise their openings on-air as well as on their websites. Check it out.
6. Take seminars and courses in marketing, promotion, public relations, publicity, and web marketing. These will give you an edge over other applicants as well as helping you hone your skills and make valuable contacts.

# PUBLIC AFFAIRS DIRECTOR

## CAREER PROFILE

**Duties:** Determines community needs; develops programming

**Alternate Title(s):** Public Service Director; Director of Community Affairs

**Salary Range:** $20,000 to $75,000+

**Employment Prospects:** Fair

**Advancement Prospects:** Fair

**Best Geographical Location(s):** Positions located throughout the country

**Prerequisites:**

**Education or Training**—College degree required or preferred by most stations

**Experience**—Experience in public relations, promotion, marketing, broadcasting, journalism, or social services helpful

**Special Skills and Personality Traits**—Communications skills; detail-oriented; personable; outgoing nature; organizational skills

## CAREER LADDER

```
┌─────────────────────────────────────┐
│      Public Affairs Director at      │
│  Larger, More Prestigious Station or │
│          On-Air Personality          │
└─────────────────────────────────────┘

┌─────────────────────────────────────┐
│       Public Affairs Director        │
└─────────────────────────────────────┘

┌─────────────────────────────────────┐
│     Public Affairs Coordinator,      │
│  Assistant Director of Public or     │
│   Community Affairs, Public Affairs  │
│ Assistant, Public Relations Assistant,│
│       or Promotion Assistant         │
└─────────────────────────────────────┘
```

## Position Description

The Federal Communications Commission (FCC) is the governmental agency that regulates radio stations. At one point, the FCC required radio stations to do a certain amount of public service programming. A number of years ago, this requirement was changed. However, despite the change, most radio stations still air a significant amount of public service programming.

The Public Affairs Director at a radio station develops the public service programming for the station based on the needs of the community. In order to do this, he or she must determine the needs of the station's target audience within the community. This may be done through a variety of research methods. The Public Affairs Director may develop questionnaires, perform surveys, send letters to community groups, or have focus groups in an effort to gather information on the community and its needs.

Once the Public Affairs Director knows the needs of the station's target audience, he or she is expected to develop programs and services to meet those specific needs. The individual will work with station management, the program

director, marketing director, and promotion director to develop the most effective, interesting, and innovative programs and services possible.

Public affairs programming serves the public interest. These shows might include, for example, programs on education, religion, government, or civic issues. It is up to the Public Affairs Director to develop these shows, determine the specific topics for each show, and find guests. In some instances, the Public Affairs Director hosts the community affairs shows. In others, he or she must find appropriate hosts for each show.

The Public Affairs Director must get information for public service announcements from community and civic groups. Public service announcements are also referred to as PSAs. They are the short announcements often heard on radio regarding upcoming community events, community news, etc.

Many Public Affairs Directors develop stock PSA forms for organizations to fill in regarding their events so all needed information is filled in and supplied. Other Public Affairs Directors may accept information through press releases, calendar notes, etc. It is up to the Public Affairs Director to determine policies regarding public service announcements.

For example, many stations set policies regarding how long in advance organizations must send in information.

The Public Affairs Director or his or her staff may take information that comes into the station for PSAs and write it in the style the station uses for these types of announcements. These will then be read by disc jockeys, hosts, news staff, and announcers at specific intervals during the broadcast day. The Public Affairs Director must keep track of each announcement so it can be logged into the daily log.

The Public Affairs Director often works with the promotion department developing promotions with local not-for-profit and community groups. These events help promote the station and its name, attracts new listening-audience members, and helps a specific cause. The event (such as a telethon) may raise money for an organization or may help collect food, toys, or clothing for the needy. Sometimes the Public Affairs Director will work with other community businesses cosponsoring events for local community organizations.

Depending on the size and structure of the station, the Public Affairs Director may also handle an array of other duties, such as writing and reporting news or various public relations and advertising responsibilities.

Additional duties of radio Public Affairs Directors may include:

- Overseeing the public affairs department staff
- Handling media and public relations functions
- Advising station staff about community affairs promotions
- Representing station at events

## Salaries
Annual earnings of radio Public Affairs Directors can vary greatly. Earnings range from $20,000 to $75,000 or more. Variables affecting earnings include the size, location, and prestige of the radio station, as well as the experience and responsibilities of the individual. Some Public Affairs Directors working in radio today may work for a group of stations all owned by the same company. Generally, those earning salaries at the higher end of the scale will be working either in major markets or will have responsibilities for more than one station.

## Employment Prospects
Employment prospects for Public Affairs Directors working in radio are fair, although individuals may have to relocate for jobs. Positions may be located throughout the country in small, midsize, and major markets.

Smaller stations often have more employee turnover because of the fact that people leave for career advancement.

## Advancement Prospects
Advancement prospects are fair for radio Public Affairs Directors. Individuals may climb the career ladder in a num-

ber of ways. The most common method is by locating similar positions with larger, more prestigious stations. Some Public Affairs Directors move into programming, public relations, marketing, or even station management. Still others become on-air radio personalities. There are also some Public Affairs Directors who find a similar position in television.

## Education and Training
Most stations require their Public Affairs Directors to hold a minimum of a four-year college degree. Good choices for majors include journalism, communications, English, public relations, marketing, advertising, social services, and liberal arts.

Courses, workshops, and seminars in public relations, writing, promotion, journalism, and radio will be helpful in honing skills and making new contacts.

## Experience, Skills, and Personality Traits
Generally, the larger the station, the more experience the individual will need for a position of this type. Experience in community affairs, broadcasting, social service, public relations, programming, or journalism is helpful.

Public Affairs Directors should enjoy working with people. Successful individuals have the ability to "know" a specific audience and how to reach it. Excellent verbal and written communications skills are needed. The ability to multitask is imperative.

## Unions and Associations
Public Affairs Directors or their stations may belong to various organizations and associations. These include the National Association of Broadcasters (NAB), the National Association of Broadcast Employees and Technicians (NABET), the American Federation of Television and Radio Artists (AFTRA), and the Public Relations Society of America (PRSA).

## Tips for Entry
1. Positions are often advertised in the newspaper classified section under the headings "Community Affairs Director," "Community Affairs," "Radio," "Broadcasting," "Public Affairs Director," and "Public Service Director."
2. Many stations also advertise their openings on-air or on their websites. Check it out.
3. Send your résumé and a short cover letter to radio stations you are interested in working for. You can never tell when an opening exists.
4. Look for internships in radio stations. These will give you on-the-job training, experience, and the opportunity to make important contacts. Contact stations to see what they offer.

# PUBLIC RELATIONS DIRECTOR

## CAREER PROFILE

**Duties:** Develops public relations strategies and campaigns for the station; handles public relations and publicity for station

**Alternate Title(s):** Director of Public Relations; P.R. Director

**Salary Range:** $22,000 to $85,000+

**Employment Prospects:** Fair

**Advancement Prospects:** Fair

**Best Geographical Location(s):** Positions located throughout the country

**Prerequisites:**

**Education or Training**—College background or degree required or preferred by most stations

**Experience**—Experience in public relations or journalism usually needed

**Special Skills and Personality Traits**—Creativity; imagination; good writing skills; command of the English language; personable; outgoing nature

## CAREER LADDER

```
┌─────────────────────────────────┐
│  Public Relations Director at    │
│  Larger, More Prestigious Station or │
│  Marketing Director              │
└─────────────────────────────────┘

┌─────────────────────────────────┐
│   Public Relations Director      │
└─────────────────────────────────┘

┌─────────────────────────────────┐
│ Assistant Public Relations Director, │
│  Publicist, or                   │
│  Assistant Promotion Director    │
└─────────────────────────────────┘
```

## Position Description

The radio station Public Relations Director is expected to help build the station's image, keeping it more visible and in the public eye. This helps attract listeners and potential advertisers.

Within the scope of the job, there are varied responsibilities and duties depending on the specific station and its size and structure. Not every station has a public relations director. In some stations, the marketing director, promotion director, or even station manager may take on the public relations responsibilities.

The Public Relations Director may work closely with a number of departments, including promotion, advertising, traffic, community relations, and programming. Together they try to develop and implement special promotions and events designed to attract media and public attention. These promotions might include contests or special events that are cosponsored by other businesses or not-for-profit organizations within the community.

The P.R. Director is expected to publicize all events at the station. He or she is responsible for writing press releases, bios, flyers, and fact sheets, as well as developing press kits for media distribution and for the public. The Director may also be responsible for writing other written materials about the station, programs, and on-air personalities. Depending on the size and structure of the station and the department, the P.R. Director may assign this task to publicists or assistants.

The P.R. Director will arrange to have publicity photos taken of on-air personalities, as well as photographs taken at special events and promotions hosted by the station.

The Public Relations Director may perform extensive research in order to determine both the audience the station is trying to reach and the best ways to garner their attention. He or she may research demographics, community needs, and other information through a variety of methods. The Director or his or her staff may, for example, develop and circulate written questionnaires, surveys, make phone calls, or have focus groups. The goal is always to attract as large a listening audience as possible.

Today many stations also have a presence on the Web. The Public Relations Director may be expected to develop and write pieces for the website, arrange for photos to be used on the Web, and help publicize the station's site.

The Public Relations Director must handle calls and correspondence from other media. In some cases, he or she will arrange for on-air personalities to be interviewed or make appearances on behalf of the station.

The Public Relations Director may be asked to represent the station at community or industry events, meetings, and promotions. The individual is also expected to act as the station's spokesperson.

Additional duties of radio Public Relations Directors may include:

• Supervising publicists, public relations assistants, and other department staff
• Generating a complete up-to-date media list
• Handling the promotion and/or community relations responsibilities of the station
• Representing the station and working with local not-for-profits to help enhance the station's image.

## Salaries

Public Relations Directors working in radio can earn between $22,000 and $85,000 or more annually. Variables affecting earnings include the size, location, and prestige of the radio station, as well as the experience and responsibilities of the individual.

In should be noted that in some cases, radio Public Relations Directors may work for a group of stations all owned by the same company. Generally, those earning salaries at the higher end of the scale will be working either in major markets or will have responsibilities for more than one station.

## Employment Prospects

Employment prospects for radio Public Relations Directors are fair, although individuals may have to relocate for jobs. Positions may be located throughout the country in small, midsize, and major markets. As noted previously, there are opportunities for individuals to work in companies that own a group of stations.

## Advancement Prospects

Advancement prospects are fair for radio Public Relations Directors. Individuals who are creative, aggressive, and hard working may climb the career ladder by locating similar positions in larger, more prestigious stations. Others may become marketing directors. Still others may strike out on their own and start their own marketing or public relations firm.

## Education and Training

Most stations require their Public Relations Directors to hold a minimum of a four-year college degree. Good choices for majors include journalism, communications, English, public relations, marketing, advertising, and liberal arts.

Courses and seminars in public relations, writing, photography, journalism, and radio will be helpful in honing skills and making new contacts.

## Experience, Skills, and Personality Traits

Generally, the larger the station, the more experience the individual will need for such a position. While most stations prefer public relations experience in radio, they often will accept public relations experience outside the broadcasting genre.

A working knowledge of public relations is needed for this position. Individuals working in radio should be outgoing, articulate, and personable. They should enjoy being around and dealing with people.

Excellent verbal and written communications skills are needed. A good command of the English language, a sense of style, and a flair for writing are essential. Creativity in both thinking and writing is mandatory.

There is often a great deal of pressure in this type of job, so the ability to work under pressure without getting flustered is necessary.

## Unions and Associations

Public Relations Directors working in radio may belong to various associations. These include the Public Relations Society of America (PRSA), the American Marketing Association (AMA), the American Advertising Federation (AAF), and Broadcast Promotion and Marketing Executives (BPME).

## Tips for Entry

1. Look for internships at radio stations. Many radio stations offer internship programs. Some are formal, others are not. These will give you on-the-job training, experience, and the opportunity to make important contacts. Contact stations to see what they offer.
2. If you can't find an internship in radio, look for one in the public relations department of another company. Your goal is to get experience.
3. Volunteer to write press releases and do P.R. for local not-for-profit or civic groups. This is another great way to obtain hands-on experience to add to your résumé.
4. Job openings are also often advertised in the newspaper classified section under headings such as "Public Relations," "Public Relations Director," "Radio," and "Broadcasting."
5. Don't forget to read trade publications. *Billboard, Broadcasting,* and *Radio and Records* often have advertisements for stations with openings.
6. Send your résumé and a short cover letter to radio stations you are interested in working for. You can never tell when an opening exists.
7. Consider a summer or part-time job working as an assistant to the public relations or promotion director of a local radio station.

# ASSISTANT DIRECTOR OF PUBLIC RELATIONS

## CAREER PROFILE

**Duties:** Assists public relations director in fulfilling public relations and publicity duties; assists in the development of public relations strategies and campaigns for radio stations; helps promote and enhance station reputation and image

**Alternate Title(s):** P.R. Assistant Director

**Salary Range:** $19,000 to $45,000+

**Employment Prospects:** Fair

**Advancement Prospects:** Fair

**Best Geographical Location(s):** Positions located throughout the country

**Prerequisites:**

**Education or Training**—College background or degree required or preferred by most stations

**Experience**—Experience in public relations or journalism usually needed

**Special Skills and Personality Traits**—Creativity; imagination; knowledge of graphics; computer competency; good writing skills; command of the English language; personable; outgoing nature

## CAREER LADDER

```
┌─────────────────────────────────────┐
│      Public Relations Director       │
└─────────────────────────────────────┘

┌─────────────────────────────────────┐
│  Assistant Public Relations Director │
└─────────────────────────────────────┘

┌─────────────────────────────────────┐
│      Public Relations Assistant      │
└─────────────────────────────────────┘
```

## Position Description

The Assistant Director of Public Relations working in a radio station is responsible for helping the station's public relations director handle public relations and publicity functions. His or her specific duties will vary, depending on the size and structure of the station.

The Assistant Director of Public Relations is expected to help the director of the department in relaying information and communications to the outside community and media. In many stations the Assistant is also responsible for handling communications and relaying information to the staff.

It is essential for radio stations to attract listeners and potential advertisers. The public relations department is responsible for helping to build the station's image and keeping it in the public eye.

The Assistant Director of Public Relations, along with others in the public relations department, often works closely with a number of departments within the station, including promotion, advertising, traffic, community relations, and programming. The goal is to develop and implement special promotions and events designed to attract media and public attention. These often include contests or special events cosponsored by other businesses or not-for-profits within the community.

The Assistant Director of P.R. helps publicize all station events. He or she may write press releases, bios, flyers, and fact sheets or supervise publicists and assistants within the department. He or she might also develop press kits for media distribution and for the public. The Assistant Director works with the department director to develop and write other materials about the station, its programming, and/or on-air personalities.

In order to be effective in determining the audience the station is trying to reach and the best way to attract their attention, the public relations director and Assistant Director must often perform extensive research. The Assistant

Director may help develop research methods, assign tasks to others in the department, or perform the research him- or herself. He or she may research demographics, community needs, and other information through written questionnaires, surveys, phone calls, or focus groups. The goal of the public relations department is always to attract as large a listening audience as possible.

Web presence is extremely important to many radio stations today. In many instances, the Assistant Director of Public Relations is responsible for finding ways to help publicize the station's site. He or she may develop and write pieces for the website or develop an entire publicity campaign to promote the website.

The individual is responsible for assisting the director in handling calls and correspondence from other media and for arranging for stories, media appearances, and interviews for on-air personalities.

It should be noted that not every station has a public relations director or even a public relations department. In some stations the public relations duties are handled by a marketing director, promotion director, station manager, or even the station owner.

The Assistant Director of Public Relations may be asked to represent the station at community or industry events, meetings, events, and promotions. The individual may be expected to act as the station's spokesperson when the public relations director is unavailable.

The Assistant Director of Public Relations at a radio station may help plan press conferences, press parties, and news conferences. He or she might also plan parties or other events for advertisers.

Additional duties of the Assistant Director of Public Relations may include:

- Assisting in the supervision of other department staff, including publicists, public relations assistants, and interns
- Helping to develop and generate complete up-to-date media lists
- Representing the station and working with local not-for-profits to help enhance the station's image

## Salaries

Assistant Public Relations Directors working in radio can earn between $19,000 and $45,000 or more annually. Variables affecting earnings include the size, location, and prestige of the radio station, as well as the experience and responsibilities of the individual.

Generally, those earning salaries at the higher end of the scale will be employed in larger stations in major markets.

## Employment Prospects

Employment prospects for radio Assistant Directors of Public Relations are fair, although individuals may have to relocate for jobs. The most opportunities for this position occur in midsize and larger stations.

In should be noted that in some cases, a director of public relations may be in charge of a group of stations owned by a media conglomerate. In these cases, an Assistant Director of Public Relations may be the on-site individual working at a specific station.

## Advancement Prospects

Advancement prospects are fair for Assistant Directors of Public Relations in radio. The most common method for career advancement is becoming a full-fledged director of public relations. Some individuals, however, climb the career ladder by locating similar positions in larger, more prestigious stations. This results in increased responsibilities and earnings.

Other individuals may strike out on their own and start their own marketing or public relations firms.

## Education and Training

Most stations require their Assistant Directors of Public Relations to hold a minimum of a four-year college degree. Good choices for majors include journalism, communications, English, public relations, marketing, advertising, and liberal arts.

Courses and seminars in public relations, writing, photography, journalism, and radio will be helpful in honing skills and making new contacts.

## Experience, Skills, and Personality Traits

As in other industries, generally, the larger the station, the more experience the individual will need for this position. While most stations prefer public relations experience in radio, many will accept public relations experience outside the broadcasting field.

A working knowledge of public relations is necessary, as are excellent communications skills. Successful individuals will be out-going, articulate, and personable. Creativity is mandatory. A good command of the English language, a sense of style, and a flair for writing are also essential. The ability to multitask is needed.

## Unions and Associations

Assistant Public Relations Directors working in radio may belong to various associations. These include the Public Relations Society of America (PRSA), the American Marketing Association (AMA), the American Advertising Federation (AAF), and Broadcast Promotion and Marketing Executives (BPME).

## Tips for Entry

1. Get experience by volunteering to do publicity for local not-for-profit and/or civic groups.
2. Look for internships in radio stations. Many radio stations offer internship programs. Some are formal, oth-

ers are not. These will give you on-the-job training, experience, and the opportunity to make important contacts. Contact stations to see what they offer.

3. If you can't find an internship in radio, look for one in the public relations department of another company. Your goal is to get experience.

4. Job openings are also often advertised in the newspaper classified section under headings such as "Public Relations," "Assistant Public Relations Director," "P.R.," "Radio," and "Broadcasting."

5. Don't forget to read trade publications. *Billboard, Broadcasting,* and *Radio and Records* often have advertisements for stations with openings.

6. Send your résumé and a short cover letter to radio stations you are interested in working for. You can never tell when an opening exists.

# PUBLICIST

## CAREER PROFILE

**Duties:** Publicizes radio station; handles publicity; writes press releases and compiles press kits;. handles public relations and publicity for station

**Alternate Title(s):** Public Relations Specialist; P.R. Rep; P.R. Representative

**Salary Range:** $18,000 to $45,000+

**Employment Prospects:** Fair

**Advancement Prospects:** Fair

**Best Geographical Location(s):** Positions may be located in areas hosting radio stations throughout the country

**Prerequisites:**

**Education or Training**—College background or degree required or preferred by most stations

**Experience**—Publicity or public relations experience helpful

**Special Skills and Personality Traits**—Creativity; imagination; good writing skills; command of the English language; personable; outgoing nature

## CAREER LADDER

```
┌─────────────────────────────────────┐
│  Publicist in Larger, More Prestigious │
│     Radio Station, Radio Station      │
│     Public Relations Director, or     │
│   P.R. Director in Other Industry     │
└─────────────────────────────────────┘

┌─────────────────────────────────────┐
│              Publicist               │
└─────────────────────────────────────┘

┌─────────────────────────────────────┐
│  Publicist in Other Industry or Intern │
└─────────────────────────────────────┘
```

## Position Description

The main function of a Publicist working at a radio station is to publicize the station. Depending on the size and structure of the station, individuals may have varied responsibilities. Some radio stations may employ PR directors and one or more Publicists. In these cases, the Publicist will work under the direction of the P.R. director. Other stations might not hire a P.R. director, opting to hire a Publicist instead. In these cases the individual will usually handle more generalized duties.

Publicists working at radio stations are expected to write stock press releases about the station. They also write news releases on special events and promotions held by the station. For example, the station may be sponsoring events such as telethons, concerts, or dances. In order to get the most publicity from the event, the Publicist must develop press releases specific to the events and distribute them to the media. The Publicist may take photographs of the events and promotions or find someone to handle the task. These too may be distributed to the media for additional publicity or might be posted on the station's website.

The radio station Publicist is often responsible for developing and putting together station press kits. These might include

stock press releases, the history of the station, fact sheets, bios for on-air personalities, photographs, schedules of special events, and other interesting and pertinent information.

These press kits are used to give and/or send to the media. The Publicist is expected to compile media lists for the general media as well as specific broadcast media.

All Publicists need to have a good working relationship with news editors, and radio is no exception. The individual must also know how to develop a good working relationship with broadcast guest coordinators and print feature editors. By doing this, he or she will be in a better position to have stories placed in print or have feature stories published. The Publicist keeps in close contact with the media to let them know about special events that should be covered, new additions to the on-air staff, etc. The Publicist working at a radio station is expected to handle calls and correspondence from other media. These might include media wanting information on station events or arranging for interviews of on-air personalities.

The Publicist must help build the station's image, keeping it in the public eye. Specific duties in this area depend to a great extent on whether there is a public relations director on staff as well. In the event there is none, the Publicist may be expected to develop a public relations campaign directed toward attracting media attention and gaining more listeners. If there is a P.R. director, the Publicist will assist in this function.

Depending on the size and structure of the station, the Publicist may work closely with various departments, including promotion, advertising, traffic, community relations, and programming. He or she will be responsible for publicizing their programs. The individual may assist in the design and implementation of programs to help bring positive attention and media exposure to the station.

One of the functions of the radio station Publicist may be to develop and write pieces for the station's website. He or she may also arrange for photos to be used on the Web and to help publicize the station's website.

The Publicist may be asked to represent the station at community or industry events, meetings, events, and promotions. The individual is also expected to act as the station's spokesperson.

Additional duties of radio station Publicists may include:

- Handling the promotion and/or community relations responsibilities of the station
- Generating a complete up-to-date media list

## Salaries

Publicists working in radio can earn between $18,000 and $45,000 or more annually. Variables affecting earnings include the size, location, and prestige of the radio station, as well as the experience and responsibilities of the individual.

In should be noted that in some cases, Publicists working in radio may work for a group of stations all owned by the same company. Generally, those earnings salaries at the higher end of the scale will be working either in major markets or will have responsibilities for more than one station.

## Employment Prospects

Employment prospects for Publicists working in radio are fair, although individuals may have to relocate for jobs. Positions may be located throughout the country in small, midsize, and major markets. As noted previously, there are opportunities for individuals to work in companies that own a group of stations.

## Advancement Prospects

Advancement prospects are fair for Publicists working in radio. Individuals who are creative, aggressive, and hard working may climb the career ladder by locating similar positions in larger, more prestigious stations. Others may become station public relations directors. Still others may start their own marketing or public relations firms or take positions as publicists in other industries.

## Education and Training

Most stations require their Publicists to hold a minimum of a four-year college degree. Good choices for majors include journalism, communications, English, public relations, marketing, advertising, and liberal arts.

Courses and seminars in public relations, writing, photography, journalism, and radio will be helpful in honing skills and making new contacts.

## Experience, Skills, and Personality Traits

Experience requirements for Publicists vary from station to station. Smaller stations may hire someone right out of college who went through an internship. Larger stations generally prefer someone with experience in either broadcasting or some other industry.

A working knowledge of publicity and public relations is needed for this position. Individuals working in radio should be outgoing, articulate, and personable. They should enjoy being around and dealing with people.

Excellent communications skills, both verbal and written, are necessary. A good command of the English language, a sense of style, and a flair for writing are essential. Creativity in both thinking and writing is mandatory.

## Unions and Associations

Publicists working in radio may belong to various associations. These include the Public Relations Society of America (PRSA), the American Marketing Association (AMA), the American Advertising Federation (AAF), and Broadcast Promotion and Marketing Executives (BPME).

## Tips for Entry

1. Many radio and television stations offer internship programs. Some are formal, others are not. These programs will give you on-the-job training, experience, and the opportunity to make important contacts. Contact stations to see what they offer.
2. If you can't find an internship in radio, look for one in the public relations department of another company. Your goal is to get experience.
3. Volunteer to write press releases and do P.R. for local not-for-profit or civic groups. This is another great way to obtain hands-on experience to add to your résumé.
4. Job openings are also often advertised in the newspaper classified section under headings such as "Publicity," "Publicist," "Public Relations," "Radio," and "Broadcasting."
5. Many stations also post their openings on their website or advertise them on-air. Check them out.
6. Send your résumé and a short cover letter to radio stations you are interested in working for. You can never tell when an opening exists.

# PUBLIC RELATIONS ASSISTANT

## CAREER PROFILE

**Duties:** Assists station's P.R. director; handles media correspondence; writes press releases

**Alternate Title(s):** Publicity Assistant; Public Relations Trainee; Publicity Trainee; P.R. Assistant

**Salary Range:** $18,000 to $33,000+

**Employment Prospects:** Fair

**Advancement Prospects:** Good

**Best Geographical Location(s):** Smaller local communities offer opportunities for small-market stations; New York City, Los Angeles, Chicago, Atlanta, etc., for major-market stations

**Prerequisites:**

**Education or Training**—College background or degree required or preferred by most stations

**Experience**—Experience in public relations or journalism helpful but not always required

**Special Skills and Personality Traits**—Creativity; good writing skills; command of the English language; personable; outgoing nature

## CAREER LADDER

```
┌─────────────────────────────────────┐
│ Assistant Public Relations Director or │
│      Public Relations Director        │
└─────────────────────────────────────┘

┌─────────────────────────────────────┐
│      Public Relations Assistant       │
└─────────────────────────────────────┘

┌─────────────────────────────────────┐
│ Entry-Level, Intern, or Other Public  │
│   Relations or Journalism Position    │
└─────────────────────────────────────┘
```

## Position Description

The main function of a Public Relations Assistant at a radio station is to help the public relations director build the station's image and keep it in the public eye in a positive manner. A good part of the job is handling a lot of the grunt work to free up the time of the P.R. director.

The Public Relations Assistant is often expected to write press releases about the happenings and events at the station. These may include things like special promotions the station is holding, contests, events, and appearances by special guests.

The Public Relations Assistant may perform research in order to get facts to write the press release. He or she may call or contact people to ask questions and make sure all dates and information going into the release are correct. Once the releases are written, they will be reviewed by the public relations director. If they are approved, the Assistant will be responsible for having copies made and sending them to the appropriate media. In many cases today, press releases are transmitted via e-mail or fax instead of, or in

addition to, by mail. The Assistant is expected to keep e-mail addresses, fax numbers, and mailing addresses of media and other pertinent people up to date.

At times the P.R. director may ask the Assistant to arrange for photographs to be taken of station events and promotions. Sometimes the Public Relations Assistant may even take pictures him- or herself.

In some smaller stations, the Public Relations Assistant may act as a secretary of sorts for the public relations director. He or she may be expected to type and copy letters, press releases, memos, envelopes, and other material. The individual might also answer the phone in the station's public relations office and route calls to the appropriate person. He or she must learn who to put through on the phone to the P.R. director and whom he or she can personally handle.

The Assistant often handles correspondence from the media as well as from fans of station personalities. He or she may send publicity photos of station personalities to fans or the media. The Assistant may be expected to write the bios of station personalities and compile press kits.

At certain smaller stations, where there is no promotion department, the Public Relations Assistant will also help promote the station. He or she might assist with and help implement contests and promotions to help attract listeners and boost the audience.

The Public Relations Assistant may represent the station or make public appearances on behalf of the station. In the same vein, he or she may set up public appearances for other station personnel, such as disc jockeys, on-air personalities, talk show hosts, news anchors, or station management.

Additional duties of radio station Public Relations Assistants may include:

- Taking photographs or arranging for photos of radio station events
- Updating program schedules and distributing them to the media
- Representing the station and working with local not-for-profits to help enhance the station's image

## Salaries

Earnings for radio Public Relations Assistants can range from approximately $18,000 to $33,000, depending on the size, location, and prestige of the station, as well as the experience and responsibilities of the individual.

## Employment Prospects

Employment prospects for radio Public Relations Assistants are fair. Positions may be located throughout the country in small, midsize, and major markets. Those with little or no experience might find positions at smaller local or regional stations. With some experience under their belt, they can often find openings in larger stations throughout the country.

## Advancement Prospects

Advancement prospects are good for creative, aggressive individuals. P.R. Assistants may climb the career ladder by locating similar positions in larger, more prestigious stations, resulting in increased earnings and responsibilities. Others advance to either a station's assistant public relations director or full-fledged public relations director. Some individuals go into the promotion end of radio and work as promotion directors.

## Education and Training

Most stations prefer or require their Public Relations Assistants to hold a college degree. Good choices for majors include journalism, communications, English, public relations, marketing, advertising, and liberal arts.

Courses and seminars in public relations, writing, and radio are offered throughout the country. These are useful for both their educational value and the opportunity to make important contacts.

## Experience, Skills, and Personality Traits

Public Relations Assistants working in radio should be articulate, personable, and outgoing. They should enjoy being around and dealing with people.

A good command of the English language, a sense of style, and a flair for writing are essential. Creativity in both thinking and writing is necessary.

The ability to multitask is needed, as is the ability to work under pressure.

## Unions and Associations

Public Relations Assistants working in radio may belong to various associations. These include the Public Relations Society of America (PRSA), the American Marketing Association (AMA), the American Advertising Federation (AAF), and the National Association of Broadcasters (NAB).

## Tips for Entry

1. Get as much experience as possible writing and doing public relations. Volunteer to write press releases and do P.R. for local not-for-profit or civic groups. This is great for hands-on experience to add to your résumé.
2. Many radio stations and associations offer internships or training programs. Internships give you on-the-job training experience and the opportunity to make important contacts.
3. Many local stations advertise openings on the air or on their websites. Check them out.
4. Job openings are also often advertised in the newspaper classified section under headings such as "Public Relations," "Public Relations Assistant," "Radio," and "Broadcasting."
5. Don't forget to read trade publications. *Billboard, Broadcasting,* and *Radio and Records* often have advertisements for stations with openings.
6. Send your résumé and a short cover letter to radio stations you are interested in working for. You can never tell when an opening exists.

# COMMUNITY RELATIONS DIRECTOR

## CAREER PROFILE

**Duties:** Cultivates and coordinates relationship between radio station and local agencies, civic, and community groups; represents station in beneficial community activities

**Alternate Title(s):** Community Relations Manager; Community Affairs Coordinator; Community Affairs Manager

**Salary Range:** $20,000 to $48,000+

**Employment Prospects:** Fair

**Advancement Prospects:** Fair

**Best Geographical Location(s):** Positions may be located in areas hosting radio stations throughout the country

**Prerequisites:**

**Education or Training**—Four-year degree preferred but not always required

**Experience**—Experience working with community and not-for-profit groups helpful

**Special Skills and Personality Traits**—People skills; creativity; good written and verbal communications skills; public speaking ability; organization

## CAREER LADDER

```
┌─────────────────────────────────┐
│  Public Relations Director or    │
│  Community Relations Director in │
│  Larger, More Prestigious        │
│  Broadcast Station               │
└─────────────────────────────────┘

┌─────────────────────────────────┐
│  Community Relations Director    │
└─────────────────────────────────┘

┌─────────────────────────────────┐
│  Community Relations Assistant,  │
│  Public Relations Assistant, or  │
│  Journalism Position             │
└─────────────────────────────────┘
```

## Position Description

The Community Relations Director of a radio station coordinates the relationship between the radio station and local agencies, civic groups, schools, community groups, political entities, and governmental agencies. In addition, the Community Relations Director must cultivate relationships with these groups. It is a great job for anyone who enjoys working with people.

As part of this job, the Community Relations Director is expected to plan and design programs to help the local community and promote a positive image of the radio station. While performing these functions, the individual must continue to be sensitive to the local community and its needs. It should be noted that in some stations, these functions are handled by the public relations director or the station manager or owner.

The Community Relations Director is responsible for representing the radio stations in beneficial community activities. The individual may work with the sponsorship of

sporting events, cultural events, and community-related programs. For example, the Community Relations Director may arrange to have the radio station sponsor a Little League team, concert, or local sports team.

The radio station Community Relations Director may develop programs or work with local community groups such as the United Way, Red Cross, or area hospitals on specific projects. The station might sponsor, for example, an on-air "heart-a-thon" for the American Heart Association and/or a local hospital.

The radio station Community Relations Director must develop new and innovative community relations programs in which the station can take a leadership role. These might include marathons, fairs, art auctions, and parades. These events keep the radio station favorably in the public eye, helping to market the station to the public.

One of the functions of the Community Relations Director is acting as the station's representative on not-for-profit organization boards and committees. The individual is often expected to be an active member of many civic and community groups.

The Community Relations Director of a radio station should have a good working relationship with the media. In this way, when the station is sponsoring a local team, helping to raise money for a worthwhile cause, or working on any other community event, the station will reap the benefits of good press coverage.

Additional duties of radio station Community Relations Directors include:

- Giving speeches on behalf of the station to local community groups
- Representing the station at community events
- Making sure the radio station maintains a good public image

## Salaries

Earnings for Community Relations Directors working at radio stations can range from $20,000 to $48,000 or more. Factors affecting earnings include the size, prestige, and location of the radio station, as well as the responsibilities and experience of the individual. Generally, the larger the station, the higher the earnings.

## Employment Prospects

Employment prospects are fair for individuals seeking this position. However it should be noted that in some stations, the responsibilities of the Community Relations Director are handled by either the public relations director, station manager, or station owner. In many cases the Community Relations Director may also handle additional responsibilities within the station.

As a rule these positions are located in radio stations or with large media groups.

## Advancement Prospects

Advancement prospects are fair once a position is obtained. There are a number of different possibilities for climbing the career ladder, depending on the individual's aspirations. Some locate similar positions in larger, more prestigious stations. Others may work in the community relations area in industries outside radio. Many individuals become radio-station public relations directors.

If the individual has developed a good working relationship with a not-for-profit organization that is seeking a director, the individual may be considered for the position.

## Education and Training

Most radio stations require or prefer their Community Relations Directors to hold a minimum of a four-year college degree. While majors vary, emphasis should be placed on courses in publicity, public relations, marketing, advertising, journalism, English, communications, writing, psychology, and sociology.

There are many seminars related to working with not-for-profit groups, community relations, public relations, and publicity that are useful in obtaining a job and excelling in it.

## Experience, Skills, and Personality Traits

It is essential in this type of position to enjoy working with people. Individuals should be community minded and have an understanding of non-for-profit, civic, and community groups.

Radio station Community Relations Directors should be outgoing, personable, pleasantly aggressive, and articulate. Good writing, organization, and planning skills are necessary. The ability to speak in front of groups is necessary.

## Unions and Associations

Community Relations Directors working in radio often are members of local civic groups, not-for-profit organizations, and service clubs. Individuals may also take advantage of opportunities offered by the Public Relations Society of America (PRSA).

## Tips for Entry

1. Send your résumé and a short cover letter to radio stations you are interested in working for.
2. Openings may be advertised in the classified section of the newspaper. Look under such classifications as "Radio," "Community Relations," and "Community Affairs."
3. Many stations advertise their openings on-air or on their websites. Check it out.
4. Join civic and not-for-profit groups and volunteer to be on committees. This will give you hands-on experience.

# COMMUNITY RELATIONS ASSISTANT

## CAREER PROFILE

**Duties:** Assists community relations staff in the cultivation and coordination of radio stations and local agencies and civic and community groups

**Alternate Title(s):** Community Relations Trainee

**Salary Range:** $15,000 to $24,000+

**Employment Prospects:** Fair

**Advancement Prospects:** Fair

**Best Geographical Location(s):** Positions may be located in areas hosting radio stations throughout the country

**Prerequisites:**

**Education or Training**—Four-year degree preferred but not always required

**Experience**—Experience working with community and not-for-profit groups helpful

**Special Skills and Personality Traits**—Computer skills; people skills; good written and verbal communications skills; organization

## CAREER LADDER

```
┌─────────────────────────────────┐
│  Community Relations Coordinator or │
│      Community Relations         │
│       Assistant Director         │
└─────────────────────────────────┘

┌─────────────────────────────────┐
│   Community Relations Assistant  │
└─────────────────────────────────┘

┌─────────────────────────────────┐
│   Entry-Level, Student, or Intern │
└─────────────────────────────────┘
```

## Position Description

Most radio stations have a relationship with local agencies, civic groups, schools, community groups, political entities, and governmental agencies. The community relations department is in charge of cultivating and coordinating the relationship between these groups and the radio station.

Very large stations may have a director, assistant director, coordinator, assistant or trainee, and other staff members. Midsize or smaller stations will generally have a much smaller community relations staff.

No matter what the size of the community relations department, their functions are twofold. The department is expected to develop and implement programs to help the local community, as well as programs that promote the radio station in a positive manner. The Community Relations Assistant helps the community relations director and his or her staff in carrying out these functions.

It should be noted that in smaller stations, the responsibilities of a community relations director might be handled by someone in public relations, marketing, or station management. In these cases, the Community Relations Assistant may handle more specific duties, helping carry out the community relations programs.

The Community Relations Assistant may fulfill an array of functions. In some cases, the Community Relations Assistant may feel like a glorified secretary. He or she may be expected to fulfill secretarial duties, such as typing letters and other correspondence, making and returning phone calls, and filing. The individual might also be responsible for keeping records of the cost of sponsorships, the cost of programs and events, media prices, etc.

The individual may help the community relations director perform research within the community to see exactly what the needs are and how the station can best serve those needs. Does the community have Little League or local sports teams? Is there a community hospital or not-for-profit organization that runs events? What is most important? What project can help the community and simultaneously promote the station in a positive manner? The Assistant may help the director do projects such as surveys or questionnaires to get this information. He or she may call community groups, ask questions, and obtain information on behalf of the director.

The individual may input information into a computer database, building a list of community groups, media, etc. Depending on the experience of the Community Relations Assistant, he or she may also be asked to help write press releases, announcements letters, or copy for print ads to advertise an event. In some instances, the individual may place ads and deliver ads and commercials to the media in time for placement. At some stations, these tasks may be handled by the advertising or public relations department.

The Assistant often does a lot of the "grunt" work, running around and doing tasks to free up the time of the director or assistant director of the department. He or she may be responsible for handling an array of details involved in the implementation and execution of events and projects handled in this department. This may involve making calls, handling correspondence, sending out bills, checking invoices, checking details, or running around to pick up things.

The Community Relations Assistant is often busiest when the community relations department is working on specific projects, such as sponsoring or taking leadership of on-air "heart-a-thons," or off-air events such as marathons, fairs, art auctions, parades, and health fairs. During these times, the Assistant often attends to many of the little details necessary to make the project a success.

These types of events keep the station in the public eye and also help local not-for-profit groups. Often the station has "remotes" from these events, where the station broadcasts from a location outside the station. During the remote, the Assistant may be responsible for finding people from the organization who agree to be interviewed on-air, putting up signage, or handling other details to make the project a success.

Generally, community relations departments of radio stations have good working relationships with the other media in the area. This is important so that when the station is sponsoring or cosponsoring an event with a local not-for-profit agency, the station will reap the benefits of good press coverage. While calendar entries and press releases may be sent out in advance, the Assistant may be assigned to contact media assignment editors right before an event, either to give them a gentle reminder about the event or to find out who is attending. He or she might also be expected to make sure the media has press releases and other information about the event, the station, etc.

While this is generally a nine-to-five position, Community Relations Assistants may need to work nights or weekends when an event is taking place.

Additional duties of radio station Community Relations Assistants include:

- Tracking tear sheets, clippings, visual cuts, and audiotapes of advertisements and commercials for events
- Tracking tear sheets, clippings, visual cuts, and audiotapes of publicity from events and projects

- Writing thank-you notes to sponsors, community leaders, and others
- Making sure contracts and agreements are signed before a promotion or event
- Acting as a buffer for the community relations director and assistant community relations director

## Salaries

Earnings for radio Community Relations Assistants vary, depending on the size and structure of the station and the experience and responsibilities of the individual. Earnings may range between $15,000 and $25,000 or more annually.

## Employment Prospects

Employment prospects for Community Relations Assistants working in radio are fair. Individuals may find positions in small, local stations as well as mid-market and major-market stations.

Smaller stations often have more employee turnover as a result of people leaving for career advancement.

## Advancement Prospects

Advancement prospects are fair for Community Relations Assistants. The most common method of career advancement is obtaining experience and moving on to become a community relations coordinator or assistant director. In some situations the Community Relations Assistant may also move on to positions in the public relations, marketing, or advertising department.

## Education and Training

While stations may prefer individuals who have a college degree or background, it is not usually a requirement. However, it should be noted that a college degree will help in career advancement. Good choices for college majors include journalism, communications, English, public relations, marketing, advertising, and liberal arts.

There are many seminars related to working with not-for-profit groups, community relations, public relations, and publicity that are useful in obtaining a job and excelling in it.

## Experience, Skills, and Personality Traits

This is often an entry-level job. However, any experience in broadcasting, journalism, or public relations is helpful in this type of position.

Individuals should be detail oriented, with good communications skills. Computer skills are generally required. Writing skills are a plus. In order to excel in this type of job, Community Relations Assistants should be personable and outgoing. It is essential to enjoy working with people. Individuals should be community minded and have an understanding of not-for-profit, civic, and community groups.

## Unions and Associations

There are no associations specific to radio Community Relations Assistants. After working in this position many individuals become members of local civic groups, not-for-profit organizations, and service clubs.

## Tips for Entry

1. Send your résumé and a short cover letter to radio stations you are interested in working for.

2. Openings may be advertised in the classified section of the newspaper. Look under such classifications as "Radio," "Community Relations," and "Community Relations Assistant."

3. Many stations advertise their openings on-air or on their websites. Check it out.

4. Internships are a great way to get experience. An internship in a radio station will give you on-the-job training, experience, and the opportunity to make important contacts. Contact stations to see what they offer.

5. Join civic and not-for-profit groups and volunteer to be on committees. This will give you hands-on experience.

# TRAFFIC

# TRAFFIC MANAGER

## CAREER PROFILE

**Duties:** Checks daily logs at station; schedules commercials; supervises and coordinates traffic department

**Alternate Title(s):** Traffic Supervisor; Traffic Coordinator; Traffic Director; Salesperson; Sales Rep; Account Rep; Sales Executive

**Salary Range:** $22,000 to $49,000+

**Employment Prospects:** Fair

**Advancement Prospects:** Fair

**Best Geographical Location(s):** Positions may be located throughout the country in small, midsize, and large radio stations

**Prerequisites:**

**Education or Training**—Educational requirements vary, from high school diploma to college background or degree

**Experience**—Experience in traffic department of broadcast station preferred

**Special Skills and Personality Traits**—Detail oriented; ability to multitask; ability to work under pressure; organization; competent with computers

## CAREER LADDER

```
┌─────────────────────────────────────┐
│        Traffic Manager at Larger,    │
│      More Prestigious Station or     │
│  Advertising Account, Executive or   │
│       Sales Representative, or       │
│      Advertising Sales Manager       │
└─────────────────────────────────────┘

┌─────────────────────────────────────┐
│           Traffic Manager            │
└─────────────────────────────────────┘

┌─────────────────────────────────────┐
│          Traffic Assistant           │
└─────────────────────────────────────┘
```

## Position Description

Radio stations are regulated by a governmental regulatory agency called the Federal Communications Commission (FCC). The FCC licenses radio and television stations that broadcast to the public. This agency requires stations to keep a log of everything aired on the station. This includes advertising and commercial spots, public service announcements, and programming information.

The radio station's traffic department is responsible for keeping these logs. The individual in charge of this department is the Traffic Manager. He or she supervises and coordinates all employees in the traffic department as well as overseeing everything happening within it.

Traffic departments vary in size, depending on the size and structure of the specific radio station. Large radio stations may have 10 or more employees. Smaller stations may have just one or two employees. In very small stations, the Traffic Manager may be the department's only employee.

The Traffic Manager is expected to schedule all the station's commercials. The individual works closely with the station's general manager, advertising sales manager, and often the owner in creating a sequence for airing commercials. This is an important task. Too many commercials, and listeners will switch stations. Too few and a station won't earn enough income.

Traffic Managers are responsible for making sure that the commercials are aired in the most effective manner. For example, individuals try not to run two commercials for competing products directly after each other.

Radio stations generally run public service announcements. These PSAs are advertisements aired by the station at no fee for not-for-profit groups or community service agencies. In many cases the FCC regulates how many PSAs must be aired in a specific time period. The Traffic Manager must be sure that these are aired so the station conforms to FCC regulations.

The Traffic Manager is expected to make sure all daily logs are typed or input into the computer. In larger departments the individual will usually assign this task to an assistant. However, in smaller stations the Traffic Manager may be responsible for handling this task him- or herself. Every commercial, public service announcement, and all programming must be listed on the log. To do this, the Traffic Manager goes over all commercial orders, ensuring that all information needed for the log is there. Every commercial, complete with the date and time it is to air, must be listed. In cases where an assistant is handling the log, the Traffic Manager is responsible for reviewing the completed daily log.

After the broadcast day, the Traffic Manager must check the daily logs to make sure all commercials that were supposed to be aired, were in fact aired. This is often done by the Traffic Manager who has all the on-air personalities and announcers check off or initial each entry as it is completed.

The Traffic Manager may, on occasion, authorize changes in the log sheet. This may occur when announcers or disc jockeys inadvertently forget to air a commercial and it was aired at a different time, or if an advertiser needs to change the date or time of a scheduled commercial. As the log sheets eventually go to the FCC for review, there is no room for error. Everything must be accounted for correctly.

The Traffic Manager must understand the station, its programming, and its advertisers in order to schedule everything effectively. Depending on the structure of the station, the Traffic Manager may be responsible to the advertising sales manager, the station's general manager, or the station owner.

Additional duties of radio station Traffic Managers may include:

- Training department employees to ensure that FCC regulations and laws are followed
- Delegating duties to traffic department employees
- Reviewing all work done by traffic department
- Reviewing commercials for content to check that copy is suitable for the station and the FCC

## Salaries

Annual earnings for Traffic Managers working in radio can range from $22,000 to $49,000 or more, depending on such factors as the size, location, and prestige of the station, as well as the experience and responsibilities of the individual.

Generally, those with more experience, working in larger stations, will have earnings at the higher end of the scale.

## Employment Prospects

Employment prospects for Traffic Managers seeking to work in radio are fair. There are many radio stations located throughout the country. As noted previously, smaller stations often have traffic departments where the Traffic Manager is the only employee. As people tend to leave for career advancement, there are often openings in these stations. Larger stations, have opportunities for individuals with more experience.

## Advancement Prospects

Advancement prospects are fair for Traffic Managers. The most common method of career advancement for Traffic Man-

agers is finding similar positions in larger, more prestigious stations. This results in increased earnings and responsibilities.

Some individuals who enjoy selling, may advance their careers by becoming advertising account executives/sales reps at larger stations. Still others become advertising sales managers.

## Education and Training

Most larger stations prefer or require their Traffic Managers to hold a four-year college degree. Smaller stations may require just a high school diploma or a two-year degree. Majors can be in almost any subject area. Good choices include communications, broadcasting, radio, advertising, business, marketing, copywriting, and communications.

## Experience, Skills, and Personality Traits

Experience requirements vary from station to station. Some smaller stations may train individuals for this job. Larger stations, as a rule, usually require experience in the traffic department.

Communications skills are essential for this position, as the Traffic Manager may need to explain and instruct others how to complete logs. Supervisory skills are necessary when overseeing a large department.

Computer competence is mandatory. Traffic Managers must also be articulate and highly organized. An understanding of the radio and advertising industry are also needed.

## Unions and Associations

Traffic Managers or their stations may be members of their specific state's broadcasting association, the American Advertising Federation (AAF), the National Association of Broadcasters (NAB), the National Association of Broadcast Employees and Technicians (NABET), the Radio and Advertising Bureau (RAB), or the National Association of Broadcasters (NAB).

## Tips for Entry

1. Many local stations advertise openings on the air or on their websites. Check them out.
2. Many radio stations and associations offer internships or training programs. Internships give you on-the-job training experience and the opportunity to make important contacts. Don't worry if you can't get an internship in the traffic department. Any experience in radio will be useful.
3. Job openings are also often advertised in the newspaper classified section under headings such as "Traffic Manager," "Radio," and "Broadcasting."
4. Don't forget to read trade publications. *Billboard, Broadcasting,* and *Radio and Records* often have advertisements for stations with openings.
5. Send your résumé and a short cover letter to radio stations in which you are interested. You can never tell when an opening exists.

# ASSISTANT TRAFFIC MANAGER

## CAREER PROFILE

**Duties:** Assists traffic manager in developing logs; checks daily logs; coordinates the scheduling of commercials; writes station identifications

**Alternate Title(s):** Assistant Traffic Supervisor; Assistant Traffic Director; Assistant Traffic/Continuity Manager

**Salary Range:** $19,000 to $27,000+

**Employment Prospects:** Fair

**Advancement Prospects:** Fair

**Best Geographical Location(s):** Positions may be located throughout the country in small, midsize, and large radio stations

**Prerequisites:**

**Education or Training**—Educational requirements vary, from high school diploma to college background or degree

**Experience**—Experience in traffic department of broadcast station preferred but not always required

**Special Skills and Personality Traits**—Detail oriented; ability to multitask ability to work under pressure; organizational skills; competent with computers

## CAREER LADDER

```
┌─────────────────────────────────┐
│        Traffic Manager          │
└─────────────────────────────────┘

┌─────────────────────────────────┐
│    Assistant Traffic Manager    │
└─────────────────────────────────┘

┌─────────────────────────────────┐
│        Traffic Assistant        │
└─────────────────────────────────┘
```

## Position Description

The Federal Communications Commission, or FCC, is a governmental agency that regulates radio and television stations broadcasting to the public. The FCC requires every radio station to keep a log of everything aired on the station. This includes advertising and commercial spots, public service announcements, and programming information.

The Assistant Traffic Manager works in the radio station's traffic department. The individual is responsible for helping the station's traffic manager develop station logs and make sure the logs are kept up to date. As keeping the logs accurate is essential to the station, this is an important task.

The Assistant Traffic Manager, who may be referred to as the Assistant Traffic/Continuity Manager, can have varied duties, depending on the size and structure of the radio station and the traffic department. In larger stations, his or her duties may be more specialized. In smaller stations, the individual often has more diverse responsibilities.

In stations with large traffic departments, the Assistant Traffic Manager is expected to help the traffic manager coordinate other employees within that department. This may include scheduling employees as well as overseeing their activities.

Commercial radio stations earn money by selling commercial space. Each commercial that is sold needs to be scheduled within the confines of a broadcast day. The scheduling of commercials is very important to the success of the station. This can be a difficult job, as commercials must be scheduled in a sequence that balances commercials with other on-air information. This includes, for example, music, news, weather, and/or other announcements. If there are too many commercials scheduled in a row, listeners may become bored and switch stations. If there are too few commercials, a station might not earn enough income. The Assistant Traffic Manager works with the traffic manager in developing a programming schedule that flows well. Additionally, the two work on developing an effective advertising schedule. For example, it would not be effective to run two ads for similar, competing products one after another.

He or she also assists the traffic manager in scheduling other on-air information. Every news break, station break, commercial, public service announcement, and program must be scheduled. Every one of these must also be logged.

The Assistant Traffic Manager is often expected to make sure all daily logs are typed or input into the computer. In some stations, he or she may assign this to another traffic employee. The Assistant Traffic Manager must then oversee and review the task, as it is important that all programming, including every commercial and public service announcement, be listed in the log.

The Assistant Traffic Manager is often assigned the task of checking daily logs to be sure all commercials that were scheduled to be aired were actually aired. In order to accomplish this task, on-air personalities and announcers are expected to check off or initial each entry as it is completed.

When announcers or disc jockeys inadvertently forget to air a commercial and air it at a different time, or if an advertiser needs to change the date or time of a scheduled commercial, it is up to either the traffic manager or Assistant Traffic Manager to authorize changes in the log sheet. As the log sheets eventually go to the FCC for review, there is no room for error. Everything must be accounted for correctly.

Additional duties of radio station Assistant Traffic Managers may include:

- Assisting in the training of department employees to ensure that FCC regulations and laws are followed
- Delegating duties to traffic department employees
- Writing station identifications
- Assisting in the review of commercials' content to check that copy is suitable for the station and the FCC

## Salaries
Annual earnings for radio Assistant Traffic Managers can range from $19,000 to $27,000 or more, depending on a number of factors. These include the size, location, and prestige of the station, as well as the experience and responsibilities of the individual. Generally, those with more experience working in larger stations will have earnings at the higher end of the scale.

## Employment Prospects
Employment prospects for Assistant Traffic Managers seeking to work in radio are fair. There are many radio stations located throughout the country. As people tend to leave for career advancement, there are often openings in these stations. Larger stations have opportunities for individuals with more experience.

## Advancement Prospects
Advancement prospects for Assistant Traffic Managers are fair. The most common method of career advancement is for the individual either to be promoted to Traffic Manager within the same station or to find a position as a traffic manager in another station.

Individuals who enjoy selling may advance their careers by becoming advertising account executives/sales reps at larger stations. Still others become advertising sales managers.

## Education and Training
Most larger stations prefer or require their Assistant Traffic Managers to hold a four-year college degree. Smaller stations may just require a high school diploma or a two-year degree. Majors can be in almost any subject area. Good choices include communications, broadcasting, radio, advertising, business, marketing, and communications.

## Experience, Skills, and Personality Traits
Experience requirements for Assistant Traffic Managers vary from station to station. Some smaller stations may hire individuals and train them for this job. Larger stations as a rule usually require experience in the traffic department.

Assistant Traffic Managers should be articulate and highly organized individuals with good communications skills. An understanding of the radio and advertising industry are needed to succeed in this job. Computer competence is mandatory.

## Unions and Associations
Assistant Traffic Managers or their stations may be members of their specific state's broadcasting association, the American Advertising Federation (AAF), the National Association of Broadcasters (NAB), the National Association of Broadcast Employees and Technicians (NABET), the Radio and Advertising Bureau (RAB), or the National Association of Broadcasters (NAB).

## Tips for Entry
1. Many radio stations and associations offer internships or training programs. Internships give you on-the-job training experience and the opportunity to make important contacts. Don't worry if you can't get an internship in the traffic department. Any experience in radio will be useful.
2. Openings are often advertised on-air as well as on a station's website.
3. Job openings are also often advertised in the newspaper classified section under headings such as "Assistant Traffic Manager," "Traffic," "Radio," and "Broadcasting."
4. Send your résumé and a short cover letter to radio stations you are interested in working for. You can never tell when an opening exists.

# TRAFFIC ASSISTANT

## CAREER PROFILE

**Duties:** Logs commercials; inputs daily commercial schedules; keeps track of advertising orders

**Alternate Title(s):** Traffic Representative; Traffic Clerk; Traffic Rep

**Salary Range:** $18,000 to $24,000+

**Employment Prospects:** Good

**Advancement Prospects:** Fair

**Best Geographical Location(s):** Positions may be located throughout the country in small, midsize, and large radio stations

**Prerequisites:**

**Education or Training**—Educational requirements vary from high school diploma to college background or degree

**Experience**—Experience in broadcasting helpful but not required

**Special Skills and Personality Traits**—Detail oriented; articulate; ability to multitask; ability to work under pressure; organizational skills; competent with computers

## CAREER LADDER

```
┌─────────────────────────────────────┐
│ Traffic Coordinator, Assistant Traffic │
│    Manager, or Traffic Manager       │
└─────────────────────────────────────┘

┌─────────────────────────────────────┐
│         Traffic Assistant            │
└─────────────────────────────────────┘

┌─────────────────────────────────────┐
│ Entry-Level, Intern, or Clerical Position │
└─────────────────────────────────────┘
```

## Position Description

The FCC is a governmental regulatory agency that licenses radio and television stations that broadcast to the public. The FCC, or Federal Communications Commission, requires stations to keep a log of everything aired on the station.

The traffic department of a radio station is responsible for keeping track of everything that is announced and put on the air during the broadcast day at a radio station. This includes advertising and commercial spots, public service announcements, and programming information.

Traffic departments might be large or small and may include a traffic manager, assistant manager, coordinator, and one or more Traffic Assistants. In smaller stations there might just be a traffic manager and a Traffic Assistant.

Responsibilities of Traffic Assistants vary depending on the size and structure of the station and the department. In larger stations, they are often assigned an area to work in by the traffic manager or supervisor of the station. In smaller stations, Traffic Assistants may be required to perform traffic responsibilities in all areas of the traffic department.

One of the responsibilities of the Traffic Assistant is typing the daily radio schedule. This is called the log. The log contains all the radio commercials and public service announcements the on-air personalities must announce during the broadcast day. Most stations are now computerized. This makes keeping a log a great deal easier, as there are often changes in the computer log. Without a computer, the Traffic Assistant must continually type and retype the schedule.

Another function of the Traffic Assistant may be reviewing radio-time sales orders. He or she must verify each order to be sure it is complete. For example, the individual must be sure that the log contains the sponsor for each commercial, as well as the date and time a commercial is supposed to air, the length, and whether it is to be done live or recorded. If information is missing, the Traffic Assistant is responsible for contacting the salesperson involved to obtain the information. The Traffic Assistant will also include the name of the on-air personality responsible for airing the commercial.

Traffic Assistants are also responsible for keeping records of advertisements to make sure all commercials are aired when they are scheduled. Many stations do this by asking each announcer or disc jockey to check off commercials and announcements as they are done and record the announcement time.

Traffic Assistants deliver and pick up completed log sheets on a daily basis. In some cases they are responsible for reviewing daily log sheets. In other situations, the traffic manager will handle this function.

In some stations, the Traffic Assistant is in charge of reviewing advertisers' requests for specific dates and times at which they want commercials to run. Traffic Assistants may be expected to deliver cassettes of commercial announcements or ad copy to the correct people, collect commercial cassettes from the studio, and store them in the correct location in the station.

Additional duties of radio Traffic Assistants may include:

- Performing clerical duties, including billing, correspondence, filing, and answering phones
- Writing copy for commercials or public service announcements
- Timing commercials recorded on tape cartridges
- Reviewing commercials for content to check whether copy is suitable for the station and the FCC

## Salaries

Annual earnings for Traffic Assistants working in radio can range from $18,000 to $24,000 or more, depending on a number of factors. These include the size, location, and prestige of the station as well as the experience and responsibilities of the individual.

Generally, those with more experience working in larger stations will have earnings at the higher end of the scale.

## Employment Prospects

Employment prospects for Traffic Assistants seeking to work in radio are good. There are many radio stations located throughout the country.

Entering the job market may be easier in smaller markets where turnover is high as a result of career advancement.

## Advancement Prospects

Advancement prospects are fair for Traffic Assistants eager to climb the career ladder. The most common method of career advancement is for individuals to become traffic coordinators, assistant traffic managers, or traffic managers in either the same or larger, more prestigious stations.

## Education and Training

Smaller stations may require just a high school diploma or a two-year degree. Larger stations may require or prefer individuals to hold a four-year degree or at least have a college background. Majors can be in almost any subject area. A college degree is useful in helping individuals who want to advance their career. Good choices include communications, broadcasting, radio, advertising, business, marketing, and communications.

Courses and seminars in broadcasting, radio, advertising, marketing, copywriting, business, and communications will all be helpful to the individual in succeeding in a career in this field.

## Experience, Skills, and Personality Traits

In some stations, this is an entry-level job. In others, individuals have moved up from intern or clerical positions.

No matter what the experience level, Traffic Assistants should be detail-oriented people who are highly organized. Typing and computer skills are essential. Good communications skills are helpful. The ability to multitask and work under pressure is a must.

## Unions and Associations

Traffic Assistants or their stations may be members of their specific state's broadcasting association, the American Advertising Federation (AAF), the National Association of Broadcasters (NAB), the National Association of Broadcast Employees and Technicians (NABET), the Radio and Advertising Bureau (RAB), or the National Association of Broadcasters (NAB).

## Tips for Entry

1. Look for internships or training programs at radio stations. Internships give you on-the-job training experience and the opportunity to make important contacts. Don't worry if you can't get an internship in the traffic department. Any experience in radio will be useful.
2. If your school has a radio club or a radio station, get involved. This gives you hands-on experience.
3. Openings are often advertised on-air or on a station's website. Check them out.
4. Job openings are also often advertised in the newspaper classified section under headings such as "Traffic Assistant," "Traffic," "Radio," and "Broadcasting."
5. If you aren't already computer competent, take courses. Most stations today are computerized.
6. Send your résumé and a short cover letter to radio stations you are interested in working for. You can never tell when an opening exists.

# ENGINEERING

# CHIEF ENGINEER

## CAREER PROFILE

**Duties:** Oversees the technical operation and maintenance of the radio station; troubleshoots; repairs equipment; keeps signal on air; supervises engineering department

**Alternate Title(s):** Director of Engineering

**Salary Range:** $22,000 to $100,000+

**Employment Prospects:** Good

**Advancement Prospects:** Fair

**Best Geographical Location(s):** Opportunities may be located throughout the country in areas hosting radio stations

**Prerequisites:**

**Education or Training**—College background or degree may be required or preferred; see text

**Experience**—Experience in engineering, electronics, etc.

**Special Skills and Personality Traits**—Working knowledge of electronics; scientific aptitude; manual dexterity; communications skills; ability to multitask

## CAREER LADDER

```
┌─────────────────────────────────────┐
│   Chief Engineer for Larger, More    │
│ Prestigious Station, Chief Engineer for │
│   Media Group, or VP of Engineering   │
└─────────────────────────────────────┘

┌─────────────────────────────────────┐
│           Chief Engineer             │
└─────────────────────────────────────┘

┌─────────────────────────────────────┐
│  Assistant Engineer, Studio Engineer, │
│      or Contract Engineer            │
└─────────────────────────────────────┘
```

## Position Description

The Chief Engineer of a radio station holds an important position. He or she is the individual ultimately responsible for keeping the station's signal on-air. The Chief Engineer is responsible for the technical operation and maintenance of the station. This may include the studios, the station itself, and the transmitter.

Troubleshooting is a big part of this job. Radio stations have a great deal of complex electronic equipment, and the Chief Engineer must make sure everything is in working order. When something breaks, the Engineer is expected to have it repaired or replaced quickly. Not doing so might mean the station's inability to broadcast. The Engineer may repair things him- or herself or may call in other engineers or repair people.

The Chief Engineer is responsible for installing new equipment in the studios and the station itself. He or she may be expected to install or supervise the installation of equipment at other locations, often in preparation for "remote" broadcasts. The station may, for example, broadcast live from a shopping mall, airing a special event the station is sponsoring. Special equipment is needed to broadcast the radio signal from outside the station, so the Chief Engineer determines what equipment is necessary and then either sets it up or has another employee handle the task.

Responsibilities of the Chief Engineer are dependent to a great extent on the size and structure of the station. At larger stations duties of the individual will be more specific than those of his or her counterpart at smaller stations.

Some radio stations may have large engineering departments employing a Chief Engineer, assistant engineers, studio engineers, transmitter engineers, maintenance engineers, and contract engineers. At other stations the Chief Engineer may be the only person in the department. While not every station has someone with this specific title, there is always someone who must handle the duties of this job. Smaller stations may utilize the services of a freelance Engineer or someone else at the station who is technically oriented.

The Chief Engineer is expected to maintain the studio equipment. If something breaks, it is his or her job to make sure it is repaired. As part of this responsibility, the individual may routinely check equipment to make sure it is in perfect working order. Employees may also report problems to the Chief Engineer, who will then troubleshoot until a solution is found.

The Chief Engineer is the liaison between operational suppliers and the station. These might include the phone company, the electric company, Internet service providers, heating and ventilation vendors, computer companies, and repair people. He or she is expected to call vendors, get quotes, and go over plans. The ultimate goal is to have things working correctly in as timely and cost-effective manner as possible.

The Chief Engineer may be responsible for analyzing technical requirements, designing the electronic systems that run the station, setting up studios, purchasing equipment, and selecting vendors. As noted, when handling these jobs he or she must make sure systems are not only efficient but cost effective as well.

In some situations, the Chief Engineer may be expected to monitor and test the performance of the station's transmitter. If repairs or adjustments are needed, he or she will make them. In these situations, the individual will also be responsible for keeping logs of both tests and repairs. This function might also be handled by a transmitter engineer.

As a result of the technical expertise of individuals in this line of work, the job may often encompass virtually everything that requires skills of this nature. He or she is often the one called upon if anything breaks or needs to be put together, from the transmitter to a new desk. This makes the Engineer a sought-out person at the station. Additional duties of radio Chief Engineers may include:

- Handling the engineering responsibilities for a number of stations in a media group
- Acting as an on-air personality
- Handling producing responsibilities
- Operating the controls during a broadcast
- Monitoring the transmitter

## Salaries

Earnings for Chief Engineers working in radio can vary tremendously, ranging from $22,000 to $100,000 or more. Variables include the size, location, prestige, and popularity of the station, as well as the experience, expertise, and responsibilities of the individual. Earnings are also dependent on the number of stations for which the individual is responsible.

In unionized situations, minimum earnings for the Chief Engineer may be negotiated and set by a union. It should be noted, however, that these are minimums. A sought-after Chief Engineer may often negotiate higher earnings.

## Employment Prospects

Employment prospects for Engineers working in radio are good. Individuals may, however, need to relocate for a position. Chief Engineers may find work in small local or regional stations, larger stations, national stations, public radio, or with media groups owning a number of stations.

## Advancement Prospects

Advancement prospects for Chief Engineers working in radio are fair. The most common method for career advancement for Chief Engineers is locating similar positions at larger, more prestigious stations. Others find employment with media groups, resulting in increased responsibilities and earnings. There are some Chief Engineers who advance through promotion to vice president of engineering. These opportunities, however, are generally only located in larger stations or with media groups.

## Education and Training

Many radio stations require their Chief Engineers to hold a minimum of a bachelor's degree. Some may waive educational requirements in lieu of experience. Majors for this position vary. Some individuals hold majors in engineering, while others have majors in communications, liberal arts, or broadcasting.

Classes, seminars, and workshops in engineering are useful, and are offered throughout the country at vocational and technical schools or by associations. The Society of Broadcast Engineers works in conjunction with a number of schools approving programs in this field. Those interested in this field who have gone through approved training often have an edge over others.

## Experience, Skills, and Personality Traits

Experience requirements for Chief Engineers vary from station to station. Generally, the larger the station, the more experience required. Many individuals break into this field by starting out at smaller stations.

Engineers working in radio should have scientific aptitude, problem-solving skills, manual dexterity, and a working knowledge of electronics.

Excellent communication skills are also necessary, as is the ability to multitask without getting flustered.

## Unions and Associations

Chief Engineers working in radio may belong to various bargaining unions and associations, depending on the specific position they hold and the station for which they work. These include the Society of Broadcast Engineers (SBE) and the National Association of Broadcast Employees and Technicians (NABET). Individuals or their stations might also be members of the National Association of Broadcasters (NAB).

## Tips for Entry

1. While certification is not always required, it illustrates professional competency and will often give you an edge over other candidates with similar qualifications.

Contact the Society of Broadcast Engineers (SBE) to get information on classes, seminars, and certification opportunities.

2. Get as much experience as possible working in broadcasting. Volunteer to work with your college radio station, join radio clubs, etc.

3. Look for classes, seminars, and workshops in the broadcast engineering field. These are useful for both their educational value and the opportunity to make important contacts.

4. Many radio stations and associations offer internships or training programs. Internships give you on-the-job training experience and another opportunity to make contacts.

5. If you can't find a formal internship program, see if you can create your own.

6. Remember that your goal is to get your foot in the door of a radio station and then move up the ladder to do what you want. Consider every job opportunity. Offer to help people in other areas when you are done with your work.

7. Many local stations advertise openings on the air as well as on their websites. Check them out.

8. Job openings are also often advertised in the newspaper classified section under headings such as "Radio," "Radio Engineer," "Broadcast Engineer," "Chief Engineer," and "Broadcasting."

# STUDIO ENGINEER

## CAREER PROFILE

**Duties:** Operates control room during broadcast; manages remote feeds; monitors sound levels; troubleshoots during broadcast

**Alternate Title(s):** Engineer

**Salary Range:** $20,000 to $65,000+

**Employment Prospects:** Fair

**Advancement Prospects:** Fair

**Best Geographical Location(s):** Opportunities may be located throughout the country in areas hosting radio stations

**Prerequisites:**

**Education or Training**—College background or degree helpful but not always required; see text

**Experience**—Experience in engineering helpful

**Special Skills and Personality Traits**—Working knowledge of electronics; scientific aptitude; manual dexterity; communications skills; ability to multitask

## CAREER LADDER

```
┌─────────────────────────────┐
│  Studio Engineer at Larger, │
│  More Prestigious Station or│
│  Assistant Chief Engineer   │
└─────────────────────────────┘

┌─────────────────────────────┐
│       Studio Engineer       │
└─────────────────────────────┘

┌─────────────────────────────┐
│ Intern, Student, or Position in │
│  Other Aspect of Radio Station  │
└─────────────────────────────┘
```

## Position Description

Studio Engineers working in radio stations are expected to ensure that the quality of each broadcast is as good as possible. Before a broadcast, the Studio Engineer must investigate the technical requirements of the programming. Will there be guests? How many microphones are needed? What types of sound effects will be used? Will there be remotes? Once the requirements are assessed, he or she is expected to make sure the necessary equipment is available and in working condition for the broadcast.

The Studio Engineer operates equipment in the broadcasting studio. This equipment regulates and controls signal strength and clarity. The Studio Engineer also operates the panels that control the source of the programming. For example, the Studio Engineer may switch from the in-studio programming to remote programming and back again.

While in smaller stations, on-air talent is responsible for playing the music, in larger stations the Studio Engineer may be the individual responsible for actually handling this function. In these situations, the Studio Engineer will also push in carts (cartridges) or tapes of

PSAs (public service announcements), commercials, or station identifications.

The Studio Engineer controls the microphones during the broadcast. He or she will monitor and adjust the sound, ensuring it is the correct level and of good quality. At times the Studio Engineer may operate equipment designed to produce special sound effects. He or she may utilize sound mixers to create special sounds or dub in specific sound effects needed for radio shows.

The Studio Engineer often communicates with the producers and on-air talent while a radio show is on-air. This is accomplished via headphones.

After a broadcast, the Studio Engineer will go over the studio, examining equipment to make sure it is in proper working order for the next broadcast. Depending on the size and structure of the station, the Studio Engineer may be responsible for repairing equipment as well.

At some stations the Studio Engineer is responsible for maintaining the studio equipment. At others this is the responsibility of the chief engineer.

Additional duties of radio Studio Engineers may include:

- Installing new equipment
- Monitoring and testing the performing of the station's transmitter
- Setting up studios

## Salaries

Earnings for radio Studio Engineers vary, ranging from $20,000 to $65,000 or more. Variables include the size, location, prestige, and popularity of the station, as well as the experience, expertise, and responsibilities of the individual.

In unionized situations, minimum earnings for Studio Engineers may be negotiated and set by a union.

## Employment Prospects

Employment prospects for Studio Engineers working in radio are fair. While there may be positions with smaller stations, most jobs are found at midsize and larger stations. Individuals may need to relocate for a position.

## Advancement Prospects

Once in the door, advancement prospects for Studio Engineers working in radio are fair. The most common method for career advancement is locating similar positions at larger, more prestigious stations. Others may climb the career ladder by advancing to such positions as assistant engineer or chief engineer.

## Education and Training

While a college education may not be required for this position, it is usually preferred. Majors for this position vary. There are some individuals who hold majors in engineering, while others have majors in communications, liberal arts, or broadcasting. Individuals may obtain education through vocational, technical, or broadcasting schools as well. Classes, seminars, and workshops in broadcast engineering are also useful. The Society of Broadcast Engineers works in conjunction with a number of schools approving programs in this field. Those interested in this field who have gone through approved training often have an edge over others. Radio stations may waive educational requirements in lieu of experience.

## Experience, Skills, and Personality Traits

Experience requirements for Studio Engineers vary from station to station. Generally, the larger the station, the more experience required. Many individuals break into this field at smaller stations. Others may obtain experi-

ence by working at their college radio station or through internships.

Studio Engineers working in radio need good communications skills and the ability to multitask without getting flustered. A working knowledge of the broadcast studio and electronics, scientific aptitude with problem-solving skills, and manual dexterity are all mandatory.

## Unions and Associations

Studio Engineers working in radio may belong to various bargaining unions and associations depending on the specific position they hold and the station for which they are working. These include the Society of Broadcast Engineers (SBE) and the National Association of Broadcast Employees and Technicians (NABET). Individuals or their stations might also be members of the National Association of Broadcasters (NAB).

## Tips for Entry

1. If you are still in school, get involved with your school or college radio station. The experience you obtain will be valuable.
2. As noted, while certification is not always required, it illustrates professional competency. It will often provide an edge over other candidates with similar qualifications. Contact the Society of Broadcast Engineers (SBE) to get information on classes, seminars, and certification opportunities.
3. Look for classes, seminars, and workshops in the broadcast engineering field. These are useful for both their educational value and the opportunity to make important contacts.
4. Many radio stations and associations offer internships or training programs. Internships give you on-the-job training experience and another opportunity to make contacts.
5. If you can't find a formal internship program, see if you can create your own.
6. Remember that your goal is to get your foot in the door of a radio station and then move up the ladder to do what you want. Consider every job opportunity. Offer to help people in other areas when you are done with your work.
7. Many stations advertise openings on the air or on their websites. Check them out.
8. Job openings are also often advertised in the newspaper classified section under headings such as "Radio Show Engineer," "Radio," "Radio Engineer," "Broadcast Engineer," "Studio Engineer," and "Broadcasting."

# PRODUCTION AND PROGRAM

# PROGRAM DIRECTOR

## CAREER PROFILE

**Duties:** Selects format, programs, and schedule for radio station; may also act in the capacity of the music director

**Alternate Title(s):** P.D.

**Salary Range:** $25,000 to $100,000+

**Employment Prospects:** Fair

**Advancement Prospects:** Fair

**Best Geographical Location(s):** Smaller local communities offer opportunities for small-market stations; New York City, Los Angeles, Chicago, Atlanta, etc., for major-market stations

**Prerequisites:**

**Education or Training**—College degree or broadcast-school training may be preferred

**Experience**—Hands-on training in radio station helpful

**Special Skills and Personality Traits**—Knowledge of radio stations; understanding of radio industry; ability to supervise, hire, and fire; responsible

## CAREER LADDER

```
┌─────────────────────────────────────┐
│   Program Director for Larger,       │
│   More Prestigious Radio Station     │
└─────────────────────────────────────┘

┌─────────────────────────────────────┐
│          Program Director            │
└─────────────────────────────────────┘

┌─────────────────────────────────────┐
│    Music Director or Disc Jockey     │
└─────────────────────────────────────┘
```

## Position Description

The Program Director of a radio station holds an important position in terms of the success of a radio station. He or she is responsible for selecting the station's format and programming. The ultimate goal of the Program Director is to make the station reach the largest audience possible.

In certain stations, the Program Director may also work as the music director. In this case, he or she will be responsible for selecting music for the station's playlist. In other situations the Program Director may also have his or her own show, working as a disc jockey or an on-air personality.

The Program Director (or P.D.) is responsible for everything that is said or played at the station. If a station is sold or is not doing well, the Program Director is expected to revise the station format.

In order to be successful at this task, the Program Director must look at the demographics of the area, as well as the formats of other stations in the listening proximity. The individual may, for example, choose country, pop, hard rock, oldies, Top 40, MOR (middle of the road), AC (adult contemporary), classical, jazz, dance-oriented, UC (urban contemporary), all-news, or talk radio.

The Program Director must have complete knowledge of the community his or her station serves. This information will help the Program Director recommend the type of format likely to attract the most listeners. In radio, the larger the audience, the higher the ratings. Ratings determine advertising and commercial rates, which is how commercial radio stations derive income.

After the Program Director determines the format, he or she must decide what type of shows will be best. He or she is also responsible for determining what kind of public service shows should be aired, the hosts, and when they should be aired in the broadcast schedule. The Program Director is also expected to decide the best times to air news and weather reports, community affairs announcements, etc.

The Program Director is often responsible for hiring, supervising, and terminating disc jockeys and on-air personalities. In some cases at larger stations, the owner or human resources director will handle this responsibility, either personally or with the assistance of the P.D.

An important responsibility of the Program Director at a radio station is developing a segue. The segue is the way that records are rotated in relation to other records, commercials, and announcements. For example, a station might play a Top 40 tune, then a ballad, have a commercial, another Top 40 tune and an oldie; then the cycle would start over again. Program Directors who develop effective segues can keep an audience interested and excited. A boring segue can prompt listeners to switch to another station.

Program Directors in music-oriented stations often meet with record promoters, who visit the station in hopes of getting their clients on the station's playlist. If the station has no music director, the Program Director usually makes up a new playlist every week or two. In cases where the station does have a music director, the individual will approve the playlist.

The Program Director is generally responsible either to the station manager or the owner. He or she often works long hours. The P.D. may come in early, stay late, or be expected to help with station promotions. One of the most satisfying parts of the job of the P.D. is seeing the station's ratings increase.

Additional duties of a Program Director may include:

- Communicating the image of the station that he or she wants disc jockeys and on-air personalities to project
- Attending station community events
- Evaluating the effectiveness of the station's format

## Salaries

Earnings for Programs Directors vary greatly, depending on the size of the station, its location, and popularity. Earnings also are dependent on the experience and responsibilities of the individual. Salaries can range from $25,000 to $100,000-plus annually. Salaries at the lower end of the scale are for individuals without a great deal of experience or those working in smaller stations. Those with a great deal of experience or those working in large stations in major markets will earn the most.

## Employment Prospects

While almost every radio station in the country has a Program Director, the responsibilities might be combined with that of a music director or a disc jockey. In some stations, the station owner assumes the duties of the Program Director.

Employment prospects are fair for individuals seeking positions in smaller stations. Experience helps attain a job in a middle or major market, although finding a position becomes more difficult as stations get larger.

## Advancement Prospects

Advancement prospects for Program Directors are fair. Individuals often start off at a small station, and after obtaining experience they move on to a similar position at a larger or more prestigious station. The ability to show an increase in ratings at a previous station can help the individual climb the career ladder.

Some Program Directors take the career path of moving into station management. Opportunities for this type of career advancement, however, are poor.

## Education and Training

Educational requirements vary for such positions as Program Director. Most stations today prefer a college degree in communications or broadcasting. It should be noted, however, that a degree will not guarantee a job. It will, however, give candidates with similar qualifications a leg up.

There are also a number of radio broadcasting, vocational, and trade schools located around the country that offer broadcast training.

## Experience, Skills, and Personality Traits

Most Program Directors began their careers as disc jockeys. Many have had experience working at college radio stations or other stations before obtaining their position.

It is essential to the success of the Program Director that he or she have the ability to understand the type of market their station is trying to reach. Individuals who work at stations geared toward music must have a working knowledge of music and be up on trends. Those working at news or talk-radio stations similarly need an understanding of those areas in order to be successful.

## Unions and Associations

Program Directors may belong to the National Association of Broadcasters (NAB). They may also be members of the American Federation of Television and Radio Artists (AFTRA) and the National Association of Broadcast Employees and Technicians (NABET).

## Tips for Entry

1. Get experience working at your college radio station.
2. A job as a disc jockey at a local station is also great experience.
3. Many stations offer internship programs. This is a good way to obtain experience and make valuable contacts.
4. Openings and positions are often advertised in the classified section of newspapers. Look under headings such as "Radio," "Broadcasting," "Program Director," and "Music."
5. Many stations also advertise openings right on the air or on their websites. Check them out.
6. Send your résumé with a cover letter to radio stations. You can never tell when an opening might be available.
7. Don't forget to read trade publications. *Billboard, Broadcasting,* and *Radio and Records* often have advertisements from stations with openings.

# PROGRAMMING ASSISTANT

## CAREER PROFILE

**Duties:** Helps the program director at a station fulfill his or her functions; performs clerical and administrative duties

**Alternate Title(s):** P.D. Assistant, Trainee

**Salary Range:** $12,000 to $24,000+

**Employment Prospects:** Fair

**Advancement Prospects:** Fair

**Best Geographical Location(s):** Areas hosting radio stations; smaller local communities offer opportunities for small-market stations; New York City, Los Angeles, Chicago, Atlanta, etc., for major-market stations

**Prerequisites:**

**Education or Training**—College degree or background, or broadcast school training may be preferred

**Experience**—Hands-on training at radio station helpful but not required

**Special Skills and Personality Traits**—People skills; good written and verbal communications skills; organizational skills; computer skills; knowledge of radio stations

## CAREER LADDER

```
┌─────────────────────────────────┐
│   Disc Jockey, Show Host,        │
│   Assistant Producer,            │
│   Advertising Sales Executive, etc. │
└─────────────────────────────────┘

┌─────────────────────────────────┐
│   Programming Assistant          │
└─────────────────────────────────┘

┌─────────────────────────────────┐
│   Entry-Level or Student         │
└─────────────────────────────────┘
```

## Position Description

Radio stations don't just decide to play country music one day, pop the next, hard rock after that, oldies after that, and then go into a total talk format. Stations today depend on a program director, along with the station manager and/or owner, to help select the format and programming for the station. This is an integral part of the success of any station. The station's format and programming draw listeners to tune in and advertisers to buy space.

The job of the programming director can be immense. Many stations employ one or more Programming Assistants to help the program director fulfill his or her responsibilities. Duties of the individual will vary depending on the specific size and structure of the station and the programming department, as well as the experience of the individual.

The Programming Assistant may fulfill an array of functions. In some cases, the individual, like others in assistant positions, may feel like a glorified secretary. He or she may be expected to fulfill secretarial duties such as typing letters and other correspondence, making and returning phone

calls, and filing. The individual might also be responsible for keeping records of department costs.

Programming Assistants, like all other assistants, are expected to do a lot of the "grunt" work, running around and doing tasks to free up the time of the program director and others in the department. He or she may be responsible for handling an array of details involved in the implementation and execution of the programming of the station. This may involve making calls, handling correspondence, checking details, or taking care of odd jobs.

Programming of a radio station involves many things. To begin with, a format for the station must be chosen. What type of music will the station primarily play? Will the station have an all-talk or news format? The format is generally chosen by the type that will be most effective in an area. In order to determine the most effective format, the program director must do extensive research.

The Programming Assistant will often help in this research. He or she might, for example, interview people about their radio listening habits, the type of music they enjoy, or if they like interactive radio. This may be done in person or on the phone.

The Programming Assistant may be responsible for collating questionnaires and surveys the programming department has developed. The individual then may be expected to address envelopes and fill them with the collated questionnaires, which need to be sent out. As questionnaires and surveys come back the Programming Assistant is often responsible for inputting results into the computer and then tabulating them. As Programming Assistants gain more experience, they may be allowed to assist in the development of questionnaires and surveys. It should be noted that once a format is chosen, programming departments often check the effectiveness of that format to be sure the demographics of their listeners hasn't changed. If a format isn't working for a radio station, it will often be changed.

Part of the job of the programming department involves determining what types of shows will work on the station. In radio, the larger the audience and the higher the ratings, the better the advertising rates will be. The Programming Assistant may compile lists of current or potential programs, and current or potential hosts. He or she may input program schedules into the computer and print out copies and distribute them to the appropriate people within the station. If the programming director is working on a new talk, news, or public affairs show, the Programming Assistant may be expected to sit in on meetings taking notes. At the request of the programming director, the individual may place calls to program hosts and producers. He or she may also be asked to schedule meetings between producers, hosts, other departments, or the station management.

The programming department is responsible for developing a segue. The segue is the manner in which records are rotated in relation to other records, commercials, and announcements on the station. As the programming director develops segues to see what will work the best, the Programming Assistant may be expected to input the information into the computer. Once a segue is chosen, he or she will print it out and distribute it as instructed.

In stations where the program director is also working as the music director, the Programming Assistant will be expected to help in that area as well. He or she may be asked to compile and type the weekly playlists of music the director has chosen and distribute it to disc jockeys and others in the station. The individual might also act as a buffer between promotion people from record companies who visit the radio station in an effort to have the station add their client's music added to the station playlist.

Additional duties of a Programming Assistant may include:

- Sending out contracts or letters of agreement to freelance show hosts
- Making sure agreements are signed
- Acting as buffer for the program director

## Salaries

Earnings for Programming Assistants vary greatly, depending on the size of the station, its location, and popularity. Earnings also depend on the experience and responsibilities of the individual. Salaries can begin at approximately $12,000 and go up to $24,000 or more.

## Employment Prospects

Employment prospects are fair for Programming Assistants. Most opportunities will be found with midsize and larger stations. In smaller stations the position of Programming Assistant may be coupled with that of other assistant duties. For example, the individual may be expected to be an administrative assistant to station management or its sales and/or programming staff.

## Advancement Prospects

Advancement prospects for Programming Assistants are fair. Advancement will depend, however, on the individual's career aspirations. Some may obtain this position and decide they want to go into the on-air talent area of radio. Others may determine that they want to go into production or advertising sales. As this is an entry-level position at most stations, the idea is for an individual to get as much experience as possible to determine an area of interest.

## Education and Training

Educational requirements vary for this position. Many stations will accept a high school diploma. Others prefer their employees to have a college background or degree. Whether or not a station requires a college degree, it should be noted that for those seeking a career in radio, a degree will be helpful in career advancement.

There are also a number of radio broadcasting, vocational, and trade schools located around the country that offer broadcasting training.

## Experience, Skills, and Personality Traits

As noted this is usually an entry-level position. Any experience in college radio or broadcasting will be useful. A variety of skills are necessary in this type of position. Organizational skills and the ability to multitask are essential. Computer skills are also needed. Those with good written and verbal communication skills who get along with others will do well. A basic knowledge of radio and the broadcasting industry is useful.

## Unions and Associations

There are a number of organizations and associations that may offer helpful information to Programming Assistants. These include the National Association of Broadcasters

(NAB) and the National Association of Broadcast Employees and Technicians (NABET).

## Tips for Entry

1. If you are in college, get experience working in your college radio station.
2. Most program directors started out as disc jockeys, talk show hosts, or announcers. If becoming a program director is your goal, look for a job as a disc jockey, on-air personality, announcer, or talk show host at a local station.
3. An internship program is the best way to obtain experience and make valuable contacts. Call or write radio stations to see if they offer internship programs. Sometimes, even if they don't have a formal program, your college adviser can put one together where you will end up getting college credit for the experience.
4. Openings and positions are often advertised in the classified section of newspapers. Look under headings such as "Radio," "Broadcasting," "Programming Assistant," and "Program Assistant."
5. Many stations also advertise openings right on the air or on their websites. Check them out.
6. Send your résumé with a cover letter to radio stations. You can never tell when an opening might be available.

# MUSIC DIRECTOR

## CAREER PROFILE

**Duties:** Selects music for specific programs on radio station; develops station playlist

**Alternate Title(s):** MD

**Salary Range:** $25,000 to $95,000+

**Employment Prospects:** Fair

**Advancement Prospects:** Fair

**Best Geographical Location(s):** Smaller local communities offer opportunities for small-market stations; New York City, Los Angeles, Chicago, Atlanta, etc., for major-market stations

**Prerequisites:**

**Education or Training**—College degree or broadcast-school training may be preferred

**Experience**—Hands-on training at radio station helpful; experience as disc jockey

**Special Skills and Personality Traits**—Knowledge of workings of radio station; understanding of music industry; ability to supervise others; responsible

## CAREER LADDER

```
┌─────────────────────────────────────────┐
│  Program Director or Music Director      │
│  in Larger, More Prestigious Station     │
└─────────────────────────────────────────┘

┌─────────────────────────────────────────┐
│            Music Director                │
└─────────────────────────────────────────┘

┌─────────────────────────────────────────┐
│  Disc Jockey or Assistant Music Director │
└─────────────────────────────────────────┘
```

## Position Description

Every time you listen to a radio station and hear the different songs being played, you are hearing the work of the station's Music Director. The Music Director of a radio station is the individual responsible for selecting music for specific programs heard on the station. He or she works closely with the program director in making sure the station attracts as many listeners as possible.

Depending on the size of the station, the Music Director may also be the program director. He or she might also have his or her own show and work as a disc jockey.

Music Directors have various duties depending on the format being utilized by the station and the duties of the program director. The Music Director often meets with record company promoters screening new tunes. The Music Director and the program director then discuss which tunes could potentially be a hit when they air them in their market.

It is the responsibility of the Music Director to assist the program director in many of the music-related activities. The individual will help the program director research the market, determine the kind of audience the station plays to, and determine what the audience wants to hear. With this

information, he or she can get a feel for the station listeners' likes and dislikes.

The Music Director often visits or talks to the managers of the major music stores in the area. These meetings help him or her find out what is hot in singles and album releases in the area.

The Music Director is often expected to help choose new disc jockeys. At times, the Music Director will work with the program director in training new disc jockeys and helping them adjust to the station's procedures. This is often done by listening to air checks, which are short tapes of the different on-air personalities recorded at various times in their shift.

Additional duties of a Music Director may include:

- Assisting in the selection of new disc jockeys
- Taking part in station promotions
- Making special appearances on behalf of the station

## Salaries

Earnings for Music Directors vary greatly, depending on the size of the station, its location, and popularity. Earnings also are dependent on the experience and responsibilities of the individual. Salaries can range from $25,000 to $95,000-plus annually. Salaries at the lower end of the scale are for individuals without a great deal of experience or those working in smaller stations. Those with a great deal of experience or those working for large stations in major markets will earn the most.

## Employment Prospects

Employment prospects are not great for Music Directors. Many radio stations do not employ a Music Director. They choose instead to combine the responsibilities of the Music Director with those of the program director.

Employment prospects are better for individuals seeking positions in smaller or midsize stations. After obtaining some experience, Music Directors often find it easier to find a position in a larger station.

## Advancement Prospects

Advancement prospects for Music Directors are fair. Individuals often start off at a small station and after obtaining experience move on to a similar position at a larger or more prestigious station. Some become program directors.

## Education and Training

Educational requirements vary for positions as Music Directors. While there is no formal educational requirement, most stations prefer or require a college degree or broadcasting school training. There are a number of radio broadcasting, vocational, and trade schools located around the country that offer broadcasting training. Courses in communications, journalism, music, and broadcasting are helpful.

## Experience, Skills, and Personality Traits

Most Music Directors begin their careers as disc jockeys. During this time period they often have the opportunity to prove their expertise at selecting music and putting shows together. Many individuals obtain experience working at college radio stations or other stations before landing the position as a Music Director.

Music Directors, as a rule, like music. They enjoy listening to music and have the knack of knowing what will be hot before it is.

## Unions and Associations

Music Directors may belong to the National Association of Broadcasters (NAB). They may also be members of the American Federation of Television and Radio Artists (AFTRA) and the National Association of Broadcast Employees and Technicians (NABET).

## Tips for Entry

1. Get experience working in your college radio station.
2. A job as a disc jockey at a local station is also great experience.
3. Many stations offer internship programs. This is a good way to obtain experience and make valuable contacts. It is not unusual for a station to hire an intern after graduation.
4. Openings and positions are often advertised in the classified section of newspapers. Look under headings such as "Radio," "Broadcasting," "Music Director," and "Music."
5. Many stations also advertise openings right on the air or on their websites. Check them out.
6. Send your résumé with a cover letter to radio stations. You can never tell when an opening might be available.
7. Don't forget to read trade publications. *Billboard, Broadcasting,* and *Radio and Records* often have advertisements for stations with openings.

# PRODUCER, RADIO SHOW

## CAREER PROFILE

**Duties:** Creates compelling, intriguing, and entertaining radio shows; plans various aspects of radio show; coordinates production elements; develops show ideas; writes scripts; brings good story ideas to table

**Alternate Title(s):** Executive Producer

**Salary Range:** $20,000 to $85,000+

**Employment Prospects:** Fair

**Advancement Prospects:** Fair

**Best Geographical Location(s):** Opportunities may be located throughout the country

**Prerequisites:**

**Education or Training**—College background or degree required or preferred by most stations

**Experience**—Experience in broadcasting required

**Special Skills and Personality Traits**—Understanding and knowledge of broadcast industry; communications skills; creativity; writing skills; ability to multitask

## CAREER LADDER

```
┌─────────────────────────────────────┐
│       Producer for Larger,          │
│  More Prestigious Show or Station   │
└─────────────────────────────────────┘

┌─────────────────────────────────────┐
│        Producer, Radio Show         │
└─────────────────────────────────────┘

┌─────────────────────────────────────┐
│       Associate Producer or         │
│         Guest Coordinator           │
└─────────────────────────────────────┘
```

## Position Description

Depending on the size and structure of radio stations, the disc jockey or on-air personality may be the only individual involved in putting a radio show on the air. Some stations may have a large number of employees in addition to the on-air talent. These may include guest coordinators, researchers, directors, and Producers.

The Producer's ultimate goal is to make each radio show he or she produces compelling, intriguing, and entertaining. The Producer works behind the scenes putting together radio shows so they flow easily.

The Producer has many responsibilities, stemming from his or her primary responsibility—coordinating the production aspects of the radio show. Different types of shows will have different types of challenges. Live shows, for example, will have challenges different from taped ones. If you make a mistake in a taped show, it can often be fixed. A Producer does not have the same luxury with a live show.

The Producer must determine the answers to a number of questions in order to do his or her job effectively. For example, will the disc jockey or on-air talent ask for calls from the listening audience? If so, a telephone setup must be in place.

Will the show utilize more than one on-air personality? If so, two microphones and two sets of earphones must be on hand. The specific responsibilities of each DJ must also be determined. Will the show use guests? How will guests fit into the scheduled programming? Will guests be in the studio with the host or will they need to use a telephone hookup? The Producer must address these and any other technical issues.

The Producer is expected to determine the direction of the show so it interests the intended audience. This task is often done in conjunction with the program director. For example, what type of morning show will attract the most listeners? Should the show be humorous or just give information? Many morning shows have two disc jockeys bantering back and forth. Some may have a traffic reporter joking with the listeners from the air. Will guests attract more listeners? How will everything go together?

A great deal of the job of the Radio Show Producer is done before the show goes on the air. He or she may hold brainstorming sessions with others involved in the show to come up with ideas for making the show more interesting. It is his or her responsibility to bring entertaining and interesting content to the table, developing themes and coming up with different ideas. Is a celebrity coming to town? Can the Producer get him or her to call in and say hello? Is there a big concert coming to the area? Will people be standing in line to get precious tickets? Can the Producer get someone to call who is standing on line to get a blow by blow account of what the experience is like? What types of guests will add to the show? The Producer must constantly come up with new and innovative ideas.

The Producer is often responsible for booking guests for the radio show. Depending on the specific show, these may include recording stars, celebrities, politicians, authors, and newsmakers. Producers may book nationally recognized guests or those who are less known. The Producer is expected to preinterview guests to ensure they are right for the show and prepare them for the interview.

Not every guest is live in the studio. Some guests appear on radio shows via telephone hookups. The Producer must make sure guests know exactly when the station will call, how long interviews will be, the names of the on-air personalities, and the subject matter to be covered. In the same vein, the Producer may provide the DJ or on-air personality with a bio of the guest and possible questions to ask.

The Producer is also expected to plan and coordinate the various aspects of the talk show. For example, what type of music will lead in and lead out of each show? What sound effects will be needed?

The Producer may have a number of writing duties. He or she may write introductions to the show, short bios of guests, scripts, etc.

The Producer is responsible for directing and supervising everyone who is involved in the production of the show. Depending on the specific show structure, he or she may have one or more assistants working on projects.

If the show has call-ins, the Producer may be the one answering the phones and screening calls while the show is on-air. He or she may obtain the caller's name and question and/or comments before putting the call through to the DJ. The individual may feed the information to the host by means of computer technology or just write it down. In some stations other employees handle this task.

It is the Producer's responsibility to make sure everything goes smoothly during the show. He or she must make sure the studio is set up correctly. If, for example, guests will be on the show, the Producer makes sure there are enough chairs and headphones available for everyone. After a show has ended, the Producer may make calls, do paperwork, or straighten up the studio for the next show.

Additional duties of Radio Show Producers may include:

- Being the disc jockey or on-air talent for a show
- Producing radio news or sports programming
- Producing radio commercials

## Salaries

Earnings for radio Producers can vary tremendously, ranging from $20,000 to $85,000 or more. Variables include the size,

location, prestige, and popularity of the station, as well as the experience, expertise, and responsibilities of the individual.

In some stations minimum earnings are negotiated and set by a union. It should be noted, however, that these are minimums. A Producer working on a popular show can usually negotiate higher earnings.

## Employment Prospects

Employment prospects for Producers working in radio are fair. It's important to note that not every radio show has a Producer. In smaller stations the on-air talent, assistants, or engineers may handle production.

Openings may be located throughout the country. Producers may find work in small local or regional stations, larger stations, national stations, public radio, or syndicated shows. The most opportunities will exist in midsize and major-market areas hosting radio stations.

## Advancement Prospects

Advancement prospects for Producers working in radio are fair. Individuals may climb the career ladder in a number of ways. After obtaining experience, Producers may locate similar jobs at larger, more prestigious stations or produce more prestigious shows.

## Education and Training

Most radio stations require their Producers to hold a four-year college degree or a certificate from a broadcasting school. Good choices for majors include communications, broadcasting, journalism, English, public relations, marketing, advertising, and liberal arts.

## Experience, Skills, and Personality Traits

Experience requirements vary from station to station for Radio Show Producers. Broadcast experience of some type is usually needed. Many Producers started out as interns, assistants, guest coordinators, or on-air talent themselves.

Producers working in radio should be personable, with the ability to multitask. Creativity is essential to this type of position. The ability to think quickly and make decisions is mandatory.

Excellent verbal and written communication skills are needed, as is the ability to work with different types of personalities.

## Unions and Associations

Radio Show Producers may belong to various bargaining unions and associations, depending on the specific position they hold and the station for which they are working. These include the National Association of Broadcast Employees and Technicians (NABET), the American Federation of Television and Radio Artists (AFTRA), and the Writers

Guild of America (WGA). Individuals or their stations might also be members of the National Association of Broadcasters (NAB).

## Tips for Entry

1. Get as much experience as possible working in broadcasting. Volunteer to work with your college radio station, join radio clubs, etc.
2. Look for classes, seminars, and workshops in the broadcasting industry. These are useful for both their educational value and the opportunity to make important contacts.
3. Many radio stations and associations offer internships or training programs. Internships give you on-the-job training experience and another opportunity to make contacts.
4. If you can't find a formal internship program, see if you can create your own.
5. Remember that your goal is to get your foot in the door of a radio station and then move up the ladder to do what you want. Consider every job opportunity. Offer to help people in other areas when you are done with your work.
6. Many local stations advertise openings on the air or on their websites. Check them out.
7. Job openings are also often advertised in the newspaper classified section under headings such as "Radio Show Producer," "Radio," "Producer-Radio," "Morning Drive Time Producer," and "Broadcasting."

# PRODUCER, RADIO TALK SHOW

## CAREER PROFILE

**Duties:** Plans various aspects of radio talk show; coordinates production elements; develops show ideas; writes scripts; locates and books potential guests; brings good story ideas to table

**Alternate Title(s):** Executive Producer

**Salary Range:** $20,000 to $85,000+

**Employment Prospects:** Fair

**Advancement Prospects:** Fair

**Best Geographical Location(s):** Opportunities may be located throughout the country; the most opportunities will be located in areas hosting all-talk or news formats

**Prerequisites:**

**Education or Training**—College background or degree required or preferred by most stations

**Experience**—Experience in broadcasting required

**Special Skills and Personality Traits**—Understanding and knowledge of broadcast industry; communications skills; creativity; writing skills; ability to multitask

## CAREER LADDER

```
┌─────────────────────────────┐
│   Producer for Larger, More │
│  Prestigious Talk Show or for│
│     Syndicated Talk Show     │
└─────────────────────────────┘

┌─────────────────────────────┐
│   Producer, Radio Talk Show  │
└─────────────────────────────┘

┌─────────────────────────────┐
│     Associate Producer or    │
│       Guest Coordinator      │
└─────────────────────────────┘
```

## Position Description

There are an array of radio talk shows on the air covering a variety of subjects. Some may be general in nature. Others might discuss areas such as business, cooking, film, music, or politics. Some talk shows are live while others are taped in advance.

When most people listen to radio talk shows, they don't consider what it took to get the show on the air. Most of us think about is whether or not we enjoyed the show or got anything out of it. Behind the scenes, however, there is a great deal of work involved in putting together radio talk shows so that they are enjoyable to listen to and just seem to flow. The individual responsible for a talk show's success is the Radio Talk Show Producer. It should be noted that in some situations, the Talk Show Producer is also the talk-show host.

Within the scope of the job, the Talk Show Producer has many responsibilities. The individual's main function is to plan and coordinate all production aspects of the talk show.

When producing a radio talk show, there are a number of questions the Producer must think about. Will the show be live or taped? Will the host ask for calls from the listening audience? Will the show use guests? Will guests be in the studio with the host or will they need to use a telephone hook-up? The Producer must address these and other questions to attend to technical issues.

The Producer must determine the direction of the show and the intended audience. Once all this is complete, the Producer is expected to plan and coordinate the various aspects of the talk show. For example, what type of music will lead in and lead out of each show? The Producer may go through various pieces of music and songs to find just the right one. Sometimes the Producer commissions a songwriter to write lyrics for the show. In other situations the Producer may ask the copywriter to develop lyrics that work with a short piece of music.

The Producer is expected to develop shows. It is his or her responsibility to bring compelling content and good story ideas to the table. He or she may develop themes or come up with different ideas for each show that are related to the talk show's focus in some manner. Often the Producer and show host will hold brainstorming sessions to come up with new and innovative ideas for shows.

Once an idea for a show is conceived, the Producer must develop the show more fully. What will be the focus of the show? What points will be covered? Should guests be used? Which guests would be best? Where are the potential guests located? Will they be willing to be on the show? What about alternatives? For shows using guests, one of the important functions of the Producer is booking those guests. In some cases, a guest coordinator handles this function.

Once guests are booked, the Producer often preinterviews them. During this time, the Producer obtains information about the individual to give to the show host.

The Producer often does a great deal of research in the development of the show. He or she may interview people, read articles or books, talk to experts, or browse the Internet to get information. He or she then takes the important points and puts them in writing for the show host to review. In this manner, the show host is prepared with accurate information to do a show.

The Producer may have a number of writing duties. He or she may write introductions to the show, short bios of guests, possible probing questions for the host to ask, or scripts. Creative Producers are able to develop new and innovative ways to tell stories.

The Producer is responsible for directing and supervising everyone involved in the production of the show. Depending on the specific show structure, he or she may have one or more assistants working on projects.

If the talk show has call-ins, the Producer may be the one answering the phones and screening calls while the show is on the air. They may obtain the caller's name and question and/or comments before putting the call through to the host. They may feed the information to the host by means of computer technology or just write it down. In some stations other employees handle this task.

It is the Producer's responsibility to make sure everything goes smoothly during the show. He or she must make sure the studio is set up correctly. If, for example, guests will be on the show, the Producer makes sure there are enough chairs and headphones available for everyone.

As a rule, the Talk Show Producer functions behind the scenes. One of the downsides of the job is that if the show does well, credit may be given to the host. If the show does poorly, the blame is often on the Producer. Many Talk Show Producers, however, feel that knowing that they were responsible for putting together a great show is worth it.

Additional duties of Radio Talk Show Producers may include:

- Hosting the show
- Producing nontalk radio programming
- Producing radio news reports

## Salaries

Earnings for Radio Talk Show Producers can vary tremendously. The range can run between $20,000 and $85,000 or more. Variables include the size, location, prestige, and popularity of the station and the specific talk show, as well as the experience, expertise, and responsibilities of the individual.

In some stations, minimum earnings are negotiated and set by a union. It should be noted, however, that these are minimums. A Talk Show Producer working on a popular show can usually negotiate higher earnings.

In some cases, Radio Talk Show Producers syndicate a show. In these situations, earnings will depend on the number of stations buying the show.

## Employment Prospects

Employment prospects for Radio Talk Show Producers are fair. Openings may be located throughout the country. Talk Show Producers may find work in small local or regional stations, larger stations, national stations, public radio, or as noted previously, have their own syndicated shows. The most opportunities will exist in areas hosting radio stations with all-talk or news formats.

## Advancement Prospects

Advancement prospects for Radio Talk Show Producers are fair. Individuals may climb the career ladder in a number of ways. After obtaining experience, some Producers locate similar jobs at larger, more prestigious stations or produce more prestigious shows. In some cases, the talk show or the show's host builds a following and moves to a more prestigious station or syndicates the show. Often when this happens, the show host will take the Producer with him or her. This results in increased responsibilities and earnings.

## Education and Training

Most radio stations require their Producers to hold a four-year college degree. Good choices for majors include communications, broadcasting, journalism, English, public relations, marketing, advertising, and liberal arts.

## Experience, Skills, and Personality Traits

Experience requirements vary from station to station and show to show for Radio Talk Show Producers. Broadcast experience of some type is usually needed.

Some Producers have worked in the news department before obtaining their position. Others worked as Producers for other types of shows. Still others were guest coordinators or assistant producers. Some had been talk show hosts themselves.

Talk Show Producers need to be personable individuals with an ability to multitask without getting flustered. These is often a great deal of pressure in this type of job. The ability to think and make decisions quickly is essential. This is especially important if the individual is producing a live show.

Excellent communications skills, both verbal and written, are necessary. The ability to work with different types of personalities is also necessary. Creativity is mandatory in this position.

## Unions and Associations

Radio Talk Show Producers may belong to various bargaining unions and associations, depending on the specific position they hold and the station for which they are working. These include the National Association of Broadcast Employees and Technicians (NABET), the American Federation of Television and Radio Artists (AFTRA), and the Writers Guild of America (WGA). Individuals or their stations might also be members of the National Association of Broadcasters (NAB).

## Tips for Entry

1. Get as much experience as possible working in broadcasting. Volunteer to work with your college radio station, join radio clubs, etc.
2. Many radio stations and associations offer internships or training programs. Internships give you on-the-job training experience and the opportunity to make important contacts.
3. If you can't find a formal internship program, see if you can create your own.
4. Remember that your goal is to get your foot in the door of a radio station and then move up the ladder to do what you want. Consider every job opportunity. Offer to help people in other areas when you are done with your work.
5. Try to find a mentor at the station where you work or volunteer. He or she can help you reach your goals.
6. Many local stations advertise openings on the air or on their websites. Check them out.
7. Job openings are also often advertised in the newspaper classified section under headings such as "Talk Show Producer," "Radio," "Radio Talk Show Producer," and "Broadcasting."
8. Don't forget to read trade publications. *Billboard, Broadcasting,* and *Radio and Records* often have advertisements for stations with openings.

# GUEST COORDINATOR

## CAREER PROFILE

**Duties:** Locates and schedules guests for radio news or talk show

**Alternate Title(s):** Guest Booker

**Salary Range:** $20,000 to $45,000+

**Employment Prospects:** Fair

**Advancement Prospects:** Fair

**Best Geographical Location(s):** Opportunities may exist throughout the country in areas with radio stations hosting talk shows

**Prerequisites:**

**Education or Training**—College degree required or preferred by most stations

**Experience**—Experience in production helpful

**Special Skills and Personality Traits**—Communication skills; organizational skills; persuasiveness; people skills

## CAREER LADDER

```
┌─────────────────────────────────────┐
│  Guest Coordinator for Larger,       │
│  More Prestigious Show or            │
│  Station or Producer                 │
└─────────────────────────────────────┘

┌─────────────────────────────────────┐
│  Guest Coordinator                   │
└─────────────────────────────────────┘

┌─────────────────────────────────────┐
│  Production Assistant                │
└─────────────────────────────────────┘
```

## Position Description

Radio stations often have a variety of different types of programming throughout the day. In addition to music, stations often host an array of news and talk shows. In addition to the show host, many news and talk shows have guests as well.

Finding the perfect guest for a radio show is a talent. The individual in charge of handling this task may differ, depending on the specific station and show. Sometimes it is the show host him- or herself who books the guests. In other situations, the producer may be in charge of that task. Some radio shows have Guest Coordinators.

Guest Coordinators are expected to find appropriate guests for radio shows. It is their responsibility to locate and book guests who will help make the show interesting and compelling. Finding just the right guest depends on the show. Generally, the host or producer develops ideas for one or a series of upcoming shows. They then determine the direction the show will follow. After that, they decide what types of guests will make the show more appealing. This is where the Guest Coordinator comes in.

For example, a radio station may have a daily show on health and fitness. The host and/or the producer may decide that they will do a weeklong series of shows on getting in shape. One show might focus on doing aerobic exercise.

Another might be on eating healthier. Still another might be on walking. The fourth day they might do a show on seniors getting in shape, and the final day of the series might be on making changes slowly. Once the focus of the shows are worked out, the producer will talk to the Guest Coordinator about possible guests.

The Guest Coordinator then must get to work finding people who can make each show more exciting and interesting. For this particular series, for example, the Guest Coordinator might seek out personal trainers, aerobic instructors, nutritionists, authors, physicians, motivational speakers, and representatives from senior organizations.

Just because someone is an expert in a specific field does not mean they will be a good guest. Nothing is worse on radio than dead air. Guest Coordinators make sure potential guests not only speak clearly and understandably but are also comfortable behind a microphone. Guest Coordinators often preinterview potential guests to ensure they are knowledgeable about a specific subject and to get their views.

Sometimes the Guest Coordinator knows of people who might be appropriate. Many individuals in this position build and keep lists of potential guests and their subject areas. There are also annual periodicals listing guests and subjects in which they are experts. Guest Coordinators often find guest possibilities in articles in newspapers and magazines, on television, or even on another radio station.

While guests are usually not paid to appear on radio talk shows, there are literally thousands of people who want to be guests. Some want to share their opinion. Others may seek the recognition. Many want the publicity for their project.

As a result, many people write letters to Guest Coordinators requesting to be considered as potential guests. In some cases, the people write themselves. In other cases, press agents, publicists, public relations people, et al., send letters, press kits, and additional information touting the expertise of their clients.

Guest Coordinators spend a great deal of time going through the correspondence sent to them and filing information that may be useful for future shows. They also spend time on the phone speaking to publicists or potential guests. Sometimes individuals seeking radio exposure call Guest Coordinators to query their interest or follow up on material that has been sent.

Depending on the size and structure of the station and the specific show, the Guest Coordinator may get local, regional, or nationally recognized guests. He or she always tries to get guests who will make listeners want to tune in to the station.

Once a Guest Coordinator locates guests, he or she must make sure the individuals are available on the date needed. Guest Coordinators often give desired guests a number of possible dates to ensure availability. In many instances, Guest Coordinators prepare and send confirmation letters to guests, detailing dates, times, and subject matter.

Guest Coordinators may ask for background information on guests, including bios, press kits, and books they may have written. They are expected to review the material and extract information to give to the producer and/or the host. Guest Coordinators may be responsible for writing biographical information or developing fact sheets for the host to use during his or her interview.

The Guest Coordinator often calls guests a day or two before they are to appear on a show to confirm once again that the guest will be available. Depending on the setup of the specific show, guests may appear live or via a phone hookup. This means that the guest might be at home in New York during the show, while the station is in California. To avoid problems, it is essential that the Guest Coordinator tell each guest the exact time and time zone in which the show will be aired.

Within the scope of their job, Guest Coordinators often perform a number of other tasks. They may be expected to keep files of guest information, including where they can be contacted, their areas of expertise, and the dates they appeared on shows. Guest Coordinators may also be responsible for having guests sign release forms before they appear on shows. Some Guest Coordinators arrange to have tapes made of the shows in which guests appeared.

Depending on the specific station, Guest Coordinators may be responsible for booking the guests on one or more shows. They may be responsible for finding guests for talk shows, news shows, or even music shows.

Additional duties of radio Guest Coordinators may include:

- Assisting in the development of show ideas
- Arranging to have a car pick up show guests
- Making travel arrangements for guests coming into town
- Conducting preshow interviews

## Salaries

Annual earnings for Guest Coordinators working in radio can range from $20,000 to $45,000 or more. Factors affecting earnings include the size, location, prestige, and popularity of the station and the show the individual works on, as well as the experience, expertise, and responsibilities of the individual.

## Employment Prospects

Employment prospects for Guest Coordinators seeking to work in radio are fair. It should be noted that at smaller stations, the Guest Coordinator may handle booking guests as well as other production responsibilities. The best opportunities will be located in areas hosting large radio stations with talk shows, all-talk-show formats, or well-syndicated talk shows.

## Advancement Prospects

Advancement prospects for Guest Coordinators are fair. Individuals who have a broad contact base and consistently book interesting guests that help "make" the show will be in demand. There are two common methods of career advancement in this area. The first is that individuals find similar positions with larger, more prestigious shows or at larger, more prestigious stations. Other Guest Coordinators climb the career ladder by becoming producers.

## Education and Training

Most stations require Guest Coordinators to have a college degree. Good majors for this type of career include communications, journalism, liberal arts, broadcasting, or English.

## Experience, Skills, and Personality Traits

Experience requirements vary from station to station for Guest Coordinators. Generally, the smaller the station, the less experience will be required. Many Guest Coordinators worked as production assistants before their current position. Others may have had internships in the production department or worked in radio news.

Guest Coordinators should be organized, persuasive individuals with good communications skills. The ability to make people feel comfortable is essential. People skills and the ability to multitask are mandatory.

## Unions and Associations

Guest Coordinators working in radio may belong to various organizations and associations, depending on the specific position they hold and the station for which they are working. These include the National Association of Broadcast Employees and Technicians (NABET) and the Writers Guild of America (WGA). Individuals or their stations might also be members of the National Association of Broadcasters (NAB).

## Tips for Entry

1. Get as much experience as possible working in broadcasting. Volunteer to work with your college radio station, join radio clubs, etc.
2. Many radio stations and associations offer internships or training programs. Internships give you on-the-job training experience and the opportunity to make important contacts.

3. Many local stations advertise openings on the air as well as on their website. Check them out.
4. Job openings are also often advertised in the newspaper classified section under headings such as "Guest Coordinator," "Radio," "Radio Talk-Show Guest Coordinator," and "Broadcasting."
5. Don't forget to read trade publications. *Billboard, Broadcasting,* and *Radio and Records* often have advertisements for stations with openings.
6. Consider sending your résumé with a letter to radio stations, inquiring about openings. Remember to request that your résumé be kept on file if there are no current openings.
7. Even though you may need to perform other responsibilities, it is usually easier to find a position in a smaller market than a larger one. Find a job, get some experience, and climb the career ladder.

# MUSIC LIBRARIAN

**Duties:** Catalogs music, recordings, etc. at radio station; performs research or reference work pertaining to music

**Alternate Title(s):** Record Librarian

**Salary Range:** $19,000 to $38,000+

**Employment Prospects:** Poor

**Advancement Prospects:** Fair

**Best Geographical Location(s):** Positions may be located throughout the country in areas hosting radio stations

**Prerequisites:**

**Education or Training**—Bachelor's degree in library science; music history, or theory

**Experience**—Experience as a record librarian assistant is helpful

**Special Skills and Personality Traits**—Interest in music recordings; library research training; organizational skills; communications skills

```
┌────────────────────────────────┐
│    Music Librarian at Larger,  │
│    More Prestigious Station or │
│    Music Library Administrator │
└────────────────────────────────┘

┌────────────────────────────────┐
│        Music Librarian         │
└────────────────────────────────┘

┌────────────────────────────────┐
│   Student or Library Assistant │
└────────────────────────────────┘
```

## Position Description

Radio stations often have a vast library of records, cassettes, CDs, and reel-to-reel tapes. This music must be kept in an orderly fashion so that when someone at the station needs a particular piece of music, it can be located easily.

An interesting position available with some radio stations is that of a Music Librarian. Music Librarians, also known as Record Librarians, combine their skills as librarians with their knowledge of music.

The Music Librarian is responsible for cataloging all the musical materials. In addition to the records, cassettes, CDs, and tapes, this might also include books or other information on music-oriented subjects. The Music Librarian catalogs the music, much like librarians in traditional libraries catalog books.

The Music Librarian also often utilizes computers to make this task easier. He or she may compile a large database of every piece of music the station has in place. In this manner, when a program director, music director, producer, or disc jockey needs something, it is easily located.

In many cases, the Music Librarian is responsible for pulling the records, tapes, cassettes, etc., the disc jockey or music director has chosen before shows. Some radio sta-

tions have programming where they ask listeners to request music they want to hear. During these live shows, Music Librarians are often the ones expected to pull the requested music from the station's music library. A computerized library database means that a comprehensive search can be done in seconds. Otherwise, trying to find a particular piece of music on short notice could be a nightmare.

After shows, the Music Librarian may be responsible for putting used records, tapes, and cassettes back in their proper locations. He or she is expected to keep track of any broken, scratched or warped records or CDs, as well as any broken or stretched tapes that need replacement.

Music Librarians may also perform reference work, looking up or locating information needed for station employees. This may be done using a variety of methods, including going through books, periodicals, databases, and the Internet.

The Music Librarian often works with the station manager, program director, and music director in choosing, ordering, and purchasing new music. Depending on the station, the Music Librarian may help choose or recommend music for commercials or programs. For example, a producer may put together a new talk show and require lead-in music. The Music Librarian may be called upon to give his or her suggestions.

Generally, Music Librarians working in radio stations are responsible to the program director, music director, or station manager.

Additional duties of Music Librarians working in radio stations may include:

- Locating hard-to-find music
- Keeping track of all music until it is returned
- Cataloging commercial tapes
- Cataloging music that comes into the station from record labels and independent distributors

## Salaries

Annual earnings for Music Librarians can range from approximately $19,000 to $38,000 or more. Factors affecting earnings include the size, prestige, and location of the specific station. Other factors affecting earnings include the experience and responsibilities of the individual.

## Employment Prospects

Employment prospects for radio Music Librarians are poor, and competition is stiff for positions. While every radio station has someone who handles the responsibilities of this position, not every station employs a Music Librarian. In some stations the music director, disc jockey, secretary, or administrative assistant may take on the general duties of this position.

## Advancement Prospects

Once on the job, advancement prospects are fair for Music Librarians in radio. The most common method of advancement for most individuals in this field is to find a similar position with a larger or more prestigious station. Some may move on to a similar position in television or the film industry. Depending on career aspirations, some Music Librarians may also seek work in conservatories or the music division of a large college.

## Education and Training

In order to become a Music Librarian, individuals generally need a bachelor's degree in either music theory, history, or library sciences. Some positions may prefer a master's degree in either music or library sciences. These would generally be at very large stations, however.

## Experience, Skills, and Personality Traits

Many Music Librarians worked in libraries before and during their training. Some also have experience working in a radio station.

Music Librarians must be very organized individuals with good memories. Research skills are necessary. Individuals should have a love of music and an interest in music and recordings. Interpersonal skills are helpful to succeed in this position.

## Unions and Associations

Music Librarians may belong to a number of associations that provide education and networking opportunities and professional support. These include the American Library Association (ALA), the Special Libraries Association (SLA), and the Music Library Association (MLA).

## Tips for Entry

1. Many radio stations and associations offer internships or training programs. Internships give you on-the-job training experience and the opportunity to make important contacts.
2. Competition is often stiff for these positions. It is to your advantage to secure as much education as possible and take specialized courses in specific areas. Try to become an expert in at least one specialty.
3. A position as a library assistant while you are still in school will be good experience. If you can find a position as an assistant in a radio station, even better.
4. Many local stations advertise openings on the air or on their websites. Check them out.
5. Job openings are also often advertised in the newspaper classified section under headings such as "Music Librarian," "Record Librarian," "Radio," "Broadcasting," and "Radio Sales."
6. Don't forget to read trade publications. *Billboard, Broadcasting,* and *Radio and Records* often have advertisements for stations with openings.
7. Send your résumé and a short cover letter to radio stations you are interested in working for. You can never tell when an opening exists.

# PROMOTION

# PROMOTION DIRECTOR

## CAREER PROFILE

**Duties:** Develops and implements promotions to help enhance the station's image and attract listeners

**Alternate Title(s):** Director of Promotion; Promotion Manager; Promotion and Special Projects Director

**Salary Range:** $22,000 to $80,000+

**Employment Prospects:** Fair

**Advancement Prospects:** Fair

**Best Geographical Location(s):** Positions located throughout the country

**Prerequisites:**

**Education or Training**—College degree required or preferred by most stations

**Experience**—Experience in public relations, promotion, marketing, broadcasting, or journalism helpful

**Special Skills and Personality Traits**—Creativity; imagination; good communications skills; persuasive; writing skills; personable; outgoing nature

## CAREER LADDER

```
┌─────────────────────────────────┐
│   Promotion Director at Larger,  │
│   More Prestigious Station or    │
│      Director of Marketing       │
└─────────────────────────────────┘

┌─────────────────────────────────┐
│       Promotion Director         │
└─────────────────────────────────┘

┌─────────────────────────────────┐
│     Promotion Coordinator,       │
│  Assistant Promotion Director, or│
│       Promotion Assistant        │
└─────────────────────────────────┘
```

## Position Description

The Promotion Director at a radio station is responsible for developing and implementing station promotions and special events. There are many radio stations from which people can choose to listen. Many make their choices by picking out stations that play the type of music they enjoy. Others may like the programming or the on-air personalities. In an attempt to attract more listeners, as well as add excitement to programming, radio stations often offer a variety of promotions, contests, and special events. These are designed to help enhance the station's image and attract listeners.

The Promotion Director will have varied duties, depending on the size and structure of the station in which he or she works. In larger stations, the individual may be responsible for an entire department of people. In smaller stations, he or she may work alone or with one or two assistants.

The Promotion Director is responsible not only for developing interesting and effective promotions but also implementing them as well. These might include a variety of contests, sweepstakes, and special events.

Many of the promotions at radio stations involve contests and sweepstakes. Some of these are small giveaways, while others can be very large. For example, the Promotion Director may design a giveaway where if a listener calls in and is the right number caller, he or she wins a radio station T-shirt, a CD, concert tickets, cash, or even a brand-new automobile. Some radio stations even have been known to give away the land to build a home on or a new prefab home.

Sometimes, when an organization owns more than one station, the Promotion Director will be responsible for handling the promotions for the entire group of stations. Often in these situations, the stations are quite different, resulting in the need for different types of promotions. For example, a group may own one station oriented toward country music, one oriented toward oldies music, and yet another geared toward hard-rock music. Promotions for the country music station may revolve around contests, giving away tickets to major country music concerts. The oldies station may have a contest giving away cash, and the hard-rock music station may be running a contest for a band to get a shot at a recording contract.

Savvy Promotion Directors are creative. If one of the station's on-air personalities is getting married, the Promotion Director might see if he or she can persuade the personality to have the ceremony and the reception in public as a promotion. The listening audience is invited to the wedding. The Promotion Director might, for example, plan the ceremony and reception at an advertiser's shopping center, hotel, or even in the park. Depending on the station's advertisers, he or she might have a jewelry store donate the ring, a bridal store donate the dress, a men's clothing store donate a tux, a restaurant throw in the food, and a travel agency give the happy couple—and perhaps a lucky listener and spouse—a honeymoon trip. The promotion might begin at the time the couple announces their engagement and go through their wedding ceremony and honeymoon trip. If no on-air personality is getting married, the Promotion Director might run a contest to find a lucky listener who wants to tie the knot in public.

Developing the ideas is just the beginning. Once the Promotion Director comes up with the ideas, he or she will often put them in writing for approval by the station management. All types of things must be considered. These include the correct time of year to run the specific promotion, any state or federal laws and regulations that must be adhered to, rules and regulations for participants, the cost of the promotion, and how it will be implemented. The Promotion Director will often find sources for prizes to lower the cost of promotions. In many instances, companies donate or contribute merchandise and services in exchange for commercial space.

At many stations, the Promotion Director is responsible for developing opportunities to sponsor events for community organizations. These might include health fairs, marathons and runs, fund-raising telethons and events, or other entertainment programs.

The Promotion Director may arrange appearances for station personalities at events or on other media. The individual may set up interviews with magazines or newspapers or other broadcast media for feature stories on on-air personalities. In some cases, these duties may be carried out by the public relations department instead.

The Promotion Director works closely with the advertising department to find new ways to increase the listening audience, which in turn increases advertising revenues.

Additional duties of radio station Promotion Directors may include:

• Overseeing and supervising the promotion department staff
• Handling media and public relations functions
• Advising station staff about promotions
• Helping to develop promotion packages for potential advertisers

## Salaries

Annual earnings of radio Promotion Directors can range between $22,000 and $80,000 or more. Variables affecting earnings include the size, location, and prestige of the radio station, as well as the experience and responsibilities of the individual. Some Promotion Directors may work for a group of stations all owned by the same company. Generally, those earnings salaries at the higher end of the scale will be working either in major markets or will have responsibilities for more than one station.

## Employment Prospects

Employment prospects for radio Promotion Directors are fair, although individuals may have to relocate for jobs. Positions may be located throughout the country in small, midsize, and major markets. Smaller stations tend to have more employee turnover because people leave for career advancement.

## Advancement Prospects

Advancement prospects are fair for Promotion Directors in radio. Individuals who are creative, aggressive, and hard working may climb the career ladder by locating similar positions with larger, more prestigious stations or with media groups owning more than one station. Others may find similar positions in the television end of broadcasting.

Some Promotion Directors advance by locating positions as radio station marketing directors.

## Education and Training

Most stations require their Promotion Directors to hold a minimum of a four-year college degree. Good choices for majors include journalism, communications, English, public relations, marketing, advertising, and liberal arts.

Courses, workshops, and seminars in public relations, writing, promotion, journalism, and radio will be helpful in honing skills and making new contacts.

## Experience, Skills, and Personality Traits

Generally, the larger the station, the more experience the individual will need for a position. While most stations prefer public relations, advertising, and/or promotion experience in radio, they will often accept similar experience outside the broadcasting genre.

A working knowledge of advertising, promotion and public relations is needed to be successful in this type of position. Individuals should be very creative with excellent communication skills.

There is often a great deal of pressure in this type of job, so the ability to work under pressure without getting flustered is necessary.

## Unions and Associations

Promotion Directors working in radio may belong to various associations. These include the Public Relations Society of America (PRSA), the American Marketing Association (AMA), the American Advertising Federation (AAF), and Broadcast Promotion and Marketing Executives (BPME).

## Tips for Entry

1. Look for internships at radio stations. These will give you on-the-job training, experience, and the opportunity to make important contacts. Contact stations to see what they offer.

2. If you can't find an internship in radio, look for one in the public relations, promotion, or advertising department of another company. Your goal is to get experience.

3. Job openings are often advertised in the newspaper classified section under headings such as "Promotion," "Promotion Director," "Radio," "Broadcasting," and "Radio."

4. Don't forget to read trade publications. *Billboard, Broadcasting,* and *Radio and Records* often have advertisements for stations with openings.

5. Send your résumé and a short cover letter to radio stations you are interested in working for. You can never tell when an opening exists.

# ASSISTANT PROMOTION DIRECTOR

## CAREER PROFILE

**Duties:** Assists in the development and implementation of promotions to help enhance the station's image and attract listeners

**Alternate Title(s):** Assistant Director of Promotion; Assistant Director of Promotion and Special Projects

**Salary Range:** $20,000 to $65,000+

**Employment Prospects:** Fair

**Advancement Prospects:** Fair

**Best Geographical Location(s):** Positions located throughout the country

**Prerequisites:**

**Education or Training**—College degree required or preferred by most stations

**Experience**—Experience in public relations, promotion, marketing, broadcasting, or journalism helpful

**Special Skills and Personality Traits**—Creativity; imagination; good communications skills; persuasiveness; writing skills; personable; outgoing nature

## CAREER LADDER

```
┌─────────────────────────────────────┐
│         Promotion Director          │
└─────────────────────────────────────┘

┌─────────────────────────────────────┐
│     Assistant Promotion Director     │
└─────────────────────────────────────┘

┌─────────────────────────────────────┐
│       Promotion Coordinator or       │
│        Promotion Assistant           │
└─────────────────────────────────────┘
```

## Position Description

It is essential to a radio station to attract the largest audience possible. This is done by building an interest in and increasing the visibility of the station. In order to accomplish these feats, radio stations use a variety of promotions, special events, and attractions. The Assistant Promotion Director working at a radio station is responsible for helping the director of the department develop and implement these promotions and special events.

It's often difficult to come up with interesting, creative, and unique promotions. The Assistant Promotion Director works with the promotion director in coming up with these ideas. The two individuals may have brainstorming sessions to develop ideas that may attract new listeners and advertisers, as well as gain the attention of the public and the media.

Promotions may include a variety of contests, sweepstakes, special events, and more. In some instances, the promotion may involve the station solely. In other instances, the promotion may involve a tie-in with advertisers, community organizations, or civic groups. Sometimes the promotions involve the radio station's sponsorship of community events such as telethons, marathons, or entertainment extravaganzas.

No matter what the promotion, they all take a great deal of time, energy, and effort to implement. The Assistant Promotion Director is expected to help implement the promotions and events from the development phase through fruition.

In some situations, media conglomerates own more than one radio station. In these cases, the Assistant Promotion Director and the promotion director will work together in the main office, developing promotions for all the stations. The Assistant Director may then go to each individual station to help them implement the programs.

Both promotion directors and Assistant Promotion Directors must be very creative to be successful. But developing the ideas for the promotions is just the beginning. Once the promotion department comes up with the ideas, either the Assistant Promotion Director or the promotion director must put them in writing for approval by the station management. Once approved, the Assistant Director will work with the promotion director in finding sources for prizes and finding additional ways to lower the cost of the promotion.

Depending on the size and structure of the station, the Assistant Promotion Director may be responsible for developing and writing press releases, announcements, advertisements, or commercials to help publicize the promotion. In other situations, the Assistant may work with the station publicist, public relations director, and advertising department to handle these functions.

Additional duties of radio station Assistant Promotion Directors may include:

- Supervising the promotion department staff
- Advising station staff about promotions
- Helping to develop promotion packages for potential advertisers

### Salaries

Annual earnings of radio Assistant Promotion Directors range between $20,000 to $65,000 or more annually. Variables affecting earnings include the size, location, and prestige of the radio station, as well as the experience and responsibilities of the individual.

It should be noted that Assistant Promotion Directors may work for a group of stations all owned by the same company. Generally, those earning salaries at the higher end of the scale will be working either in major markets or will have responsibilities for more than one station.

### Employment Prospects

Employment prospects for radio Assistant Promotion Directors are fair, although individuals may have to relocate for jobs. Positions may be located throughout the country in small, midsize, and major markets.

Smaller stations often have more employee turnover because people leave for career advancement. As noted, individuals may also find employment working for a media conglomerate or a group of stations.

### Advancement Prospects

Advancement prospects are fair for Assistant Promotion Directors working in radio. The most common method of career advancement is to get some experience and then move up to become a full-fledged promotion director.

### Education and Training

Most stations require or prefer their Assistant Promotion Directors to hold a minimum of a four-year college degree.

Good choices for majors include journalism, communications, English, public relations, marketing, advertising, and liberal arts.

Courses, workshops, and seminars in public relations, writing, promotion, journalism, and radio will be helpful in honing skills and making new contacts.

### Experience, Skills, and Personality Traits

Many individuals obtain experience in this field as promotion assistants. Others work in the marketing or public relations department.

Generally, the larger the station, the more experience the individual will need for a position. While most stations prefer public relations, advertising, and/or promotion experience in radio, often they will accept similar experience outside the broadcasting genre. A working knowledge of advertising, promotion, and public relations is needed to be successful in this type of position. Individuals should be very creative with excellent communications

### Unions and Associations

Assistant Promotion Directors may belong to various associations. These include the Public Relations Society of America (PRSA), the American Marketing Association (AMA), the American Advertising Federation (AAF), and Broadcast Promotion and Marketing Executives (BPME).

### Tips for Entry

1. Internships are a great way to get experience. An internship in a radio station will give you on-the-job training, experience, and the opportunity to make important contacts. Contact stations to see what they offer.
2. If you can't find an internship in radio, look for one in the public relations, promotion, or advertising department of another company. Your goal is to get experience.
3. Job openings are often advertised in the newspaper classified section under headings such as "Promotion," "Assistant Promotion Director," "Broadcasting," and "Radio."
4. Send your résumé and a short cover letter to radio stations you are interested in working for. You can never tell when an opening exists.
5. Many radio stations advertise their openings on-air or on their websites. Check it out.

# PROMOTION ASSISTANT

## CAREER PROFILE

**Duties:** Assists the promotion staff in the implementation of radio station promotions and events

**Alternate Title(s):** Promo Assistant; Promotion Coordinator; Promotion Trainee

**Salary Range:** $15,000 to $25,000+

**Employment Prospects:** Fair

**Advancement Prospects:** Fair

**Best Geographical Location(s):** Positions located throughout the country

**Prerequisites:**

**Education or Training**—College degree or background may be preferred but not always required

**Experience**—Experience in promotion, public relations, marketing, broadcasting, or journalism helpful but not usually required

**Special Skills and Personality Traits**—Computer literate; detail oriented; imaginative; good communications skills; writing skills; personable; outgoing nature

## CAREER LADDER

```
┌─────────────────────────────────────┐
│   Assistant Promotion Director      │
└─────────────────────────────────────┘

┌─────────────────────────────────────┐
│      Promotion Assistant            │
└─────────────────────────────────────┘

┌─────────────────────────────────────┐
│      Entry-Level, Intern,           │
│ Secretarial Position, or College Student │
└─────────────────────────────────────┘
```

## Position Description

A radio station's Promotion Assistant is responsible for helping the promotion staff in the development and implementation of the station's promotions. Duties of the Promotion Assistant vary, depending on the specific station as well as the experience of the individual.

The Promotion Assistant might be expected to fulfill secretarial duties such as typing letters, other correspondence, returning phone calls, keeping records of the cost of promotions, and checking media prices.

Many stations advertise their promotions in a variety of media in addition to the radio station. This might include local daily, weekly, or biweekly newspapers; magazines; television; and even billboards. The Promotion Assistant may be in charge of calling advertising representatives from the various media to get advertising rates, packages, and specials.

Depending on the experience of the Promotions Assistant, he or she may be asked to help write ad copy or do rough layouts for print ads to advertise a promotion. The individual may be expected to place ads, purchase space on television, and deliver ads and commercials to the media in

time for placement. In some stations, this might be handled by the advertising department.

The Promotion Assistant is often responsible for checking billings, authorizing payments, and keeping accurate records of promotion expenses.

At times, the Promotion Assistant may sit in on brainstorming sessions with the promotion director and assistant director. As he or she obtains more experience, the individual may offer suggestions for promotions and events as well as their implementation.

The Promotion Assistant is often expected to do a great deal of the "grunt" work. He or she may be responsible for handling an array of details involved in the implementation and execution of each event. This may involve making calls, handling correspondence, sending out bills, checking invoices, checking details, and running around to pick up things.

At some stations, the Promotion Assistant may also help write press releases, blurbs, and announcements publicizing and promoting the event.

At times, the Promotion Assistant may seem like a glorified secretary. However, the successful Promotion Assistant does as much as possible to learn the ropes. In this manner, he or she can climb the career ladder.

Additional duties of radio station Promotion Assistants may include:

- Tracking tear sheets, clippings, visual cuts, and audio-tapes of advertisements and commercials for promotions
- Writing thank-you notes to sponsors
- Making sure contracts and agreements are signed before a promotion or event
- Acting as a buffer for the promotion director and assistant promotion director

## Salaries

Earnings for radio Promotion Assistants vary, depending on the size and structure of the station and the experience and responsibilities of the individual. Earnings may range between $15,000 and $25,000 or more annually.

## Employment Prospects

Employment prospects for radio Promotion Assistants are fair. Individuals may find positions in small local stations as well as mid-market and major-market stations.

Smaller stations often have more employee turnover because people leaving for career advancement.

## Advancement Prospects

Advancement prospects are fair for hard-working, creative Promotion Assistants. The most common method of career advancement is obtaining experience and moving on to become a promotion assistant director. In some situations, the Promotion Assistant may also move on to positions in the public relations, marketing, or advertising departments.

## Education and Training

While stations may prefer individuals who have a college degree or background, it is not usually a requirement. However, it should be noted that a college degree will help in career advancement. Good choices for college majors include journalism, communications, English, public relations, marketing, advertising, and liberal arts.

Courses, workshops, and seminars in public relations, writing, promotion, journalism, and radio will be helpful in honing skills and making new contacts.

## Experience, Skills, and Personality Traits

At many stations, this is an entry-level job. Any experience in broadcasting, journalism, or public relations is helpful in this type of job.

Individuals should be detail oriented, creative, and imaginative with good communications skills. Writing skills are a plus. Promotion Assistants who are personable and outgoing do well in radio.

## Unions and Associations

Promotion Assistants may belong to various associations, including the Public Relations Society of America (PRSA), the American Marketing Association (AMA), the American Advertising Federation (AAF), and Broadcast Promotion and Marketing Executives (BPME).

## Tips for Entry

1. There is quite a bit of turnover in these positions. Consider sending your résumé and a cover letter to a number of radio stations, asking that your résumé be kept on file.
2. Internships are a great way to get experience. An internship in a radio station will give you on-the-job training, experience, and the opportunity to make important contacts. Contact stations to see what they offer.
3. If you can't find an internship in radio, look for one in the public relations, promotion, or advertising department of another company. Your goal is to get experience.
4. Job openings are often advertised in the newspaper classified section under headings such as "Promotion," "Promotion Assistant," "Broadcasting," and "Radio."
5. Many radio stations advertise their openings on-air or on their websites. Check it out.

# PUBLIC RADIO

# DIRECTOR OF FUND-RAISING AND DEVELOPMENT

## CAREER PROFILE

**Duties:** Coordinates the annual giving activities, capital campaigns, deferred-giving opportunities, and corporate sponsorships for a public radio station

**Alternate Title(s):** Fund-raising Director; Development Director; Director of Fund-raising; Director of Development

**Salary Range:** $25,000 to $110,000+

**Employment Prospects:** Poor

**Advancement Prospects:** Good

**Best Geographical Location(s):** Opportunities may be located throughout the country in areas hosting public radio stations

**Prerequisites:**

**Education or Training**—Minimum of a bachelor's degree required by most stations

**Experience**—Fund-raising and development experience; experience with not-for-profits

**Special Skills and Personality Traits**—Understanding and knowledge of not-for-profit organizations and broadcast industry; communications skills; creativity; writing skills; ability to multitask; persuasiveness; organizational skills

## CAREER LADDER

```
┌─────────────────────────────────────────┐
│  Director of Fund-raising and            │
│  Development for Larger, More            │
│  Prestigious Public Radio or Television  │
│  Station, Director of Fund-raising and   │
│  Development for Not-for-Profit in Other │
│  Industry, or Business Manager           │
└─────────────────────────────────────────┘

┌─────────────────────────────────────────┐
│  Director of Fund-Raising and            │
│  Development                             │
└─────────────────────────────────────────┘

┌─────────────────────────────────────────┐
│  Assistant Director of Fund-raising and  │
│  Development, Assistant Director of       │
│  Corporate Sponsorship, or               │
│  Corporate Sponsorship Coordinator       │
└─────────────────────────────────────────┘
```

## Position Description

Commercial radio stations make money by selling commercial space. Each commercial spot sold means additional income for the station. Public radio stations don't sell commercial space. Instead, they are funded by donations, grants, and corporate sponsors. The individual in charge of obtaining these funds at a public radio station is called the Director of Fund-Raising and Development. Depending on the size and structure of the station, there may also be an assistant director, director of corporate sponsorship, assistant director of corporate sponsorship, director of volunteer activities, assistant director of volunteer activities, and a variety of staff members.

The Director of Fund-raising and Development in a public radio station holds a very important position. The viability of the station depends to a great extent on how well the individual does his or her job. Within the scope of the position, the Director of Fund-raising and Development has a number of responsibilities.

The individual is expected to lead and direct the fund-raising efforts of the public radio station. He or she must develop strategies for obtaining the financial support of individuals and businesses. The Director may raise funds through a variety of methods, including personal solicitations, direct mail, and telemarketing.

The Director may also raise funds through on-air fund-raising events. During these events, the individual may develop special programming to spotlight the need for financial support. Today many public radio stations also utilize the Internet to raise funds. The Director of Fund-raising and Development may additionally put together balls, dinners, cocktail parties, or other special events to help raise funds for the station.

A large amount of money for public radio is raised through foundations, grants, corporations, endowments, and planned gifts. The individual may be responsible for cultivating corporate sponsors and businesses to underwrite special projects or may oversee a director of corporate sponsorship who handles these duties. The Director of Fund-raising and Development must also know how to write and apply for grants, develop proposals, and follow up in order to receive the largest amount of funds possible.

In order to reach people who are interested in the cause, the Director of Fund-raising and Development must often perform a great deal of research. He or she may develop and utilize questionnaires and surveys to locate potential station supporters. Once the individual has developed a list, he or she will use it to make supporters aware of fund-raising efforts.

Public radio, like many other not-for-profit organizations, depends on the services of volunteers. The Director of Fund-raising and Development may be expected to coordinate the efforts of the volunteers, although some stations have a director of volunteers who handles this function.

The Director of Fund-raising and Development is expected to act as a liaison between all donors, potential donors, and corporate sponsors and the station's management and board of directors. The individual must inform management and the board of any situations or occurrences affecting donors.

The Director of Fund-raising and Development is always on the lookout for new donors, new corporate sponsors, and new fund-raising ideas. He or she must also constantly build and maintain the relationship with current and potential donors and sponsors.

Additional duties of the Director of Fund-raising and Development at a public radio station may include:

- Representing the station at public or private functions
- Setting goals and developing budgets
- Developing and creating literature and marketing pieces for fund-raising
- Working with volunteers
- Managing and directing the staff of the fund-raising development office
- Overseeing capital fund-raising campaigns

## Salaries

Salaries for Directors of Fund-raising and Development at public radio stations can vary tremendously. Earnings may range from $25,000 to $110,000 or more. Variables include the size, location, prestige, and popularity of the station, as well as the experience, responsibilities, and track record of the individual.

## Employment Prospects

Employment prospects are fair for Directors of Fund-raising and Development in public radio. As noted, this is an important position in public radio. While there are a limited number of public radio stations in the country, they depend on fund-raising to survive. Individuals who have a proven track record will always be in demand. Individuals may need to relocate for positions.

## Advancement Prospects

Advancement prospects for Directors of Fund-raising and Development in public radio are good. Advancement opportunities are based to a great extent on career aspirations. Individuals might climb the career ladder by locating similar positions with larger, more prestigious public radio or television stations. Others find fund-raising and development positions with large not-for-profit groups outside the public broadcasting world.

There are also Directors of Fund-raising and Development who climb the career ladder by becoming the station's general or business manager.

## Education and Training

A minimum of a four-year college degree is required for this position. Good choices for majors include communications, broadcasting, journalism, English, public relations, marketing, advertising, and liberal arts.

Seminars and workshops on fund-raising, development, planned giving, capital campaigns, sales, and marketing will be useful.

## Experience, Skills, and Personality Traits

Generally, the larger the public radio station, the more experience required for the position of Director of Fund-raising and Development. Some stations will take individuals with a proven track record in fund-raising and development outside the public radio/public television area. Other stations prefer candidates with public broadcasting experience.

The Director of Fund-raising and Development needs a full understanding of public radio, as well as a working knowledge of fund-raising, corporate giving, foundation solicitation, marketing, and public relations.

The individual in this position should be personable, persuasive, enthusiastic, and creative, with a lot of people skills. The ability to work with different types of personalities is necessary.

The Director of Fund-raising and Development must have the ability to multitask without getting flustered. There is often a great deal of pressure in this type of job. The ability to think and make decisions quickly is essential. The ability to relate to others is essential. Communications skills, both verbal and written, are also needed.

## Unions and Associations

The Director of Fund-raising and Development working in a public radio station may belong to various associations, depending on the specific position held and the station they work for. These include Public Radio International (PRI), the National Society of Fund Raising Executives (NSFRE), and the Council for the Advancement and Support of Education (CASE).

## Tips for Entry

1. Fund-raising experience is essential to this position. Volunteer to be on the fund-raising committee or, better yet, to be the fund-raising chairperson of a local not-for-profit organization or civic group.
2. If you live in an area with a public radio or television station, volunteer during their fund-raising drives. This will give you great experience and help you make contacts within the industry.
3. Get experience working in broadcasting if possible. Volunteer with your college radio station, join radio clubs, etc.
4. Send your résumé with a short cover letter to public radio or television stations, asking if there are openings for assistants.
5. Both commercial and public radio stations often offer internships or training programs. Internships are another way to get on-the-job training experience and the opportunity to make important contacts.
6. If you can't find a formal internship program, see if you can create your own.
7. Many stations advertise openings on the air or on their websites. Check them out.
8. Job openings are also often advertised in the newspaper classified section under headings such as "Director of Fund-raising and Development," "Director of Fund-raising," "Public Radio," and "Public Broadcasting."
9. Don't forget to look on some of the employment sites on the Web. Start with some of the more popular ones, such as www.hotjobs.com and www.monster.com and go from there.

# ASSISTANT DIRECTOR OF FUND-RAISING AND DEVELOPMENT

## CAREER PROFILE

**Duties:** Assists the director of fund-raising and development in the coordination of annual giving activities and corporate sponsorships at public radio station

**Alternate Title(s):** Assistant Fund-raising Director; Assistant Development Director; Assistant Director of Fund-raising; Assistant Director of Development

**Salary Range:** $22,000 to $42,000+

**Employment Prospects:** Fair

**Advancement Prospects:** Fair

**Best Geographical Location(s):** Opportunities may be located throughout the country in areas hosting public radio stations

**Prerequisites:**

**Education or Training**—Minimum of bachelor's degree required by most stations

**Experience**—Fund-raising and development experience; experience with nonprofits

**Special Skills and Personality Traits**—Understanding and knowledge of not-for-profit organizations and broadcast industry; communications skills; creativity; writing skills; ability to multitask; persuasiveness; organizational skills

## CAREER LADDER

```
┌─────────────────────────────────────┐
│             Director of             │
│   Fund-raising and Development      │
└─────────────────────────────────────┘

┌─────────────────────────────────────┐
│        Assistant Director of        │
│   Fund-Raising and Development      │
└─────────────────────────────────────┘

┌─────────────────────────────────────┐
│        Assistant Director of        │
│    Corporate Sponsorship or         │
│  Corporate Sponsorship Coordinator  │
└─────────────────────────────────────┘
```

## Position Description

Commercial radio stations are for-profit organizations. They derive their income by selling commercial spots to advertisers. Public radio stations, on the other hand, are not-for-profit organizations. Their funding comes from a combination of donations, grants, and corporate sponsors.

The director of fund-raising and development at a public radio station is in charge of developing programs to obtain these funds. As the public radio station's existence depends on public and private funding, it can often be a massive project. Many public radio stations also employ an Assistant Director of Fund-raising and Development to help the director perform his or her duties.

Depending on the size and structure of the station, the staff in this department may also include a director of corporate sponsorship, assistant director of corporate sponsorship, director of volunteer activities, assistant director of volunteer activities, a newsletter and publications editor, and a variety of others.

The Assistant Director of Fund-raising and Development in a public radio station may have an array of responsibilities, depending on the specific station. His or her main responsibility is to help the director of the department raise money for the station. This includes helping to develop fund-raising programs for the station. These may include an array of large- and small-scale projects. For example, the station might hold huge annual fund-raising drives where people are asked to become members of the station, featuring on-air telethons and special programming. Many public radio stations develop century clubs or other annual giving and sustaining campaigns.

Smaller fund-raising projects might include auctions, art sales, concerts, dinner dances, house tours, theatrical events, and bake sales. The concept is to find as many ways to raise money from the public as possible. In developing programs, the director and Assistant Director may try to reach a variety of market segments. In this manner, people from different parts of the community will have the opportunity to participate and donate. Once programs and special events have been developed, the Assistant Director of Fund-raising and Development is expected to help with the implementation. Depending on the size of the staff and the number of volunteers, the individual may be responsible for actually implementing projects him- or herself or may just supervise others in the department.

The implementation of special events and projects can be a huge undertaking. It may involve finding a location for an event, making phone calls to ensure good attendance, finding businesses to donate prizes, locating guest speakers, planning menus, and finding chairpersons.

Depending on the size and structure of the specific public radio station, the Assistant Director's job may be multifunctional. For example, the business manager may also be the acting director of fund-raising. In these cases, the Assistant Director of Fund-raising and Development may handle more specific duties.

In the same vein, public radio stations without an actual marketing or public relations director may expect the Assistant Director of Fundraising and Development to handle the public relations, publicity, and marketing duties as well. He or she may be responsible for writing a report for the department regarding the progress of fund-raising projects and efforts, press releases, etc.

The Assistant Director of Fund-raising and Development may be assigned the task of cultivating potential station donors. To accomplish this task, the individual will often attend luncheons, dinners, meetings, parties, and other affairs on behalf of the station. The Assistant Director may also be asked to speak to groups about the station and its fund-raising efforts.

In public radio stations where there is no grant writer, the Assistant Director may be responsible for seeking out grants offered by the government or private foundations. He or she may just locate the grants or also may be responsible for writing grant proposals.

If the station does not have a director of corporate sponsorship, the Assistant Director may be responsible for helping to cultivate corporate sponsorships as well. These sponsorships often underwrite programs the station has undertaken.

Public radio, like many other not-for-profit institutions, depends on the services of volunteers. The Assistant Director of Fund-raising and Development is expected to help coordinate the efforts of the volunteers. In some stations, there is a director of volunteers who handles this function.

Additional duties of the Assistant Director of Fund-raising and Development at a public radio station may include:

- Keeping records of donor management and resource development
- Sending acknowledgements and thank-you letters to donors
- Assisting in the development and creation of literature and marketing pieces for fund-raising
- Working with volunteers
- Assisting with capital fund-raising campaigns

## Salaries

Salaries for Assistant Directors of Fund-raising and Development at public radio stations can vary tremendously. Earnings may range from $22,000 to $42,000 or more. Variables include the size, location, prestige, and popularity of the station, as well as the experience, responsibilities, and track record of the individual.

## Employment Prospects

Employment prospects are fair for Assistant Directors of Fund-raising and Development. While there are a limited number of public radio stations in the country, they depend on fund-raising to survive. Individuals who have a proven track record will always be in demand. Individuals may need to relocate for positions.

## Advancement Prospects

Advancement prospects for Assistant Directors of Fund-raising and Development in public radio are fair. Advancement opportunities are based to a great extent on career aspirations. Individuals might climb the career ladder by locating similar positions in larger, more prestigious public radio or television stations or by becoming a full-fledged director of fund-raising and development for a station. Some individuals find fund-raising and development positions for large not-for-profit groups outside the public broadcasting world.

## Education and Training

A minimum of a four-year college degree is required for this position. Good choices for majors include communications, broadcasting, journalism, English, public relations, marketing, advertising, and liberal arts.

Seminars and workshops on fund-raising, development, planned giving, capital campaigns, sales, and marketing will be useful.

## Experience, Skills, and Personality Traits

Experience requirements vary for this position. Generally, the larger the station, the more experience will be required. Some individuals have fund-raising experience outside the public radio/public television area. The Assistant Director of Fund-raising and Development should have an understanding of public radio as well as a working knowledge of fund-raising, corporate giving, foundation solicitation, marketing, and public relations.

Assistant Directors of Fund-raising and Development in public radio should be creative, enthusiastic, and motivated. People skills are needed. The ability to work with different types of personalities is also necessary.

The Assistant Director of Fund-raising and Development needs great communication skills, both verbal and written, as well as marketing, public relations, and advertising skills.

## Unions and Associations

The Assistant Director of Fund-raising and Development working at a public radio station may belong to various associations, including the National Society of Fund-Raising Executives (NSFRE) and the Council for the Advancement and Support of Education (CASE).

## Tips for Entry

1. Volunteer to be on the fund-raising committee of a local not-for-profit organization or civic group.

2. If you live in an area with a public radio or television station, volunteer during their fund-raising drives. This will give you great experience and help you make contacts within the industry.

3. Get experience working in broadcasting.

4. Send your résumé with a short cover letter to public radio or television stations, asking if there are openings as assistants.

5. Both commercial and public radio stations often offer internships or training programs. Internships are another way to get on-the-job training experience and the opportunity to make important contacts.

6. If you can't find a formal internship program, see if you can create your own.

7. Many stations advertise openings on the air and on their websites. Check them out.

8. Job openings are also often advertised in the newspaper classified section under headings such as "Assistant Director of Fund-raising and Development," "Assistant Director of Fund-raising," "Public Radio," and "Public Broadcasting."

# DIRECTOR OF CORPORATE SPONSORSHIP

## CAREER PROFILE

**Duties:** Cultivates corporate sponsors; oversees staff in corporate sponsorship department

**Alternate Title(s):** Corporate Sponsorship Director

**Salary Range:** $22,000 to $85,000+

**Employment Prospects:** Poor

**Advancement Prospects:** Fair

**Best Geographical Location(s):** Opportunities may be located throughout the country in areas hosting public radio stations

**Prerequisites:**

**Education or Training**—Minimum of bachelor's degree required by most stations

**Experience**—Experience in corporate sponsorship, media sales, fund-raising, and development

**Special Skills and Personality Traits**—Understanding and knowledge of broadcast industry; communications skills; creativity; writing skills; ability to multitask

## CAREER LADDER

```
┌─────────────────────────────────────────┐
│ Director of Corporate Sponsorship for   │
│ Larger, More Prestigious Public Radio    │
│ or Television Station, Director of       │
│ Corporate Sponsorship in Other           │
│ Industry, or Director of Fund-raising    │
│ and Development                          │
└─────────────────────────────────────────┘

┌─────────────────────────────────────────┐
│ Director of Corporate Sponsorship        │
└─────────────────────────────────────────┘

┌─────────────────────────────────────────┐
│ Assistant Director of Corporate          │
│ Sponsorship, Media Sales Director, or    │
│ Corporate Sponsorship Coordinator        │
└─────────────────────────────────────────┘
```

## Position Description

Commercial radio stations derive the majority of their income by selling commercial space to advertisers. Public radio stations, on the other hand, are funded by donations, grants, and corporate sponsors. The individual in charge of obtaining corporate sponsors in public radio stations is called the Director of Corporate Sponsorship.

There are many reasons companies become corporate sponsors of public radio. Some believe in the cause of public radio or its programming. Others want to improve their public image. Some want to keep their name in the public eye in a positive manner.

Corporate sponsors may encompass a variety of companies in an array of industries. Depending on the size, structure, and prestige of a station, corporate sponsors may be very large national companies or smaller local or regional firms.

The function of the Director of Corporate Sponsorship at a public radio station is to cultivate corporate donors. Individuals are expected to seek out new companies to become corporate sponsors, as well as maintain relationships with current donors.

On a certain level, this position is much like a director of sales at a private station. The Director of Corporate Sponsorship locates corporations and then "sells" them sponsorships. At larger stations, the Director may have a staff of representatives. In smaller stations, the individual may work alone.

The Director of Corporate Sponsorship may develop relationships with corporate sponsors in a number of ways. In many situations, the individual or his or her staff works directly with the senior management of corporations. In other situations, they may work with account executives from advertising agencies representing corporations. In order to sell corporate sponsorships, the individual must explain the value of becoming a corporate sponsor for the station, as well as develop marketing materials, including station facts, demographics, and programming.

Sometimes the Director of Corporate Sponsorship attends luncheons, dinners, meetings, parties, and other affairs to meet potential donors. While the Director of Corporate Sponsorship may be low-key during these functions, he or she will be busy collecting business cards, making contacts, and introducing him- or herself. Once the individual is on a more familiar basis with corporate contacts, he or she may make calls, write letters, or send marketing materials in hopes of setting up appointments.

The Director of Corporate Sponsorship is expected to develop long- and short-term strategies to secure sponsorships and underwriting revenue. These strategies must include the manner in which the plan will be successfully implemented. The individual may, for example, find a corporate sponsor to underwrite a specific program aired on the station. He or she may turn that into funding for a new show as well.

The Director of Corporate Sponsorship will often be responsible for developing budgets. He or she may be expected to perform research to determine what monies are needed to fund specific programming at the station and then find donors who might be interested in the related projects.

The individual will often work under the director of fund-raising and development. In some cases, the two are the same.

The Director of Corporate Sponsorship may develop sales and marketing materials which will help increase either national, regional, or local revenues. He or she may, for example, develop sponsorship guides detailing amounts of funding needed for specific projects. Other marketing materials might include reports, sales letters, brochures, visual aides, and additional materials.

The Director of Corporate Sponsorship may develop and give presentations to groups to further explain sponsorship, underwriting, and funding opportunities.

Once sponsorships are obtained, the Director will be expected to make sure contracts and clearances have been signed. For example, the Director must make sure that the sponsor approves of the on-air tag line. If the station has a website, the individual must also be sure that corporate logos are correct.

The Director of Corporate Sponsorship is expected to maintain a relationship with corporate sponsors. He or she may provide reports to the sponsor detailing demographics, audience numbers, comments, and any other pertinent information.

The Director of Corporate Sponsorship must always be on the lookout for enhanced sponsorship opportunities. For example, if the station has created a weekly gospel program, the Director may attempt to get a gospel record label to underwrite the show.

Additional duties of the Director of Corporate Sponsorship at a public radio station may include:

- Representing the station at public or private functions
- Developing budgets
- Setting sponsorship goals
- Working with volunteers
- Overseeing staff

## Salaries

Salaries for Directors of Corporate Sponsorship for public radio can vary tremendously, depending on the size and structure of the station. Earnings can range between $22,000 and $85,000 or more. Variables include the size, location, prestige, and popularity of the station, as well as the experience and responsibilities of the individual.

## Employment Prospects

Employment prospects for Directors of Corporate Sponsorship in public radio are poor. There are only a limited number of public radio stations in the country and not every station has this position. That does not mean that it is impossible to get into this position—but it is difficult. Individuals who have a proven track record will always be in demand. The most opportunities will exist in areas hosting large public radio stations.

## Advancement Prospects

Advancement prospects for Directors of Corporate Sponsorship are based to a great extent on career aspirations. Individuals may advance by locating similar positions at larger, more prestigious public radio stations. They might also find similar positions at public television stations. Some individuals go into corporate sponsorship in other industries outside public broadcasting.

Some Directors of Corporate Sponsorship advance by becoming the director of fund-raising and development at a public radio or television station or other not-for-profit organization.

## Education and Training

A minimum of a four-year college degree is required for this position. Good choices for majors include communications, broadcasting, journalism, English, public relations, marketing, advertising, and liberal arts.

Seminars and workshops on fund-raising, development, sales, marketing, etc., are useful.

## Experience, Skills, and Personality Traits

Experience requirements vary from station to station for this position. Generally, the larger the public radio station, the more experience required. Types of experience vary as well. Some individuals have worked in public radio or television as assistant directors in corporate sponsorship before their current position. Others worked in corporate sponsorship in other industries. Some individuals have experience in media sales in commercial radio or television or various areas of fund-raising.

The Director of Corporate Sponsorship working in public radio should be a personable individual with excellent people skills and communication skills, both verbal and written. The ability to work with different types of personalities is also necessary.

There is often a great deal of pressure in this type of job. The individual in this position needs to be able to think quickly and multitask without getting flustered. Creativity, marketing and sales skills, and the ability to motivate both a sales team and corporate sponsors are essential.

## Unions and Associations

Directors of Corporate Sponsorship working in public radio may belong to various associations, depending on the specific position held and the station they work for. These include the National Society of Fund Raising Executives (NSFRE), the Council for the Advancement and Support of Education (CASE), and the Writers Guild of America (WGA). Individuals or their stations might also be members of the National Association of Broadcasters (NAB).

## Tips for Entry

1. Get as much experience as possible working in broadcasting. Volunteer to work with your college radio station, join radio clubs, etc.
2. If you live in an area with a public radio or television station, consider volunteering during their fund-raising drives. This looks great on your résumé, as well as being a great way to get experience and make important contacts.
3. Many radio stations and associations offer internships or training programs. Internships are another way to get on-the-job training experience and the opportunity to make important contacts.
4. If you can't find a formal internship program, see if you can create your own.
5. Many stations advertise openings on the air as well as on their websites. Check them out.
6. Job openings are also often advertised in the newspaper classified section under headings such as "Director of Corporate Sponsorship," "Fund-Raising," "Radio," "Public Radio," and "Broadcasting."
7. Don't forget to look on some of the employment sites on the web. Start with some of the more popular ones, such as www.hotjobs.com and www.monster.com, and go from there.
8. Get experience selling radio advertising in a commercial station.

# PUBLICATION MANAGER

## CAREER PROFILE

**Duties:** Develops and writes internal and external publications for public radio station

**Alternate Title(s):** Director of Publications

**Salary Range:** $22,000 to $45,000+

**Employment Prospects:** Fair

**Advancement Prospects:** Fair

**Best Geographical Location(s):** Opportunities may be located throughout the country in areas hosting public radio stations

**Prerequisites:**

**Education or Training**—Four-year college degree

**Experience**—Writing and editing experience

**Special Skills and Personality Traits**—Understanding and knowledge of not-for-profit organizations and broadcast industry; communications skills; creativity; writing skills; ability to multitask; excellent writing and editing skills; layout and graphic skills

## CAREER LADDER

```
┌─────────────────────────────────────┐
│ Publication Manager at Larger, More  │
│   Prestigious Public Radio Station or│
│      Director of Publications or     │
│ Marketing in Public Broadcasting or  │
│           Other Industry             │
└─────────────────────────────────────┘

┌─────────────────────────────────────┐
│        Publication Manager           │
└─────────────────────────────────────┘

┌─────────────────────────────────────┐
│   Newsletter Editor, Copywriter,     │
│      Journalist, or Publicist        │
└─────────────────────────────────────┘
```

## Position Description

Public radio stations often utilize a variety of publications to make the community, potential and current donors, and corporate sponsors aware of fund-raising efforts, events, and other happenings. These might include both internal and external publications such as newsletters, events sheets, fund-raising reports, news releases, advertisements, pamphlets, letters, and leaflets. Many stations employ a Publication Manager to handle the development and completion of these internal and external publications.

The specific responsibilities of the Publication Manager will vary from station to station, depending on a station's size and structure. He or she may work with individuals involved in public relations, marketing, and fund-raising. At very large public radio stations, there may be a staff of copywriters, editors, researchers, et al. At smaller stations, the Publication Manager may be expected to research, write, and lay out publications him- or herself.

Whatever the publication, it needs to be done on a timely basis. If a station newsletter highlighting a big fund-raising drive comes out late, the station will lose money. It is essen-

tial that the Publication Manager set timetables for projects. He or she is expected to develop schedules for copywriters, printers, graphic designers, and any other individuals involved in the preparation of the publications. The individual must make sure that projects are not only assigned but finished on time.

Some public radio stations do not have the funding to employ a staff of writers, artists, or public relations specialists full time. They may depend instead on the services of freelancers. In these instances, the Publication Manager is responsible for finding freelancers to handle specific projects. In some situations, the Publication Manager may be the person responsible for all the writing.

Within the scope of the job, the Publication Manager may be expected to write specific publications him- or herself or may be asked to develop publications for various departments within the station. The individual may write outlines for specific publications or assign the task to an assistant or other writer.

The Publication Manager is expected to edit the copy of writers and check facts for accuracy. If the individual is working with graphic designers or photographers, he or she must explain exactly what types of graphics are needed.

As part of the job, the Publications Manager will be expected to estimate budgets for specific publications. What will the total cost of an annual report be? What will pamphlets cost? What are the costs of monthly newsletters? In order to determine this information, the Publication Manager may write or call vendors to get bids or quotes on projects. Once the cost is determined and approved, it is up to the Publication Manager to bring the project in at or under budget.

Publication Managers should have an understanding and knowledge of the printing industry. The individual is expected to choose paper stock, type styles, and graphic formats for each publication. There are many different types, weights, and colors of paper available. There are also thousands of different type styles and varieties. While this might not seem like an important function, it is essential. For example, if the paper stock is too heavy, it may cost more to send through the mail. If a type is difficult to read, people might not be able to see an important message. If paper is the wrong size, it may be difficult to send through the mail effectively.

With today's computerized desktop publishing, Publication Managers can now prepare many publication projects "in-house," turning out printer-ready mechanicals. With this in mind, it is essential that the Publication Manager be computer competent. This is especially important in stations where volunteers are utilized to help with publication writing and graphics.

Additional duties of a Publication Manager working at a public radio station may include:

- Handling public relations, marketing, and advertising duties
- Writing speeches for station management
- Assisting in the development and creation of literature and marketing pieces for fund-raising
- Working with volunteers

## Salaries

Salaries for Publication Managers at public radio stations can vary tremendously. Earnings may range from $22,000 to $45,000 or more. Variables include the size, location, prestige, and popularity of the station as well as the experience, responsibilities, and track record of the individual.

## Employment Prospects

Employment prospects are fair for Publication Managers at public radio stations. While there are a limited number of public radio stations in the country, most put out various types of publications. Individuals may need to relocate for positions.

It should be noted that this may be a freelance position at some stations.

## Advancement Prospects

Advancement prospects for the Publication Managers at public radio stations are fair. Advancement opportunities are based to a great extent on the individual's career aspirations. Individuals might climb the career ladder by locating similar positions in larger, more prestigious public radio or television stations. Some find similar positions in other industries outside public broadcasting. Still others become the director of public relations or marketing, either in public broadcasting or another industry.

## Education and Training

A minimum of a four-year college degree is required for this position. Good choices for majors include communications, broadcasting, journalism, English, public relations, marketing, advertising, and liberal arts.

Seminars and workshops in any type of writing, editing, newsletter production, desktop publishing, graphics and layout, or marketing, etc., will be useful.

## Experience, Skills, and Personality Traits

Publication Managers should have some sort of experience working with publications. Some individuals have experience as journalists, reporters, or in publicity or public relations. Generally, the larger the station, the more experience will be required.

Publication Managers need to be excellent writers with a strong command of the English language. Editing skills are needed. A working knowledge of grammar, spelling, and word usage is essential. An understanding and sense of graphic style and layout are also necessary. Desktop publishing experience is mandatory. A working knowledge of desktop publishing software such as Pagemaker and Quark is needed.

Publication Managers working in public radio should be creative, articulate individuals with supervisory skills.

## Unions and Associations

Publication Managers working in public radio may belong to various associations, depending on the specific position held and the station they work for. These include the Public Relations Society of America (PRSA), International Association of Business Communicators (IABC), Women in Communications, Inc. (WIC), National Society of Fund Raising Executives (NSFRE), and the Council for the Advancement and Support of Education (CASE).

## Tips for Entry

1. Get as much writing experience as possible. If you are still in school, volunteer to work on your school newspaper or yearbook.

2. Job openings are also often advertised in the newspaper classified section under headings such as "Publication Manager," "Publications Editor," "Public Radio," and "Public Broadcasting."

3. If you live in an area with a public radio or television station, volunteer to work in their publications department. This will give you great experience and help you make contacts within the industry.

4. Send your résumé with a short cover letter to public radio or television stations, asking if there are openings. Remember to request that your résumé be kept on file.

5. Many stations advertise openings on the air as well as on their websites. Check them out.

# NEWSLETTER EDITOR

## CAREER PROFILE

**Duties:** Develops and writes newsletter for public radio station

**Alternate Title(s):** Publication Editor

**Salary Range:** $21,000 to $38,000+

**Employment Prospects:** Fair

**Advancement Prospects:** Fair

**Best Geographical Location(s):** Opportunities may be located throughout the country in areas hosting public radio stations

**Prerequisites:**
**Education or Training**—Four-year college degree
**Experience**—Writing and editing experience
**Special Skills and Personality Traits**—Editing skills; writing skills; communications skills; creativity; ability to multitask; layout and graphic skills

## CAREER LADDER

```
┌─────────────────────────────────┐
│  Newsletter Editor at Larger, More │
│  Prestigious Public Radio Station or │
│       in Other Industry or         │
│       Publication Manager          │
└─────────────────────────────────┘

┌─────────────────────────────────┐
│       Newsletter Editor           │
└─────────────────────────────────┘

┌─────────────────────────────────┐
│  Copywriter or Journalist or Publicist │
└─────────────────────────────────┘
```

## Position Description

Many public radio stations put out regular newsletters to inform potential and current donors and corporate sponsors about station happenings and events. The individual in charge of the public radio station newsletter is the Newsletter Editor.

It is the Newsletter Editor's responsibility to ensure that the public radio station's newsletter is the best it can be in both appearance and content.

The specific responsibilities of a Newsletter Editor varies from station to station, depending on station size and structure. At very large public radio stations, there may be a staff of publication manager, copywriters, researchers, graphic designers, photographers, et al. At smaller stations, the Newsletter Editor may be the only one involved in the preparation of the newsletter.

One of the main functions of the Newsletter Editor is to determine the content of the newsletter. He or she must decide what types of articles, columns, photographs, and additional information will be included in each issue of the newsletter.

Articles, stories, and columns may be written by staff writers, freelancers, or volunteers. Photographers, art directors and graphic designers may be full-time, part-time, free-

lancers, or volunteers. The Newsletter Editor is expected to assign projects to all of these individuals working on the newsletter. He or she is also responsible for supervising these individuals, ensuring that they turn in assigned work on a timely basis. It must be noted that in some instances, especially smaller public radio stations, the Newsletter Editor will be expected to write most if not all of the copy him- or herself.

Once the articles have been turned in, the Newsletter Editor must read and edit them. If necessary, he or she may need to do rewrites as well. The Editor then must determine where in the newsletter the articles, columns, and graphics will fit best.

Most newsletters today are set up with desktop publishing software on the computer. Once everything is in place, the newsletter may either be printed in-house or the camera-ready mechanical or disk will be sent to a professional printer.

The Editor is responsible for making sure that the newsletter is accurate, looks graphically pleasing, and is done on time. He or she may be responsible to the publications manager, public relations, marketing, or fund-raising and development director or station manager.

Additional duties of the Newsletter Editor working at a public radio station may include:

- Handling public relations, marketing, and advertising duties
- Writing editorials
- Assisting in the development and creation of literature and marketing pieces for fund-raising
- Working with volunteers

## Salaries

Earnings for Newsletter Editors at public radio stations can range from $21,000 to $38,000 or more. Variables include the size and location of the station as well as the experience, responsibilities, and track record of the individual. Generally, those working at larger public radio stations will earn more than their counterparts at smaller stations.

## Employment Prospects

Employment prospects are fair for Newsletter Editors seeking to work at public radio stations. Individuals may need to relocate for positions.

It should be noted that at smaller stations this may be either a part-time or freelance position.

## Advancement Prospects

Advancement prospects for Newsletter Editors at public radio stations are fair. Some Newsletter Editors find similar positions with larger, more prestigious public radio or television stations. Others find similar positions in various other industries, either in the not-for-profit sector or private industry. Some individuals locate a position as the publication manager at public radio stations. Others may move into public relations, publicity, or marketing positions.

## Education and Training

A minimum of a four-year college degree is required for this position. Good choices for majors include communications, broadcasting, journalism, English, public relations, marketing, advertising, and liberal arts.

Seminars and workshops in any type of writing, editing, newsletter production, desktop publishing, graphics, or layout will be helpful.

## Experience, Skills, and Personality Traits

Newsletter Editors need writing and editing experience. This may be obtained working as a journalist or reporter or in publicity or public relations. Some Newsletter Editors just starting out may have worked on their college newspaper or small-town weeklies before their position. Others obtained experience through internships.

Individuals need to have communication skills, editing skills, and be excellent writers. A good command of the English language, grammar, spelling, and word usage is essential. An understanding and sense of graphic style, layout, and desktop publishing are also necessary. Individuals should be creative and articulate, with the ability to multitask.

## Unions and Associations

Newsletter Editors working in public radio may belong to various associations, including the Public Relations Society of America (PRSA), the International Association of Business Communicators (IABC), Women in Communications, Inc. (WIC), the National Society of Fund-Raising Executives (NSFRE), and the Council for the Advancement and Support of Education (CASE).

## Tips for Entry

1. Writing experience is essential to this job. If you are still in school, volunteer to work on your school newspaper or yearbook.
2. Put together a portfolio of your best writing samples. Bring it to interviews to illustrate your skills and style.
3. To get editing experience, consider volunteering to edit a newsletter for a not-for-profit or civic organization.
4. Job openings are also often advertised in the newspaper classified section under headings such as "Newsletter Editor," "Publication Editor," "Public Radio," and "Public Broadcasting."
5. If you live in an area with a public radio or television station, volunteer to work in their publications department. This will give you great experience and help you make contacts within the industry.
6. Send your résumé with a short cover letter to public radio or television stations, asking if there are openings. Remember to request that your résumé be kept on file.
7. Many stations advertise openings on the air as well as on their websites. Check them out.

# RADIO STATION WEBSITES

# WEBMASTER

## CAREER PROFILE

**Duties:** Designs website for radio station; creates content for site; manages and maintains site

**Alternative Title(s):** Website Administrator

**Salary Range:** $28,000 to $150,000+

**Employment Prospects:** Good

**Advancement Prospects:** Good

**Best Geographical Location(s):** Positions located throughout the country

**Prerequisites:**
**Education or Training**—Education and training requirements vary
**Experience**—Experience designing, creating, and maintaining websites necessary
**Special Skills and Personality Traits**—Creative; computer skills; Internet savvy; knowledge of HTML and other programming languages; graphic and layout skills

## CAREER LADDER

```
┌─────────────────────────────────┐
│   Webmaster for Larger, More    │
│ Prestigious Station or Company or│
│      Webmaster Consultant       │
└─────────────────────────────────┘

┌─────────────────────────────────┐
│           Webmaster             │
└─────────────────────────────────┘

┌─────────────────────────────────┐
│   Webmaster in Other Industry   │
└─────────────────────────────────┘
```

## Position Description

The World Wide Web is changing the way many companies are doing business. More and more radio stations are jumping on the Web bandwagon. The individual in charge of creating and putting together a website is a Webmaster.

A Webmaster has many responsibilities. Depending on the situation, he or she may work alone or may assign tasks to assistants, content producers, copywriters, graphic designers, et al.

One of the first things a Webmaster may do is find a host for the site. For a station (or any company) to have a website, they must rent a space or location on the Web. This may be done by obtaining a host. The station pays the host for the right to place their site on-line on the host's space. In some instances, the station and the host are one.

In order for people to be able to locate the radio station's website, it must have a Web address. This is called the domain name. The Webmaster will work with the station management to develop a web address that people can remember and is available. Sometimes the Web address is the station's call letters; sometimes the Web address is the station's name or a saying people associate with the station, such as Mix 97 or Cool Radio.

The Webmaster must discuss the direction and goals of the station with management.

Does the management just want a website to have a web presence? Do they want people to be able to listen to the station while on-line via the Internet? Many stations today have websites with this option so that an individual around the corner or around the world can listen to a station. Does the station management want to have a site where they can sell products or advertising? Do they want news scrolling as it occurs? After the Webmaster discerns what the station management wants, he or she can get to work.

The Webmaster is responsible for developing and creating the station's website on the World Wide Web (WWW). He or she must design the site so it is exciting and easy to use. The Webmaster must be sure that pages on the website open easily and quickly. If they don't, people often leave the site and surf to another location.

The Webmaster will develop the site and add pictures of products, animation, and other graphics.

The individual may manipulate images to the proper size and format, because if an image is too large it will slow down the loading of a web page on an individual's computer. If an image is too small, it may be difficult to see clearly. The Webmaster must therefore know how many graphics to add and size them properly to make each page graphically pleasing, yet quick to open.

The Webmaster often develops a system for people to search for something on the site. He or she may program pop-up windows, features, shopping carts, secure-payment systems, or other functions, depending on the station's use for the site.

If the station's website sells advertising, potential advertisers will want to know how many people visit. Every time an individual visits a webpage, it is called a hit. The more people who visit a site, the better chance they will see an advertisement. The Webmaster may build in technology to see how many people visit the site, how long they stay, and what webpages they look at on the site.

Developing and designing the website is just one part of the job of the Webmaster. He or she is additionally responsible for the continued management and maintenance of the site.

In order to keep a website fresh and timely, the Webmaster may change the homepage and update other parts of the site. Sometimes the site content changes daily. The Webmaster must make changes and remove untimely content.

Websites are created in special languages so they can be displayed on the Internet. Text, for example, is converted into a language called HTML. This stands for Hypertext Markup Language. Other languages may be used as well. The Webmaster must know how to format the special languages.

Part of the job of the Webmaster is to monitor the site on a continuing basis. Every time new content or a link is added, the individual must be sure everything on the site is working and all links are accurate. This may be done by the Webmaster or may be assigned to an assistant.

Other duties of a Webmaster for a radio station include:

- Developing Web content
- Making sure the site is user-friendly
- Responding to inquiries from browsers having problems with the site
- Handling problems with the site
- Finding the best way to present information and graphics

## Salaries

Annual earnings for radio station Webmasters may range from $28,000 to $150,000 or more annually. Variables include the location, size, and prestige of the station and the specific site, as well as the responsibilities, experience, and reputation of the individual.

Webmasters who have a proven track record for developing creative sites that attract attention will earn the highest salaries.

It should be noted that some stations hire consultants to handle their websites. These individuals may earn between $50 and $200 or more per hour.

## Employment Prospects

Employment prospects are good for Webmasters seeking to work at radio stations and getting better every day. Depending on the experience of the individual, he or she might work for smaller-market stations as well as mid-market and major-market stations throughout the country.

One of the neat things about being a Webmaster is that because of the nature of the job, some employers may allow their Webmasters to telecommute all or part of the time. Individuals may also find part-time or consulting positions.

## Advancement Prospects

Webmasters working for radio stations may advance their careers in a number of ways. Those who build websites that consistently attract visitors will have no trouble climbing the career ladder. The most common method of career advancement for Webmasters is locating similar positions with larger or more prestigious radio stations or on-line retailers or other on-line sites. This will result in increased responsibilities and earnings. Some Webmasters decide to strike out on their own and begin consulting firms.

## Education and Training

Education and training requirements vary for Webmasters working for radio stations. Many Webmasters are self-taught. Some have taken classes. Others have college backgrounds or degrees in computers, programming, programming languages, graphics, web authoring, and the Internet.

However it is learned, Webmasters must know HTML. It is also necessary to know other programming languages, such as Cold Fusion, PERL, and Active Server Pages. Knowing how to integrate databases is a plus.

It is essential that Webmasters update their skills by self-study and/or classes, seminars, and workshops to keep up with changes in technology.

## Experience, Skills, and Personality Traits

Experience requirements depend, to a great extent, on the size and prestige of the station. Smaller stations just starting a website may not require Webmasters with a great deal of experience as long as they demonstrate that they are effective. Larger, more prestigious stations will generally want their Webmasters to have a proven track record and experience.

Individuals must have total competence with web dynamics, HTML authorship, and other programming languages. While some graphic work is outsourced or done by graphic designers within the company, graphic talent is necessary.

Webmasters additionally need excellent verbal and written communications skills. Creativity is essential. A knowledge of the broadcasting industry is helpful.

## Unions and Associations

Individuals interested in learning more about careers in the field may obtain additional information by contacting the

Internet Professionals Association (IPA) and the National Association of Webmasters (NAW).

## Tips for Entry

1. Positions may be located in the classified section of newspapers. Look under headings such as "Webmaster," "Radio Careers," "Broadcasting," "Radio Webmaster," and "Web Careers." Also look for ads under specific radio station names.
2. Many stations also advertise their openings on-air or on their websites. Check them out.
3. Look for a job on-line. Start with the more popular job sites, such as www.hotjobs.com and www.monster.com and go from there.
4. Get experience putting together websites for not-for-profit organizations or civic groups. Don't forget to add your name as the creator and Webmaster.
5. Look for internships in radio stations. These will give you on-the-job training, experience, and the opportunity to make important contacts. Contact stations to see what they offer.
6. Don't forget to read trade publications. *Billboard, Broadcasting,* and *Radio and Records* often have advertisements for stations with openings.
7. Send your résumé and a short cover letter to radio stations you are interested in working for. You can never tell when an opening exists.

# WEBSITE MARKETING MANAGER

## CAREER PROFILE

**Duties:** Develops and implements marketing plans and campaigns for radio station's website; handles day-to-day marketing functions; plans and implements special events; oversees advertising and public relations program

**Alternate Title(s):** Website Marketing Director

**Salary Range:** $24,000 to $45,000+

**Employment Prospects:** Fair

**Advancement Prospects:** Fair

**Best Geographical Location(s):** Jobs may be located throughout the country in areas hosting radio stations

**Prerequisites:**

**Education or Training**—College degree preferred but not always required

**Experience**—Marketing, merchandising, publicity, public relations or advertising experience, and Internet experience necessary

**Special Skills and Personality Traits**—Creativity; good verbal and written communications skills; Internet savvy; understanding of radio industry

## CAREER LADDER

```
┌─────────────────────────────────────────┐
│ Marketing Manager for Larger, More       │
│ Prestigious Radio Website, Station       │
│ Marketing Director, or Marketing         │
│ Director in Other Industry               │
└─────────────────────────────────────────┘

┌─────────────────────────────────────────┐
│ Website Marketing Manager                │
└─────────────────────────────────────────┘

┌─────────────────────────────────────────┐
│ Assistant Website Marketing Manager      │
│ or Marketing Manager                     │
│ in Other Industry                        │
└─────────────────────────────────────────┘
```

## Position Description

Many radio stations have jumped on the bandwagon and created a presence on the Web. A radio station website promotes the station, lists station events and news, and in some cases allows listeners to tune in to the station over the Internet.

While most of the money radio stations earn has traditionally been generated through the selling of commercial space on the air, today many stations also utilize their website to augment earnings by selling advertising space on the site.

With all this in mind, for many stations their website can be very important. With so many sites available, how does any website attract visitors to their site? As in traditional business, a website must also market its presence. The Website Marketing Manager for a radio station has an important job. He or she is responsible for finding ways to market the site and the station to potential advertisers and potential station listeners.

Responsibilities may vary, depending on the size and structure of the station and its website. In some stations, a marketing director will handle all the marketing functions, including that of the website. More and more, however, stations are hiring Website Marketing Managers whose sole job is marketing the station's website. The manner in which this is accomplished can be the success or failure of the site.

The radio station Website Marketing Manager is responsible for developing the concepts and campaigns that will determine how the site will be marketed. The individual is expected to determine the most effective techniques and programs to market the site and its contents. To do this, the individual will work closely with the station marketing director, station manager, and/or station owner.

As part of this job, the Marketing Manager must plan and coordinate the site's marketing goals and objectives. How will people know the website is on-line? How will they know the web address? Who will the site be marketed to? Who are they trying to attract? Marketing a website is slightly different from marketing a traditional business. Visitors to on-line sites can come from virtually anywhere in the world.

It is essential that the Marketing Manager find ways to include the web address in as many places as possible. One obvious advantage for a radio station is that its DJs and announcers can constantly promote the site's web address on the air. The more people hear a web address, the more likely they are to remember it and visit to see what's happening on the site.

The radio station Website Marketing Manager must also be sure that the station's Web address, or URL, is added to all television commercials, print advertisements, billboards, stationery, etc. This helps keep the name and address of the station in the public eye.

Often Marketing Managers advertise the radio station's site on other websites. They may do this via banner ads, the advertisements where an individual need only click on the banner and it takes the person to the site of the advertiser.

The Marketing Manager is often expected to do research to obtain information about people visiting the site. He or she may prepare questionnaires or surveys to be placed on the site. In order to entice people to answer questionnaires, the Website Marketing Manager may offer a gift or entry into a sweepstakes.

Radio station Website Marketing Managers must come up with innovative ideas to try to attract new visitors to the site. In many situations, the Website Marketing Manager may work with the station's promotion department, developing contests, sweepstakes, and other promotions that can be entered on-line. People will then have an incentive to go to the station's website. The more people who visit the website and the more "hits" the site gets, the more the station can charge for on-line advertisements.

Once people log on to the website to enter the contest, the hope is they will return to the site to browse or listen to the station. To accomplish this, many Marketing Managers run contests that visitors can enter daily. This means visitors have an incentive to visit the radio station website daily and hopefully be attracted to something of interest on the site.

Another reason Website Marketing Managers use sweepstakes is to help build mailing lists. When people enter contests they usually provide their name, address, phone number, age, and e-mail address. Additional information may be gathered that may be helpful in targeting the site to visitors and the station to listeners.

Marketing Managers also use sweepstakes to build lists for e-mail newsletters. These newsletters are useful for informing station listeners about station events, shows, and promotions.

The Marketing Manager who can come up with innovative and creative ideas might get the attention of media journalists or others doing articles or stories on interesting websites. Depending on which media show a story ends up on, the attention generated can lead to thousands of website hits.

Depending on the size and structure of the station, the Marketing Manager may work with the station's marketing, advertising, public relations, and promotion departments. In some situations, the Marketing Director may also be responsible for handling the public relations and advertising functions of the website.

Additional duties of the Website Marketing Manager for a radio station might include:

- Handling the marketing, public relations, and advertising duties for the station itself
- Developing marketing budgets
- Designing and developing marketing materials
- Developing and providing advertising content for the site

## Salaries

Annual earnings for radio station Website Marketing Managers can range from $24,000 to $45,000 or more. Variables affecting earnings include the location, size, and prestige of the specific station and website, as well as the experience and responsibilities of the individual.

## Employment Prospects

While this is a fairly new position, employment prospects are fair and getting better. As more stations see the potential of a great website, prospects will improve. Jobs can be located throughout the country.

## Advancement Prospects

Radio station Website Marketing Managers have a number of options for career advancement. Some individuals get experience, prove themselves, and move on to positions at larger or more prestigious stations or station websites. This results in increased responsibilities and earnings.

Other individuals may climb the career ladder by moving into positions as Marketing Directors in other industries. Still other individuals strike out on their own and start their own marketing firms.

## Education and Training

Generally, larger, more prestigious or better-known stations will require their Marketing Managers to hold a minimum of a four-year college degree. Good choices for majors include public relations, advertising, journalism, marketing, liberal arts, English, communications, and business. While smaller stations may prefer a college degree, they may not make it a requirement.

Courses and seminars in marketing, public relations, publicity, promotion, the broadcast industry, and web marketing are also helpful.

## Experience, Skills, and Personality Traits

Radio station Website Marketing Managers must be web savvy. Communications skills, both written and verbal, are essential. Individuals should be creative, innovative, ambitious, articulate, and highly motivated. Marketing Managers also need to be energetic, with the ability to handle many details and projects at one time without getting flustered and stressed.

A knowledge of publicity, promotion, public relations, advertising, and various research techniques is also necessary.

## Unions and Associations

Radio station Website Marketing Managers may belong to a number of trade associations that provide support and guidance. These might include the American Marketing Association (AMA), the Marketing Research Association (MRA), and the Public Relations Society of America (PRSA).

## Tips for Entry

1. Positions may be advertised in the classified ad section of newspapers. Look under such headings as "Marketing," "Marketing Manager," "Website Marketing," "Radio Station Marketing," and "Radio Website Marketing Manager."

2. Send your résumé and a cover letter to radio stations you are interested in working for. Ask that your résumé be kept on file.

3. Look for jobs on-line. Check out sites such as www.hotjobs.com and www.monster.com to get started. Go from there.

4. Many radio stations advertise their openings on-air as well as on their websites. Check it out.

5. Take seminars and courses in marketing, promotion, public relations, publicity, and web marketing. These will give you an edge over other applicants, as well as help you hone your skills and make valuable contacts.

# WEBSITE CONTENT PRODUCER

## CAREER PROFILE

**Duties:** Develops and creates content for radio station website; researches and writes articles for website

**Alternative Title(s):** Website Content Editor

**Salary Range:** $28,000 to $75,000

**Employment Prospects:** Fair

**Advancement Prospects:** Good

**Best Geographical Location(s):** Positions located throughout the country

**Prerequisites:**

**Education or Training**—Education and training requirements vary

**Experience**—Writing and editing experience helpful

**Special Skills and Personality Traits**—Good command of the English language; excellent writing skills; creative; Internet savvy

## CAREER LADDER

```
┌─────────────────────────────────────┐
│  Website Content Producer for Larger,│
│  More Prestigious Station or Company │
│         in Other Industry            │
└─────────────────────────────────────┘

┌─────────────────────────────────────┐
│      Website Content Producer        │
└─────────────────────────────────────┘

┌─────────────────────────────────────┐
│        Journalist or Writer          │
└─────────────────────────────────────┘
```

## Position Description

Radio station websites allow radio stations to have a presence on the Web. The website also gives a station another avenue for presenting itself. In order to make websites interesting, many stations employ Website Content Producers.

The main function of the Website Content Producer is to create and develop interesting and unique content for the station's site. Individuals in this position are responsible for researching and writing engaging stories and articles in a variety of areas and categories. Their job is similar to that of a combination of a print journalist and editor.

Depending on the size and extent of a station's website, there may be more than one Content Producer. One may handle events, another may handle news, and yet another may be responsible for writing business stories. It all depends on how comprehensive the station wants their site to be.

Stations hosting large sites may have a senior or executive Website Content Producer. He or she may then be responsible for overseeing the work of the other Content Producers.

The radio station Website Content Producer is often responsible for overseeing staff copywriters and graphic artists. Some Content Producers are also responsible for finding and retaining freelancers to write articles on specific subjects or specific areas. A Content Producer in charge of an entire radio station website may find writers to do stories on, for example, business, local government, consumer affairs, health related issues, and entertainment. Once they get the stories, the Content Producer will be responsible for editing them and giving them to the webmaster to put on-line.

Radio station Website Content Producers may develop pieces on various subjects. Depending on the specific area the Website Content Producer is responsible for, he or she may be expected to develop and maintain relationships with news, community, commerce, and other organizations. These relationships will help the individual create unique and appealing content.

The radio station Website Content Producer may be responsible for covering local and/or station events. He or she may interview people, arrange for photos, and obtain other information to make the on-line stories interesting.

One of the great things about the Internet is that it can be interactive. With this in mind, the Content Producer may develop surveys, questionnaires, or other pieces to involve those visiting the site.

In some instances, the interactive part of the site may be related to what is occurring on the air at the specific time.

For example, sometimes the on-air personality may be discussing a specific subject and ask people to go to the website to give their opinion. Within minutes, the voice of the listeners can be tabulated and discussed on-air.

While there are sites that take stories right from the print media, creating pieces for the Web is often slightly different. Many Web stories are shorter to keep the interest of those reading them.

The radio station Website Content Producer is often responsible for getting pictures, animation, and other graphics to make the content more appealing. He or she may utilize the services of graphic artists, photographers, or others to accomplish this task. The individual may work with the webmaster to find images that will look good but not affect the ease of opening the site.

In order to keep the site fresh, radio station Website Content Producers may be responsible for daily updates. In situations where a station is owned by a media conglomerate, the Website Content Producer may be responsible for developing content for the websites of more than one station.

Other duties of radio station Website Content Producers include:

• Staying up-to-date with radio station events
• Responding to inquiries from people who visit the site
• Finding the best way to present information and graphics
• Handling webcams and chats
• Handling on-line contests and promotions

## Salaries

Annual earnings for radio station Website Content Producers range from $20,000 to $75,000 or more annually. Variables include the location, size, and prestige of the station and the specific site, as well as the responsibilities, experience, and reputation of the individual.

It should be noted that some stations hire consultants to handle the content on their websites. These individuals may earn between $15 and $50 or more per hour or may be paid on a per-project basis.

## Employment Prospects

Employment prospects are fair for radio station Website Content Producers and are getting better every day. Depending on the experience of the individual, he or she might work for smaller market stations as well as mid-market and major-market stations throughout the country.

One of the neat things about being a Website Content Producer is that due to the nature of the job, some employers may allow individuals to telecommute all or part of the time. Individuals may also find part-time or consulting positions.

## Advancement Prospects

Radio station Website Content Producers may advance their careers in a number of ways. The most common method of advancement is locating a similar position at a larger, more prestigious station, resulting in increased responsibilities and earnings. Individuals working in a specific area of website content producing may be promoted to executive content producer. Some radio station Website Content Producers find similar positions in other industries.

## Education and Training

Education and training requirements vary for radio station Website Content Producers. Most stations today prefer that people in this position have a minimum of a four-year college degree. Good choices for majors include journalism, communications, English, public relations, marketing, or liberal arts.

Courses, workshops, and seminars in public relations, writing, promotion, journalism, and radio will be helpful in honing skills and making new contacts.

While it may not be required, individuals who know HTML (a programming language) may have a leg up on other candidates.

## Experience, Skills, and Personality Traits

Experience requirements depend, to a great extent, on the size and prestige of the station. Smaller stations just starting a website may not require their Content Producer to have a great deal of experience, as long as he or she demonstrates competency. Generally, the larger the station and more extensive their site, the more experience that will be required.

Writing and editing experience will be useful, no matter what the capacity. Individuals need a good command of the English language, great writing skills, and creativity. Editing skills are also necessary. A knowledge of the broadcasting industry is helpful. Those who are Web savvy have an advantage.

Website Content Producers should have the ability to multitask and work under pressure without getting flustered. People skills are mandatory in this position.

## Unions and Associations

Individuals interested in learning more about careers in the field may obtain additional information by contacting the Internet Professionals Association (IPA). They may also belong to radio station and journalism associations.

## Tips for Entry

1. Positions may be located in the classified section of newspapers. Look under headings such as "Radio Website Content Producer," "Website Content Manager," "Radio Careers," "Broadcasting," "Radio," and "Web Careers." Also look for ads under specific radio station names.
2. Many stations also advertise their openings on-air or on their website. You might want to check it out.

3. This is the perfect type of job to look for on-line. Start with the more popular job sites such as www.hotjobs.com and www.monster.com and go from there.

4. Get as much experience writing as you can. If you are still in school, get involved in your school newspaper and/or website.

5. Consider a part-time job for a local newspaper to get some writing experience and to build up your contact list.

6. Look for internships in radio stations. These will give you on-the-job training, experience, and the opportunity to make important contacts. Contact stations to see what they offer.

7. Send your résumé and a short cover letter to radio stations you are interested in working for. You can never tell when an opening exists.

8. Don't forget to read trade publications. *Billboard, Broadcasting,* and *Radio and Records* often have advertisements for stations with openings.

# WEBSITE GRAPHIC DESIGNER

## CAREER PROFILE

**Duties:** Designs and creates graphics for radio station website

**Alternative Title(s):** Graphic Artist

**Salary Range:** $23,000 to $45,000+

**Employment Prospects:** Fair

**Advancement Prospects:** Fair

**Best Geographical Location(s):** Positions located throughout the country in areas hosting radio stations

**Prerequisites:**

**Education or Training**—Education and training requirements vary

**Experience**—Graphic artist experience; experience working with websites

**Special Skills and Personality Traits**—Creativity; artistic ability; computer skills; Internet savvy; graphic and layout skills

## CAREER LADDER

```
┌─────────────────────────────────────┐
│  Website Graphic Designer Consultant │
│  or Website Graphic Designer for     │
│  Larger, More Prestigious Station    │
│  or Company                          │
└─────────────────────────────────────┘

┌─────────────────────────────────────┐
│     Website Graphic Designer         │
└─────────────────────────────────────┘

┌─────────────────────────────────────┐
│    Graphic Artist in Other Industry  │
└─────────────────────────────────────┘
```

## Position Description

Radio station websites serve a number of functions. Websites give the station a presence on the Web. They also help to promote the station, offering browsers the opportunity to find information they might have heard on-air, as well as additional information. Radio station websites also give the station another avenue for earning advertising revenue.

In order to help make their website more attractive, many stations employ Website Graphic Designers. The function of these individuals is to design graphics to create the most attractive website possible.

Website Graphic Designers often work with the webmaster. Within the scope of the job, they are expected to find the best way to present information and graphics. It should be noted that in some instances, the Graphic Designer is also the webmaster.

The Graphic Designer is expected to develop a layout for the website. What colors should the background be? What should go where? What types of graphics should be used? There are countless options.

Part of the job of the Graphic Designer may be choosing the size, kind, and color of fonts to use on the website. The Website Graphic Designer must also choose background colors and styles. In choosing fonts, colors, and background, the Graphic Designer must keep in mind that things often appear differently on different computers or browsers. Some people have huge displays on their computers. Others may have 12-inch screens. The Graphic Designer will often try out various types, backgrounds, and layouts on different browsers to see how they look and to ensure they will be easy to read.

When designing the website, the individual tries to keep the design of all the site pages tied together. This means the station's name, graphics, and logos will look similar on each page. The reason for this is so visitors to the site will be able to easily identify the station.

The Website Graphic Designer may utilize a variety of pictures, photos, animation, computer-generated images, and other types of graphics. The individual may manipulate images to the proper size and format. This is necessary because if an image is too large it will slow down the loading of a web page on an individual's computer. If an image is too small, it may be difficult to see clearly. The Graphic Designer may work with the webmaster to determine how many graphics can be added and what the proper size is to make each page graphically pleasing yet quick to open.

While most of the money radio stations earn is generated through the selling of on-air commercial space, many stations now utilize their website to augment earnings by selling advertising space on the site. Website Graphic Designers may be expected to design or create an array of different types of ads for advertisers. They may, for example, create banner advertisements. These are the ads which, when clicked on, go directly to the advertiser's site. The Website Graphic Designer may incorporate advertisers logos into on-line ads or create logos for those who don't have one in place.

In order to keep a website fresh and timely, the Graphic Designer may be expected to regularly change the graphics or design of the homepage and update other parts of the site.

Depending on the size and structure of the station website, there may be one or more Graphic Designers. In some stations, the Website Graphic Designer may also be responsible for handling the graphic needs of the station. He or she might, for example, develop the art work for station logos, advertisements, promotional and marketing material, etc.

Other duties of radio station Website Graphic Designers may include:

- Developing web content
- Making sure the site is user-friendly
- Handling webmaster duties
- Handling graphic design projects for the radio station itself

## Salaries

Annual earnings for radio station Website Graphic Designers range from $23,000 to $45,000 or more. Factors affecting earnings include the location, size, and prestige of the station and the specific site, as well as the responsibilities, experience, and reputation of the individual.

It should be noted that some stations hire consultants to handle the graphic design of their websites. These individuals may earn between $10 and $100 or more per hour.

## Employment Prospects

Employment prospects are fair for radio station Website Graphic Designers. More and more stations are realizing the importance of an attractive website.

Depending on the experience of the individual, he or she might work for smaller-market stations as well as mid-market and major-market stations throughout the country.

Some Radio Station Website Graphic Designers may work part time or on a consulting basis.

## Advancement Prospects

Advancement prospects for radio station Website Graphic Designers are fair. Advancement will depend to a great extent on the talent of the individual and his or her career aspirations.

Some Graphic Designers climb the career ladder by finding similar positions working for larger or more prestigious radio stations. This results in increased responsibilities and earnings. Other individuals may land jobs as art directors in radio or in another industry. Many Graphic Designers strike

out on their own and become consultants. There are also Website Graphic Designers who learn more about building websites and become webmasters.

## Education and Training

Education and training requirements vary for radio station Website Graphic Designers. Some Graphic Designers are self-taught. Some have taken classes. Many stations require or prefer an applicant to have a four-year college degree in fine arts or commercial art or an art school background.

A good portfolio demonstrating that the individual possesses the required skills can often land a job in lieu of education. A portfolio or "book" made up of the individual's best work is usually necessary in order to show samples and illustrate skills.

Courses or seminars in advertising or HTML may prove useful.

## Experience, Skills, and Personality Traits

Experience requirements depend, to a great extent, on the size and prestige of the station. Smaller stations just starting a website may not require that their Graphic Designers have a great deal of experience as long as they illustrate competence. Larger, more prestigious stations may want their Website Graphic Designers to have more experience. As noted, a good portfolio can often get an individual a job, even if their experience is limited.

Radio station Website Graphic Designers should be artistic individuals with a lot of creativity. Graphic talent is essential, as is the ability to develop eye-catching graphics.

As most of the work is done on the computer, computer skills and the ability to use appropriate software programs are mandatory. A basic knowledge of the broadcasting industry and advertising is helpful.

## Unions and Associations

Radio station Website Graphic Designers may belong to a number of trade associations that offer professional guidance, education, and information. These might include the American Advertising Federation (AAF), the Art Director Club, Inc. (ADC), the One Club, the Society of Illustrators (SOI), the Graphic Artists Guild (GAG), and the American Institute of Graphic Arts (AIGA).

Individuals interested in learning more about careers in the field may obtain additional information by contacting the Internet Professionals Association (IPA).

## Tips for Entry

1. Your portfolio can help you get a job. Start working on it now. A good portfolio can give you an edge over other applicants. In many instances, it can take the place of educational requirements. Make sure your

portfolio includes some work relevant to graphic design on the Web, even if you have to do samples. Take your portfolio to every job interview.

2. Positions may be located in the classified section of newspapers. Look under headings such as "Website Graphic Designer," "Radio Careers," "Broadcasting," "Graphic Designer-Radio Website," "Website Graphic Artists," and "Web Careers." Also look for ads under specific radio station names.

3. Many stations advertise their openings on-air or on their websites. Check it out.

4. Get experience doing graphics for websites by volunteering to handle the task for not-for-profit organiza-tions or civic groups. Don't forget to add your name as the Graphic Designer.

5. Look for internships in radio stations. These will give you on-the-job training, experience, and the opportunity to make important contacts. Contact stations to see what they offer.

6. Send your résumé and a short cover letter to radio stations you are interested in working for. You can never tell when an opening exists.

7. Join trade associations. Many have student memberships. Others offer critique sessions on improving your portfolio. All of them will help you make important contacts.

# ADVERTISING SALES REPRESENTATIVE— RADIO STATION WEBSITE

## CAREER PROFILE

**Duties:** Sells advertising space on radio station website; services current accounts; brings in new accounts

**Alternate Title(s):** Sales Representative; Salesman; Saleswoman; Advertising Account Executive; Salesperson; Sales Rep; Account Rep; Sales Executive

**Salary Range:** $18,000 to $85,000+

**Employment Prospects:** Good

**Advancement Prospects:** Good

**Best Geographical Location(s):** Positions may be located throughout the country in small, midsize, and large radio stations

**Prerequisites:**

    **Education or Training**—College background or degree required or preferred by some stations

    **Experience**—Experience in sales helpful but not always required

    **Special Skills and Personality Traits**—Sales skills; persuasiveness; articulate; self-motivated; aggressiveness; personable; outgoing nature

## CAREER LADDER

```
┌─────────────────────────────────────────┐
│  Sales Manager or Sales Representative    │
│  for Larger, More Prestigious Station     │
│  Website or Station                       │
└─────────────────────────────────────────┘

┌─────────────────────────────────────────┐
│  Sales Representative—Radio Station       │
│  Website                                  │
└─────────────────────────────────────────┘

┌─────────────────────────────────────────┐
│  Entry-Level or                           │
│  Sales Position in Other Industry         │
└─────────────────────────────────────────┘
```

## Position Description

Radio stations, like other businesses, are now seeking a presence on the Web. The website serves to promote the station, as well as list station events and news. While most of the money radio stations earn is generated through the selling of commercial space on the air, many stations also utilize their website to augment earnings by selling advertising space on the site.

The person in charge of selling the advertising on the station's website is called an Advertising Sales Representative. He or she might also be referred to as an advertising account representative, salesperson, or ad rep.

At some stations, the individual who sells the commercial air space may also be the person who sells ad space on the website. At other stations, these may be two separate positions.

Depending on the size and structure of the station's website, there may be one or more Advertising Sales Representatives assigned to sell ads on the website. Once assigned accounts, the Sales Rep is expected to call or visit the advertisers on a regular basis to determine when they want to advertise.

While selling air space on radio stations is a known commodity to many advertisers, some are not familiar with the exposure they will get on a station's website. The Advertising Sales Rep must have a full knowledge not only of the station but also of the website. He or she may, for example, need to explain the demographics of people who are visiting the site to show potential advertisers how advertising can benefit them.

In order to entice new advertisers to try advertising on the website, the Sales Rep may offer a variety of promotions and discounts. The website Advertising Sales Rep must be aware of all the promotions the station is running to best service his or her accounts. Many stations put together packages where an advertiser gets a certain number of "spots" or commercials on-air while running advertisements on the site. It is the responsibility of the Sales Rep to explain various promotions, discounts, and package rates to advertisers and potential advertisers.

Many website Ad Sales Representatives also offer suggestions for copy or ad content. Web advertising has options and limitations differing from traditional print ads. Many stations sell "banner ads" on the site, where a visitor need only hit the banner on the site to be taken to the advertiser's site.

As large graphics may slow down a site, ad graphics must be specially sized and created to allow the website and the ad to open quickly. Otherwise visitors may not wait around to see what the advertisement says.

Website Advertising Sales Reps must determine how long advertisers want to run specific ads and when advertisers want ads changed. One of the great things about advertising on-line is that ads can be changed quickly. The Sales Rep is responsible for knowing which ads need to be put up on the site and when.

As the station website becomes more prominent, customers may call the station to get more information about the station, its demographics, and advertising and commercial rates. When calls regarding potential advertising come in, the sales manager usually refers them to the appropriate Advertising Sales Rep.

The Rep is then expected to call them or send out advertising kits with rate cards; informational sheets on the station, the website, and demographics; testimonials from other advertisers, etc. In some cases, the Rep will schedule an appointment with the potential client to discuss advertising needs. As noted previously, the Sales Representative may offer special discounts to new advertisers in order to get them to try advertising on the station website to see its effectiveness.

One of the major responsibilities of website Advertising Sales Reps is bringing in new business. The individual may make what is known as "cold" calls to potential advertisers. These calls are made to people who may or may not have advertised on the station, but not on the website. Often these potential advertisers have not expressed an interest in advertising on the website at all. After identifying him- or herself and the station affiliation, the Account Rep attempts to set up an appointment to tell the potential advertiser more about the station, the website, and advertising opportunities. Not every call will result in an appointment. Sales Reps must have the ability to accept rejection without taking it personally.

Many radio stations provide training sessions for the entire sales staff. These may be in-house or may be offered by an outside training force. Advertising Sales Reps are expected to attend these training sessions and seminars as well as weekly staff meetings. During these meetings the sales manager may make suggestions regarding selling, offer helpful sales techniques, and discuss advertising specials and promotions the station is offering.

The Advertising Sales Representative must stay up-to-date on various rates, discounts, and packages the station offers for both on-air and website advertising. He or she should be able to explain all of these to advertisers in an easy-to-understand manner.

Many successful Advertising Representatives help develop marketing and advertising ideas for current or potential customers. Individuals also often brainstorm with clients to come up with effective advertising ideas. The more effective ads are, the more commercial space customers will purchase.

Website Advertising Sales Representatives, like all other sales reps, are expected to keep accurate records of advertisements sold, billings, etc. Individuals must write orders and make sure they get to the appropriate department at the radio station. In many situations, the Sales Reps are responsible for obtaining client approval of copy and commercials before putting them up on the site.

Those who are successful in this line of work continually check with clients to make sure they are happy with their ads, are being billed properly, and to see if they want to buy additional advertisements.

Advertising Sales Reps must know how to set priorities and organize the work day. They may work in the field or from their desk, making calls to current and potential clients. While individuals may work normal business hours, they may arrange sales calls after hours, in the evening or on weekends.

Additional duties of radio website Advertising Sales Representatives include:

- Selling on-air commercials
- Working with clients' graphic designers or marketing staff
- Working with clients' advertising agencies
- Representing the station at events

## Salaries

Annual earnings for website Advertising Sales Representatives at radio stations can range from $18,000 to $85,000 or more depending on a number of variables. These include the size, prestige, and location of the radio station and its website. Other variables include the sales ability of the Advertising Account Representative. Individuals who sell more, earn more.

The reason many people love this type of job so much is that the sky is the limit on earnings. Most Advertising Sales Representatives are paid on a commission basis. This means that for every dollar of advertising that an individual sells, he or she receives a percentage as part of his or her salary. Percentages can vary from station to station and might range from 10% to 20%, with the average commission about 15%.

Some stations offer a weekly or monthly draw against salary to Advertising Sales Representatives. They do this for a number of reasons—the first of which is to help beginning Sales Representatives get into the swing of selling. The second is to adjust the take-home pay of individuals in case they had a "bad" week or month.

## Employment Prospects

Individuals who are sales oriented, aggressive, and hard working are always in demand for all sales positions. Employment prospects for radio station website Advertising Sales Representatives are good and getting better all the time. More and more radio stations have websites to enhance their image and give them a Web presence.

Jobs may be located throughout the country in small, midsize, and major-market radio.

## Advancement Prospects

Advancement prospects are good for radio station website Advertising Sales Representatives. Some individuals move up the career ladder by selling more ads, which increases their income considerably. Others may find similar positions working for larger, more prestigious stations with larger websites. Individuals may also sell commercial space on the air.

Some Advertising Sales Representatives are also promoted to assistant sales managers or full-fledged sales managers at the same or another radio station.

## Education and Training

Most stations prefer or require their Advertising Sales Representatives to hold a college degree or at least have a college background. Courses that might prove useful in selling include advertising, sales, business, English, psychology, sociology, writing, and communications. Seminars and workshops offered through private groups or trade associations may also be useful to the individual in honing sales skills.

Educational requirements may be waived by the station if the applicant is eager, aggressive, and shows potential for selling.

## Experience, Skills, and Personality Traits

Radio station website Advertising Sales Representatives should be articulate, personable, and outgoing. Individuals should enjoy being around and dealing with people. Individuals need to be pleasantly aggressive. Sales skills are essential.

Self-motivation and the ability to work without constant supervision are mandatory. Individuals must be able to plan out their work day, make appointments and calls, and go to appointments without someone looking over their shoulder.

The ability to work with numbers is helpful in figuring out costs and rates of ads and packages. A general knowledge of the radio industry and the Internet is useful.

## Unions and Associations

Advertising Account Representatives or their stations may be members of their specific state's broadcasting association, the American Advertising Federation (AAF), the National Association of Broadcasters (NAB), the National Association of Broadcast Employees and Technicians (NABET), and/or the Radio and Advertising Bureau (RAB).

## Tips for Entry

1. Many radio stations and associations offer internships or training programs. Internships give you on-the-job training experience and the opportunity to make important contacts.
2. Get as much selling experience as possible. You might, for example, want to volunteer to sell ads for a journal for local not-for-profit or civic groups. This is great hands-on experience to add to your résumé.
3. Many local stations advertise openings on the air as well as on their websites. Check them out.
4. Job openings are also often advertised in the newspaper classified section under headings such as "Advertising Sales Representatives," "Advertising," "Radio," "Broadcasting," "Website Sales," Radio Sales," and "Broadcasting Sales."
5. Send your résumé and a short cover letter to radio stations you are interested in working for. You can never tell when an opening exists.

# APPENDIXES

# APPENDIX I
# DEGREE PROGRAMS

## A. COLLEGES AND UNIVERSITIES OFFERING MAJORS IN BROADCASTING

The following is a state-by-state listing of selected four-year schools offering degrees in broadcasting. School names, addresses, phone numbers, Web addresses, and e-mail addresses are included when available.

The author does not endorse any one school over another. Use this list as a beginning. Check the latest edition of *Love-joy's College Guide*—found in the reference section of libraries or in guidance counseling centers—for additional schools offering degrees in this field.

### ALABAMA

**Alabama State University**
915 South Jackson Street
Montgomery, AL 36104
**Phone:** (334) 229-4291
http://www.alasu.edu

**Auburn University**
Auburn University, AL 36849-5145
**Phone:** (334) 844-4080 or (800)
   AUBURN9 (toll-free in Alabama)
**E-mail:** admissions@auburn.edu
http://www.auburn.edu/admissions

**Spring Hill College**
4000 Dauphin Street
Mobile, AL 36608-1791
**Phone:** (251) 380-3030 or
   (800) SHC-6704
**Fax:** (251) 460-2186
**E-mail:** admit@shc.edu

**University of Alabama**
Box 870132
Tuscaloosa, AL 35487-0132
**Phone:** (205) 348-5666 or
   (800) 933-BAMA
**Fax:** (205) 348-9046
**E-mail:** admissions@ua.edu

**University of Montevallo**
Montevallo, AL 35115-6000
**Phone:** (205) 665-6030
**E-mail:** admissions@montevallo.edu
http://www.montevallo.edu

### ARIZONA

**Arizona State University**
Box 870112
Tempe, AZ 85287-0112
**Phone:** (480) 965-7788
**Fax:** (480) 965-3610
**E-mail:** ugradinq@asu.edu
http://www.asu.edu

**Northern Arizona University**
Box 4084
Flagstaff, AZ 86011-4084
**Phone:** (888) MORE-NAU (toll-free)
**E-mail:** undergraduate.admissions@nau.
   edu
http://www4.nau.edu/uadmissions/admis/
   home.htm

**University of Arizona**
P.O. Box 210040
Tucson, AZ 85721-0040
**Phone:** (520) 621-3237
**Fax:** (520) 621-9799
**E-mail:** appinfo@arizona.edu
http://www.ualr.edu/www/index.htmlx

### ARKANSAS

**Arkansas State University**
P.O. Box 1630
State University, AR 72467
**Phone:** (870) 972-3024
**E-mail:** admissions@chickasaw.astate.edu
http://www.astate.edu

**Harding University**
Station A, Box 12255
Searcy, AR 72149
**Phone:** (501) 279-4407 or (800) 477-4407
**Fax:** (501) 279-4129
**E-mail:** admissions@harding.edu
http://www.harding.edu

**John Brown University**
Siloam Springs, AR 72761-2121
**Phone:** (877) JBU-INFO (toll-free)
**Fax:** (501) 524-4196
**E-mail:** jbuinfo@acc.jbu.edu
http://www.jbu.edu

**University of Arkansas at Little Rock**
2801 South University Avenue
Little Rock, AR 72204-1099
**Phone:** (501) 569-3127 or (800) 482-8892
**Fax:** (501) 569-8915
http://www.ualr.edu/www/index.htmlx

### CALIFORNIA

**Biola University**
13800 Biola Avenue
La Mirada, CA 90639-0001
**Phone:** (800) OK-BIOLA (toll-free)
**E-mail:** admissions@biola.edu
http://www.biola.edu

**California State University, Chico**
Chico, CA 95929-0722
**Phone:** (530) 898-4879 or (800) 542-4426
**Fax:** (530) 898-6456
**E-mail:** info@csuchico.edu
http://www.csuchico.edu

**California State University, Fresno**
5150 North Maple Avenue, M/S JA 57
Fresno, CA 93740-8026
**Phone:** (559) 278-2261
**Fax:** (559) 278-4812
**E-mail:** donna_mills@csufresno.edu
http://www.csufresno.edu

**California State University, Fullerton**
P.O. Box 6900
Fullerton, CA 92834-6900
**Phone:** (714) 278-2370
http://www.fullerton.edu

**California State University, Long Beach**
1250 Bellflower Boulevard
Long Beach, CA 90840
**Phone:** (562) 985-4641
http://www.csulb.edu

**California State University, Los
   Angeles**
5151 State University Drive
Los Angeles, CA 90032-8530

**Phone:** (323) 343-3839
**E-mail:** admission@calstatela.edu
http://www.calstatela.edu

**California State University, Northridge**
18111 Nordhoff Street
Northridge, CA 91330-8207
**Phone:** (818) 677-3777
**Fax:** (818) 677-3766
**E-mail:** admissions.records@csun.edu
http://www.csun.edu

**Master's College**
21726 Placerita Canyon Road
Santa Clarita, CA 91321-1200
**Phone:** (661) 259-3540 Ext. 3363
**Fax:** (661) 288-1037 (enrollment)
**E-mail:** enrollment@masters.edu
http://www.masters.edu

**San Diego State University**
5500 Campanile Drive
San Diego, CA 92182-7455
**Phone:** (619) 594-6886
**Fax:** (619) 594-1250
**E-mail:** admissions@sdsu.edu
http://www.sdsu.edu

**San Francisco State University**
1600 Holloway Avenue
Administration 154
San Francisco, CA 94132
**Phone:** (415) 338-2037
**Fax:** (415) 338-7196
**E-mail:** ugadmit@sfsu.edu
http://www.sfsu.edu

**San Jose State University**
One Washington Square
San Jose, CA 95192-0001
**Phone:** (408) 924-2000
**Fax:** (408) 924-2050
**E-mail:** contact@sjsu.edu
http://www.sjsu.edu

**University of California, Los Angeles**
405 Hilgard Avenue
Los Angeles, CA 90095
**Phone:** (310) 825-3101
**E-mail:** ugadm@saonet.ucla.edu
http://www.ucla.edu

**University of La Verne**
1950 Third Street
La Verne, CA 91750
**Phone:** (909) 392-2800
**Fax:** (909) 392-2714
**E-mail:** admissions@ulv.edu
http://www.ulv.edu

**University of San Francisco**
2130 Fulton Street
San Francisco, CA 94117-1046
**Phone:** (415) 422-6563 or (800) CALL-
  USF (toll-free outside California)
**Fax:** (415) 422-2217
**E-mail:** admission@usfca.edu
http://www.usfca.edu

**University of Southern California**
University Park
Los Angeles, CA 90089-0911
**Phone:** (213) 740-1111
http://www.usc.edu

**Vanguard University of Southern
  California**
55 Fair Drive
Costa Mesa, CA 92626
**Phone:** (714) 556-3610 Ext. 327 or
  (800) 722-6279
**Fax:** (714) 966-5471
**E-mail:** admissions@vanguard.edu
http://www.vanguard.edu

## COLORADO

**Colorado State University**
Fort Collins, CO 80523-1020
**Phone:** (970) 491-6909
http://www.colostate.edu

**Mesa State College**
P.O. Box 2647
Grand Junction, CO 81502-2647
**Phone:** (970) 248-1875 or
  (800) 982-MESA
**Fax:** (970) 248-1973
**E-mail:** admissions@mesastate.edu
http://www.mesastate.edu

**University of Southern Colorado**
2200 Bonforte Boulevard
Pueblo, CO 81001
**Phone:** (719) 549-2461 or (877) 872-9653
**Fax:** (719) 549-2419
**E-mail:** info@uscolo.edu
http://www.uscolo.edu

**Western State College of Colorado**
Gunnison, CO 81231
**Phone:** (800) 876-5309 (toll-free)
**E-mail:** talbers@western.edu
http://www.western.edu

## CONNECTICUT

**Sacred Heart University**
5151 Park Avenue
Fairfield, CT 06825-1000

**Phone:** (203) 371-7880
**E-mail:** guastellek@sacredheart.edu
http://www.sacredheart edu

## DISTRICT OF COLUMBIA

**Gallaudet University**
800 Florida Avenue, NE
Washington, DC 20002-3625
**Phone:** (202) 651-5750 or (800) 995-0550
**Fax:** (202) 651-5774
**E-mail:** admissions@gallua.gallaudet.edu
http://www.gallaudet.edu

**George Washington University**
Office of Admissions
2121 I Street, NW
Suite 201
Washington, DC 20052
**Phone:** (202) 994-6040
**E-mail:** gwadm@gwu.edu
http://www.gwu.edu/~go2gw

## FLORIDA

**Barry University**
11300 Northeast Second Avenue
Miami Shores, FL 33161-6695
**Phone:** (305) 899-3100
**Fax:** (305) 899-2971
**E-mail:** admissions@mail.barry.edu
http://www.barry.edu/success

**Florida State University**
Tallahassee, FL 32306-2400
**Phone:** (850) 644-6200
**Fax:** (850) 644-0197
**E-mail:** admissions@admin.fsu.edu
http://admissions.fsu.edu

**University of Central Florida**
P.O. Box 160111
Orlando, FL 32816-0111
**Phone:** (407) 823-3000
**E-mail:** admission@mail.ucf.edu
http://www.ucf.edu

**University of Florida**
P.O. Box 114000
Gainesville, FL 32611-4000
**Phone:** (352) 392-1365
**E-mail:** freshmen@ufl.edu
http://www.ufl.edu

**University of Miami**
P.O. Box 248025
1252 Memorial Drive
Coral Gables, FL 33146-4616
**Phone:** (305) 284-4323

**Fax:** (305) 284-2507
**E-mail:** admission@miami.edu
http://www.miami.edu/UMH/CDA/
    UMH_Main

## GEORGIA

**Georgia Southern University**
GSU P.O. Box 8024, Building #805
Forest Drive
Statesboro, GA 30460
**Phone:** (912) 681-5391
**Fax:** (912) 486-7240
**E-mail:** admissions@gasou.edu
http://www.gasou.edu

**Toccoa Falls College**
P.O. Box 800-899
Toccoa Falls, GA 30598
**Phone:** (706) 886-6831 Ext. 5380
**Fax:** (706) 282-6012
**E-mail:** admissions@tfc.edu
http://www.tfc.edu

**Valdosta State University**
Valdosta, GA 31698
**Phone:** (229) 333-5791 or
    (800) 618-1878 Ext. 1
**Fax:** (229) 333-5482
**E-mail:** admissions@valdosta.edu
http://www.gasou.edu

## IDAHO

**University of Idaho**
Admissions Office
P.O. Box 444264
Moscow, ID 83844-4264
**Phone:** (208) 885-6326 or (888) 884-3246
**Fax:** (208) 885-9119
**E-mail:** admappl@uidaho.edu
http://www.uihome.uidaho.edu

## ILLINOIS

**Chicago State University**
95th Street at King Drive
Chicago, IL 60628
**Phone:** (773) 995-2513
**E-mail:** ug-admissions@csu.edu
http://www.csu.edu

**Columbia College Chicago**
600 South Michigan Avenue
Chicago, IL 60605
**Phone:** (312) 344-7130
**Fax:** (312) 344-8024
**E-mail:** admissions@colum.edu
http://www.colum.edu

**Northwestern University**
P.O. Box 3060
Evanston, IL 60204-3060
**Phone:** (847) 491-7271
**E-mail:** ug-admission@northwestern.edu
http://www.northwestern.edu

**Olivet Nazarene University**
One University Avenue
Bourbonnais, IL 60914
**Phone:** (815) 939-5203
**E-mail:** admissions@olivet.edu
http://www.olivet.edu

**Quincy University**
1800 College Avenue
Quincy, IL 62301-2699
**Phone:** (217) 228-5210 or
    (800) 688-HAWK (4295) (toll-free)
**E-mail:** admissions@quincy.edu
http://www.quincy.edu

**Southern Illinois University Carbondale**
Carbondale, IL 62901-4710
**Phone:** (618) 536-4405
**Fax:** (618) 453-3250
**E-mail:** admrec@siu.edu
http://www.siuc.edu

## INDIANA

**Indiana State University**
Terre Haute, IN 47809
**Phone:** (812) 237-2121
**E-mail:** admisu@amber.indstate.edu
http://www.indstate.edu

**Indiana University Bloomington**
300 North Jordan Avenue
Bloomington, IN 47405-1106
**Phone:** (812) 855-0661 or
    (812) 855-0661 (toll-free)
**Fax:** (812) 855-5102
**E-mail:** iuadmit@indiana.edu
http://www.indiana.edu

## IOWA

**Buena Vista University**
610 West Fourth Street
Storm Lake, IA 50588
**Phone:** (800) 383-9600 (toll-free)
**E-mail:** admissions@bvu.edu
http://www.bvu.edu

**Drake University**
2507 University Avenue
Des Moines, IA 50311
**Phone:** (515) 271-3181

**Fax:** (515) 271-2831
http://www.choose.drake.edu

**Grand View College**
1200 Grandview Avenue
Des Moines, IA 50316-1599
**Phone:** (515) 263-2810
**Fax:** (515) 263-2974
**E-mail:** admiss@gvc.edu
http://www.gvc.edu

**St. Ambrose University**
518 West Locust Street
Davenport, IA 52803
**Phone:** (563) 333-6300
**E-mail:** admit@sau.edu
http://www.sau.edu

## KANSAS

**Fort Hays State University**
600 Park Street
Hays, KS 67601-4099
**Phone:** (785) 628-5830 or
    (800) 628-FHSU (toll-free)
**Fax:** (785) 628-4187
**E-mail:** tigers@fhsu.edu
http://www.fhsu.edu

**University of Kansas**
1502 Iowa Street
Lawrence, KS 66045-1910
**Phone:** (785) 864-3911 or
    (888) 686-7323 (toll-free)
**Fax:** (785) 864-5006
**E-mail:** adm@ku.edu

**Washburn University of Topeka**
1700 SW College Avenue
Topeka, KS 66621
**Phone:** (785) 231-1010 Ext. 1293 or
    (800) 332-0291 (toll-free)
**Fax:** (785) 231-1089
**E-mail:** zzhansen@acc.washburn.edu
http://www.washburn.edu/index3.html

## KENTUCKY

**Fort Hays State University**
600 Park Street
Hays, KS 67601-4099
**Phone:** (785) 628-5830 or
    (800) 628-FHSU (toll-free)
**Fax:** (785) 628-4187
**E-mail:** tigers@fhsu.edu
http://www.eku.edu

**Murray State University**
P.O. Box 9
Murray, KY 42071-0009

**Phone:** (270) 762-3035 or
   (800) 272-4678 (toll-free)
**Fax:** (270) 762-3050
**E-mail:** admissions@murraystate.edu
http://www.eku.edu

**Northern Kentucky University**
Highland Heights, KY 41099
**Phone:** (859) 572-5220
**E-mail:** admitnku@nku.edu
http://www.nku.edu

**University of Kentucky**
100 W.D. Funkhouser Building
Lexington, KY 40506-0054
**Phone:** (859) 257-2000 or
   (800) 432-0967 (toll-free)
**E-mail:** admissio@uky.edu
http://www.uky.edu

**Western Kentucky University**
1 Big Red Way
Bowling Green, KY 42101-3576
**Phone:** (270) 745-4241 or
   (800) 495-8463 (toll-free)
**Fax:** (270) 745-6133
**E-mail:** admission@wku.edu
http://www.wku.edu

## MAINE

**New England School of
   Communications**
1 College Circle
Bangor, ME 04401
**Phone:** (207) 941-7176 Ext. 1093 or
   (888) 877-1876
**Fax:** (207) 947-3987
**E-mail:** info@nescom.edu
http://www.nescom.org

## MASSACHUSETTS

**Boston University**
121 Bay State Road
Boston, MA 02215
**Phone:** (617) 353-2300
**E-mail:** admissions@bu.edu
http://www.bu.edu/admissions

**Curry College**
Milton, MA 02186
**Phone:** (617) 333-2210
**Fax:** (617) 333-2114
**E-mail:** curryadm@curry.edu
http://www.curry.edu

**Eastern Nazarene College**
Quincy, MA 02170
**Phone:** (617) 745-3000 or
   (800) 88-ENC-88 (toll-free)

**E-mail:** admissions@enc.edu
http://www.enc.edu

**Emerson College**
120 Boylston Street
Boston, MA 02116-4624
**Phone:** (617) 824-8600
**Fax:** (617) 824-8906
**E-mail:** admission@emerson.edu
http://www.emerson.edu

**Hampshire College**
Amherst, MA 01002-5001
**Phone:** (413) 559-5471
**E-mail:** admissions@hampshire.edu
http://www.hampshire.edu

**Northeastern University**
150 Richards Hall
360 Huntington Avenue
Boston, MA 02115
**Phone:** (617) 373-2200
**E-mail:** admissions@neu.edu
http://www.neu.edu

## MICHIGAN

**Olivet College**
Olivet, MI 49076
**Phone:** (616) 749-7635
**E-mail:** admissions@olivetcollege.edu
http://www.olivetcollege.edu

**Western Michigan University**
1903 West Michigan Avenue
Kalamazoo, MI 49008-5720
**Phone:** (269) 387-2000 or
   (800) 400-4WMU (toll-free)
http://www.wmich.edu

## MINNESOTA

**Bemidji State University**
Deputy-102
Bemidji, MN 56601
**Phone:** (218) 755-2040; (800) 475-2001
   (in-state, toll-free) (800) 652-9747
   (out-of-state, toll-free)
**Fax:** (218) 755-2074
**E-mail:** admissions@bemidjistate.edu
http://www.bemidjistate.edu

**Northwestern College**
3003 Snelling Avenue North
St. Paul, MN 55113-1598
**Phone:** (651) 631-5209 or
   (800) 827-6827 (toll-free)
**Fax:** (651) 631-5680
**E-mail:** admissions@nwc.edu
http://www.nwc.edu

**Southwest State University**
1501 State Street
Marshall, MN 56258-1598
**Phone:** (507) 537-6286 or
   (800) 642-0684 (toll-free)
**Fax:** (507) 537-7154
**E-mail:** shearerr@southwest.msus.edu
http://www.southwest.msus.edu

**Winona State University**
P.O. Box 5838
Winona, MN 55987
**Phone:** (507) 457-5100 or
   (800) DIAL-WSU (toll-free)
**Fax:** (507) 457-5620
**E-mail:** admissions@vax2.winona.msus.
   edu
http://www.winona.edu

## MISSOURI

**Central Missouri State University**
Warrensburg, MO 64093
**Phone:** (800) SAY-CMSU (toll-free)
**Fax:** (660) 543-8517
**E-mail:** admit@cmsuvmb.cmsu.edu
http://www.cmsu.edu

**Lindenwood University**
209 South Kingshighway
St. Charles, MO 63301-1695
**Phone:** (636) 949-4949
**Fax:** (636) 949-4989
http://www.lindenwood.edu

**Stephens College**
Columbia, MO 65215
**Phone:** (573) 876-7207
**Fax:** (573) 876-7237
**E-mail:** apply@stephens.edu
http://www.stephens.edu

**Webster University**
470 East Lockwood
St. Louis, MO 63119-3194
**Phone:** (314) 968-6991 or
   (800) 75-ENROLL (toll-free)
**E-mail:** admit@webster.edu
http://www.webster.edu

**William Woods University**
1 University Avenue
Fulton, MO 65251-1098
**Phone:** (573) 592-4221
**E-mail:** admissions@williamwoods.edu
http://www.williamwoods.edu

## MONTANA

**University of Montana–Missoula**
Missoula, MT 59812-0002

**Phone:** (406) 243-6266 or
(800) 462-8636 (toll-free)
**Fax:** (406) 243-5711
**E-mail:** admiss@selway.umt.edu
http://www.umt.edu

## NEBRASKA

**Hastings College**
800 North Turner Avenue
Hastings, NE 68901-7696
**Phone:** (402) 461-7316 or
(800) 532-7642 (toll-free)
**Fax:** (402) 461-7490
**E-mail:** admissions@hastings.edu
http://www.hastings.edu

**University of Nebraska at Omaha**
6001 Dodge Street
Omaha, NE 68182
**Phone:** (402) 554-2416 or
(800) 858-8648 (toll-free)
**Fax:** (402) 554-3472
http://www.unomaha.edu/home.html

## NEW HAMPSHIRE

**Franklin Pierce College**
20 College Road
Rindge, NH 03461-0060
**Phone:** (603) 899-4050 or
(800) 437-0048 (toll-free)
**Fax:** (603) 899-4394
**E-mail:** admissions@fpc.edu
http://www.fpc.edu

## NEW JERSEY

**Montclair State University**
Department of Broadcasting
Upper Montclair, NJ 07043
**Phone:** (973) 655-7870
**E-mail:** sandersd@mail.montclair.edu
http://www.montclair.edu/Pages/
Broadcasting/index.html

**Rider University**
2083 Lawrenceville Road
Lawrenceville, NJ 08648-3099
**Phone:** (609) 896-5042
**E-mail:** admissions@rider.edu
http://www.rider.edu

## NEW YORK

**Brooklyn College of the City University
of New York**
2900 Bedford Avenue
Brooklyn, NY 11210

**Phone:** (718) 951-5001
**E-mail:** adminqry@brooklyn.cuny.edu
http://www.brooklyn.cuny.edu

**Buffalo State**
Moot Hall 110
1300 Elmwood Avenue
Buffalo, NY 14222-1095
**Phone:** (716) 878-4017
**Fax:** (716) 878-6100
**E-mail:** admissio@buffalostate.edu
http://www.buffalostate.edu/prospect

**Fordham University**
Office of Undergraduate Admission
Thebaud Hall
441 East Fordham Road
New York, NY 10458-9993
**Phone:** (800) FORDHAM (367-3426)
(toll-free)
**E-mail:** enroll@fordham.edu
http://www.fordham.edu

**Ithaca College**
100 Job Hall
Ithaca, NY 14850-7020
**Phone:** (800) 429-4274 (toll-free)
**Fax:** (607) 274-1900
**E-mail:** admission@ithaca.edu
http://www.ithaca.edu

**Long Island University, Brooklyn
Campus**
1 University Plaza
Brooklyn, NY 11201
**Phone:** (718) 488-1011
http://www.liu.edu

**Long Island University, C.W. Post
Campus**
720 Northern Boulevard
Brookville, NY 11548-1300
**Phone:** (516) 299-2900 or
(800) LIU-PLAN (toll-free)
**Fax:** (516) 299-2137
**E-mail:** enroll@cwpost.liu.edu
http://www.liu.edu/cwpost

**Mercy College**
555 Broadway
Dobbs Ferry, NY 10522
**Phone:** (914) 674-7600 or
(800) MERCY-NY (toll-free)
**E-mail:** admissions@mercy.edu
http://www.mercy.edu

**New York University**
22 Washington Square North
New York, NY 10011

**Phone:** (212) 998-4500
http://www.nyu.edu/ugadmissions

**State University of New York College at
Brockport**
350 New Campus Drive
Brockport, NY 14420-2915
**Phone:** (585) 395-2751
**E-mail:** admit@brockport.edu
http://www.brockport.edu

**State University of New York at
Fredonia**
Fredonia, NY 14063
**Phone:** (716) 673-3251
**E-mail:** admissions.office@fredonia.edu
http://www.fredonia.edu

**State University of New York at New
Paltz**
75 South Manheim Boulevard
Suite 1
New Paltz, NY 12561-2499
**Phone:** (845) 257-3200 or
(888) 639-7589 (toll-free)
**Fax:** (845) 257-3209
**E-mail:** admissions@newpaltz.edu

**Syracuse University**
Syracuse, NY 13244
**Phone:** (315) 443-3611
http://admissions.syracuse.edu

## NORTH CAROLINA

**Campbell University**
P.O. Box 546
Buies Creek, NC 27506
**Phone:** (910) 893-1320
**E-mail:** adm@mailcenter.campbell.edu
http://www.campbell.edu

## NORTH DAKOTA

**Minot State University**
500 University Avenue West
Minot, ND 58707-0002
**Phone:** (701) 858-3346 or
(800) 777-0750 Ext. 3350 (toll-free)
**Fax:** (701) 839-6933
**E-mail:** askmsu@misu.nodak.edu
http://www.minotstateu.edu

## OHIO

**Ashland University**
Ashland, OH 44805
**Phone:** (419) 289-5052
**Fax:** (419) 289-5999

**E-mail:** auadmsn@ashland.edu
http://www.ashland.edu

**Bowling Green State University**
Bowling Green, OH 43402
**Phone:** (419) 372-BGSU or
    (866) CHOOSE-BGSU (toll-free)
**Fax:** (419) 372-6955
**E-mail:** choosebgsu@bgnet.bgsu.edu
http://www.bgsu.edu

**Cedarville University**
251 North Main Street
Cedarville, OH 45314
**Phone:** (800) CEDARVILLE
    (800-233-2784, toll-free)
**E-mail:** admissions@cedarville.edu
http://www.cedarville.edu

**Kent State University**
P.O. Box 5190
Kent, OH 44242-0001
**Phone:** (330) 672-2444 or
    (800) 988-KENT (toll-free)
**E-mail:** kentadm@kent.edu
http://www.kent.edu

**Marietta College**
Marietta, OH 45750-4005
**Phone:** (800) 331-7896 (toll-free)
**E-mail:** admit@marietta.edu
http://www.marietta.edu

**Otterbein College**
Westerville, OH 43081
**Phone:** (614) 823-1500
**E-mail:** uotterb@otterbein.edu

**University of Cincinnati**
P.O. Box 210091
Cincinnati, OH 45221-0091
**Phone:** (513) 556-1100
**Fax:** (513) 556-1105
**E-mail:** admissions@uc.edu
http://www.admissions.uc.edu

**University of Dayton**
300 College Park
Dayton, OH 45469-1300
**Phone:** (937) 229-4411
**E-mail:** admission@udayton.edu
http://admission.udayton.edu

**Youngstown State University**
One University Plaza
Youngstown, OH 44555
**Phone:** (330) 941-2000
**Fax:** (330) 941-3674
**E-mail:** enroll@ysu.edu
http://www.ysu.edu

## OKLAHOMA

**Cameron University**
2800 West Gore Boulevard
Lawton, OK 73505
**Phone:** (580) 581-2837 or
    (888) 454-7600 (toll-free)
**Fax:** (580) 581-5514
**E-mail:** admiss@cua.cameron.edu
http://www.cameron.edu

**Oklahoma Baptist University**
Box 61174
Shawnee, OK 74804
**Phone:** (405) 878-2033 or
    (800) 654-3285 (toll-free)
**Fax:** (405) 878-2046
**E-mail:** admissions@mail.okbu.edu
http://www.okbu.edu

**Oklahoma Christian University**
Box 11000
Oklahoma City, OK 73136-1100
**Phone:** (405) 425-5050 or
    (800) 877-5010 (toll-free)
**Fax:** (405) 425-5208
**E-mail:** info@oc.edu
http://www.oc.edu

**University of Oklahoma**
1000 Asp Avenue
Norman, OK 73019
**Phone:** (405) 325-2151 or
    (800) 234-6868 (toll-free)
**Fax:** (405) 325-7124
**E-mail:** admrec@ou.edu
http://www.ou.edu

## OREGON

**George Fox University**
Newberg, OR 97132-2697
**Phone:** (800) 765-4369 Ext. 2240
    (toll-free)
**E-mail:** admissions@georgefox.edu
http://www.georgefox.edu

**Pacific University**
2043 College Way
Forest Grove, OR 97116
**Phone:** (503) 359-2218
**E-mail:** admissions@pacificu.edu
http://www.pacificu.edu

**University of Oregon**
Eugene, OR 97403-1217
**Phone:** (541) 346-3201 or
    (800) BE-A-DUCK (toll-free)
**E-mail:** uoadmit@uoregon.edu
http://admissions.uoregon.edu

## PENNSYLVANIA

**Gannon University**
109 University Square
Erie, PA 16541
**Phone:** (814) 871-7240 or (800)
    GANNON-U (426-6668, toll-free)
**Fax:** (814) 871-5803
**E-mail:** admissions@gannon.edu
http://www.gannon.edu

**La Salle University**
1900 West Olney Avenue
Philadelphia, PA 19141-1199
**Phone:** (215) 951-1500 or
    (800) 328-1910 (toll-free)
**Fax:** (215) 951-1656
**E-mail:** admiss@lasalle.edu
http://www.lasalle.edu

**Lock Haven University of Pennsylvania**
Lock Haven, PA 17745
**Phone:** (570) 893-2027
**E-mail:** admissions@lhup.edu
http://www.lhup.edu

**Marywood University**
2300 Adams Avenue
Scranton, PA 18509
**Phone:** (570) 348-6234
**Fax:** (570) 961-4763
**E-mail:** ugadm@marywood.edu
http://www.marywood.edu

**Mercyhurst College**
Admissions
501 East 38th Street
Erie, PA 16546-0001
**Phone:** (814) 824-2202
**E-mail:** admissions@mercyhurst.edu
http://www.mercyhurst.edu

**Point Park College**
201 Wood Street
Pittsburgh, PA 15222-1984
**Phone:** (412) 392-3430
**Fax:** (412) 392-3902
**E-mail:** enroll@ppc.edu
http://www.ppc.edu

**Waynesburg College**
Waynesburg, PA 15370
**Phone:** (724) 852-3248
**E-mail:** admissions@waynesburg.edu
http://waynesburg.edu

## SOUTH DAKOTA

**University of South Dakota**
414 East Clark Street
Vermillion, SD 57069

**Phone:** (605) 677-5434 or
(877) 269-6837 (toll-free)
**Fax:** (605) 677-6753
**E-mail:** admiss@usd.edu
http://www.usd.edu

**University of Sioux Falls**
Sioux Falls, SD 57105
**Phone:** (605) 331-6600 or
(800) 888-1047 Ext. 6 (toll-free)
**Fax:** (605) 331-6615
**E-mail:** admissions@usiouxfalls.edu
http://www.usiouxfalls.edu

## TENNESSEE

**Belmont University**
1900 Belmont Boulevard
Nashville, TN 37212
**Phone:** (615) 460-6785 or
(800) 56ENROLL (toll-free)
**Fax:** (615) 460-5434
**E-mail:** buadmission@belmont.edu
http://www.belmont.edu

**Freed-Hardeman University**
158 East Main Street
Henderson, TN 38340-2399
**Phone:** (731) 989-6651 or
(800) 630-3480 (toll-free)
**Fax:** (731) 989-6047
**E-mail:** admissions@fhu.edu
http://www.fhu.edu

**Milligan College**
P.O. Box 210
Milligan College, TN 37682
**Phone:** (423) 461-8730
**Fax:** (423) 461-8982
**E-mail:** admissions@milligan.edu
(general); visits@milligan.edu
(for visits)
http://www.milligan.edu

**Union University**
1050 Union University Drive
Jackson, TN 38305-3697
**Phone:** (800) 33-UNION (toll-free)
**E-mail:** info@uu.edu
http://www.uu.edu

## TEXAS

**Southern Methodist University**
P.O. Box 750181
Dallas, TX 75275-0181
**Phone:** (214) 768-2058 or
(800) 323-0672 (toll-free)

**Fax:** (214) 768-0103
**E-mail:** enrol_serv@mail.smu.edu
http://www.smu.edu

**Texas Christian University**
2800 South University Drive
Fort Worth, TX 76129
**Phone:** (817) 257-7490 or
(800) TCU-FROG (toll-free)
**Fax:** (817) 257-7268
**E-mail:** frogmail@tcu.edu
http://www.tcu.edu

**University of Houston**
Houston, TX 77204-2023
**Phone:** (713) 743-1010 Option 2
http://www.uh.edu

## UTAH

**Weber State University**
1137 University Circle
3750 Harrison Boulevard
Ogden, UT 84408-1137
**Phone:** (801) 626-6050 or
(800) 848-7770 (toll-free)
**Fax:** (801) 626-6744
**E-mail:** admissions@weber.edu
http://weber.edu

## VERMONT

**Castleton State College**
Castleton, VT 05735
**Phone:** (802) 468-1213
**Fax:** (802) 468-1476
**E-mail:** info@castleton.edu
http://www.castleton.edu

## WASHINGTON

**Eastern Washington University**
Cheney, WA 99004
**Phone:** (509) 359-2397
**Fax:** (509) 359-6692
**E-mail:** admissions@mail.ewu.edu
http://www.ewu.edu

**Pacific Lutheran University**
Tacoma, WA 98447
**Phone:** (800) 274-6758 (toll-free)
**Fax:** (253) 536-5136
http://www.plu.edu

**Walla Walla College**
204 South College Avenue
College Place, WA 99324

**Phone:** (509) 527-2327 or
(800) 541-8900 (toll-free)
**Fax:** (509) 527-2397
**E-mail:** info@wwc.edu
http://www.wwc.edu

**Washington State University**
Pullman, WA 99164
**Phone:** (509) 335-5586 or
(888) 468-6978 (toll-free)
**Fax:** (509) 335-7468
**E-mail:** ir@wsu.edu
http://www.wsu.edu

## WEST VIRGINIA

**Salem International University**
Salem, WV 26426
**Phone:** (304) 782-5336
**E-mail:** admissions@salemiu.edu
http://www.salemiu.edu

## WISCONSIN

**University of Wisconsin–Madison**
716 Langdon Street
Madison, WI 53706-1400
**Phone:** (608) 262-3961
**Fax:** (608) 262-7706
**E-mail:** on.wisconsin@mail.admin.wisc.
edu
http://www.wisc.edu

**University of Wisconsin–Oshkosh**
Oshkosh, WI 54901-8602
**Phone:** (920) 424-0202
**Fax:** (920) 424-1098
**E-mail:** oshadmuw@uwosh.edu
http://www.uwosh.edu

**University of Wisconsin–River Falls**
410 South Third Street
River Falls, WI 54022-5001
**Phone:** (715) 425-3500
**Fax:** (715) 425-0676
**E-mail:** admit@uwrf.edu
http://www.uwrf.edu

**University of Wisconsin–Superior**
**Belknap and Catlin**
P.O. Box 2000
Superior, WI 54880-4500
**Phone:** (715) 394-8230
**Fax:** (715) 394-8407
**E-mail:** admissions@uwsuper.edu
http://www.uwsuper.edu

## B. COLLEGES AND UNIVERSITIES OFFERING MAJORS IN PUBLIC RELATIONS

The following is a listing of selected four-year schools offering degrees in public relations. They are grouped by state. School names, addresses, phone numbers, Web addresses, and e-mail admission addresses are included where available.

The author does not endorse any one school over another. Use this list as a beginning. More colleges are granting degrees in this area every year. Check the latest edition of *Lovejoy's* (found in the reference section of libraries or in guidance counseling centers) for additional schools offering degrees in this field.

### ALABAMA

**Auburn University**
202 Martin Hall
Auburn University, AL 36849
**Phone:** (334) 844-4000
**E-mail:** admissions@auburn.edu
http://www.auburn.edu

**Spring Hill College**
4000 Dauphin Street
Mobile, AL 36608
**Phone:** (334) 380-4000
**E-mail:** admit@shc.edu
http://www.shc.edu

**University of Alabama**
Box 870132
Tuscaloosa, AL 35487
**Phone:** (205) 348-6010
**E-mail:** uaadmit@enroll.ua.edu
http://www.ua.edu

**University of North Alabama**
UNA—Box 5121
Florence, AL 35632
**Phone:** (256) 765-4100
**E-mail:** admis1@unanov.una.edu
http://www.una.edu

### ALASKA

**University of Alaska–Anchorage**
3211 Providence Drive
Anchorage, AK 99508
**Phone:** (907) 786-1800
**E-mail:** ayenrol@uaa.alaska.edu
http://www.uaa.alaska.edu

### ARIZONA

**Northern Arizona University**
P.O. Box 4084
Flagstaff, AZ 86011
**Phone:** (520) 523-9011
**E-mail:** undergraduate.admissions@nau.edu
http://www.nau.edu
http://www.bsu.edu

### ARKANSAS

**Harding University**
900 E. Center
Searcy, AR 72149
**E-mail:** admissions@harding.edu
http://www.harding.edu

**John Brown University**
2000 W. University Street
Siloam Springs, AR 72761
**Phone:** (501) 524-3131
**E-mail:** jbuinfo@acc.jbu.edu
http://www.jbu.edu

### CALIFORNIA

**California State University—Stanislaus**
801 W. Monte Vista Avenue
Turlock, CA 95382
**Phone:** (209) 667-3122
**E-mail:** Outreach_Help_Desk@stan.csustan.edu
http://www.csustan.edu

**Pacific Union College**
One Angwin Avenue
Angwin, CA 94508
**Phone:** (707) 965-6336
**E-mail:** enroll@puc.edu
http://www.puc.edu

**Pepperdine University**
24255 Pacific Coast Highway
Malibu, CA 90263
**Phone:** (310) 456-4000
**E-mail:** admission-seaver@pepperdine.edu
http://www.pepperdine.edu

**Point Loma Nazarene University**
3900 Lomaland Drive
San Diego, CA 92106
**Phone:** (619) 849-2200
**E-mail:** admissions@ptloma.edu
http://www.ptloma.edu

**San Jose State University**
One Washington Square
San Jose, CA 95192
**Phone:** (408) 924-1000
**E-mail:** info@soar.sjsu.edu
http://www.sjsu.edu

**University of Southern California**
University Park
Los Angeles, CA 90089
**Phone:** (213) 740-2311
**E-mail:** admapp@enroll1.usc.edu
http://www.usc.edu

### COLORADO

**Colorado State University**
Colorado State University
Fort Collins, CO 80523
**Phone:** (970) 491-1101
**E-mail:** admissions@colostate.edu
http://www.colostate.edu

### CONNECTICUT

**Quinnipiac University**
Mount Carmel Avenue
Hamden, CT 06518
**Phone:** (203) 582-8200
**E-mail:** admissions@quinnipiac.edu
http://www.quinnipiac.edu

### DELAWARE

**Delaware State University**
1200 N. Dupont Highway
Dover, DE 19901
**Phone:** (302) 857-6060
**E-mail:** dadmiss@dsc.edu
http://www.dsc.edu

### DISTRICT OF COLUMBIA

**American University**
4400 Massachusetts Avenue, NW
Washington, DC 20016
**Phone:** (202) 885-1000
**E-mail:** afa@american.edu
http://www.american.edu

### FLORIDA

**Barry University**
11300 N.E. Second Avenue
Miami Shores, FL 33161
**Phone:** (305) 899-3000
**E-mail:** admissions@mail.barry.edu
http://www.barry.edu

**Florida A&M University**
Tallahassee, FL 32307
**E-mail:** bcox2@famu.edu
http://www.famu.edu

**Florida State University**
Tallahassee, FL 32306
**Phone:** (850) 644-2525
**E-mail:** admissions@admin.fsu.edu
http://www.fsu.edu

**University of Central Florida**
4000 Central Florida Boulevard
Orlando, FL 32816
**Phone:** (407) 823-2000
**E-mail:** admission@mail.ucf.edu
http://www.ucf.edu

**University of Florida**
201 Criser Hall
Gainesville, FL 32611
**Phone:** (352) 392-3261
**E-mail:** freshman@ufl.edu
http://www.ufl.edu

**University of Miami**
P.O. Box 248025
Coral Gables, FL 33124
**Phone:** (305) 284-2211
**E-mail:** admission@miami.edu
http://www.miami.edu

## GEORGIA

**Augusta State University**
2500 Walton Way
Augusta, GA 30904-2200
**Phone:** (706) 737-1400
**E-mail:** admissio@aug.edu
http://www.aug.edu

**Columbus State University**
4225 University Avenue
Columbus, GA 31907
**Phone:** (706) 568-2001
**E-mail:** admissions@colstate.edu
http://www.colstate.edu

**Georgia Southern University**
P.O. Box 8033
Statesboro, GA 30460
**Phone:** (912) 681-5611
**E-mail:** admissions@gasou.edu
http://www.gasou.edu

**Shorter College**
315 Shorter Avenue
Rome, GA 30165
**Phone:** (706) 291-2121
**E-mail:** admissions@shorter.edu
http://www.shorter.edu

**Toccoa Falls College**
P.O. Box 800-899
Toccoa Falls, GA 30598
**Phone:** (706) 886-6831
**E-mail:** admissions@toccoafalls.edu
http://www.toccoafalls.edu

**University of Georgia**
212 Terrell Hall
Athens, GA 30602
**Phone:** (706) 542-3000
**E-mail:** undergrad@admissions.uga.edu
http://www.uga.edu

## HAWAII

**Hawaii Pacific University**
1164 Bishop Street
Honolulu, HI 96813
**Phone:** (808) 544-0200
**E-mail:** admissions@hpu.edu
http://www.hpu.edu

## IDAHO

**Northwest Nazarene University**
623 Holly Street
Nampa, ID 83686
**Phone:** (208) 467-8011
**E-mail:** Admissions@nnu.edu
http://www.nnu.edu

**University of Idaho**
P.O. Box 443151
Moscow, ID 83844-3151
**Phone:** (208) 885-6111
**E-mail:** admappl@uidaho.edu
http://www.uidaho.edu/index-ext.shtml

## ILLINOIS

**Bradley University**
1501 W. Bradley Avenue
Peoria, IL 61625
**Phone:** (309) 676-7611
**E-mail:** admissions@bradley.edu
http://www.bradley.edu

**Columbia College**
600 S. Michigan Avenue
Chicago, IL 60605-1996
**Phone:** (312) 344-1600
**E-mail:** admissions@popmail.colum.edu
http://www.colum.edu

**Illinois State University**
Campus Box 2200
Normal, IL 61790-2200
**Phone:** (309) 438-2111

**E-mail:** ugradadm@ilstu.edu
http://www.ilstu.edu

**McKendree College**
701 College Road
Lebanon, IL 62254-1299
**Phone:** (618) 537-4481
**E-mail:** scordon@atlas.mckendree.edu
http://www.mckendree.edu

**Monmouth College**
700 E. Broadway
Monmouth, IL 61462
**Phone:** (309) 457-2131
**E-mail:** admit@monm.edu
http://www.monm.edu

**North Central College**
30 N. Brainard Street
P.O. Box 3063
Naperville, IL 60566
**Phone:** (630) 637-5100
**E-mail:** ncadm@noctrl.edu
http://www.noctrl.edu

**Roosevelt University**
430 S. Michigan Avenue
Chicago, IL 60605
**Phone:** (312) 341-3500
**E-mail:** applyRU@roosevelt.edu
http://www.roosevelt.edu

## INDIANA

**Ball State University**
2000 University Avenue
Muncie, IN 47306
**E-mail:** askus@wp.bsu.edu

**Indiana University-Purdue University—Fort Wayne**
2101 E. Coliseum Boulevard
Fort Wayne, IN 46805
**Phone:** (219) 481-6100
**E-mail:** ipfwadms@ipfw.edu
http://www.ipfw.edu

**University of Southern Indiana**
8600 University Boulevard
Evansville, IN 47712
**Phone:** (812) 464-8600
**E-mail:** enroll@usi.edu
http://www.usi.edu

## IOWA

**Drake University**
2507 University Avenue
Des Moines, IA 50311
**Phone:** (515) 271-2011

E-mail: admitinfo@acad.drake.edu
http://www.drake.edu

**Loras College**
1450 Alta Vista
Dubuque, IA 52001
**Phone:** (319) 588-7100
**E-mail:** adms@loras.edu
http://www.loras.edu

**Mount Mercy College**
1330 Elmhurst Drive, NE
Cedar Rapids, IA 52402
**Phone:** (319) 363-8213
**E-mail:** admission@mmc.mtmercy.edu
http://www.mtmercy.edu

**University of Northern Iowa**
1227 W. 27th Street
Cedar Falls, IA 50614
**Phone:** (319) 273-2311
**E-mail:** admissions@uni.edu
http://www.uni.edu/index.html

## KENTUCKY

**Eastern Kentucky University**
521 Lancaster Avenue
Richmond, KY 40475
**Phone:** (859) 622-1000
**E-mail:** admissions@eku.edu
http://www.eku.edu

**Murray State University**
15th and Main Streets
Murray, KY 42071
**E-mail:** phil.bryan@murraystate.edu
http://www.murraystate.edu

**Western Kentucky University**
One Big Red Way
Bowling Green, KY 42101
**Phone:** (270) 745-0111
**E-mail:** admission@wku.edu
http://www.wku.edu

## LOUISIANA

**University of Louisiana—Lafayette**
P.O. Drawer 41008
Lafayette, LA 70504
**Phone:** (337) 482-1000
**E-mail:** enroll@louisiana.edu
http://www.usl.edu

**Louisiana State University—
    Shreveport**
One University Place
Shreveport, LA 71115

**Phone:** (318) 797-5000
**E-mail:** admissions@pilot.Isus.edu
http://www.Isus.edu

## MASSACHUSETTS

**Boston University**
121 Bay State Road
Boston, MA 02215
**Phone:** (617) 353-2000
**E-mail:** admissions@bu.edu
http://www.bu.edu

**Emerson College**
120 Boylston Street
Boston, MA 02116
**Phone:** (617) 824-8500
**E-mail:** admission@emerson.edu
http://www.emerson.edu

**Northeastern University**
360 Huntington Avenue
Boston, MA 02115
**Phone:** (617) 373-2000
**E-mail:** admissions@neu.edu
http://www.neu.edu

**Simmons College**
300 The Fenway
Boston, MA 02115
**E-mail:** ugadm@simmons.edu
http://www.simmons.edu

**Suffolk University**
Eight Ashburton Place
Beacon Hill
Boston, MA 02108
**Phone:** (617) 573-8000
**E-mail:** admission@admin.suffolk.edu
http://www.suffolk.edu

## MICHIGAN

**Andrews University**
Berrien Springs, MI 49104
**Phone:** (800) 253-2874
**E-mail:** enroll@andrews.edu
http://www.andrews.edu

**Central Michigan University**
105 Warriner
Mount Pleasant, MI 48859
**Phone:** (517) 774-4000
**E-mail:** cmuadmit@cmich.edu
http://www.cmich.edu

**Eastern Michigan University**
Ypsilanti, MI 48197
**Phone:** (734) 487-1849

**E-mail:** undergraduate.admissions@
    emich.edu
http://www.emich.edu

**Ferris State University**
901 State Street
Big Rapids, MI 49307
**Phone:** (231) 591-2000
**E-mail:** admissions@ferris.edu
http://www.ferris.edu

**Grand Valley State University**
One Campus Drive
Allendale, MI 49401
**Phone:** (616) 895-6611
**E-mail:** go2gvsu@gvsu.edu
http://www.gvsu.edu

**Madonna University**
36600 Schoolcraft Road
Livonia, MI 48150
http://www.munet.edu

**Northern Michigan University**
1401 Presque Isle Avenue
Marquette, MI 49855
**Phone:** (906) 227-1000
**E-mail:** admiss@nmu.edu
http://www.nmu.edu

**Wayne State University**
656 W. Kirby
Detroit, MI 48202
**Phone:** (313) 577-2424
**E-mail:** admissions@wayne.edu
http://www.wayne.edu

**Western Michigan University**
1201 Oliver Street
Kalamazoo, MI 49008
**Phone:** (616) 387-1000
**E-mail:** ask-wmu@wmich.edu
http://www.wmich.edu

## MINNESOTA

**Concordia College—Moorhead**
901 S. Eighth Street
Moorhead, MN 56562
**Phone:** (218) 299-4000
**E-mail:** admissions@cord.edu
http://www.cord.edu

**Metropolitan State University**
700 E. Seventh Street
St. Paul, MN 55106
**Phone:** (651) 772-7779
**E-mail:** admission@metrostate.edu
http://www.metrostate.edu

**St. Cloud State University**
720 S. Fourth Avenue
St. Cloud, MN 56301
**Phone:** (320) 255-2244
**E-mail:** scsu4u@stcloudstate.edu
http://www.stcloudstate.edu

**St. Mary's University of Minnesota**
700 Terrace Heights
Winona, MN 55987
**Phone:** (507) 452-4430
**E-mail:** admissions@smumn.edu
http://www.smumn.edu

**Winona State University**
P.O. Box 5838
Winona, MN 55987
**Phone:** (800) 342-5978
**E-mail:** admissions@vax2.winona.msus.
   edu
http://www.winona.msus.edu

## MISSISSIPPI

**Mississippi University for Women**
W. Box 1600
Columbus, MS 39701
**Phone:** (662) 329-4750
**E-mail:** admissions@muw.edu
http://www.muw.edu

## MISSOURI

**Central Missouri State University**
Administration Building
Warrensburg, MO 64093
**Phone:** (660) 543-4111
**E-mail:** admit@cmsu1.cmsu.edu
http://www.cmsu.edu

**Fontbonne College**
6800 Wydown Boulevard
St. Louis, MO 63105
**E-mail:** pmusen@fontbonne.edu
http://www.fontbonne.edu

**Northwest Missouri State University**
800 University Drive
Maryville, MO 64468
**E-mail:** admissions@mail.nwmissouri.edu
http://www.nwmissouri.edu

**Rockhurst University**
1100 Rockhurst Road
Kansas City, MO 64110-2561
**Phone:** (816) 501-4000
**E-mail:** admission@rockhurst.edu
http://www.rockhurst.edu

**St. Louis University**
221 N. Grand Boulevard
St. Louis, MO 63103
**Phone:** (314) 977-2222
**E-mail:** admitme@slu.edu
http://www.slu.edu

**Stephens College**
1200 E. Broadway
Box 2121
Columbia, MO 65215
**Phone:** (573) 442-2211
**E-mail:** apply@sc.stephens.edu
http://www.stephens.edu

**Webster University**
470 E. Lockwood Avenue
St. Louis, MO 63119
**E-mail:** admit@webster.edu
http://www.webster.edu

## MONTANA

**Carroll College**
1601 N. Benton Avenue
Helena, MT 59625
**E-mail:** enroll@carroll.edu
http://www.carroll.edu

**Montana State University—Billings**
1500 N. 30th Street
Billings, MT 59101
**Phone:** (406) 657-2011
**E-mail:** admissions@msubillings.edu
http://www.msubillings.edu

## NEBRASKA

**Bellevue University**
1000 Galvin Road, South
Bellevue, NE 68005
**Phone:** (402) 291-8100
**E-mail:** bellevue_u@scholars.bellevue.edu
http://www.bellevue.edu

**College of St. Mary**
1901 S. 72nd Street
Omaha, NE 68124
**Phone:** (402) 399-2400
**E-mail:** enroll@csm.edu
http://www.csm.edu

**Creighton University**
2500 California Plaza
Omaha, NE 68178
**E-mail:** admissions@creighton.edu
http://www.creighton.edu

**Doane College**
1014 Boswell Avenue
Crete, NE 68333
**Phone:** (402) 826-2161
**E-mail:** admissions@doane.edu
http://www.doane.edu

**University of Nebraska—Kearney**
905 W. 25th Street
Kearney, NE 68849
**Phone:** (308) 865-8441
**E-mail:** admissionsug@unk.edu
http://www.unk.edu

## NEW HAMPSHIRE

**Rivier College**
420 Main Street
Nashua, NH 03060
**E-mail:** rivadmit@rivier.edu
http://www.rivier.edu

## NEW YORK

**Buffalo State College**
1300 Elmwood Avenue
Buffalo, NY 14222
**E-mail:** admissio@buffalostate.edu
http://www.buffalostate.edu

**College of New Rochelle**
Castle Place
New Rochelle, NY 10805
**Phone:** (914) 654-5000
**E-mail:** admission@cnr.edu
http://www.cnr.edu

**College of St. Rose**
432 Western Avenue
Albany, NY 12203
**Phone:** (800) 637-8556
**E-mail:** admit@rosnet.strose.edu
http://www.strose.edu

**CUNY—Lehman College**
250 Bedford Park Boulevard, West
Bronx, NY 10468
**Phone:** (718) 960-8000
**E-mail:** enroll@lehman.cuny.edu
http://www.lehman.cuny.edu

**Ithaca College**
100 Job Hall
Ithaca, NY 14850-7020
**Phone:** (607) 274-3124
**E-mail:** admission@ithaca.edu
http://www.ithaca.edu

**Keuka College**
Keuka Park, NY 14478
**Phone:** (315) 536-4411

**E-mail:** admissions@mail.keuka.edu
http://www.keuka.edu

**Long Island University—C.W. Post Campus**
720 Northern Boulevard
Brookville, NY 11548-1300
**Phone:** (516) 299-2000
**E-mail:** enroll@cwpost.liu.edu
http://www.liu.edu

**Mount St. Mary College**
330 Powell Avenue
Newburgh, NY 12550
**Phone:** (914) 561-0800
**E-mail:** mtstmary@msmc.edu
http://www.msmc.edu

**SUNY—Oswego**
7060 State Route 104
Oswego, NY 13126
**E-mail:** admiss@oswego.edu
http://www.oswego.edu

**Syracuse University**
201 Tolley Administration Building
Syracuse, NY 13244
**Phone:** (315) 443-1870
**E-mail:** orange@syr.edu
http://www.syracuse.edu
Apply Online via CollegeLink

**Utica College of Syracuse University**
1600 Burrstone Road
Utica, NY 13502
**E-mail:** admiss@utica.ucsu.edu
http://www.utica.edu

## NORTH CAROLINA

**Appalachian State University**
Boone, NC 28608
**Phone:** (828) 262-2000
**E-mail:** admissions@appstate.edu
http://www.appstate.edu

**East Carolina University**
Fifth Street
Greenville, NC 27858
**E-mail:** admis@mail.ecu.edu
http://www.ecu.edu

**Elon College**
2700 Campus Box
Elon College, NC 27244
**Phone:** (336) 584-9711
**E-mail:** admissions@elon.edu
http://www.elon.edu

**Mars Hill College**
100 Athletic Street
Mars Hill, NC 28754
**E-mail:** admissions@mhc.edu
http://www.mhc.edu

**North Carolina A&T State University**
1601 E. Market Street
Greensboro, NC 27411
**Phone:** (336) 334-7500
**E-mail:** uadmit@ncat.edu
http://www.ncat.edu

**University of North Carolina—Greensboro**
1000 Spring Garden Street
Greensboro, NC 27412
**Phone:** (336) 334-5243
**E-mail:** undergrad_admissions@uncg.edu
http://www.uncg.edu/adm

## OHIO

**Ashland University**
401 College Avenue
Ashland, OH 44805
**Phone:** (419) 289-4142
**E-mail:** auadmsn@ashland.edu
http://www.ashland.edu

**Bowling Green State University**
110 McFall Center
Bowling Green, OH 43403
**Phone:** (419) 372-2531
**E-mail:** admissions@bgnet.bgsu.edu
http://www.bgsu.edu

**Capital University**
2199 E. Main Street
Columbus, OH 43209
**Phone:** (614) 236-6011
**E-mail:** admissions@capital.edu
http://www.capital.edu

**David N. Myers College**
112 Prospect Avenue
Cleveland, OH 44115
**Phone:** (216) 696-9000
**E-mail:** admissions@dnmyers.edu
http://www.dnmyers.edu

**Heidelberg College**
310 E. Market Street
Tiffin, OH 44883
**E-mail:** admission@heidelberg.edu
http://www.heidelberg.edu

**Kent State University**
P.O. Box 5190
Kent, OH 44242

**Phone:** (330) 672-2121
**E-mail:** kentadm@Admissions.Kent.edu
http://www.kent.edu

**Marietta College**
215 Fifth Street
Marietta, OH 45750
**Phone:** (740) 376-4643
**E-mail:** admit@marietta.edu
http://www.marietta.edu

**Ohio University**
Athens, OH 45701
**Phone:** (740) 593-1000
**E-mail:** frshinfo@ohiou.edu
http://www.ohiou.edu

**Otterbein College**
College Avenue and Grove Street
Westerville, OH 43081
**Phone:** (614) 890-3000
**E-mail:** uotterb@Otterbein.edu
http://www.otterbein.edu

**Ursuline College**
2550 Lander Road
Pepper Pike, OH 44124
**Phone:** (440) 449-4200
**E-mail:** joakley@ursuline.edu
http://www.ursuline.edu

**Wright State University**
3640 Colonel Glenn Highway
Dayton, OH 45435
**Phone:** (937) 775-3300
**E-mail:** admissions@wright.edu
http://www.wright.edu

**Youngstown State University**
One University Plaza
Youngstown, OH 44555
**Phone:** (330) 742-3000
**E-mail:** enroll@ysu.edu
http://www.ysu.edu

## OKLAHOMA

**Oklahoma Baptist University**
500 W. University
Shawnee, OK 74804
**Phone:** (405) 275-2850
**E-mail:** admissions@mail.okbu.edu
http://www.okbu.edu

**Oklahoma Christian University**
Box 11000
Oklahoma City, OK 73136
**Phone:** (405) 425-5000

**E-mail:** Kyle.Wray@oc.edu
http://www.oc.edu

**Oral Roberts University**
7777 S. Lewis
Tulsa, OK 74171
**Phone:** (918) 495-6161
**E-mail:** admissions@oru.edu
http://www.oru.edu

**University of Oklahoma**
660 Parrington Oval
Norman, OK 73019
**Phone:** (405) 325-0311
**E-mail:** admrec@ouwww.ou.edu
http://www.ou.edu

## OREGON

**Marylhurst University**
17600 Pacific Highway & Hwy. 43
P.O. Box 261
Marylhurst, OR 97036-0261
**Phone:** (800) 634-9982
**E-mail:** admissions@marylhurst.edu
http://www.marylhurst.edu

**University of Oregon**
1217 University of Oregon
Eugene, OR 97403
**E-mail:** uoadmit@oregon.uoregon.edu
http://www.uoregon.edu

**University of Portland**
5000 N. Willamette Boulevard
Portland, OR 97203
**Phone:** (503) 943-7911
**E-mail:** admissio@up.edu
http://www.up.edu

**Western Baptist College**
5000 Deer Park Drive, SE
Salem, OR 97301
**Phone:** (503) 581-8600
**E-mail:** admissions@wbc.edu
http://www.wbc.edu

## PENNSYLVANIA

**Duquesne University**
600 Forbes Avenue
Pittsburgh, PA 15282
**Phone:** (412) 396-6000
**E-mail:** admissions@duq.edu
http://www.duq.edu

**Mansfield University of Pennsylvania**
Alumni Hall
Mansfield, PA 16933

**Phone:** (570) 662-4000
**E-mail:** admissns@mnsfld.edu
http://www.mansfield.edu

**Pennsylvania State University—**
**University Park**
University Park Campus
University Park, PA 16802
**E-mail:** admissions@psu.edu
http://www.psu.edu

**Marywood University**
2300 Adams Avenue
Scranton, PA 18509
**Phone:** (570) 348-6211
**E-mail:** ugadm@ac.marywood.edu
http://www.marywood.edu

**Point Park College**
201 Wood Street
Pittsburgh, PA 15222
**Phone:** (800) 321-0129
**E-mail:** enroll@ppc.edu
http://www.ppc.edu

**University of Pittsburgh—Bradford**
300 Campus Drive
Bradford, PA 16701
**Phone:** (800) 872-1787
**E-mail:** admissions@www.upb.pitt.edu
http://www.upb.pitt.edu

**Westminster College**
South Market Street
New Wilmington, PA 16172
**Phone:** (724) 946-8761
**E-mail:** admis@westminster.edu
http://www.westminster.edu

**York College of Pennsylvania**
Country Club Road
York, PA 17405-7199
**Phone:** (717) 846-7788
**E-mail:** admissions@ycp.edu
http://www.ycp.edu

## RHODE ISLAND

**University of Rhode Island**
Green Hall
Kingston, RI 02881
**Phone:** (401) 874-1000
**E-mail:** uriadmit@uri.edu
http://www.uri.edu

## SOUTH CAROLINA

**University of South Carolina—**
**Columbia**
Columbia, SC 29208

**Phone:** (803) 777-7000
**E-mail:** admissions-ugrad@sc.edu
http://www.sc.edu

## TENNESSEE

**David Lipscomb University**
3901-4001 Granny White Pike
Nashville, TN 37204
**Phone:** (800) 333-4358
**E-mail:** admissions@lipscomb.edu
http://www.lipscomb.edu

**Middle Tennessee State University**
1301 E. Main Street
CAB Room 205
Murfreesboro, TN 37132
**Phone:** (615) 898-2300
**E-mail:** admissions@mtsu.edu
http://www.mtsu.edu

**Southern Adventist University**
P.O. Box 370
Collegedale, TN 37315
**Phone:** (423) 238-2111
**E-mail:** admissions@southern.edu
http://www.southern.edu

## TEXAS

**Southern Methodist University**
P.O. Box 750296
Dallas, TX 75275
**Phone:** (214) 768-2000
**E-mail:** ugadmission@smu.edu
http://www.smu.edu

**Texas Christian University**
2800 S. University Drive
Fort Worth, TX 76129
**E-mail:** frogmail@tcu.edu
http://www.tcu.edu

**Texas Tech University**
Box 42013
Lubbock, TX 79409
**Phone:** (806) 742-2011
**E-mail:** nsr@ttu.edu
http://www.texastech.edu

**University of Houston**
4800 Calhoun Road
Houston, TX 77004
**Phone:** (713) 743-1000
**E-mail:** admissions@uh.edu
http://www.uh.edu

**West Texas A&M University**
P.O. Box 60999
Canyon, TX 79016

**Phone:** (806) 651-2000
**E-mail:** apifer@mail.wtamu.edu
http://www.wtamu.edu

## VIRGINIA

**Hampton University**
Tyler Street
Hampton, VA 23668
**E-mail:** admissions@hamptonu.edu
http://www.hamptonu.edu

**Virginia Commonwealth University**
821 W. Franklin Street
Richmond, VA 23284
**Phone:** (804) 828-0100
**E-mail:** ugrad@vcu.edu
http://www.vcu.edu

## WASHINGTON

**Central Washington University**
400 E. Eighth Avenue
Ellensburg, WA 98926
**Phone:** (509) 963-1111
**E-mail:** cwuadmis@cwu.edu
http://www.cwu.edu

**Eastern Washington University**
MS 148
Cheney, WA 99004
**Phone:** (509) 359-6200
**E-mail:** admissions@mail.ewu.edu
http://www.ewu.edu

**Gonzaga University**
502 E. Boone Avenue
Spokane, WA 99258
**Phone:** (509) 328-4220
**E-mail:** Ballinger@gu.gonzaga.edu
http://www.gonzaga.edu

**Washington State University**
French Administration Building
Pullman, WA 99164
**E-mail:** admiss@wsu.edu
http://www.wsu.edu

## WISCONSIN

**Cardinal Stritch University**
6801 N. Yates Road
Milwaukee, WI 53217
**Phone:** (414) 410-4000
**E-mail:** admityou@stritch.edu
http://www.stritch.edu

**Concordia University Wisconsin**
12800 N. Lake Shore Drive
Mequon, WI 53097
**E-mail:** admission@cuw.edu
http://www.cuw.edu

**Marquette University**
P.O. Box 1881
Milwaukee, WI 53201
**Phone:** (414) 288-7250
**E-mail:** admissions@marquette.edu
http://www.marquette.edu

**Mount Mary College**
2900 N. Menomonee River Parkway
Milwaukee, WI 53222
**Phone:** (414) 258-4810
**E-mail:** admiss@mtmary.edu
http://www.mtmary.edu

## WEST VIRGINIA

**West Virginia Wesleyan College**
59 College Avenue
Buckhannon, WV 26201
**Phone:** (304) 473-8000
**E-mail:** admissions@wvwc.edu
http://www.wvwc.edu

# C. COLLEGES AND UNIVERSITIES OFFERING MAJORS IN ADVERTISING

The following is a listing of selected four-year schools offering degrees in advertising. They are grouped by state. School names, addresses, phone numbers, Web addresses, and e-mail addresses are included when available.

The author does not endorse any one school over another. Use this list as a beginning. More colleges are granting degrees in this area every year. Check the latest edition of *Lovejoy's* (found in the reference section of libraries or in guidance counseling centers) for additional schools offering degrees in this field.

## ALABAMA

**Spring Hill College**
4000 Dauphin Street
Appendix I-C (adv. colleges)
Mobile, AL 36608
**Phone:** (334) 380-4000
**E-mail:** admit@shc.edu
http://www.shc.edu

**University of Alabama**
Box 870132
Tuscaloosa, AL 35487
**Phone:** (205) 348-6010
**E-mail:** uaadmit@enroll.ua.edu
http://www.ua.edu

## ARIZONA

**Harding University**
900 E. Center
Searcy, AR 72149
**E-mail:** admissions@harding.edu
http://www.harding.edu

**Northern Arizona University**
P.O. Box 4084
Flagstaff, AZ 86011-4084
**Phone:** (520) 523-9011
**E-mail:** undergraduate.admissions@nau.
    edu
http://www.nau.edu

## ARKANSAS

**University of Arkansas—Little Rock**
2801 S. University Avenue
Little Rock, AR 72204
**Phone:** (501) 569-3000
http://www.ualr.edu

## CALIFORNIA

**Art Center College of Design**
1700 Lida Street
Pasadena, CA 91103
**Phone:** (626) 396-2200

**E-mail:** admissions@artcenter.edu
http://www.artcenter.edu

**College of Notre Dame**
1500 Ralston Avenue
Belmont, CA 94002
**E-mail:** admiss@cnd.edu
http://www.cnd.edu

**National University**
11255 N. Torrey Pines Road
La Jolla, CA 92037
**Phone:** (619) 563-7100
**E-mail:** advisor@nu.edu
http://www.nu.edu

**Pepperdine University**
24255 Pacific Coast Highway
Malibu, CA 90263
**Phone:** (310) 456-4000
**E-mail:** admission-seaver@pepperdine.edu
http://www.pepperdine.edu

**San Jose State University**
One Washington Square
San Jose, CA 95192
**Phone:** (408) 924-1000
**E-mail:** info@soar.sjsu.edu
http://www.sjsu.edu

## COLORADO

**University of Colorado—Boulder**
Regent Admin. Center, Room 125
Campus Box 6
Boulder, CO 80309
**Phone:** (303) 492-1411
**E-mail:** apply@colorado.edu
http://www.colorado.edu

## CONNECTICUT

**Quinnipiac University**
Mount Carmel Avenue
Hamden, CT 06518
**Phone:** (203) 582-8200
**E-mail:** admissions@quinnipiac.edu
http://www.quinnipiac.edu

## FLORIDA

**Barry University**
11300 N.E. Second Avenue
Miami Shores, FL 33161
**Phone:** (305) 899-3000
**E-mail:** admissions@mail.barry.edu
http://www.barry.edu

**Florida State University**
Tallahassee, FL 32306
**Phone:** (850) 644-2525
**E-mail:** admissions@admin.fsu.edu
http://www.fsu.edu

**University of Central Florida**
4000 Central Florida Boulevard
Orlando, FL 32816
**Phone:** (407) 823-2000
**E-mail:** admission@mail.ucf.edu
http://www.ucf.edu

**University of Florida**
201 Criser Hall
Gainesville, FL 32611
**Phone:** (352) 392-3261
**E-mail:** freshman@ufl.edu
http://www.ufl.edu

**University of Miami**
P.O. Box 248025
Coral Gables, FL 33124
**Phone:** (305) 284-2211

**E-mail:** admission@miami.edu
http://www.miami.edu

## GEORGIA

**Augusta State University**
2500 Walton Way
Augusta, GA 30904
**Phone:** (706) 737-1400
**E-mail:** admissio@aug.edu
http://www.aug.edu

**University of Georgia**
212 Terrell Hall
Athens, GA 30602
**Phone:** (706) 542-3000
**E-mail:** undergrad@admissions.uga.edu
http://www.uga.edu

## HAWAII

**Hawaii Pacific University**
1164 Bishop Street
Honolulu, HI 96813
**Phone:** (808) 544-0200
**E-mail:** admissions@hpu.edu
http://www.hpu.edu

## ILLINOIS

**Bradley University**
1501 W. Bradley Avenue
Peoria, IL 61625
**Phone:** (309) 676-7611
**E-mail:** admissions@bradley.edu
http://www.bradley.edu

**University of Illinois—Urbana-
  Champaign**
901 W. Illinois
Urbana, IL 61801
**Phone:** (217) 333-1000
**E-mail:** admissions@oar.uiuc.edu
http://www.uiuc.edu

## INDIANA

**Ball State University**
2000 University Avenue
Muncie, IN 47306
**E-mail:** askus@wp.bsu.edu
http://www.bsu.edu

**University of Southern Indiana**
8600 University Boulevard
Evansville, IN 47712
**Phone:** (812) 464-8600
**E-mail:** enroll@usi.edu
http://www.usi.edu

## IOWA

**Clarke College**
1550 Clarke Drive
Dubuque, IA 52001
**Phone:** (319) 588-6300
**E-mail:** admissions@clarke.edu
http://www.clarke.edu

**Drake University**
2507 University Avenue
Des Moines, IA 50311
**Phone:** (515) 271-2011
**E-mail:** admitinfo@acad.drake.edu
http://www.drake.edu

**Iowa State University**
100 Alumni Hall
Ames, IA 50011
**Phone:** (515) 294-4111
**E-mail:** admissions@iastate.edu
http://www.iastate.edu

## KANSAS

**University of Kansas**
1502 Iowa
Lawrence, KS 66045
**Phone:** (785) 864-2700
**E-mail:** adm@ukans.edu
http://www.ukans.edu

## KENTUCKY

**University of Kentucky**
206 Administration Building
Lexington, KY 40506
**E-mail:** admissio@pop.uky.edu
http://www.uky.edu

**Western Kentucky University**
One Big Red Way
Bowling Green, KY 42101
**Phone:** (270) 745-0111
**E-mail:** admission@wku.edu
http://www.wku.edu

## MASSACHUSETTS

**Boston University**
121 Bay State Road
Boston, MA 02215
**Phone:** (617) 353-2000
**E-mail:** admissions@bu.edu
http://www.bu.edu

**Emerson College**
120 Boylston Street
Boston, MA 02116
**Phone:** (617) 824-8500

**E-mail:** admission@emerson.edu
http://www.emerson.edu

**Endicott College**
376 Hale Street
Beverly, MA 01915
**Phone:** (978) 927-0585
**E-mail:** admissio@endicott.edu
http://www.endicott.edu

**Northeastern University**
360 Huntington Avenue
Boston, MA 02115
**Phone:** (617) 373-2000
**E-mail:** admissions@neu.edu
http://www.neu.edu

**Western New England College**
1215 Wilbraham Road
Springfield, MA 01119
**Phone:** (413) 782-3111
**E-mail:** ugradmis@wnec.edu
http://www.wnec.edu

## MICHIGAN

**Ferris State University**
901 State Street
Big Rapids, MI 49307
**Phone:** (231) 591-2000
**E-mail:** admissions@ferris.edu
http://www.ferris.edu

**Grand Valley State University**
One Campus Drive
Allendale, MI 49401
**Phone:** (616) 895-6611
**E-mail:** go2gvsu@gvsu.edu
http://www.gvsu.edu

**Michigan State University**
East Lansing, MI 48824
**Phone:** (517) 355-1855
**E-mail:** admis@msu.edu
http://www.msu.edu

**Western Michigan University**
1201 Oliver Street
Kalamazoo, MI 49008
**Phone:** (616) 387-1000
**E-mail:** ask-wmu@wmich.edu
http://www.wmich.edu

## MINNESOTA

**Concordia College—Moorhead**
901 S. Eighth Street
Moorhead, MN 56562
**Phone:** (218) 299-4000

**E-mail:** admissions@cord.edu
http://www.cord.edu

**Winona State University**
P.O. Box 5838
Winona, MN 55987
**Phone:** (800) 342-5978
**E-mail:** admissions@vax2.winona.msus.
   edu
http://www.winona.msus.edu

## MISSISSIPPI

**University of Mississippi**
P.O. Box 1848
University, MS 38677
**Phone:** (662) 915-7211
**E-mail:** admissions@olemiss.edu
http://www.olemiss.edu

**University of Southern Mississippi**
Box 5167 Southern Station
Hattiesburg, MS 39406
**Phone:** (601) 266-4000
**E-mail:** admissions@USM.EDU
http://www.usm.edu

## MISSOURI

**Northwest Missouri State University**
800 University Drive
Maryville, MO 64468
**E-mail:** admissions@mail.nwmissouri.edu
http://www.nwmissouri.edu

**Stephens College**
1200 E. Broadway
Box 2121
Columbia, MO 65215
**Phone:** (573) 442-2211
**E-mail:** apply@sc.stephens.edu
http://www.stephens.edu

**University of Missouri—Columbia**
305 Jesse Hall
Columbia, MO 65211
**Phone:** (573) 882-2121
**E-mail:** mu4u@missouri.edu
http://www.missouri.edu

**Webster University**
470 E. Lockwood Avenue
St. Louis, MO 63119
**E-mail:** admit@webster.edu
http://www.webster.edu

## NEBRASKA

**University of Nebraska—Lincoln**
14th and R Streets
Lincoln, NE 68588

**Phone:** (402) 472-7211
**E-mail:** nuhusker@unl.edu
http://www.unl.edu

**University of Nebraska—Omaha**
6001 Dodge Street
Omaha, NE 68182
**Phone:** (402) 554-2800
**E-mail:** unoadm@unomaha.edu
http://www.unomaha.edu

## NEW HAMPSHIRE

**Franklin Pierce College**
College Road
P.O. Box 60
Rindge, NH 03461
**Phone:** (603) 899-4000
**E-mail:** admissions@fpc.edu
http://www.fpc.edu

**New Hampshire College**
2500 N. River Road
Manchester, NH 03106
**Phone:** (603) 668-2211
**E-mail:** admission@nhc.edu
http://www.nhc.edu

## NEW JERSEY

**Rider University**
2083 Lawrenceville Road
Lawrenceville, NJ 08648
**Phone:** (609) 896-5000
**E-mail:** admissions@rider.edu
http://www.rider.edu

**Thomas Edison State College**
101 W. State Street
Trenton, NJ 08608
**E-mail:** admissions@call.tesc.edu
http://www.tesc.edu

## NEW YORK

**College of New Rochelle**
Castle Place
New Rochelle, NY 10805
**Phone:** (914) 654-5000
**E-mail:** admission@cnr.edu
http://www.cnr.edu

**CUNY—Baruch College**
17 Lexington Avenue
New York, NY 10010
**E-mail:** admissions@baruch.cuny.edu
http://www.baruch.cuny.edu

**New York Institute of Technology**
P.O. Box 8000
Old Westbury, NY 11568
**Phone:** (516) 686-7516
**E-mail:** admissions@nyit.edu
http://www.nyit.edu

**Syracuse University**
201 Tolley Administration Building
Syracuse, NY 13244
**Phone:** (315) 443-1870
**E-mail:** orange@syr.edu
http://www.svracuse.edu

## NORTH CAROLINA

**Appalachian State University**
Boone, NC 28608
**Phone:** (828) 262-2000
**E-mail:** admissions@appstate.edu
http://www.appstate.edu

## OHIO

**Columbus College of Art and Design**
107 N. Ninth Street
Columbus, OH 43215
**Phone:** (614) 224-9101
**E-mail:** admissions@ccad.edu
http://www.ccad.edu

**Kent State University**
P.O. Box 5190
Kent, OH 44242
**Phone:** (330) 672-2121
**E-mail:** kentadm@Admissions.Kent.edu
http://www.kent.edu

**Marietta College**
215 Fifth Street
Marietta, OH 45750
**Phone:** (740) 376-4643
**E-mail:** admit@marietta.edu
http://www.marietta.edu

**Ohio University**
Athens, OH 45701
**Phone:** (740) 593-1000
**E-mail:** frshinfo@ohiou.edu
http://www.ohiou.edu

**University of Akron**
302 Buchtel Common
Akron, OH 44325
**Phone:** (330) 972-7111
**E-mail:** InfoReq@uakron.edu
http://www.uakron.edu

**Youngstown State University**
One University Plaza
Youngstown, OH 44555
**Phone:** (330) 742-3000
**E-mail:** enroll@ysu.edu
http://www.ysu.edu

## OKLAHOMA

**University of Oklahoma**
660 Parrington Oval
Norman, OK 73019
**Phone:** (405) 325-0311
**E-mail:** admrec@ouwww.ou.edu
http://www.ou.edu

## OREGON

**Portland State University**
P.O. Box 751
Portland, OR 97207
**Phone:** (503) 725-3000
**E-mail:** askadm@ess.pdx.edu
http://www.pdx.edu

**University of Oregon**
1217 University of Oregon
Eugene, OR 97403
**E-mail:** uoadmit@oregon.uoregon.edu
http://www.uoregon.edu

## PENNSYLVANIA

**Duquesne University**
600 Forbes Avenue
Pittsburgh, PA 15282
**Phone:** (412) 396-6000
**E-mail:** admissions@duq.edu
http://www.duq.edu

**Marywood University**
2300 Adams Avenue
Scranton, PA 18509
**Phone:** (570) 348-6211
**E-mail:** ugadm@ac.marywood.edu
http://www.marywood.edu

**Pennsylvania State University—
    University Park**
University Park Campus
University Park, PA 16802
**E-mail:** admissions@psu.edu
http://www.psu.edu

**Point Park College**
201 Wood Street
Pittsburgh, PA 15222
**Phone:** (800) 321-0129
**E-mail:** enroll@ppc.edu
http://www.ppc.edu

**Waynesburg College**
51 W. College Street
Waynesburg, PA 15370
**Phone:** (724) 627-8191
**E-mail:** admissions@waynesburg.edu
http://waynesburg.edu

## SOUTH CAROLINA

**University of South Carolina—
    Columbia**
Columbia, SC 29208
**Phone:** (803) 777-7000
**E-mail:** admissions-ugrad@sc.edu
http://www.sc.edu

## TENNESSEE

**Union University**
1050 Union University Drive
Jackson, TN 38305
**Phone:** (901) 668-1818
**E-mail:** info@uu.edu
http://www.uu.edu

**University of Tennessee—Knoxville**
800 Andy Holt Tower
Knoxville, TN 37996
**Phone:** (865) 974-1000
**E-mail:** admissions@utk.edu
http://www.utk.edu

## TEXAS

**Sam Houston State University**
1700 Sam Houston Avenue
Huntsville, TX 77341
**Phone:** (936) 294-1111
**E-mail:** adm_jbc@shsu.edu
http://www.shsu.edu

**Southern Methodist University**
P.O. Box 750296
Dallas, TX 75275
**Phone:** (214) 768-2000
**E-mail:** ugadmission@smu.edu
http://www.smu.edu

**Texas Christian University**
2800 S. University Drive
Fort Worth, TX 76129
**E-mail:** frogmail@tcu.edu
http://www.tcu.edu

**Texas Tech University**
Box 42013
Lubbock, TX 79409
**Phone:** (806) 742-2011
**E-mail:** nsr@ttu.edu
http://www.texastech.edu

**Texas Woman's University**
Box 425587
Denton, TX 76204
**Phone:** (940) 898-2000
**E-mail:** admissions@twu.edu
http://www.twu.edu

**University of Houston**
4800 Calhoun Road
Houston, TX 77004
**Phone:** (713) 743-1000
**E-mail:** admissions@uh.edu
http://www.uh.edu

**University of Texas—Austin**
Main Building, Room 7
Austin, TX 78712
**Phone:** (512) 471-3434
**E-mail:** frmn@uts.cc.utexas.edu
http://www.utexas.edu

**West Texas A&M University**
P.O. Box 60999
Canyon, TX 79016

**Phone:** (806) 651-2000
**E-mail:** apifer@mail.wtamu.edu
http://www.wtamu.edu

## VIRGINIA

**Hampton University**
Tyler Street
Hampton, VA 23668
**E-mail:** admissions@hamptonu.edu
http://www.hamptonu.edu

**Virginia Commonwealth University**
821 W. Franklin Street
Richmond, VA 23284
**Phone:** (804) 828-0100
**E-mail:** ugrad@vcu.edu
http://www.vcu.edu

## WASHINGTON

**Washington State University**
French Administration Building
Pullman, WA 99164

**E-mail:** admiss@wsu.edu
http://www.wsu.edu

## WEST VIRGINIA

**Concord College**
1000 Vermillion Street
Athens, WV 24712
**Phone:** (304) 384-3115
**E-mail:** admissions@concord.edu
http://www.concord.edu

## WISCONSIN

**Marquette University**
P.O. Box 1881
Milwaukee, WI 53201
**Phone:** (414) 288-7250
**E-mail:** admissions@marquette.edu
http://www.marquette.edu

# APPENDIX II
# TRADE ASSOCIATIONS, UNIONS, AND OTHER ORGANIZATIONS

The following is a selected listing of trade associations, unions, and organizations discussed in this book. There are also a number of other associations listed that might be of use to you.

Addresses, phone numbers, fax numbers, websites, and e-mail addresses are included when available to help you get in touch with any of the organizations.

Many of the associations have branch offices located throughout the country. By contacting an organization's headquarters or accessing their website, you can find phone numbers and addresses of local branches.

Use this listing to help you find internships, explore job opportunities, and obtain other useful information.

**Academy of Television Arts and Sciences (ATAS)**
5220 Lankershim Boulevard
North Hollywood, CA 91601
**Phone:** (818) 754-2800
**Fax:** (818) 761-2827
**E-mail:** webmaster@emmys.org
http://www.emmys.org

**American Advertising Federation (AAF)**
1101 Vermont Avenue NW
Suite 500
Washington, DC 20005-6306
**Phone:** (202) 898-0089
**Fax:** (202) 898-0159
**E-mail:** aaf@aaf.org
http://www.aaf.org

**American Federation of Television and Radio Artists (AFTRA)**
260 Madison Avenue
New York, NY 10016-2402
**Phone:** (212) 532-0800
**Fax:** (212) 532-2242
**E-mail:** aftra@aftra.com
http://www.aftra.com

**American Institute of Certified Public Accountants (AICPA)**
1211 Avenue of the Americas
New York, NY 10036-8775
**Phone:** (212) 596-6200 or
(888) 777-7077 (toll-free)
**Fax:** (212) 596-6213
**Telex(es):** 70 3396
**E-mail:** committee@aicpa.org
http://www.aicpa.org

**American Institute of Graphic Arts (AIGA)**
164 5th Avenue
New York, NY 10010
**Phone:** (212) 807-1990 or
(800) 548-1634 (toll-free)
**Fax:** (212) 807-1799
**E-mail:** comments@aiga.org
http://www.aiga.org

**American Library Association (ALA)**
50 E. Huron Street
Chicago, IL 60611
**Phone:** (312) 944-7298 or
(800) 545-2433 (toll-free)
**Fax:** (312) 440-9374
**E-mail:** ala@ala.org
http://www.ala.org

**American Marketing Association**
311 S. Wacker Drive
Suite 5800
Chicago, IL 60606
**Phone:** (312) 542-9000 or
(800) 262-1150 (toll-free)
**Fax:** (312) 542-9001
**E-mail:** info@ama.org
http://www.ama.org

**American Meteorological Society (AMS)**
45 Beacon Street
Boston, MA 02108-3693
**Phone:** (617) 227-2425
**Fax:** (617) 742-8718
http://www.ametsoc.org/AMS

**American Sportscasters Association (ASA)**
5 Beekman Street
Suite 814
New York, NY 10038

**Phone:** (212) 227-8080
**Fax:** (212) 571-0556
**E-mail:** Ischwa8918@aol.com
http://www.americansportscasters.com

**American Women in Radio and Television (AWRT)**
1595 Spring Hill Road
Suite 330
Vienna, VA 22182-2228
**Phone:** (703) 506-3290
**Fax:** (703) 506-3266
**E-mail:** info@awrt.org
http://www.awrt.org

**American Women in Radio and Television, Austin**
c/o Tracy Walker, President
LBJS Broadcasting
8309 N. IH 35
Austin, TX 78753
**Phone:** (512) 832-4041
**Fax:** (512) 832-4081
**E-mail:** twalker@lbjs.com
http://www.awrtaustin.org

**American Women in Radio and Television, Bay Area Media Network**
c/o Lynne Conlan, President
WMOR-TV
7201 E. Hillsborough Avenue
Tampa, FL 33610
**Phone:** (813) 740-3206
**Fax:** (813) 626-1961
**E-mail:** lconlan@hearst.com
http://bamnawrt.org

**American Women in Radio and Television, Bluegrass**
c/o Terri Carpenter, President

WLEX-TV
P.O. Box 1457
Lexington, KY 40591-1457
**Phone:** (859) 226-7642
**Fax:** (859) 254-1272
**E-mail:** tcarpenter@wlextv.com

**American Women in Radio and Television, Buckeye of Central Ohio**
c/o Brenda Spencer, Account Executive
Blue Chip Broadcasting
1500 W. 3rd Avenue
Suite 300
Columbus, OH 43212
**Phone:** (614) 487-1444
**E-mail:** bspencer@bluechipbroadcasting.
org

**American Women in Radio and Television, Central Florida**
c/o Kelley Lesperance, President
WESH-TV—Channel 2
1021 N. Wymore Road
Winter Park, FL 32789
**Phone:** (407) 539-7936
**Fax:** (407) 539-7950
**E-mail:** klesperance@hearst.com

**American Women in Radio and Television, Central Florida Media Network**
P.O. Box 940591
Maitland, FL 32794
**Phone:** (407) 263-7689
**Fax:** (407) 852-5955
**E-mail:** tmccommon@msn.com

**American Women in Radio and Television, Charlotte**
c/o Don Irons, Jr., President
Media Power, Inc.
5009 Monroe Road
Charlotte, NC 28205-7847
**Phone:** (704) 567-1000
**Fax:** (704) 567-8193

**American Women in Radio and Television, Chicago**
c/o Dawn Smith, National Director of
  Marketing
Metro Networks
Merchandise Mart, No. 1547
Chicago, IL 60654
**Phone:** (312) 467-2900
**E-mail:** dawn_smith@metronetworks.com

**American Women in Radio and Television, Dallas/Fort Worth**
c/o Teresa Novak, President

KDAF, WB33
8001 John Carpenter Fwy.
Dallas, TX 75247
**Phone:** (214) 252-3411
**Fax:** (214) 252-3440
**E-mail:** tcnovak@tribune.com

**American Women in Radio and Television, Golden Gate**
c/o Jayne Patterson Sanchez, President
KCSM FM 91.1
855 Fremont Street No. 1
Menlo Park, CA 94025-5051
**Phone:** (650) 291-0045
**Fax:** (650) 854-9257
**E-mail:** jaynesanchez@yahoo.com

**American Women in Radio and Television, Greater Palm Beaches**
c/o Pam Triolo, President
First Impressions Creative Services, Inc.
205 Worth Avenue, No. 201
Palm Beach, CA 33480
**Phone:** (561) 655-2031
**Fax:** (561) 655-2084

**American Women in Radio and Television, Houston**
P.O. Box 980908
Houston, TX 77098
**Phone:** (713) 663-8790
http://www.awrthouston.org

**American Women in Radio and Television, Indiana**
c/o Emily Mantel, President
Network Indiana
One Emmis Plaza
Indianapolis, IN 46204
**Phone:** (317) 684-4174
**Fax:** (317) 684-2022

**American Women in Radio and Television, Kentucky**
c/o Rosiland A. Jones, President
Blue Chip Broadcasting
520 S. 4th Avenue
Louisville, KY 40202
**Phone:** (502) 625-1241
**Fax:** (502) 625-1255
**E-mail:** rjones@bluechipbroadcasting.com

**American Women in Radio and Television, Nashville**
c/o Michelle Dube, President
WKRN-TV
441 Murfreesboro Road
Nashville, TN 37210
**Phone:** (615) 369-7266

**Fax:** (615) 244-2114
**E-mail:** michelledube@wkrn.com

**American Women in Radio and Television, Nebraska**
c/o Ruth McCully, President
KSRZ/KESY
11128 John Galt Boulevard, No. 192
Omaha, NE 68137-2321
**Phone:** (402) 556-6700
**Fax:** (402) 556-9427

**American Women in Radio and Television, New York City**
c/o Lynne Grasz, President/CEO
Grasz Communications
130 W. 67th Street
Suite 25-C
New York, NY 10023-5914
**Phone:** (212) 873-5014
**E-mail:** lmgrasz@aol.com

**American Women in Radio and Television, New York State Capital District**
c/o Heather DeForge, President
WXXA-FOX 23, WEDG UPN 4
28 Corporate Circle
Albany, NY 12203
**Phone:** (518) 862-2323
**Fax:** (518) 862-0865
**E-mail:** heatherdeforge@clearchannel.com

**American Women in Radio and Television, Northeast Area**
c/o Audrey Tanzer, Director
165 E 72nd Street, Apartment 10-D
New York, NY 10021
**Phone:** (212) 628-1262
**Fax:** (212) 628-6391
**E-mail:** ttanzart@aol.com

**American Women in Radio and Television, Oklahoma City**
c/o Annetta Abbott, Account Executive
KWTV News 9
7401 N Kelley Avenue
Oklahoma City, OK 73111
**Phone:** (405) 841-9929
**Fax:** (405) 841-9926
**E-mail:** abbott@kwtv.com

**American Women in Radio and Television, Phoenix**
c/o Laurel Lawton, President
KPNX-TV
1101 N. Central Avenue
Phoenix, AZ 85004
**Phone:** (602) 257-6518

**Fax:** (602) 257-6664
**E-mail:** llawton@kpnx.com

**American Women in Radio and
    Television, San Antonio**
c/o Carole Van Buren, President
KSMG-MAGIC 105.3—Cox Radio
8930 Four Winds Drive No. 500
San Antonio, TX 78239
**Phone:** (210) 646-0105
**Fax:** (210) 646-9711
**E-mail:** carole.vanburen@cox.com

**American Women in Radio and
    Television, South Central Area**
c/o Joanne May, Director
WFAA-TV
606 Young Street
Dallas, TX 75202-4810
**Phone:** (214) 977-6719
**Fax:** (214) 977-6560
**E-mail:** jmay@wfaa.com

**American Women in Radio and
    Television, Southeast Area**
c/o Tracy A. Moore, Director
RCP Limited
270 Brevard Avenue
Cocoa, FL 32922
**Phone:** (312) 635-8724
**E-mail:** rcptm@yourlink.net

**American Women in Radio and
    Television, Southern California
    (AWRT)**
c/o Marida Petitjean, President
P.O. Box 7132
Burbank, CA 91510
**Phone:** (323) 964-2740
http://www.awrtla.org

**American Women in Radio and
    Television, Southern Colorado**
c/o Karen Gonzalez, President
KILO-FM/The Eagle
1805 E. Cheyenne Road
Colorado Springs, CO 80906
**Phone:** (719) 955-1311
**Fax:** (719) 634-5837
**E-mail:** karen@kilo943.com

**American Women in Radio and
    Television Triangle**
c/o Janice F. Sharp, SPHR
Capitol Broadcasting Company Inc.
711 Hillsborough Street
Raleigh, NC 27603
**Phone:** (919) 890-6012
**Fax:** (919) 890-6011
**E-mail:** jsharp@cbc-raleigh.com

**American Women in Radio and
    Television, Tucson**
c/o Katrina Noble, Media Director
326 S. Wilmot Road No. c-200
Tucson, AZ 85711
**Phone:** (520) 745-8221
**Fax:** (520) 745-5540
**E-mail:** katrina@adwiz.com

**American Women in Radio and
    Television, Tulsa**
c/o Alison O'Rear, President
KOTV
302 S. Frankfort
Tulsa, OK 74120
**Phone:** (918) 732-6004
**Fax:** (918) 732-6016
**E-mail:** aorear@kotv.com

**American Women in Radio and
    Television, Twin Cities**
c/o Carrie De Net, Media Director
Gallagher Media, Inc.
2626 E. 82nd Street No. 201
Minneapolis, MN 55425
**Phone:** (952) 853-2266
**Fax:** (952) 853-2262
**E-mail:** carrie@gallaghermedia.net

**American Women in Radio and
    Television, Washington, D.C.**
c/o Patricia Spurlock, President
National Association of Broadcasters
1771 N Street, NW
Washington, DC 20036
**Phone:** (202) 429-5309
**Fax:** (202) 775-2157
**E-mail:** pspurlock@nab.org

**American Women in Radio and
    Television, Western Area**
c/o Cindy Ramirez, Director
AZStarnet
5447 E. 18th Street
Tucson, AZ 85711
**Phone:** (520) 795-6993
**Fax:** (520) 795-6941
**E-mail:** cramirezl@mindspring.com

**American Women in Radio and
    Television, Western Michigan**
c/o Suzin Vandercook Claver, President
TCI Media Services
965 Century SW
Grand Rapids, MI 49503
**Phone:** (616) 247-3600
**Fax:** (616) 247-1169
**E-mail:** vandercook.suzin@tci.com

**American Women in Radio and
    Television, New York Chapter**
234 5th Avenue
Suite 417
New York, NY 10001
**Phone:** (212) 481-3038
**Fax:** (212) 481-3071

**Arkansas Broadcasters Association
    (ABA)**
2024 Arkansas Valley Drive
Suite 403
Little Rock, AR 72212
**Phone:** (501) 227-7564
**Fax:** (501) 223-9798
http://www.arkbroadcasters.org

**Art Directors Club (ADC)**
106 W. 29th Street
New York, NY 10001
**Phone:** (212) 643-1440
**Fax:** (212) 643-4266
**E-mail:** messages@adcny.org
http://www.adcny.org

**Associated Press Broadcasters (APB)**
c/o Jim Williams
1825 K Street, NW
Suite 800
Washington, DC 20006-1202
**Phone:** (202) 736-1100 or
    (800) 821-4747 (toll-free)
**Fax:** (202) 736-1107
**E-mail:** info@abroadcaster.org

**Association for Women in Sports
    Media (AWSM)**
P.O. Box 726
Farmington, CT 06034-0726
**Fax:** (817) 390-7210
**E-mail:** info@awsmonline.org
http://www.awsmonline.org

**Association of America's Public
    Television Stations (AAPTS)**
1350 Connecticut Avenue NW
Suite 200
Washington, DC 20036
**Phone:** (202) 887-1700
**Fax:** (202) 293-2422
**E-mail:** john@apts.org
http://www.apts.org

**Association of Broadcasting Doctors**
P.O. Box 15
Sindalthorpe House
Ely CB7 4SG, United Kingdom
**Phone:** 44 1353 688456
**Fax:** 13 53 688451

**E-mail:** abd@soundplanltd.
netscapeonline.co.uk
http://www.broadcasting-doctor.org/
index.htm

**Association of Catholic T.V. and Radio**
**Syndicators (ACTRS)**
518 S. Alandele Avenue
Los Angeles, CA 90036
**Phone:** (213) 938-4861
**Fax:** (213) 933-8578
**E-mail:** mhop511311@aol.com

**Association of Fundraising**
**Professionals (AFP)**
1101 King Street
Suite 700
Alexandria, VA 22314
**Phone:** (703) 684-0410 or
(800) 666-FUND (toll-free)
**Fax:** (703) 684-0540
**E-mail:** mnilsen@afpnet.org
http://www.afpnet.org

**Association of Independent Radio**
**Stations (AIRS)**
c/o Fleishman-Hillard Saunders
15 Fitzwilliam Query
Dublin 4, Ireland
**Phone:** 353 1 6188444

**Association of Internet Professionals**
**(AIP)**
2629 Main Street, No. 136
Santa Monica, CA 90405
**Phone:** (866) AIP-9700 (toll-free)
**Fax:** (501) 423-2248
**E-mail:** khalbeck@association.org
http://www.association.org

**Association of Private Broadcasters**
**(APB)**
Zelena 14A
CS-160 00 Prague, Czech Republic
**Phone:** 42 2 9317722
**Fax:** 42 2 315455
**E-mail:** zelenka@comp.cz

**Black Broadcasters Alliance (BBA)**
3474 William Penn Hwy.
Pittsburgh, PA 15235
**Phone:** (412) 829-9788
**Fax:** (412) 829-0313
**E-mail:** e-mail@thebba.org
http://www.thebba.org

**Black College Radio Organization**
P.O. Box 3191
Atlanta, GA 30302

**Phone:** (404) 523-6136
**Fax:** (404) 523-5467
**E-mail:** bcrmail@blackcollegeradio.com
http://www.blackcollegeradio.com

**Broadcasters' Foundation**
7 Lincoln Avenue
Greenwich, CT 06830
**Phone:** (203) 862-8577
**Fax:** (203) 629-5739
**E-mail:** ghastings@
broadcastersfoundation.org
http://broadcastersfoundation.org

**Broadcast Promotion and Marketing**
**Executives – Now PROMAX**
**International**
2029 Century Park East
Suite 555
Los Angeles, CA 90067-2906
**Phone:** (310) 788-7600
**Fax:** (310) 788-7616
http://www.promax.org

**Canadian Association of Broadcast**
**Representatives (Association**
**Canadienne des Representants en**
**Radiofussion)**
c/o CTV Television Inc.
9 Channel Nine Ct.
Scarborough, ON, Canada M1S 4B5
**Phone:** (416) 332-4311
**Fax:** (416) 332-4453

**Canadian Association of Ethnic Radio**
**Broadcasters (CAERB)**
622 College Street
Toronto, ON, Canada M6G 1B6
**Phone:** (416) 531-9991 or
(800) 882-8425 (toll-free)
**Fax:** (416) 531-5274
**E-mail:** info@chinradio.com
http://www.chinradio.com

**Canadian Society for Independent**
**Radio Production (CSIRP)**
242 Westhaven Crescent
Ottawa, ON, Canada K1Z 7G3
**Phone:** (613) 791-9542
http://www.csirp.org

**Council for Advancement and Support**
**of Education (CASE)**
1307 New York Avenue, NW
Suite 1000
Washington, DC 20005
**Phone:** (202) 328-2273
**Fax:** (202) 387-4973
**E-mail:** info@case.org
http://www.case.org

**Council on Employee Benefits (CEB)**
4910 Moorland Lane
Bethesda, MD 20814
**Phone:** (301) 664-5940
**Fax:** (301) 664-5944
**E-mail:** vschieber@ceb.org
http://www.ceb.org

**Country Radio Broadcasters (CRB)**
819 18th Avenue South
Nashville, TN 37203
**Phone:** (615) 327-4487
**Fax:** (615) 329-4492
**E-mail:** info@crb.org
http://www.crb.org

**Friends of Public Radio—Arizona**
c/o Susan Edwards
2323 W. 14th Street
Tempe, AZ 85281-6950

**Graphic Artists Guild (GAG)**
90 John Street
Suite 403
New York, NY 10038-3202
**Phone:** (212) 791-3400 or
(800) 500-2627 (toll-free)
**Fax:** (212) 791-0333
**E-mail:** pr@gag.org
http://www.gag.org

**International Association of**
**Administrative Professionals (IAA)**
10502 NW Ambassador Drive
P.O. Box 20404
Kansas City, MO 64195-0404
**Phone:** (816) 891-6600
**Fax:** (816) 891-9118
**E-mail:** service@iaap-hq.org
http://www.iaap-hq.org

**International Association of**
**Broadcasting (IAB/AIR) (Association**
**Internacional de Radiodifusion)**
Brandzen 1961/402
11200 Montevideo, Uruguay
**Phone:** 598 2 4088121 598 2 4088129
**E-mail:** mail@alrlab.com

**International Association of Business**
**Communicators (IABC)**
1 Hallidie Plaza
Suite 600
San Francisco, CA 94102-2818
**Phone:** (415) 544-4700
**Fax:** (415) 544-4747
**E-mail:** service centre@iabc com
http://www.iabc.com

**International Radio and Television Society Foundation (IRTSF)**
420 Lexington Avenue
Suite 1714
New York, NY 10170
**Phone:** (212) 867-6650
**Fax:** (212) 867-6653
http://www.irts.org

**Kansas Association of Broadcasters (KAB)**
1916 SW Sieben Ct.
Topeka, KS 66611-1656
**Phone:** (913) 235-1307
**Fax:** (785) 233-3052
**E-mail:** harriet@kab.net
http://www.kab.net

**Low Power Radio Association (LPRA)**
c/o Walker Mitchell Ltd., Secretariat
Brearley Hall
Halifax HX2 6HS, United Kingdom
**Phone:** 44 1422 886463
**Fax:** 44 1422 886950
**E-mail:** info@lpra.org
http://www.lpra.org

**Maine Association of Broadcasters**
128 State Street
Augusta, ME 04330
**Phone:** (207) 623-3870

**Marketing Research Association (MRA)**
1344 Silas Deane Hwy.
Suite 306
P.O. Box 230
Rocky Hill, CT 06067-0230
**Phone:** (860) 257-4008
**Fax:** (860) 257-3990
**E-mail:** email@mra-net.org

**Media Rating Council**
200 W. 57th Street
Suite 204
New York, NY 10019
**Phone:** (212) 765-0200
**Fax:** (212) 765-1868

**Michigan Association of Broadcasters (MAB)**
819 N. Washington
Lansing, MI 48906
**Phone:** (517) 484-7444
**Fax:** (517) 484-5810
**E-mail:** mab@michmab.com
http://www.michmab.com

**Mississippi Association of Broadcasters**
855 S. Pear Orchard Road
Suite 403
Ridgeland, MS 39157
**Phone:** (601) 957-9121
**Fax:** (601) 957-9175
**E-mail:** jlett2@earthlink.net

**Missouri Broadcasters Association (MBA)**
P.O. Box 104445
Jefferson City, MO 65110-4445
**Phone:** (573) 636-6692
**Fax:** (573) 634-8258
**E-mail:** mba@mbaweb.org
http://www.mbaweb.org

**Music Library Association (MLA)**
8551 Research Way
Suite 180
Middleton, WI 53562-3567
**Phone:** (608) 836-5825
**Fax:** (608) 831-8200
**E-mail:** mla@areditions.com
http://www.musiclibraryassoc.org

**National Academy of Television Arts and Sciences (NATAS)**
111 W. 57th Street
Suite 1020
New York, NY 10019
**Phone:** (212) 586-8424
**Fax:** (212) 246-8129
**E-mail:** natashq@aol.com
http://www.emmyonline.org

**National Association of African-American Sportswriters and Broadcasters**
308 Deer Park Avenue
Dix Hills, NY 11746
**Phone:** (631) 462-3933
**E-mail:** cldavis@suffolk.library.us

**National Association of Black Owned Broadcasters (NABOB)**
1155 Connecticut Avenue, NW, 6th Floor
Washington, DC 20036
**Phone:** (202) 463-8970
**Fax:** (202) 429-0657
**E-mail:** info@abs.net
http://www.nabob.org

**National Association of Broadcast Employees and Technicians—Communications Workers of America (NABET-CWA)**
501 3rd Street, NW, 8th Floor
Washington, DC 20001
**Phone:** (202) 434-1254
**Fax:** (202) 434-1426
**E-mail:** nabet@nabetcwa.org
http://www.nabetcwa.org

**National Association of Broadcasters**
1771 N Street, NW
Washington, DC 20036-2891
**Phone:** (202) 429-5300 or
(800) 368-5644 (toll-free)
**Fax:** (202) 429-5406
**E-mail:** Nabpubs@nab.org
http://www.nab.org/nabstore

**National Association of Farm Broadcasters (NAFB)**
26 E. Exchange Street, No. 307
St. Paul, MN 55101
**Phone:** (651) 224-0508
**Fax:** (651) 224-1956
**E-mail:** info@nafb.com
http://www.nafb.com

**National Association of Minority Media Executives**
1921 Gallows Road, No. 600
Vienna, VA 22182
**Phone:** (703) 893-2410 or (703) 288-6501; (888) 968-7658 (toll-free)
**Fax:** (703) 893-2414
**E-mail:** nammeexecutivedirector@worldnet.att.net
http://www.namme.org

**National Association of Press Agencies**
41 Lansdowne Crescent
Leamington Spa CV32 4PR, United Kingdom
**Phone:** 44 1926 424181
**Fax:** 44 1926 424760
http://www.napa.org.uk

**National Association of Radio and Telecommunications Engineers (NARTE)**
167 Village Street
Medway, MA 02053
**Phone:** (508) 533-8333 or
(800) 89-NARTE (toll-free)
**Fax:** (508) 533-3815
**E-mail:** narte@narte.org
http://www.narte.org

**National Association of State Radio Networks (NASRN)**
6060 N. Central Expy.
Suite 644
Dallas, TX 75206
**Phone:** (214) 363-0844
**Fax:** (214) 363-0892
http://www.statenets.com

**National Broadcast Association for Community Affairs**
270 Brevard Avenue
Cocoa, FL 32922

Phone: (407) 635-8709
Fax: (407) 635-1979
E-mail: nbaca@yourlink.net
http://www.nbaca.org

**National Conference of Editorial Writers (NCEW)**
6223 Executive Boulevard
Rockville, MD 20852
Phone: (301) 984-3015
Fax: (301) 231-0026
E-mail: ncewhqs@erols.com
http://www.ncew.org

**National Federation of Community Broadcasters (NFCB)**
Fort Mason Center, Building D
San Francisco, CA 94123
Phone: (415) 771-1160
Fax: (415) 771-4343
E-mail: comments@nfcb.org
http://www.nfcb.org

**National Federation of Press Women (NFPW)**
P.O. Box 5556
Arlington, VA 22205-0056
Phone: (703) 534-2500 or
    (800) 780-2715 (toll-free)
Fax: (703) 534-5731
E-mail: presswomen@aol.com
http://www.nfpw.org

**National Press Club (NPC)**
National Press Building
529 14th Street, NW, 13th Floor
Washington, DC 20045
Phone: (202) 662-7500
Fax: (202) 662-7512
E-mail: info@npcpress.org
http://www.press.org

**National Public Radio (NPR)**
635 Massachusetts Avenue, NW
Washington, DC 20001
Phone: (202) 513-2000 or
    (877) 677-8398 (toll-free)
Fax: (202) 513-3329
E-mail: ombudsman@npr.org
http://www.npr.org

**National Religious Broadcasters**
7839 Ashton Avenue
Manassas, VA 20109
Phone: (703) 330-7000
Fax: (703) 330-6996
http://www.nrb.org

**National Society of Accountants (NSA)**
1010 N. Fairfax Street
Alexandria, VA 22314-1574
Phone: (703) 549-6400 or
    (800) 966-6679 (toll-free)
Fax: (703) 549-2984
E-mail: ifelski@nsacct.org
http://www.nsacct.org

**National Society of Fund Raising Executives—Greater Detroit Chapter**
c/o Association Management
    Professionals, Inc.
3319 Greenfield Road, No. 321
Dearborn, MI 48120
Phone: (313) 271-7543
http://www.afpdetroit.org/index.htm

**National Society of Fund Raising Executives—Greater New York Chapter**
c/o Ann L. Woodfield, Executive Director
250 W. 57th Street
Suite 2301
New York, NY 10107-2399
Phone: (212) 265-7838
Fax: (212) 265-4974

**National Society of Fund Raising Executives—Greater Washington, D.C., Area Chapter**
c/o Jan Sapp
4424 Montgomery Avenue
Suite 201
Bethesda, MD 20814-4409
Phone: (301) 657-3265
Fax: (301) 654-3739

**National Sportscasters and Sportswriters Association (NSSA)**
322 E. Innes Street
Salisbury, NC 28144
Phone: (704) 633-4275
Fax: (704) 633-2027

**Nebraska Broadcasters Association**
12020 Shamrock Plaza
Suite 200
Omaha, NE 68154
Phone: (402) 778-5178
E-mail: dp@ne-ba.org
http://www.ne-ba.org

**New Jersey Broadcasters Association**
348 Applegarth Road
Monroe Township, NJ 08831
Phone: (609) 860-0111
Fax: (609) 860-0110

E-mail: proberts@njba.com
http://www.njba.com

**North American Broadcasters Association (NABA)**
P.O. Box 500, Station A
Toronto, ON, Canada M5W 1E6
Phone: (416) 598-9877
Fax: (416) 598-9774
E-mail: info@nabanet
http://www.nabanet.com

**North Carolina Association of Broadcasters**
150 Fayetteville Street Mall, 1610
P.O. Box 627
Raleigh, NC 27602
Phone: (919) 821-7300
Fax: (919) 839-0304
E-mail: ncbrdcast@aol.com
http://www.ncbroadcast.com

**Ohio Association of Broadcasters (OAB)**
88 E. Broad Street
Suite 1180
Columbus, OH 43215
Phone: (614) 228-4052 or
    (614) 228-4053
Fax: (614) 228-8133
E-mail: oab@oab.org

**Professional Secretaries International, Anacacho Chapter**
c/o Inzia Miller, President
17302 Saule Lane
San Antonio, TX 78232

**PROMAX International**
2029 Century Park East
Suite 555
Los Angeles, CA 90067-2906
Phone: (310) 788-7600
Fax: (310) 788-7616
http://www.promax.org

**Public Broadcasting Management Association**
P.O. Box 50008
Columbia, SC 29250
Phone: (803) 799-5517
Fax: (803) 771-4831
E-mail: chuck@ploma.org

**Public Radio News Directors (PRNDI)**
c/o WSKG
P.O. Box 3000
Binghamton, NY 13902
Phone: (607) 729-0100
Fax: (607) 729-7328

**E-mail:** wskg_mail@wskg.pbs.org
http://www.wskg.com

**Public Radio Programmer's**
**Association (PRPD)**
517 Ocean Front Walk
Suite 10
Venice, CA 90291
**Phone:** (310) 664-1591
**Fax:** (310) 664-1592
**E-mail:** info@prpd.org
http://www.prpd.org

**Public Relations Society of America**
**(PRSA)**
33 Irving Plaza, 3rd Floor
New York, NY 10003-2376
**Phone:** (212) 995-2230
**E-mail:** hq@prsa.org
http://www.prsa.org

**Radio Advertising Bureau (RAB)**
1320 Greenway Drive, No. 500
Irving, TX 75038
**Phone:** (212) 681-7200 or
(800) 232-3131 (toll-free)
**Fax:** (212) 681-7223
**E-mail:** gfries@rab.com

**Radio and Television News Directors'**
**Association Canada (RTNDA)**
2175 Sheppard Avenue E
Suite 310
North York, ON, Canada M2J 1W8
**Phone:** (416) 756-2213 or
(877) 25-RTNDA (toll-free)
**Fax:** (416) 491-1670
**E-mail:** rtnda@taylorenterprises.com
http://www.rtndacanada.com

**Radio Marketing Bureau (RAB)**
146 Yorkville Avenue
Toronto, ON, Canada M5R 1C2
**Phone:** (416) 922-5757 or
(800) ONR-ADIO (toll-free)
**E-mail:** info@rmb.ca
http://www.rmb.ca

**Radio Talk Show Hosts Association**
c/o Carol Nashe
2791 S. Buffalo Drive
Las Vegas, NV 89117
**E-mail:** carol@talkshowhosts.com
http://www.talkshowhosts.com

**Radio-Television Correspondents**
**Association (RTCA)**
c/o Senate Radio- TV Gallery
U.S. Capitol, Rm. S-325
Washington, DC 20510

**Phone:** (202) 224-6421
**Fax:** (202) 224-4882

**Radio-Television News Directors**
**Association (RTNDA)**
1600 K Street, NW
Suite 700
Washington, DC 20006-2838
**Phone:** (202) 659-6510 or
(800) 80-RTNDA (toll-free)
**Fax:** (202) 223-4007
**E-mail:** rtnda@rtnda.org
http://rtnda.org

**Society for Human Resource**
**Management (SHRM)**
1800 Duke Street
Alexandria, VA 22314-3499
**Phone:** (703) 548-3440 or
(800) 283-7476 (toll-free)
**Fax:** (703) 535-6497
**E-mail:** shrm@shrm.org
http://www.shrm.org

**Society of Broadcast Engineers (SBE)**
9247 N Meridian Street
Suite 305
Indianapolis, IN 46260
**Phone:** (317) 846-9000
**Fax:** (317) 846-9120
**E-mail:** jporay@sbe.org
http://www.sbe.org

**Society of Broadcast Engineers,**
**Chapter 68 (SBE)**
P.O. Box 55181
Birmingham, AL 35255
http://www.broadcast.net/sbe68

**Society of Broadcast Engineers,**
**Connecticut Valley Chapter 14 (SBE)**
8445 Keystone Crossing
Suite 140
Indianapolis, IN 46240
**Phone:** (317) 253-1640

**Society of Broadcast Engineers,**
**Northeastern Pennsylvania Chapter**
**2 (SBE)**
200 W. Main Street
Nanticoke, PA 18634-1407
**E-mail:** mrutkowski@usnetway.com

**Society of Illustrators (SI)**
128 E. 63rd Street
New York, NY 10021-7303
**Phone:** (212) 838-2560
**Fax:** (212) 838-2561
**E-mail:** sil901@aol.com
http://www.societyillustrators.org

**South Carolina Broadcasters Association**
c/o Shani White
One Harbison Way
Suite 112
Columbia, SC 29210
**Phone:** (803) 732-1186
**Fax:** (803) 732-4085
**E-mail:** scba@scba.net
http://scba.net

**South Dakota Broadcasters Association**
**(SDBA)**
106 W. Capitol Avenue, No. 7
P.O. Box 1037
Pierre, SD 57501
**Phone:** (605) 224-1034
**Fax:** (605) 224-7426
http://www.sdba.org

**Southern California Broadcasters**
**Association (SCBA)**
5670 Wilshire Boulevard
Suite 1370
Los Angeles, CA 90036-5609
**Phone:** (323) 938-3100
**Fax:** (323) 938-8600
**E-mail:** radio@scba.com
http://www.scba.com

**Special Libraries Association (SLA)**
1700 18th Street, NW
Washington, DC 20009-2514
**Phone:** (202) 234-4700
**Fax:** (202) 265-9317
**E-mail:** sla@sla.org
http://www.sla.org

**Station Representatives Association**
**(SRA)**
16 W. 77th Street No. 9-E
New York, NY 10024-5126
**Phone:** (212) 362-8868
**Fax:** (212) 362-4999
**E-mail:** srajerry@aol.com

**Southern Gospel Radio Partners**
c/o Mike Martin
302 Depot Street
Suite A
Delhi, LA 71232-2816

**Texas Association of Broadcasters**
c/o Ann Arnold, Executive Director
502 E. 11th Street
Austin, TX 78701
**Phone:** (512) 322-9944
**Fax:** (512) 322-0522
**E-mail:** tab@tab.org
http://www.tab.org

**Virginia Association of Broadcasters (VAB)**
630 Country Green Lane
Charlottesville, VA 22902-6478
**Phone:** (804) 977-3716
**Fax:** (804) 979-2439
**E-mail:** easter@esinet.net
http://www.vab.net

**Western Public Radio (WPR)**
Fort Mason Center, Building D
San Francisco, CA 94123

**Wisconsin Public Radio Association**
c/o Patty Stockdale
821 University Avenue
Madison, WI 53706-1412
**Phone:** (608) 263-1235

**Women in Communications Foundation (WCF)**
355 Lexington Avenue, 17th Floor
New York, NY 10017
**Phone:** (212) 297-2133
**Fax:** (212) 370-9047
**E-mail:** eileenast@aol.com
http://www.nywici.org/foundation

**World Organization of Webmasters**
9580 Oak Pkwy.
Suite 7-177
Folsom, CA 95630
**Phone:** (916) 608-1597
**Fax:** (916) 987-3022
**E-mail:** info@joinwow.org
http://www.joinwow.org

**Writers Guild of America—West**
7000 West Third Street
Los Angeles, CA 90048-4329
**Phone:** (323) 951-4000 or
    (800) 548-4532 (toll-free)
**Fax:** (323) 782-4800
http://www.wga.org

# APPENDIX III
# RADIO STATIONS

The following is a selected listing of radio stations throughout the country, arranged alphabetically by state. Radio stations of various sizes and an array of formats have been included. There are many stations that have not been listed because of space limitations. Additional stations may be located at your local library, in directories such as *Gale's Directory of Media and Broadcasting*. Listings of radio stations may also be located in the yellow pages of phone books.

Use this list as a starting point to find internships, explore job opportunities, and obtain additional useful information. The addresses, phone and fax numbers, websites, e-mail addresses, and formats of radio stations have been included where available.

## ALABAMA

**WAAX-AM**
6510 Whorton Bend Road
Gadsden, AL 35901
**Phone:** (256) 543-9229
**Fax:** (256) 543-3279
http://waax570.com
**Format:** Talk, News, Sports

**WAFN-FM**
P.O. Box 4148
Huntsville, AL 35815
**Phone:** (256) 586-9300 or
    (800) 867-9270 (toll-free)
**Fax:** (256) 586-9301
**E-mail:** funradio@hiwaay.net
**Format:** Oldies

**WAPI-AM**
244 Goodwin Crest Drive
Suite 300
Birmingham, AL 35205
**Phone:** (205) 942-1004
**Fax:** (205) 942-8959
**E-mail:** wapi 107.com
http://www.wapi1070.com
**Format:** News, Talk

**WAPR-FM**
P.O. Box 870370
Tuscaloosa, AL 35487-0370
**Phone:** (205) 348-6644
**Fax:** (205) 348-6648
**E-mail:** apr@apr.org
http://www.wual.ua.edu
**Format:** Public Radio

**WAVD-AM**
1209 N. Danville Road SW
Decatur, AL 35601
**Phone:** (205) 353-1400
**Fax:** (205) 353-0363

**E-mail:** tarnold@wavd.com
http://www.wavd.com
**Format:** Talk, News, Sports

**WAWV-FM**
P.O. Box 629
Sylacauga, AL 35150
**Phone:** (205) 245-3281
**Fax:** (256) 245-4355
**E-mail:** thev983@mindspring.com
http://www.thev983.com
**Format:** Adult Contemporary

**WBAM-FM**
4101 A Wall Street
Montgomery, AL 36106
**Phone:** (334) 244-1170
**Fax:** (334) 279-9563
**E-mail:** pd@star989.com
http://www.star989.com
**Format:** Top 40, Adult Contemporary

**WBHM-FM**
650 11th Street S.
Birmingham, AL 35233
**Phone:** (205) 934-2606
**Fax:** (205) 934-5075
**E-mail:** info@wbhm.org
http://www.wbhm.org
**Format:** Hot Country

**WBHY-AM**
P.O. Box 1328
Mobile, AL 36633-1328
**Phone:** (334) 473-8488
**E-mail:** power88@goforth.org
http://www.goforth.org
**Format:** Talk

**WERC-AM**
530 Beacon Pkw. W.
Suite 600
Birmingham, AL 35209

**Phone:** (205) 439-9600
**Fax:** (205) 439-8190
http://www.werc960am.com
**Format:** News, Talk

**WGAD-AM**
823 Forrest Avenue
P.O. Box 1350
Gadsden, AL 35902
**Phone:** (205) 546-1611
**Fax:** (205) 547-9062
**E-mail:** wgad@cybertyme.com
http://www.wgad.com
**Format:** News, Sports, Talk

**WGRW-FM**
P.O. Box 2555
Anniston, AL 36202
**Fax:** (256) 237-1102
**E-mail:** jon@graceradio.com
http://www.graceradio.com
**Format:** Talk

**WJLD-AM**
1449 Spaulding Ishkooda Road
Birmingham, AL 35211
**Phone:** (205) 942-1776
**Fax:** (205) 942-4814
**E-mail:** wjld@juno.com
http://www.wjld1400.com
**Format:** Blues, Talk, Gospel

**WKAC-AM**
P.O. Box 1083
Athens, AL 35611
**Phone:** (205) 232-6827
**E-mail:** wkac@companet.net
http://www.wkac1080.com
**Format:** Oldies, Country

**WJOX-AM**
244 Goodwin Crest Drive
Suite 300
Birmingham, AL 35209

**Phone:** (205) 942-6690
**Fax:** (205) 942-8959
**E-mail:** wjox.sports@citcomm.com
http://www.wjox690.com
**Format:** Sports

**WKUL-FM**
P.O. Box 803
Cullman, AL 35056
**Phone:** (205) 734-0183
**Fax:** (205) 739-2999
**E-mail:** wkul@wkul.com
**Format:** Contemporary Country, Talk

**WKXN-FM**
P.O. Box 369
Greenville, AL 36037
**Phone:** (334) 382-6555
**Fax:** (334) 382-7770
**E-mail:** wkxn@wkxn.com
http://www.wkxn.com
**Format:** Urban Contemporary

**WNTM-AM**
P.O. Box 160587
Mobile, AL 36616
**Phone:** (334) 479-4333
**Fax:** (334) 479-3418
**E-mail:** wntm@capitolweb.com
http://www.capitolweb.com
**Format:** News, Talk

**WLAY-FM**
620 E. 2nd Street
Muscle Shoals, AL 35661
**Phone:** (205) 383-2525
**Fax:** (205) 381-1450
http://www.wlay.com
**Format:** Country

**WLDX-AM**
733 Columbus Street E.
P.O. Box 189
Fayette, AL 35555
**Phone:** (205) 932-3318
**Fax:** (205) 932-3318
**E-mail:** wldx@wldx.com
http://www.wldx.com

**WLDX-AM**
733 Columbus Street E.
P.O. Box 189
Fayette, AL 35555
**Phone:** (205) 932-3318
**Fax:** (205) 932-3318
**E-mail:** wldx@wldx.com
http://www.wldx.com

**WLWI-FM**
1 Commerce Street
Suite 300
Montgomery, AL 36104-3542
**Phone:** (334) 240-9274
**Fax:** (334) 240-9219
http://www.colonialbroadcasting.com
**Format:** Country

**WNTM-AM**
P.O. Box 160587
Mobile, AL 36616
**Phone:** (334) 479-4333
**Fax:** (334) 479-3418
**E-mail:** wntm@capitolweb.com
http://www.capitolweb.com
**Format:** News, Talk

**WVNN-AM**
P.O. Box 389
Athens, AL 35611
**Phone:** (205) 232-3911
**Fax:** (205) 232-6842
**E-mail:** wvnn@wvnn.com
http://wvnn.com
**Format:** Talk, News

**WQPR-FM**
Box 870370
Tuscaloosa, AL 35487-0370
**Phone:** (205) 348-6644 or
    (800) 654-4262 (toll-free)
**Fax:** (205) 348-6648
http://www.apr.org
**Format:** Public Radio, News, Jazz,
    Classical

**WRAX-FM**
244 Goodwin Crest Drive
Suite 300
Birmingham, AL 35209
**Phone:** (205) 945-4646
**Fax:** (205) 942-3175
http://www.wrax.com
**Format:** Alternative, New Music,
    Progressive

# ALASKA

**KABN-AM**
2509 Eide Street
Suite 6
Anchorage, AK 99503
**Phone:** (907) 277-5652
**Fax:** (907) 344-5728
**E-mail:** x-fm@chugach.net
**Format:** Talk

**KADX-FM**
2509 Eide Street
Suite 6
Anchorage, AK 99503
**Phone:** (907) 277-5652
**Fax:** (907) 344-5728
**E-mail:** x-fm@chugach.net

**KAKN-FM**
P.O. Box 214
Naknek, AK 99633
**Phone:** (907) 246-7492
**Fax:** (907) 246-7462
**E-mail:** kakn@bristolbay.com
**Format:** Religious, Easy Listening

**KATB-FM**
6401 E. Northern Lights Boulevard
Anchorage, AK 99504
**Format:** Religious

**KAXX-AM**
2509 Eide Street
Suite 6
Anchorage, AK 99503
**Phone:** (907) 277-5652
**Fax:** (907) 344-5728
**E-mail:** x-fm@chugach.net
**Format:** Sports

**KBRJ-FM**
11259 Tower Road
Anchorage, AK 99515
**Phone:** (907) 344-2200
**Fax:** (907) 349-3299
**Format:** Hot Country

**KBRW-FM**
1695 Okpik Street
P.O. Box 109
Barrow, AK 99723
**Phone:** (907) 852-6811
**Fax:** (907) 852-2274
http://kbrw.org
**Format:** Public Radio, Educational

**KCAM-AM**
Box 249
Glennallen, AK 99588
**Phone:** (907) 822-3434
**Fax:** (907) 822-3761
**E-mail:** kcam@alaska.net
http://www.kcam.org
**Format:** Country, Religious

**KCBF-AM**
1060 Aspen Street
Fairbanks, AK 99709
**Phone:** (907) 451-5910

**Fax:** (907) 451-5999
**E-mail:** kcbf@akradio.com
http://www.akradio.com
**Format:** Country

**KENI-AM**
800 E. Diamond Bluff
Suite 3-320
Anchorage, AK 99515
**Phone:** (907) 522-1515
**Fax:** (907) 349-6801
**Format:** Talk, News

**KFAR-AM**
1060 Aspen Street
Fairbanks, AK 99709-5501
**Phone:** (907) 451-5910
**Fax:** (907) 451-5999
**E-mail:** kfar@akradio.com
**Format:** Talk, News, Public Radio

**KFQD-AM**
9200 Lake Otis Pkwy.
Anchorage, AK 99507
**Phone:** (907) 344-9622
**Fax:** (907) 349-7326
**E-mail:** kfqd@ corcom.com
http://www.kfqd.com
**Format:** News

**KGOT-FM**
500 L Street, No. 200
Anchorage, AK 99501-5909
**Phone:** (907) 272-5945
**Fax:** (907) 272-5055
**E-mail:** kgot@alaskanet.com
http://www.alaskanet.com/kgot
**Format:** Contemporary Hit Radio (CHR)

**KIAM-AM**
Box 474
Nenana, AK 99760
**Phone:** (907) 832-5426
**Fax:** (907) 832-5450
**E-mail:** akradio@mtaonline.net,
    vfcm@mtaonline.net
http://www.vfcm.org
**Format:** Religious

**KINY-AM**
1107 W. 8th Street, No. 2
Juneau, AK 99801
**Phone:** (907) 586-1800
**Fax:** (907) 586-3266
**E-mail:** kiny@ptialaska.net
http://www.juneau.com
**Format:** Adult Contemporary, Full
    Service

**KJNO-AM**
3161 Channel Drive
Suite 2
Juneau, AK 99801
**Phone:** (907) 586-3630
**Fax:** (907) 463-3685
**E-mail:** kjno@micronet.net
**Format:** Talk, Sports

**KLAM-AM**
P.O. Box 60
Cordova, AK 99574
**Phone:** (907) 424-3796
**Fax:** (907) 424-3737
**Format:** News

**KMXT-FM**
620 Egan Way
Kodiak, AK 99615
**Phone:** (907) 486-3181
**Fax:** (907) 486-2733
**E-mail:** kmxt@ptialaska.net
http://www.ptialaska.net/~kmxt
**Format:** Public Radio

**KRUA-FM**
3211 Providence Drive
Anchorage, AK 99508
**Phone:** (907) 786-6800
**Fax:** (907) 786-6806
**E-mail:** aykrua@uaa.alaska.edu
http://www.netcasting.krua

**KSRM-AM**
40960 K-Beach Road
Kenai, AK 99611
**Phone:** (907) 283-5811
**Fax:** (907) 283-9177
**E-mail:** radiokenai@gci.net
**Format:** Talk, Adult Contemporary, News

**KSUA-FM**
307 Constitution Hall
University of Alaska, Fairbanks
Fairbanks, AK 99775
**Phone:** (907) 474-7054
**Fax:** (907) 474-6314
**E-mail:** fyksua@uaf.edu
http://www.uaf.edu/ksua
**Format:** Alternative, New Music,
    Progressive

**KSTK-FM**
202 St. Michaels Street
P.O. Box 1141
Wrangell, AK 99929
**Phone:** (907) 874-2345 or
    (800) 874-KSTK (toll-free)
**Fax:** (907) 874-3293

**E-mail:** kstkfm@seapac.net
http://seapac.net/~kstkfm
**Format:** Full Service, Public Radio

**KSUP-FM**
1107 W. 8th Street, No. 2
Juneau, AK 99801
**Phone:** (907) 586-1063
**Fax:** (907) 586-3266
**E-mail:** ksup@ptialaska.net
http://www.ptialaska.net/~ksup
**Format:** Album-Oriented Rock (AOR),
    Adult Album Alternative

**KTNA-FM**
P.O. Box 300
Talkeetna, AK 99676
**Phone:** (907) 733-1700
**E-mail:** ktnaprogramming@yahoo.com
http://www.ktna.org
**Format:** Eclectic

**KUAC-FM**
University of Alaska
P.O. Box 775620
Fairbanks, AK 99775-5620
**Phone:** (907) 474-7491
**Fax:** (907) 474-5064
**E-mail:** kuac@uaf.edu
http://www.kuac.org
**Format:** Public Radio, News, Classical,
    Jazz

**KWVV-FM**
P.O. Box 109
Homer, AK 99603
**Phone:** (907) 235-6000
**Fax:** (907) 235-6683
**E-mail:** kwavefm@xyz.net
**Format:** Adult Contemporary

**KYUK-AM**
640 Radio Street
Pouch 468
Bethel, AK 99559
**Phone:** (907) 543-3131 or
    (800) 478-3640 (toll-free)
**Fax:** (907) 543-3130
**Format:** Eclectic, Adult Contemporary,
    Country, Oldies, Blues, Talk, News,
    Sports, Jazz, Classical

## ARIZONA

**KAAA-AM**
2534 Hualapai Mountain Road
Kingman, AZ 86401
**Phone:** (520) 753-2537 or
    (888) 867-9470 (toll-free)
**Fax:** (520) 753-1551

E-mail: sunny@kingsman.com
Format: News, Talk

**KATO-AM**
Drawer L
Safford, AZ 85548
Phone: (520) 428-1230
Fax: (520) 428-1311
Format: News, Talk, Sports

**KAZM-AM**
P.O. Box 1525
Sedona, AZ 86339
Phone: (520) 282-4154
Fax: (520) 282-2230
Format: Talk, News, Sports,
    Contemporary Hit Radio

**KCFY-FM**
P.O. Box 1669
Yuma, AZ 85366
Phone: (520) 341-9730
Fax: (520) 341-9099
E-mail: main@kcfyfmmail.com
http://www.kcfyfm.com
Format: Contemporary Christian

**KCUZ-AM**
301-B E. Highway 70
P.O. Box 1330
Safford, AZ 85548
Phone: (928) 428-0916 or
    (888) 591-7797 (toll-free)
Fax: (928) 428-7797
E-mail: kfmm@eaznet.com
http://www.kfmmradio.com
Format: Country, Sports, News

**KEDJ-FM**
4745 N. 7th Street, No. 410
Phoenix, AZ 85014
Phone: (602) 266-1360
Fax: (602) 263-4820
http://www.edge106.com
Format: Alternative, New Music,
    Progressive

**KESZ-FM**
5555 N. 7th Avenue
Phoenix, AZ 85013
Phone: (602) 207-9999
Fax: (602) 207-3177
E-mail: kez@azfamily.com
http://www.azfamily.com
Format: Adult Contemporary

**KFLT-AM**
7355 N. Orade, No. 102
P.O. Box 36868
Tucson, AZ 85740

Phone: (520) 797-3700
Fax: (520) 797-3375
E-mail: kflt@flc.org
Format: Talk, News, Middle-of-the-Road
    (MOR), Religious

**KFNN-AM**
4800 N. Central Avenue
Phoenix, AZ 85012-1722
Phone: (602) 241-1510 or
    (800) 293-KFNN (toll-free)
Fax: (602) 241-1540
E-mail: kfnnradio@juno.com
Format: Talk, News

**KFYI-AM**
645 E. Missouri Avenue
Suite 119
Phoenix, AZ 85012-1370
Phone: (602) 258-6161
Fax: (602) 817-1199
E-mail: kfyi.com
Format: News, Talk

**KGCB-FM**
5025 N. US Highway 89
Prescott, AZ 86301-8103
Phone: (520) 776-0909 or
    (800) 720-0909 (toll-free)
Fax: (520) 776-1736
E-mail: kgcb@primenet.com
http://www.kgcb.org
Format: Religious, Adult
    Contemporary

**KHYT-FM**
575 W. Roger Road
Tucson, AZ 85705
Phone: (520) 887-1000
Fax: (520) 887-7585
http://www.khit.com
Format: Classic Rock

**KJOK-AM**
949 S. Avenue B
Yuma, AZ 85364
Phone: (520) 782-4321
Fax: (520) 343-1710
E-mail: kjok1400@juno.com
Format: Full Service, News, Sports,
    Talk, Oldies

**KLPX-FM**
1920 W. Copper Drive
Tucson, AZ 85745
Phone: (520) 622-6711
Fax: (520) 624-3226
E-mail: 96@klpx.com
http://www.klpx.com

**KLPZ-AM**
816 6th Street
Parker, AZ 85344
Phone: (520) 669-9274 or
    (800) 448-1380 (toll-free)
Fax: (520) 669-9300
E-mail: klpz@redrivernet.com
Format: Contemporary Country, News,
    Talk

**KMXP-FM**
645 E. Missouri Avenue
Suite 360
Phoenix, AZ 85012
Phone: (602) 260-0969
http://www.mix969.com
Format: Adult Contemporary

**KMXZ-FM**
3438 N. Country Club
Tucson, AZ 85716
Phone: (520) 795-1490
Fax: (520) 327-2260
http://mixfm.com
Format: Adult Contemporary

**KMYL-AM**
8611 N. Black Canyon Hwy. 206
Phoenix, AZ 85021-4188
Phone: (602) 995-9555
Fax: (602) 995-3390
E-mail: kmyl@uswest.net
http://www.kmyl.com
Format: Oldies

**KNOT-AM**
116 S. Alto Street
P.O. Box 151
Prescott, AZ 86302
Phone: (602) 445-6880
Fax: (602) 445-6852
E-mail: knot@mwaz.com
Format: Big Band, Nostalgia

**KNST-AM**
3202 N. Oracle Road
Tucson, AZ 85710
Phone: (520) 618-2100
Fax: (520) 618-2135
http://www.knst.com
Format: Talk, Sports, News

**KOAZ-FM**
575 W. Roger Road
Tucson, AZ 85705
Phone: (520) 887-1000
Fax: (520) 887-7585
http://www.koaz.com
Format: Jazz, Soft Rock

**KOHT-FM**
889 W. El Puente Lane
Tucson, AZ 85713
**Phone:** (520) 623-6429
**Fax:** (520) 622-2680
**Format:** Contemporary Hit Radio

**KPXQ-AM**
2425 E. Camelback, No. 570
Phoenix, AZ 85016
**Phone:** (602) 955-9600
**Fax:** (602) 955-7860
http://www.kpxq1360.com
**Format:** Talk, Religious

**KQNA-AM**
P.O. Box 26523
Prescott Valley, AZ 86312
**Phone:** (520) 445-8289 or
    (800) 264-5449 (toll-free)
**Fax:** (520) 775-4188
**E-mail:** sanford@kppv.com
http://www.kqna.com

**KXAM-AM**
4725 N. Scottsdale Road
Suite 234
Scottsdale, AZ 85251
**Phone:** (480) 423-1310
**Fax:** (480) 423-3867
**E-mail:** kxam@phnx.uswest.net
**Format:** Talk

# ARKANSAS

**KASU-FM**
104 Cooley Drive
Arkansas State University
Box 2160
State University, AR 72467
**Phone:** (870) 972-2200 or (800) 643-8269
    (toll-free)
**Fax:** (870) 972-2997
**E-mail:** kasu@kiowa.astate.edu
http://www.kasu.astate.edu
**Format:** Classical, Jazz, News, Folk,
    New Age, Blues

**KCAC-FM**
327 Stewart Street, S.W.
Camden, AR 71701
**Phone:** (870) 836-5289
**Fax:** (870) 836-9369
**E-mail:** kcac89@mail.cei.net
http://www.cei.net/~kcac89
**Format:** Alternative, New Music,
    Progressive

**KCDI-FM**
P.O. Box 491
Bryant, AR 72089
**Phone:** (501) 332-6981
**Fax:** (501) 332-6984
**E-mail:** listeners@kdifm.com
http://www.kcdifm.com
**Format:** Hot Country

**KCXY-FM**
P.O. Box 956
Camden, AR 71701
**Phone:** (870) 836-9567
**Fax:** (870) 836-9500
**E-mail:** y95@y95.net
http://www.y95.net
**Format:** Contemporary Country

**KDEL-FM**
P.O. Box 40
Arkadelphia, AR 71923
**Phone:** (870) 246-4561
**Fax:** (870) 246-4562
**E-mail:** kvrckdel@ezclick.net
http://www.kvrckdel.com
**Format:** Contemporary Country

**KDQN-FM**
Box 311
De Queen, AR 71832
**Phone:** (870) 642-2446
**Fax:** (870) 642-2442
http://numberonecountry.yahoo.com

**KERX-FM**
24 S. Express Street
Paris, AR 72855
**Phone:** (501) 963-8362 or
    (877) 953-9953 (toll-free)
**Fax:** (501) 963-8461
http://www.pearsonbroadcasting.com
**Format:** Classic Rock

**KFFA-AM**
Box 430
Helena, AR 72342
**Phone:** (501) 338-8331
**Fax:** (501) 338-8332
http://www.kingbiscuit.com
**Format:** Talk, Information, Blues, Sports,
    Music of Your Life

**KHGG-AM**
P.O. Box 573
Fort Smith, AR 72902-0573
**Phone:** (501) 288-1047
**Fax:** (501) 288-0942
**E-mail:** fox46@ipa.net
**Format:** Sports Talk

**KHOZ-AM**
P.O. Box 430
Harrison, AR 72602
**Phone:** (870) 741-2301 or
    (800) 553-6103 (toll-free)
**Fax:** (870) 741-3299
**E-mail:** khoz@cswnet.com
**Format:** Talk, Adult Contemporary

**KKPT-FM**
2400 Cottondale Lane
Little Rock, AR 72202
**Phone:** (501) 664-9410
**Fax:** (501) 664-5871
http://www.kkpt.com
**Format:** Classic Rock

**KKRN-FM**
700 Wellington Hills Road
Little Rock, AR 72211
**Phone:** (501) 401-0200
**Fax:** (501) 401-0365
http://www.karnnewsradio.com
**Format:** News, Talk

**KLRG-AM**
1403 Main Street
North Little Rock, AR 72114-4128
**Phone:** (501) 376-1063
**Fax:** (501) 374-6381
**E-mail:** info@klrg.com
http://www.klrg.com
**Format:** Gospel, Urban Contemporary

**KOCY-FM**
1309 Twin Oaks Avenue
Jonesboro, AR 72401
**Phone:** (870) 933-0044 or
    (888) 410-5336 (toll-free)
**Fax:** (870) 933-9652
http://www.kozyfm.com
**Format:** Adult Contemporary

**KOZY-FM**
P.O. Box 540
Jonesboro, AR 72403
**Phone:** (870) 933-0044 or
    (888) 410-5336 (toll-free)
**Fax:** (870) 933-9652
http://www.kozyfm.com
**Format:** Sports

**KQAR-FM**
10800 Colonel Glenn Road
Little Rock, AR 72204
**Phone:** (501) 217-5000
**Fax:** (501) 372-7787
http://www.q100fm.com
**Format:** Top 40

**KSSN-FM**
10800 Colonel Glenn Road
Little Rock, AR 72204-8017
**Phone:** (501) 217-5000
**Fax:** (501) 374-0808
http://www.kssn.com
**Format:** Contemporary Country

**KTLO-AM**
620 Hwy. 5 N.
P.O. Box 2010
Mountain Home, AR 72654-2010
**Phone:** (870) 425-3101
**Fax:** (870) 424-4314
**E-mail:** news@ktlo.com
http://www.ktlo.com
**Format:** Country

**KUAR-FM**
2801 S. University Avenue
Little Rock, AR 72204
**Phone:** (501) 569-8485
**Fax:** (501) 569-8488
**E-mail:** kuar@ualr.edu
http://www.kuar.org
**Format:** News, Information

**KVLO-FM**
700 Wellington Hills Road
Little Rock, AR 72211
**Phone:** (501) 401-0200
**Fax:** (501) 401-0349
http://www.k-love.com
**Format:** Adult Contemporary

**KVRC-AM**
P.O. Box 40
Arkadelphia, AR 71923
**Phone:** (870) 246-4561
**Fax:** (870) 246-4562
**E-mail:** kvrckdel@ezclick.com
http://www.kvkckdel.com
**Format:** Contemporary Country

**KXAR-AM**
P.O.Box 320
Hope, AR 71801-0320
**Phone:** (501) 777-3601
**Fax:** (501) 777-3535
**Format:** Talk, Country

**KXRJ-FM**
Department of Journalism
Arkansas Tech University
Department of Journalism
Russellville, AR 72801
**Phone:** (501) 964-0890
**Fax:** (501) 964-0899
**E-mail:** kxrj@mail.atu.edu

http://broadcast.atu.edu
**Format:** Jazz, Album-Oriented Rock
(AOR), Classical, News

**KZNG-AM**
125 Corporate Terrace
Hot Springs, AR 71913
**Phone:** (501) 525-9700
**Fax:** (501) 525-9739
**E-mail:** worpdaddy@direclynx.net
**Format:** Talk, News

# CALIFORNIA

**KABC-AM**
3321 S. La Cienega Boulevard
Los Angeles, CA 90016-3114
**Phone:** (310) 840-4900
**Fax:** (310) 840-4977
**Format:** Talk

**KALW-FM**
500 Mansell
San Francisco, CA 94134
**Phone:** (415) 841-4121
**E-mail:** kalwradio@aol.com
**Format:** Public Radio, Talk, Ethnic,
News, Eclectic

**KACD-FM**
1424 Lincoln Bovlevard
Santa Monica, CA 90401-2745
**Phone:** (310) 899-6999
**E-mail:** comments@channel103.com
http://www.channel1031.com
**Format:** Urban Contemporary

**KATY-FM**
27450 Ynez Road
Suite 316
Temecula, CA 92591
**Phone:** (909) 506-1222
**Fax:** (909) 506-1213
**E-mail:** katy@ez2.net
http://www.katyfm.com
**Format:** Adult Contemporary

**KBAY-FM**
190 Park Center Plaza
Suite 200
San Jose, CA 95113-2223
**Phone:** (408) 287-5775 or
(888) 558-5229 (toll-free)
**Fax:** (408) 278-6394
http://www.kbay.com
**Format:** Adult Contemporary

**KBIG-FM**
7755 Sunset Boulevard
Los Angeles, CA 90046

**Phone:** (213) 874-7700 or
(800) 524-4104 (toll-free)
**Fax:** (213) 874-4276
**E-mail:** kbig104@aol.com
http://www.kbig104.com
**Format:** Adult Contemporary

**KBLX-FM**
55 Hawthorne Street
Suite 900
San Francisco, CA 94105
**Phone:** (415) 284-1029
**Fax:** (415) 764-4959
**E-mail:** info@kblx.com
http://www.kblx.com
**Format:** Jazz, Adult Contemporary

**KBOQ-FM**
2511 Garden Road
Suite C-150
Monterey, CA 93940
**Phone:** (831) 656-9550
**Fax:** (831) 656-9551
**E-mail:** info@kbach.com
http://www.kbach.com
**Format:** Classical

**KCBS-FM**
6121 Sunset Boulevard
Los Angeles, CA 90028
**Phone:** (213) 460-3293
**Fax:** (213) 463-9270
**E-mail:** vandyked@la.cbs.com
http://www.arrowfm.com
**Format:** Classic Rock

**KCWR-FM**
1900 Pico Boulevard
Santa Monica, CA 90405
**Phone:** (310) 450-5183
**Fax:** (310) 450-3855
**E-mail:** mail@kcrw.org
http://www.kcrw.org
**Format:** Public Radio, News, Eclectic,
Progressive, New Music, Talk

**KDAR-FM**
P.O. Box 5626
Oxnard, CA 93031-5626
**Phone:** (805) 485-8881
**Fax:** (805) 656-5330
**E-mail:** info@kdar.com
http://www.kdar.com
**Format:** Religious, Talk

**KFBK-AM**
1440 Ethan Way
Suite 200
Sacramento, CA 95825

**Phone:** (916) 924-3901
**Fax:** (916) 921-5555
**Format:** News, Talk

**KFI-AM**
610 S. Ardmore Avenue
Los Angeles, CA 90005
**Phone:** (213) 385-0101
**Fax:** (213) 385-7076
**Format:** Talk

**KFMB-AM**
7677 Engineer Road
San Diego, CA 92111
**Phone:** (619) 495-7536 or
    (800) 455-KFMB (toll-free)
**Fax:** (619) 279-7676
**E-mail:** kfmb@cts.com
http://www.760kfmb.com
**Format:** Talk

**KFOG-FM**
55 Hawthorne Street
Suite 1100
San Francisco, CA 94105
**Phone:** (415) 817-KFOG
**Fax:** (415) 995-6867
http://www.kfog.com
**Format:** Album-Oriented Rock (AOR)

**KFRC-AM**
500 Washington Street, 2nd Floor
San Francisco, CA 94111-2919
**Phone:** (415) 391-9970
**Fax:** (415) 951-2329
http://www.kfrc.com
**Format:** Oldies

**KGB-FM**
5745 Kearny Villa Road
Suite M
San Diego, CA 92123-1136
**Phone:** (858) 565-6006
**Fax:** (858) 277-1015
**E-mail:** jaysisbell@101kgb.com
http://www.101kgb.com
**Format:** Classic Rock

**KGBY-FM**
1440 Ethan Way
Suite 200
Sacramento, CA 95825
**Phone:** (916) 929-5325 or
    (800) 870-KGBY (toll-free)
**Fax:** (916) 925-9292
**E-mail:** funandgames@y92.com
http://www.y92.com
**Format:** Adult Contemporary

**KGO-AM**
900 Front Street
San Francisco, CA 94111-1450
**Phone:** (415) 954-8100
**Fax:** (415) 362-5827
**Format:** News, Talk

**KLSX-FM**
3580 Wilshire Boulevard
Los Angeles, CA 90010
**Phone:** (213) 383-4222
**Fax:** (213) 386-3649
http://realradio.com
**Format:** Full Service

**KNX-AM**
6121 Sunset Boulevard
Los Angeles, CA 90028-6455
**Phone:** (213) 460-3000
**Fax:** (213) 460-3339
**Format:** News

**KOST-FM**
610 S. Ardmore Avenue
Los Angeles, CA 90005
**Phone:** (213) 427-1035 or
    (800) 929-5678 (toll-free)
**Fax:** (213) 385-0281
**Format:** Adult Contemporary

**KRLA-AM**
3580 Wilshire Boulevard
Los Angeles, CA 90010
**Phone:** (213) 383-4222
**Fax:** (213) 386-3679
**Format:** Oldies

**KSCA-FM**
1645 N. Vine Street
Suite 200
Los Angeles, CA 90028
**Phone:** (213) 860-0480
**Fax:** (213) 468-5337

**KZLA-FM**
7755 Sunset Boulevard
Los Angeles, CA 90046
**Phone:** (323) 882-8000 or
    (800) 977-1939 (toll-free)
**Fax:** (323) 874-9494
http://www.kzla.net, http://www.kzla.com
**Format:** Country

# COLORADO

**KATR-FM**
804 S. Ash
Yuma, CO 80759
**Phone:** (970) 848-3525

**Fax:** (970) 332-4172
**E-mail:** krdzkatr@plains.net
http://www.plains.net/krdzkatr
**Format:** Hot Country

**KBCO-AM**
8975 E. Kenyon Avenue
Denver, CO 80237
**Phone:** (303) 694-6300
**Fax:** (303) 694-4919
**Format:** Talk

**KBZS-AM**
2808 North Avenue
Suite 440
Grand Junction, CO 81501-5130
**Phone:** (970) 242-5787
**Fax:** (970) 245-6585
**E-mail:** radiobuzz@radiobuzz.com
http://www.radiobuzz.com
**Format:** Talk

**KCKK-AM**
1095 S. Monaco Pkwy.
Denver, CO 80224
**Phone:** (303) 321-0950
**Fax:** (303) 321-3383
http://www.16kicks.com
**Format:** Country

**KCOL-AM**
1612 Laporte Avenue
Fort Collins, CO 80522
**Phone:** (970) 482-5991
**Fax:** (970) 482-5994
http://www.kcol.com
**Format:** News, Talk

**KCSJ-AM**
3305 N. Elizabeth
Pueblo, CO 81008
**Phone:** (719) 543-5900
**Fax:** (719) 543-7609
**E-mail:** kcsj@rm11.com
http://www.puebloradio.com
**Format:** News, Sports, Talk

**KDUR-FM**
CUB 239
College Union Building
Fort Lewis College
Durango, CO 81301-3920
**Phone:** (303) 247-7262
**Fax:** (303) 247-7487
http://www.fortlewis.edu/kdur

**KEKB-FM**
315 Kennedy Avenue
Grand Junction, CO 81501

**Phone:** (970) 243-3699
**Fax:** (970) 243-0567
http://www.coloradowest.com
**Format:** Contemporary Country, Sports

**KIIX-AM**
1612 Laporte Avenue
P.O. Box 2047
Fort Collins, CO 80522
**Phone:** (970) 482-5991
**Fax:** (970) 482-5994
http://1410kiix.com
**Format:** Sports

**KILO-FM**
Box 2080
Colorado Springs, CO 80901
**Phone:** (719) 634-4896
**Fax:** (719) 634-5837
http://www.kilo943.com
**Format:** Album-Oriented Rock (AOR)

**KJCD-FM**
1095 S. Monaco Pkwy.
Denver, CO 80224
**Phone:** (303) 321-0950
**Fax:** (303) 321-3383
http://www.cd1043.com
**Format:** Jazz

**KKCS-AM**
3515 N. Chestnut Street
Colorado Springs, CO 80907-4101
**Phone:** (719) 633-9200
**Fax:** (719) 667-1831
**E-mail:** webmaster@hottalk1460.com
http://www.hottalk1460.com
**Format:** Talk

**KKFM-FM**
6605 Corporate Drive
Suite 130
Colorado Springs, CO 80919-1977
**Phone:** (719) 593-2700
**Fax:** (719) 593-2727
http://kkfm.com
**Format:** Classic Rock

**KKLI-FM**
2864 S. Circle Drive
Suite 150
Colorado Springs, CO 80906
**Phone:** (719) 540-9200
**Fax:** (719) 579-0882
**E-mail:** kkli@kkli.com
http://www.kkli.com
**Format:** Adult Contemporary

**KKMG-FM**
6805 Corporate Drive
Suite 130
Colorado Springs, CO 80919-1977
**Phone:** (719) 593-2700
**Fax:** (719) 593-2727
http://989magicfm.com
**Format:** Contemporary Hit Radio
    (CHR), Urban Contemporary

**KKXK-FM**
Box 970
Montrose, CO 81402
**Phone:** (970) 249-4546
**Fax:** (970) 249-2229
**E-mail:** staff@kubckkxk.com
http://www.coloradoradio.com
**Format:** Contemporary Country

**KMSA-FM**
1175 Texas Avenue
Grand Junction, CO 81502
**Phone:** (970) 248-1240
**Fax:** (970) 248-1708
**E-mail:** jared@rustyhoot.com
http://www.kmsa.com
**Format:** Alternative, New Music,
    Progressive

**KMTS-FM**
1322 1/2 Grand
Glenwood Springs, CO 81601
**Phone:** (970) 945-9124
**Fax:** (970) 945-5409
**E-mail:** kmts@kmts.com
http://www.kmts.com
**Format:** Country

**KOA-AM**
4695 S. Monaco Street
Denver, CO 80237
**Phone:** (303) 713-8000
**Fax:** (303) 713-8424
http://www.850koa.com
**Format:** News, Talk, Sports

**KPAW-FM**
1612 Laporte Avenue
Fort Collins, CO 80521
**Phone:** (970) 482-5991
**Fax:** (970) 482-5994
**E-mail:** info@kpaw.com
http://www.kpaw.com
**Format:** Classic Rock

**KSIR-AM**
231 Main Street
Fort Morgan, CO 80701
**E-mail:** ksir@henge.com

http://www.ksir.com
**Format:** Sports, Talk, Agricultural

**KVOR-AM**
6805 Corporate Drive
Suite 130
Colorado Springs, CO 80919
**Phone:** (719) 593-2700
**Fax:** (719) 593-2727
http://kvor.com
**Format:** News, Talk

**KVRH-AM**
7600 County Road
Suite 120
Salida, CO 81201
**Phone:** (719) 539-2575
**Fax:** (719) 539-4851
**E-mail:** kvrh@kurh.com
http://www.kvrh.com

**KWUF-AM**
P.O. Box 780
Pagosa Springs, CO 81147
**Phone:** (970) 264-1400
**Fax:** (970) 264-1063
**E-mail:** kwuf@frontier.net
**Format:** Country, Talk, Sports

**KWYD-AM**
490 Willow Spring Road
Fountain, CO 80817-2722
**Phone:** (877) 612-7330 (toll-free)
**E-mail:** kwyd@email.com
http://www.kwyd.com
**Format:** Talk, Gospel, Religious

**KYBG-FM**
5660 Greenwood Plaza Boulevard
Suite 400
Englewood, CO 80111
**Phone:** (303) 721-9210
**Fax:** (303) 721-1435
**Format:** Sports, Talk

## CONNECTICUT

**WATR-AM**
1 Broadcast Lane
Waterbury, CT 06706
**Phone:** (203) 755-1121
**Fax:** (203) 574-3025
**Format:** News, Talk, Music of Your Life

**WAXK-FM**
7 Governor Winthrop Boulevard
New London, CT 06320
**Phone:** (860) 443-1980
**Fax:** (860) 444-7970

http://www.waxk.fm
**Format:** Alternative, New Music, Progressive

**WCCC-AM**
1039 Asylum Avenue
Hartford, CT 06105
**Phone:** (860) 525-1069 or
(866) 233-8468 (toll-free)
**Fax:** (860) 246-9084
http://www.beethoven.com
**Format:** Classical

**WCCC-FM**
1039 Asylum Avenue
Hartford, CT 06105
**Phone:** (860) 525-1069
**Fax:** (860) 246-9084
http://www.wccc.com
**Format:** Soft Rock

**WDRC-AM**
869 Blue Hills Avenue
Bloomfield, CT 06002
**Phone:** (860) 243-1115
**Fax:** (860) 286-8257
**E-mail:** mulligan@wdrc.com
http://www.wdrc.com
**Format:** Adult Contemporary, Sports

**WDRC-FM**
869 Blue Hills Avenue
Bloomfield, CT 06002
**Phone:** (860) 243-1115
**Fax:** (860) 286-8257
**E-mail:** mulligan@wdrc.com
http://www.drcfm.com
**Format:** Oldies

**WEBE-FM**
2 Lafayette Square
Bridgeport, CT 06604
**Phone:** (203) 333-9108 or
(800) WEB-E108 (toll-free)
**Fax:** (203) 333-9107
http://www.webe108.com
**Format:** Adult Contemporary

**WELI-AM**
495 Benham Street
Hamden, CT 06514
**Phone:** (203) 281-9600
**E-mail:** weli@weli.com

**WELI-AM**
495 Benham Street
Hamden, CT 06514
**Phone:** (203) 281-9600
**E-mail:** weli@weli.com
**Format:** News, Talk

**WEZN-FM**
440 Wheelers Farms Road
Suite 302
Milford, CT 06460
**Phone:** (203) 783-8200
**Fax:** (203) 783-8383
**E-mail:** star999.com
http://star999.com
**Format:** Adult Contemporary

**WFIF-AM**
90 Kay Avenue
Milford, CT 06460-5421
**Phone:** (203) 878-5915
**E-mail:** wfif@aol.com
http://www.lifechangingradio.com
**Format:** Religious, Talk

**WGCH-AM**
1490 Dayton Avenue
Greenwich, CT 06830-1490
**Phone:** (203) 869-1490
**Fax:** (203) 869-3636
**E-mail:** webmaster@wgch.com
http://www.wgcham.com
**Format:** News, Talk, Sports

**WGSK-FM**
1014 Monroe Turnpike
Monroe, CT 06468
**Phone:** (203) 268-9667
**E-mail:** staff@wmnr.org
http://wmnr.org
**Format:** Classical, Big Band, Nostalgia, Folk

**WHUS-FM**
Box U-8R
2110 Hillside Road
Storrs Mansfield, CT 06269-3008
**Phone:** (860) 486-4007
**Fax:** (860) 486-2955
**E-mail:** whusfm@uconnvm.uconn.edu
http://whusfm.sauf.uconn.edu
**Format:** Eclectic, Alternative, New Music, Progressive

**WKCI-FM**
P.O. Box 85
New Haven, CT 06501
**Phone:** (203) 248-8814
**Fax:** (203) 281-2795
http://www.kc101.com
**Format:** Contemporary Hit Radio

**WKWL-FM**
P.O. Box 1031
New London, CT 06320-1031
**Phone:** (860) 442-5328

**Fax:** (860) 442-6532
**E-mail:** wkwl@hallradio.com
http://www.kool101fm.com
**Format:** Oldies

**WLIS-AM**
77 Springbrook Road
P.O. Drawer W
Old Saybrook, CT 06475
**Phone:** (203) 388-1420
**Fax:** (203) 388-2931
**E-mail:** radio@wlis.com
http://www.wlis.com
**Format:** Full Service, News, Sports, Soft Rock

**WMRD-AM**
P.O. Box 1150
Middletown, CT 06457
**Phone:** (860) 347-9673
**Fax:** (860) 347-7704
**E-mail:** radio@wliswmrd.net
http://www.wliswmrd.net
**Format:** Full Service

**WNHU-FM**
300 Orange Avenue
West Haven, CT 06516
**Phone:** (203) 934-8888
**Fax:** (203) 931-6055
**E-mail:** wnhu@charger.newhaven.edu
http://www.wnhu.org
**Format:** New Age, Jazz, Ethnic, Folk, Heavy Metal, Alternative/New Music/Progressive, Rap

**WPKT-FM**
240 New Britain Avenue
P.O. Box 6240
Hartford, CT 06106
**Phone:** (860) 278-5310
**Fax:** (860) 244-9624
http://www.wnpr.org
**Format:** Public Radio, Classical

**WPLR-FM**
440 Wheelers Farms Road
Suite 302
Milford, CT 06460
**Phone:** (203) 783-8202
http://www.wplr.com
**Format:** Album-Oriented Rock (AOR)

**WQQQ-FM**
P.O. Box 446
Lakeville, CT 06039
**Phone:** (860) 435-3333 or
(877) 733-1033 (toll-free)
**Fax:** (860) 435-3334

**E-mail:** info@wqqq.com
http://www.wqqq.com
**Format:** Adult Contemporary

**WSUB-AM**
7 Governor Winthrop Boulevard
New London, CT 06320-4360
**Phone:** (860) 443-1980
**Fax:** (860) 444-7970
http://www.wsub.com
**Format:** Talk, News, Sports

**WSHU-FM**
5151 Park Avenue
Fairfield, CT 06432-1023
**Phone:** (203) 371-7989 or
    (800) 937-6045 (toll-free)
**Fax:** (203) 371-7991
http://www.wshu.org
**Format:** Public Radio, Classical, News,
    Folk, New Age

**WSUB-AM**
7 Governor Winthrop Boulevard
New London, CT 06320-4360
**Phone:** (860) 443-1980
**Fax:** (860) 444-7970
http://www.wsub.com
**Format:** Talk, News, Sports

**WWUH-FM**
200 Bloomfield Avenue
West Hartford, CT 06117
**Phone:** (860) 768-4703
**Fax:** (860) 768-5701
**E-mail:** wwuh@hartford.edu
http://www.wwuh.org
**Format:** Eclectic, Ethnic, News, Folk,
    Talk, Jazz

# DELAWARE

**WAFL-FM**
P.O. Box 808
Milford, DE 19963-0808
**Phone:** (302) 422-7575
**Fax:** (302) 422-3069
**E-mail:** staff@dol.net
http://www.eagle977.com
**Format:** Adult Contemporary

**WDEL-AM**
2727 Shipley Road
P.O. Box 7492
Wilmington, DE 19803
**Phone:** (302) 478-2700 or
    (800) 544-1150 (toll-free)
**Fax:** (302) 478-0100
**E-mail:** wdel@wdel.com

http://www.wdel.com
**Format:** News, Talk

**WDOV-AM**
5595 W. Denney's Road
Dover, DE 19904
**Phone:** (302) 674-1410
**Fax:** (302) 674-8621
**E-mail:** mail@wdov.com
**Format:** News, Talk

**WDSD-FM**
5595 Denneys Road
Dover, DE 19904-1362
**Phone:** (302) 734-5816
**Fax:** (302) 674-8621
**E-mail:** mail@wdsd.com
http://www.wdsd.com
**Format:** Country

**WDTS-AM**
Delaware Tech
P.O. Box 610
Georgetown, DE 19947
**Phone:** (302) 856-5400
**Fax:** (302) 858-5461
**Format:** Blues, Classic Rock

**WGMD-FM**
Box 530
Rehoboth Beach, DE 19971
**Phone:** (302) 945-2050
**Fax:** (302) 945-3781
**E-mail:** listen@wgmd.com
**Format:** Full Service

**WILM-AM**
1215 French Street
Wilmington, DE 19801
**Phone:** (302) 656-9800
**Fax:** (302) 655-1450
**Format:** News

**WJBR-FM**
3001 Philadelphia Pike
Claymont, DE 19703
**Phone:** (302) 765-1160 or
    (800) 275-9527 (toll-free)
**Fax:** (302) 765-1192
**E-mail:** info@wjbr.com
http://www.wjbr.com
**Format:** Adult Contemporary

**WJIC-AM**
704 N. King Street
Suite 604
Wilmington, DE 19801-3535
**E-mail:** wjic@water.waterw.com
http://www.delcom.com/wjicj
**Format:** News, Talk

**WJKS-FM**
First Federal Plaza Building
704 King Street
Suite 604
Wilmington, DE 19801
**Phone:** (302) 622-8895
**Fax:** (302) 622-8678
http://www.wjks1017.com
**Format:** Urban Contemporary

**WJPX-AM**
1039 S. Dual Hwy.
Seaford, DE 19973
**Phone:** (302) 629-6636
**Fax:** (302) 846-9898
**Format:** Adult Contemporary

**WJWL-AM**
701 N. Dupont Hwy.
Georgetown, DE 19947
**Phone:** (302) 856-2567
**Fax:** (302) 856-6839
**Format:** Big Band/Nostalgia

**WMPH-FM**
5201 Washington Street
Wilmington, DE 19809-2198
**Phone:** (302) 762-7199
**Fax:** (302) 762-7042
**E-mail:** radio@wmph.org;
    news@wmph.org
http://www.wmph.org

**WNRK-AM**
496 Walther Road
Box 8152
Newark, DE 19702
**Phone:** (302) 737-5200
**Fax:** (302) 737-7466
**Format:** Full Service, Oldies

**WYUS-AM**
P.O. Box 808
Milford, DE 19963
**Phone:** (302) 422-7575
**Fax:** (302) 422-3069
**Format:** Latino

**WMPH-FM**
5201 Washington Street
Wilmington, DE 19809-2198
**Phone:** (302) 762-7199
**Fax:** (302) 762-7042
**E-mail:** radio@wmph.org;
    news@wmph.org
http://www.wmph.org

**WOCM-FM**
P.O. Box 379
Selbyville, DE 19975

**Phone:** (302) 436-9725
**Fax:** (302) 436-9726
**E-mail:** ocean98wocm@netzero.net
**Format:** Adult Album Alternative

**WQVL-AM**
400 Walker Road
P.O. Box 553
Dover, DE 19901
**Phone:** (302) 730-1600
**Fax:** (302) 730-9398
**E-mail:** heaven 1600@juno.com
**Format:** Gospel, Religious

**WRDX-FM**
3001 Philadelphia Drive
Claymont, DE 19703
**Phone:** (302) 792-9739 or
    (888) 383-9739 (toll-free)
**Fax:** (302) 792-8329
**E-mail:** mail@wrdx.com
http://www.wrdx.com
**Format:** Classic Rock

**WRKE-FM**
Q-Tone Broadcasting Corp.
63 Atlantic Avenue
Rte. 1, Box 24
Ocean View, DE 19970-9801
**Phone:** (302) 539-2600
**Format:** Top 40

**WSTW-FM**
2727 Shipley Road
P.O. Box 7492
Wilmington, DE 19803
**Phone:** (302) 478-2700 or
    (800) 544-9370 (toll-free)
**Fax:** (302) 478-0100
**E-mail:** wstw@wstw.com
http://www.wstw.com

**WVUD-FM**
University of Delaware
Perkins Student Center
Newark, DE 19716
**Phone:** (302) 831-2701
**Fax:** (302) 831-1399
**E-mail:** wvudmusic@udel.edu;
    ud-wvud@udel.edu
http://www.wvud.org
**Format:** Eclectic, Full Service

**WSUX-FM**
1039 S. Dual Hwy.
Seaford, DE 19973
**Phone:** (302) 629-6636
**Fax:** (302) 846-9898
**Format:** Adult Contemporary

**WVUD-FM**
University of Delaware
Perkins Student Center
Newark, DE 19716
**Phone:** (302) 831-2701
**Fax:** (302) 831-1399
**E-mail:** wvudmusic@udel.edu,
    ud-wvud@udel.edu
http://www.wvud.org
**Format:** Eclectic, Full Service

**WXPZ-FM**
P.O. Box K
Milford, DE 19963
**Phone:** (302) 424-1013 or
    (800) 314-1013 (toll-free)
**Fax:** (302) 424-2358
**E-mail:** lightfm@wxpz.com
http://www.wxpz.com
**Format:** Contemporary Christian

**WYUS-AM**
P.O. Box 808
Milford, DE 19963
**Phone:** (302) 422-7575
**Fax:** (302) 422-3069
**Format:** Latino

# DISTRICT OF COLUMBIA

**WAMU-FM**
American University/Brandywine
    Building
Washington, DC 20016-8082
**Phone:** (202) 885-1200
**E-mail:** feedback@wamu.org
**Format:** News, Information, Talk, Folk,
    Bluegrass

**WASH-FM**
3400 Idaho Avenue, NW
Washington, DC 20016
**Phone:** (202) 895-5000
**Fax:** (202) 895-5103
**Format:** Adult Contemporary

**WDCU-FM**
4200 Connecticut Avenue, NW
Washington, DC 20008
**Phone:** (202) 274-5090
**Fax:** (202) 274-6174
**Format:** Jazz, Public Radio

**WETH-FM**
P.O. Box 2626
Washington, DC 20013
http://www.weta.org
**Format:** Public Radio Classical News

**WGMS-FM**
3400 Idaho Avenue, NW
Washington, DC 20016-3069
**Phone:** (202) 895-5000
**Fax:** (202) 895-4168
**E-mail:** classical@wgms.com
http://www.wgms.com
**Format:** Classical

**WHUR-FM**
529 Bryant Street, NW
Washington, DC 20059
**Phone:** (202) 806-3500
**Fax:** (202) 806-3522
**Format:** Urban Contemporary, Adult
    Contemporary

**WJZW-FM**
4400 Jenifer Street, NW
Washington, DC 20015-2113
**Phone:** (202) 686-3100
**Format:** Jazz

**WKYS-FM**
4001 Nebraska Avenue, NW
Washington, DC 20016-2733
**Phone:** (202) 686-9300
**Fax:** (202) 686-2028
**Format:** Adult Contemporary,
    Contemporary Hit Radio (CHR)

**WMAL-AM**
4400 Jenifer Street, NW
Washington, DC 20015-2113
**Phone:** (202) 686-3100
**Fax:** (202) 537-0009
**Format:** Full Service

**WMMJ-FM**
400 H Street, NE
Washington, DC 20002
**Phone:** (202) 675-4800
**Fax:** (202) 675-4842
**Format:** Oldies

**WPFW-FM**
2390 Champlain Street, NW, 2nd Floor
Washington, DC 20009
**Phone:** (202) 588-0999
**Fax:** (202) 588-0561
**E-mail:** bmwpfw@aol.com
**Format:** Jazz, Ethnic, News

**WQPO-FM**
P.O. Box 752
Harrisonburg, VA 22801
**Phone:** (540) 434-0331
**Fax:** (540) 434-7087
**E-mail:** wqpo@valley.radio.com
**Format:** Adult Contemporary

**WRQX-FM**
4400 Jenifer Street, NW
Washington, DC 20015-2113
**Phone:** (202) 686-3100
**Fax:** (202) 364-9668
**Format:** Adult Contemporary

**WTOP-AM**
3400 Idaho Avenue, NW
Washington, DC 20016-3046
**Phone:** (202) 895-5000
**Fax:** (202) 895-5140
**Format:** News, Sports

**WYCB-AM**
1025 Vermont Avenue, NW
Suite 1030
Washington, DC 20005
**Phone:** (202) 737-6400
**Fax:** (202) 638-3027
**Format:** Gospel, Religious

**WZHF-AM**
5513 Connecticut Avenue, NW
Washington, DC 20015
**Phone:** (202) 362-8330
**Fax:** (202) 966-2679
**Format:** Country

# FLORIDA

**WAFC-FM**
116 Commercio Street
P.O. Box 2109
Clewiston, FL 33440
**Phone:** (813) 983-6106
**Fax:** (813) 983-6109
**E-mail:** robbiec@gate.net
http://www.radiofiesta.com
**Format:** Contemporary Country

**WAJD-AM**
7120 SW 24th Avenue
Gainesville, FL 32607-3705
**Phone:** (352) 331-2200 or (800) 330-1053
 (toll-free)
**Fax:** (352) 331-0401
**E-mail:** kiss1053@aol.com
http://www.kiss1053
**Format:** Public Radio

**WAMR-AM**
282 N. Auburn Road
Venice, FL 34292
**Phone:** (941) 480-9267
**Fax:** (941) 488-4159
http://www.1320wamr.com
**Format:** Sports

**WAMR-FM**
2828 Coral Way
Miami, FL 33145-3204
**Phone:** (305) 441-2073
**Fax:** (305) 445-8908
**E-mail:** info@wamr.com
http://www.wamr.com
**Format:** Adult Contemporary, Ethnic,
 Latino

**WAMT-AM**
3909 Champion Road
Titusville, FL 32796
**Phone:** (407) 264-1060
**Format:** News, Talk

**WAPE-FM**
9090 Hogan Road
Jacksonville, FL 32216-4648
**Phone:** (904) 642-1055
**Fax:** (904) 641-3297
**E-mail:** wape951.com
http://www.wape951.com
**Format:** Contemporary Hit Radio
 (CHR)

**WAVS-AM**
6360 SW 41st Place
Davie, FL 33314
**Phone:** (954) 584-1170 or
 (888) 854-9660 (toll-free)
**Fax:** (954) 581-6441
**E-mail:** isd@wavs1170.com
http://www.wavs1170.com
**Format:** Ethnic

**WAXE-AM**
P.O. Box 850093
Port St. Lucie, FL 34985-0093
**Phone:** (561) 567-1055
**Fax:** (561) 595-0214
**E-mail:** waxe@bloomberg.net
**Format:** News, Talk

**WBGG-FM**
194 NW 187th Street
Miami, FL 33169
**Phone:** (305) 654-9494
http://www.big106.com
**Format:** Classic Rock

**WBZE-FM**
P.O. Box 3168
Tallahassee, FL 32315-3168
**Phone:** (850) 201-3000
**Fax:** (850) 561-8903
http://www.989breeze.com
**Format:** Adult Contemporary

**WBZT-AM**
4763 10th Avenue N.
P.O. Box 20389
West Palm Beach, FL 33416
**Phone:** (407) 965-9211
**Fax:** (407) 965-9233
**Format:** News, Talk, Sports

**WCCF-AM**
4810 Deltona Drive
Punta Gorda, FL 33950
**Phone:** (813) 639-1188 or (800) 749-9290
 (toll-free)
**Fax:** (813) 639-6742
**Format:** Talk

**WCOA-AM**
P.O. Box 12487
Pensacola, FL 32573-2487
**Phone:** (904) 478-6011
**Fax:** (904) 478-3971
**Format:** News, Talk

**WCRM-AM**
3448 Canal Street
Fort Myers, FL 33916-6513
**Phone:** (941) 332-1350
**Fax:** (941) 332-8890
**Format:** Gospel, Ethnic

**WDBO-AM**
4192 John Young Pkwy.
Orlando, FL 32804
**Phone:** (407) 295-5858
**Fax:** (407) 291-4879
**Format:** Talk, News, Sports

**WDCF-AM**
37905 WDCF Drive
Dade City, FL 33525
**Phone:** (904) 567-1350
**Fax:** (904) 567-5532
**Format:** Country

**WDSR-AM**
3507 S. Marion Street
P.O. Box 3299
Lake City, FL 32056
**Phone:** (904) 752-1340
**Fax:** (904) 755-9369
**E-mail:** wnfb@mix943.com
http://www.mix943.com
**Format:** Sports, Talk

**WEBY-AM**
7179 Printers Alley
Milton, FL 32583
**Phone:** (850) 983-2242
**Fax:** (850) 983-3231
**Format:** News, Talk

**WELE-AM**
432 S. Nova Road
Ormond Beach, FL 32174
**Phone:** (904) 677-4122
**Fax:** (904) 677-4123
**E-mail:** info@wele.com
http://www.wele.com
**Format:** Sports, News, Talk

**WENG-AM**
1355 S. River Road
P.O. Box 2908
Englewood, FL 34295
**Phone:** (941) 474-3231
**Fax:** (941) 475-2205
**E-mail:** radio@thewave1530am.com
**Format:** Talk, News, Sports

**WEOW-FM**
5450 MacDonald Avenue
Key West, FL 33041-2523
**Phone:** (305) 296-7511
**Fax:** (305) 296-0358
**E-mail:** info@keysradio.net
http://www.keysradio.net
**Format:** Contemporary Hit Radio (CHR)

**WFLA-AM**
4002A Gandy Boulevard
Tampa, FL 33611
**Phone:** (813) 839-9393
**Fax:** (813) 831-3299
http://970wfla.com
**Format:** News, Talk

**WFLZ-FM**
4002A Gandy Boulevard
Tampa, FL 33611
**Phone:** (813) 839-9393
**Fax:** (813) 831-3299
http://www.933flz.com
**Format:** Contemporary Hit Radio (CHR)

**WFOY-AM**
1 Radio Road
St. Augustine, FL 32084
**Phone:** (904) 829-3416
**Fax:** (904) 829-8051
**E-mail:** wfoy@aug.com
**Format:** Talk, News

**WFSQ-FM**
1600 Red Barber Plaza
Tallahassee, FL 32310
**Phone:** (904) 487-3086 or
    (800) 829-8809 (toll-free)
**Fax:** (904) 487-3293
**E-mail:** wfsufm@wfsu.org
http://www.wfsu.org
**Format:** Classical

**WFTW-AM**
P.O. Box 2347
Fort Walton Beach, FL 32549-2347
**Phone:** (850) 243-7676
**Fax:** (850) 664-0203
**E-mail:** wftw@radiopeople.net
http://www.wftw.com
**Format:** News, Talk, Information

**WFYV-FM**
9090 Hogan Road
Jacksonville, FL 32216-4648
**Phone:** (904) 642-1055
**Fax:** (904) 641-3297
**E-mail:** rock@wfyv105.com
http://www.wfyvi.com
**Format:** Classic Rock

**WNDB-AM**
126 W. International Speedway Boulevard
Daytona Beach, FL 32114
**Phone:** (904) 257-1150
**Fax:** (904) 239-0966
http://www.wndb.com
**Format:** Talk, News, Sports

**WKIQ-AM**
14624 US Highway 441
Tavares, FL 32778-4315
**Phone:** (352) 357-1240
**Fax:** (352) 357-4250
http://www.wkiq.com,
    http://www.graveline.com
**Format:** Talk, News, Sports

# GEORGIA

**WABE-FM**
740 Bismark Road, NE
Atlanta, GA 30324-4102
**Phone:** (678) 686-0321
**Fax:** (678) 686-0356
http://www.wabe.org
**Format:** Public Radio, News, Classical

**WCLK-FM**
111 James P. Brawley Drive, SW
Atlanta, GA 30314-4207
**Phone:** (404) 880-8273
**Fax:** (404) 880-8869
http://www.cau-wclk.com
**Format:** Public Radio, Jazz

**WKLS-FM**
1819 Peachtree Road, NE
Suite 700
Atlanta, GA 30309-1849
**Phone:** (404) 325-0960
**Fax:** (404) 325-8715
**E-mail:** 96rock.com

http://www.96rock.com
**Format:** Album-Oriented Rock (AOR),
    Classic Rock

**WKXC-FM**
1776 Briarcliff Road, NE
Atlanta, GA 30306
http://www.kicks99.com
**Format:** Country

**WLTA-AM**
2970 Peachtree Road, NW
Suite 700
Atlanta, GA 30305
**Phone:** (404) 365-0970
**Fax:** (404) 816-0748
**E-mail:** wniv@wniv.com
http://www.wniv.com
**Format:** Talk

**WDMG-AM**
620 E. Ward Street
Douglas, GA 31533-3915
**Phone:** (912) 389-0995
**Fax:** (912) 383-8552
**Format:** News, Talk, Sports, Classic Rock

**WMJE-FM**
P.O. Box 10
Gainesville, GA 30503
**Phone:** (770) 532-9921 or
    (800) 273-0103 (toll-free)
**Fax:** (770) 532-0506
**E-mail:** radiocenter@applied.com
http://www.wdun.com
**Format:** Adult Contemporary

**WNIV-AM**
2970 Peachtree Road
Suite 700
Atlanta, GA 30305
**Phone:** (404) 365-0970
**Fax:** (404) 816-0748
**E-mail:** wniv@wniv.com
http://www.wniv.com
**Format:** Talk

**WOBB-FM**
P.O. Box 3106
Albany, GA 31706-3106
**Phone:** (912) 439-9704 or
    (800) 567-1003 (toll-free)
**Fax:** (912) 439-1509
http://www.bloowobb.com
**Format:** Country

**WNNX-FM**
780 Johnson Ferry Road, NE, Floor 5
Atlanta, GA 30342-1436

Phone: (404) 266-0997
Fax: (404) 364-5855
http://www.com/99X
Format: Alternative/New
     Music/Progressive

**WPAX-AM**
117 Remington Avenue
Thomasville, GA 31792
Phone: (912) 226-1240
Fax: (912) 226-1361
E-mail: lenrob@rose.net
http://www.wpaxradio.com
Format: News, Middle-of-the-Road
     (MOR), Big Band/Nostalgia, Easy
     Listening

**WPCH-FM**
1819 Peachtree Road, NE
Suite 700
Atlanta, GA 30309
Phone: (404) 367-0949
Fax: (404) 362-9490
http://www.peach949.com
Format: Soft Rock

**WQBZ-FM**
7080 Industrial Hwy.
Macon, GA 31206-7538
Phone: (912) 781-1063
Fax: (912) 781-6711
E-mail: taylor@hom.net
http://q106.fm
Format: Album-Oriented Rock (AOR)

**WQXI-AM**
1 Capital City Plaza
3350 Peachtree Road
Penthouse Suite
Atlanta, GA 30326
Phone: (404) 261-2970
Fax: (404) 365-9026
E-mail: inewkirk@wqxi.com
http://www.wqxi.com
Format: Sports, Talk

**WRFC-AM**
1010 Tower Place
Bogart, GA 30622
Phone: (706) 549-6222
Fax: (706) 353-1967
E-mail: athens96@aol.com
http://www.wrfc.com
Format: News, Talk, Sports

**WRHQ-FM**
110 E. June Street
Savannah, GA 31404
Phone: (912) 234-1053

Fax: (912) 354-6600
E-mail: qualityrockatwrhq.com
http://www.wrhq.com
Format: Adult Contemporary

**WRLD-FM**
1353 13th Avenue
Columbus, GA 31901-2347
Phone: (706) 596-4627 or
     (877) WRLD-953 (toll-free)
Fax: (706) 596-4600
http://www.wrldfm.com
Format: Oldies

**WSTE-FM**
340 Jesse Jewell Pky.
Suite 525
Gainesville, GA 30501
Phone: (770) 534-8106
Fax: (770) 534-2614
http://www.south106.com
Format: Country

**WSTR-FM**
3350 Peachtree Road
Penthouse Suite
Atlanta, GA 30326
Phone: (404) 261-2970
Fax: (404) 365-9026
http://www.star94.com
Format: Contemporary Hit Radio (CHR)

**WZGC-FM**
1100 Johnson Ferry Road
Suite 593
Atlanta, GA 30342
Phone: (404) 851-9393
Fax: (404) 843-3541
E-mail: zmail@z93.com
http://www.293.com
Format: Classic Rock

**WEAS-AM**
2515 Abercorn Street
Savannah, GA 31401
Phone: (912) 234-7264
Fax: (912) 233-7247
E-mail: thefan@weas.com
http://www.weas.com
Format: Sports, Talk

**WDUN-AM**
1102 Thompson Bridge Road
P.O. Box 10
Gainesville, GA 30503
Phone: (770) 532-9921 or
     (800) 552-WDUN (toll-free)
Fax: (770) 532-0506
E-mail: radiocenter@applied.com

http://www.wdun.com
Format: News, Talk, Sports

**WGOR-FM**
P.O. Box 211045
Augusta, GA 30917-1594
Phone: (706) 855-9494
Fax: (706) 860-9343
E-mail: wqac@wqac.com
http://www.gabn.net/coolfm
Format: Oldies

**WJCL-FM**
214 Television Circle
Savannah, GA 31406-4519
Phone: (912) 921-0965 or
     (800) 365-0549 (toll-free)
Fax: (912) 921-2218
E-mail: kix96@wce.com
http://www.kix965.com
Format: Country, Hot Country

**WKLS-FM**
1819 Peachtree Road, NE
Suite 700
Atlanta, GA 30309-1849
Phone: (404) 325-0960
Fax: (404) 325-8715
http://www.96rock.com
Format: Album-Oriented Rock (AOR),
     Classic Rock

# HAWAII

**KAIM-AM**
560 N. Nimitz Hwy.
Suite 109
Honolulu, HI 96817-5330
Phone: (808) 533-0065 or
     (800) 435-5246 (toll-free)
Fax: (808) 524-2104

**KAIM-FM**
560 N. Nimitz Hwy.
Suite 109
Honolulu, HI 96817-5330
E-mail: kaim@kaimradio.org
Format: Contemporary Christian

**KAOI-FM**
1900 Main Street
Wailuku, HI 96793-1707
Phone: (808) 244-9145
Format: Album-Oriented Rock (AOR),
     Contemporary Hit Radio (CHR)

**KAQA-FM**
P.O. Box 825
Hanalei, HI 96714

**Phone:** (808) 826-7774
**Fax:** (808) 826-7977
**E-mail:** kkcr@hawaiian.net
http://www.kkcr.org
**Format:** Public Radio

**KCCN-AM**
900 Fort Street
Suite 700
Honolulu, HI 96813
**Phone:** (808) 536-2728
**Format:** Ethnic

**KCCN-FM**
900 Fort Street
Suite 400
Honolulu, HI 96813
**Phone:** (808) 536-2728
**Fax:** (808) 536-2528
**E-mail:** kccn@kestrok.com
http://www.kestrok.com/~kccn
**Format:** Ethnic, Adult Contemporary,
    Eclectic, Reggae, Hawaiian

**KCIF-FM**
P.O. Box 1060
Hilo, HI 96721
**Phone:** (808) 935-7434
**Fax:** (808) 961-6022
http://home1.gte.net/keif/index.htm
**Format:** Religious

**KFMN-FM**
P.O. Box 1566
Lihue, HI 96766-5566
**Phone:** (808) 246-1197
**Fax:** (808) 246-9697
**E-mail:** kfmn@gte.net
**Format:** Adult Contemporary

**KGU-AM**
560 N. Nimitz Hwy.
Suite 114-13
Honolulu, HI 96817
**Phone:** (808) 533-0065
**Fax:** (808) 528-5467
**E-mail:** admin@kgu.com
http://www.kgu.com
**Format:** Sports

**KHLO-AM**
913 Kanuelehua
Hilo, HI 96720-5116
**Phone:** (808) 935-1952
**Fax:** (808) 935-0396
**Format:** Oldies

**KHPR-FM**
738 Kaheka Street
Honolulu, HI 96814

**Phone:** (808) 955-8821
**Fax:** (808) 942-5477
**E-mail:** hpr@lava.net
**Format:** Information, Classical

**KHWI-FM**
688 Kinoole Street
Hilo, HI 96720
**Phone:** (808) 935-6858
**Fax:** (808) 969-7949
**Format:** Album-Oriented Rock (AOR)

**KIFO-AM**
738 Kaheka Street
Honolulu, HI 96814
**Phone:** (808) 955-8821
**Fax:** (808) 942-5477
**E-mail:** lpr@lcva.net
**Format:** News, Information

**KIKI-AM**
650 Iwilei Road
Suite 400
Honolulu, HI 96817-5319
**Phone:** (808) 531-4602
**Fax:** (808) 531-4606
**Format:** Contemporary Hit Radio (CHR)

**KIKI-FM**
650 Iwilei Road
Suite 400
Honolulu, HI 96817-5319
**Phone:** (808) 531-4602
**Fax:** (808) 531-4606
**Format:** Contemporary Hit Radio (CHR)

**KIPA-AM**
688 Kinoole Street
Hilo, HI 96720
**Phone:** (808) 935-6858
**Fax:** (808) 969-7949
**Format:** Middle-of-the-Road (MOR)

**KIPO-FM**
738 Kaheka Street
Honolulu, HI 96814
**Phone:** (808) 955-8821
**Fax:** (808) 942-5477
**E-mail:** hpr@lpr@lava.net
**Format:** Classical, Information, Jazz

**KISA-AM**
904 Kohou Street
Suite 204
Honolulu, HI 96817
**Phone:** (808) 841-4555
**Fax:** (808) 841-4855
**Format:** Adult Contemporary, Ethnic

**KKBG-FM**
913 Kanoelehua Avenue
Hilo, HI 96720
**Phone:** (808) 961-0651
**Fax:** (808) 935-0396
**Format:** Contemporary Hit Radio
    (CHR), Adult Contemporary

**KKCR-FM**
P.O. Box 825
Hanalei, HI 96714
**Phone:** (808) 826-7774
**Fax:** (808) 876-7977
**E-mail:** kkcr@hawaiian.net
http://www.kkcr.org
**Format:** Public Radio

**KKUA-FM**
738 Kaheka Street
Honolulu, HI 96814
**Phone:** (808) 955-8821
**Fax:** (808) 942-5477
**E-mail:** hpr@lava.net
**Format:** Public Radio, Classical, News

**KLHT-AM**
1190 Nuuanu Avenue
Honolulu, HI 96817
**Phone:** (808) 524-1040
**Fax:** (808) 524-0998
**E-mail:** klht@hawaii.rr.com
**Format:** Religious

**KLHT-AM**
1190 Nuuanu Avenue
Honolulu, HI 96817
**Phone:** (808) 524-1040
**Fax:** (808) 524-0998
**E-mail:** klht@hawaii.rr.com
**Format:** Religious

**KMVI-AM**
311 Ano Street
Kahului, HI 96732-1304
**Phone:** (808) 877-5566
**Fax:** (808) 877-2137
**Format:** Adult Contemporary, Ethnic,
    Religious

**KMVI-FM**
311 Ano Street
Kahului, HI 96732-1304
**Phone:** (808) 877-5566
**Fax:** (808) 877-2137
**Format:** Classic Rock

**KNDI-AM**
1734 S. King Street
Honolulu, HI 96826

**Phone:** (808) 946-2844 or
   (800) 649-5634 (toll-free)
**Fax:** (808) 947-3531
**Format:** Ethnic, Religious

**KNUI-AM**
311 Ano Street
Kahului, HI 96732-1304
**Phone:** (808) 877-5566
**Fax:** (808) 871-0666
**Format:** Adult Contemporary, News,
   Sports

**KNUI-FM**
311 Ano Street
Kahului, HI 96732-1304
**Phone:** (808) 877-5566
**Fax:** (808) 871-0666
**Format:** Adult Contemporary

**KODB-FM**
1833 Kalakaua Avenue
Street 500
Honolulu, HI 96815
**Phone:** (808) 591-9369
**Fax:** (808) 591-9349
**Format:** Contemporary Hit Radio (CHR)

**KOHO-AM**
500 Ala Moana Boulevard
Suite 400
Honolulu, HI 96813
**Phone:** (808) 585-8899
**Fax:** (808) 951-1170
**Format:** Oldies

**KPOA-FM**
311 Ano Street
Kahului, HI 96732
**Phone:** (808) 877-5566
**Fax:** (808) 871-0666
**E-mail:** kpoa@mauigateway.com
http://kpoa.com
**Format:** Ethnic

**KPOI-FM**
1833 Kalakaua Avenue
Suite 500
Honolulu, HI 96815
**Phone:** (808) 591-9369
**Fax:** (808) 591-9349
**E-mail:** http://www.kpoi.net
**Format:** Alternative/New
   Music/Progressive

**KQMQ-FM**
711 Kapiolani Boulevard
Suite 1193
Honolulu, HI 96814

**Phone:** (808) 591-9369
**Fax:** (808) 591-9349
**E-mail:** kqmqaatshula.net
**Format:** Contemporary Hit Radio (CHR)

# IDAHO

**KACH-AM**
1133 E. Glendale Road
Preston, ID 83263
**Phone:** (208) 852-1340
**Fax:** (208) 852-1342
**E-mail:** kach@nstep.net
**Format:** Oldies

**KADQ-FM**
90 S. First W.
Box 66
Rexburg, ID 83440
**Phone:** (208) 356-7323
**Fax:** (208) 356-7324
**E-mail:** kadq@cyberhighway.net
**Format:** Adult Contemporary, News,
   Sports

**KATW-FM**
403 C Street
Lewiston, ID 83501
**Phone:** (208) 743-6564
**Fax:** (208) 798-0110
**Format:** Adult Contemporary

**KAWZ-FM**
4002 N. 3300 E.
Kimberly, ID 83341
**Phone:** (208) 734-4357 or (800) 357-4226
   (toll-free)
**Fax:** (208) 736-1958
**E-mail:** csn@calvarychapel.com
**Format:** Religious, Contemporary
   Christian

**KBBK-AM**
120 South 300 West
Rupert, ID 83350
**Phone:** (208) 436-4757
**Fax:** (208) 436-3050
**E-mail:** supertalk1230@hotmail.com
**Format:** Public Radio

**KBGN-AM**
3303 E. Chicago
Caldwell, ID 83605
**Phone:** (208) 459-3635
**E-mail:** kbgn@kbgnradio.com
**Format:** Religious

**KBOI-AM**
1419 W. Bannock
Boise, ID 83702

**Phone:** (208) 336-3670 or
   (800) 649-3670 (toll-free)
**Fax:** (208) 336-3734
**Format:** Full Service, Adult Contemporary

**KBRV-AM**
P.O. Box 777
Soda Springs, ID 83276-0777
**Phone:** (208) 547-4012
**Fax:** (208) 547-3775
**Format:** Country, Talk, News, Sports

**KBSM-FM**
c/o KBSU-FM
Boise State University
1910 University Drive
Boise, ID 83725
**Phone:** (208) 426-3663
**Fax:** (208) 344-6631
http://www.idbsu.edu/bsuradio
**Format:** Public Radio, Classical, News

**KBSY-FM**
1910 University Drive
Boise, ID 83725
**Phone:** (208) 426-3663
**Fax:** (208) 344-6631
http://www.idbsu.edu/bsuradio
**Format:** News, Information

**KBXL-FM**
1477 S. Five Mile Road
Boise, ID 83709-1308
**Phone:** (208) 377-3790
**Fax:** (208) 377-3792
**Format:** Contemporary Christian, Talk

**KCDA-FM**
2211 E. Sprague
Spokane, WA 99202
**Phone:** (509) 534-3636
**Fax:** (509) 534-7640
Contact: John H. Rook
**Format:** Country

**KCID-AM**
P.O. Box 968
Caldwell, ID 83606-0968
**Phone:** (208) 459-3608
**Fax:** (208) 454-1490
**Format:** Adult Contemporary, Sports,
   Latino

**KCIR-FM**
1446 Filer Avenue, E.
Twin Falls, ID 83301-4121
**Phone:** (208) 734-5777
**Fax:** (208) 734-0331
http://www.sosnetwork.org

**Format:** Talk, Educational, Adult
  Contemporary, Religious

**KCIX-FM**
827 Park Boulevard
Suite 201
Boise, ID 83712-7782
**Phone:** (208) 344-6363
**Fax:** (208) 385-7385
**Format:** Adult Contemporary

**KCLK-AM**
403 C Street
Lewiston, ID 83501
**Phone:** (208) 743-6564
**Fax:** (208) 798-0110
**E-mail:** Kclkam@aol.com;
  bike2426@aol.com
**Format:** Sports, Talk

**KFXD-AM**
1109 Main Street
Boise, ID 83702
**Phone:** (208) 344-6363
http://www.kfxd.com
**Format:** Country

**KGEM-AM**
5601 Cassia
Boise, ID 83705
**Phone:** (208) 344-3511
**Fax:** (208) 336-3264
**Format:** Big Band/Nostalgia, Oldies

**KIZN-FM**
1419 W. Bannock
Boise, ID 83702
**Phone:** (208) 336-3670 or
  (800) 574-9292 (toll-free)
**Fax:** (208) 336-3734
**E-mail:** justiceid@efortress.com
http://www.kizn.com
**Format:** Contemporary Country

**KJOT-FM**
5601 Cassia
Boise, ID 83705
**Phone:** (208) 344-3511
**Fax:** (208) 336-3264
http://www.j105.com
**Format:** Classic Rock

**KKGL-FM**
1419 West Bannock Street
Boise, ID 83702
**Phone:** (208) 336-3670
**Fax:** (208) 336-3736
http://www.kkgl.com
**Format:** Classic Rock

**KLCE-FM**
765 S. Woodruff
Box 51097
Idaho Falls, ID 83405
**Phone:** (208) 522-5523
**Fax:** (208) 785-0184
**E-mail:** klce-jb@srv.net
**Format:** Adult Contemporary

**KLER-AM**
Box 32
Orofino, ID 83544
**Phone:** (208) 476-5702
**Fax:** (208) 476-5703
**E-mail:** klerorofino@clearwater.net
**Format:** Country

**KLIX-AM**
415 Park Avenue
P.O. Box 1259
Twin Falls, ID 83303-1259
**Phone:** (208) 733-7512
**Fax:** (208) 733-7525
**Format:** Talk, News

**KLLP-FM**
259 Contor Avenue
Idaho Falls, ID 83401
**Phone:** (208) 524-5900
http://www.kllp.com
**Format:** Soft Rock, Adult Contemporary

**KLTB-FM**
827 E. Park Boulevard
Suite 201
Boise, ID 83712
**Phone:** (208) 344-6363
**Fax:** (208) 385-7385
**Format:** Oldies

**KOFC-FM**
1419 W. Bannock
Boise, ID 83702
**Phone:** (208) 336-3670
**Fax:** (208) 336-3734
http://www.98kqfc.com
**Format:** Contemporary Country

**KUOI-FM**
University of Idaho
Student Union Building
Moscow, ID 83843
**Phone:** (208) 885-6433
**Fax:** (208) 885-2222
**E-mail:** kuoi@uidaho.edu
http://kuoi.com
**Format:** Alternative/New
  Music/Progressive

**KXLT-FM**
1109 Main Street
Suite 570
Boise, ID 83702
**Phone:** (208) 376-6363
http://www.lite108.com
**Format:** Adult Contemporary, Soft Rock

**KZMG-FM**
1419 W. Bannock
Boise, ID 83702
**Phone:** (208) 336-3670
**Fax:** (208) 336-3734
http://www.kzmg.com
**Format:** Adult Contemporary

## ILLINOIS

**WAUG-FM**
Augustana College
639-38th Street
Rock Island, IL 61201
**Phone:** (309) 794-7513
**Fax:** (309) 794-7511
http://search.augustana.edu/augieweb/
  campus/studentorgs/waug
**Format:** Eclectic

**WBNQ-FM**
P.O. Box 8
236 Greenwood Avenue
Bloomington, IL 61702
**Phone:** (309) 829-1221
**Fax:** (309) 827-8071
http://www.wbnq.com
**Format:** Adult Contemporary

**WBVN-FM**
P.O. Box 1126
Marion, IL 62959
**Phone:** (618) 997-1500
**Fax:** (618) 997-3194
**E-mail:** wbvn@midwest.net
http://www.wbvn.org
**Format:** Adult Contemporary, Religious

**WBWN-FM**
236 Greenwood Avenue
Bloomington, IL 61704
**Phone:** (309) 829-1221
**Fax:** (309) 662-8598
**E-mail:** wbwn@wbwn.com
http://www.wbwn.com
**Format:** Hot Country

**WCBU-FM**
1501 W. Bradley Avenue
Peoria, IL 61625
**Phone:** (309) 677-3690

**Fax:** (309) 677-3462
**E-mail:** wcbu@bradley.edu
http://www.bradley.edu/irt/wcbu
**Format:** Public Radio, Classical, News

**WCCQ-FM**
1520 N. Rock Run Drive
Joliet, IL 60435
**Phone:** (815) 729-4400
**Fax:** (815) 729-4444
**E-mail:** fmwccq@aol.com
http://www.wccq.com
**Format:** Country, Contemporary Country

**WCFL-FM**
1802 N. Division Street
Suite 403
Morris, IL 60450
**Phone:** (815) 942-4400 or
    (800) 520-WCFL (toll-free)
**Fax:** (815) 942-4401
**E-mail:** wcfl@xnet.com
http://www.wcfl.com
**Format:** Contemporary Christian

**WCIC-FM**
3263 Court Street
Pekin, IL 61554
**Phone:** (309) 353-9191
**Fax:** (309) 353-1141
**E-mail:** wcic@dpc.net
http://www.wcicfm.com
**Format:** News

**WCKG-FM**
2 Prudential Plaza
Suite 1059
Chicago, IL 60601
**Phone:** (312) 240-7900
**Fax:** (312) 565-3181
**Format:** Talk

**WDBX-FM**
224 N. Washington
Carbondale, IL 62901
**Phone:** (618) 529-5900
**Fax:** (618) 529-3692
**E-mail:** wdbx@globaleyes.net
http://www.wdbx.org
**Format:** Eclectic

**WDCB-FM**
College of DuPage
425 22nd Street
Glen Ellyn, IL 60137
**Phone:** (630) 942-4200
**Fax:** (630) 942-2788
http://www.cod.edu/wdcb
**Format:** Public Radio, Folk, Jazz, News

**WDMJ-AM**
P.O. Box 700
845 W. Washington Street
Marquette, MI 49855
**Phone:** (906) 225-1313
**Fax:** (906) 225-1324
http://www.wjpd.com
**Format:** News, Talk, Sports

**WDNL-FM**
1501 N. Washington
Danville, IL 61832
**Phone:** (217) 442-1700
**Fax:** (217) 431-1489
**E-mail:** carolw@soltec.net
http://www.wdnlfm.com
**Format:** Adult Contemporary

**WDWS-AM**
2301 S. Neil Street Road
Box 3939
Champaign, IL 61826-3939
**Phone:** (217) 351-5300
**Fax:** (217) 351-5385
**E-mail:** wdws@prairienet.org
http://www.wdws.com
**Format:** Talk, News, Sports

**WEAI-FM**
E. Old State Road
P.O. Box 1180
Jacksonville, IL 62650
**Phone:** (217) 243-2800
http://www.weai.com
**Format:** Oldies, Adult Contemporary

**WEFT-FM**
113 N. Market Street
Champaign, IL 61820-4004
**Phone:** (217) 359-9338
**E-mail:** weft@prairienet.org
http://www.prairienet.org/weft
**Format:** Public Radio

**WGEM-AM**
513 Hampshire Street
Quincy, IL 62301
**Phone:** (217) 228-6600 or
    (800) 728-6600 (toll-free)
**Fax:** (217) 228-6670
**E-mail:** manager@wgem.com
http://wgem.com
**Format:** News, Sports, Information

**WGFA-AM**
1950 North Road
Watseka, IL 60970
**Phone:** (815) 432-4955
**Fax:** (815) 432-4957

**E-mail:** 941fm@wgfaradio.com
http://www.wgfaradio.com
**Format:** Big Band/Nostalgia, Easy
    Listening

**WGFA-FM**
1950 North Road
Watseka, IL 60970
**Phone:** (815) 432-4955
**Fax:** (815) 432-4957
**E-mail:** mmartin@wgfaradio.com
http://www.wgfaradio.com
**Format:** Adult Contemporary

**WGFB-FM**
4570 Rockton Road
P.O. Box 345
Rockton, IL 61072
**Phone:** (815) 624-2603
**Fax:** (815) 624-7777
http://b103fm.com
**Format:** Adult Contemporary

**WGLT-FM**
Campus P.O. Box 8910
Normal, IL 61761
**Phone:** (309) 438-2255
**Fax:** (309) 438-7870
**E-mail:** wglt@ilstu.edu
http://www.wglt.org
**Format:** Jazz, Blues, News

**WGN-AM**
435 N. Michigan Avenue
Chicago, IL 60611-4001
**Phone:** (312) 222-4700
**Fax:** (312) 222-5165
**E-mail:** wgnradio@tribune.com
http://wgnradio.com
**Format:** News, Talk

**WHMS-FM**
2301 S. Neil Street Road
Box 3939
Champaign, IL 61826-3939
**Phone:** (217) 351-5300
**Fax:** (217) 351-5385
**E-mail:** 975@whms.com
http://www.whms.com
**Format:** Adult Contemporary

**WJMK-FM**
180 N. Michigan Avenue
Suite 1200
Chicago, IL 60601
**Phone:** (312) 977-1800
**Fax:** (312) 855-1043
**E-mail:** wjmk.com
http://wjark.com
**Format:** Oldies

**WLUW-FM**
820 Michigan Avenue
Chicago, IL 60611
**Phone:** (312) 915-6558
**Fax:** (312) 915-7095
**E-mail:** wluwradio@luc.edu
http://www.wluw.org
**Format:** Alternative/New
    Music/Progressive

**WNND-FM**
One Prudential Plaza
Suite 2780
Chicago, IL 60601
**Phone:** (312) 297-5100
**Fax:** (312) 297-5111
http://windy 100.com
**Format:** Adult Contemporary

**WOUI-FM**
3300 S. Federal Street
Chicago, IL 60616
**Phone:** (312) 567-3087
**Fax:** (312) 567-8930
**E-mail:** wov:@charlie.acc.iit.edu;
    woui@charlie.acc.iit.edu
http://www.iit.edu~ovi
**Format:** Alternative/New
    Music/Progressive, Urban
    Contemporary, Album-Oriented Rock
    (AOR)

**WSCR-AM**
4949 W. Belmont Avenue
Chicago, IL 60641
**Phone:** (773) 777-1700
**Fax:** (773) 777-5994
http://www.wscr670am.com
**Format:** Sports

**WVON-AM**
3350 S. Kedzie Avenue
Chicago, IL 60623
**Phone:** (773) 247-6200
**Fax:** (773) 247-5336
**E-mail:** wvon@ix.netcom.com
http://www.wvon.com
**Format:** Talk

**WXRT-FM**
4949 W. Belmont Avenue
Chicago, IL 60641
**Phone:** (773) 777-1700
**Fax:** (773) 777-5031
**E-mail:** comments@wxrt.com
http://www.wxrt.com
**Format:** Album-Oriented Rock (AOR)

**WYLL-AM**
Box 56889
Chicago, IL 60656
**Phone:** (847) 956-5030
**Fax:** (847) 956-5040
http://www.wyll.com
**Format:** Religious, Talk

**WZRD-FM**
5500 North Street Louis Avenue
Chicago, IL 60625
**Phone:** (773) 583-4050
**Fax:** (773) 794-6205
**E-mail:** wzrd@imagescape.com
http://www.imagescape.com/wzrd
**Format:** Eclectic

## INDIANA

**KFAV-FM**
P.O. Box 545
Frankfort, IN 46041
**E-mail:** kwrekfav@kasparradio.com
http://www.kfav.com
**Format:** Hot Country

**WAOR-FM**
237 W. Edison Road
Suite 200
Mishawaka, IN 46545-3103
**E-mail:** waor@waor.com
http://www.waor.com
**Format:** Classic Rock

**WAOV-AM**
P.O Box 217
Vincennes, IN 47591
**Phone:** (812) 882-6060
**Fax:** (812) 885-2604
http://waovam.com
**Format:** News, Talk, Sports

**WAWC-FM**
10129 N. 800 E.
Syracuse, IN 46567
**Phone:** (219) 457-8181 or
    (800) 779-1094 (toll-free)
**Fax:** (219) 457-4488
**E-mail:** wawasee@wawasee103.com
http://www.wawasee103.com
**Format:** Classic Rock

**WAWK-AM**
931 East Avenue
Kendallville, IN 46755
**Phone:** (219) 347-2400
**Fax:** (219) 347-2524
**E-mail:** wawk@locl.net
http://www.wawk.com
**Format:** Oldies

**WAXI-FM**
1215 Wabash Avenue
Terre Haute, IN 47807-3311
**Phone:** (812) 234-9770
**Fax:** (812) 238-1576
**E-mail:** waxi@waxi.com
http://www.waxi.com
**Format:** Oldies, News, Sports

**WAZY-FM**
P.O. Box 1410
Lafayette, IN 47902-1410
**Phone:** (765) 474-1410
**Fax:** (765) 474-3442
http://www.wazy.com
**Format:** Contemporary Hit Radio
    (CHR)

**WBAA-AM**
1740 Elliott Hall of Music
West Lafayette, IN 47907-1740
**Phone:** (317) 494-5920 or
    (866) WBAA-101 (toll-free)
**Fax:** (317) 496-1542
**E-mail:** mail@wbaa.org
http://www.wbaa.purdue.edu/wbaa
**Format:** Public Radio, Talk, Jazz, News,
    Eclectic, Classical

**WBAA-FM**
1740 Purdue University
West Lafayette, IN 47907
**Phone:** (765) 494-5920
**Fax:** (765) 496-1542
**E-mail:** mail@wbaa.org
http://www.wbaa.org
**Format:** Classical

**WBCL-FM**
1025 W. Rudisill Boulevard
Fort Wayne, IN 46807
**Phone:** (219) 745-0576
**Fax:** (219) 745-2001
**E-mail:** wbcl@wbcl.org
http://www.wbcl.org
**Format:** Religious

**WBCY-FM**
1025 W. Rudisill Boulevard
Fort Wayne, IN 46807
**Phone:** (219) 745-0576
**Fax:** (219) 745-2001
**E-mail:** wbcl@wbcl.org
http://www.wbcl.org
**Format:** Religious

**WBRI-AM**
4802 E. 62nd Street
Indianapolis, IN 46220

**Phone:** (317) 255-5484
**Fax:** (317) 255-4452
http://ww.wbriam.com
**Format:** Talk, News, Information,
    Southern Gospel

**WBTU-FM**
2100 Goshen Road
Suite 232
Fort Wayne, IN 46808
**Phone:** (219) 482-9288
**Fax:** (219) 482-8655
**E-mail:** wbtu@wbtu.com
http://www.wbtu.com
**Format:** Contemporary Country

**WBYR-FM**
P.O. Box 80397
Fort Wayne, IN 46898-0397
**Phone:** (219) 471-5100
**Fax:** (219) 471-5224
**E-mail:** wbyr@wbyr.com
http//www.wbyr.com
http://www.989thebear.com
**Format:** Album-Oriented Rock (AOR)

**WBYT-FM**
1 Edison Ctr.
Suite 200
237 Edison Road
Mishawaka, IN 46545
**Phone:** (219) 258-5483
**Fax:** (219) 258-0930
**E-mail:** b100@b100.com
http://b100.com
**Format:** Country

**WCBK-FM**
P.O. Box 1577
Martinsville, IN 46151
**Phone:** (317) 342-3394
**Fax:** (317) 342-5020
http://www.scican.net/~wcbk/
**Format:** Country

**WCSI-AM**
3212 Washington Street
Columbus, IN 47203
**Phone:** (812) 372-4448
http://www.columbusin/wcsi.com
**Format:** News, Talk, Sports

**WEDM-FM**
Walker Career Ctr.
9651 E. 21st Street
Indianapolis, IN 46229
**Phone:** (317) 532-6301
**Fax:** (317) 532-6199
**Format:** Adult Contemporary

**WEJE-FM**
2000 Lower Huntington Road
Fort Wayne, IN 46819
**Phone:** (219) 747-1511
**Fax:** (219) 747-3999
**E-mail:** extreme963@hotmail.com
http://www.extreme963.com
**Format:** Alternative/New
    Music/Progressive

**WENS-FM**
One Emmis Plaza
40 Monument Plaza
Suite 600
Indianapolis, IN 46204
**Phone:** (317) 266-9700
**Fax:** (317) 634-1618
http://www.wens.com
**Format:** Adult Contemporary

**WERK-AM**
8510 S. State Road 3
Muncie, IN 47302-8710
**Phone:** (765) 289-9375 or
    (888) 289-9375 (toll-free)
**Fax:** (765) 286-3493
**E-mail:** wade@netusal.net
http://www.werkfm.com

**WERK-FM**
8510 S. State Road 3
Muncie, IN 47302-8787
**Phone:** (765) 289-9375 or
    (888) 289-9375 (toll-free)
**Fax:** (765) 286-3493
http://www.werkfm.com
**Format:** Oldies

**WFLQ-FM**
P.O. Box 100
French Lick, IN 47432
**Phone:** (812) 936-9100
**Fax:** (812) 936-9495
**E-mail:** wflqfm@smithville.net
http://wflq.com
**Format:** Country, Sports

**WFMS-FM**
6810 N. Shadeland Avenue
Indianapolis, IN 46220-4236
**Phone:** (317) 842-9550
**Fax:** (317) 577-3361
**E-mail:** person@wfms.com
http://wfms.com
**Format:** Country

**WFRN-FM**
P.O. Box 307
Elkhart, IN 46515

**Phone:** (219) 875-5166 or
    (800) 933-0501 (toll-free)
**Fax:** (219) 875-6662
**E-mail:** moore@wfrn.com
http://www.wfrn.com
**Format:** Contemporary Christian

**WGLD-FM**
8120 Knue Road
Indianapolis, IN 46250
**Phone:** (317) 842-9550
**Fax:** (317) 577-3361
**Format:** Oldies

**WHHH-FM**
6264 LaPas Trail
Indianapolis, IN 46268
**Phone:** (317) 239-9696
**Fax:** (317) 328-3870
**Format:** Contemporary Hit Radio (CHR)

**WHJE-FM**
520 E. Main Street
Carmel, IN 46032
**Phone:** (317) 846-7721
**Fax:** (317) 571-4066
http://www.whje.com
**Format:** Alternative/New
    Music/Progressive, Classic Rock

**WHTI-FM**
9821 S. 800 West
Daleville, IN 47334
**Phone:** (765) 378-2080
**Fax:** (765) 378-2090
**E-mail:** waxt@astralite.com
http://www.whitfm.com
**Format:** Adult Contemporary

**WHUT-AM**
36 S. Pennsylvania Street
Suite 200
Indianapolis, IN 46204-3627
**Phone:** (765) 644-1255 or
    (800) 452-9997 (toll-free)
**Fax:** (765) 644-1775
**Format:** Big Band/Nostalgia

**WIBC-AM**
9292 N. Meridian Street
Indianapolis, IN 46260
**Phone:** (317) 844-7200
**Fax:** (317) 846-1081
**E-mail:** wibc.com
http://www.wibc.com
**Format:** Talk, News, Sports

**WIKY-FM**
1162 Mt. Auburn Road
P.O. Box 3848
Evansville, IN 47736

**Phone:** (812) 424-8284
**Fax:** (812) 426-7928
http://www.wiky.com
**Format:** Adult Contemporary

**WIMS-AM**
6405 Olcott Avenue
Hammond, IN 46320
**Phone:** (219) 844-1230
http://www.wimstalk.com
**Format:** Talk

**WIRE-FM**
P.O. Box 68920
Indianapolis, IN 46268-0920
**Phone:** (317) 482-4427
**Format:** Country

**WKAM-AM**
P.O. Box 497
Goshen, IN 46526
**Phone:** (219) 533-1460 or
    (800) 977-7847 (toll-free)
**Fax:** (219) 534-3698
**E-mail:** wkam@wkam.com
http://www.wkam1460.com

**WKAM-AM**
P.O. Box 497
Goshen, IN 46526
**Phone:** (219) 533-1460 or
    (800) 977-7847 (toll-free)
**Fax:** (219) 534-3698
**E-mail:** wkam@wkam.com
http://www.wkam1460.com

**WKHY-FM**
711 N. Earl Avenue
P.O. Box 7093
Lafayette, IN 47904
**Phone:** (765) 448-1566
**Fax:** (765) 448-1348
http://www.wkhy.com
**Format:** Classic Rock, Album-Oriented
    Rock (AOR)

**WKUZ-FM**
P.O. Box 342
Wabash, IN 46992
**Phone:** (219) 563-4111
**Fax:** (219) 563-4425
http://www.wkuz.com
**Format:** Country

**WNDE-AM**
6161 Fall Creek Road
Indianapolis, IN 46220
**Phone:** (317) 257-7565
**Fax:** (317) 253-6501

http://www.wnde.com
**Format:** Sports, Talk

**WNOU-FM**
One Emmis Plaza
40 Monument Circle
Suite 600
Indianapolis, IN 46204
**Phone:** (317) 684-6532
**Fax:** (317) 684-2021
http://www.radionow931.com
**Format:** Classic Rock

**WNSN-FM**
300 W. Jefferson Boulevard
South Bend, IN 46601
**Phone:** (219) 239-4230
**Fax:** (219) 239-4231
http://www.wsbt.com
**Format:** Adult Contemporary

**WOWO-AM**
2915 Maples Road
Fort Wayne, IN 46816
**Phone:** (219) 447-5511 or
    (800) 333-1190 (toll-free)
**Fax:** (219) 447-7546
http://www.wowo.com
**Format:** News, Talk

**WRZQ-FM**
825 Washington Street
Columbus, IN 47201
**Phone:** (812) 379-1077
**Fax:** (812) 375-2555
**E-mail:** qmix@qmix.com
http://www.qmix.com
**Format:** Adult Contemporary

**WSBT-AM**
202 S. Michigan Street
Suite 700
South Bend, IN 46601
**Phone:** (219) 239-4230
**Fax:** (219) 239-4231
http://www.wsbt.com
**Format:** News, Talk

# IOWA

**KALA-FM**
518 W. Locust Street
Davenport, IA 52803-2898
**Phone:** (319) 333-6219 or
    (800) 728-2586 (toll-free)
**Fax:** (319) 333-6218
http://cs.sau.edu/~kala
**Format:** Jazz, Urban Contemporary,
    Alternative/New Music/Progressive

**KBOE-FM**
Highway 63 N.
P.O. Box 380
Oskaloosa, IA 52577
**Phone:** (515) 673-3493
**Fax:** (515) 673-3495
**E-mail:** kboe@lisco.com
http://www.lisco.com/kboe
**Format:** Country

**KCCK-FM**
6301 Kirkwood Boulevard SW
Cedar Rapids, IA 52406
**Phone:** (319) 398-5446 or
    (800) 373-5225 (toll-free)
**Fax:** (319) 398-5492
**E-mail:** kcck@inav.net
http://www.kcck.org
**Format:** Jazz, Blues, Information

**KCJJ-AM**
Box 2118
Iowa City, IA 52244
**Phone:** (319) 354-1242
**Fax:** (319) 354-1921
**E-mail:** kcjjam@aol.com
http://www.kcjj.com
**Format:** Adult Contemporary, News,
    Sports

**KCLN-AM**
1853 442nd Avenue
Clinton, IA 52732
**Phone:** (563) 243-1390 or (800) 895-8436
    (toll-free)
**Fax:** (563) 243-4567
**E-mail:** kcln@clinton.net
http://kcln.clinton.net
**Format:** Big Band/Nostalgia, Oldies,
    Agricultural

**KCNZ-AM**
721 Shirley Street
P.O. Box 248
Cedar Falls, IA 50613
**Phone:** (319) 277-1918 or (800) 913-9479
    (toll-free)
**Fax:** (319) 277-5202
**E-mail:** kcnz@kcnzam.com
http://www.kcnzam.com
**Format:** News, Talk, Sports

**KCPS-AM**
208 Jefferson Street
P.O. Box 946
Burlington, IA 52601
**Phone:** (319) 754-6698
**E-mail:** kcps@aol.com
http://www.listen.to/kcps
**Format:** News, Talk, Sports

**KCRG-AM**
2nd Avenue at 5th Street SE
Box 816
Cedar Rapids, IA 52401
**Phone:** (319) 395-9999
**Fax:** (319) 398-8378
**E-mail:** 9online@kcrg.com
http://www.kcrg.com
**Format:** News

**KCRR-FM**
501 Sycamore Street
Suite 300
Waterloo, IA 50703-4651
**Phone:** (319) 833-4800
**Fax:** (319) 833-4866
**E-mail:** kcrr@kcrr.com
http://www.kcrr.com
**Format:** Classic Rock

**KDFR-FM**
P.O. Box 57023
Des Moines, IA 50317
**Phone:** (515) 262-0449
**E-mail:** kdfr@familyradio.com
http://www.familyradio.com
**Format:** Religious

**KGGY-FM**
P.O. Box 1280
Dubuque, IA 52004-1280
**Phone:** (319) 557-8888 or (800) 790-1023
   (toll-free)
**Fax:** (319) 557-7424
http://www.kggy.com
**Format:** Classic Rock

**KGLO-AM**
P.O. Box 1300
Mason City, IA 50402-1300
**Phone:** (641) 423-1300 or (800) 747-2346
   (toll-free)
**Fax:** (641) 423-2906
**E-mail:** tamiramon@clearchannel.com
http://www.netms.net/showcase/kgkifx
**Format:** Adult Contemporary, News, Full
   Service

**KHKE-FM**
University of Northern Iowa
Cedar Falls, IA 50614-0359
**Phone:** (319) 273-6400 or (800) 772-2440
   (toll-free)
**Fax:** (319) 273-2682
**E-mail:** kuni@uni.edu
http://www.khke.org
**Format:** Public Radio, Jazz, Classical

**KIA-FM**
341 Yorktown Pike
Box 1300
Mason City, IA 50401
**Phone:** (641) 423-1300 or (800) 747-2346
   (toll-free)
**Fax:** (641) 423-2906
**E-mail:** tamiramon@clearchannel.com
http://www.netins.net/showcase/kgkifx
**Format:** Country

**KIIK-FM**
57 1/2 S. Court
Fairfield, IA 52556
**Phone:** (515) 472-4191
**Fax:** (515) 472-2071
http://www.kmcdkick96.com
**Format:** Oldies

**KIWR-FM**
1700 College Road
Council Bluffs, IA 51503
**Phone:** (712) 325-3254
**Fax:** (712) 325-3391
**E-mail:** theriver897@hotmail.com
http://www.webradio.com
**Format:** Public Radio, Alternative/New
   Music/Progressive

**KLMJ-FM**
1509 4th Street NE
P.O. Box 495
Hampton, IA 50441
**Phone:** (515) 456-5656
**Fax:** (515) 456-5655
**E-mail:** klmj@klmj.com
http://www.klmj.com
**Format:** Adult Contemporary,
   Contemporary Country, News, Sports

**KLTI-FM**
1416 Locust Street
Des Moines, IA 50309
**Phone:** (515) 280-1350 or (800) 333-1041
   (toll-free)
**Fax:** (515) 280-3011
**E-mail:** klti@netins.net
http://lite1041.com
**Format:** Adult Contemporary

**KLYF-FM**
1801 Grand Avenue
Des Moines, IA 50309
**Phone:** (515) 242-3500
http://www.klyf.com
**Format:** Adult Contemporary, Soft Rock

**KMCD-AM**
57 1/2 S. Court
Fairfield, IA 52556

**Phone:** (515) 472-4191 or (888) 337-2346
   (toll-free)
**Fax:** (515) 472-2071
**E-mail:** kmcdkick@ffradio.com
http://www.kmcdkick96.com
**Format:** Country, News, Talk

**KMXD-FM**
1801 Grand Avenue
Des Moines, IA 50309-3362
**Phone:** (515) 242-3500
**Fax:** (515) 242-3798
http://mixradio.com
**Format:** Adult Contemporary

**KOEL-FM**
501 Sycamore Street
Suite 300
Waterloo, IA 50703-4651
**Phone:** (319) 833-4800
**Fax:** (319) 833-4866
**E-mail:** koel@koel.com
http://www.koel.com
**Format:** Country

**KRNI-AM**
c/o KUNI-FM
University of Northern Iowa
Cedar Falls, IA 50614-0359
**Phone:** (319) 273-6400 or (800) 772-2440
   (toll-free)
**Fax:** (319) 273-2682
**E-mail:** kuni@uni.edu
http://www.kuniradio.org
**Format:** Public Radio, Eclectic

**KRNL-FM**
Cornell College
810 Commons Circle
Mount Vernon, IA 52314
**Phone:** (319) 895-4431
**Fax:** (319) 895-5188
**E-mail:** krnl@cornell-iowa.edu
http://www.cornell-iowa.edu/krnl
**Format:** Eclectic

**KRUI-FM**
129 Grand Avenue Ct.
Iowa City, IA 52242
**Phone:** (319) 335-9525
**Fax:** (319) 335-9526
**E-mail:** krui@uiowa.edu
http://www.uiowa.edu/~krui
**Format:** Urban Contemporary,
   Alternative/New Music/Progressive

**KSFT-FM**
1113 Nebraska Street
Sioux City, IA 51105

**Phone:** (712) 258-5595
**Fax:** (712) 252-2430
http://www.soft107.com
**Format:** Adult Contemporary, Soft Rock

**KSTZ-FM**
1416 Locust Street
Des Moines, IA 50309
**Phone:** (515) 280-1350 or (800) 255-1025
    (toll-free)
**Fax:** (515) 280-3011
**E-mail:** kstz1025@aol.com
http://www.star1025.com
**Format:** Adult Contemporary

**KUNI-FM**
University of Northern Iowa
Cedar Falls, IA 50614-0359
**Phone:** (319) 273-6400 or (800) 772-2440
    (toll-free)
**Fax:** (319) 273-2682
**E-mail:** kuni@.uni.edu
http://www.kuniradio.org
**Format:** Public Radio, Adult
    Contemporary, Ethnic, Eclectic, Urban
    Contemporary, Classical

**KWBG-AM**
724 Story Street, 2nd Floor
Boone, IA 50036
**Phone:** (515) 432-2046
**Fax:** (515) 432-1448
**E-mail:** kwbg@willinet.net
http://www.kwbg.com
**Format:** Information

**KWOF-AM**
3232 Osage Road
Waterloo, IA 50703
**Phone:** (319) 236-5700 or
    (800) 774-5963 (toll-free)
**Fax:** (319) 236-8777
**E-mail:** christianhits@mail.com
**Format:** Religious, Contemporary
    Christian

**KXNO-AM**
1801 Grand Avenue
Des Moines, IA 50309
**Phone:** (515) 242-3500
**Fax:** (515) 242-3798
http://www.kxno.com
**Format:** Sports

**KZAT-FM**
303 McClellan Street
Tama, IA 52339
**Phone:** (641) 484-5958 or
    (888) 484-5955 (toll-free)

**Fax:** (641) 484-5962
**E-mail:** kzat@kzat.com
http://www.kzat.com
**Format:** Classic Rock

# KANSAS

**KANS-FM**
1811 W. 6th Avenue
Emporia, KS 66801
**Phone:** (316) 343-9393 or
    (800) 356-KANS (toll-free)
**Fax:** (316) 342-7617
**E-mail:** kans@ksradio.com
http://www.ksradio.com
**Format:** Oldies

**KANU-FM**
Broadcasting Hall
University of Kansas
Lawrence, KS 66045
**Phone:** (785) 864-4530 or
    (877) 526-8365 (toll-free)
**Fax:** (785) 864-5278
http://www.ukans.edu/cwis/units/kanufm/
    public_html
**Format:** Public Radio

**KBLS-FM**
5008 Skyway Drive
Manhattan, KS 66503
**Phone:** (785) 823-1111
**E-mail:** ebclink.com
http://www.ebcinc.com
**Format:** Adult Contemporary

**KCHZ-FM**
11900 College Boulevard
Suite 320
Overland Park, KS 66210
**Phone:** (913) 696-3700
http://www.channelz95.com
**Format:** Contemporary Hit Radio
    (CHR)

**KFH-AM**
2120 N. Woodlawn
Suite 352
Wichita, KS 67208-1847
**Phone:** (316) 685-2121
**Fax:** (316) 685-3314
**E-mail:** kfh@cis.compuserve.com
http://ourworld.compuserve.
    com/homepages/kfh
**Format:** Talk

**KHCA-FM**
103 N. 3rd
Manhattan, KS 66502

**Phone:** (785) 537-9595
**Fax:** (785) 537-2955
**E-mail:** angel95@kansas.net
http://www.tfsksu.net/~angel95
**Format:** Contemporary Christian

**KHCC-FM**
815 N. Walnut
Suite 300
Hutchinson, KS 67501-6217
**Phone:** (316) 662-6646
**E-mail:** webmaster@radiokansas.org
http://www.radiokansas.org
**Format:** Public Radio, News, Classical,
    New Age

**KHCD-FM**
815 N. Walnut
Suite 300
Hutchinson, KS 67501-6217
**Phone:** (316) 662-6646
**E-mail:** webmaster@radiokansas.org
http://www.radiokansas.org
**Format:** Public Radio, News, Classical,
    New Age

**KHOK-FM**
5501 10th Street
Box 48
Great Bend, KS 67530
**Phone:** (316) 792-3647
**Fax:** (316) 792-3649
**E-mail:** http://www@eagleradio.net
**Format:** Hot Country

**KHYM-FM**
P.O. Box 991
Meade, KS 67864
**Phone:** (316) 873-2991
**Fax:** (316) 873-2755
**E-mail:** kjil@kjil.com
http://www.kjil.com
**Format:** Gospel

**KICT-FM**
4200 N. Old Lawrence Road
Wichita, KS 67219-3211
**Phone:** (316) 722-5600
**Fax:** (316) 773-5310
**E-mail:** staff@t95.com
http://www.t95.com
**Format:** Album-Oriented Rock (AOR)

**KJIL-FM**
P.O. Box 991
Meade, KS 67864
**Phone:** (316) 873-2991
**Fax:** (316) 873-2755
**E-mail:** kjil@kjil.com

http://www.kjil.com
**Format:** Contemporary Christian

**KJLS-FM**
107 W. 13th
Box 728
Hays, KS 67601
**Phone:** (785) 628-1064 or
  (800) 681-9102 (toll-free)
**Fax:** (785) 628-1822
http://www.mix103fm.com
**Format:** Adult Contemporary

**KLOE-AM**
Box 569
Broadcast Plaza
Goodland, KS 67735
**Phone:** (785) 899-3062
**Fax:** (785) 899-3062
**E-mail:** kloe@goodland.ixks.com
http://www.kloe.com
**Format:** Full Service, News, Country,
  Talk

**KLZR-FM**
3125 W. 6th Street
Lawrence, KS 66049-3101
**Phone:** (913) 843-1320
**Fax:** (913) 841-1320
**E-mail:** 1059@lazer.com
http:www.lazer.com
Contact(s): Hawk Booth, General
**Format:** Classic Rock

**KMBZ-AM**
4935 Belinder Road
Westwood, KS 66205-1937
**Phone:** (913) 677-8998
**Fax:** (913) 677-8901
http://www.kmbz.com
**Format:** News, Sports, Talk

**KMKF-FM**
2414 Casement Road
P.O. Box 1350
Manhattan, KS 66502-0011
**Phone:** (785) 776-1350 or
  (800) 559-1350 (toll-free)
**Fax:** (785) 539-1000
http://www.purerock.com
**Format:** Album-Oriented Rock (AOR)

**KNCK-AM**
Rte. 1 W. 11th Street
Box 629
Concordia, KS 66901
**Phone:** (913) 243-1414
http://1390knck.com
**Format:** News, Sports

**KNGM-FM**
815 Graham Street
Emporia, KS 66801
**Phone:** (316) 343-9292 or
  (888) 808-8034 (toll-free)
**E-mail:** kngm@freeyellow.com
http://www.freeyellow.com/members/kngm
**Format:** Religious, Contemporary
  Christian

**KNSS-AM**
2120 N. Woodlawn
Suite 352
Wichita, KS 67208
**Phone:** (316) 685-2121
**Fax:** (316) 634-5190
**E-mail:** dwilson@entercom.com
http://www.1240knss.com
**Format:** News, Talk

**KOFO-AM**
P.O. Box 16
Ottawa, KS 66067
**Phone:** (913) 242-1220
**Fax:** (913) 242-1442
**E-mail:** kofo@kofo.com
http://www.kofo.com
**Format:** Country

**KQNS-FM**
1321 W. Crawford
Salina, KS 67401
**Phone:** (913) 826-9636
**Fax:** (913) 826-9789
**E-mail:** kqns@midkan.com
http://www.mid-kan.com/star95
**Format:** Contemporary Hit Radio (CHR)

**KQRC-FM**
4935 Belinder
Westwood, KS 66205
**Phone:** (913) 677-8998
**Fax:** (913) 677-7510
http://www.989therock.com
**Format:** Album-Oriented Rock (AOR)

**KRSL-AM**
Box 666
Russell, KS 67665
**Phone:** (785) 483-3121
**Fax:** (785) 483-6511
**E-mail:** wayne@krsl.com
http://www.krsl.com
**Format:** Adult Contemporary

**KRWV-FM**
1811 W. 6th Avenue
Emporia, KS 66801
**Phone:** (316) 343-9393 or (800) 356-5267
  (toll-free)

**Fax:** (316) 342-7617
**E-mail:** krwv@ksradio.com
http://www.ksradio.com
**Format:** Adult Contemporary Soft Rock

**KSAJ-FM**
P.O. Box 80
Salina, KS 67402
**Phone:** (785) 263-7111
**Fax:** (785) 263-0166
http://www.ebcinc.com
**Format:** Oldies

**KSAL-AM**
P.O. Box 80
Salina, KS 67402-0080
**Phone:** (785) 823-1111 or (800) 608-1150
  (toll-free)
**Fax:** (785) 823-2034
**E-mail:** csanders@informatics.net
http://www.ebcinc.com
**Format:** Talk, News, Agricultural, Sports

**KUDL-FM**
4935 Belinder
Westwood, KS 66205
**Fax:** (913) 677-8981
http://www.kudl.com
**Format:** Adult Contemporary

**KVGB-AM**
P.O. Box 609
Great Bend, KS 67530
**Phone:** (316) 792-3647 or (888) 782-3647
  (toll-free)
**Fax:** (316) 792-3649
http://www.eagleradio.net
**Format:** News, Talk, Sports

**KVGB-FM**
P.O. Box 609
Great Bend, KS 67530
**Phone:** (316) 792-3647 or
  (888) 792-3647 (toll-free)
**Fax:** (316) 792-3649
http://www.eagleradio.net
**Format:** Classic Rock

**KVOE-FM**
P.O. Box 968
Emporia, KS 66801-0968
**Phone:** (316) 342-1400
**Fax:** (316) 342-0804
http://www.kvoe@kvoe.com
**Format:** Country

**KXTR-AM**
4935 Belinder
Westwood, KS 66205

**Phone:** (913) 677-8998
**Fax:** (913) 677-7530
http://www.kxtrlive.com
**Format:** Classical

**KYYS-FM**
4935 Belinder
Westwood, KS 66205
**Phone:** (913) 677-8998
**Fax:** (913) 677-8050
http://www.kyys.com
**Format:** Classic Rock

**WDAF-AM**
4935 Belinder
Westwood, KS 66205
**Phone:** (913) 677-8998
**Fax:** (913) 677-8080
http://www.wdaf.com
**Format:** Country

# KENTUCKY

**WAMZ-FM**
520 W. Chestnut
Louisville, KY 40202
**Phone:** (502) 582-7840
**Fax:** (502) 582-7837
**Format:** Contemporary Country

**WBBE-AM**
2601 Nicholasville Road
Lexington, KY 40503-3307
**Format:** Big Band/Nostalgia

**WCGW-AM**
3270 Blazer Pkwy.
Suite 102
Lexington, KY 40509
**Phone:** (859) 264-9700
**Fax:** (859) 264-9705
**E-mail:** kcn1000@aol.com
**Format:** Southern Gospel

**WDJX-FM**
520 S. 4th
Louisville, KY 40202
**Phone:** (502) 625-1220
**Fax:** (502) 625-1253
http://wdjx.com
**Format:** Contemporary Hit Radio (CHR)

**WDXL-AM**
Box 170
Lexington, KY 38351
**Phone:** (901) 968-3500 or
    (800) 301-9930 (toll-free)
**Fax:** (901) 968-0380
**Format:** Country

**WFIA-AM**
612 4th Avenue
Suite 200
Louisville, KY 40202
**Phone:** (502) 583-4811
**Fax:** (502) 583-4820
**Format:** Religious

**WFLE-FM**
RR. 3, No. 1 Radio Drive
Fleming County Industrial Park
Flemingsburg, KY 41041
**Phone:** (606) 849-4433
**Fax:** (606) 845-9353
**Format:** Country

**WFPK-FM**
619 S. 4th Street
Louisville, KY 40202-2403
**Phone:** (502) 574-1640
**Fax:** (502) 574-1671
**E-mail:** wfpk@iglou.com
**Format:** Adult Album Alternative

**WFPL-FM**
619 4th Street
Louisville, KY 40202-2403
**Phone:** (502) 574-1640
**Fax:** (502) 574-1671
**E-mail:** webmaster@wfpl.org
**Format:** Public Radio, News, Talk

**WGKS-FM**
1500 Greendale Road
Lexington, KY 40511
**Phone:** (606) 233-1515
**Fax:** (606) 233-1517
**Format:** Adult Contemporary

**WHAS-AM**
4000 No. 1 Radio Drive
Louisville, KY 40218
**Phone:** (502) 479-2222
**Fax:** (502) 479-2224
**E-mail:** kcarls84@yahoo.com
**Format:** News, Talk

**WHKW-FM**
520 W. Chestnut Street
Louisville, KY 40202-2235
**E-mail:** info@whkw.com
http://www.whkw.com
**Format:** Contemporary Country

**WJIE-FM**
P.O. Box 197309
Louisville, KY 40259
**Phone:** (502) 968-1220 or (800) 433-8958
    (toll-free)

**Fax:** (502) 962-3143
http://www.wjie.org
**Format:** Contemporary Christian

**WKJK-AM**
4000 1 Radio Drive
Louisville, KY 40218
**Phone:** (502) 479-2222
**Fax:** (502) 479-2225
**E-mail:** info@wkjk.com
http://www.wkjk
**Format:** Adult Contemporary,
    Middle-of-the-Road (MOR)

**WKQQ-FM**
2601 Nicholasville Road
Lexington, KY 40503-3307
**Phone:** (606) 252-6694
**Fax:** (606) 225-0981
**Format:** Classic Rock

**WLAP-AM**
2601 Nicholasville Road
Lexington, KY 40503-3307
**Phone:** (859) 422-1000 or (800) 606-4263
    (toll-free)
**Fax:** (859) 299-9527
http://www.wlap.com
**Format:** Talk, News

**WLKY-AM**
P.O. Box 1897
Louisville, KY 40201
**Phone:** (502) 587-0970 or (800) 848-0318
    (toll-free)
**Format:** Top 40

**WLLV-AM**
2001 W. Broadway
Suite 13
Louisville, KY 40203-3551
**Phone:** (502) 581-1240
**Fax:** (502) 583-4301
**Format:** Gospel

**WMXL-FM**
2601 Nicholasville Road
Lexington, KY 40503
**Phone:** (859) 422-1000
**Fax:** (859) 422-1038
**E-mail:** wmxl.com
http://www.wmxl.com
**Format:** Adult Contemporary

**WNAI-AM**
P.O. Box 197309
Louisville, KY 40259-7309
**E-mail:** wnairadio@hotmail.com
http://www.wnai.com
**Format:** News, Talk, Sports

**WQMF-FM**
4000 Radio Drive
Suite 1
Louisville, KY 40218
**Phone:** (502) 896-4400
**Fax:** (502) 896-1496
**Format:** Classic Rock

**WRKA-FM**
612 S. 4th Street
Louisville, KY 40202-2460
**Phone:** (502) 423-9752
**Fax:** (502) 423-0231
**Format:** Oldies

**WSOH-FM**
P.O. Box 36005
Louisville, KY 40233-6005
**Phone:** (812) 246-0200
**Fax:** (502) 246-0200
http://www.lifetalk.net/wsoh
**Format:** Talk, Religious

**WTFX-FM**
4000 Radio Drive
Suite 1
Louisville, KY 40218
**Phone:** (502) 479-2222
**Fax:** (502) 479-2234
**Format:** Album-Oriented Rock (AOR)

**WTKT-FM**
2601 Nicholasville Road
Lexington, KY 40503-3307
**Format:** Oldies

**WTMT-AM**
162 W. Broadway
Louisville, KY 40202-2135
**Phone:** (502) 583-6200
**Fax:** (502) 589-2979
**Format:** Sports

**WUOL-FM**
Strickler Hall
University of Louisville
Louisville, KY 40292
**Phone:** (502) 852-6467
**Fax:** (502) 852-1621
**E-mail:** notes@wuol.org
http://wuol.org
**Format:** Classical

**WUKY-FM**
University of Kentucky
340 McVey Hall
Lexington, KY 40506
**Phone:** (859) 257-3221
**Fax:** (859) 257-6291

**E-mail:** wuky913@ukcc.uky.edu
http://wuky.uky.edu
**Format:** Adult Album Alternative, News

**WVLK-AM**
P.O. Box 1559
Lexington, KY 40507-1621
**Phone:** (606) 253-5900
**Fax:** (606) 253-5903
**E-mail:** wvlkam.com
http://www.wvlkam.com
**Format:** Full Service

**WVLK-FM**
Broadway & Vine, 3rd Floor
Lexington, KY 40507
**Phone:** (606) 253-5900
**Fax:** (606) 253-5903
**E-mail:** k93@mis.net

**WXXA-AM**
4000 1 Radio Drive
Louisville, KY 40218
**Phone:** (502) 479-2222
**Fax:** (502) 479-2224
http://www.xtrasports790.com
**Format:** Sports

## LOUISIANA

**KEDM-FM**
225 Stubbs Hall
Monroe, LA 71209-6805
**Phone:** (318) 342-5556 or (800) 256-4085
   (toll-free)
**Fax:** (318) 342-5570
**E-mail:** kedm@ulm.edu
http://kedm.org
**Format:** News, Classical, Jazz, New Age

**KEEL-AM**
6341 Westport Avenue
Shreveport, LA 71129-2498
**Phone:** (318) 688-1130
**Fax:** (318) 687-8574
http://710keel.com
**Format:** News, Talk

**KEUN-AM**
330 W. Laurel Avenue
Eunice, LA 70535
**Phone:** (318) 457-3041
**Fax:** (318) 457-3081
http://keunworldwide.com
**Format:** Country, Sports, News, Cajun

**KJAE-FM**
Box 1323
Leesville, LA 71496-1323

**Phone:** (318) 238-1956
**Fax:** (318) 238-9283
**E-mail:** kjae@leesville.com
http://www.leesville.com/kjae
**Format:** Country

**KJJB-FM**
330 W. Laurel Avenue
Eunice, LA 70535-3306
**Phone:** (318) 457-3041
**Fax:** (318) 457-3081
http://keunworldwide.com
**Format:** Country

**KKND-FM**
929 Howard Avenue
New Orleans, LA 70113
**Phone:** (504) 679-7300
**Fax:** (504) 679-7342
http://www.1067theend.com
**Format:** Alternative/New
   Music/Progressive

**KLEB-AM**
11603 Hwy. 308
P.O. Box 1350
Larose, LA 70373
**Phone:** (504) 798-7792
**Fax:** (504) 798-7793
**E-mail:** klrz@mobiletel.com
http://www.rajuncajunradio.com
**Format:** Cajun

**KLIL-FM**
Hwy. I
P.O. Box 365
Moreauville, LA 71355
**Phone:** (318) 985-2929
**Fax:** (318) 985-2995
**E-mail:** klil@kricket.net
http://www.klil.com
**Format:** Adult Contemporary, Oldies

**KHOM-FM**
1001 Howard Avenue
Suite 4200
New Orleans, LA 70113
**Phone:** (504) 524-5158
**Fax:** (504) 522-6544
**Format:** Contemporary Hit Radio (CHR)

**KKND-FM**
929 Howard Avenue
New Orleans, LA 70113
**Phone:** (504) 679-7300
**Fax:** (504) 679-7342
http://www.1067theend.com
**Format:** Alternative/New
   Music/Progressive

**KMEZ-FM**
1450 Poydras Street
New Orleans, LA 70112
**Phone:** (504) 593-2171
**Fax:** (504) 593-1865
**Format:** Urban Contemporary

**KOGM-FM**
P.O. Box 1150
Opelousas, LA 70570
**Phone:** (337) 942-2633
**Fax:** (337) 942-2635
**E-mail:** kslokogm@bellsouth.net
http://www.kslokogm-fm.com
**Format:** Oldies

**KQKI-FM**
128 Pluto Street
Morgan City, LA 70380
**Phone:** (504) 395-2853
**Fax:** (504) 395-5094
**E-mail:** kqki@cajun.net
http://www.kqki.com
**Format:** Country, Ethnic, French

**KQXL-FM**
650 Wooddale Boulevard
Baton Rouge, LA 70806
**Phone:** (225) 926-1106
**Fax:** (225) 928-1602
http://www.q106dot5.com
**Format:** Urban Contemporary

**KRRQ-FM**
3225 Ambassador Caffery
Lafayette, LA 70506
**Phone:** (337) 981-0106
**Fax:** (337) 988-0443
http://www.krrq.com
**Format:** Urban Contemporary

**KRUF-FM**
6341 Westport Avenue
Shreveport, LA 71129
**Phone:** (318) 688-1130
**Fax:** (318) 687-8574
http://k945.com
**Format:** Contemporary Hit Radio (CHR)

**KRVQ-FM**
208 N. Thomas Drive
Shreveport, LA 71107
**Phone:** (318) 222-0636
**Fax:** (318) 222-2957
http://www.river102.com
**Format:** Oldies

**KSYR-FM**
208 N. Thomas
Shreveport, LA 71107

**Phone:** (318) 222-0636
**Fax:** (318) 222-2957
http://www.star957fm.com
**Format:** Adult Contemporary

**KTLN-FM**
2000 Lakeshore Drive
New Orleans, LA 70148
**Phone:** (504) 280-7000 or (800) 286-7002
  (toll-free)
**Fax:** (504) 280-6061
**E-mail:** wwno@uno.edu
http://www.wwno.org
**Format:** Classical, Public Radio

**KWKH-AM**
6341 Westport Avenue
Shreveport, LA 71129
**Phone:** (318) 688-1130
**Fax:** (318) 687-8574
http://am1130thefan.com
**Format:** Sports

**KXKS-FM**
6341 Westport Avenue
Shreveport, LA 71129-2498
**Phone:** (318) 688-1130
**Fax:** (318) 687-8574
http://www.kisscountry937.com
**Format:** Country

**WBBE-FM**
650 Wooddale Boulevard
Baton Rouge, LA 70806
**Phone:** (225) 926-1106
**Fax:** (225) 928-1606
http://www.bl03.fm
**Format:** Adult Contemporary

**WBOK-AM**
1639 Gentilly Boulevard
New Orleans, LA 70119-2100
**Phone:** (504) 943-4600
**Fax:** (504) 944-4662
**Format:** Religious

**WBSN-FM**
3939 Gentilly Boulevard
New Orleans, LA 70126
**Phone:** (504) 816-8000 or (888) 480-3600
  (toll-free)
**Fax:** (504) 816-8580
**E-mail:** chair@lifesongs.com
http://www.christianrockradio.com
**Format:** Adult Contemporary, Religious

**WBYU-AM**
1515 Street Charles Avenue
New Orleans, LA 70130-4445

**Phone:** (504) 522-1450
**Fax:** (504) 528-9244
**Format:** Easy Listening

**WCKW-FM**
P.O. Box 5905
Metairie, LA 70009
**Phone:** (504) 831-8811
**Fax:** (504) 831-8885
**E-mail:** rook923@wckw.com
http://www.wckw.com
**Format:** Album-Oriented Rock (AOR)

**WEMX-FM**
650 Wooddale Boulevard
Baton Rouge, LA 70806
**Phone:** (225) 926-1106
**Fax:** (225) 928-1606
http://www.max94one.com
**Format:** Urban Contemporary

**WKJN-FM**
9737 N. Winston Avenue
Baton Rouge, LA 70804-2531
**Phone:** (504) 292-9556
**Fax:** (504) 291-6420
http://www.challengernet/kajun103
**Format:** Contemporary Country

**WNOE-AM**
529 Bienville Street
New Orleans, LA 70130-2290
**Phone:** (504) 529-1212
**Fax:** (504) 525-1011
**Format:** Contemporary Country

**WSHO-AM**
1001 Howard Avenue
Suite 4304
New Orleans, LA 70113-2045
**Phone:** (504) 527-0800
**Fax:** (504) 527-0881
**E-mail:** wsho@cis.compuserve.com
http://www.wsho.com
**Format:** Talk, Religious, Contemporary
  Christian

**WWOZ-FM**
P.O. Box 51840
New Orleans, LA 70151-1840
**Phone:** (504) 568-1239
**Fax:** (504) 558-9332
**E-mail:** mailhost@wwoz.org
http://www.wwoz.org
**Format:** Jazz, Blues, World Beat

**WYLD-AM**
2228 Gravier Street
New Orleans, LA 70119

Phone: (504) 827-6000
Fax: (504) 827-6048
E-mail: email@am940mail.com
http://www.am940.com
Format: Religious, Contemporary
  Christian, Gospel

# MAINE

## WABI-AM
27 State Street
Bangor, ME 04401
Phone: (207) 947-9100
Fax: (207) 947-2346
E-mail: b97hits@b97hits.com
Format: Oldies, Middle-of-the-Road
  (MOR)

## WABK-FM
150 Whitten Road
Augusta, ME 04330-6021
Phone: (207) 582-3303
Fax: (207) 582-8144
Format: Oldies

## WALZ-FM
105 Main Street
Machias, ME 04654
Phone: (207) 255-8321
Format: Country, Easy Listening

## WBCI-FM
122 Main Street
Topsham, ME 04086-1220
Phone: (207) 725-9224
Fax: (207) 725-2686
E-mail: wbci@qwi.net
Format: Talk

## WBFB-FM
12 Acme Road
Suite 207
Brewer, ME 04412-1546
Phone: (207) 989-7364
Fax: (207) 989-8321
Format: Contemporary Country

## WBLM-FM
1 City Center
Portland, ME 04101
Phone: (207) 774-6364
Fax: (207) 774-8707
Format: Album-Oriented Rock (AOR),
  Classic Rock

## WBOR-FM
1 College Street
Brunswick, ME 04011
Phone: (207) 725-3210

E-mail: wbor@polar.bowdoin.edu
http://www.bowdoin.edu/~wbor/index.html
Format: Alternative/New
  Music/Progressive

## WBPW-FM
P.O. Box 312
Presque Isle, ME 04769
Phone: (207) 769-6600
Fax: (207) 764-5274
E-mail: wqhr@agate.net
Format: Hot Country

## WCYI-FM
One City Center
Portland, ME 04101
Phone: (207) 774-6364
Fax: (207) 774-8707
http://www.wcyy.com
Format: Classic Rock

## WCDQ-FM
Box 631
Sanford, ME 04073
Phone: (207) 324-7271
Fax: (207) 324-2464
E-mail: wcdq@wcdq.com

## WCME-FM
P.O. Box 159
Skowhegan, ME 04976
Phone: (207) 474-5171 or
  (800) 635-7355 (toll-free)
Fax: (207) 474-3299
Format: Contemporary Country

## WCXU-FM
152 E. Green Ridge Road
Caribou, ME 04736
Phone: (207) 473-7513 or
  (800) 622-9298 (toll-free)
Fax: (207) 472-3221
E-mail: channelxradio@yahoo.com
Format: Adult Contemporary

## WCXX-FM
152 E. Green Ridge Road
Caribou, ME 04736
Phone: (207) 473-7513 or
  660-WCXU (toll-free)
Fax: (207) 472-3221
E-mail: channelxradio@yahoo.com
Format: Adult Contemporary

## WCYI-FM
One City Center
Portland, ME 04101
Phone: (207) 774-6364
Fax: (207) 774-8707

http://www.wcyy.com
Format: Alternative/New
  Music/Progressive

## WDME-FM
P.O. Box 98
Dover Foxcroft, ME 04426
Phone: (207) 564-2642
Fax: (207) 564-8905
E-mail: wdme@kynd.net
http://www.zoneradio.com
Format: Adult Contemporary, Sports,
  News, Information

## WEBB-FM
52 Western Avenue
Augusta, ME 04330
Phone: (207) 623-4735
Fax: (207) 626-5948
http://www.b985.fm
Format: Contemporary Country

## WGAN-AM
420 Western Avenue
South Portland, ME 04106
Phone: (207) 774-4561
Fax: (207) 774-3788
E-mail: gan56.com
Format: Talk, News

## WGUY-FM
108 Elm Street
Newport, ME 04953
Phone: (207) 368-1021 or (888) 266-2146
  (toll-free)
Fax: (207) 368-3299
Format: Oldies

## WHCF-FM
P.O. Box 5000
Bangor, ME 04401
Phone: (207) 947-2751 or (800) 947-2577
  (toll-free)
Fax: (207) 947-0010
E-mail: fm885@telplus.net
http://www.teleplus.net/whcf
Format: Religious, Talk

## WHOU-FM
P.O. Box 40
Houlton, ME 04730
Phone: (207) 532-3600
Fax: (207) 521-0056
E-mail: whoufm@webtv.net
Format: Adult Contemporary, Public
  Radio

## WMME-FM
52 Western Avenue
Augusta, ME 04330

**Phone:** (207) 623-4735
**Fax:** (207) 626-5948
http://www.92moose.fm
**Format:** Contemporary Hit Radio
   (CHR)

**WMSJ-FM**
P.O. Box 287
Freeport, ME 04032-0287
**Phone:** (207) 865-3448
**Fax:** (207) 865-1763
**E-mail:** wmsj@wmsj.org
http://www.wmsj.org
**Format:** Contemporary Christian

**WNHQ-FM**
482 Congress Street
Suite 501
Portland, ME 04101
**Phone:** (207) 773-8900
http://www.fnxradio.com
**Format:** Alternative/New
   Music/Progressive

**WOZI-FM**
U.S. Rte. 1
Presque Isle, ME 04769
**Phone:** (207) 769-6600
**Fax:** (207) 764-5274
http://www.oldies 1019.com
**Format:** Oldies

**WQCB-FM**
49 Acme Road
P.O. Box 100
Brewer, ME 04412
**Phone:** (207) 989-5631
**Fax:** (207) 989-5685
**E-mail:** q1065@midmaine.com
http://www.telplus.net/q1065
**Format:** Country

**WRBC-FM**
339 Bates College
Lewiston, ME 04240
**Phone:** (207) 777-7532
**Fax:** (207) 786-6035
**E-mail:** wrbc@abacus.bates.edu
http://www.bates.edu/wrbc
**Format:** Eclectic

**WRED-FM**
P.O. Box 1978
Portland, ME 04104
**Phone:** (207) 284-9600
**Fax:** (207) 283-1234
**E-mail:** mail@redhot95.com
http://www.redhot95.com
**Format:** Contemporary Hit Radio (CHR)

**WTPN-FM**
1 City Center
Portland, ME 04101
**Phone:** (207) 774-6364
**Fax:** (207) 774-8707
http://www.989thepoint.com
**Format:** Adult Contemporary

# MARYLAND

**WAAI-FM**
P.O. Box 1495
Cambridge, MD 21613
**Phone:** (410) 754-3032
**Fax:** (410) 228-0130
**E-mail:** waai@intercom.net
http://www.mtslive.com
**Format:** Country

**WARK-AM**
880 Commonwealth Avenue
Hagerstown, MD 21740-6881
**Phone:** (301) 733-4500 or (800) 222-9279
   (toll-free)
**Fax:** (301) 733-0040
**E-mail:** sales@warx.com
http://www.warx.com
**Format:** Talk, Oldies

**WARX-FM**
880 Commonwealth Avenue
Hagerstown, MD 21740
**Phone:** (301) 733-4500 or (800) 222-9279
   (toll-free)
**Fax:** (301) 733-0040
http://www.warx.com
**Format:** Oldies

**WBAL-AM**
3800 Hooper Avenue
Baltimore, MD 21211
**Phone:** (410) 467-3000 or (800) 467-9225
   (toll-free)
**Fax:** (410) 338-6483
http://www.wbal.com
**Format:** News, Talk, Sports

**WBIG-FM**
11300 Rockville Pike
Suite 905
Rockville, MD 20852
**Phone:** (301) 468-1800 or
   (800) 493-0236 (toll-free)
**Fax:** (301) 770-0236
**E-mail:** oldie@mindspring.com
http://www.oldies100.com
**Format:** Oldies

**WBIS-AM**
1081 Bay Ridge
Annapolis, MD 21404
**Phone:** (410) 269-0700
**Fax:** (410) 269-0692
**Format:** News, Talk

**WCBC-AM**
35 Baltimore Street
Cumberland, MD 21502
**Phone:** (301) 724-5000
**Fax:** (301) 722-8336
**E-mail:** staff@wcbc1270am.com
**Format:** Talk, Adult Contemporary,
   News, Sports, Oldies

**WCBM-AM**
11 Music Fair Road
Owings Mills, MD 21117
**Phone:** (410) 356-3003
**Fax:** (410) 581-0150
**Format:** Talk

**WCEI-AM**
306 Port Street
Easton, MD 21601-4101
**Phone:** (410) 822-3301
**Fax:** (410) 822-0576
http://wceiradio.com
**Format:** Talk, Big Band/Nostalgia, Easy
   Listening

**WCTR-AM**
P.O. Box 700
Chestertown, MD 21620-0700
**Phone:** (410) 778-1530
**Fax:** (410) 778-4800
**E-mail:** wctr 1530am@friendly.net
**Format:** Talk, News, Sports, Adult
   Contemporary, Agricultural

**WEAA-FM**
Hillen Road & Coldspring Lane
Baltimore, MD 21251
**Phone:** (443) 885-4526
**Fax:** (410) 319-3798
**Format:** Public Radio, Gospel, Urban
   Contemporary, Jazz, Talk

**WFMD-AM**
P.O. Box 151
Frederick, MD 21705
**Phone:** (301) 663-4181
**Fax:** (301) 663-5494
**E-mail:** nt930@aol.com
**Format:** News, Talk

**WHAG-AM**
1250 Maryland Avenue
Hagerstown, MD 21740-7244

**Phone:** (301) 797-7300
**Format:** Talk, Sports, News

**WHFS-FM**
8201 Corporate Drive
Suite 550
Hyattsville, MD 20785
**Phone:** (301) 306-0991 or
    (800) 321-WHFS (toll-free)
**Fax:** (301) 731-0431
http://www.whfs.com
**Format:** Alternative/New
    Music/Progressive

**WJEJ-AM**
1135 Haven Road
Hagerstown, MD 21742
**Phone:** (301) 739-2323 or (800) 265-0057
    (toll-free)
**Fax:** (301) 797-7408
**Format:** Full Service, Easy Listening,
    Talk, Adult Contemporary, Oldies

**WJHU-FM**
2216 N. Charles Street
Baltimore, MD 21218
**Phone:** (410) 516-9548
**Fax:** (410) 516-1976
**E-mail:** mail@wjhu.org
http://www.wjhu.org

**WJTM-FM**
P.O. Box 205
Braddock Heights, MD 21714
**Phone:** (301) 662-9090
**Fax:** (301) 371-8888
http://www.wjtm.org
**Format:** Gospel

**WLAC-AM**
55 Music Square W.
Nashville, TN 37203-3207
**Phone:** (615) 256-0555 or
    (800) 688-WLAC (toll-free)
**Fax:** (615) 242-4826
**E-mail:** 1510@wlac.com
http://www.wlac.com
**Format:** News, Talk, Sports

**WLIF-FM**
One W. Pennsylvania Avenue
Suite 850
Baltimore, MD 21204
**Phone:** (410) 823-1570
**Fax:** (410) 821-5482
http://wliffm.com
**Format:** Adult Contemporary

**WLOJ-AM**
116 S. Business Plaza
New Bern, NC 28562-8959
**Phone:** (919) 633-1144
**Format:** Contemporary Hit Radio
    (CHR), Gospel, Talk, Sports

**WMDM-AM**
P.O. Box 600
Lexington Park, MD 20653
**Phone:** (301) 475-8383
**Fax:** (301) 475-7832
**Format:** News, Talk

**WMZQ-FM**
1801 Rockville Pike, 6th Floor
Rockville, MD 20852
**Phone:** (301) 231-8231 or (800) 505-0098
    (toll-free)
**Fax:** (301) 984-4895
http://www.wmzqfm.com
**Format:** Country

**WNAV-AM**
236 Admiral Drive
Annapolis, MD 21401
**Phone:** (410) 263-1430 or (888) 345-9628
    (toll-free)
**Fax:** (410) 268-5360
**E-mail:** wnav@toad.net
http://www.wnav.com
**Format:** Full Service, Adult
    Contemporary

**WNTR-AM**
516 White Avenue
Cumberland, MD 21502
**Phone:** (301) 759-3600
**Fax:** (301) 777-5404
**E-mail:** wrogwntr@miworld.net
http://www.wntr.com
**Format:** News, Sports, Talk,
    Information

**WOCT-FM**
600 Washington Avenue
Suite 201
Baltimore, MD 21204
**Phone:** (410) 825-1043
**Fax:** (410) 583-5557
http://www.woctfm.com
**Format:** Classic Rock

**WOL-AM**
5900 Pricess Garden Pkwy.
Suite 800
Lanham, MD 20706
**Phone:** (301) 306-1111

**Fax:** (301) 306-1149
**Format:** News, Talk

**WQJZ-FM**
P.O. Box 269
Salisbury, MD 21803
**Phone:** (410) 742-3212
**Fax:** (410) 548-1543
**E-mail:** dtgm@wqjz.com
http://www.wqjz.com
**Format:** Jazz

**WRNR-FM**
112 Main Street, 3rd Floor
Annapolis, MD 21401
**Phone:** (410) 626-0103
**Fax:** (410) 267-7634
**E-mail:** info@wrnr.com
http://www.wrnr.com
**Format:** Alternative/New
    Music/Progressive

**WROG-FM**
516 White Avenue
Cumberland, MD 21502
**Phone:** (301) 777-5400
**Fax:** (301) 777-5404
**E-mail:** wrogwntr@miworld.net
http://www.wrog.com
**Format:** Country

**WSER-AM**
192 Maloney Road
Elkton, MD 21921
**Phone:** (410) 398-3883
**Fax:** (410) 392-9882
**Format:** News, Talk

**WTEM-AM**
11300 Rockville Pike
Suite 707
Rockville, MD 20852-3089
**Phone:** (301) 231-7798
**Fax:** (301) 881-8030
**Format:** Sports, Talk

**WTHU-AM**
10 Radio Lane
Thurmont, MD 21788-1645
**Phone:** (301) 271-2188
**Format:** News, Talk

**WWRC-AM**
8121 Georgia Avenue
Silver Spring, MD 20910-4933
**Phone:** (301) 587-4900
**Fax:** (301) 587-5759
**Format:** Talk

## MASSACHUSETTS

**WARA-AM**
45 West Street
Attleboro, MA 02703
**Phone:** (508) 222-9272
**Fax:** (508) 222-8284
**E-mail:** talk@am1320wara.com
**Format:** Talk, News, Sports

**WBEC-AM**
211 Jason Street
Pittsfield, MA 01201-5907
**Phone:** (413) 499-3333
**Fax:** (413) 442-1590
**Format:** Full Service, News, Talk

**WBET-AM**
60 Main Street
Brockton, MA 02301
**Phone:** (508) 587-2400
**Fax:** (508) 587-4786
**Format:** News, Talk

**WBOQ-FM**
8 Enon Street
Beverly, MA 01915
**Phone:** (978) 927-1049 or
    (800) 370-1049 (toll-free)
**Fax:** (978) 921-2635
**E-mail:** wbach@wbach.com
http://www.wbach.com
**Format:** Classical, Jazz

**WBSM-AM**
22 Sconticut Neck Road
Fairhaven, MA 02719
**Phone:** (508) 993-1767
**Fax:** (508) 999-1420
**Format:** Talk, News

**WBZ-AM**
1170 Soldiers Field Road
Boston, MA 02134-1092
**Phone:** (617) 787-7000
**Fax:** (617) 787-7060
**Format:** News, Talk

**WCCM-AM**
462 Merriman Street
Methuen, MA 01844
**Phone:** (978) 683-7171
**Fax:** (978) 687-1180
http://www.800wccm.com
**Format:** News, Talk, Music of Your Life

**WCAI-FM**
P.O. Box 82
Woods Hole, MA 02543

**Phone:** (508) 548-9600
**E-mail:** cainan@wgbh.org
**Format:** Talk, News

**WCAP-AM**
243 Central Street
Lowell, MA 01852
**Phone:** (508) 454-0404
**Fax:** (508) 458-9124
**Format:** News, Talk

**WCAT-AM**
660 E. Main Street
P.O. Box 90
Orange, MA 01364
**Phone:** (508) 544-2321
**Format:** Talk, News

**WCCM-AM**
462 Merriman Street
Methuen, MA 01844
**Phone:** (978) 683-7171
**Fax:** (978) 687-1180
http://www.800wccm.com
**Format:** News, Talk, Music of Your Life

**WEIM-AM**
762 Water Street
P.O. Box 727
Fitchburg, MA 01420
**Phone:** (978) 343-3766
**Fax:** (978) 345-6397
**E-mail:** news@weim.com
http://www.weim.com
**Format:** Sports, Adult Contemporary,
    News, Talk

**WERS-FM**
120 Boylston Street
Boston, MA 02116
**Phone:** (617) 824-8891
**Fax:** (617) 824-8804
**E-mail:** music@wers.org
http://www.wers.org
**Format:** Eclectic

**WESX-AM**
P.O. Box 710
Salem, MA 01970
**Phone:** (508) 744-1230
**Fax:** (508) 744-1853
**E-mail:** 1230wesx@yahoo.com
**Format:** Big Band/Nostalgia, Oldies,
    Adult Contemporary, Talk, News,
    Sports

**WEZE-AM**
P.O. Box 9121
North Quincy, MA 02171

**Phone:** (617) 328-0880 or
    (888) 659-0590 (toll-free)
**Fax:** (617) 328-0375
**E-mail:** family590590@aol.com
http://www.weze.net
**Format:** Religious, Talk

**WFNX-FM**
25 Exchange Street
Lynn, MA 01901
**Phone:** (617) 595-6200
**Fax:** (617) 595-3810
**E-mail:** fnx@fnxradio.com
http://www.fnxradio.com
**Format:** Alternative/New
    Music/Progressive

**WGBH-FM**
125 Western Avenue
Boston, MA 02134
**Phone:** (617) 492-2777
**Fax:** (617) 864-7927
http://www.wgbh.org
**Format:** Classical, Jazz, Folk, News,
    Public Radio

**WGAO-FM**
99 Main Street
Franklin, MA 02038
**Phone:** (508) 528-4210
**Fax:** (508) 541-1922
**Format:** Contemporary Christian, Eclectic,
    Album-Oriented Rock (AOR), Classic
    Rock, Alternative/New
    Music/Progressive

**WGFP-AM**
27 Douglas Road
Webster, MA 01570
**Phone:** (508) 943-9400
**Fax:** (508) 943-0405
**Format:** News, Talk

**WHYN-FM**
1331 Main Street
Springfield, MA 01103
**Phone:** (413) 781-1011
http://www.mix931fm.com
**Format:** Adult Contemporary

**WILD-AM**
90 Warren Street
Boston, MA 02119
**Phone:** (617) 427-2222
**Fax:** (617) 427-2677
http://www.wildam1090.com
**Format:** Urban Contemporary, Adult
    Contemporary

**WKOX-AM**
100 Mt. Wayte Avenue
Framingham, MA 01702-5705
**Phone:** (508) 820-2400
**Fax:** (508) 820-2458
**Format:** News, Talk, Ethnic

**WINQ-FM**
3 Central Street
Winchendon, MA 01475
**Phone:** (508) 297-3698
**Fax:** (508) 297-9970
**E-mail:** staff@winqfm.com
http://www.winqfm.com
**Format:** Contemporary Hit Radio (CHR)

**WKPE-AM**
426 North Street
Hyannis, MA 02601-5132
**Phone:** (508) 255-3220
**Fax:** (508) 255-9787
**E-mail:** rock1047@rock1047.com
http://www.rock1047.com
**Format:** Album-Oriented Rock (AOR)

**WKPE-FM**
426 North Street
Hyannis, MA 02601-5132
**Phone:** (508) 255-3220 or
    (800) 497-1047 (toll-free)
**Fax:** (508) 255-9787
**E-mail:** wkpefm@ix.netcom.com
http://www.rock1047.com
**Format:** Album-Oriented Rock (AOR)

**WMNB-FM**
Box 707
North Adams, MA 01247
**Phone:** (413) 663-6567
**Fax:** (413) 662-2143
**E-mail:** wnaw@bcn.net
http://www.wmnbfm.com
**Format:** Easy Listening

**WMRC-AM**
258 Main Street
P.O. Box 421
Milford, MA 01757
**Phone:** (508) 473-1490
**Fax:** (508) 478-2200
http://www.uwmrc.com
http://www.wmrc@dfront.com
**Format:** Full Service, Adult
    Contemporary

**WNNZ-AM**
1331 Main Street
Suite 5
Springfield, MA 01103-1621

**Phone:** (413) 736-6400 or
    (800) 736-4640 (toll-free)
**Fax:** (413) 858-1958
**Format:** Talk

**WMVY-FM**
Box 1148
Vineyard Haven, MA 02568
**Phone:** (508) m693-5000
**Fax:** (508) 693-8211
**E-mail:** wmvy@mvyradio.com
http://www.mvyradi
**Format:** Album-Oriented Rock (AOR),
    Classical, Jazz

**WORC-FM**
250 Commercial Street
Worcester, MA 01608
**Phone:** (508) 752-1045
**Fax:** (508) 793-0824
http://www.oldies989.com
**Format:** Oldies

**WNKS-FM**
116 Huntington Avenue
Boston, MA 02116
http://www.kiss951.com
**Format:** Contemporary Hit Radio (CHR)

**WOMR-FM**
14 Center Street
P.O. Box 975
Provincetown, MA 02657
**Phone:** (508) 487-2106 or
    (800) 921-9667 (toll-free)
**Fax:** (508) 487-5524
**E-mail:** info@womr.org
http://www.womr.org
**Format:** Eclectic, Blues, Jazz, Folk,
    Classical, Bluegrass, Oldies, World
    Beat

**WORC-AM**
108 Grove Street
Suite 17A
Worcester, MA 01605-2629
**Phone:** (508) 799-0581
**Fax:** (508) 756-4851
**Format:** Talk

**WPEP-AM**
41 Taunton Green
Taunton, MA 02780-3233
**Phone:** (508) 822-1570
**Format:** News, Talk

**WRKO-AM**
20 Guest Street
Boston, MA 02135-2040

**Phone:** (617) 236-6800
**Fax:** (617) 236-6889
**Format:** Talk

**WSAR-AM**
1 Home Street
Somerset, MA 02725
**Phone:** (508) 678-9727
**Fax:** (508) 673-0310
**E-mail:** general@wsar.com
http://www.wsar.com
**Format:** News, Talk, Sports

**WSSS-FM**
116 Huntington Avenue
Boston, MA 02116
http://www.wsss.com
**Format:** Oldies, Contemporary Hit Radio
    (CHR)

**WTAG-AM**
P.O. Box 58, West Side Station
Worcester, MA 01602
**Phone:** (508) 795-0580
**Fax:** (508) 757-1779
**Format:** Talk, Sports

**WVNE-AM**
70 James Street
Suite 201
Worcester, MA 01603-1000
**Phone:** (508) 831-9863
**Fax:** (508) 831-7964
**E-mail:** wvne@aol.com
http://www.lifechangingradio.com
**Format:** Religious, Talk

**WWFX-FM**
250 Commercial Street
Worcester, MA 01608
**Phone:** (508) 752-1045
**Fax:** (508) 793-0624
http://www.thefoxfm.com
**Format:** Oldies

**WXTK-FM**
851 Rte. 28
South Yarmouth, MA 02664
**Phone:** (508) 862-6397 or
    (888) 998-5951 (toll-free)
**Fax:** (508) 760-5353
**Format:** News, Talk

## MICHIGAN

**WABJ-AM**
121 W. Maumee Street
Adrian, MI 49221
**Phone:** (517) 265-1500

**Fax:** (517) 263-4525
**E-mail:** wabj@dmci.net
http://www.radiofriends.com
**Format:** News, Talk

**WBCK-AM**
390 Golden Avenue
Battle Creek, MI 49015
**Phone:** (616) 963-5555
**Fax:** (616) 963-5185
http://www.battlecreekradio.com
**Format:** News, Talk, Information

**WBFH-FM**
4200 Andover Road
Bloomfield Hills, MI 48302
**Phone:** (248) 645-4740
**Fax:** (248) 645-4744
**E-mail:** wbfh@hotmail.com
http://www.iwbfh.fm
**Format:** Top 40, Classic Rock,
    Educational

**WBFX-FM**
77 Monroe Center
Suite 1000
Grand Rapids, MI 49503
**Phone:** (616) 459-1919
**Fax:** (616) 242-9373
**E-mail:** web@101thefoxrocks.com
http://www.101thefoxrocks.com
**Format:** Classic Rock

**WBLV-FM**
Blue Lake Fine Arts Camp
Rt. 2
Twin Lake, MI 49457
**Phone:** (616) 894-2616
**E-mail:** radio@bluelake.org
http://www.bluelake.org
**Format:** Public Radio, Classical, Jazz,
    News

**WBXX-FM**
390 Golden Avenue
Battle Creek, MI 49015
**Phone:** (616) 963-5555
**Fax:** (616) 963-4245
http://www.wbxxb95.com
**Format:** Adult Contemporary

**WBYB-FM**
745 S. Garfield Avenue
Traverse City, MI 49685
**Phone:** (616) 947-0003 or
    (888) 442-8943 (toll-free)
**Fax:** (616) 947-4290
http://www.10943.com
**Format:** Country

**WCMM-FM**
2025 US 41 West
Marquette, MI 49855
**Phone:** (906) 288-9702 or
    (800) 947-9266 (toll-free)
**Fax:** (906) 228-9717
**E-mail:** wcmm@upmail.com
http://www.wcmm.com
**Format:** Country

**WCRZ-FM**
3338 E. Bristol Road
Flint, MI 48501
**Phone:** (810) 743-1080
**Fax:** (810) 742-5170
http://www.wcrz.com
**Format:** Adult Contemporary

**WCSX-FM**
1 Radio Plaza
Detroit, MI 48220
**Phone:** (248) 398-7600
**Fax:** (248) 542-8800
http://www.wcsx.com
**Format:** Classic Rock

**WDEO-AM**
24 Frank Lloyd Wright Drive
Ann Arbor, MI 48106
**Phone:** (734) 930-5200
**Fax:** (734) 930-3101
**E-mail:** hroot@rc.net
http://www.wdeo.net
**Format:** Talk, Religious

**WDFN-AM**
2930 E. Jefferson
Detroit, MI 48207
**Phone:** (313) 259-5440
**Fax:** (313) 259-1885
**E-mail:** wuggiefan@aol.com
http://www.wdfn.com
**Format:** Sports

**WDMJ-AM**
P.O. Box 700
845 W. Washington Street
Marquette, MI 49855
**Phone:** (906) 225-1313
**Fax:** (906) 225-1324
http://www.wjpd.com
**Format:** News, Talk, Sports

**WDOW-FM**
P.O. Box 150
Dowagiac, MI 49047
**Phone:** (616) 782-5106
**Fax:** (616) 782-5107
http://www.wvhq.com
**Format:** Adult Contemporary

**WDZZ-FM**
6317 Taylor Drive
Flint, MI 48507-4683
**Phone:** (810) 767-7300
**Fax:** (810) 238-7310
**E-mail:** wdzzfm@aol.com
http://www.wdzz.com
**Format:** Urban Contemporary

**WHTC-AM**
P.O. Box 1467
Holland, MI 49422
**Phone:** (616) 392-3121
**Fax:** (616) 392-8066
**E-mail:** whtc@whtc.com
http://www.whtc.com
**Format:** Full Service

**WIAA-FM**
Interlochen Center for the Arts
Interlochen, MI 49643
**Phone:** (616) 276-4400 or
    (800) 441-9422 (toll-free)
**Fax:** (616) 276-4417
**E-mail:** ipr@interlochen.k12.mi.us
http://www.interlochen.k12.mi.us/ipr
**Contact(s):** Thom Paulson, General Mgr.
**Format:** Classical

**WIAN-AM**
P.O. Box 700
845 W. Washington Street
Marquette, MI 49855
**Phone:** (906) 225-1313
**Fax:** (906) 225-1324
http://www.wjpd.com
**Format:** News, Talk, Sports

**WIBM-AM**
1700 Glenshire Drive
Jackson, MI 49201
**Phone:** (517) 787-9546
**Fax:** (517) 787-7517
**E-mail:** wkhm@wkhm.com
http://www.espnradio1450.com
**Format:** Sports

**WILZ-FM**
1740 Champagne Drive
Saginaw, MI 48604
**Phone:** (517) 776-2100
**Fax:** (517) 776-2121
http://www.wheelz.com
**Format:** Classic Rock

**WJR-AM**
2100 Fisher Building
Detroit, MI 48202

**Phone:** (313) 875-4440 or
   (800) 859-0957 (toll-free)
**Fax:** (313) 875-9022
http://www.wjr.net
**Format:** News, Talk

**WKFR-FM**
4154 Jennings Drive
P.O. Box 50911
Kalamazoo, MI 49005
**Phone:** (616) 344-0111
**Fax:** (616) 344-4223
**E-mail:** wkfr@wkfr.com
http://www.wkfr.com
**Format:** Top 40

**WKLQ-FM**
60 Monroe Center, NW
Suite 1000
Grand Rapids, MI 49503
**Phone:** (616) 774-8461
**Fax:** (616) 774-0351
http://www.wklq.com
**Format:** Classic Rock

**WKMI-AM**
4154 Jennings Drive
P.O. Box 50911
Kalamazoo, MI 49005-0911
**Phone:** (616) 344-0111
**Fax:** (616) 344-4223
**E-mail:** radio@wkmi.com;
   news@wkmi.com
http://www.wkmi.com
**Format:** Talk

**WKQZ-FM**
3190 Christy Way
Suite No. 5
Saginaw, MI 48603
**Phone:** (517) 695-5115
**Fax:** (517) 695-5376
http://www.z93kqz.fm
**Format:** Album-Oriented Rock (AOR),
   Classic Rock

**WLAV-FM**
60 Monroe Center
Grand Rapids, MI 49503
**Phone:** (616) 456-5461
**Fax:** (616) 451-3299
http://www.wlav.com
**Format:** Classic Rock

**WLCS-FM**
851 W. Laketon Avenue
Muskegon, MI 49441-2964
**Phone:** (231) 759-0544
**Fax:** (231) 759-3410

**E-mail:** eagleoldies@bear.com
http://www.eagleoldiesbear.com
**Format:** Oldies

**WLHT-FM**
P.O. Box 96
Grand Rapids, MI 49501
**Phone:** (616) 451-4800
**Fax:** (616) 451-0113
http://www.wlht.com
**Format:** Adult Contemporary

**WMKM-AM**
1514 E. Jefferson
Detroit, MI 48207
**Phone:** (313) 393-1044
**Fax:** (313) 393-1878
**E-mail:** wmkm@prodigy.net
**Format:** Gospel

**WMUZ-FM**
12300 Radio Plaza
Detroit, MI 48228
**Phone:** (313) 272-3434
**Fax:** (313) 272-5045
**E-mail:** sales@wmuz.com

**WMUZ-FM**
12300 Radio Plaza
Detroit, MI 48228
**Phone:** (313) 272-3434
**Fax:** (313) 272-5045
**E-mail:** sales@wmuz.com

**WMXD-FM**
645 Griswold
Detroit, MI 48226
**Phone:** (313) 965-2000
**Fax:** (313) 965-9970
**Format:** Adult Contemporary, Urban
   Contemporary

**WOMC-FM**
2201 Woodward Heights Boulevard
Detroit, MI 48220
**Phone:** (248) 546-9600
**Fax:** (248) 546-5446
**Format:** Oldies

**WPLT-FM**
2100 Fisher Building
Detroit, MI 48202
**Phone:** (313) 871-3030
**Fax:** (313) 875-9636
**E-mail:** planet963@planet963.com
http://www.963theplanet.com

**WQBH-AM**
Penobscot Building
Detroit, MI 48226

**Phone:** (313) 965-4500
**Fax:** (313) 965-4608
**Format:** Urban Contemporary, Blues,
   Jazz

**WRIF-FM**
One Radio Plaza
Detroit, MI 48220
**Phone:** (248) 547-0101
**Fax:** (248) 542-8800
**Format:** Album-Oriented Rock (AOR)

## MINNESOTA

**BRAT-FM**
108 Main W.
Sleepy Eye, MN 56085
**Phone:** (507) 794-3149 or
   (800) 444-5685 (toll-free)
**Fax:** (507) 794-4990
**E-mail:** radioone@ic.new-ulm.mn.us
http://www.radiooneminnesota.com
**Format:** Adult Contemporary

**KBEM-FM**
1555 James Avenue
Minneapolis, MN 55411
**Phone:** (612) 668-1735
**Fax:** (612) 668-1766
**E-mail:** kbem@mpls.k12.mn.us
http://www.mpls.k12.mn.us/kbem/index.
   html
**Format:** Information, Jazz

**KCCD-FM**
Concordia College
901 S. 8th Street
Moorhead, MN 56562
**Phone:** (218) 299-3666
**Fax:** (218) 299-3418
http://www.mpr.org
**Format:** News, Information

**KDHL-AM**
601 Central Avenue
Box 30
Faribault, MN 55021-0030
**Phone:** (507) 334-0061 or
   (800) 369-5345 (toll-free)
**Fax:** (507) 334-7057
**E-mail:** kdhl@radiominnesota.com
http://www.radiominnesota.com
**Format:** Oldies, Country, News,
   Information

**KDIZ-AM**
2000 Elm Street SE
Minneapolis, MN 55414
**Phone:** (612) 617-4000

**Fax:** (612) 676-8214
**E-mail:** brian.alker@abc.com

**KDIZ-AM**
2000 Elm Street SE
Minneapolis, MN 55414
**Phone:** (612) 617-4000
**Fax:** (612) 676-8214
**E-mail:** brian.alker@abc.com
**Format:** Contemporary Hit Radio (CHR)

**KDXL-FM**
6425 W. 33rd Street
Street Louis Park, MN 55426
**Phone:** (612) 928-6149
**Fax:** (612) 928-6206
**Format:** Alternative/New
    Music/Progressive, Hip Hop, Top 40

**KEEY-FM**
7900 Xerxes Avenue S.
Suite 102
Minneapolis, MN 55431
**Phone:** (612) 820-4200
**Fax:** (612) 820-4241
**E-mail:** k102@k102.com
http://www.k102.com
**Format:** Country

**KFAN-AM**
P.O. Box 20731
Minneapolis, MN 55420-0731
**Format:** Sports

**KFMC-FM**
1371 W. Lair Road
P.O. Box 491
Fairmont, MN 56031
**Phone:** (507) 235-5595
**Fax:** (507) 235-3299
**E-mail:** kfmc@beucomm.net
http://www.kfmc.com
**Format:** Adult Contemporary,
    Contemporary Hit Radio (CHR)

**KFML-FM**
16405 Haven Road
Little Falls, MN 56345-6400
**Phone:** (320) 632-2992
**Fax:** (320) 632-2571
**E-mail:** fallsradio@fallsnet.com
http://www.fallsradio.com
**Format:** Adult Contemporary, Oldies

**KKBJ-AM**
2115 Washington Avenue S.
Bemidji, MN 56601
**Phone:** (218) 751-7777
**Fax:** (218) 759-0658
**E-mail:** kkbjwbji@northernnet.com

http://www.mnradio.com
**Format:** Talk

**KKCK-FM**
1414 E. College Drive
Marshall, MN 56258
**Phone:** (507) 532-2282
**Fax:** (507) 532-3739
http://marshallradio.net
**Format:** Top 40

**KKEQ-FM**
Hwy. 2 E.
P.O. Box 606
Fosston, MN 56542-0606
**Phone:** (218) 435-1919 or
    (800) 435-1071 (toll-free)
**Fax:** (218) 435-1480
**E-mail:** q107@gvtel.com
http://www.christianradio.com/q107
**Format:** Adult Contemporary, Religious

**KLBB-AM**
331 S. 11th Street
Minneapolis, MN 55404-1006
**Phone:** (612) 321-7200 or
    (800) 879-3462 (toll-free)
**Fax:** (612) 321-7202
**Format:** Big Band/Nostalgia

**KLQL-FM**
P.O. Box 599
Hwy. 16 E
Luverne, MN 56156
**Phone:** (507) 283-4444
**Fax:** (507) 283-4445
**E-mail:** tenews@k101.net
http://www.k101.net
**Format:** Country, Agricultural

**KMOJ-FM**
501 Bryant Avenue N.
Minneapolis, MN 55405
**Phone:** (612) 377-0594
**Fax:** (612) 377-6919
http://www.kmoj.com
**Format:** Urban Contemporary

**KNFX-AM**
1530 Greenview Drive SW
Suite 200
Rochester, MN 55902
**Phone:** (507) 288-3888
**Fax:** (507) 288-7815
http://www.wchestersquare.com
**Format:** News

**KNOW-FM**
45 E. 7th Street
St. Paul, MN 55101

**Phone:** (612) 290-1500
**Fax:** (612) 290-1260
**E-mail:** mail@mpr.org
http://www.mpr.org
**Format:** News, Public Radio

**KQQL-FM**
60 S 6th Street
Suite 930
Minneapolis, MN 55402-4409
**Phone:** (612) 333-8118
**Fax:** (612) 333-1616
**E-mail:** kool108@usinternet.com
**Format:** Oldies

**KQRS-FM**
2000 SE Elm Street
Minneapolis, MN 55414
**Phone:** (612) 617-4000
**Fax:** (612) 676-8292
http://www.92kqrs.com
**Format:** Album-Oriented Rock (AOR)

**KRBR-FM**
715 E. Central Entrance
Duluth, MN 55811
**Phone:** (218) 722-4321
**Fax:** (218) 722-5423
http://www.krbr.com

**KRCH-FM**
1530 Greenview Drive, SW
Suite 200
Rochester, MN 55902
**Phone:** (507) 288-3888
**Fax:** (507) 288-7815
http://www.radiominnesota.com
**Format:** Classic Rock

**KSGS-AM**
7001 France Avenue, S.
Suite 200
Minneapolis, MN 55435-4202
**Phone:** (612) 836-1041
**Fax:** (612) 915-9781
**Format:** Urban Contemporary

**KSTP-FM**
3415 University Avenue
Minneapolis, MN 55414
**Phone:** (612) 642-4141
**Fax:** (612) 642-4142
**Format:** Adult Contemporary

**KWEB-AM**
1530 Greenview Drive, SW
Suite 200
Rochester, MN 55902
**Phone:** (507) 288-3888

**Fax:** (507) 288-7815
http://www.wchestersquare.com
**Format:** Talk, Agricultural, News, Sports

**KXLP-FM**
1807 Lee Boulevard
North Mankato, MN 56003
**Phone:** (507) 388-2900
**Fax:** (507) 345-4675
**E-mail:** @kysmkxlpradio.com
http://www.kxzpradio.com
**Format:** Classic Rock

**KXXR-FM**
2000 SE Elm Street
Minneapolis, MN 55414
**Phone:** (612) 617-4000
**Fax:** (612) 676-8293
http://www.93x.com
**Format:** Rock

**KYSM-AM**
1807 Lee Boulevard
North Mankato, MN 56003
**Phone:** (507) 388-2900
**Fax:** (507) 345-4675
http://www.kysmradio.com
**Format:** Oldies

**KYSM-FM**
1807 Lee Boulevard
North Mankato, MN 56003
**Phone:** (507) 388-2900
**Fax:** (507) 345-4675
http://www.kysmradio.com
**Format:** Country

## MISSISSIPPI

**KAIN-AM**
P.O. Box 17833 Tracetown
Beltline Hwy.
Natchez, MS 39122
**Phone:** (601) 446-8803
**Fax:** (601) 446-8803
**Format:** News, Talk

**KUUZ-FM**
P.O. Box 1794
Greenville, MS 38702-1794
**Phone:** (601) 332-0025 or
(800) 844-8979 (toll-free)
**Fax:** (601) 332-0038
**Format:** Contemporary Country

**KZYQ-FM**
P.O. Box 5395
Greenville, MS 38704
**Phone:** (662) 378-4103

**Fax:** (662) 332-3103
**E-mail:** star@deltaradio.net
http://www.deltaradio.net
**Format:** Adult Contemporary

**WABG-AM**
P.O. Box 408
Greenwood, MS 38930
**Phone:** (601) 453-7822
**Fax:** (601) 455-3311
**E-mail:** wabgradio@wabg.com
**Format:** Country, Talk

**WACR-AM**
1910 14th Avenue N.
P.O. Box 1078
Columbus, MS 39703
**Phone:** (601) 328-1050
**Fax:** (601) 328-1054
**Format:** Religious, Urban
Contemporary

**WADI-FM**
1608 S. John Street
Corinth, MS 38834
**Phone:** (662) 287-3101
**Fax:** (662) 287-9262
**Format:** Contemporary Country

**WAFM-FM**
521 Hwy. 278 W.
P.O. Box 458
Amory, MS 38821
**Phone:** (601) 256-9726
**Format:** Oldies

**WBBV-FM**
P.O. Box 820537
Vicksburg, MS 39182
**Phone:** (601) 638-0101
**Fax:** (601) 638-0869
**Format:** Country

**WDBT-FM**
1375 Beasley Road
Jackson, MS 39206
**Phone:** (601) 982-1062
http://95.5thebeat.com
**Format:** Top 40

**WDMS-FM**
1383 Picket Street
Greenville, MS 38701
**Phone:** (601) 334-4559 or
(888) 808-8644 (toll-free)
**Fax:** (601) 332-1315
**E-mail:** wdms@tecinfo.com
http://www.tecinfo.com./~wdms
**Format:** Contemporary Country

**WDTL-FM**
P.O. Box 1438
Cleveland, MS 38732
**Phone:** (662) 846-0929
**Fax:** (662) 843-1410
**E-mail:** wdtl@deltaradio.net
http://www.deltaradio.net
**Format:** Country

**WIQQ-FM**
Unit 39, Delta Plaza Mall
Hwy. 1 S.
Greenville, MS 38701
**Phone:** (662) 378-2617
**Fax:** (662) 378-8341
**E-mail:** wiqq@bellsouth.net
http://www.wiqq.com
http://www.tecifo.com/~wiqq
**Format:** Contemporary Hit Radio (CHR)

**WJDX-AM**
1375 Beasley Road
Jackson, MS 39206
**Phone:** (601) 982-1062
http://www.wjdx.com
**Format:** Sports, Talk

**WKNN-FM**
P.O. Box 4606
Biloxi, MS 39535
**Phone:** (228) 388-2323
**Fax:** (228) 388-2362
**E-mail:** greggory@amfm.com
http://www.k99fm.com
**Format:** Country

**WJNT-AM**
P.O. Box 1248
Jackson, MS 39215
**Phone:** (601) 366-1150
**Fax:** (601) 366-1627
**E-mail:** contactus@wjnt.com
http://www.wjnt.com
**Format:** News, Talk

**WKNN-FM**
P.O. Box 4606
Biloxi, MS 39535
**Phone:** (228) 388-2323
**Fax:** (228) 388-2362
**E-mail:** greggory@amfm.com
http://www.k99fm.com
**Format:** Country

**WLNF-FM**
P.O. Box 939
Gulfport, MS 39501
**Phone:** (228) 867-9953 or
(888) 548-3953 (toll-free)

**Fax:** (228) 868-0095
**E-mail:** studio@live95fm.com
http://www.live95fm.com
**Format:** Contemporary Hit Radio (CHR)

**WMAB-FM**
c/o Public Radio in Mississippi
3825 Ridgewood Road
Jackson, MS 39211-6463
**Phone:** (601) 432-6565 or
    (800) 472-2580 (toll-free)
**Fax:** (601) 432-6746
**E-mail:** prm@etv.state.ms.us
http://www.npr.org/members/prm
**Format:** Classical, News, Information,
    New Age

**WMAE-FM**
c/o Public Radio in Mississippi
3825 Ridgewood Road
Jackson, MS 39211
**Phone:** (601) 432-6565 or
    (800) 472-2580 (toll-free)
**Fax:** (601) 432-6746
**E-mail:** prm@etv.state.ms.us
http://www.npr.org/members
**Format:** News, Bluegrass, Classical,
    Folk

**WMAH-FM**
c/o Public Radio in Mississippi
3825 Ridgewood Road
Jackson, MS 39211-6463
**Phone:** (601) 432-6565
**Fax:** (601) 432-6746
**E-mail:** prm@etv.state.ms.us
http://www.npr.org/members
**Format:** Classical, News

**WMAO-FM**
c/o Public Radio in Mississippi
3825 Ridgewood Road
Jackson, MS 39211-6463
**Phone:** (601) 432-6565 or
    (800) 472-2580 (toll-free)
**Fax:** (601) 432-6746
**E-mail:** prm@etv.state.ms.us
http://www.npr.org/members
**Format:** Classical, News

**WMAU-FM**
c/o Public Radio in Mississippi
3825 Ridgewood Road
Jackson, MS 39211-6463
**Phone:** (601) 432-6565
**Fax:** (601) 432-6747
**E-mail:** prm@etv.state.ms.us
http://www.npr.org/members
**Format:** Classical, News

**WMAV-FM**
c/o Public Radio in Mississippi
3825 Ridgewood Road
Jackson, MS 39211
**Phone:** (601) 432-6565 or
    (800) 472-2580 (toll-free)
**Fax:** (601) 432-6746
**E-mail:** prm@etv.state.ms.us
http://www.npr.org/members
**Format:** Classical, News

**WMAW-FM**
c/o Public Radio in Mississippi
3825 Ridgewood Road
Jackson, MS 39211
**Phone:** (601) 982-6565 or
    (800) 472-2580 (toll-free)
**Fax:** (601) 982-6746
**E-mail:** prm@etv.state.ms.us
http://www.npr.org/members
**Format:** Public Radio, Full Service

**WMJY-FM**
P.O. Box 4606
Biloxi, MS 39535
**Phone:** (228) 388-2323
**Fax:** (228) 388-2362
**E-mail:** magic937.com
http://www.magic937.com
**Format:** Adult Contemporary

**WMPN-FM**
c/o Public Radio in Mississippi
3825 Ridgewood Road
Jackson, MS 39211
**Phone:** (601) 432-6565 or
    (800) 472-2580 (toll-free)
**Fax:** (601) 432-6746
**E-mail:** prm@etv.state.ms.us
http://www.npr.org/members
**Format:** News, Classical

**WNIX-AM**
Delta Plaza Mall, Unit 39
Hwy. 1 S.
Greenville, MS 38701
**Phone:** (662) 378-2617
**Fax:** (662) 378-8341
**E-mail:** wigg@bellsouth.net;
    wnix@tecinfo.com
http://www.wiqq.com
http://www.tecinfo.com/~wiqq
**Format:** Oldies

**WOKK-FM**
3436 Highway 45N
Meridian, MS 39301
**Phone:** (601) 693-2661
**Fax:** (601) 483-0826

**E-mail:** 97okk@wokk.com
http://www.wokk.com
**Format:** Country

**WQJQ-FM**
1375 Beasley Road
Jackson, MS 39206
**Phone:** (601) 982-1062
http://www.wqjq.com
**Format:** Oldies

**WQYZ-FM**
P.O. Box 1209
Biloxi, MS 39533-1209
**Phone:** (228) 374-8800
**Fax:** (228) 872-0670
**E-mail:** q92@wqyz.com
http://www.wqyz.com

**WRPM-AM**
Progress Road
Box 352
Poplarville, MS 39470
**Phone:** (601) 795-4900 or
    (800) 934-9776 (toll-free)
**Fax:** (601) 795-0277
**E-mail:** tcvaugh@ibm.net
http://www.com.poplarville
**Format:** Southern Gospel

**WUMS-FM**
Student Media Center
Farley Hall
University, MS 38677
**Phone:** (601) 232-7566
**Fax:** (601) 232-5703
**E-mail:** wusm@usm.edu
http://www.wusm.usm.edu
**Format:** Alternative/New
    Music/Progressive

**WVMI-AM**
P.O. Box 4606
Biloxi, MS 39535
**Phone:** (601) 388-2323
**Fax:** (601) 388-2362
**Format:** News, Talk

## MISSOURI

**KALM-AM**
P.O. Box 15
Thayer, MO 65791
**Phone:** (417) 264-7211
**Fax:** (417) 264-7212
**E-mail:** kkountr.com
http://www.kkountry.com
**Format:** News, Sports, Agricultural,
    Information

**KBXR-FM**
503 Old 63 North
Columbia, MO 65201
**Phone:** (573) 449-1520
**Fax:** (573) 449-7770
**E-mail:** bxr@bxr.com
http://www.bxr.com
**Format:** Adult Album Alternative

**KCLQ-FM**
18785 Finch Road
Lebanon, MO 65536
**Phone:** (417) 532-2962
**Fax:** (417) 532-5184
http://www.kclq.com
**Format:** Country

**KDHX-FM**
3504 Magnolia
St. Louis, MO 63118
**Phone:** (314) 664-3955
**Fax:** (314) 664-1020
**E-mail:** bhacker@kdhx.org
http://www.kdhx.org
**Format:** Eclectic

**KDKD-FM**
2201 N. Antioch Road
P.O. Box 448
Clinton, MO 64735-0448
**Phone:** (816) 885-6141
**Fax:** (816) 885-4801
http://www.kdkd.com
**Format:** Contemporary Country

**KEZK-FM**
3100 Market Street
St. Louis, MO 63103-2528
**Phone:** (314) 531-0000
**Fax:** (314) 289-9789
**E-mail:** kezk.com
http://kezk.com
**Format:** Adult Contemporary

**KFAL-AM**
1805 Westminster
Fulton, MO 65251-0581
**Phone:** (573) 642-3341 or
(800) 769-5274 (toll-free)
**Fax:** (573) 642-3343
**E-mail:** kfal@sockets.net
http://www.kfal.com
**Format:** Contemporary Country

**KFMZ-FM**
1101 E. Walnut
P.O. Box 1268
Columbia, MO 65205
**Phone:** (573) 874-3000
**Fax:** (573) 443-1460

**E-mail:** kfmz@socket is.net
http://www.983thebuzz.com
**Format:** Alternative/New
Music/Progressive

**KFNS-AM**
7711 Carondelet
Suite 304
St. Louis, MO 63105
**Phone:** (314) 727-2160
**Fax:** (314) 727-7696
http://www.kfns.com
**Format:** Easy Listening, Sports

**KFUO-FM**
88 Founders Lane
St. Louis, MO 63105
**Phone:** (314) 725-0099 or
(800) 844-0524 (toll-free)
**Fax:** (314) 725-3801
http://www.classic99.com
**Format:** Classical

**KGMY-FM**
1856 Glenstone
Springfield, MO 65804
**Phone:** (417) 890-5555
http://www.clearchannel.com/radio/
**Format:** Country

**KIXQ-FM**
1309 S. Monroe Avenue
Joplin, MO 64801-3629
**Phone:** (417) 624-1025
**Fax:** (417) 781-6842
**E-mail:** onair@hiy1025.com
http://www.hix1025.com
**Format:** Country

**KJAB-FM**
621 W. Monroe
Mexico, MO 65265
**Phone:** (573) 581-8606 or
(800) 371-5522 (toll-free)
**Fax:** (573) 581-8606
**E-mail:** kjab@ktis.net
http://www.kjab.com
**Format:** Southern Gospel, Talk

**KJLU-FM**
820 Chestnut Street
Jefferson City, MO 65102-0029
**Phone:** (573) 681-5301
**Fax:** (573) 681-5299
http://www.lincolnu.edu/~kjlu
**Format:** Jazz, Urban Contemporary

**KKCA-FM**
1805 Westminster
Fulton, MO 65251-0581

**Phone:** (573) 642-3341 or
(800) 769-5274 (toll-free)
**Fax:** (573) 642-3343
**E-mail:** kkca@sockets.net
http://www.kkca.com
**Format:** Oldies

**KKFI-FM**
P.O. Box 32250
Kansas City, MO 64171-5250
**Phone:** (816) 931-3122
**Fax:** (816) 931-7078
**E-mail:** kkfi901@aol.com
http://www.gazlay.com/kkfi
**Format:** Public Radio, Full Service,
Eclectic

**KKLH-FM**
319-B W. Battlefield
Springfield, MO 65807
**Phone:** (417) 886-5677
**Fax:** (417) 886-2155
**E-mail:** wklh@kklh.fm
http://www.kklh.com
**Format:** Classic Rock

**KKOZ-FM**
306 2nd
Box 386
Ava, MO 65608
**Phone:** (417) 683-4193 or
(800) 683-4191 (toll-free)
**E-mail:** jcorum@getgoin.net
http://www.kkoz.com,
http://kkoz.com
**Format:** Country, News, Sports,
Agricultural

**KLFJ-AM**
601A E. Battlefield Street
PMB 253
Springfield, MO 65807-4865
**Phone:** (417) 831-5535
**Fax:** (417) 831-5544
**E-mail:** klfj@dialus.com
http://www.talk1550.com
**Format:** Talk, News, Sports

**KLIK-AM**
3605 Country Club Drive
Jefferson City, MO 65109
**Phone:** (573) 556-5555
**Fax:** (573) 893-8330
http://www.klik1240.com
**Format:** Full Service, Country

**KLJC-FM**
15800 Calvary Road
Kansas City, MO 64147-1341

**Phone:** (816) 331-8700 or
    (800) 466-5552 (toll-free)
**Fax:** (816) 331-4474
**E-mail:** kljc@kljc.org
http://www.kljc.org
**Format:** Religious

**KLPW-AM**
Box 623
Washington, MO 63090
**Phone:** (636) 583-5155
**Fax:** (636) 583-1644
**E-mail:** klpwam@klpw.com
http://www.klpw.com
**Format:** Talk, News

**KMAL-FM**
P.O. Box 69
Sikeston, MO 63801-0069
**Phone:** (573) 276-5625
**Fax:** (573) 276-2282
**E-mail:** kmal@sheltonbbs.com
http://www.kmal.com
**Format:** Adult Contemporary, News,
    Sports

**KMAM-AM**
800 E. Nursery Street
Butler, MO 64730
**Phone:** (660) 679-4191
**Fax:** (660) 679-4193
**E-mail:** point97@infi.net
http://www.fm92radio.com
**Format:** Country, Religious, News,
    Agricultural

**KMMO-FM**
P.O. Box 128
Marshall, MO 65340
**Phone:** (816) 886-7422
**Fax:** (816) 886-6291
**E-mail:** kmmo@mvrlin.com
http://www.kmmo@murlin.com
**Format:** News, Sports, Contemporary
    Country, Agricultural

**KMOE-FM**
800 E. Nursery Street
Butler, MO 64730
**Phone:** (660) 679-4191
**Fax:** (660) 679-4193
http://www.fm92radio.com
**Format:** Country, Religious

**KMOX-AM**
1 Memorial Drive
St. Louis, MO 63102
**Phone:** (314) 621-2345
**Fax:** (314) 444-3230

http://www.kmox.basic.net
**Format:** News, Talk, Sports

**KNRX-FM**
4240 Blue Ridge Boulevard
Suite 820
Kansas City, MO 64133
**Phone:** (816) 353-7600
**Fax:** (816) 353-2300
**E-mail:** pennyb@2957.net
http://k107fm.com
**Format:** Oldies

**KOMC-AM**
202 Courtney Street
Branson, MO 65616
**Phone:** (417) 334-6003
**Fax:** (417) 334-7141
**E-mail:** krzk@mail.tri-lakes.net
http://www.branson.com
**Format:** Big Band/Nostalgia

**KOPN-FM**
915 E. Broadway
Columbia, MO 65201-4857
**Phone:** (573) 874-1139 or
    (800) 895-5676 (toll-free)
**Fax:** (573) 499-1662
**E-mail:** mail@kopn.org
http://www.kopn.org
**Format:** News, Talk

**KOQL-FM**
503 Old 63 Hwy.
Columbia, MO 65201
**Phone:** (573) 443-1524 or
    (800) 786-1061 (toll-free)
**Fax:** (573) 449-7770
**E-mail:** kool@kool1061.com
http://www.koql.com
**Format:** Oldies

**KOSP-FM**
319-B East Battlefield
Springfield, MO 65807
**Phone:** (417) 886-5677
**Fax:** (417) 886-2155
**E-mail:** kosp@kosp.fm
http://www.kosp.com
**Format:** Oldies

# MONTANA

**KALS-FM**
P.O. Box 9710
Kalispell, MT 59904-2710
**Phone:** (406) 752-5257
**Fax:** (406) 752-3416
**E-mail:** kals@kals.com
http://kals.com

**KATL-AM**
810 S. Haynes Avenue
P.O. Box 700
Miles City, MT 59301-0700
**Phone:** (406) 232-7700 or
    (800) 473-5285 (toll-free)
**Fax:** (406) 232-2281
**E-mail:** katlradio@mcn.net
**Format:** Adult Contemporary

**KATQ-AM**
112 3rd Avenue
Suite E
Plentywood, MT 59254-2223
**Phone:** (406) 765-1480
**Fax:** (406) 765-2357
**E-mail:** katq@nemontel.net
**Format:** Full Service, Agricultural,
    Country

**KBBB-FM**
P.O. Box 1276
Billings, MT 59103
**Phone:** (406) 252-9577
http://www.bee 104.com
**Format:** Adult Contemporary

**KBEV-FM**
610 N. Montana Street
Dillon, MT 59725
**Phone:** (406) 683-2800
**Fax:** (406) 683-9480
**E-mail:** deadair@mcn.net
**Format:** Country, Adult Contemporary

**KBGA-FM**
University of Montana
University Center
Missoula, MT 59812
**Phone:** (406) 243-6758
**Fax:** (406) 243-6428
**E-mail:** kbga@selway.umt.edu
http://www.kbga.org
**Format:** Alternative/New
    Music/Progressive

**KBLG-AM**
2075 Central Avenue
Billings, MT 59102
**Phone:** (406) 652-8400 or
    (800) 406-1743 (toll-free)
**Fax:** (406) 652-4899
**E-mail:** newsradio91@kblg.com;
    mtmorningreport@canwetalk.com
http://www.kblg.com
**Format:** Talk, Sports, News

**KBLL-AM**
1400 11th Avenue
Helena, MT 59601

**Phone:** (406) 442-6620
**Fax:** (406) 442-6161
**Format:** News, Talk

**KBMG-FM**
217 N. 3rd Street
Suite L
Hamilton, MT 59840-2471
**Phone:** (406) 363-3010
**Fax:** (406) 363-6436
**E-mail:** klyq@montana.com
http://www.magic96radio.com

**KBOZ-AM**
5445 Johnson Road
P.O. Box 20
Bozeman, MT 59715
**Phone:** (406) 586-5466
**Fax:** (406) 587-8201
**Format:** Country

**KCAP-AM**
110 Broadway
Helena, MT 59601-4232
**Phone:** (406) 442-4490
**Fax:** (406) 442-7356
**E-mail:** kcap@uswest.net
http://www.kcap.com
**Format:** Talk, Sports, News

**KGGL-FM**
P.O. Box 4106
Missoula, MT 59806
**Phone:** (406) 728-9399
**Fax:** (406) 721-3020
**E-mail:** eagle93@montana.com
http://www.eagle93.com
**Format:** Country

**KCGM-FM**
c/o Prarie Communications, Inc.
P.O. Box 220
Scobey, MT 59263
**Phone:** (406) 487-2293
**Fax:** (406) 487-5922
**Format:** Country, Contemporary
    Country, Agricultural

**KCTR-FM**
27 N. 27th Street
Penthouse Suite
P.O. Box 1276
Billings, MT 59101
**Phone:** (406) 248-7827
**Fax:** (406) 252-9577
**Format:** Contemporary Country

**KDBM-AM**
610 N. Montana Street
Dillon, MT 59725

**Phone:** (406) 683-2800
**Fax:** (406) 683-9480
**E-mail:** deadair@mcn.net
**Format:** Country

**KDWG-AM**
27 N. 27th Street
Penthouse Suite
Billings, MT 59103
**Phone:** (406) 248-7827
**Fax:** (406) 252-9577
**Format:** Contemporary Country

**KEIN-AM**
3313 15th Street NE
P.O. Box F
Black Eagle, MT 59414-0237
**Phone:** (406) 761-1310
**Fax:** (406) 454-3775
**Format:** Country

**KERR-AM**
581 N. Reservoir Road
Polson, MT 59860-9730
**Phone:** (406) 883-5255 or
    (800) 766-7105 (toll-free)
**Fax:** (406) 883-4441
**Format:** Country

**KGEZ-AM**
P.O. Box 169
Kalispell, MT 59903-0169
**Phone:** (406) 752-2600
**Fax:** (406) 257-0459
**E-mail:** kgez@digisys.net
**Format:** Oldies

**KGGL-FM**
P.O. Box 4106
Missoula, MT 59806
**Phone:** (406) 728-9399
**Fax:** (406) 721-3020
**E-mail:** eagle93@montana.com
http://www.eagle93.com
**Format:** Country

**KGHL-AM**
222 N. 32nd Street 10th Floor
Billings, MT 59101-1911
**Phone:** (406) 656-1410 or
    (800) 735-1187 (toll-free)
**Fax:** (406) 656-0110
**Format:** Country

**KGLT-FM**
330 Sub, Box 174240
Bozeman, MT 59717-4240
**Phone:** (406) 994-3001
**Fax:** (406) 994-1987

**E-mail:** wwwkglt@montana.edu
http://www.montana.edu/wwwkglt
**Format:** Eclectic

**KGRZ-AM**
P.O. Box 4106
Missoula, MT 59806
**Phone:** (406) 728-1450
**Fax:** (406) 721-3020
**Format:** Sports, Talk

**KHKR-FM**
Box 4111
Helena, MT 59604
**Phone:** (406) 449-4251
**Fax:** (406) 443-7577
**E-mail:** khkr@uswest.net
http://www.khkr.com
**Format:** Contemporary Country

**KIDX-FM**
222 N. 32nd Street 10th Floor
Billings, MT 59101-1911
**Phone:** (406) 656-1410 or
    (800) 735-1187 (toll-free)
**Fax:** (406) 656-0110
**Format:** Hot Country

**KKRY-FM**
508 Main Street
Box 1426
Miles City, MT 59301
**Phone:** (406) 232-5626
**Fax:** (406) 425-4497
**E-mail:** kmcm@mcn.net

**KKRY-FM**
508 Main Street
Box 1426
Miles City, MT 59301
**Phone:** (406) 232-5626
**Fax:** (406) 425-4497
**E-mail:** kmcn@mcn.net

**FLFM-FM**
P.O. Box 3309
Great Falls, MT 59403
**Phone:** (406) 761-7600
**Fax:** (406) 761-5511
http://www.klfmfm.com
**Format:** Oldies, Classic Rock

**KMON-AM**
20 3rd Street, N.
Great Falls, MT 59401
**Phone:** (406) 761-7600
**Fax:** (406) 761-5511
http://www.kmon.com
**Format:** Country, Agricultural

**KMTX-FM**
Box 1183-59624
Helena, MT 59624
**Phone:** (406) 442-0400
**Fax:** (406) 442-0491
**E-mail:** sales@kmtxradio.com
**Format:** Adult Contemporary

**KOFI-AM**
317 1st Avenue, E.
Box 608
Kalispell, MT 59901
**Phone:** (406) 755-6690
**Fax:** (406) 752-5078
**E-mail:** kofi@kofiradio.com
http://www.kofiradio.com
**Format:** News, Talk, Oldies

**KOFI-FM**
317 1st Avenue, E.
P.O. Box 608
Kalispell, MT 59901
**Phone:** (406) 755-6690
**Fax:** (406) 752-5078
**E-mail:** county104.fm.com
http://www.kofiradio.com
**Format:** Contemporary Country

**KYYA-FM**
2075 Central Avenue
Billings, MT 59102-4596
**Phone:** (406) 652-8400
**Fax:** (406) 652-4899
http://www.sunbrook.com/y93/
http://www.y93.com
**Format:** Adult Contemporary

**KZMT-FM**
110 E. Broadway Street
Helena, MT 59601-4232
**Phone:** (406) 442-4490
**Fax:** (406) 442-7356
**E-mail:** kzmt@uswest.net
**Format:** Classic Rock

# NEBRASKA

**KAAQ-FM**
1210 W. 10th Street
P.O. Box 600
Alliance, NE 69301
**Phone:** (308) 762-1400 or
(800) 584-9310 (toll-free)
**Fax:** (308) 762-7804
**E-mail:** kcow@bbc.net
http://www.doubleqcountry.com

**KAAQ-FM**
1210 W. 10th Street
P.O. Box 600
Alliance, NE 69301

**Phone:** (308) 762-1400 or
(800) 584-9310 (toll-free)
**Fax:** (308) 762-7804
**E-mail:** kcow@bbc.net
http://www.doubleqcountry.com
**Format:** Country

**KBBX-AM**
11128 John Galt Boulevard
Suite 192
Omaha, NE 68137-2321
**Phone:** (402) 556-6700
**Fax:** (402) 556-9427
http://www.KBBX.com
**Format:** Urban Contemporary

**KCNE-FM**
P.O. Box 83111
Lincoln, NE 68501
**Phone:** (402) 472-3611
**Fax:** (402) 472-2403
**E-mail:** nprn@unl.edu
http://www.net.unl.edu
**Format:** Classical, News

**KEFM-FM**
105 S. 70th Street
Omaha, NE 68132-3325
**Phone:** (402) 558-9696
**Fax:** (402) 558-3158
http://omahasmix96.com
**Format:** Adult Contemporary

**KELN-FM**
P.O. Box 248
North Platte, NE 69103
**Phone:** (308) 532-1120 or
(877) 532-1120 (toll-free)
**Fax:** (308) 532-0458
**E-mail:** hot97@nponline.net
http://www.hot97keln.com
**Format:** Adult Contemporary

**KEXL-FM**
P.O. Box 789
Norfolk, NE 68702
**Phone:** (402) 371-0780
**Fax:** (402) 371-6303
**E-mail:** wjagkexl@wjag.com
http://www.wjag.com
**Format:** Adult Contemporary, News,
Sports

**KFRX-FM**
6900 Van Dorn Street
Suite 11
Lincoln, NE 68506-2882
**Phone:** (402) 483-5100
**Fax:** (402) 483-4095

http://www.lincnet.com
**Format:** Contemporary Hit Radio (CHR)

**KGBI-FM**
831 Pine Street
Omaha, NE 68108
**Phone:** (402) 449-2900
**Fax:** (402) 449-2825
**E-mail:** kgbi@thebridge.fm
http://www.thebridge.fm
**Format:** Religious

**KGOR-FM**
5010 Underwood Avenue
Omaha, NE 68132
**Phone:** (402) 556-2323
**Fax:** (402) 556-8937
**E-mail:** oldies@kgor.com
http://www.kgor.com
**Format:** Oldies

**KIOD-FM**
106 W. 8th Street
Box 939
McCook, NE 69001
**Phone:** (308) 345-1981 or (888) 752-9105
(toll-free)
**Fax:** (308) 345-7202
**E-mail:** news@coyote105.com
http://www.coyote105.com
**Format:** Contemporary Country

**KIOS-FM**
3230 Burt Street
Omaha, NE 68131
**Phone:** (402) 557-2777
**Fax:** (402) 557-2559
http://www.kios.org
**Format:** Public Radio, Classical, Jazz

**KJLT-AM**
P.O. Box 709
North Platte, NE 69103
**Phone:** (308) 582-5515
http://www.nque.com/kjlt
**Format:** Religious

**KJLT-FM**
P.O. Box 709
North Platte, NE 69103
**Phone:** (308) 582-5515
http://www.nque.com/kjlt
**Format:** Religious

**KKAR-AM**
5011 Capitol Avenue
Omaha, NE 68132-2921
**Phone:** (402) 342-2000
**Fax:** (402) 342-5874

http://www.kkar.com
**Format:** News, Sports, Talk

**KMNE-FM**
P.O. Box 83111
Lincoln, NE 68501
**Phone:** (402) 472-3611
**Fax:** (402) 472-2403
**E-mail:** nprn@unl.edu
http://www.net.unl.edu
**Format:** Classical, News

**KMOR-FM**
P.O. Box 532
Scottsbluff, NE 69363
**Phone:** (308) 632-5667 or (800) 592-5667
　(toll-free)
**Fax:** (308) 635-1905
http://www.tracybroadcasting.com
**Format:** Contemporary Hit Radio
　(CHR)

**KNGN-AM**
R.R. 3, Box 1360
McCook, NE 69001
**Phone:** (308) 345-2006 or (800) 767-1360
　(toll-free)
**Fax:** (308) 345-2052
**E-mail:** goodnews@nebi.com
http://www.christianlink.com/kngn
**Format:** Religious

**KOAQ-AM**
P.O. Box 1263
Scottsbluff, NE 69361
**Phone:** (308) 635-2690 or (800) 592-5667
　(toll-free)
**Fax:** (308) 635-1905
http://www.tracybroadcasting.com
**Format:** Oldies

**KOLT-AM**
P.O. Box 660
Scottsbluff, NE 69363
**Phone:** (308) 632-5667
**Fax:** (308) 632-6452
http://www.tracybroadcasting.com
**Format:** Talk

**KOOQ-AM**
P.O. Box 248
North Platte, NE 69103
**Phone:** (308) 532-1120 or (877) 532-1120
　(toll-free)
**Fax:** (308) 532-0458
**E-mail:** oldiesradio@nponline.net
http://www.oldiesradio.com
**Format:** Oldies, Agricultural, News

**KPNE-FM**
P.O. Box 83111
Lincoln, NE 68501
**Phone:** (402) 472-3611
**Fax:** (402) 472-2403
**E-mail:** nprn@unl.edu
http://www.net.unl.edu
**Format:** Classical, News

**KPNO-FM**
109 S. 2nd
Norfolk, NE 68701
**Phone:** (402) 379-3677
**Fax:** (402) 379-3662
**E-mail:** kpno@newsnet.com
http://www.kpno.org
**Format:** Religious

**KQKQ-FM**
5011 Capitol Avenue
Omaha, NE 68132-2921
**Phone:** (402) 342-2000
**Fax:** (402) 342-5874
http://www.sweet98.com
**Format:** Contemporary Hit Radio (CHR)

**KRKU-FM**
1811 West O
Box 333
McCook, NE 69001
**Phone:** (308) 345-5400
**Fax:** (308) 345-4720
http://www.k-rock985.com
**Format:** Classic Rock

**KRNE-FM**
P.O. Box 83111
Lincoln, NE 68501
**Phone:** (402) 472-3611
**Fax:** (402) 472-2403
**E-mail:** nprn@unl.edu
http://www.net.unl.edu
**Format:** Classical, News

**KRVN-AM**
P.O. Box 880
Lexington, NE 68850-0880
**Phone:** (308) 324-2371
**Fax:** (308) 324-5786
**E-mail:** krvnam@krvn.com
http://www.krvn.com
**Format:** Country, Agricultural, News,
　Sports

**KRVN-FM**
P.O. Box 880
Lexington, NE 68850-0880
**Phone:** (308) 324-2371
**Fax:** (308) 324-5786

**E-mail:** krvnam@krvn.com
http://www.krvnfm.com
**Format:** Adult Contemporary, News,
　Sports

**KSDZ-FM**
Box 390
Gordon, NE 69343
**Phone:** (308) 282-2500
**Fax:** (308) 282-0061
http://www.broadcastmusic.com
**Format:** Hot Country, Oldies

**KSLI-FM**
4630 Antelope Creek Road
Suite 200
Lincoln, NE 68506
**Phone:** (402) 484-8000
**Fax:** (402) 489-9989
http://kiss104fm.net
**Format:** Top 40

**KSRZ-FM**
11128 John Galt Boulevard
Suite 192
Omaha, NE 68137-2321
**Phone:** (402) 592-5300
**Fax:** (402) 331-1348
http://www.104star.com
**Format:** Adult Contemporary

**KSWN-FM**
P.O. Box 939
McCook, NE 69001
**Phone:** (308) 345-1100 or (877) 825-5939
　(toll-free)
**Fax:** (308) 345-7202
**E-mail:** coyote@ns.nque.com
http://www.theprairie.net
**Format:** Talk, News

**KTGL-FM**
4630 Antelope Creek Road
Suite 200
Lincoln, NE 68506-5581
**Phone:** (402) 484-8000
**Fax:** (402) 489-9607
**E-mail:** ktgl@ktgl.com
http://ktgl.com
**Format:** Classic Rock

## NEVADA

**KBAD-AM**
P.O. Box 26629
Las Vegas, NV 89126-0629
**Phone:** (702) 876-1460
**Fax:** (702) 876-6685
**Format:** Sports

**KCEP-FM**
330 W. Washington Street
Las Vegas, NV 89106-3327
**Phone:** (702) 648-4218
**Fax:** (702) 647-0803
**Format:** Blues, Urban Contemporary

**KDOT-FM**
2900 Sutro Street
Reno, NV 89512
**Phone:** (702) 329-9261
**Fax:** (702) 323-1450
**Format:** Alternative/New
Music/Progressive

**KDOX-AM**
Commercial Arts Building
953 E. Sahara
Suite 255
Las Vegas, NV 89104
**Phone:** (702) 732-1664 or (888) 410-9864
(toll-free)
**Fax:** (702) 732-3060
**Format:** Latino, Adult Contemporary

**KDWN-AM**
1 Maine Street
Las Vegas, NV 89101
**Phone:** (702) 385-7212 or (800) 338-8255
(toll-free)
**Fax:** (702) 385-7990
http://www.kdawn.com
**Format:** Talk, News, Sports

**KENO-AM**
4660 S. Decatur Boulevard
Las Vegas, NV 89103
**Phone:** (702) 876-1460
**Fax:** (702) 876-6685
**E-mail:** lotusup@wizard.com
**Format:** News

**KFMS-FM**
1130 E. Desert Inn Road
Las Vegas, NV 89109-2812
**Phone:** (702) 732-7753
**Fax:** (702) 732-4890
**Format:** Country

**KGVN-FM**
595 E. Plumb Lane
Reno, NV 89503
**Phone:** (775) 789-6700
**Fax:** (775) 789-6767
http://www.937thegroove.com
**Format:** Oldies

**KHIT-AM**
2900 Sutro Street
Reno, NV 89512

**Phone:** (775) 329-9261
**Fax:** (775) 323-1450
**Format:** Country

**KISF-FM**
1455 E. Tropicana
Suite 650
Las Vegas, NV 89119
**Phone:** (702) 795-1035
**Fax:** (702) 798-1738
**E-mail:** kiss@kiss1035.com
http://www.intermind.net/kedg

**KJUL-FM**
1455 E. Tropicana Avenue
Suite 800
Las Vegas, NV 89119-6522
**Phone:** (702) 730-0300
**Fax:** (702) 730-8447
**E-mail:** kjvl@kjul.com

**KKLZ-FM**
4305 S. Industrial Road
Suite 120
Las Vegas, NV 89103
**Phone:** (702) 739-9600
**Fax:** (702) 739-0083
**Format:** Classic Rock

**KKVV-AM**
3185 S. Highland Drive
Suite 13
Las Vegas, NV 89109
**Phone:** (702) 731-5588
**Fax:** (702) 731-5851
**E-mail:** kkvvradio@aol.com
http://www.kkvv.com
**Format:** Contemporary Christian, Talk

**KNHK-FM**
595 E. Plumb Lane
Reno, NV 89502
**Phone:** (775) 789-6700
**Fax:** (775) 789-6767
http://www.hawkfm.com
**Format:** Classic Rock

**KNPR-FM**
5151 Boulder Hwy.
Las Vegas, NV 89122
**Phone:** (702) 456-6695
**Fax:** (702) 458-2787
**E-mail:** knpr@accessnv.com
**Format:** Public Radio, News, Classical

**KODS-FM**
300 E. 2nd Street, 14th Floor
Reno, NV 89501-1500
**Phone:** (702) 829-1964

**Fax:** (702) 825-3183
**Format:** Oldies

**KNUU-AM**
1455 E. Tropicana Avenue
Suite 550
Las Vegas, NV 89119
**Phone:** (702) 735-8644
**Fax:** (702) 735-8184
**Format:** Talk, News

**KOMP-FM**
4660 S. Decatur Boulevard
Las Vegas, NV 89103
**Phone:** (702) 876-1460
**Fax:** (702) 876-6685
**E-mail:** komp@wizard.com;
lotusup@wizard.com
**Format:** Album-Oriented Rock (AOR)

**KOZZ-FM**
Box 9870
Reno, NV 89507
**Phone:** (775) 329-9261
**Fax:** (775) 323-1450
http://www.kozzradio.com
**Format:** Classic Rock

**KPLY-AM**
300 E. 2nd Street, 14th Floor
Reno, NV 89501-1500
**Phone:** (702) 829-1964
**Fax:** (702) 825-3183
**Format:** Sports, News

**KPTT-AM**
2900 Sutro Street
Reno, NV 89512
**Phone:** (702) 329-9261
**Fax:** (702) 323-1450
**Format:** Sports, Talk, News

**KRJC-FM**
1250 LaMoille Hwy.
Suite 1045
Elko, NV 89801
**Phone:** (775) 738-9895
**Fax:** (775) 753-8085
http://www.krjc.com
**Format:** Country, News, Sports

**KRNV-FM**
300 S. Wells Avenue
Suite 12
Reno, NV 89502
**Phone:** (775) 333-1017
**Fax:** (775) 333-9046
http://www.krnv.com
**Format:** News, Talk

**KRZQ-FM**
2395 Tampa Street
Reno, NV 89512
**Phone:** (775) 333-1023
**Fax:** (775) 333-0101
http://www.krzq.com

**KSHP-AM**
2400 S. Jones Boulevard
Suite 3
Las Vegas, NV 89148
**Phone:** (702) 221-1200
**Fax:** (702) 221-2285
**E-mail:** mail@kshp.com
http://www.kshp.com
**Format:** News, Talk

**KTKR-AM**
3305 West Mountain Road
Suite 60
Las Vegas, NV 89102
**E-mail:** ticketsports.com
http://www.ticketsports.com
**Format:** Sports

**KUNR-FM**
Mail Stop 294
University of Nevada
Reno, NV 89557
**Phone:** (775) 327-5867
**Fax:** (775) 784-1381
**E-mail:** kunr@unr.edu
http://www.kunr.org
**Format:** Classical, Jazz, News, Talk

**KWNR-FM**
1130 E. Desert Inn Road
Las Vegas, NV 89109
**Phone:** (702) 798-4004
**Fax:** (702) 733-0433
**Format:** Contemporary Country

**KXNT-AM**
6655 W. Sanara
Suite D-208
Las Vegas, NV 89102
**Phone:** (702) 364-8400
**Fax:** (702) 889-7384
**E-mail:** am840kxnt@aol.com;
    gjspittle@cbs.com
http://www.kxnt.com
**Format:** News, Talk

# NEW HAMPSHIRE

**WASR-AM**
P.O. Box 900
73 Varney Road
Wolfeboro, NH 03894-0900

**Phone:** (603) 569-1420
**Fax:** (603) 569-1900
**E-mail:** wkpp@worldpath.net
**Format:** News, Middle-of-the-Road
    (MOR)

**WBHG-FM**
P.O. Box 7326
Gilford, NH 03247
**Phone:** (603) 524-1323 or
    (800) 368-7664 (toll-free)
**Fax:** (603) 528-5185
**E-mail:** radioman@metrocast.net
**Format:** Classic Rock

**WBNC-AM**
196 E. Main Street
P.O. Box 2008
Conway, NH 03818
**Phone:** (603) 447-5988
**Fax:** (603) 447-3655
**E-mail:** office@wbnc.com
http://www.valley1045.com
**Format:** Oldies

**WBNC-FM**
196 E. Main Street
P.O. Box 2008
Conway, NH 03818
**Phone:** (603) 447-5988
**Fax:** (603) 447-3655
**E-mail:** office@wbnc.com
http://www.valley1045.com
**Format:** Oldies

**WBYY-FM**
P.O. Box 400
Dover, NH 03820
**Phone:** (603) 742-0987 or
    (888) 441-9876 (toll-free)
**Fax:** (603) 742-0448
**Format:** Adult Contemporary

**WCFR-AM**
31 Hanover Street
Suite 4
Lebanon, NH 03766-1312
**Format:** Big Band/Nostalgia

**WCFR-FM**
31 Hanover Street
Suite 4
Lebanon, NH 03766-1312
**Format:** Adult Contemporary

**WDCR-AM**
P.O. Box 957
Hanover, NH 03755
**Phone:** (603) 646-3313

**Fax:** (603) 643-7655
**E-mail:** wdcr-wfrd@dartmouth.edu
http://www.wfrd.com
**Format:** Alternative/New
    Music/Progressive, Heavy Metal, Jazz

**WEVO-FM**
207 N. Main Street
Concord, NH 03301-5003
**Phone:** (603) 228-8910
**Fax:** (603) 224-6052
http://www.NHPR.org
**Format:** News, Classical, Folk, Jazz

**WFRD-FM**
P.O. Box 957
Hanover, NH 03755-0957
**Phone:** (603) 646-3313
**Fax:** (603) 643-7655
**E-mail:** wdcr-wfrd@dartmouth.edu
http://www.wfrd.com
**Format:** Album-Oriented Rock (AOR)

**WGIN-AM**
815 LaFayette Road
Portsmouth, NH 03801
http://www.clearchannel.com/radio
**Format:** Sports, News, Talk

**WGIP-AM**
815 LaFayette Road
Portsmouth, NH 03801
http://www.clearchannel.com/radio
**Format:** Sports, News, Talk

**WJYY-FM**
7 Perley Street
P.O. Box 1923
Concord, NH 03302-1923
**Phone:** (603) 228-9036
**Fax:** (603) 224-7280
**E-mail:** jyy105@aol.com
http://www.wjyy.com
**Format:** Adult Contemporary

**WKBK-AM**
13 Lamson Street
Keene, NH 03431
**Phone:** (603) 352-6113
**Fax:** (603) 357-4582
http://wkbkwxod.com
**Format:** News, Talk

**WKNE-AM**
P.O. Box 466
Keene, NH 03431
**Phone:** (603) 352-9230
**Fax:** (603) 357-3926
**E-mail:** am1290@wkne.com

http://www.wkcne.com
**Format:** News, Classic Rock

**WKNE-FM**
P.O. Box 466
Keene, NH 03431
**Phone:** (603) 352-9230
**Fax:** (603) 357-3926
**E-mail:** fm1037@wkne.com
http://www.wkne.com
**Format:** Adult Contemporary

**WKNH-FM**
229 Main Street
Keene State College
Keene, NH 03431
**Phone:** (603) 358-2421
**Fax:** (603) 358-2417
http://www.wknh.com
**Format:** Alternative/New
    Music/Progressive

**WMWV-FM**
196 E. Main Street
P.O. Box 2008
Conway, NH 03818
**Phone:** (603) 447-5988
**Fax:** (603) 447-3655
**E-mail:** office@wmwv.com
http://www.wmwv.com
**Format:** Adult Album Alternative

**WNNH-FM**
501 South Street
Concord, NH 03301
**Phone:** (603) 225-1160 or
    (800) 228-WNNH (toll-free)
**Fax:** (603) 225-5938
**E-mail:** oldies99@wnnh.com
http://www.wnrh.com
**Format:** Oldies

**WNTK-AM**
P.O. Box 2295
New London, NH 03257
**Phone:** (603) 526-9464
**Fax:** (603) 526-9372
**E-mail:** wntk1020@aol.com
http://wntk.com
**Format:** Talk

**WNTK-FM**
250 Newport Road
P.O. Box 2295
New London, NH 03257
**Phone:** (603) 448-0500
**Fax:** (603) 526-9372
**E-mail:** info@wntk.com
http://www.wntk.com
**Format:** Talk

**WPCR-FM**
CUBANNEX
Plymouth State College
Plymouth, NH 03264
**Phone:** (603) 535-2242
**Fax:** (603) 535-2783
http://wpcr.plymouth.edu
**Format:** Album-Oriented Rock (AOR),
    Eclectic

**WPKQ-FM**
2617 White Mountain Hwy.
P.O. Box 1888
North Conway, NH 03860
**Phone:** (603) 356-7500
**Fax:** (603) 356-6222
http://www.wpkq.com
**Format:** Contemporary Country

**WSAK-FM**
292 Middle Road
P.O. Box 576
Dover, NH 03820-4901
**Phone:** (603) 749-9750
**Fax:** (603) 749-1459
http://www.shark1053.com
**Format:** Classic Rock

**WTSV-AM**
Rtes. 12 and 103
P.O. Box 1230
Claremont, NH 03743
**Phone:** (603) 542-7735
**Fax:** (603) 542-8721
**E-mail:** valleysam@aol.com
http://www.scoreradio.com
**Format:** Sports, Talk

**WUNH-FM**
University of New Hampshire
Memorial Union Building
Durham, NH 03824
**Phone:** (603) 862-2541
**Fax:** (603) 862-2543
**E-mail:** info@wunh.unh.edu
http://www.wunh.unh.edu
**Format:** Full Service, Alternative/New
    Music/Progressive

**WWNH-AM**
P.O. Box 69
Dover, NH 03820
**Phone:** (603) 742-8575 or
    (800) 805-8815 (toll-free)
**Fax:** (603) 743-6444
**E-mail:** info@loveradio.net
http://www.loveradio.net
**Format:** Gospel, Adult Contemporary

**WXOD-FM**
P.O. Box 707
Keene, NH 03431
**Phone:** (603) 352-6113
**Fax:** (603) 357-4582
**E-mail:** info@wkbkwxod.com
http://wkbkwxod.com
**Format:** Oldies

**WXXK-FM**
31 Hanover Street
Suite 4
Lebanon, NH 03766
**Phone:** (603) 448-5229
**Fax:** (603) 448-5231
http://www.kixx.com
**Format:** Contemporary Country

**WZID-FM**
500 Commercial Street
Manchester, NH 03101
**Phone:** (603) 669-5777
**Fax:** (603) 669-4641
**E-mail:** raydionh@wzid.com
http://www.wzid.com
**Format:** Adult Contemporary

## NEW JERSEY

**WBGO-FM**
54 Park Plaza
Newark, NJ 07102
**Phone:** (201) 624-8880
**Fax:** (201) 824-8888
**E-mail:** jazz88@wbgo.org
http://wbgo.org
**Format:** Jazz

**WBJB-FM**
Brookdale Community College
Lincroft, NJ 07738
**Phone:** (908) 224-2490
**E-mail:** wbjb@shell.monmouth.com
http://www.monmouth.com/~wbjb
**Format:** Jazz, Adult Contemporary,
    News

**WBNJ-FM**
2922 Atlantic Avenue
Suite 201
Atlantic City, NJ 08401
**Phone:** (609) 348-4040
**Fax:** (609) 348-1303
**Format:** Adult Contemporary

**WBZC-FM**
County Rte. 530
Pemberton, NJ 08068

**Phone:** (609) 894-9311
**Fax:** (609) 894-9440
http://www.wbzc.org
**Format:** Eclectic, Information

**WCSX-FM**
1 Radio Plaza
Detroit, MI 48220
**Phone:** (248) 398-7600
**Fax:** (248) 542-8800
http://www.wcsx.com
**Format:** Classic Rock

**WDHA-FM**
55 Horsehill Road
Cedar Knolls, NJ 07927
**Phone:** (973) 538-1250
**Fax:** (973) 538-3060
**E-mail:** wdha@ix.netcom.com
http://www.wdhafm.com
**Format:** Album-Oriented Rock (AOR),
    Blues

**WFDQ-FM**
1000 River Road
Teaneck, NJ 07666
**Phone:** (201) 692-2103
http://alpha.fdu.edu/~emmert/wfdq/
    wfdqinfo.htm
**Format:** Alternative/New
    Music/Progressive, Hip Hop, Blues,
    Eclectic

**WFME-FM**
289 Mt. Pleasant Avenue
West Orange, NJ 07052
**Phone:** (973) 736-3600
**Fax:** (973) 736-4832
**E-mail:** wfme@aol.com
http://www.familyradio.com
**Format:** Religious

**WFMU-FM**
P.O. Box 2011
Jersey City, NJ 07303
**Phone:** (201) 200-9368
**E-mail:** wfmu@wfmu.org
http://www.wfmu.org
**Format:** Full Service, Eclectic, Talk

**WGLS-FM**
Rowan University
Glassboro, NJ 08028
**Phone:** (856) 863-9457
**Fax:** (856) 256-4704
**E-mail:** wgls@rowan.edu
http://wgls.rowan.edu
**Format:** Classic Rock, Talk

**WHCY-FM**
33 Newton-Sparta Road
Newton, NJ 07860
**Phone:** (973) 383-3400
**Fax:** (973) 383-2432
**E-mail:** whcy@aol.com
http://www.whcy.com
**Format:** Contemporary Hit Radio (CHR)

**WIBG-AM**
3328 Simpson Avenue
Ocean City, NJ 08226
**Phone:** (609) 398-1020
**Fax:** (609) 398-3736
**E-mail:** wibg@juno.com
http://www.wibg.com
**Format:** Contemporary Christian

**WJRZ-FM**
22 W. Water Street
P.O. Box 100
Toms River, NJ 08754
**Phone:** (732) 240-7200
**Fax:** (732) 505-8700
http://www.wjrz.com
**Format:** Country

**WKOE-FM**
950 Tilton Road
Suite 200
Northfield, NJ 08225
**Phone:** (609) 645-9797
**Fax:** (609) 272-9228
**E-mail:** johnd@atlanticcityradio.com
http://www.shorefm.com
**Format:** Adult Contemporary

**WKXW-FM**
218 Ewingville Road
P.O. Box 5698
Trenton, NJ 08638
**Phone:** (609) 882-4600 or
    (800) 876-9599 (toll-free)
**Fax:** (609) 883-6684
**E-mail:** nj1015@nj1015.com
http://www.nj1015.com
**Format:** Oldies, News, Talk

**WMGQ-FM**
78 Veronica Avenue
Somerset, NJ 08873
**Phone:** (732) 249-2600
**Fax:** (732) 249-9010
http://www.wm6qfm.com
**Format:** Adult Contemporary

**WMID-AM**
2922 Atlantic Avenue
Suite 201
Atlantic City, NJ 08401

**Phone:** (609) 348-4040
**Fax:** (609) 348-1303
**Format:** Adult Contemporary

**WSAX-FM**
2922 Atlantic Avenue
Suite 201
Atlantic City, NJ 08401
**Phone:** (609) 348-4040
**Fax:** (609) 348-1303
**Format:** Jazz

**WMVB-AM**
415 N. High Street
Millville, NJ 08332-3006
http://www.wmvb.net
**Format:** News, Talk, Information

**WOBM-FM**
P.O. Box 927
Toms River, NJ 08754-0927
**Phone:** (732) 269-0927
**Fax:** (732) 269-9292
http://www.wobm.com
**Format:** Adult Contemporary

**WPRB-FM**
P.O. Box 342
Princeton, NJ 08542
**Phone:** (609) 258-3655
**Fax:** (609) 258-1806
**E-mail:** wprb@princeton.edu
http://www.wprb.com
**Format:** Alternative/New
    Music/Progressive, Classical, Jazz,
    Sports

**WPSC-FM**
300 Pompton Road
Wayne, NJ 07470
**Phone:** (973) 720-3331
**Fax:** (973) 720-2483
**E-mail:** hitradio@frontier.willpaterson.edu
http://gindy.wilpaterson.edu
**Format:** Adult Contemporary, Top 40

**WPST-FM**
619 Alexander Road, 3rd Floor
Princeton, NJ 08540-6003
**Phone:** (609) 419-0300
**Fax:** (609) 419-0143
http://www.wpst.com
**Format:** Contemporary Hit Radio (CHR)

**WPUR-FM**
950 Tilton Road
Suite 200
Northfield, NJ 08225
**Phone:** (609) 645-9797

**Fax:** (609) 272-9228
http://www.catcoutnry1073.com
**Format:** Contemporary Country,
Country

**WRAT-FM**
1731 F Street
South Belmar, NJ 07719
**Phone:** (201) 681-3800
**Fax:** (201) 681-5995
**E-mail:** production@wrat.com
http://www.wrat.com
**Format:** Album-Oriented Rock (AOR)

**WRSU-FM**
126 College Avenue
New Brunswick, NJ 08903
**Phone:** (908) 932-7800
**Fax:** (908) 932-1768
http://www.cybercomm.net/~dsun
**Format:** Alternative/New
Music/Progressive, Jazz, Ethnic

**WSOU-FM**
400 S. Orange Avenue
South Orange, NJ 07079
**Phone:** (973) 761-9768 or
(800) 895-9768 (toll-free)
**Fax:** (973) 761-7593
**E-mail:** wsou@lanmail.shu.edu
http://www.wsou.net
**Format:** Album-Oriented Rock (AOR)

**WTSR-FM**
Kendall Hall
The College of New Jersey
Trenton, NJ 08650-4700
**Phone:** (609) 771-3200
**Fax:** (609) 637-5113
**E-mail:** wtsr@trenton.edu
http://trenton.edu/~wtsr
**Format:** Alternative/New
Music/Progressive, Folk, Jazz, Adult
Contemporary, Gospel

**WWFM-FM**
P.O. Box B
Trenton, NJ 08690
**Phone:** (609) 587-8989 or
(800) 622-WWFM (toll-free)
**Fax:** (609) 586-4533
**E-mail:** wwfm@wwfm.org
http://www.wwfm.org
**Format:** Public Radio, Classical

**WWNJ-FM**
1200 Old Trenton Road
P.O. Box B
Trenton, NJ 08690

**Phone:** (609) 587-8989 or
(800) 622-WWFM (toll-free)
**Fax:** (609) 586-4533
**E-mail:** wwfm@thecore.com
http://www.wwfm.org
**Format:** Classical, Public Radio

**WZBZ-FM**
2922 Atlantic Avenue
Suite 201
Atlantic City, NJ 08401
**Phone:** (609) 348-4040
**Fax:** (609) 348-1303
**Format:** Top 40

## NEW MEXICO

**KABR-AM**
P.O. Box 907
Magdalena, NM 87825
**Phone:** (505) 854-2632
**Fax:** (505) 854-2545
**Format:** News, Ethnic

**KALQ-FM**
P.O. Box 179
Alamosa, CO 81101-0179
**Phone:** (719) 589-6644
**Fax:** (719) 589-0993
**Format:** Adult Contemporary

**KAMQ-AM**
121 S. Canal
Suite C
P.O. Box 1952
Carlsbad, NM 88220
**Phone:** (505) 887-5323
**Fax:** (505) 887-5451
**E-mail:** undrtkr@caverns.com
http://www.kdoveradio.com
**Format:** Contemporary Christian

**KANW-FM**
2020 Coal Avenue SE
Albuquerque, NM 87106
**Phone:** (505) 242-7163
http://kanw.com

**KATK-FM**
714 N. Canyon
Carlsbad, NM 88220
**Phone:** (505) 885-2151
**Fax:** (505) 887-5691
**E-mail:** katk@carlsbadnm.com
**Format:** Country

**KBCQ-FM**
P.O. Box 670
Roswell, NM 88201

**Phone:** (505) 622-6450
**Fax:** (505) 622-9041
**E-mail:** tj@kbcq.com
http://www.kbcq.com
**Format:** Contemporary Hit Radio (CHR)

**KBOM-FM**
2600-A Camino Entrada
Santa Fe, NM 87505
**Phone:** (505) 471-1067
**Fax:** (505) 473-2667
**Format:** Oldies

**KBQI-FM**
2700 San Pedre, NE
Albuquerque, NM 87110
**Phone:** (505) 830-6400
http://www.clearchannel.com/radio
**Format:** Country

**KCCC-AM**
930 N. Canal
Carlsbad, NM 88220
**Phone:** (505) 887-5521
**Fax:** (505) 885-5481
**E-mail:** kccc@carlsbadnm.com
**Format:** News, Talk

**KCDY-FM**
1609 Radio Boulevard
P.O. Box 1538
Carlsbad, NM 88220
**Phone:** (505) 887-7563
**Fax:** (505) 887-7000
**Format:** Adult Contemporary

**KCKN-AM**
P.O. Box 670
Roswell, NM 88202
**Phone:** (505) 622-6450
**Fax:** (505) 622-9041
**E-mail:** tj@kbcq.com
**Format:** News, Talk, Adult
Contemporary

**KCLV-FM**
2112 Thornton
P.O. Box 1907
Clovis, NM 88101
**Phone:** (505) 763-4401
**Fax:** (505) 769-2564
**Format:** Country

**KENW-FM**
Eastern New Mexico University
52 Broadcast Center
Portales, NM 88130
**Phone:** (505) 562-2112
**Fax:** (505) 562-2590

E-mail: kenwfm@enmu.edu
http://www.kenw.org
**Format:** Classical, Easy Listening, News,
    Educational, Jazz

**KKSS-FM**
8009 Marble Avenue, NE
Albuquerque, NM 87110
**Phone:** (505) 262-1142
**Fax:** (505) 262-9211
http://www.kiss973.com
**Format:** Contemporary Hit Radio (CHR)

**KLSK-FM**
2700 San Pedro Drive, NE
Suite 104
Albuquerque, NM 87110-3333
**Phone:** (505) 830-6400 or (800) 436-1041
    (toll-free)
**Fax:** (505) 830-6517
**E-mail:** comments@eagle104.com
http://www.eagle104.com

**KLYT-FM**
4001 Osuna Road NE
Albuquerque, NM 87109-4422
**Phone:** (505) 293-8300
**Fax:** (505) 296-1331
**E-mail:** klyt@klyt.org
http://www.klyt.org/klyt
**Format:** Contemporary Christian

**KMTH-FM**
Eastern New Mexico University
Portales, NM 88130
**Phone:** (505) 562-2112
**Fax:** (505) 562-2590
**E-mail:** kenwfm@enmu.edu
http://www.kenw.org
**Format:** Classical, Educational, Easy
    Listening, News, Jazz

**KMXQ-FM**
834 Hwy. 60 West
P.O. Box 699
Socorro, NM 87801
**Phone:** (505) 835-1286
**Fax:** (505) 835-2015
**E-mail:** kmxq@rt66.com
http://www.kmxq.com/kmxq
**Format:** Country

**KNMI-FM**
2103 W. Main Street
Box 1230
Farmington, NM 87401
**Phone:** (505) 325-0255 or
    (888) 889-5664 (toll-free)
**Fax:** (505) 325-9035

E-mail: knmi@hotmail.com
http://www.verticalradio.org
**Format:** Adult Contemporary, Album-
    Oriented Rock (AOR), Alternative/New
    Music/Progressive, Hip Hop

**KPEK-FM**
2700 San Pedro, NE
Albuquerque, NM 87110
**Phone:** (505) 830-6400
http://www.1003thepeak.com
**Format:** Album-Oriented Rock (AOR)

**KPZA-FM**
1 Radio Square
619 N. Turner
Hobbs, NM 88240
**Phone:** (505) 397-4969
**Fax:** (505) 393-4310
**E-mail:** gerald@1radiosquare.com
http://www.1radiosquare.com
**Format:** Latino

**KSCQ-FM**
1560 N. Corbin Street
P.O. Box 2577
Silver City, NM 88062
**Phone:** (505) 538-3396 or (888) 388-4116
    (toll-free)
**Fax:** (505) 388-1759
**E-mail:** kscq@gilanet.com
http://www.gilnet.com/kscq
**Format:** Adult Contemporary

**KSFQ-FM**
1401 Maclovia
Santa Fe, NM 87501
**Phone:** (505) 989-3338
http://www.clearchannel.com/radio
**Format:** Adult Contemporary

**KSYU-FM**
2700 San Pedro, NE
Albuquerque, NM 87110
**Phone:** (505) 830-6400
http://www.sunny951.com
**Format:** Contemporary Hit Radio (CHR)

**KTAO-FM**
P.O. Box 1844
Taos, NM 87571
**Phone:** (505) 758-5826
**Fax:** (505) 758-8430
http://www.ktao.com
**Format:** Adult Album Alternative

**KTEG-FM**
2700 San Pedro, NE
Albuquerque, NM 87110

**Phone:** (505) 830-6400
http://www.clearchannel.com/radio
**Format:** Alternative/New
    Music/Progressive

**KTEK-FM**
New Mexico Tech
Student Activities Center, Rm. 212
Socorro, NM 87801
**Phone:** (505) 835-6013
**Fax:** (505) 835-5285
**E-mail:** ktek@nmt.edu
http://www.nmt.edu/~ktek
**Format:** Eclectic

**KTZO-FM**
500 4th Street, NW
Albuquerque, NM 87102
**Phone:** (505) 767-6700
**Fax:** (505) 767-6767
http://www.1033thezone.com
**Format:** Alternative/New
    Music/Progressive, Adult Album
    Alternative

**KUNM-FM**
University of New Mexico
Campus Boulevard & Girard Boulevard,
    NE
Albuquerque, NM 87131
**Phone:** (505) 277-4806
**Fax:** (505) 277-8004
**E-mail:** kunm@unm.edu
http://kunm.unm.edu
**Format:** Public Radio, Eclectic, Full
    Service

**KZIA-AM**
Eastern New Mexico University
Campus Union Building, 2nd Floor
Portales, NM 88130
http://members.xoom.com/_XMCM/kzia/
    welcome.htm
**Format:** Eclectic, Alternative/New
    Music/Progressive

**KZZX-FM**
Box 618
Alamogordo, NM 88311
**Phone:** (505) 437-4440
**Fax:** (505) 434-2586
**E-mail:** cathykzzx@hotmail.com
http://www.ktalkkzzx.com
**Format:** Country

# NEW YORK

**WABC-AM**
2 Penn Plaza
New York, NY 10121

**Phone:** (212) 613-3800 or
   (800) 848-9222 (toll-free)
**Fax:** (212) 613-3868
**Format:** Talk

**WADO-AM**
666 3rd Avenue
New York, NY 10017
**Phone:** (212) 687-9236
**Fax:** (212) 599-2161
**E-mail:** 70743,3305@compuserve.com
http://www.buymedia.com
**Format:** Latino, News, Talk

**WAMC-FM**
318 Central Avenue
Albany, NY 12206
**Phone:** (518) 465-5233 or (800) 323-9262
   (toll-free)
**Fax:** (518) 432-6974
**E-mail:** mail@wamc.org
http://www.wamc.org
**Format:** Public Radio, Folk, News,
   Classical

**WAXQ-FM**
1180 Avenue of the Americas
New York, NY 10036
**Phone:** (212) 575-1043
**Fax:** (212) 302-7814
http://www.classicq104.com
**Format:** Classic Rock

**WBBF-FM**
500 B Forman Building
Rochester, NY 14604-1727
**Phone:** (716) 423-2900
**Fax:** (716) 325-5139
**Format:** Oldies

**WBLS-FM**
3 Park Avenue
New York, NY 10016
**Phone:** (212) 447-1000 or (800) 545-1075
   (toll-free)
**Fax:** (212) 447-5194
http://www.wbls.com
**Format:** Urban Contemporary

**WBVE-FM**
349 W. Commercial Street
Suite 2695
East Rochester, NY 14445
**Phone:** (716) 586-2263
**Fax:** (716) 586-0098
Format: Adult Contemporary

**WCBS-AM**
51 W. 52nd Street
New York, NY 10019

**Phone:** (212) 975-4321
**Fax:** (212) 975-4674
**Format:** News

**WCBS-FM**
1515 Broadway, 40th Floor
New York, NY 10036-8900
**Phone:** (212) 846-5100 or
   (800) 367-1101 (toll-free)
**Format:** Oldies

**WCDW-FM**
495 Court Street, 2nd Floor
Binghamton, NY 13904
**Phone:** (607) 772-1005
**Fax:** (607) 772-2945
**E-mail:** geoequinox@aol.com
**Format:** Alternative/New
   Music/Progressive

**WFLY-FM**
P.O. Box 12279
Albany, NY 12212
http://wakeupfly.aol.com
**Format:** Contemporary Hit Radio
   (CHR)

**WGY-AM**
One Washington Square
Albany, NY 12205
**Phone:** (518) 452-4800
**Fax:** (518) 452-4855
http://www.wgy.com
**Format:** News, Talk

**WGRF-FM**
464 Franklin Street
Buffalo, NY 14202
**Phone:** (716) 881-4555
**Fax:** (716) 884-2931
**Format:** Classic Rock

**WHEN-AM**
500 Plum Street
Suite 100
Syracuse, NY 13204-1401
**Phone:** (315) 472-9797
**Fax:** (315) 472-2323
**E-mail:** sports620@dreamscape.com
http://sybercuse.com/sportsmonster
**Format:** Sports

**WINS-AM**
888 7th Avenue
New York, NY 10106
**Phone:** (212) 397-1010
**Fax:** (212) 247-7918
**Format:** News

**WGRF-FM**
464 Franklin Street
Buffalo, NY 14202
**Phone:** (716) 881-4555
**Fax:** (716) 884-2931
**Format:** Classic Rock

**WHTT-AM**
225 Delaware Avenue
Suite 1A
Buffalo, NY 14202-2108
**Phone:** (716) 881-4555
**Fax:** (716) 844-2931
**Format:** Eclectic, Oldies

**WKNY-AM**
718 Broadway
Kingston, NY 12401
**Phone:** (914) 331-1490
**Fax:** (914) 331-9569
**Format:** Adult Contemporary, Soft Rock

**WLTW-FM**
1515 Broadway, 40th Floor
New York, NY 10036
**Phone:** (212) 258-7000
**Fax:** (212) 764-2734
**Format:** Adult Contemporary

**WNEW-FM**
888 7th Avenue, 10th Floor
New York, NY 10006
**Phone:** (212) 489-1027
**Fax:** (212) 489-1623
http://1027blink.com
**Format:** Adult Contemporary

**WNTQ-FM**
1064 James Street
Syracuse, NY 13203-2704
**Phone:** (315) 446-9090
**Fax:** (315) 446-1614
**Format:** Contemporary Hit Radio
   (CHR)

**WNYC-AM**
1 Centre Street
New York, NY 10007
**Phone:** (212) 669-7800
**Fax:** (212) 609-3312
**Format:** Public Radio, Information,
   News, Talk

**WOR-AM**
1440 Broadway
New York, NY 10018
**Phone:** (212) 642-4500 or (800) 321-0710
   (toll-free)
**Fax:** (212) 642-4486

http://www.wor710.com
**Format:** Talk

**WPDH-FM**
P.O. Box 416
Poughkeepsie, NY 12602
**Phone:** (914) 471-1500 or
    (800) 527-7597 (toll-free)
**Fax:** (914) 454-1204
**Format:** Classic Rock

**WPKF-FM**
20 Tucker Drive
Poughkeepsie, NY 12603
**Phone:** (845) 471-2300
**Fax:** (845) 471-2683
**Format:** Contemporary Hit Radio
    (CHR), Urban Contemporary

**WPLJ-FM**
2 Penn Plaza, 17th Floor
New York, NY 10121
**Phone:** (212) 613-8900 or
    (800) 553-WPLJ (toll-free)
**Fax:** (212) 947-1340
**Format:** Top 40

**WQXR-FM**
122 5th Avenue
New York, NY 10011
**Phone:** (212) 633-7600
**Fax:** (212) 633-7666
http://www.wqxr.com
**Format:** Classical

**WRKS-FM**
395 Hudson Street, 7th Floor
New York, NY 10014
**Phone:** (212) 242-9870
**Fax:** (212) 929-8559
**Format:** Urban Contemporary

**WWVY-FM**
P.O. Box 1071
New York, NY 10156-1071
**Phone:** (800) 219-Y107
**Fax:** (800) Y107-FAX
http://www.newcountryy107.com
**Format:** Contemporary Country

## NORTH CAROLINA

**WAGR-AM**
5102 Durham Chapel Hill Boulevard
Durham, NC 27707-3311
**Phone:** (910) 739-3394
**Fax:** (910) 671-1812
**E-mail:** wjsk@vacationtime.net
http://www.vacationtime.net/wjsk
**Format:** Country

**WAHD-FM**
804 E. Millbrook Road
Raleigh, NC 27609-5352
**Phone:** (919) 855-9243
**Fax:** (919) 833-9243
**E-mail:** smoothjazz@clink.net
http://www.wahdfm.com
**Format:** Jazz

**WBT-FM**
One Julian Price Plaza
Charlotte, NC 28208
**Phone:** (704) 374-3500 or
    (800) 928-1110 (toll-free)
**Fax:** (704) 374-3777
http://www.wbt.com
**Format:** News, Talk

**WDLX-AM**
Box 1707
Washington, NC 27889
**Phone:** (919) 946-2162 or
    (800) 260-0933 (toll-free)
**Fax:** (919) 946-0330
http://www.theArrow.com
**Format:** News, Talk

**WDTF-AM**
3012 Highwoods Boulevard
Suite 200
Raleigh, NC 27604-1031
**Phone:** (919) 855-9383
**Fax:** (919) 875-1126
http://www.570wdtf.com
**Format:** Religious, Contemporary
    Christian

**WEGO-AM**
P.O. Box 126
Concord, NC 28026-0126
**Phone:** (704) 788-9346
**Fax:** (704) 784-4652
**E-mail:** wego@1410wego.com
http://www.1410wego.com
**Format:** Classic Rock, Sports

**WFLB-FM**
1338 Bragg Boulevard
Fayetteville, NC 28302
**Phone:** (910) 486-0965
**Fax:** (910) 323-5635
http://www.oldies965.com
**Format:** Oldies

**WFNZ-AM**
1520 South Boulevard
Charlotte, NC 28203
**Phone:** (704) 319-9360 or (800) 570-9610
    (toll-free)

**Fax:** (704) 319-3933
http://www.wfnz.com
**Format:** Sports

**WGQR-FM**
512 Peanut Road
P.O. Box 458
Elizabethtown, NC 28337
**Phone:** (910) 862-2000
**Fax:** (910) 872-0100
**E-mail:** wgqr1057@carolina.net
http://www.wgqr1057.com
**Format:** Oldies

**WHKP-AM**
1450 7th Avenue, E.
P.O. Box 2470
Hendersonville, NC 28793
**Phone:** (704) 693-9061
**Fax:** (704) 696-9329
**E-mail:** 1450@whkp.com
http://www.whkp.com
**Format:** Full Service, Contemporary Hit
    Radio (CHR)

**WHNC-AM**
601 Henderson Street
P.O. Box 336
Oxford, NC 27565
**Phone:** (919) 693-4121
**Fax:** (919) 693-9054
**E-mail:** wcbqwhnc@gloryroad.net
http://www.gloryroad.net/wcbq
**Format:** Gospel

**WHQR-FM**
254 N. Front Street
Wilmington, NC 28401-3920
**Phone:** (910) 343-1640 or (866) 343-1138
    (toll-free)
**Fax:** (910) 251-8693
**E-mail:** whgr@wilmington.net
http://whqr.wilmington.org
**Format:** Public Radio, News, Eclectic

**WIKS-FM**
207 Glenburnie Drive
New Bern, NC 28561-2815
**Phone:** (252) 633-1500
**Fax:** (252) 633-0718
http://www.kiss102.com
**Format:** Urban Contemporary

**WJSK-FM**
5102 Durham Chapel Hill Boulevard
Durham, NC 27707-3311
**Phone:** (910) 738-4771
**Fax:** (910) 671-1812

**E-mail:** wjsk@vacationtime.net
http://www.vacationtime.net/wjsk
**Format:** Country

**WKOO-FM**
P.O. Box Drawer 1126
Jacksonville, NC 28541
**Phone:** (910) 455-5300 or (800) 553-5665
    (toll-free)
**Fax:** (910) 455-3112
**E-mail:** geezloiz@onslowonline.net
**Format:** Oldies

**WKXB-FM**
122 Cinema Drive
Wilmington, NC 28405
**Phone:** (910) 772-6300
**Fax:** (910) 772-6310
http://jammin999.com

**WKXR-AM**
1119 Eastview Drive
Asheboro, NC 27203
**Phone:** (336) 625-2187
**E-mail:** wkxr@atomic.net
http://www.wkxr.com
**Format:** Country

**WKXU-FM**
Box 1119
Burlington, NC 27216
**Phone:** (336) 584-0126 or (800) 272-6404
    (toll-free)
**Fax:** (336) 584-0739
**E-mail:** wpcmsales@netpath.net;
    wildcat@netpath.net
http://www.country101.com
http://www.newcountrykix.com
**Format:** Country

**WLYT-FM**
801 Woodridge Center Drive
Charlotte, NC 28217
**Phone:** (704) 714-9444
http://www.clearchannel.com/radio
**Format:** Adult Contemporary

**WNAA-FM**
NC A&T State University
Price Hall
Suite 200
Greensboro, NC 27411
**Phone:** (336) 334-7936
**Fax:** (336) 334-7960
**E-mail:** wnaafm@ncat.edu
http://wnaalive.ncat.edu
**Format:** Jazz, Urban Contemporary,
    Eclectic, Gospel

**WNCU-FM**
P.O. Box 19875
Durham, NC 27707
**Phone:** (919) 560-9628
**Fax:** (919) 530-7975
**E-mail:** info@wncu.com
http://www.wncu.com
**Format:** Public Radio, Educational, Jazz,
    Information, News

**WQDR-FM**
3012 Highwoods Boulevard
Suite 201
Raleigh, NC 27604
**Phone:** (919) 876-6464 or (800) 233-9470
    (toll-free)
**Fax:** (919) 790-8893
http://www.wqdr.net
**Format:** Contemporary Country

**WRAL-FM**
Box 10100
Raleigh, NC 27605
**Phone:** (919) 890-6101 or (800) 849-6101
    (toll-free)
**Fax:** (919) 890-6146
**E-mail:** mixonline@wralfm.com
http://www.wralfm.com
**Format:** Adult Contemporary

**WRCM-FM**
P.O. Box 17069
Charlotte, NC 28227
**Phone:** (704) 821-9293 or (877) 972-6624
    (toll-free)
**Fax:** (704) 821-9285
**E-mail:** wrcm@wrcm.org
http://www.wrcm.org
**Format:** Contemporary Christian, Adult
    Contemporary

**WRDU-FM**
3100 Smoketree Ct.
Suite 700
Raleigh, NC 27604-1050
**Phone:** (919) 876-1061
**Fax:** (919) 876-2929
**Format:** Classic Rock, Album-Oriented
    Rock (AOR)

**WRFX-FM**
915 E. 4th
Charlotte, NC 28204
**Phone:** (704) 338-9970
**Fax:** (704) 342-3813
**Format:** Classic Rock

**WRMT-AM**
2940 Raleigh Road
P.O. Box 4005
Rocky Mount, NC 27803-0005

**Phone:** (919) 442-8091
**Fax:** (919) 977-6664
**E-mail:** wsay@rockymountnc.com
**Format:** Sports

**WRNS-AM**
Rte. 2, Box 182
Kinston, NC 28501
**Phone:** (252) 522-4141 or
    (888) 682-9767 (toll-free)
**Fax:** (252) 523-4877
**E-mail:** wrns@wrns.com
**Format:** Contemporary Country

**WRSF-FM**
Box 1418
Nags Head, NC 27959
**Phone:** (252) 441-1024
**Fax:** (252) 441-2109
http://www.ecri.net
**Format:** Hot Country

**WRSN-FM**
3100 Smoketree Ct.
Suite 700
Raleigh, NC 27604
**Phone:** (919) 878-1500
**Fax:** (919) 876-8578
http://www.sunny939.com
**Format:** Adult Contemporary, Soft
    Rock

**WSJS-AM**
875 W. Fifth Street
P.O. Box 3018
Winston-Salem, NC 27101-2505
**Phone:** (910) 727-8826
**Fax:** (910) 777-3915
**E-mail:** wsjsgov.@mr.infi.net
**Format:** News, Talk

**WSOC-FM**
4015 Stuart Andrew Boulevard
P.O. Box 30247
Charlotte, NC 28230
**Phone:** (704) 522-1103
**Fax:** (704) 523-4800
**E-mail:** chahn@wsocfm.com
http://www.wsocfm.com
**Format:** Contemporary Country

## NORTH DAKOTA

**KBMR-AM**
Box 1233
Bismarck, ND 58502
**Phone:** (701) 255-1234 or
    (800) 766-5267 (toll-free)
**Fax:** (701) 222-1131

**E-mail:** kbur@aol.com
**Format:** Country

**KBMW-AM**
P.O. Box 1115
Wahpeton, ND 58074
**Phone:** (701) 642-8747
**Fax:** (701) 642-9501
**Format:** Country

**KBQQ-FM**
P.O. Box 1686
Minot, ND 58702-1686
**Phone:** (701) 852-0301 or
    (800) 659-1284 (toll-free)
**Fax:** (701) 852-4400
**Format:** Classic Rock

**KBTO-FM**
Hwy. 5 W.
P.O. Box 28
Bottineau, ND 58318
**Phone:** (701) 228-5151 or
    (800) 827-1614 (toll-free)
**Fax:** (701) 228-2483
**Format:** Country

**KBYZ-FM**
P.O. Box 1377
Bismarck, ND 58502
**Phone:** (701) 663-6411
**Fax:** (701) 663-8790
**Format:** Classic Rock

**KCND-FM**
c/o Prairie Public Radio
1814 N. 15th Street
Bismarck, ND 58501
**Phone:** (701) 224-1700 or
    (800) 359-5566 (toll-free)
**Fax:** (701) 224-0555
**E-mail:** ppr@pol.org
**Format:** Public Radio, News, Classical,
    Jazz

**KCAD-FM**
20th Street SW
Box 1478
Dickinson, ND 58601
**Phone:** (701) 227-1876
http://www.ndba.org/stations/kcadfm.html
**Format:** Country

**KDSU-FM**
207 N 5th Street
Fargo, ND 58102
**Phone:** (701) 241-6900
**Fax:** (701) 241-1893
**E-mail:** ppr@prairiepublic.org

http://www.ndpr.org
**Format:** Public Radio, Classical, News,
    Jazz

**KDSU-FM**
207 N 5th Street
Fargo, ND 58102
**Phone:** (701) 241-6900
**Fax:** (701) 241-1893
**E-mail:** ppr@prairiepublic.org
http://www.ndpr.org
**Format:** Public Radio, Classical, News,
    Jazz

**KFBN-FM**
P.O. Box 107
Fargo, ND 58107-0107
**Phone:** (701) 298-8877
**Format:** Contemporary Christian

**KFGO-AM**
1020 S. 25th Street
Fargo, ND 58103
**Phone:** (701) 237-5972
**Fax:** (701) 237-0980
http://www.kfgo.com
**Format:** News, Talk, Sports,
    Agricultural

**KFGO-FM**
1020 S. 25th Street
Fargo, ND 58108-2312
**Phone:** (701) 237-5346
**Fax:** (701) 235-4042
http://www.moosecountry 1019.com
**Format:** Country

**KFJM-FM**
Box 8117
Grand Forks, ND 58202
**Phone:** (701) 777-2577
**Fax:** (701) 777-4263
**Format:** Alternative/New
    Music/Progressive, Classical

**KMAV-FM**
P.O. Box 216
Mayville, ND 58257
**Phone:** (701) 786-2335
**Fax:** (701) 786-2268
http://www.kmav1520am.com
**Format:** Country

**KQLX-FM**
1206 S. Main
P.O. Box 1008
Lisbon, ND 58054
**Phone:** (701) 683-5287 or (800) 726-8965
    (toll-free)

**Fax:** (701) 683-9029
**E-mail:** kqlxradio@mlgc.com
http://www.kqlx.com
**Format:** Country

**KRVI-FM**
1020 25th Street, S.
Fargo, ND 58103
**Phone:** (701) 237-5346
http://www.river95.com
**Format:** Adult Contemporary, Soft Rock

**KRVI-FM**
1020 25th Street, S.
Fargo, ND 58103
**Phone:** (701) 235-9999
**Fax:** (701) 235-4042
http://www.theriver951.com
**Format:** Soft Rock

**WDAY-AM**
Box 2466
Fargo, ND 58108
**Phone:** (701) 237-6500
**Fax:** (701) 241-5373
**E-mail:** 1becker@i29.net
http://www.in-forum.com
**Format:** News, Talk

**KHND-AM**
P.O. Box 6
Harvey, ND 58341
**Phone:** (701) 324-4848 or (800) 375-9661
    (toll-free)
**Fax:** (701) 324-2043
**E-mail:** khnd@ndak.net
**Format:** Contemporary Country

**KLTA-FM**
2501 13th Avenue S.W.
Suite 201
Fargo, ND 58103
**Phone:** (701) 237-4500
**Fax:** (701) 235-9082
**Format:** Adult Contemporary

**KLTC-AM**
129 3rd Avenue, E., No. KRRB
Dickinson, ND 58601-5231
**Phone:** (701) 227-1876
**Fax:** (701) 227-1959
**Format:** Full Service, Country,
    Agricultural

**KLXX-AM**
Box 1377
Bismarck, ND 58502-1377
**Phone:** (701) 663-6411
**Fax:** (701) 663-8790
**Format:** Big Band/Nostalgia, Sports

**KMPR-FM**
c/o Prairie Public Radio
1814 N. 15th Street
Bismarck, ND 58501
**Phone:** (701) 224-1700
**Fax:** (701) 224-0555
**Format:** Public Radio, News, Classical,
  Jazz

**KNOX-AM**
P.O. Box 13638
Grand Forks, ND 58208-3638
**Phone:** (701) 775-4611 or (800) 726-0092
  (toll-free)
**Fax:** (701) 772-0540
**Format:** Talk, Agricultural, News

**KOVC-AM**
232 3rd Street, NE
Box 994
Valley City, ND 58072
**Phone:** (701) 845-1490
**Fax:** (701) 845-1245
**E-mail:** dcountry@daktel.com
**Format:** Country

**KPOK-AM**
P.O. Box 829
Bowman, ND 58623
**Phone:** (701) 523-3883
**Format:** Country, Agricultural

# OHIO

**WAKW-FM**
6275 Collegevue Plaza
Cincinnati, OH 45224-1959
**Phone:** (513) 542-9393 or (888) 542-9393
  (toll-free)
**Fax:** (513) 542-9333
**E-mail:** wakw@eos.net
http://www.wakw.com
**Format:** Contemporary Christian

**WAPS-FM**
65 Steiner Avenue
Akron, OH 44301
**Phone:** (330) 761-3099
**Fax:** (330) 761-3240
**E-mail:** airstaff@wapsfm.com;
  alillie@akron.k12.oh.us
http://www.wapsfm.com
http://www.913thesummit.com
**Format:** Adult Album Alternative

**WBBI-FM**
1906 Highland Avenue
Cincinnati, OH 45219
http://www.wbbi.com
**Format:** Country, Contemporary Country

**WBZX-FM**
1458 Dublin Road
Columbus, OH 43215
**Phone:** (614) 481-7800
**Fax:** (614) 481-8070
**E-mail:** mail@wbzx.com
http://www.wbzx.com
**Format:** Album-Oriented Rock (AOR)

**WCBE-FM**
540 Jack Gibbs Boulevard
Columbus, OH 43215
**Phone:** (614) 365-5555
**Fax:** (614) 365-5060
**E-mail:** wcbe@wcbe.org
http://www.wcbe.org
**Format:** Jazz, Blues, Alternative/New
  Music/Progressive, Public Radio,
  News

**WCIN-AM**
3540 Reading Road
Cincinnati, OH 45229
**Phone:** (513) 281-7180 or (800) 733-6051
  (toll-free)
**Fax:** (513) 281-6125
http://www.1480wcin.com

**WCKY-AM**
1111 St. Gregory Street
Cincinnati, OH 45202
**Phone:** (513) 421-9724
**Fax:** (513) 655-9700
**Format:** Sports, Talk

**WCLR-FM**
P.O. Box 1206
Dayton, OH 45401-1206
**Phone:** (937) 259-2111
**Fax:** (937) 259-2168
**E-mail:** coxradio@erinet.com
**Format:** Oldies

**WCLT-FM**
674 Jacksontown Road SE
Box 5150
Newark, OH 43058-5150
**Phone:** (740) 345-4004
**Fax:** (740) 345-5775
**E-mail:** wclt@wclt.com
http://www.wclt.com
**Format:** Country

**WCLV-FM**
26501 Renaissance Pkwy.
Cleveland, OH 44128
**Phone:** (216) 464-0900
**Fax:** (216) 464-2206
**E-mail:** wclv@wclv.com

http://www.wclv.com
**Format:** Classical

**WCPN-FM**
3100 Chester Avenue
Suite 300
Cleveland, OH 44114-4617
**Phone:** (216) 432-3700
**Fax:** (216) 432-3681
**E-mail:** comments@wcpn.org
http://www.wcpu.org
**Format:** Jazz, Information, News, Public
  Radio

**WCPZ-FM**
1640 Cleveland Road
Sandusky, OH 44870
**Phone:** (419) 625-1010 or (800) 589-1027
  (toll-free)
**Fax:** (419) 625-1348
http://wcpz.com
**Format:** Adult Contemporary

**WDFM-FM**
118 Clinton Street
Defiance, OH 43512
**Phone:** (419) 782-9336
**Fax:** (419) 784-0306
**E-mail:** wdfm@bright.net
http://www.bright.net/wdfm
**Format:** Adult Contemporary

**WDPS-FM**
441 River Corridor Drive
Dayton, OH 45402
**Phone:** (513) 223-0906
**Fax:** (513) 262-3744
**Format:** Eclectic

**WEBN-FM**
1111 St. Gregory
Cincinnati, OH 45202
**Phone:** (513) 621-9326 or
  (800) 749-WEBN (toll-free)
**Fax:** (513) 749-3299
http://www.webn.com
**Format:** Album-Oriented Rock (AOR)

**WFUN-AM**
3226 Jefferson Road
P.O. Box 738
Ashtabla, OH 44004
**Phone:** (216) 993-2126
**Fax:** (216) 992-2658
**E-mail:** wfun@ashtebula.net;
  wfun@wfunam97.com
http://www.wfunam97.com
**Format:** Talk, News, Sports

**WGLE-FM**
136 N. Huron Street
Box 30
Toledo, OH 43604
**Phone:** (419) 243-3091 or (800) 243-9483
  (toll-free)
**Fax:** (419) 243-9711
**Format:** Public Radio, Classical, News,
  Information

**WGRR-FM**
3656 Edwards Road
Cincinnati, OH 45208
**Phone:** (513) 321-8900
**Fax:** (513) 321-1175
**Format:** Oldies

**WGTZ-FM**
717 E. David Road
Dayton, OH 45429
**Phone:** (937) 294-5858
**Fax:** (937) 297-5233
http://www.wgtz.com
**Format:** Contemporary Hit Radio (CHR)

**WGUC-FM**
1223 Central Pkwy.
Cincinnati, OH 45214-2889
**Phone:** (513) 241-8282
**Fax:** (513) 241-8456
**E-mail:** wguc.org
http://www.wguc.org
**Format:** Public Radio, Classical

**WGNZ-AM**
P.O. Box 1100
Dayton, OH 45405-0875
**Phone:** (937) 454-9000
**Fax:** (937) 454-1980
**E-mail:** wgnz@good-news.org
www.good-news.org
**Format:** Gospel

**WGTZ-FM**
717 E. David Road
Dayton, OH 45429
**Phone:** (937) 294-5858
**Fax:** (937) 297-5233
http://www.wgtz.com
**Format:** Contemporary Hit Radio (CHR)

**WGXM-FM**
2251 Timber Lane
Dayton, OH 45414
**Phone:** (513) 275-8434
**Fax:** (513) 278-5888
**Format:** Country, Soft Rock,
  Alternative/New Music/Progressive

**WHIO-AM**
1414 Wilmington Avenue
Dayton, OH 45420-1568
**Phone:** (513) 259-2111
**Fax:** (513) 259-2168
**Format:** Talk, News

**WHOT-FM**
4040 Simon Road
Youngstown, OH 44512
**Phone:** (330) 783-1000
**Fax:** (330) 783-0060
**E-mail:** whot@aol.com
http://www.hot101.com
**Format:** Contemporary Hit Radio
  (CHR)

**WING-FM**
717 E. David Road
Dayton, OH 45429
**Phone:** (937) 294-5858
**Fax:** (937) 297-5233
**E-mail:** kgc@erinet.com
http://www.wingfm.com
**Format:** Classic Rock

**WIOT-FM**
125 S. Superior Street
Toledo, OH 43602
**Phone:** (419) 241-8321
**Fax:** (419) 244-7631
**E-mail:** wiot@wiot.com
http://www.wiot.com
**Format:** Album-Oriented Rock (AOR)

**WIZF-FM**
7030 Reading Road
Suite 316
Cincinnati, OH 45237-3839
**Phone:** (513) 351-5900
**Fax:** (513) 351-0020
**Format:** Urban Contemporary

**WJER-FM**
646 Boulevard
Dover, OH 44622-2027
**Phone:** (330) 343-7755
**Fax:** (330) 364-4538
**E-mail:** wjer@tusco.net
http://www.tusco.net/wjer
**Format:** Adult Contemporary

**WKRC-AM**
1111 St. Gregory Street
Cincinnati, OH 45202
**Phone:** (513) 241-1550
**Fax:** (513) 723-9221
**Format:** Talk, News

**WKRQ-FM**
1906 Highland Avenue
Cincinnati, OH 45219-3161
**Phone:** (513) 763-5686
**Fax:** (513) 763-5541
**E-mail:** q102cincy@aol.com
**Format:** Contemporary Christian

**WKXA-FM**
551 Lake Cascades Pkwy.
Findlay, OH 45840
**Phone:** (419) 422-4545
**Fax:** (419) 422-6736
**E-mail:** wkxa@wkxa.com
http://www.wkxa.com
**Format:** Top 40, Adult Contemporary

**WMJI-FM**
6200 Oak Tree Boulevard, 4th Floor
Cleveland, OH 44131-2510
**Phone:** (216) 520-2600 or (800) 669-1057
  (toll-free)
**Fax:** (216) 524-2600
http://www.wmji.com
**Format:** Oldies

## OKLAHOMA

**KBEL-AM**
P.O. Box 418
Idabel, OK 74745
**Phone:** (580) 286-6642 or (877) 329-8279
  (toll-free)
**Fax:** (580) 286-6643
http://www.kbelsports.com
**Format:** Sports, Talk

**KBEL-FM**
P.O. Box 418
Idabel, OK 74745
**Phone:** (580) 286-6642 or (877) 329-8279
  (toll-free)
**Fax:** (580) 286-6643
**E-mail:** kbel1967@yahoo.com
http://www.kbelcountry.com
**Format:** Country

**KCCU-FM**
Administration Building
2800 West Gore Boulevard
Lawton, OK 73505
**Phone:** (580) 581-2425 or (888) 454-7800
  (toll-free)
**Fax:** (580) 581-5571
**E-mail:** kccu@cameron.edu
http://www.kccu.org
**Format:** Jazz, Easy Listening, Classical,
  News

**KDKR-FM**
P.O. Box 1924
Tulsa, OK 74101
**Phone:** (918) 455-5693
**Fax:** (918) 455-0411
**E-mail:** mail@oasisnetwork.org
http://www.oasisnetwork.org
**Format:** Religious, Southern Gospel

**KECO-FM**
220 S. Pioneer Road
P.O. Box 945
Elk City, OK 73648
**Phone:** (405) 225-9696 or (800) 297-5326
   (toll-free)
**Fax:** (405) 225-9699
**E-mail:** keco@itlnet.net
http://www.kecofm.com
**Format:** Country

**KEYB-FM**
808 N. Main
P.O. Box 1077
Altus, OK 73522
**Phone:** (580) 482-1555
**Fax:** (580) 482-8353
**E-mail:** keyb@keyb.net
http://www.keyb.net
**Format:** Country

**KGOU-FM**
780 Van Vleet Oval
Norman, OK 73019
**Phone:** (405) 325-5468
**Fax:** (405) 325-7129
http://www.kgou.org
**Format:** News, Talk, Blues

**KGWA-AM**
Box 3128
Enid, OK 73702
**Phone:** (580) 234-4230
**Fax:** (580) 234-2971
http://www.kgwa960.com
**Format:** News, Talk

**KGWA-AM**
Box 3128
Enid, OK 73702
**Phone:** (580) 234-4230
**Fax:** (580) 234-2971
http://www.kgwa960.com
**Format:** News, Talk

**KIMY-FM**
Box 221
Watonga, OK 73772-0221
**Phone:** (580) 623-4777

**Fax:** (580) 623-4997
http://www.my93.com
**Format:** Country

**KKBS-FM**
P.O. Box 1756
Guymon, OK 73942
**Phone:** (580) 338-5493
**Fax:** (580) 338-0717
**E-mail:** kibbs@brightok.net
http://www.kkbs.com
**Format:** Classic Rock, Agricultural

**KKWD-FM**
4045 NW 64th Street
Suite 600
Oklahoma City, OK 73116
**Phone:** (405) 848-0100
**Fax:** (405) 843-5288
http://www.wild979.com
**Format:** Contemporary Hit Radio (CHR)

**KLAW-FM**
626 SW D Avenue
Lawton, OK 73501
**Phone:** (580) 581-3600
**Fax:** (580) 357-2880
**E-mail:** klaw@sirinet.net
http://www.klaw.com
**Format:** Country

**KMGZ-FM**
1421 Great Plains Boulevard
Suite C
Box 7953
Lawton, OK 73506-1953
**Phone:** (580) 536-9530 or (888) 624-4295
   (toll-free)
**Fax:** (580) 536-FAXX
**E-mail:** kmgz@sirinet.net
http://kmgz.com
**Format:** Contemporary Hit Radio (CHR)

**KMOD-FM**
5801 E. 41st Street
Suite 900
Tulsa, OK 74135
**Phone:** (918) 664-2810
**Fax:** (918) 665-0555
http://www.kmod.com
**Format:** Album-Oriented Rock (AOR),
   Classic Rock

**KNYD-FM**
P.O. Box 1924
Tulsa, OK 74101
**Phone:** (918) 455-5693
**Fax:** (918) 455-0411
**E-mail:** mail@oasisnetwork.org

http://www.oasisnetwork.org
**Format:** Religious, Middle-of-the-Road
   (MOR)

**KOMA-FM**
820 SW 4th Street
Moore, OK 73160
**Phone:** (405) 794-4000
**Fax:** (405) 793-0514
**E-mail:** koma@compuserve.com
http://www.komaradio.com
**Format:** Oldies

**KOZO-FM**
P.O. Box 1924
Tulsa, OK 74101
**Phone:** (918) 455-5693
**Fax:** (918) 455-0411
**E-mail:** mail@oasisnetwork.org
http://www.oasisnetwork.org
**Format:** Religious, Middle-of-the-Road
   (MOR)

**KQSR-FM**
50 Penn Place
Suite 1000
Oklahoma City, OK 73118
**Phone:** (405) 840-5271
**Fax:** (405) 842-1315
http://www.kqsr947.com
**Format:** Adult Contemporary, Soft Rock

**KQTZ-FM**
1515 N. Broadway
Hobart, OK 73651
**Phone:** (405) 726-5656 or (800) 401-2686
   (toll-free)
**Fax:** (405) 726-2222
http://www.kq106.com
**Format:** Hot Country

**KRAV-FM**
7136 S. Yale, 5th Floor
Tulsa, OK 74133
**Phone:** (918) 491-9696
**Fax:** (918) 493-5385
**E-mail:** krav96@ix.netcom.com
http://www.krav.com
**Format:** Adult Contemporary

**KRKZ-FM**
212 W. Cypress
P.O. Box 577
Altus, OK 73521-0577
**Phone:** (405) 482-1450 or (800) 401-2686
   (toll-free)
**Fax:** (405) 482-3420
http://www.krkz.com
**Format:** Classic Rock

**KSEO-AM**
P.O. Box 190
Durant, OK 74702
**Phone:** (580) 924-3100
**Fax:** (580) 920-1426
http://www.redriverok.com/klbckseo
**Format:** Adult Contemporary, Oldies

**KTJS-AM**
1515 N. Broadway
Hobart, OK 73651
**Phone:** (580) 726-5656 or (800) 299-5657
  (toll-free)
**Fax:** (580) 726-2222
**E-mail:** chadfuchs@ktjs.com
http://www.ktjs.com
**Format:** News, Sports, Country,
  Religious, Agricultural, Easy
  Listening

**KTLS-FM**
1150 North Hills Centre
Ada, OK 74820
**Phone:** (580) 332-2211
**Fax:** (580) 436-1629
http://ktlsradio.com
**Format:** Classic Rock

**KTRT-AM**
P.O. Box 1270
Tulsa, OK 74101-1270
**Phone:** (918) 234-1270
**Fax:** (918) 341-1411
http://www.ktrt.com
**Format:** Talk, Sports

**KVOO-AM**
4590 E. 29th
Tulsa, OK 74114-6208
**Phone:** (918) 743-7814
**Fax:** (918) 743-7613
http://www.kvoo.com
**Format:** Country

**KWHW-AM**
212 W. Cypress
P.O. Box 577
Altus, OK 73521-0577
**Phone:** (405) 482-1450 or
  (800) 401-2686 (toll-free)
**Fax:** (405) 462-3420
http://www.kwhw.com

**KYLV-FM**
P.O. Box 11000
Oklahoma City, OK 73136-1100
**E-mail:** klove@klove.com
http://www.klove.com
**Format:** Contemporary Christian

**KZCD-FM**
626 SW D Avenue
Lawton, OK 73501
**Phone:** (580) 581-3600
**Fax:** (580) 357-2880
**E-mail:** z94@sirinet.net
http://www.z94.com
**Format:** Album-Oriented Rock (AOR)

**WWLS-FM**
4045 NW 64th
Suite 600
Oklahoma City, OK 73116
**Phone:** (405) 848-0100
**Fax:** (405) 843-5288
http://www.thesportsanimal.com
**Format:** Sports

# OREGON

**KAGI-AM**
1250 Siskiyou Boulevard
Ashland, OR 97520
**Phone:** (541) 552-6301
**E-mail:** jpr@jeffnet.org
http://www.jeffnet.org
**Format:** Talk, News

**KAGO-AM**
P.O. Box 339
Klamath Falls, OR 97601-0350
**Phone:** (541) 882-2551
**Fax:** (541) 883-6141
**E-mail:** kagoam@newnw.com
http://www.kagoradio.com
**Format:** Talk, News

**KAJO-AM**
600 Roguelea Lane
P.O. Box 230
Grants Pass, OR 97526
**Phone:** (503) 476-6608
**Fax:** (503) 476-4018
**E-mail:** kajo@kajo.com
http://www.kajo.com
**Format:** Middle-of-the-Road (MOR),
  Big Band/Nostalgia, Full Service

**KBDN-FM**
P.O. Box 250
Coquille, OR 97423
**Phone:** (541) 396-2141
**Fax:** (541) 396-2143
**E-mail:** mainoffice@kshr.com
http://www.kshr.com
**Format:** Classic Rock

**KBND-AM**
711 NE Butler Road
Bend, OR 97701-8083

**Phone:** (503) 382-5263
**Fax:** (503) 388-0456
**E-mail:** kbnd@kbnd.com
http://www.kbnd.com
**Format:** News, Sports, Talk

**KBPS-AM**
515 NE 15th Avenue
Portland, OR 97232
**Phone:** (503) 916-5828
**Fax:** (503) 916-2642
http://www.kbps.org
**Format:** Public Radio, Educational,
  Classical, Eclectic

**KBPS-FM**
515 NE 15th
Portland, OR 97232
**Phone:** (503) 916-5828
**Fax:** (503) 916-2642
**E-mail:** kbps@kbps.org
http://www.allclassical.org
**Format:** Classical

**KDCO-FM**
P.O. Box 478
Coos Bay, OR 97420
**Phone:** (541) 269-0935 or (800) 833-9211
  (toll-free)
**Fax:** (541) 269-9376
**E-mail:** oldies@ucinet.com
http://www.kdcq.com
**Format:** Oldies

**KEUG-FM**
P.O. Box 3088
Portland, OR 97228
**Phone:** (541) 767-9000 or (800) 488-6397
  (toll-free)
**Fax:** (541) 942-1991
http://lite-fm.com
**Format:** Easy Listening

**KEX-AM**
4949 SW Macadam Avenue
Portland, OR 97201
**Phone:** (503) 225-1190 or (800) 345-1190
  (toll-free)
**Fax:** (503) 227-5873
**E-mail:** cswan@1190kex.com
http://www.1190kex.com
**Format:** Full Service

**KFXX-AM**
0700 SW Bancroft Street
Portland, OR 97201
**Phone:** (503) 223-1441 or (800) 932-5399
  (toll-free)
**Fax:** (503) 223-6909

http://www.kfxx.com
**Format:** Sports, News, Talk

**KGON-FM**
0700 SW Bancroft Street
Portland, OR 97201
**Phone:** (503) 223-1441 or (800) 222-9236
    (toll-free)
**Fax:** (503) 223-6909
**E-mail:** anyone@kgon.com
http://www.kgon.com
**Format:** Classic Rock

**KIFS-FM**
3624 Avion Drive
Medford, OR 97504
**Phone:** (541) 772-4174
**Fax:** (541) 858-5416
http://www.107kiss.com
**Format:** Contempoary Hit Radio (CHR)

**KLCC-FM**
4000 E. 30th Avenue
Eugene, OR 97405
**Phone:** (541) 726-2224 or (800) 922-3682
    (toll-free)
**Fax:** (541) 744-3962
**E-mail:** klcc@lanec.edu
http://www.klcc.org
**Format:** Public Radio, Eclectic

**KMHD-FM**
26000 SE Stark
Gresham, OR 97030
**Phone:** (503) 491-7271 or (800) 487-5643
    (toll-free)
**Fax:** (503) 491-6999
http://www.kmhd.org
**Format:** Jazz

**KOAC-AM**
Oregon State University
239 Covell Hall
Corvallis, OR 97331
**Phone:** (541) 737-4311
**Fax:** (541) 737-4314
http://www.opb.org
**Format:** Public Radio, News,
    Information

**KPDQ-AM**
5110 SE Stark Street
Portland, OR 97215
**Phone:** (503) 231-7800
**Fax:** (503) 238-7202
**E-mail:** kpdq@easystreet.com
http://www.kpdq.com
**Format:** Religious, Talk

**KPDQ-FM**
5110 SE Stark Street
Portland, OR 97215
**Phone:** (503) 231-7800
**Fax:** (503) 238-7202
http://www.kpdq.com
**Format:** Religious

**KRTA-AM**
1257 N. Riverside
Suite 10
Medford, OR 97501
**Phone:** (503) 772-0322
**Fax:** (503) 772-4233
http://www.krta.com
**Format:** Latino, Adult Contemporary

**KSOR-FM**
1250 Siskiyou Boulevard
Ashland, OR 97520
**Phone:** (541) 552-6301
**E-mail:** jpr@jeffnet.org
http://www.jeffnet.org
**Format:** Public Radio, News, Classical

**KSRV-AM**
P.O. Box 129
Ontario, OR 97914
**Phone:** (541) 889-8651
**Fax:** (541) 889-8733
**E-mail:** ksrv@cyberhighway.net;
    ksrv@ksrv.com; adds@ksrv.com
http://www.ksrv.com
**Format:** News, Talk

**KSTE-FM**
4949 SW Macadam Avenue
Portland, OR 97201
**Phone:** (503) 467-1059 or (866) 445-1059
    (toll-free)
http://star1059.com
**Format:** Alternative/New
    Music/Progressive

**KSTE-FM**
4949 SW Macadam Avenue
Portland, OR 97201
**Phone:** (503) 467-1059 or (866) 445-1059
    (toll-free)
http://star1059.com
**Format:** Alternative/New
    Music/Progressive

**KTBR-FM**
P.O. Box 1760
Roseburg, OR 97470
**Phone:** (541) 572-8255
**Fax:** (541) 672-4827
**E-mail:** ktbr@wanweb.net
**Format:** Talk

**KWBY-AM**
1665 James Street
P.O. Box 158
Woodburn, OR 97071-0158
**Phone:** (503) 981-9400
**Fax:** (503) 981-3561
http://radio-fiesta.com
**Format:** Ethnic

**KXIX-FM**
P.O. Box 5068
Bend, OR 97708
**Phone:** (541) 382-5611
**Fax:** (541) 389-7885
http://www.x94.com
**Format:** Alternative/New
    Music/Progressive

**KYKN-AM**
P.O. Box 1430
Salem, OR 97308
**Phone:** (503) 390-3014
**Fax:** (503) 390-3728
http://www.kykn.com
**Format:** News, Talk, Sports

**KZZE-FM**
3624 Avion Drive
Medford, OR 97504
**Phone:** (541) 857-0340
**Fax:** (541) 858-5416
http://www.kzze.net
**Format:** Album-Oriented Rock (AOR)

## PENNSYLVANIA

**KDKA-AM**
1 Gateway Center
Pittsburgh, PA 15222
**Phone:** (412) 575-2200
**Fax:** (412) 575-2874
**E-mail:** kdkaradio.com
http://www.kdkaradio.com
**Format:** News, Talk

**WBAX-AM**
149 Penn Avenue
Scranton, PA 18503
**Phone:** (570) 346-6555
**Fax:** (570) 346-6038
**E-mail:** wejl@wejl-wbax.com
http://www.wejl-wbax.com
**Format:** Sports

**WBHD-FM**
600 Baltimore Drive, 2nd Floor
Wilkes Barre, PA 18702
**Phone:** (570) 824-9000
**Fax:** (570) 820-0520

http://www.97bht.com
**Format:** Top 40

**WBHV-FM**
2551 Park Center Boulevard
State College, PA 16801-3007
**Phone:** (814) 237-4959
**Fax:** (814) 234-1659
**E-mail:** b103fm.com
http://www.b103fm.com

**WBHV-FM**
2551 Park Center Boulevard
State College, PA 16801-3007
**Phone:** (814) 237-4959
**Fax:** (814) 234-1659
**E-mail:** b103fm.com
http://www.b103fm.com

**WBSX-FM**
600 Baltimore Drive
Wilkes Barre, PA 18702
**Phone:** (570) 824-9000
**Fax:** (570) 820-0520
**E-mail:** 937x@citcomm.com
http://www.937x.com
**Format:** Album-Oriented Rock (AOR)

**WBXQ-FM**
4000 5th Avenue
Altoona, PA 16602
**Phone:** (814) 944-9320
**Fax:** (814) 944-9350
**E-mail:** bohradi858@aol.com
http://www.wbxq.com
**Format:** Classic Rock

**WCCS-AM**
P.O. Box 1020
Indiana, PA 15701
**Phone:** (724) 349-WCCS
**Fax:** (724) 479-3500
**E-mail:** mbertig@wpia.net
http://www.1160wccs.com
**Format:** Full Service, Adult Contemporary

**WCTO-FM**
2158 Avenue C
Bethlehem, PA 18017
**Phone:** (610) 266-7600
**Fax:** (610) 231-0400
http://www.catcountry96.fm
**Format:** Contemporary Country

**WDNH-FM**
575 Grove Street
Honesdale, PA 18431
**Phone:** (717) 253-1616
**Fax:** (717) 253-6297

http://www.infocow.net
**Format:** Adult Contemporary

**WDVE-FM**
200 Fleet Street
Pittsburgh, PA 15220
**Phone:** (412) 937-1441
**Fax:** (412) 937-0323
http://www.due.com
**Format:** Album-Oriented Rock (AOR)

**WEAE-AM**
400 Ardmore Boulevard
Pittsburgh, PA 15221
**Phone:** (412) 731-1250
**Fax:** (412) 244-4596
http://www.espnradio 1250.com
**Format:** News, Talk, Sports

**WEEU-AM**
34 N. 4th Street
Reading, PA 19601-3996
**Phone:** (610) 376-7335 or
   (800) 323-8800 (toll-free)
**Fax:** (610) 376-7756
**E-mail:** weeuradio@aol.com
http://www.weeu.com
**Format:** Full Service, Talk

**WEJL-AM**
149 Penn Avenue
Scranton, PA 18503
**Phone:** (717) 346-6555
**Fax:** (717) 346-6038
http://www.wejc-wbax
**Format:** Sports

**WESA-AM**
5706 Woodmont Street
Pittsburgh, PA 15217-1208
**Phone:** (412) 483-6551
**Fax:** (412) 483-9251
**E-mail:** 98@dp.net
**Format:** Talk, News, Sports, Oldies

**WFIL-AM**
117 Ridge Pike
Lafayette Hill, PA 19444
**Phone:** (610) 941-9560 or
   (800) 560-WFIL (toll-free)
**Fax:** (610) 828-8879
http://www.wfil.com
**Format:** Talk, Religious

**WGBI-AM**
P.O. Box 729
Pittston, PA 18640
**Phone:** (717) 883-9800
**Fax:** (717) 883-9851

http://www.wilk@micxroserve.net
**Format:** News, Talk, Sports

**WILP-AM**
305 Highway 315
Pittston, PA 18640-3985
**Phone:** (717) 455-9979
**Fax:** (717) 636-2877
http://www.thewilknetwork.com
**Format:** Talk, News

**WHAT-AM**
2471 N. 54th Street
Philadelphia, PA 19131
**Phone:** (215) 581-5161
**Fax:** (215) 581-5185
**Format:** Urban Contemporary, Talk

**WHYY-FM**
150 N. 6th Street
Philadelphia, PA 19106
**Phone:** (215) 351-1200
**Fax:** (215) 351-1211
http://www.whyy.org
**Format:** Public Radio, News, Talk,
   Information

**WILP-AM**
305 Highway 315
Pittston, PA 18640-3985
**Phone:** (717) 455-9979
**Fax:** (717) 636-2877
http://www.thewilknetwork.com
**Format:** Talk, News

**WIP-AM**
441 N. 5th Street
Philadelphia, PA 19123
**Phone:** (215) 922-5000
**Fax:** (215) 922-2434
**Format:** Sports

**WJJZ-FM**
440 Domino Lane
Philadelphia, PA 19128
**Phone:** (215) 508-1200 or (800) 667-1106
   (toll-free)
**E-mail:** wjjz@pond.com
**Format:** Jazz

**WKDU-FM**
3210 Chestnut Street
Philadelphia, PA 19104
**Phone:** (215) 895-5920
**Fax:** (215) 895-1414
**Format:** Jazz, Ethnic, Religious, Urban
   Contemporary, Alternative/New
   Music/Progressive

**WLTJ-FM**
650 Smithfield Street
Pittsburgh, PA 15222
**Phone:** (412) 316-3342
**Fax:** (412) 316-3387
**E-mail:** info@wltj.com
**Format:** Adult Contemporary

**WMMR-FM**
Independence Mall E.
Philadelphia, PA 19106
**Phone:** (215) 238-8000
**Fax:** (215) 238-4737
**Format:** Album-Oriented Rock (AOR)

**WOGL-FM**
City Avenue & Monument Road
Philadelphia, PA 19131
**Phone:** (215) 668-5910
**Fax:** (215) 668-5929
**Format:** Oldies

**WORD-FM**
7 Parkway Ctr.
Pittsburgh, PA 15220-3702
**Phone:** (412) 937-1500 or (800) 320-8255
(toll-free)
**Fax:** (412) 937-1576
http://www.wordfm.com
**Format:** Contemporary Christian Talk

**WRDR-FM**
1080 N. Delaware Avenue
Suite 500
Philadelphia, PA 19125-4330
**Format:** Adult Contemporary

# RHODE ISLAND

**WADK-AM**
140 Thames Street
P.O. Box 367
Newport, RI 02840
**Phone:** (401) 846-1540 or (888) 421-0993
(toll-free)
**Fax:** (401) 846-1598
**E-mail:** wadk1540am@edgenet.net
**Format:** Talk, News, Jazz

**WADK-AM**
140 Thames Street
P.O. Box 367
Newport, RI 02840
**Phone:** (401) 846-1540 or (888) 421-0993
(toll-free)
**Fax:** (401) 846-1598
**E-mail:** wadk1540am@edgenet.net
**Format:** Talk, News, Jazz

**WARV-AM**
19 Luther Avenue
Warwick, RI 02886
**Phone:** (401) 737-0700
**Fax:** (401) 737-1604
**E-mail:** warv@aol.com
http://www.lifechangingradio.com
**Format:** Religious

**WBSR-FM**
P.O. Box 1930
Providence, RI 02912-1930
**Phone:** (401) 863-9600
http://www.brown.edu/students/wbsr/
about.html
**Format:** Eclectic, Sports, Information

**WCVY-FM**
40 Reservoir Road
Coventry, RI 02816-9532
**Phone:** (401) 821-8540
**Fax:** (401) 822-9492
**E-mail:** wcvyfm@aol.com
**Format:** Classic Rock, Alternative/New
Music/Progressive

**WDOM-FM**
Providence College
Joseph Hall
Suite 106
Providence, RI 02918
**Phone:** (401) 865-2460
**Fax:** (401) 865-2822
http://www.broadcastamerica.com
**Format:** Jazz, Alternative/New
Music/Progressive, Classical, Top 40,
Urban Contemporary, Country

**WFIF-AM**
90 Kay Avenue
Milford, CT 06460-5421
**Phone:** (203) 878-5915
**E-mail:** wfif@aol.com
http://www.lifechangingradio.com
**Format:** Religious, Talk

**WHJJ-AM**
115 Eastern Avenue
East Providence, RI 02914
**Phone:** (401) 438-6110
**Fax:** (401) 438-3520
**Format:** Talk, News

**WHJY-FM**
115 Eastern Avenue
East Providence, RI 02914
**Phone:** (401) 438-6110
**Fax:** (401) 438-3520
**E-mail:** whjy@aol.com
**Format:** Album-Oriented Rock (AOR)

**WJHD-FM**
Portsmouth Abbey School
Cory's Lane
Portsmouth, RI 02871
**Phone:** (401) 683-4756
**Format:** Eclectic

**WJJF-AM**
26 Woody Hill Road
Hope Valley, RI 02832
**Phone:** (401) 539-8502
**Format:** Country

**WJMF-FM**
Bryant College
1150 Douglas Pike
Box 6
Smithfield, RI 02917
**Phone:** (401) 232-6044
**Fax:** (401) 232-6748
**E-mail:** wjmp@acad.bryant.edu
**Format:** Alternative/New
Music/Progressive

**WLKW-AM**
1502 Wampanoag
East Providence, RI 02915
**Phone:** (401) 433-4200
**Fax:** (401) 433-1183
**Format:** Big Band/Nostalgia

**WNRI-AM**
786 Diamond Hill Road
Woonsocket, RI 02895
**Phone:** (401) 769-6925
**Fax:** (401) 762-0442
**Format:** Talk, Adult Contemporary

**WOTB-FM**
140 Thames Street
Newport, RI 02840
**Phone:** (401) 846-6900
**Fax:** (401) 846-1548
**Format:** Jazz

**WPJB-FM**
P.O. Box 5555
Wakefield, RI 02880
**Format:** Adult Contemporary

**WPRO-AM**
1502 Wampanoag Trail
East Providence, RI 02915
**Phone:** (401) 433-4200
**Fax:** (401) 433-5967
**E-mail:** wpro@ids.net
**Format:** Talk, News

**WPRO-FM**
1502 Wampanoag Trail
East Providence, RI 02915
**Phone:** (401) 433-4200
**Fax:** (401) 433-5967
**E-mail:** wprofm@aol.com
**Format:** Top 40

**WQRI-FM**
Roger Williams University
One Old Ferry Road
Bristol, RI 02809
**Phone:** (401) 254-3283
**E-mail:** wqri@alpha.rwu.edu
http://wqri.rwu.edu
**Format:** Alternative/New
    Music/Progressive

**WRBU-FM**
88 Benevolent Street
Providence, RI 02906
**Phone:** (401) 272-9550 or
    (800) 659-9550 (toll-free)
**Fax:** (401) 272-WRBU
http://www.wbru.com
**Format:** Alternative/New
    Music/Progressive, Jazz, Urban
    Contemporary

**WRIU-FM**
R.I. Memorial Union, Rm. 362
Kingston, RI 02881
**Phone:** (401) 789-4949
**Fax:** (401) 874-4349
**Format:** Eclectic

**WSKO-AM**
1502 Wampanoag Trail
East Providence, RI 02915
**Phone:** (401) 433-4200
**Fax:** (401) 433-1183
http://www.790thescore.com
**Format:** Sports

**WSNE-FM**
75 Oxford Street
Providence, RI 02905-4722
**Phone:** (401) 438-9300
**Fax:** (401) 434-4243
**Format:** Adult Contemporary

**WWBB-FM**
75 Oxford Street
Suite 302
Providence, RI 02905
**Phone:** (401) 781-9979
**Fax:** (401) 781-9329
**Format:** Oldies

**WWKX-FM**
110 Central Avenue
Pawtucket, RI 02861-2262
**Phone:** (401) 723-1063
**Fax:** (401) 725-8209
http://www.kix106fm.com
**Format:** Contemporary Hit Radio (CHR)

**WWLI-FM**
1502 Wampanoag Trail
East Providence, RI 02915
**Phone:** (401) 272-1105
**Fax:** (401) 453-5483
**E-mail:** lite105@lite105.com
**Format:** Adult Contemporary

**WWRX-FM**
150 Chestnut Street
Providence, RI 02903
**Phone:** (401) 273-6397
**Fax:** (401) 272-8712
http://www.fnxradio.com
**Format:** Alternative/New
    Music/Progressive

**WXIN-FM**
600 Mount Pleasant Avenue
Student Union, Rm. 309
Providence, RI 02908
**Phone:** (401) 456-8288
**Fax:** (401) 456-8541
**Format:** News, Talk, Eclectic

**WZRA-FM**
1502 Wampanoag Trail
East Providence, RI 02916
**Phone:** (401) 433-4200
**Fax:** (401) 433-1183
http://www.z100providence.com
**Format:** Contemporary Hit Radio (CHR)

**WZRI-FM**
1502 Wampanoag Trail
East Providence, RI 02916
**Phone:** (401) 433-4200
**Fax:** (401) 433-1183
http://www.z100providence.com
**Format:** Contemporary Hit Radio (CHR)

## SOUTH CAROLINA

**WAHT-AM**
202 Lawrence Road
Box 1560
Clemson, SC 29631
**Phone:** (803) 654-1560 or
    (800) 499-1049 (toll-free)
**Fax:** (803) 654-3300
**E-mail:** waht@carol.net

http://www.wahtam.com
**Format:** Gospel

**WALC-FM**
950 Houston Northcutt Boulevard
Suite 201
Mt. Pleasant, SC 29465
**Phone:** (843) 884-2534
**Fax:** (843) 884-6096
http://www.alicefm.com
**Format:** Adult Contemporary

**WARQ-FM**
P.O. Box 9127
Columbia, SC 29221-9127
**Phone:** (803) 772-5600
**Fax:** (803) 695-8605
**E-mail:** rock935@act.com
http://www.ward.com
**Format:** Alternative/New
    Music/Progressive

**WAVE-FM**
1 Street Augustine Plaza
Hilton Head Island, SC 29928
**Phone:** (803) 785-9569
**Fax:** (803) 842-3369
**E-mail:** email@106.9wave.com
http://www.106.9wave.com
**Format:** Contemporary Hit Radio (CHR)

**WCCP-FM**
202 Laurence Road
P.O. Box 1560
Clemson, SC 29631
**Phone:** (803) 654-1560 or (800) 499-1049
    (toll-free)
**Fax:** (803) 654-9328
**E-mail:** wccp@carol.net
http://www.wccpfm.com
**Format:** Sports

**WFBC-FM**
501 Rutherford Street
Greenville, SC 29609
**Phone:** (803) 271-9200
**Fax:** (803) 242-1567
http://www.wfbcfm.com
**Format:** Contemporary Hit Radio (CHR)

**WGOG-FM**
P.O. Box 10
Walhalla, SC 29691
**Phone:** (864) 638-3616
**Fax:** (864) 638-6810
**E-mail:** wgog@netmds.com
http://www.wgog.com
**Format:** Oldies

**WGUS-AM**
500 Carolina Springs Road
North Augusta, SC 29841-9437
**Phone:** (803) 279-1977
http://www.clearchannel.com/radio
**Format:** News, Talk

**WJMX-FM**
P.O. Box 103000
Florence, SC 29501-3000
**Phone:** (803) 667-9569
**Fax:** (803) 664-2869
**E-mail:** wjmx@southtech.net
http://www.wjmx.com
**Format:** Top 40

**WKZQ-AM**
1116 Ocaca Street
Myrtle Beach, SC 29577
**Phone:** (843) 448-4735
**Fax:** (843) 626-2508
http://www.wkzq.net
**Format:** Album-Oriented Rock (AOR)

**WLFJ-FM**
2420 Wade Hampton Boulevard
Greenville, SC 29615
**Phone:** (803) 292-6040 or
     (800) 849-8930 (toll-free)
**Fax:** (803) 292-8428
**E-mail:** hisradio@hisradio.org
http://www.hisradio.org
**Format:** Educational, Contemporary
     Christian Religious

**WLGI-FM**
1272 Williams Hill Road
Hemingway, SC 29554
**Phone:** (803) 558-9100
**Fax:** (803) 558-9114
**E-mail:** wlgi@usbnc.org
http://www.bci.org/radiobahaiusa
**Format:** Jazz, Oldies, Alternative/New
     Music/Progressive, Gospel

**WLXC-FM**
1801 Charleston Hwy.
Suite J
Cayce, SC 29033
**Phone:** (803) 796-7600
**Fax:** (803) 796-5502
http://www.kiss985fm.com
**Format:** Urban Contemporary

**WMUU-AM**
920 Wade Hampton Boulevard
Greenville, SC 29609
**Phone:** (864) 242-6240
**Fax:** (864) 370-3829

**E-mail:** wmuu@bju.edu
http://www.wmuu.com
**Format:** Religious

**WMUU-FM**
920 Wade Hampton Boulevard
Greenville, SC 29609
**Phone:** (864) 242-6240
**Fax:** (864) 370-3829
**E-mail:** wmuu@bju.edu
http://www.wmuu.com
**Format:** Easy Listening

**WMYI-FM**
7 N. Laurens Street
Suite 700
Greenville, SC 29601-2744
**Phone:** (864) 235-1025 or (888) 860-3366
     (toll-free)
**Fax:** (864) 271-3830
http://www.wmyi.com
**Format:** Adult Contemporary

**WNKT-FM**
1 Orange Grove Road
Charleston, SC 29407-3732
**Phone:** (843) 566-1100
**Fax:** (843) 529-1933
**E-mail:** brothermud@aol.com;
     spin45rpm@aol.com;
     catfish@gtemail.net
http://www.catcountry1075.com
**Format:** Country

**WNOK-FM**
316 Greystone Boulevard
Columbia, SC 29210-8007
**Phone:** (803) 771-0105
**Fax:** (803) 799-4367
http://www.wnok.com
**Format:** Contemporary Hit Radio (CHR)

**WPLS-FM**
Furman University
Box 28573
Greenville, SC 29613
**Phone:** (803) 294-3045
**Fax:** (803) 294-3001
**E-mail:** wplsfm@hotmail.com
http://s9000.furman.edu/~adams/wpls
**Format:** Alternative/New
     Music/Progressive

**WRCM-FM**
P.O. Box 17069
Charlotte, NC 28227
**Phone:** (704) 821-9293 or (877) 972-6624
     (toll-free)
**Fax:** (704) 821-9285

**E-mail:** wrcm@wrcm.org
http://www.wrcm.org
**Format:** Contemporary Christian, Adult
     Contemporary

**WRHI-AM**
P.O. Box 307
Rock Hill, SC 29731-6307
**Phone:** (803) 324-1340
**Fax:** (803) 324-2860
**E-mail:** 1340@wrhi.com
http://www.wrhi.com
**Format:** Talk, Adult Contemporary,
     News, Eclectic

**WRHM-FM**
P.O. Box 307
Rock Hill, SC 29731-6307
**Phone:** (803) 324-1071
**Fax:** (803) 324-2860
**E-mail:** sales@fm 107.com
http://fm107.com
**Format:** Contemporary Country, Sports

**WRJA-FM**
1101 George Rogers Boulevard
Columbia, SC 29201-4761
**Phone:** (803) 737-3420 or (800) 922-5437
     (toll-free)
**Fax:** (803) 737-3552
**E-mail:** gasque@scetv.org
http://www.scetv.state.sc.us/scetv
**Format:** Public Radio, Jazz, News

**WROQ-FM**
7 N. Laurens Street
Suite 700
Greenville, SC 29601
**Phone:** (864) 242-0101 or (888) 257-0058
     (toll-free)
**Fax:** (864) 298-0067
**E-mail:** radio@wroq.com
http://www.wroq.com
**Format:** Classic Rock

**WSBF-FM**
Box 2156 University Station
Clemson, SC 29632
**Phone:** (864) 656-4010
**Fax:** (864) 656-4011
**E-mail:** wsbf@clemson.edu
http://www.wsbf.clemson.edu
**Format:** Alternative/New
     Music/Progressive

**WSPX-FM**
P.O. Box 1546
Orangeburg, SC 29115

**Phone:** (803) 536-1710
**Fax:** (803) 531-1089
**E-mail:** bbinc@oburg.net
http://www.boswellbroadcasting.com
**Format:** Sports

**WSSL-FM**
7 N. Laurens Street
Suite 700
Greenville, SC 29601
**Phone:** (864) 242-1005 or (800) 248-0863
  (toll-free)
**Fax:** (864) 271-3830
http://www.wsslfm.com
**Format:** Hot Country

**WSUY-FM**
1 Orange Grove Road
Charleston, SC 29407
**Phone:** (843) 556-5660
**Fax:** (843) 763-0304
http://www.sunny969.com
**Format:** Adult Contemporary

**WTCB-FM**
P.O. Box 5106
Columbia, SC 29250
**Phone:** (803) 796-7600
**Fax:** (803) 796-9291
http://www.wtcbfm.com
**Format:** Adult Contemporary

**WTMA-AM**
P.O. Box 30909
Charleston, SC 29417
**Phone:** (843) 556-5660 or (800) 737-1250
  (toll-free)
**Fax:** (843) 763-0304
http://www.wtma.com
**Format:** News, Talk

**WYBB-FM**
59 Windermere Boulevard
Charleston, SC 29407-7411
**Phone:** (843) 769-4799
**Fax:** (843) 769-4797
http://www.98rock.net
**Format:** Classic Rock

**WYFG-FM**
6150 Canons Campground Road
Cowpens, SC 29330
**Phone:** (864) 487-5836
**Fax:** (864) 487-5836
**E-mail:** wyfg@aol.com
http://www.amen.net/bbn
**Format:** Religious

# SOUTH DAKOTA

**KAOR-FM**
University of South Dakota
414 East Clark
Vermillion, SD 57069-2390
**Phone:** (605) 677-5049
**Fax:** (605) 677-4025
**E-mail:** kaor@sunfish.usd.edu
**Format:** Alternative/New
  Music/Progressive

**KAWK-FM**
437 Montgomery Street
P.O. Box 804
Custer, SD 57730
**Phone:** (605) 673-5327
**Fax:** (605) 673-3079
**Format:** Oldies

**KBFO-FM**
3980 S. Dakota Street
Aberdeen, SD 57402
**Phone:** (605) 225-1560
http://www.clearchannel.com/radio
**Format:** Adult Contemporary

**KBRK-AM**
P.O. Box 97
Brookings, SD 57006
**Phone:** (605) 692-1430
**Fax:** (605) 692-4441
**E-mail:** kbrk@brookings.net
http://www.kbrk@brookings.net
**Format:** Middle-of-the-Road (MOR),
  News, Sports

**KBRK-FM**
P.O. Box 97
Brookings, SD 57006
**Phone:** (605) 692-1430
**Fax:** (605) 692-4441
**E-mail:** kbrk@brookings.net
http://www.b937@brookings.net
**Format:** Adult Contemporary

**KCUE-AM**
474 Guernsey Lane
Red Wing, MN 55066
**Phone:** (612) 388-7151
**Fax:** (612) 388-7153
**Format:** News, Talk, Country

**KDLO-FM**
Box 952
Watertown, SD 57201
**Phone:** (605) 882-1597 or (800) 952-3569
  (toll-free)
**Fax:** (605) 886-6757
**Format:** Contemporary Country

**KDSD-FM**
Cherry & Dakota Streets
P.O. Box 5000
Vermillion, SD 57069
**Phone:** (605) 677-5861 or (800) 456-0766
  (toll-free)
**Fax:** (605) 677-5010
**Format:** Classical, News, Jazz

**KDSJ-AM**
745 Main
Deadwood, SD 57732
**Phone:** (605) 578-1826
**Fax:** (605) 578-1827
http://www.kdsj980.com
**Format:** News, Oldies

**KELO-AM**
500 S. Phillips
Sioux Falls, SD 57104
**Phone:** (605) 331-5350
**Fax:** (605) 336-0415
**E-mail:** keloam@home.com
**Format:** News, Talk

**KELO-FM**
500 S. Phillips
Sioux Falls, SD 57104
**Phone:** (605) 331-5350
**Fax:** (605) 336-0415
**E-mail:** kelofm@mmi.net
**Format:** Adult Contemporary

**KEZV-FM**
2827 E. Colorado Boulevard
Spearfish, SD 57783-9759
**Phone:** (605) 642-5747
**Format:** Soft Rock, Adult Contemporary

**KFXS-FM**
Box 8205
Rapid City, SD 57709
**Phone:** (605) 348-1100
**Fax:** (605) 348-8121
**Format:** Classic Rock

**KGFX-AM**
214 W. Pleasant Drive
Pierre, SD 57501
**Phone:** (605) 224-8686
**Fax:** (605) 224-8984
**E-mail:** mascomm@iw.net
**Format:** Country, News, Agricultural

**KGIM-AM**
349 Berkshire Plaza
Box 306
Aberdeen, SD 57401

**Phone:** (605) 229-3636 or
    (800) 777-1420 (toll-free)
**Fax:** (605) 229-4849
**E-mail:** phcountry@midco.net
**Format:** Country, Full Service,
    Agricultural, Adult Contemporary

**KIMM-AM**
P.O. Box 8164
Rapid City, SD 57709
**Phone:** (605) 348-1100
**Fax:** (605) 348-8121
**Format:** Country

**KINI-FM**
P.O. Box 419
St. Francis, SD 57572
**Phone:** (605) 747-2291
**Fax:** (605) 747-5791
**E-mail:** kinifm@gwtc.net
http://www.wgtc.net/kinifm
**Format:** Eclectic, News

**KJAM-AM**
101 S. Egan Avenue
Madison, SD 57042
**Phone:** (605) 256-4514 or
    (800) 529-0032 (toll-free)
**Fax:** (605) 256-6477
**E-mail:** kjam@hcpd.com
http://www.kjamradio.com
**Format:** Contemporary Country, News

**KKLS-AM**
2100 S. Seventh Street
Rapid City, SD 57701
**Phone:** (605) 343-6161
**Fax:** (605) 343-9012
**E-mail:** kkmk@rapidnet.com
http://www.kkmk.rapidnet.com
**Format:** Oldies

**KKLS-FM**
3205 S. Meadow
Sioux Falls, SD 57106
**Phone:** (605) 361-0300
**Fax:** (605) 361-5410
http://www.hot1047.com
**Format:** Contemporary Hit Radio (CHR)

**KKMK-FM**
2100 S. 7th Street
Rapid City, SD 57701
**Phone:** (605) 343-6161
**Fax:** (605) 343-9012
**E-mail:** kkmk@rapidnet.com
http://www.kkmk.rapidnet.com
**Format:** Adult Contemporary

**KLND-FM**
HC61 Box 1
Mc Laughlin, SD 57642
**Phone:** (605) 823-4661
**Fax:** (605) 823-4660
**E-mail:** klnd@westriv.com
http://www.klnd.org
**Format:** Ethnic

**KMXC-FM**
2600 S. Spring Avenue
Sioux Falls, SD 57105
**Phone:** (605) 339-9999
**Fax:** (605) 339-2735
**Format:** Contemporary Hit Radio (CHR)

**KOKK-AM**
1835 Dakota S.
P.O. Box 931
Huron, SD 57350
**Phone:** (605) 352-1933
**Fax:** (605) 352-0911
**E-mail:** kokk@kokk.com
**Format:** Contemporary Country

**KOTA-AM**
518 1/2 St. Joe
P.O. Box 1760
Rapid City, SD 57709
**Phone:** (605) 342-2000
**Fax:** (605) 342-7305
http://kotaradio.rapidnet.com
**Format:** News, Talk

**KSDR-AM**
3 E. Kemp
Suite 300
Watertown, SD 57201
**Phone:** (605) 886-5747 or
    (800) 234-5793 (toll-free)
**Fax:** (605) 886-2121
http://www.ksdr.com
**Format:** Talk

**KSDR-FM**
3 E. Kemp
Suite 300
P.O. Box 1480
Watertown, SD 57201
**Phone:** (605) 886-5747 or (800) 274-5793
    (toll-free)
**Fax:** (605) 886-2121
**E-mail:** ksdr@ksdr.com
http://www.ksdr.com
**Format:** Country

**KSFS-AM**
P.O. Box 667
Crooks, SD 57020-0667

**Phone:** (605) 333-9646
**Fax:** (605) 335-8428
**E-mail:** thezone@dakotaconnect.com
http://www.ksfs.com
**Format:** Sports

**KTEQ-FM**
501 E. St. Joseph Street
Rapid City, SD 57701
**Phone:** (605) 394-2231
**E-mail:** kteq@zoop.org
http://www.kteq.org
**Format:** Eclectic, Alternative/New
    Music/Progressive

**KVHT-FM**
231 Broadway
Yankton, SD 57078
**Phone:** (605) 665-2600
**Fax:** (605) 665-8875
**E-mail:** mix106@kvht.com
**Format:** Adult Contemporary, Top 40

**KWAT-AM**
921 9th Avenue, SE
Box 950
Watertown, SD 57201
**Phone:** (605) 886-8444
**Fax:** (605) 886-9306
**Format:** Talk, Adult Contemporary

**KWYR-AM**
346 Main Street
Box 491
Winner, SD 57580
**Phone:** (605) 842-3333 or (800) 388-5997
    (toll-free)
**Fax:** (605) 842-3875
**E-mail:** 937radio@gwtc.net
http://www.kwtr.com
**Format:** Contemporary Country, News,
    Sports, Agricultural

**KXRB-AM**
3205 S. Meadow
Sioux Falls, SD 57106
**Phone:** (605) 361-0300
**Fax:** (605) 361-5410
**Format:** Country

**KYNT-AM**
Box 628
Yankton, SD 57078-0628
**Phone:** (605) 665-7892
**Fax:** (605) 665-0818
**E-mail:** kyntkkya@byelectric.com
**Format:** Talk, Adult Contemporary,
    News

**KZMX-AM**
P.O. Box 611
Hot Springs, SD 57747
**Phone:** (605) 745-3637
**Fax:** (605) 745-3517
**Format:** Country

## TENNESSEE

**WASL-FM**
Box 100
Dyersburg, TN 38025
**Phone:** (901) 285-1339
**Fax:** (901) 287-0100
**E-mail:** SL100fm@usit.net
http://wasl.net
**Format:** Adult Contemporary

**WCDT-AM**
1201 S. College Street
Winchester, TN 37398
**Phone:** (931) 967-2201
**Fax:** (931) 967-2201
**E-mail:** wcdt@wcdtradio.com
http://www.wcdtradio.com/home.htm
**Format:** Full Service, News, Talk

**WCRK-AM**
204 Brown Avenue
Box 220
Morristown, TN 37815-0220
**Phone:** (423) 586-9101
**Fax:** (423) 581-7756
**E-mail:** wcrk@wcrk.com,
    news@wcak.com, wcrk@lcs.net
http://www.wcrk.com
**Format:** Adult Contemporary

**WCVQ-FM**
P.O. Box 2249
Clarksville, TN 37042
**Phone:** (931) 431-4984 or (800) 727-4108
    (toll-free)
**Fax:** (931) 431-4986
http://www.q108.com
**Format:** Adult Contemporary

**WDIA-AM**
112 Union Avenue
Memphis, TN 38103
**Phone:** (901) 529-4300
**Fax:** (901) 529-9557
**E-mail:** jmeehan@am1070wdia.com
http://www.am1979wdia.com
**Format:** Adult Contemporary, Urban
    Contemporary

**WDOD-FM**
P.O. Box 1449
Chattanooga, TN 37401-1449

**Phone:** (423) 321-6200
**Fax:** (423) 321-6270
http://www.965mtn.com
**Format:** Album-Oriented Rock (AOR)

**WDYN-FM**
1815 Union Avenue
Chattanooga, TN 37404
**Phone:** (423) 493-4383
**Fax:** (423) 493-4526
**E-mail:** wdyn@wdyn.com
http://www.wdyn.com
**Format:** Religious

**WEPG-AM**
Ash Avenue
P.O. Box 8
South Pittsburg, TN 37380
**Phone:** (423) 837-0747 or (866) 837-7577
    (toll-free)
**Fax:** (423) 837-2974
**E-mail:** wepgtv6@aol.com
http://www.starartist.com
**Format:** Country

**WFSK-FM**
1000 17th Avenue N.
Nashville, TN 37208
**Phone:** (615) 329-8754
**Fax:** (615) 329-8754
**E-mail:** wdobbins@dubois.fisk.edu
http://www.wfsk.org
**Format:** Jazz, Gospel, Talk, Information,
    Urban Contemporary

**WGFX-FM**
P.O. Box 101604
Nashville, TN 37224
**Phone:** (615) 244-9533
**Fax:** (615) 259-1271
http://www.arrow104.5com
**Format:** Oldies, Classical

**WGNS-AM**
306 S. Church
Broadcast Plaza
Murfreesboro, TN 37130-3732
**Phone:** (615) 893-5373
**E-mail:** news@145owgns.com
http://www.1450wgns.com
**Format:** News, Talk, Sports

**WGOW-AM**
P.O. Box 11202
Chattanooga, TN 37401
**Phone:** (423) 756-6141
**Fax:** (423) 266-1652
**E-mail:** wgow@chattanooga.net
http://www.chattanooga.net/radio
**Format:** News, Talk

**WHBQ-AM**
6080 Mount Moriah Road
Memphis, TN 38115-2645
**Phone:** (901) 375-9324 or (888) 360-8255
    (toll-free)
**Fax:** (901) 375-4454
**E-mail:** mail@sports56whbq.com
http://www.flinn.com
**Format:** Sports

**WHRK-FM**
112 Union Avenue
Memphis, TN 38103
**Phone:** (901) 529-4300
**Fax:** (901) 529-9557
**E-mail:** jmeehan@k97fm.com
http://www.k97fm.com
**Format:** Urban Contemporary

**WHRS-FM**
630 Mainstream Drive
Nashville, TN 37228-1204
**Phone:** (615) 760-2903
**Fax:** (615) 760-2904
http://www.wpln.org
**Format:** Classical, News, Public Radio

**WIVK-FM**
Box 11167
Knoxville, TN 37939
**Phone:** (865) 588-6511
**Fax:** (865) 588-3725
http://www.wivk.com
**Format:** Country

**WJOC-AM**
722 S. Germantown Road
Chattanooga, TN 37412
**Phone:** (423) 861-0800 or
    (888) 988-WJOC (toll-free)
**Fax:** (423) 861-2299
**E-mail:** wjoc1490@aol.com
http://www.wjoc1490.com
**Format:** Contemporary Christian

**WKNQ-FM**
P.O. Box 241880
Memphis, TN 38124
**Phone:** (901) 325-6544 or (800) 766-9566
    (toll-free)
**Fax:** (901) 325-6506
**E-mail:** wknofm@wknofm.org
http://www.wknofm.org
**Format:** News, Talk

**WLAC-AM**
55 Music Square, W.
Nashville, TN 37203-3207
**Phone:** (615) 256-0555 or
    (800) 688-WLAC (toll-free)

**Fax:** (615) 242-4826
**E-mail:** 1510@wlac.com
http://www.wlac.com
**Format:** News, Talk, Sports

**WLOK-AM**
363 S. 2nd Street
Memphis, TN 38103
**Phone:** (901) 527-9565
**Fax:** (901) 528-0335
**E-mail:** staff@wlok.com
http://www.wlok.com
**Format:** Gospel, News, Talk

**WMBW-FM**
P.O. Box 73026
Chattanooga, TN 37407
**Phone:** (615) 629-8900 or (800) 621-9629
(toll-free)
**Fax:** (615) 629-0021
**E-mail:** 76117.1031@compuserve.com
http://www.moody.edu
**Format:** Religious

**WMC-FM**
1960 Union Avenue
Memphis, TN 38104
**Phone:** (901) 726-0469
**Fax:** (901) 272-9186
http://www.wmcstations.com
**Format:** Adult Contemporary

**WMFS-FM**
1632 Sycamore View
Memphis, TN 38134
**Phone:** (901) 383-9637
**Fax:** (901) 373-1478
http://www.wmfs.com
**Format:** Album-Oriented Rock (AOR)

**WNOX-AM**
P.O. Box 11167
Knoxville, TN 37939-1167
**Phone:** (865) 558-9900
**Fax:** (865) 558-4218
http://www.newstalk99.com
**Format:** Talk, News

**WNOX-FM**
P.O. Box 11167
Knoxville, TN 37939-1167
**Phone:** (865) 558-9900
**Fax:** (865) 558-4218
http://www.newstalk99.com
**Format:** Talk, News

**WNQM-AM**
1300 WWCR Avenue
Nashville, TN 37218

**Phone:** (615) 255-1300 or (800) 238-5576
(toll-free)
**Fax:** (615) 255-1311
**E-mail:** wwcr@aol.com
http://www.wwcr.com/wnqm.htm
**Format:** Religious

**WNRQ-FM**
10 Music Circle E.
Nashville, TN 37203
**Phone:** (615) 256-0555
http://www.1059.com
**Format:** Classic Rock

**WPTN-AM**
698 S. Willow Avenue
P.O. Box 3146
Cookeville, TN 38502
**Phone:** (931) 526-7144 or (800) 264-7144
(toll-free)
**Fax:** (931) 528-8400
**E-mail:** mikedyer@clearchannel.com
http://www.midtenn.net/780
**Format:** News, Oldies

**WQAK-FM**
Box 100
Union City, TN 38261
**Phone:** (901) 885-6106
**Fax:** (901) 885-0250
**E-mail:** sales@realrockradio.com
**Format:** Talk

**WREC-AM**
203 Beale Street
Memphis, TN 38103
**Phone:** (901) 578-1160
**Fax:** (901) 525-8054
**E-mail:** wrecradio@aol.com
http://www.wrecradio.com
**Format:** Talk, Sports, News

## TEXAS

**KAEZ-FM**
1616 S. Kentucky C400
Amarillo, TX 79109
**Phone:** (806) 353-4037
**Fax:** (806) 353-4665
**E-mail:** kaez@thebreeze1057.com
http://broadcastamerica.com
**Format:** Adult Contemporary,
Contemporary Christian

**KAHK-FM**
911 W. Anderson Lane
Suite 107
Austin, TX 78757

**Phone:** (512) 419-1077 or (888) 438-1077
(toll-free)
**Fax:** (512) 419-9328
**E-mail:** 1077thehawk@1077thehawk.com
http://1077thehawk.com
**Format:** Contemporary Hit Radio (CHR)

**KAMX-FM**
4301 Westbank Drive
Suite B-350
Austin, TX 78746
**Phone:** (512) 327-9595
**Fax:** (512) 329-6252
http://www.mix947.com
**Format:** Adult Contemporary,
Alternative/New Music/Progressive

**KANJ-FM**
2424 S. Boulevard
Houston, TX 77098
**Phone:** (888) 777-KHCB
http://www.khcb.org
**Format:** Religious

**KAYD-FM**
3130 Blanchette Street
P.O. Box 870
Beaumont, TX 77704
**Phone:** (409) 833-9421
**Fax:** (409) 833-9296
**E-mail:** kayd@kayd.com
http://www.kayd.com
**Format:** Contemporary Country

**KBUS-FM**
P.O. Box 690
Paris, TX 75461
**Phone:** (903) 785-1068
**Fax:** (903) 785-6874
**E-mail:** carephil@kbusmail.com
http://www.kbus.com
**Format:** Contemporary Hit Radio (CHR)

**KCOR-AM**
1777 NE Loop 410, 4th Floor
San Antonio, TX 78217-5209
http://www.kcor.com
**Format:** Latino

**KCYY-FM**
8122 Datapoint Drive
Suite 500
San Antonio, TX 78229
**Phone:** (210) 615-5400
**Fax:** (210) 615-5300
**E-mail:** steve.giuttari@cox.com
http://www.y100fm.com
**Format:** Country

**KEAN-FM**
3911 S. 1st Avenue
Abilene, TX 79605
**Phone:** (915) 676-7711
**Fax:** (915) 676-3851
http://www.keanradio.com
**Format:** Contemporary Country

**KEGL-FM**
14001 N. Dallas Pkwy.
Suite 1210
Dallas, TX 75240
**Phone:** (972) 869-9700
**Fax:** (972) 263-9710
**E-mail:** 97-1kegl@computek.net
http://www.kegl.com
**Format:** Album-Oriented Rock (AOR)

**KIKK-FM**
24 Greenway Plaza
Suite 1900
Houston, TX 77046-2419
**Phone:** (713) 881-5100
**Fax:** (713) 881-5271
**Format:** Country

**KILT-AM**
24 Greenway Plaza
Suite 1900
Houston, TX 77046-2419
**Phone:** (713) 881-5100
**Fax:** (713) 881-5271
**Format:** Sports

**KILT-FM**
24 Greenway Plaza
Suite 1900
Houston, TX 77046-2419
**Phone:** (713) 881-5100
**Fax:** (713) 881-5271
**Format:** Country

**KKBQ-AM**
11 Greenway Plaza
Suite 2022
Houston, TX 77046
**Phone:** (713) 961-0093
**Fax:** (713) 963-1293
**E-mail:** kkbq@neosoft.com

**KLBJ-FM**
8309 N. 1H-35
Austin, TX 78753
**Phone:** (512) 832-4000
**Fax:** (512) 832-4081
http://www.klbj.com
**Format:** Album-Oriented Rock (AOR)

**KLIF-AM**
3500 Maple at Turtle Creek
Suite 1600
Dallas, TX 75219
**Phone:** (214) 526-2400 or (800) 537-5759
(toll-free)
**Fax:** (214) 520-4343
**E-mail:** klif-js@ix.netcom.com
http://www.klif.com
**Format:** Talk

**KNON-FM**
4415 San Jacinto
Dallas, TX 75204
**Phone:** (214) 828-9500
**Fax:** (214) 823-3051
http://www.knon.org
**Format:** Full Service

**KPLX-FM**
3500 Maple at Turtle Creek
Suite 1600
Dallas, TX 75219
**Phone:** (214) 526-2400
**Fax:** (214) 520-4343
**Format:** Contemporary Country

**KRBV-FM**
7901 Carpenter Frwy.
Dallas, TX 75247
**Phone:** (214) 630-3011
**Fax:** (214) 688-7760
**Format:** Contemporary Hit Radio (CHR)

**KSLR-AM**
9601 McAllister Fwy.
Suite 1200
San Antonio, TX 78216
**Phone:** (210) 344-8481 or (877) 630-5757
(toll-free)
**Fax:** (210) 340-1213
**E-mail:** genmgr@kslr.com
http://www.kslr.com
**Format:** Talk, Adult Contemporary,
Religious

**KSMG-FM**
8930 Fourwinds Drive
Suite 500
San Antonio, TX 78239
**Phone:** (210) 646-0105
**Fax:** (210) 646-9711
**E-mail:** http://www.magic105.com
**Format:** Adult Contemporary

**KTFA-FM**
27 Sawyer Street
P.O. Box 22257
Beaumont, TX 77720-2257

**Phone:** (409) 832-9250
**Fax:** (409) 832-5686
**E-mail:** manager@ktfa.com
http://www.ktfa.com
**Format:** Religious, Contemporary
Christian

**KTRH-AM**
510 Lovett Boulevard
Houston, TX 77006
**Phone:** (713) 526-5874
**Fax:** (713) 630-3666
http://www.ktrh.com
**Format:** Talk, News, Sports

**KUT-FM**
Communication Building B
The University of Texas
Austin, TX 78712
**Phone:** (512) 471-1631 or (800) 344-9588
(toll-free)
**Fax:** (512) 471-3700
http://www.kut.org
**Format:** Public Radio

**KVIC-FM**
3613 N. Main Street
Victoria, TX 77901
**Phone:** (512) 576-6111
**Fax:** (512) 572-0014
**E-mail:** kvic@icsi.net
http://www.thenumberone.com
**Format:** Adult Contemporary

**KVLY-FM**
901 E. Pike
Weslaco, TX 78596
**Phone:** (210) 964-1548
**Fax:** (210) 968-1643
http://www.kvly.com
**Format:** Adult Contemporary

**KVST-FM**
1212 S. Frazier
Conroe, TX 77301
**Phone:** (409) 788-1035
**Fax:** (409) 788-2525
**E-mail:** kvst@kvst.com
http://www.kvst.com
**Format:** Country

**KWBU-FM**
P.O. Box 97124
Waco, TX 76798-7124
**Phone:** (254) 710-3426
**Fax:** (254) 710-3874
http://www.kwbu.org
**Format:** Public Radio, Classical

**KWRD-FM**
6400 N. Beltline Road
Suite 110
Irving, TX 75063
**Phone:** (214) 561-9673 or (800) 949-5973
(toll-free)
**Fax:** (214) 561-9662
**E-mail:** theword@thewordfm.com
http://www.thewordfm.com
**Format:** Religious, Talk

**KXRI-FM**
1220 S. Georgia
Amarillo, TX 79102
**Phone:** (806) 371-0444 or (800) 974-2471
(toll-free)
**Fax:** (806) 372-1615
**E-mail:** aldenw@juno.com
http://www.airl
**Format:** Religious

**KYKS-FM**
P.O. Box 2209
Lufkin, TX 75901
**Phone:** (936) 639-4455
**Fax:** (936) 639-4647
http://www.kicks105.com
**Format:** Contemporary Country

**KZSP-FM**
5009 Padre Boulevard
Suite 16
South Padre Island, TX 78597
**Phone:** (956) 761-2270
**Fax:** (956) 761-1656
http://www.love953.com
**Format:** Jazz

**WBAP-AM**
2221 East Lamar Boulevard
Suite 400
Arlington, TX 76006
**Phone:** (817) 695-1820
**Fax:** (817) 695-0014
http://wbap.com
**Format:** News, Talk

# UTAH

**KALL-AM**
2801 S. Decker Lake Drive
West Valley City, UT 84119
**Phone:** (801) 908-1300
**Fax:** (801) 908-1389
**Format:** News, Talk, Sports

**KARB-FM**
Hwy. 6, Box 875
Price, UT 84501

**Phone:** (801) 637-1167 or
(800) 748-4169 (toll-free)
**Fax:** (801) 637-1177
**Format:** Country

**KBEE-FM**
434 Bear Cat Drive
Salt Lake City, UT 84115
**Phone:** (801) 485-6700
**Fax:** (801) 487-5369
http://www.b987.com
**Format:** Adult Contemporary

**KBRE-FM**
P.O. Box 819
Cedar City, UT 84721-0858
**Phone:** (435) 586-5273
**Fax:** (435) 588-0437
**E-mail:** b949@interspan.com
**Format:** Contemporary Hit Radio
(CHR)

**KBYU-FM**
C302 Harris Fine Arts Center
Brigham Young University
Provo, UT 84602
**Phone:** (801) 378-8450
**Fax:** (801) 378-5300
**E-mail:** kbyu@byu.edu
http://www.kbyu.byu.edu
**Format:** Public Radio, Classical

**KCNR-AM**
434 Bear Cat Drive
Salt Lake City, UT 84115-2520
**Phone:** (801) 485-6700
**Fax:** (801) 487-5369
**Format:** News

**KEOT-FM**
P.O. Box 1450
St. George, UT 84771-1450
**Phone:** (435) 628-1000
**Fax:** (435) 628-6636
http://www.keot.com
**Format:** Country

**KEYY-AM**
307 S. 1600 W.
Provo, UT 84601-3932
**Phone:** (801) 374-5210
**Fax:** (801) 374-2910
**E-mail:** mail@keyy.com
http://www.keyy.com
**Format:** Contemporary Christian

**KFAM-AM**
1171 SW Temple
Salt Lake City, UT 84101

**Phone:** (801) 295-0700
**Fax:** (801) 532-7500
**Format:** Easy Listening

**KFNZ-AM**
434 Bear Cat Drive
Salt Lake City, UT 84115
**Phone:** (801) 485-6700
**Fax:** (801) 487-5369
**Format:** News

**KGNT-FM**
2072 N. Main
P.O. Box 6280
Logan, UT 84341-6280
**Phone:** (435) 753-2200
**Fax:** (435) 753-8211
**E-mail:** country@thegiant.com
http://www.thegiant.com
**Format:** Country

**KISN-FM**
2801 Decker Lake Drive
Salt Lake City, UT 84119-2330
**Phone:** (801) 262-9797
**Fax:** (801) 262-9772
**Format:** Contemporary Hit Radio
(CHR)

**KKAT-FM**
2801 Decker Lake Drive
Salt Lake City, UT 84119-2330
**Phone:** (801) 533-0102
**Fax:** (801) 521-5018
**Format:** Contemporary Country

**KLO-AM**
4155 Harrison Boulevard
Suite 206
Ogden, UT 84403-2463
**Phone:** (801) 627-1430
**Fax:** (801) 627-0317
**Format:** News, Talk, Sports

**KMUT-FM**
2801 Decker Lake Drive
Salt Lake City, UT 84119-2330
**Phone:** (801) 262-9797
**Fax:** (801) 265-2843
**E-mail:** mountain@xmission.com
http://www.mountain1057.com
**Format:** Soft Rock

**KMXU-FM**
Box 40
Manti, UT 84642
**Phone:** (801) 835-7301
**Fax:** (801) 835-2250
**Format:** Easy Listening

**KNFL-FM**
2072 N. Main
P.O. Box 6280
Logan, UT 84341-6280
**Phone:** (435) 279-8855
**Fax:** (435) 753-8211
**E-mail:** classics@thekar.com
http://www.thekar.com
**Format:** Oldies, Soft Rock

**KRFD-FM**
P.O. Box 1450
St. George, UT 84771-1450
**Phone:** (435) 893-8100
**Fax:** (435) 628-6636
http://www.krfd.com
**Format:** Soft Rock

**KSL-AM**
KSL Broadcast House
5 Triad Center
Salt Lake City, UT 84110-1160
**Phone:** (801) 575-7600
**Fax:** (801) 575-7625
**E-mail:** talk@ksl.com
http://www.ksl.com
**Format:** News, Talk

**KSNN-FM**
750 W. Ridgeview Drive
St. George, UT 84770
**Phone:** (801) 673-3579
**Fax:** (801) 673-8900
**Format:** Adult Contemporary

**KSOP-FM**
P.O. Box 25548
Salt Lake City, UT 84125
**Phone:** (801) 972-1043
**Fax:** (801) 974-0868
**E-mail:** ksop@ksopcountry.com
http://www.ksopcountry.com
**Format:** Country, Contemporary Country

**KSUU-FM**
350 West 200 South
Cedar City, UT 84720
**Phone:** (801) 586-7975
**Fax:** (801) 865-8352
http://www.suu.edu
**Format:** Public Radio, Alternative/New
  Music/Progressive

**KSVC-AM**
450 East 400 South
P.O. Box 37
Richfield, UT 84701
**Phone:** (801) 896-4456
**Fax:** (801) 896-9333

http://www.ksvcradio.com
**Format:** News, Talk

**KTKK-AM**
10348 S. Redwood Road
South Jordan, UT 84095
**Phone:** (801) 253-4883 or (800) 482-5563
  (toll-free)
**Fax:** (801) 253-9085
**E-mail:** ktkk.com
http://www.ktkk.com
**Format:** Talk, News

**KTSP-AM**
P.O. Box 1450
St. George, UT 84771-1450
**Phone:** (435) 628-1000
**Fax:** (435) 628-6636
**E-mail:** legacy1@infowest.com
http://www.ktsp.com
**Format:** Sports

**KUER-FM**
101 S. Wasatch Drive
Rm. 270
Salt Lake City, UT 84112-1791
**Phone:** (801) 581-6625 or (800) 444-8638
  (toll-free)
**Fax:** (801) 581-6758
**E-mail:** fm90@media.utah.edu
http://www.kuer.org
**Format:** Public Radio, Jazz, News

**KVNU-AM**
1350 North 200 West
P.O. Box 267
Logan, UT 84321-0267
**Phone:** (435) 752-5141
**Fax:** (435) 753-5555
**E-mail:** al@cvradio.com
http://www.61kvnu.com
**Format:** Talk, Sports, News

**KXRK-FM**
515 S. 700 E.
Suite 1-C
Salt Lake City, UT 84103-2801
**Phone:** (801) 521-9696
**Fax:** (801) 364-1811
http://www.kxrk-fm96.3
**Format:** Alternative/New
  Music/Progressive

**KZEZ-FM**
Box 473
Fillmore, UT 84631
**Phone:** (435) 864-4500
**Fax:** (435) 743-7519

http://www.kzez.com
**Format:** Adult Contemporary

**WWVZ-FM**
55 N. 3rd W.
P.O. Box 1160
Salt Lake City, UT 84110
**Phone:** (801) 663-5400
http://www.thez.com
**Format:** Contemporary Hit Radio (CHR)

## VERMONT

**WBTN-AM**
P.O. Box 560
Bennington, VT 05201
**Phone:** (802) 442-6321
**Fax:** (802) 442-3112
**E-mail:** knkomalley@juno.com
http://www.mainstreetvermont.com/wbtn
**Format:** News, Talk, Sports, Full Service

**WBTZ-FM**
P.O. Box 999
Burlington, VT 05402
**Phone:** (802) 860-2465
**Fax:** (802) 860-1818
**E-mail:** mailbag@999thebuzz.com
http://www.999thebuzz.com
**Format:** Alternative/New
  Music/Progressive

**WCVR-FM**
P.O. Box 249
Randolph Center, VT 05061
**Phone:** (802) 728-4411 or (800) 743-9287
  (toll-free)
**Fax:** (802) 728-4013
**E-mail:** country@wcvr.com
http://www.wcvr.com
**Format:** Country

**WEQX-FM**
P.O. Box 1027
Manchester, VT 05254
**Phone:** (802) 362-4800
**Fax:** (802) 362-5555
**E-mail:** eqx@weqx.com
http://www.weqx.com
**Format:** Alternative/New
  Music/Progressive

**WEZF-FM**
1500 Hegeman Avenue
Colchester, VT 05446
**Phone:** (802) 655-0093
http://www.star929.com
**Format:** Adult Contemporary

**WFAD-AM**
Box 150
Middlebury, VT 05753
**Phone:** (802) 388-1490
**Fax:** (802) 338-9236
**Format:** Full Service, Adult
    Contemporary

**WGMT-FM**
Box 97
Lyndonville, VT 05851
**Phone:** (802) 626-9800
**Fax:** (802) 626-8500
**Format:** Adult Contemporary

**WGTK-FM**
P.O. Box 590
Middlebury, VT 05753
**Phone:** (802) 388-4101 or (800) 877-5101
    (toll-free)
**Fax:** (802) 388-1723
**Format:** Classic Rock

**WIKE-AM**
Farrant Street
P.O. Box 377
Newport, VT 05855
**Format:** Country

**WIUV-FM**
Campus Ctr.
Castle State College
Castleton, VT 05735
**Format:** Alternative/New
    Music/Progressive

**WJJR-FM**
The Opera House
P.O. Box 30
Rutland, VT 05702
**Phone:** (802) 775-7500
**Fax:** (802) 775-7555
**E-mail:** mix981.com
**Format:** Adult Contemporary

**WJOY-AM**
P.O. Box 4489
Burlington, VT 05406
**Phone:** (802) 658-1230
**Fax:** (802) 862-0786
**E-mail:** wjoy@hallradio.com
**Format:** Big Band/Nostalgia

**WJSC-FM**
Johnson State College
Johnson, VT 05656
**Phone:** (802) 635-1355
**Fax:** (802) 635-1202
**Format:** Public Radio, Eclectic

**WKDR-AM**
388A Shelburne Road
South Burlington, VT 05401
**Phone:** (802) 863-8255
**E-mail:** wkdr@together.net
http://www.burlingtonut.com
**Format:** Talk, News

**WKVT-AM**
P.O. Box 1490
Brattleboro, VT 05302
**Phone:** (802) 254-2343
**Fax:** (802) 254-6683
**E-mail:** wkvtnews@together.net
http://www.wkvt.com
**Format:** News, Talk

**WKVT-FM**
P.O. Box 1490
Brattleboro, VT 05302-1490
**Phone:** (802) 254-2343
**Fax:** (802) 254-6683
**E-mail:** kvtsales@together.net
http://www.wknt.com
http://www.wkvt.com
**Format:** Classic Rock

**WKXE-FM**
Box 910
White River Junction, VT 05001
**Phone:** (802) 295-3093
**Fax:** (802) 295-3095
**Format:** Album-Oriented Rock (AOR)

**WLFE-FM**
P.O. Box 712
St. Albans, VT 05478-0712
**Phone:** (802) 524-2133
**Fax:** (802) 527-1450
**E-mail:** WLFE@together.net
**Format:** Country

**WMNM-FM**
Box 150
Middlebury, VT 05753
**Phone:** (802) 388-9236
**Format:** Oldies

**WMTT-FM**
Rte. 100, Box 850
West Dover, VT 05356
**Phone:** (802) 464-1111
**Fax:** (802) 464-1112
http://www.theriver.cc
**Format:** Adult Album Alternative

**WNCS-FM**
169 River Street
Box 551
Montpelier, VT 05602

**Phone:** (802) 223-2396
**Fax:** (802) 223-1520
**E-mail:** pointfm@together.not

**WRMC-FM**
Middlebury College
Drawer 29
Middlebury, VT 05753
**Phone:** (802) 443-6324
**Fax:** (802) 443-5108
**E-mail:** wcmc@panther.middlebury.edu
http://www.middlebury.edu/~wrmc
**Format:** Full Service

**WNHV-AM**
Box 910
White River Junction, VT 05001
**Phone:** (802) 295-3093
**Fax:** (802) 295-3095
**Format:** Easy Listening

**WNKV-FM**
Concord Avenue
P.O. Box 249
St. Johnsbury, VT 05819
**Phone:** (802) 748-2362
**Fax:** (802) 748-2361
**Format:** Contemporary Country

**WNYV-FM**
P.O. Box 568
East Poultney, VT 05741
**Phone:** (802) 287-9031
**Format:** Oldies, Adult Contemporary,
    Contemporary Country

**WOKO-FM**
P.O. Box 4489
Burlington, VT 05406
**Phone:** (802) 658-1230 or (800) 554-9890
    (toll-free)
**Fax:** (802) 862-0786
**E-mail:** woko@hallradio.com
**Format:** Country

**WRUV-FM**
Billings Student Center
UVM
Burlington, VT 05405
**Phone:** (802) 656-0796
**Fax:** (802) 656-2281
**E-mail:** wruv@zoo.uvm.edu
http://www.uvm.edu/~wruv
**Format:** Eclectic

**WRVT-FM**
The Public Radio Center
20 Troy Avenue
Colchester, VT 05446

**Phone:** (802) 655-9451
**Fax:** (802) 655-2799
http://www.vprnet.org
**Format:** Public Radio, Jazz, News, Classical

**WVPR-FM**
The Public Radio Center
20 Troy Avenue
Colchester, VT 05446
**Phone:** (802) 655-9451
**Fax:** (802) 655-2799
http://www.vprnet.org
**Format:** Public Radio, Classical, Jazz, News

**WVPS-FM**
20 Troy Avenue
Colchester, VT 05446
**Phone:** (802) 655-9451
**Fax:** (802) 655-2799
http://www.vprnet.org
**Format:** Public Radio, Jazz, News, Classical

**WWPV-FM**
Winooski Park
Box 274
Colchester, VT 05439
**Phone:** (802) 654-2334
http://www.personalweb.smcvt.edu/wwpr
**Format:** Eclectic, Alternative/New Music/Progressive

**WWWT-AM**
P.O. Box 249
Randolph Center, VT 05061
**Phone:** (802) 728-4411 or (800) 743-9287 (toll-free)
**Fax:** (802) 728-4013
**E-mail:** country@wcvr.com
http://www.wcvr.com
**Format:** Adult Contemporary

# VIRGINIA

**WABN-FM**
396 Old 11 Ct.
Suite A
Abingdon, VA 24210
**Phone:** (703) 628-4422
**Fax:** (703) 628-9847
**E-mail:** wabn@naxs.com
http://www.eva.org/radio/wabn.htm
**Format:** Contemporary Hit Radio (CHR)

**WABS-AM**
1901 N. Moore Street
Suite 200
Arlington, VA 22209

**Phone:** (703) 807-2266 or (877) 534-0780 (toll-free)
**Fax:** (703) 807-2248
**E-mail:** comment@wava.com
http://www.wabs.com
**Format:** Adult Contemporary, Religious

**WAGE-AM**
711 WAGE Drive, SW
Leesburg, VA 20175-3418
**Phone:** (703) 777-1200
**Fax:** (703) 777-7431
**E-mail:** wage@wage.com
http://www.wage.com
**Format:** Full Service, Country

**WAPP-FM**
P.O. Box 3300
Winchester, VA 22604
**Phone:** (540) 667-2224
**Fax:** (540) 722-3295
http://www.applecountry.fm
**Format:** Country

**WAZR-FM**
123 E. Court Street
P.O. Box 10
Woodstock, VA 22664
**Phone:** (540) 459-8810 or (800) 459-8810 (toll-free)
**Fax:** (540) 459-5834
**E-mail:** wazr@wazt.com
http://infl.com/waz
**Format:** Big Band/Nostalgia

**WBOP-FM**
1790-10 E. Market Street
Harrisonburg, VA 22801
**Phone:** (540) 432-1063 or (800) 296-9267 (toll-free)
**Fax:** (540) 433-9267
**E-mail:** wbop@rica.net
http://www.wbopfm.com
**Format:** Classic Rock

**WBYM-AM**
2845 N. Armistead Avenue
Hampton, VA 23666
**Phone:** (757) 766-9262
**Fax:** (757) 766-7439
**E-mail:** wbym@arro.net
http://www.wbym@arro.net
**Format:** Country

**WCMS-FM**
5589 Greenwich Road
Suite 200
Virginia Beach, VA 23462
**Phone:** (757) 424-1050

**Fax:** (757) 424-3479
**E-mail:** wcms@norfolk.infi.net
http://www.pilotonline.com/wcms
**Format:** Contemporary Country

**WEMC-FM**
Eastern Mennonite University
1200 Park Road
Harrisonburg, VA 22802-2462
**Phone:** (540) 432-4288
**Fax:** (540) 432-4444
**E-mail:** wemc@emu.edu
http://www.emu.edu/wemc
**Format:** Jazz, Classical, World Beat

**WETA-FM**
2775 S. Quincy Street
Arlington, VA 22206-2236
**Phone:** (703) 998-2790
**Fax:** (703) 824-7288
**E-mail:** radio@weta.com
http://www.weta.org
**Format:** Public Radio, News, Classical

**WFAX-AM**
161-B Hillwood Avenue
Falls Church, VA 22046
**Phone:** (703) 532-1220
**Fax:** (703) 533-7572
**E-mail:** wfax@erols.com
http://www.wfaxam.com
**Format:** Religious

**WFLS-FM**
616 Amelia Street
Fredericksburg, VA 22401
**Phone:** (540) 373-1500 or (800) 735-9393 (toll-free)
**Fax:** (540) 374-5525
http://www.flstarweb.com/wfls/wfls.htm
**Format:** Country

**WFQX-FM**
381 Spinning Wheel Lane
Winchester, VA 22603
**Phone:** (540) 662-5101 or (800) 993-FROG (toll-free)
**Fax:** (540) 662-8610
**E-mail:** thefrog@v.shallink.com
http://www.993thefrog.com
**Format:** Adult Contemporary, Top 40

**WGGM-AM**
4301 W. Hundred Road
Chester, VA 23831
**Phone:** (804) 717-2000
**Fax:** (804) 717-2009
**E-mail:** hoffmancommunication@erols.com

http://www.oneplace.com
**Format:** Religious

**WGH-AM**
5589 Greenwich Road
Virginia Beach, VA 23462
**Phone:** (757) 671-1000
**Fax:** (757) 671-1010
http://www.thescor1310.com
**Format:** Sports

**WHEO-AM**
3824 Wayside Road
Stuart, VA 24171
**Phone:** (540) 694-3114
**Fax:** (540) 694-2241
**E-mail:** wheo@sitestar.net
http://www.mtview.net
**Format:** Country, Talk

**WHRO-FM**
5200 Hampton Boulevard
Norfolk, VA 23508
**Phone:** (757) 889-9400
**Fax:** (757) 489-0007
**E-mail:** bluse@whro.org
http://www.whro.org
**Format:** Public Radio, Classical

**WHRV-FM**
5200 Hampton Boulevard
Norfolk, VA 23508
**Phone:** (757) 889-9400
**Fax:** (757) 489-0007
**E-mail:** rjones@whro.org
http://www.whro.org
**Format:** Public Radio, News, Eclectic

**WINA-AM**
1140 Rose Hill Drive
Charlottesville, VA 22903-5128
**Phone:** (804) 977-3030
**Fax:** (804) 977-3775
**E-mail:** mail@wina.com
http://www.wina.com
**Format:** News, Talk

**WINC-AM**
520 N. Pleasant Valley Road
Box 3300
Winchester, VA 22604
**Phone:** (703) 667-2224
**Fax:** (703) 722-3295
http://www.winc.@visuallink.com
**Format:** Talk, News

**WKDE-FM**
P.O. Box 390
Altavista, VA 24517

**Phone:** (804) 369-5588
**Fax:** (804) 369-1632
**E-mail:** info@kdcountry.com
http://www.kdcountry.com
**Format:** Country

**WKHK-FM**
300 Arboretum Plaza
Suite 590
Richmond, VA 23236
**Phone:** (804) 330-5700
**Fax:** (804) 330-5714
http://www.k95.com
**Format:** Country

**WKLR-FM**
1011 Boulder Springs Drive
Richmond, VA 23225
**Phone:** (804) 330-7123
**Fax:** (804) 330-4780
http://www.965theplanet.com
**Format:** Oldies, Classic Rock

**WKOC-FM**
999 Waterside Drive
Suite 500
Norfolk, VA 23510
**Phone:** (757) 640-8500
**Fax:** (757) 640-8552
**Format:** Adult Album Alternative

**WLTK-FM**
166 Main Street
P.O. Box 337
Broadway, VA 22815
**Phone:** (540) 896-8933
**Fax:** (540) 896-1448
**E-mail:** wbtx-wltk@rica.net
http://www.wltk.net
**Format:** Religious, Contemporary
Christian

**WMEV-FM**
2151 Old Lake Road
Marion, VA 24354-6230
**Phone:** (703) 783-3151
**Fax:** (703) 783-3152
**E-mail:** fm94@netva.com
http://www.fm94.com
**Format:** Country

**WMXH-FM**
Hwy. 211 W.
P.O. Box 387
Luray, VA 22835
**Phone:** (540) 743-5167 or
    (877) 649-1057 (toll-free)
**Fax:** (540) 743-9522

**E-mail:** wlcc&wraa@rica.net
http://www.mix107.com
**Format:** Hot Country

**WNRN-FM**
2125 Ivy Road
Suite L
Charlottesville, VA 22903
**Phone:** (804) 971-4096 or
    (877) 881-9676 (toll-free)
**Fax:** (804) 971-6562
**E-mail:** wnrn@cstone.net
http://www.wnrn.cstone.net
**Format:** Adult Album Alternative

**WODI-AM**
1230 Radio Road
Brookneal, VA 24528-3141
**Phone:** (804) 376-1230
**Fax:** (804) 376-9634
**E-mail:** wodi@lynchburg.net
http://www.lynchburg.net/wodi
**Format:** Oldies, Talk

**WODU-AM**
Old Dominion University
2102 Webb Center
Norfolk, VA 23529
**Phone:** (757) 683-3441
http://www.odu/edu/~wodu
**Format:** Alternative/New
    Music/Progressive, Eclectic

**WRCL-FM**
812 Moorefield Park Drive
Suite 300
Richmond, VA 23236
**Phone:** (804) 330-5700
**Fax:** (804) 330-4079
http://www.cool1065.com
**Format:** Oldies

**WREL-AM**
P.O. Drawer 902
Lexington, VA 24450
**Phone:** (703) 463-2161
**Fax:** (540) 463-9524
**E-mail:** info@wrel.com
http://www.wrel.com
**Format:** News, Talk, Sports

**WRIC-FM**
P.O. Box 838
Richlands, VA 24641
**Phone:** (540) 964-4066
**Fax:** (540) 963-4927
**E-mail:** wric@netscape.net
http://www.wricfm.com
**Format:** Classic Rock

# WASHINGTON

**KAEP-FM**
1601 E. 57th Avenue
Spokane, WA 99223
**Phone:** (509) 448-1000
**Fax:** (509) 448-7015
http://www.1057thepeak.com
**Format:** Alternative/New
Music/Progressive

**KAFE-FM**
2340 E. Sunset Drive
Bellingham, WA 98226
**Phone:** (360) 734-5233
**Fax:** (360) 734-5697
**E-mail:** kafe@kafe.com
http://www.kafe.com
**Format:** Soft Rock

**KASB-FM**
10416 SE Kilmarnock
Bellevue, WA 98004-6698
**Phone:** (425) 456-7121
**E-mail:** zujkow@belnet.bellevue.k12.wa.
us
http://listen.at/kasb
**Format:** Sports, Alternative/New
Music/Progressive

**KBCS-FM**
3000 Landerholm Circle, SE
Bellevue, WA 98007
**Phone:** (425) 564-2427
**E-mail:** kbcs@ctc.edu
http://www.kbcs-fm.org
**Format:** Full Service, Jazz, Blues,
Bluegrass, Folk, World Beat

**KBLE-AM**
2737 77th Avenue, SE
Suite 207
Mercer Island, WA 98040-2832
**E-mail:** operations@kble.com
http://www.kble.com
**Format:** Religious

**KBTB-FM**
190 Queen Anne Avenue, N.
Seattle, WA 98109
**Phone:** (206) 494-2000
**Fax:** (206) 494-2297
http://www.957thebeat.com
**Format:** Adult Contemporary

**KCMS-FM**
19303 Fremont Avenue, N.
Seattle, WA 98133

**Phone:** (206) 546-7350 or
(877) 275-1093 (toll-free)
**Fax:** (206) 546-7372
**E-mail:** comments@spirit1053.com
http://www.spirit1053.com
**Format:** Religious, Contemporary
Christian

**KCWU-FM**
400 E. 8th Avenue
Ellensburg, WA 98926-7594
**Phone:** (509) 963-2282
**Fax:** (509) 963-1688
http://www.cwu.edu/~kcwu/stationinfo.
html
**Format:** Educational, Information

**KDRK-FM**
P.O. Box 30013
Spokane, WA 99223
**Phone:** (509) 448-8300
**Fax:** (509) 448-7015
**E-mail:** edwards@kdrk.com
http://www.kdrk.com
**Format:** Contemporary Country

**KEGX-FM**
830 N. Columbia Center Boulevard
Suite B-2
Kennewick, WA 99336-7713
**Phone:** (509) 783-0783
**Fax:** (509) 735-8627
http://www.kegx.com
**Format:** Classic Rock

**KGDN-FM**
P.O. Box 31000
Spokane, WA 99223
**Phone:** (509) 783-8600
**Fax:** (509) 448-3811
**E-mail:** kgdn@kgdn.com
http://www.kgdn.com
**Format:** Religious

**KGRG-FM**
12401 SE 320th Street
Auburn, WA 98092
**Phone:** (253) 833-9111
**Fax:** (253) 288-3398
**E-mail:** tkrause@grcc.ctc.edu
http://www.kgrg.com
**Format:** Alternative/New
Music/Progressive

**KGSG-FM**
P.O. Box 2852
Pasco, WA 99301
**Phone:** (509) 547-5196 or
(888) 353-KGSG (toll-free)

**Fax:** (509) 547-5203
**E-mail:** info@kgsg.com
http://www.kgsg.com
**Format:** Southern Gospel

**KIOK-FM**
830 N. Columbia Center Boulevard
Suite B2
Kennewick, WA 99336
**Phone:** (509) 783-0783
**Fax:** (509) 735-8627
**E-mail:** kiok@oneworld.owt.com
http://www.kiok949.com
**Format:** Country

**KISW-FM**
712 Aurora Avenue, N.
Seattle, WA 98109
**Phone:** (206) 285-7625
**Fax:** (206) 282-7018
http://www.klsw.com
**Format:** Album-Oriented Rock (AOR)

**KITI-FM**
1133 Kresky Road
Centralia, WA 98531
**Phone:** (360) 736-1355
**Fax:** (360) 736-4761
http://www.live95.com
**Format:** Top 40, Soft Rock

**KIXI-AM**
12011 NE 1st Street
Suite 206
Bellevue, WA 98005
**Phone:** (425) 653-9462 or
(800) 491-KIXI (toll-free)
**Fax:** (425) 653-1088
**E-mail:** AM880KIXI@aol.com
http://www.kixi.com
**Format:** Oldies

**KKDZ-AM**
1334 1st Avenue
Suite 150
Seattle, WA 98101-2003
**Phone:** (206) 382-1250
http://www.kson.com
**Format:** Country

**KLFE-AM**
2815 2nd Avenue
Suite 550
Seattle, WA 98121
**Phone:** (206) 443-8200
**Fax:** (206) 777-1133
**E-mail:** info@kgnw.com
http://www.kqnw.com
**Format:** Talk

**KMPS-AM**
1000 Dexter Avenue, N.
Suite 100
Seattle, WA 98109
**Phone:** (206) 805-1090
**Fax:** (206) 805-0911
http://www.kiss106.com
**Format:** Country

**KMTT-FM**
1100 Olive Way
Suite 1650
Seattle, WA 98101-1827
**Phone:** (206) 233-1037 or (800) 676-5688
     (toll-free)
**Fax:** (206) 233-8979
http://www.kmtt.com

**KNHC-FM**
10750 30th Avenue NE
Seattle, WA 98125
**Phone:** (206) 366-7815
**Fax:** (206) 421-5018
**E-mail:** c895fm@hotmail.com
http://www.c895fm.com
**Format:** Contemporary Hit Radio
     (CHR), Adult Album Alternative

**KOMO-AM**
1809 7th Avenue
Suite 200
Seattle, WA 98101
**Phone:** (206) 223-5700
**Fax:** (206) 516-3160
**E-mail:** comments@komoradio.com
http://www.komoradio.com
**Format:** News, Talk

**KONA-AM**
2823 W. Lewis
Pasco, WA 99301
**Phone:** (509) 547-1618
**Fax:** (509) 547-1618
**E-mail:** kona@owt.com
http://www.konradio.com/am
**Format:** Adult Contemporary, News

**KPLZ-FM**
1809 7th Avenue
Suite 200
Seattle, WA 98101
**Phone:** (206) 223-5700
**Fax:** (206) 292-1015
http://www.kplz.com
http://www.star1015.com
**Format:** Contemporary Hit Radio
     (CHR), Adult Contemporary

**KRKO-AM**
2707 Colby Avenue
Suite 1380
Everett, WA 98201
**Phone:** (425) 304-1381
**Fax:** (425) 304-1382
**E-mail:** rkonews@krko1380.com
http://www.krko1380.com
**Format:** Talk, News

**KTAC-FM**
P.O. Box 31000
Spokane, WA 99223
**Phone:** (509) 754-2000
**Fax:** (509) 754-0330
**E-mail:** ktac@ktac.com
http://www.acn-network.com
**Format:** Religious

**KUBE-FM**
351 Elliott Avenue, W.
Suite 300
Seattle, WA 98119
**Phone:** (206) 285-2295
**Fax:** (206) 286-2376
http://www.kubeg3.com
**Format:** Contemporary Hit Radio (CHR)

**KVI-AM**
1809 7th Avenue
Suite 200
Seattle, WA 98101
**Phone:** (206) 223-5700 or (888) 312-5757
     (toll-free)
**Fax:** (206) 292-3194
http://www.570kvi.com
**Format:** Public Radio, Talk

**KVTI-FM**
4500 Steilacoom Boulevard, SW
Tacoma, WA 98499-4098
**Phone:** (253) 589-5884
**Fax:** (253) 589-5797
http://www.i91.ctc.edu
**Format:** Top 40

# WEST VIRGINIA

**WAED-FM**
200 Back Fork Street
Webster Springs, WV 26288
**Phone:** (304) 847-5141
**Fax:** (304) 847-5149
**E-mail:** hardmanpastor@aol.com
**Format:** Country, Southern Gospel

**WAJR-AM**
Greer Building
1251 Earl Core Road
Morgantown, WV 26505

**Phone:** (304) 296-0029
**Fax:** (304) 296-3876
**Format:** Talk, News, Country

**WBBD-AM**
1015 Main Street
Wheeling, WV 26003
**Phone:** (304) 232-1170
**Fax:** (304) 232-0041
**Format:** Middle-of-the-Road (MOR),
     Big Band/Nostalgia

**WBRB-FM**
P.O. Box 2377
Buckhannon, WV 26201
**Phone:** (304) 472-1460
**Fax:** (304) 472-1528
**E-mail:** phillips_p@wvlink.com;
     radio@msys.net
**Format:** Country

**WBTQ-FM**
228 Randolph Avenue
Elkins, WV 26241
**Phone:** (304) 472-1400
**Fax:** (304) 472-1740
**Format:** Oldies

**WCKA-FM**
180 Main Street
Sutton, WV 26601
**Phone:** (304) 765-7373
**Fax:** (304) 765-7836
**E-mail:** boss97fm@mountain.net
http://www.theboss97fm.com
**Format:** Country

**WCLG-FM**
343 High Street
Morgantown, WV 26507
**Phone:** (304) 292-2222
**Fax:** (304) 292-2224
**E-mail:** mail@wclg.com
http://www.wclg.com
**Format:** Classical

**WCST-FM**
1010 Radio Station Road
Berkeley Springs, WV 25411
**Format:** Country, News, Sports

**WCWV-FM**
713 Main Street
Summersville, WV 26651
**Phone:** (304) 872-5202
**Fax:** (304) 872-6904
**E-mail:** wcwv@ntec.com
**Format:** Adult Contemporary, Soft Rock,
     Religious

**WDGG-FM**
401 11th Street
Suite 200
Huntington, WV 25713
**Phone:** (304) 523-8401 or (800) 777-9782
   (toll-free)
**Fax:** (304) 523-4848
**Format:** Country

**WELC-AM**
Box 949
Welch, WV 24801
**Phone:** (304) 436-2131
**Fax:** (304) 436-2132
**E-mail:** jjvsid@citlink.net
**Format:** Adult Contemporary, Religious

**WETZ-FM**
P.O. Box 10
New Martinsville, WV 26155-0010
**Phone:** (304) 455-1111
**Fax:** (304) 455-6170
**Format:** Country

**WHAJ-FM**
900 Bluefield Avenue
Bluefield, WV 24701
**Phone:** (304) 327-7114
**Fax:** (304) 325-7850
**Format:** Contemporary Hit Radio (CHR)

**WHCM-FM**
P.O. Box 798
Ripley, WV 25271-0798
**Phone:** (304) 485-6158
**Fax:** (304) 485-7365
**Format:** Country

**WHIS-AM**
900 Bluefield Avenue
Bluefield, WV 24701
**Phone:** (304) 327-7114
**Fax:** (304) 325-7850
**Format:** News, Talk, Information

**WIWS-AM**
P.O. Box 1037
Beaver, WV 25813
**Phone:** (304) 252-6452
**Fax:** (304) 255-1044
**Format:** Oldies

**WJYP-FM**
605 D Street
P.O. Box 8600
South Charleston, WV 25303
**Phone:** (304) 744-5388
**E-mail:** info@praise101.com
http://praise101.com

**Format:** News, Eclectic, Sports,
   Religious, Contemporary Christian

**WJLS-FM**
P.O. Box 5499
Beckley, WV 25802
**Phone:** (304) 253-7311
**Fax:** (304) 253-3466
**E-mail:** dawg@wjls.com
**Format:** Country

**WKEE-FM**
134 4th Avenue
P.O. Box 2288
Huntington, WV 25724
**Phone:** (304) 525-7788
**Fax:** (304) 525-6281
http://www.wkee.com
**Format:** Contemporary Hit Radio (CHR)

**WKKW-FM**
1251 Earl L. Core Road
Morgantown, WV 26505
**Phone:** (304) 296-0029
**Fax:** (304) 296-3876
http://www.wkkw.com
**Format:** Contemporary Country

**WKLP-AM**
Drawer F
Keyser, WV 26726-0180
**Fax:** (304) 788-1662
**E-mail:** wqzk@miworld.net
**Format:** Music of Your Life

**WKWS-FM**
1111 Virginia Street, E.
Charleston, WV 25301
**Phone:** (304) 342-8131
**Fax:** (304) 344-4745
**E-mail:** wkws@wkws.com
http://www.wkws.com
**Format:** Hot Country

**WQWV-FM**
P.O. Box 55
Petersburg, WV 26847
**Phone:** (304) 257-4432
**Fax:** (304) 257-9733
**E-mail:** wqwc@wqwc.com
http://www.wqwv.com
**Format:** Sports, Talk

**WRKP-FM**
2002 1st Street
Moundsville, WV 26041
**Phone:** (304) 845-1052 or (800) 376-6149
   (toll-free)
**Fax:** (304) 845-1054

http://www.wrkp.com
**Format:** Religious, Contemporary
   Christian

**WRZZ-FM**
Old Blennerhassett School
Rte. 4, Jewell Road
Box 474 A
Parkersburg, WV 26101
**Phone:** (304) 863-3319
**Fax:** (304) 863-3310
http://www.classicrock2106.com
**Format:** Classic Rock

**WSGB-AM**
180 Main Street
Sutton, WV 26601
**Phone:** (304) 765-7373
**Fax:** (304) 765-7836
**E-mail:** boss97fm@mountain.net,
   wcka@mountain.net
http://www.theboss97m.com
**Format:** Country

**WSLW-AM**
Rt. 60 Hartsrun Bot 610
White Sulphur Springs, WV 24986
**Phone:** (304) 536-1310 or (877) 536-1031
   (toll-free)
**Fax:** (304) 536-1311
http://www.wkcj-wslw.com
**Format:** Adult Contemporary, Oldies

**WVNP-FM**
600 Capitol Street
Charleston, WV 25301
**Phone:** (304) 556-4900 or
   (800) RADIO-87 (toll-free)
**Fax:** (304) 556-4981
**E-mail:** wvapr@wvpubcast.org
http://www.wvpubcast.org
**Format:** Classical, News, Jazz

**WVPB-FM**
600 Capitol Street
Charleston, WV 25301
**Phone:** (304) 556-4900 or
   (800) RADIO-87 (toll-free)
**Fax:** (304) 556-4981
**E-mail:** wvapr@wvpubcast.org
http://www.wvpubcast.org
**Format:** Classical, News, Jazz

**WVPG-FM**
600 Capitol Street
Charleston, WV 25301
**Phone:** (304) 556-4900 or
   (800) RADIO-87 (toll-free)
**Fax:** (304) 556-4981
**E-mail:** wvpub@ast.org

http://www.wvpubrad.org
**Format:** Classical, News, Jazz

**WWVU-FM**
West Virginia University
Mountainlair
P.O. Box 6446
Morgantown, WV 26506-6446
**Phone:** (304) 293-3329
**Fax:** (304) 293-7363
http://www.wvu.edu/~U92
**Format:** Alternative/New
    Music/Progressive

## WISCONSIN

**KFIZ-AM**
254 Winnebago Drive
Fond du Lac, WI 54935
**Phone:** (414) 921-1071 or (800) 266-1071
    (toll-free)
**Fax:** (414) 921-0757
**E-mail:** rhopper@kfiz.com
http://www.kfiz.com
**Format:** Talk, News, Adult
    Contemporary, Sports

**KFIZ-FM**
254 Winnebago Drive
P.O. Box 1450
Fond du Lac, WI 54935
**Phone:** (920) 921-1071 or (800) 266-1071
    (toll-free)
**Fax:** (920) 921-0757
http://www.k107.com
**Format:** Contemporary Hit Radio (CHR)

**KUWS-FM**
1800 Grand Avenue
Superior, WI 54880-2898
**Phone:** (715) 394-8530
**Fax:** (715) 394-8404
**E-mail:** kuws@iName.com
http://www.come.to/kuws
**Format:** Public Radio, News, Jazz,
    Urban Contemporary, Alternative/New
    Music/Progressive, Talk

**WAPL-FM**
2727 Radio Road
Appleton, WI 54915-3200
**E-mail:** wapl@wcinet.com
http://www.wapl.com
**Format:** Classic Rock, Alternative/New
    Music/Progressive

**WBDK-FM**
3030 Park Drive
Suite 3
Sturgeon Bay, WI 54235

**Phone:** (920) 746-9430
**Fax:** (920) 746-9433
**E-mail:** wbdk@dct.com
http://www.doorradio.com
**Format:** Public Radio

**WBSD-FM**
400 McCanna Pkwy.
Burlington, WI 53105
**Phone:** (262) 763-0195
**Fax:** (262) 763-0207
**E-mail:** wbsd@wi.net;
    wbsd@89bsd.com
http://www.2.wi.net/~wbsd
**Format:** Adult Album Alternative

**WCLQ-FM**
4111 Schofield Avenue
Suite 10
Schofield, WI 54476
**Phone:** (715) 355-5151
**Fax:** (715) 359-3128
**E-mail:** 89q@89q.org
http://www.89q.org
**Format:** Contemporary Hit Radio
    (CHR), Contemporary Christian

**WCUB-AM**
1915 Mirro Drive
P.O. Box 1990
Manitowoc, WI 54221-1990
**Phone:** (920) 683-6800 or (888) 282-9922
    (toll-free)
**Fax:** (920) 683-6807
http://cubradio.com
**Format:** Country

**WEGZ-FM**
101 W. Omaha Street
P.O. Box 207
Washburn, WI 54891
**Phone:** (715) 373-5151 or (800) 853-1059
    (toll-free)
**Fax:** (715) 373-5805
http://www.eagle106.com
**Format:** Country

**WEXT-FM**
8500 Green Bay Road
Kenosha, WI 53142
**Phone:** (414) 694-7800
**Fax:** (414) 694-7767
http://www.extremecountry.com
**Format:** Hot Country

**WFDL-FM**
210 S. Main Street
Fond du Lac, WI 54935

**Phone:** (920) 924-9697 or (800) 977-9335
    (toll-free)
**Fax:** (920) 923-1042
**E-mail:** davis@wfdl.com
http://www.wfdl.com
**Format:** Adult Contemporary

**WFHR-AM**
645 25th Avenue, N.
Wisconsin Rapids, WI 54494
**Phone:** (715) 424-1300
**Fax:** (715) 424-1347
**E-mail:** onradio@wctc.net
http://www.wfhrradio.com
**Format:** Talk, News

**WGBM-FM**
445 S. Madison Street
Green Bay, WI 54301-4126
**Phone:** (920) 465-3947 or
    (800) 947-WGBM (toll-free)
**Fax:** (920) 468-9471
**E-mail:** contact@wbm.com
http://www.wgbm.com
**Format:** Country

**WGLX-FM**
645 25th Avenue, N.
Box 8022
Wisconsin Rapids, WI 54494
**Phone:** (715) 424-1300
**Fax:** (715) 424-1347
**E-mail:** onradio@wctc.net
http://www.wglx.com
**Format:** Classic Rock

**WGNV-FM**
P.O. Box 88
Milladore, WI 54454
**Phone:** (715) 457-2988
**Fax:** (715) 457-2987
**E-mail:** wgnv@wctc.net
http://www.christianfamilyradio.net
**Format:** Religious

**WHBY-AM**
P.O. Box 1519
Appleton, WI 54913
**Phone:** (920) 733-6639
**Fax:** (920) 739-0494
**E-mail:** 1150whby@wcinet.com
http://www.whby.com
**Format:** News, Full Service, Talk, Sports

**WHDG-FM**
3616 Highway 47 North
Rhinelander, WI 54501
**Phone:** (715) 362-1975
**Fax:** (715) 362-1973

**E-mail:** 975sales@whdg.com
http://www.whdg.com
**Format:** Contemporary Country

**WHID-FM**
2420 Nicolet Drive
Green Bay, WI 54311
**Phone:** (414) 465-2444 or (800) 654-6228
(toll-free)
**Fax:** (414) 465-2576
http://www.wpr.org
**Format:** Public Radio, Talk

**WISS-AM**
P.O. Box 5
112 N. Pearl Street
Berlin, WI 54923
**Phone:** (414) 361-3551 or (888) 879-8574
(toll-free)
**Fax:** (414) 361-3737
**E-mail:** cowcountry@wissradio.com
http://www.wissradio.com
**Format:** Country

**WIZD-FM**
P.O. Box 850
Plover, WI 54467
**Phone:** (715) 344-6050 or (800) 967-1740
(toll-free)
**Fax:** (715) 341-8070
**E-mail:** wizdfm@coredcs.com
http://www.wizd.com
**Format:** Oldies

**WIZM-AM**
Box 99
La Crosse, WI 54602
**Phone:** (608) 782-1230
**Fax:** (608) 782-1170
**E-mail:** record@lax.net
http://www.dickplaza.com
**Format:** Talk

**WIZM-FM**
Box 99
La Crosse, WI 54602
**Phone:** (608) 782-1230
**Fax:** (608) 782-1170
http://www.dickplaza.com
**Format:** Top 40

**WJZI-FM**
2979 N. Mayfair Road
Milwaukee, WI 53222-4301
**Phone:** (414) 276-2040
**Fax:** (414) 276-8406
http://www.933wjzi.com
**Format:** Jazz

**WKKV-FM**
2400 S. 102nd Street
West Allis, WI 53227
**Phone:** (414) 321-1007
**Fax:** (414) 321-2231
http://www.v1oo.com
**Format:** Urban Contemporary

**WKPO-FM**
1 Parker Plaza
Suite 485
Janesville, WI 53545
**Phone:** (608) 758-9025
**Fax:** (608) 758-9550
http://www.wkpo.com
**Format:** Urban Contemporary

**WKTI-FM**
720 E. Capitol Drive
Milwaukee, WI 53201
**Phone:** (414) 967-5339 or
(800) 945-WKTI (toll-free)
**Fax:** (414) 967-5266
**E-mail:** info@wkti.com
http://www.wkti.com
**Format:** Contemporary Hit Radio
(CHR), Adult Contemporary

**WLST-FM**
N. 2880 Roosevelt Road
Marinette, WI 54143
**Phone:** (715) 735-6631
**Fax:** (715) 732-0125
http://www.live95.net
**Format:** Adult Contemporary

**WMCS-AM**
2979 N. Mayfair Road
Milwaukee, WI 53222
**Phone:** (414) 771-1021
http://www.1290wmcs.com
**Format:** Blues, Talk, News, Urban
Contemporary

**WMEQ-AM**
619 Cameron Street
Eau Claire, WI 54703
**Phone:** (715) 830-4000
http://www.clearchannel.com/radio
**Format:** Talk

**WMUR-FM**
1131 W. Wisconsin Avenue
Suite 421
Milwaukee, WI 53233
**Phone:** (414) 288-7768
**Fax:** (414) 288-1979
**E-mail:** muwmurads@vms.csd.mu.edu

http://www.mu.edu/stumedia/wmur
**Format:** Eclectic

**WMZK-FM**
120 S. Mill Street
Merrill, WI 54452
**Phone:** (715) 536-6262 or (800) 236-6266
(toll-free)
**Fax:** (715) 536-6208
**E-mail:** advertising@z104rocks.com
http://www.z104rocks.com
**Format:** Album-Oriented Rock (AOR)

**WOFM-FM**
P.O. Box 2048
Wausau, WI 54402
**Phone:** (715) 355-1614
**Fax:** (715) 359-0520
**E-mail:** wofm.com
http://www.theoldiesstation.com
**Format:** Oldies

**WOGO-AM**
2396 State Hwy. 53
Suite 1
Chippewa Falls, WI 54729
**Phone:** (715) 723-2555 or (800) 657-4600
(toll-free)
**Fax:** (715) 723-1348
**E-mail:** csteward@wwib.com
http://www.wwib.com
**Format:** Contemporary Christian, Sports

**WPFF-FM**
P.O. Box 444
Sturgeon Bay, WI 54235
**Phone:** (920) 743-7443
**E-mail:** wpff@wpff.com
http://www.wpff.com/
**Format:** Contemporary Christian,
Religious

**WPKR-FM**
2401 W. Waukau Avenue
P.O. Box 3450
Oshkosh, WI 54903
**Phone:** (920) 236-4242
**Fax:** (920) 236-4240
**E-mail:** country@wpkr.com
http://www.wpkr.com
**Format:** Country

**WRQT-FM**
P.O. Box 99
La Crosse, WI 54601
**Phone:** (608) 782-1230
**Fax:** (608) 782-1170
**E-mail:** therock@957therock.com
http://www.957therock.com
**Format:** Country

# WYOMING

**KASL-AM**
227 S. Seneca
Newcastle, WY 82701-2820
**Phone:** (307) 746-4433
**Fax:** (307) 746-4435
**E-mail:** kasl@vcn.com
**Format:** Full Service, Adult
   Contemporary, Country, Oldies

**KBBS-AM**
1221 Fort Street
Buffalo, WY 82834
**Phone:** (307) 684-7070 or (800) 735-8313
   (toll-free)
**Fax:** (307) 684-7676
**E-mail:** klgt@vcn.com
**Format:** Oldies

**KCGY-FM**
Box 1290
Laramie, WY 82070
**Phone:** (307) 745-9242 or (800) 352-5249
   (toll-free)
**Fax:** (307) 742-4576
**E-mail:** kcgy@kowbkcgy.com
http://www.broadcasting.com
**Format:** Country

**KDLY-FM**
1530 W. Main Street
Lander, WY 82520-2658
**Phone:** (307) 332-5683
**Fax:** (307) 332-5548
**E-mail:** radiol@wyoming.com
**Format:** Classic Rock

**KERM-FM**
R.R. 2, Box 40
Torrington, WY 82240
**Phone:** (307) 532-2158
**Fax:** (307) 532-2641
**Format:** Country

**KGWY-FM**
P.O. Box 1179
Gillette, WY 82717
**Phone:** (307) 686-2242
**Fax:** (307) 686-7736
**E-mail:** kgwy@kgwy.com
http://kgwy.com
**Format:** Hot Country

**KIML-AM**
Box 1009
Gillette, WY 82717-1009
**Phone:** (307) 682-4747
**Fax:** (307) 687-0568

**E-mail:** kiml@vcn.com
**Format:** Country

**KIMX-FM**
302 S. 2nd Street
Suite 202
Laramie, WY 82070
**Phone:** (307) 745-5208
**Fax:** (307) 745-8570
**Format:** Adult Contemporary

**KIQZ-FM**
2346 W. Spruce
Rawlins, WY 82301
**Phone:** (307) 324-3315
**Fax:** (307) 324-3509
**E-mail:** mtrush@trib.com
**Format:** Adult Contemporary

**KKLX-FM**
1340 Radio Drive
Worland, WY 82401
**Phone:** (307) 347-3231 or (800) 359-0232
   (toll-free)
**Fax:** (307) 347-4880
**Format:** Top 40

**KKWY-AM**
110 E. 17th Street
Suite 205
Cheyenne, WY 82001
**Phone:** (307) 635-8787
**Fax:** (307) 635-8788
**E-mail:** kwy1630@aol.com;
   kjj11370@aol.com
**Format:** Country

**KLDI-AM**
409 S. 4th Street
Laramie, WY 82070
**Phone:** (307) 745-7396
**Fax:** (307) 745-7397
**E-mail:** krqu@compuserve.com
**Format:** Country

**KLEN-FM**
1912 Capitol Avenue
Suite 300
Cheyenne, WY 82001
**Phone:** (307) 632-4400
**Fax:** (307) 632-1898
**Format:** Adult Contemporary

**KLGT-FM**
1221 Fort Street
Buffalo, WY 82834
**Phone:** (307) 684-5126 or (800) 735-8313
   (toll-free)
**Fax:** (307) 684-7676

**E-mail:** klgt@vcn.com
http://www.mallwest.com
**Format:** Hot Country

**KMER-AM**
436 Fossil Butte Drive
P.O. Box 432
Kemmerer, WY 83101-0432
**Phone:** (307) 877-4422 or
   (800) 564-KMER (toll-free)
**Fax:** (307) 877-5537
**E-mail:** kmer@hamsfork.net
**Format:** Oldies

**KMGW-FM**
150 W. Nichols
Casper, WY 82601
**Phone:** (307) 266-5252
**Fax:** (307) 235-9143
**Format:** Adult Contemporary

**KMKX-FM**
1750 Sunset
Suite B
P.O. Box 1058
Rock Springs, WY 82902
**Phone:** (307) 362-7034
**Fax:** (307) 875-4545
**E-mail:** themixx@sweetwater.net
**Format:** Classic Rock

**KMTN-FM**
645 S. Cache
P.O. Box 927
Jackson, WY 83001
**Phone:** (307) 733-4500
**Fax:** (307) 733-7773
**Format:** Album-Oriented Rock (AOR),
   Classic Rock

**KODI-AM**
2001 Mountain View Drive
P.O. Box 1210
Cody, WY 82414
**Phone:** (307) 587-4100
**Fax:** (307) 527-5045
http://broadcastamerica.com
**Format:** Talk

**KOTB-FM**
Box 190
Evanston, WY 82931-0190
**Phone:** (307) 789-8255
**Fax:** (307) 789-8521
**Format:** Contemporary Country

**KOVE-AM**
1530 Main Street
Lander, WY 82520-2658

**Phone:** (307) 332-5683
**Fax:** (307) 332-5548
**E-mail:** radiol@wyoming.com
**Format:** Country

**KOWB-AM**
Box 1290
Laramie, WY 82070
**Phone:** (307) 745-4888 or (800) 352-5249
    (toll-free)
**Fax:** (307) 742-4576
**E-mail:** y95@aol.com
**Format:** News, Talk, Sports

**KPIN-FM**
2232 Dell Range Boulevard
Cheyenne, WY 82009-4994
**Phone:** (307) 367-2000 or
    (800) USA-RULE (toll-free)
**Fax:** (307) 367-3300
**Format:** Country, Oldies

**KPOW-AM**
P.O. Box 968
912 Lane 11
Powell, WY 82435
**Phone:** (307) 754-5183
**Fax:** (307) 754-9667
**E-mail:** kpow-z92@wir.net
**Format:** Country, Sports, Agricultural

**KQSW-FM**
P.O. Box 2128
Rock Springs, WY 82902
**Phone:** (307) 362-3793
**Fax:** (307) 362-8727
**Format:** Country

**KRKK-AM**
P.O. Box 2128
Rock Springs, WY 82902

**Phone:** (307) 362-3793
**Fax:** (307) 362-8727
**Format:** Oldies

**KRQU-FM**
P.O. Box 848
Laramie, WY 82070-0848
**Phone:** (307) 745-7396
**Fax:** (307) 745-7397
**E-mail:** krqu@compuserve.com
**Format:** Classic Rock

**KRRR-FM**
1001 E. Lincoln Way
Cheyenne, WY 82001
**Phone:** (307) 638-0999
**Fax:** (307) 635-6766
**E-mail:** krrline@qwest.net
**Format:** Oldies

**KTAG-FM**
2001 Mountain View Drive
P.O. Box 1210
Cody, WY 82414
**Phone:** (307) 587-4100
**Fax:** (307) 527-5045
http://broadcastameria.com
**Format:** Adult Contemporary

**KTAK-FM**
P.O. Box 393
Riverton, WY 82501
**Phone:** (307) 856-2251
**Format:** Country

**KTRS-FM**
251 W. 1st Street
Casper, WY 82601
**Phone:** (307) 235-7000 or (800) 251-5877
    (toll-free)

**Fax:** (307) 237-5836
**Format:** Contemporary Hit Radio (CHR)

**KTRZ-FM**
P.O. Box 808
Riverton, WY 82501
**Phone:** (307) 856-2922
**Fax:** (307) 856-7552
**E-mail:** ktrz@tcinc.net
http://broadcastamerica.com
**Format:** Adult Contemporary

**KTWO-AM**
150 N. Nichols
Casper, WY 82601
**Phone:** (307) 266-5252
**Fax:** (307) 235-9143
**Format:** Country

**KUWR-FM**
Box 3984
Laramie, WY 82071-3984
**Phone:** (307) 766-4240
**Fax:** (307) 766-6184
**E-mail:** jbs@uwyo.edu
http://www.uwyo.edu/wpr
**Format:** News, Adult Album Alternative,
    Classical

**KZMQ-AM**
P.O. Box 1210
Cody, WY 82414-1210
**Phone:** (307) 587-4100
**Fax:** (307) 527-5045
**E-mail:** kzmq@tctwest.net
http://www.broadcastamerica.com
**Format:** Country, Oldies

# APPENDIX IV
# NETWORK AND MEDIA GROUP
# ON-LINE JOB BANKS

The following is a selected listing of radio network and media group on-line job bank websites. Use this listing to help start your search for internships, career opportunities, and information on radio broadcasting companies. The author does not endorse any one group over another.

**ABC (Links to local stations)**
http://www.abc.go.com

**Ackerly Group**
http://www.ackerley.com/
    ackerley_corporate/indexcareers.html

**CBS Radio (Nationwide)**
http://www.cbsradio.com

**Clear Channel Communications
    (Nationwide)**
http://www.clearcareers.com/

**Cox Communications (Nationwide)**
http://www.cox.com/coxcareer/search.asp

**Cox Radio**
http://www.coxradio.com/cxr/employ.html

**Cumulus Media**
http://www.cumulus.com/career_index.
    html

**EMMIS Communications**
http://www.emmis.com

**Entercom Communications**
http://www.entercom.com

**Gannett Co., Inc. (Nationwide)**
http://www.gannett.com/job/job.htm

**Infinity Broadcasting**
http://www.infinityradio.com/jobs

**Jefferson Pilot Communications**
http://www.jpc.com/jobs/jpcc-job.html

**Journal Broadcasting Group**
http://www.journalbroadcastgroup.com/
    jobsradio.htm

**Meredith Corporation (Nationwide)**
http://www.meredith.com

**National Public Radio (Nationwide)**
http://www.npr.org

**Public Broadcasting Service
    (Nationwide)**
http://pbs.org/stations

**Public Radio International
    (Minneapolis, MN)**
http://www.pri.org

**Public Broadcasting Service
    (Washington, DC)**
http://pbs.org/insidepbs

**Roth Multimedia**
http://www.rothmultimedia.com/radio.htm

# APPENDIX V
# RADIO CAREER WEBSITES

The following is a listing of selected career websites containing potential jobs in the radio industry. Use this list as a starting point. There are many more websites on the Internet for you to explore. The author does not endorse any one site over another. Remember to check out general career websites such as monster.com, careerbuilder.com, and hotjobs.com as well as specific radio station sites.

**AJR News Link/JobLink**
http://newslink.org

**All Access Music Group**
http://www1.allaccess.com

**American Journalism Review**
http://www.newslink.org/x-joblink.html

**The Antenna**
http://www.theantenna.com/97/jun/jobs/
    index.html

**Avalanche of Jobs for Writers**
http://www.sunoasis.com/west.html

**Broadcast Employment Services**
http://www.tvjobs.com/index_a.htm

**Broadcast Executive Directors
    Association-Job Bank**
http://www.careerpage.org/jobbank/index.
    html

**Broadcasting & Cable**
http://www.broadcastingcable.com/index.
    asp?layout=static&page=careers_cat

**California Journalism Online**
http://www.csne.org/

**Career Page: The Source for Broadcast
    Radio and Television Jobs**
http://www.careerpage.org

**Career Path**
http://www.careerpath.com

**CBA Radio Jobs Page**
http://www.cabroadcasters.org/radiojobs.
    shtml

**CNY Radio Jobs**
http://cnyradio.com/q?m=8

**Corporation for Public Broadcasting**
http://www.cpb.org/jobline/index.html

**Craig's List—Bay Area Insider**
http://www.listfoundation.org

**Current Classifieds**
http://www.current.org/jobs/index.html

**Freelance Jobs**
http://www.freelanceonline.com/jobsavail.
    html

**Gannett Jobs**
http://www.gannett.com/job/news.htm

**Inside Radio.com**
http://www.mstreet.net

**Jobs at Public Radio International**
http://www.pri.org/webfiles/jobs.html

**Louisiana Tech**
http://eb.journ.latech.edu/jobs.html

**Mediarecruiter**
http://www.mediarecruiter.com

**NAB Job Bank**
http://www.nab.org/bcc/JobBank/other

**NPR Jobs**
http://www.npr.org/inside/jobs

**OnAirJobs.com**
http://www.onairjobs.com

**Planet Media**
http://planetmedia.net

**Radio and Production—Classified**
http://radio411.com/classifieds.htm

**Radio & Records**
http://www.rronline.com

**Radio Broadcasting Report**
http://www.rbr.com/pages/jobs.asp

**Radio College—Openings for
    Producers**
http://www.radiocollege.org/rc/
    wwwboard/wwwboard.html

**Radio 411—Classified**
http://radio411.com/classifieds.htm

**Radio Gigs**
http://www.radiogigs.com

**Radio Jobs Board**
http://www.users.nwark.com/~frye/bbs/
    wwwboard.html

**Radio Star Jobs**
http://newradiostar.com/jobs.htm

**The Reporters Network**
http://www.reporters.net

**Rock Radio Gigs**
http://www.entertainmentworlds.com/
    jobs.html

**Sportscasting Jobs**
http://www.sportscastingjobs.com/

**TVandradiojobs.com**
http://tvandradiojobs.com

**UC Berkeley's Journalism School**
http://www.journalism.berkeley.edu/
    resources/jobs
http://www.journalism.berkeley.edu/jobs

# APPENDIX VI
# STATE ASSOCIATIONS OF THE NATIONAL ASSOCIATION OF BROADCASTERS (NAB)

The National Association of Broadcasters (NAB) is one of the most prominent trade associations in the broadcast industry. The following is a listing of websites of the state associations of the National Association of Broadcasters.

Use theses sites to obtain information, seek out job possibilities, and learn about internships.

Information is subject to change. For the latest information contact the National Association of Broadcasters.

**National Association of Broadcasters (NAB)**
http://www.nab.org

**Alabama**
http://www.al-broadcasters.org/jobbank.html

**Arizona**
http://www.azbroadcasters.org

**Arkansas**
http://www.arkbroadcasters.org

**California**
http://www.cabroadcasters.org

**Florida**
http://www.fab.org/tvjobs.shtml

**Georgia**
http://www.gab.org

**Illinois**
http://www.ilba.org

**Indiana**
http://www.indianabroadcasters.org

**Iowa**
http://www.iowabroadcasters.com

**Kansas**
http://www.kab.net/jobbank

**Kentucky**
http://www.kba.org

**Louisiana**
http://www.broadcasters.org

**Maine**
http://www.mab.org

**Massachusetts**
http://www.massbroadcasters.org

**MDCD (Maryland, Washington D.C., & Delaware)**
http://www.mdcd.com

**Michigan**
http://www.michmab.com

**Minnesota**
http://www.minnesotabroadcasters.com

**Missouri**
http://www.mbaweb.org

**Nebraska**
http://radiostation.com/cgi-bin/w3-msql/jobopeningshow.html

**Nevada**
http://www.nevadabroadcasters.org

**New Hampshire**
http://www.nhab.org

**New Mexico**
http://www.nmba.org

**New York**
http://www.nysbroadcastersassn.org

**North Carolina**
http://www.ncbroadcast.com/job-bank.html

**North Dakota**
http://www.ndba.org/jobbank.htm

**Oklahoma**
http://www.oabok.org/jobbank.html

**Oregon**
http://www.theoab.org

**Tennessee**
http://www.tabtn.org

**Texas**
http://www.tab.org

**Vermont**
http://www.vab.org/jobs_page.html

**Virginia**
http://www.vab.net

**West Virginia**
http://www.wvba.com/Jobs/htm

**Wisconsin**
http://www.wi-broadcasters.org/jobs/toc.htm

**Wyoming**
http://www.wyomingbroadcasting.org

# GLOSSARY

The following is a list of abbreviations and terms that will prove helpful to those interested in the radio and broadcasting industry.

**ABC** American Broadcasting Company

**AC** Adult contemporary format

**account executive** Radio station sales person or sales rep.

**actives** Station listeners who call in for contests, to make song requests, or to offer comments.

**ad lib** Spontaneous, unrehearsed comments made by on-air personalities.

**AFTRA** American Federation of Television and Radio Artists

**aircheck** A tape of a live radio broadcast.

**AMA** American Marketing Association

**amplification** The increase of the power of a radio signal.

**AM** Amplitude Modulation. A method of radio signal transmission that uses a standard broadcast band with frequencies between 535 and 1705.

**AP** Associated Press, a wire news service.

**Arbitron Ratings** A rating service for television and radio stations that illustrates the percentage of the population viewing or listening to specific shows or stations. Commercials on television and radio are often based on Arbitron ratings.

**Associated Press** AP, a wire news service.

**ASCAP** American Society of Composers, Artists, and Performers: a music licensing service.

**audition tape** A recording used by on-air personalities to illustrate their talent.

**automation** System radio stations use to play prepacked taped programming.

**AWRT** American Women in Radio and Television

**BM** "Beautiful Music," a radio format.

**BMI** Broadcast Music Incorporated, a music licensing service.

**BPME** Broadcast Promotion and Management Executives

**break** To play a new tune, CD, record, etc., before any other station.

**bulk eraser** A piece of equipment that removes the sound from recording tape so it may be reused.

**calendar listing** Dated listings sent to the media by publicists regarding upcoming events and programs. They are designed to bring events to the attention of the public.

**call letters** A radio station's identification letters, such as WABC or KABC.

**cart** The plastic cartridge containing a continuous loop of record tape. Public service announcements, commercials, etc., are often on carts.

**CASE** Council for the Advancement and Support of Education

**CD** Compact disc

**CFR** Code of Federal Regulations

**CHR** "Contemporary Hit Radio," a radio format.

**circulation** The number of copies of a newspaper or magazine that are distributed.

**commercial** Paid advertising announcements; sometimes referred to as a spot.

**co-op** Cooperative. Co-op advertising shares the expense of advertising between a manufacturer or corporation and a retailer or other local company.

**copy** Written words for advertising or announcements.

**CPB** Corporation for Public Broadcasting

**DAT** Digital audiotape

**dateline** Location information provided at the beginning of a news release indicating the specific town, city, etc., where the press or news release originated. In some instances the date may also be included.

**DBS** Direct Broadcast Satellite, a communication satellite that beams programs to receiving stations.

**dead air** Absence of on-air sound.

**deejay** Disc Jockey

**demagnetize** Removing magnetic impressions to clean audiotape.

**demographics** The statistical data making up the listening audience, such as sex, age, race, income, etc.

**DJ** Disc Jockey

**dub** To make a duplicate of a recording.

**dupe** Duplicate

**EAS** Emergency Alert System

**ENG** Electronic News Gathering

**fade** Slowly-changing volume.

**Five Ws** The Who, What, When, Where, and Why used by press people to gather and write the basic news story.

**FM** Frequency modulation, the signal transmission using 88-108 MHz band.

**format** Type of programming utilized at a radio station.

**IABC** International Association of Business Communicators

**IBEW** International Brotherhood of Electrical Workers

**ID** Identification, as in station identification.

**IPA** Internet Professionals Association

**jingle** The musical tune used in commercials or promotions.

**Jock** Disc jockey

**lead** The opening lines of a news release or feature designed to attract reader interest.

**liner cards** Cards containing written on-air promotions.

**live copy** Copy read live on the air.

**live tag** Live words added after a recorded commercial.

**local** The local in a union is the local affiliation in a particular geographic area of a national or international union. May also refer to a local television or radio station in relation to a national station.

**market** The geographic area covered by a radio station.

**master** Original recording.

**MHZ** Megahertz, an FM frequency measurement.

**mono** Single track sound.

**MOR** Middle of the road format.

**morning drive** Part of the broadcast day, usually between 6 am and 10 am.

**MRA** Marketing Research Association

**multitracking** Overdubbing.

**NAB** National Association of Broadcasters

**NABET** National Association of Broadcast Employees and Technicians

**NBC** National Broadcasting Company

**NPR** National Public Radio

**NSFRE** National Society of Fund Raising Executives

**NSSA** National Sportscasters and Sportswriters Association

**on-line** Connected to the Internet.

**packaged programming** Syndicated or prerecorded programming.

**PRSA** Public Relations Society of America

**portfolio** A collection of artwork or writing samples used to illustrate talent and potential to prospective clients or employers.

**PR** Public relations

**press kit** A promotion kit containing photographs, promotional materials and publicity, etc., on a person, product, or service. Usually used by publicists or public relations people to publicize clients.

**PSA** Public Service Announcement

**publicity peg** An interesting piece of information designed to grab the attention of a news editor.

**RAB** Radio Advertising Bureau

**rate card** Printed information giving, station's advertising rates.

**ratings** The measurement of the size of a listening audience.

**remote** Radio broadcast originating outside the station studio.

**Reuters** A wire news service.

**RPM** Revolutions per minute

**RTNDA** Radio Television News Directors Association

**SBE** Society of Broadcast Engineers

**search the net** To look for information on the Internet.

**SESAC** Society of European Stage Authors and Composers, a music licensing service.

**ship date** The actual date a manufacturer physically ships a product.

**signal** A sound transmission.

**site** A website.

**spot** Commercial.

**station ID** Radio station identification; call letters.

**stringer** Freelance news reporter.

**surf the Net** To go on-line to visit various sites on the Internet.

**syndication** Programming that goes out to a number of stations.

**trade-out** The exchange of airtime for goods or services.

**UPI** United Press International, a wire news service.

**URL** An address on the Internet.

**VOA** Voice of America

**Web** The World Wide Web

**website** A "place" on the World Wide Web.

**WGA** Writers Guild of America

**wire services** News gathering services such as UPI, AP, and Reuters that, for a fee, provide the media with news stories.

**World Wide Web** The Internet.

**WWW** World Wide Web

# BIBLIOGRAPHY

## A. BOOKS

There are thousands of books written on all aspects of radio and the broadcast industry. The books listed below are separated into general categories, and the subject matter in many overlaps with other categories.

These books can be found in bookstores or libraries. If your local library does not have the books you want, you might ask your librarian to order them for you through the interlibrary loan system.

This list is meant to be a starting point in your search for information. For other books that might interest you, look in the business or entertainment sections of bookstores and libraries. You can also check *Books in Print* (found in the reference section of libraries) for other books on these subjects.

### Advertising

Belch, George E. *Advertising & Promotion.* New York: McGraw-Hill, 2000.

Berger, Arthur Asa. *Ads, Fads & Consumer Culture.* Blue Ridge Summit, Pa.: Rowman & Littlefield Publishers, Inc., 2000.

Cohen, Barry. *The Truth About Advertising (Forget Everything You Think You Know).* Irvine, Calif.: Entrepreneur Press, 2001.

Goodstein, Scott. *Advertising & Promotions.* New York: Thomson Learning, 2001.

Institute of Practitioners in Advertising Staff. *Excellence in Advertising.* Stoneham, Mass.: Butterworth-Heinemann, 1999.

Kobliski, Kathy J. *Advertising Without An Agency.* Central Point, Ore.: PSI Research, 2001.

McAllister, Matthew. *Advertising & Consumer Culture.* Mahwah, N.J.: Lawrence Erbaum Associates, Inc., 2000.

National Register Publishing Staff. *Co-Op Advertising Programs Sourcebook.* New Providence, N.J.: National Register Publishing, 2000.

### Broadcasting

Christopher H. *Special Reports on American Broadcasting.* Manchester, N.H.: Ayer Company Publishers, Inc., 1974.

Quaal, Ward, L. *Broadcast Management: Radio and Television.* Fern Park, Fla.: Hastings House, 1976.

Smith, F. Leslie. *Perspectives on Radio and Television.* Mahwah, N.J.: Lawrence Erlbaum Associates, Inc., 1998.

### Copywriting

Kahn, Robin. *Promotional Copy.* New York: Distributed Art Publishers/D. A. P., 1994.

Lewis, Herschell Gordon. *On the Art of Writing Copy.* New York: AMACOM, 1994.

Lewis, Herschell Gordon. *Power Copywriting.* Chicago: Dartnell Corporation, 1994.

MacLoughlin, Shaun. *Writing for Radio: How to Write Plays, Features and Short Stories That Get You on Air.* Northfield, Ill.: How to Books, 2001.

Messke, Milan, D. *Copywriting for the Electronic Media: A Practical Guide.* Belmont, Calif.: Wadsworth Publishing Company, 1997.

One Club for Art and Copy Staff. *The One Show, Vol. 6: Radio, T.V. and Print's Best Ads.* New York: Robert Silver Associates, 1985.

### Engineering

Brindley, Keith. *Newnes Radio and Electronic Engineer's Pocketbook.* Boca Raton, Fla.: C R C Press LLC, 2000.

Rudman, Jack. *Radio and Television Engineer.* Lincolnwood, Ill.: National Learning Corporation, 1994.

### Human Resources

Scott, Randall. *Human Resource Management In The Electronic Media.* Westport, Conn.: Greenwood Publishing Group, Inc., 1998.

### Internet Advertising/Public Relations/Media

Columbo, George. *Capturing Customers.com.* Franklin Lakes, N.J.: Career Press Incorporated, 2001.

Middleton, Don. *Winning PR in the Wired World.* New York: McGraw-Hill, 2000.

Phillips, Michael, and Salli Raspberry. *Marketing Without Advertising.* Berkeley: Nolo.com, 1997.

Trepper, Charles. *E-Commerce Strategies: Mapping Your Organization's Success in Today's Competitive Marketplace.* Boston: Microsoft Press, 2000.

Zeff, Robin, and Brad Aronson. *Advertising on the Internet.* New York: John Wiley and Sons, 1999.

### Marketing

Rosen, Emanuel. *The Anatomy of Buzz.* New York: Doubleday, 2000.

**Media Relations**

*The Radio Power Book: Directory of Music Radio and Record Promotion—1999.* New York: Billboard Books, 1997.

**On-Air Careers**

Brewster, Bill, and Frank Broughton. *Last Night a DJ Saved My Life: The History of The Disc Jockey.* New York: Grove Atlantic, Inc., 2000.

Frazier, Skipper Lee. *Tighten Up: The Autobiography of a Houston Disc Jockey.* Victoria, British Columbia: Trafford Publishing, 2001.

Fresh, Chuck. *How to Be a DJ: Your Guide to Becoming a Radio, Nightclub or Private Party Disc Jockey.* Melbourne, Fla.: Bevard Marketing, 1999.

Harper, Laurie. *Don Sherwood: The Life and Times of The World's Greatest Disc Jockey.* Brooklyn: Prima Publishing, 1989.

Hyde, Stuart Wallace. *Television and Radio Announcing.* Boston: Houghton Mifflin Company, 2001.

Jud, Brian. *It's Showtime: How to Perform on Television and Radio.* Boulder, Colo.: Marketing Directors, Inc., 1997.

O'Donnell, Lewis B. *Announcing: Broadcast Communicating Today.* Belmont, Calif.: Wadsworth Publishing Company, 1999.

Rudman, Jack. *Announcer.* Lincolnwood, Ill.: National Learning Corporation, 1994.

Sagerian, J.M. *Everything You Need to Know to Start a Disc Jockey Service.* Sturbridge, Mass.: J.M. Sagerian, 1990.

Weisgsant, Chris. *Careers as a Disc Jockey.* New York: Rosen Publishing Group, 1999.

**Production**

Keith, Michael C. *Production in Format Radio Handbook.* Lanham, Md.: University Press of America, 1984.

**Programming**

Adams, Michael. *Introduction to Radio: Production and Programming.* New York: McGraw-Hill, 1994.

Howard, Herbert H. *Radio, TV, and Cable Programming.* Ames, Ill.: Iowa State Press, 1994.

Warren, Steve. *Radio—The Book: A Fun Practical Programming Manual and Idea Book for Program Directors & Operations Managers.* New York: MOR Media, 1992.

**Promotion**

Holsopple, Curtis R. *Handbook of Radio Publicity and Promotion.* New York: McGraw-Hill, 1990.

Keith, Michael C. *Selling Radio Direct.* St. Louis, Mo.: Elsevier Science and Technology Books, 1992.

Radio Ink Magazine Staff. *Programming and Promotion.* West Palm Beach, Fla.: Streamline Press, 1995.

Roberts, Ted E. *Practical Radio Promotions.* Saint Louis: Science & Technology Books, 1992.

*Think Big: Events Marketing for Radio.* Washington, DC: National Association of Broadcasters, 1994.

**Public Radio**

Engleman, Ralph. *Public Radio and Television in America: A Political History.* Bloomfield Hills, Mich.: Sage Publications, 1996.

Starr, Jerold M. *Air Wars: The Fight to Reclaim Public Broadcasting.* Boston: Beacon Press, 2001.

Krattenmaker, Thomas. *Regulating Broadcast Programming.* Washington, DC: American Enterprise Institute for Public Policy Research, 1994.

**Public Relations and Publicity**

Conners, Gail A. *Good News!* Thousand Oaks, Calif.: Corwin Press, Inc., 2000

Doty, Dorothy. *Publicity & Public Relations.* Hauppauge, N.Y.: Barron's Educational Series, Inc., 2001.

Field, Shelly. *Career Opportunities in Advertising and Public Relations, Third Edition.* New York: Facts On File, Inc., 2001.

Fletcher, Tana. *Getting Publicity.* Bellingham, Wash.: Self-Counsel Press, Inc., 2000.

Kohl, Susan. *Getting Attention: Leading Edge Lessons for Publicity & Marketing.* Woburn, Mass.: Butterworth-Heimann, 2000.

Middleton, Don. *Winning PR in the Wired World.* New York: McGraw-Hill, 2000.

Parkhurst, William. *How to Get Publicity.* New York: HarperCollins, 2000.

Theaker, Alison. *The Public Relations Handbook.* New York: Routeldge, 2001.

Yale, David R. *The Publicity Handbook.* Lincolnwood, Ill.: NTC Contemporary Publishing Company, 2001.

**Radio Commercials**

Book, Albert C. *The Radio and Television Commercial.* Boulder, Co.: netLibrary, Incorporated, 1996.

Cushman, Timothy J. *The 60 Second Radio Salesperson.* Barrington, N.H.: Advantage Publications, 1988.

Dickey, Lew. *The Franchise Book: Building Radio Brands.* Washington, D.C.: National Association of Broadcasters, 1994.

Doll, Bob. *Instant Revenue: Low Maintenance High Profit Radio Telemarketing.* West Palm Beach, Fla.: Streamline Press, 1998.

Fiedler, Joseph. *If You Think It's Tough to Sell, Try Buying: The Complete Guide to Effective Radio Advertising.* Mechanicsburg, Pa.: Executive Books, 1994.

Fox, Shane. *Pricing and Rate Forecasting Using Broadcast Yield Management.* Washington, D.C.: National Association of Broadcasters, 1992.

Hettinger, Herman S. *Decade of Radio Advertising.* Manchester, N.H.: Ayer Company Publishers, Inc., 1976.

Jugenheimer, Donald W. *Advertising Media: Strategy and Tactics.* Madison, Wis.: Brown & Benchmark, 1992.

Kobliski, Kathy. *Advertising Without An Agency: A Comprehensive Guide to Radio, Television, Print, Direct Mail and Outdoor Advertising for Small Business.* Irvine, Calif.: Entrepreneur Press, 2001.

Lange, Mark R. *Professional Radio Selling.* Vincennes, Ind.: Original Company, Inc:, 1987.

Oakner, Larry. *And Now a Few Laughs from Our Sponsor: The Best Fifty Years of Radio Commercials.* New York: John Wiley & Sons, 2002.

Schulberg, Pete. *Radio Advertising: The Authoritative Handbook.* Lincolnwood, Ill.: McGraw-Hill, 1994.

Smulywan, Susan. *Selling Radio: The Commercialization of American Broadcasting, 1920-1934.* Washington, D.C.: Smithsonian Institution Press, 1996.

Traverso, Debra Koontz. *How to Write a Compelling 30-Second Commercial—of Yourself!: 52 Tips to Make Your First Impression a Lasting Impression.* Frederick, Md.: Blue Island Productions, 2000.

U.S. Bureau of Foreign and Domestic Commerce Staff. *World Broadcast Advertising: Four Reports.* Manchester, N.H.: Ayer Company Publishers, 1976.

Urlacher, Marvin R. *Radio Broadcasting Sales: Making an Intangible Tangible.* Billings, Mont.: MW Publishing Company, 1989.

Weinberger, Marc G. *Effective Radio Advertising.* Boulder, Colo.: netLibrary, Incorporated, 1994.

West, Bill. *Radio Advertising 101. 5: A Step-by-Step Guide to Creating Better Radio Advertising.* West Palm Beach, Fla.: Streamline Press, 1999.

Zager, Michael. *Writing For Television and Radio Commercials: A Manual for Composers and Students.* Blue Ridge Summit, Penn.: Scarecrow Press, Inc., 2003.

## Radio—General

Barrett. *Los Angeles Radio People.* Valenda, Calif.: Db Marketing Company, 1997.

Elrod, Bruce C. *Your Hit Parade.* Ann Arbor, Mich.: Popular Culture Ink, 1994.

Floyd, Thurmon. *The Radio Dictionary.* Columbus, Ohio: Riverview Press, 1993.

Garner, Joe. *We Interrupt This Broadcast: The Events That Stopped Our Lives...from the Hindenburg Explosion to the Attacks of September 11.* Neverville, Ill.: Sourcebooks, Inc., 2002.

Herweg, Godfrey. W. *Radio's Niche Marketing Revolution: Future Sell.* Saint Louis: Science & Technology Books, 1997.

Keillor, Garrison. *WLT: A Radio Romance.* St. Paul, Minn.: Penguin/HighBridge, 1991.

Lederman, Jim. *Battle Lines: The American Media and the Intifada.* Collingdale, Penn.: DIANE Publishing Company, 2001.

Osgood, Charles. *See You on the Radio.* Waterville, Maine: Thorndike Press, 2000.

## Radio Marketing

Herweg, Godfrey. *Radio's Niche Marketing Revolution: Future Sell.* St. Louis, Mo.: Elsevier Science & Technology Books, 1997.

Radio Ink Magazine Staff. *Sales and Marketing.* West Palm Beach, Fla: Streamline Press, 1995.

## Radio News

Bliss, Edward. *Now The News: The Story of Broadcast Journalism.* New York: Columbia University Press, 1991.

Bromley, Michael. *No News Is Bad News: Radio Television and the Press.* New York: Pearson Education, 2001.

Fang, Irving. *Writing Style Differences in Newspaper, Radio and Television News.* Minneapolis, Minn.: University of Minnesota, 1991.

Miles, Donald. *Broadcast News Handbook.* Indianapolis, Ind.: Macmillan Publishing Company, Inc., 1975.

Selb, Philip. *Going Live: Getting the News Right in a Real-Time, Online World.* Blue Ridge Summit, Penn.: Rowman & Littlefield Publishers, Inc., 2002.

Wulfemeyer, K. Tim. *Radio-TV News Writing: A Workbook.* Ames, Iowa: Iowa State Press, 1995.

## Radio Ratings

Occhiogrosso, Michael G, and R. Frankel Martin. *Arbitron Replication II: A Study of the Reliability of Radio Ratings.* Chester, Md.: Fishergate Publishing Company, Inc., 1982.

Starr, Jerold M. *Air Wars: The Flight to Reclaim Public Broadcasting.* Philadelphia, Penn.: Temple University Press, 2001.

Webster, James. *Ratings Analysis: Theory and Practice of Audience Research.* Mahwah, N.J.: Lawrence Erlabaum Associates, Inc., 2000.

## Radio Station Operations

Lange, Mark R. *Radio Station Operations.* Vincennes, Ind.: Original Company, Inc., 1985.

## Radio Sports

Catsis, John R. *Sports Broadcasting.* New York: Thomson Learning, 1996.

Garner, Joe. *And the Fans Roared: The Sports Broadcasts That Kept Us on the Edge of Our Seats.* Toronto, Ontario: Sourcebooks, Inc., 2000.

Redmond, Michael. *60 Second Sells: Ninety-Nine Hot Radio Sports for Retail Business.* Jefferson, N.C.: McFarland & Company, Incorporated Publishers, 1993.

Schultz, Bradley. *Sports Broadcasting.* St. Louis, Mo.: Elsevier Science & Technology Books, 2002.

## Research

Eastman, Susan T. *Research in Media Promotion.* Mahwah, N.J.: Lawrence Erlbaum Associates, Incorporated, 2000.

## Syndicated Radio

Magliozzi, Tom. *In Our Humble Opinion: Car Talk's Click and Clack Rant and Rave.* East Rutherford, N.J.: Berkley Publishing Group, 2002.

## Talk Radio

Barker, David C. *Rushed to Judgment: Talk Radio, Persuasion and American Political Behavior.* New York: Columbia University Press, 2002.

Eisenstock, Allan. *Sports Talk: A Journey Inside the World of Sports Talk Radio.* New York: Pocket Books, 2001.

Ratner, Ellen. *1010 Ways to Get Your Progressive Issues on Talk Radio.* Washington, DC: National Press Books, 1997.

Sadow, Catherine. *On the Air: Listening to Radio Talk: Instructors Manual.* Port Melbourne, Victoria: Cambridge University Press, 1998.

Scott, Gin G. *Can We Talk? The Power and Influence of Talk Shows.* Boulder, Colo.: Da Capo Press, Inc., 1997.

## Voice-overs

Blu, Susan. *Word of Mouth: A Guide to Commercial Voice-Over Excellence.* Beverly Hills: Pomegranate Press, Limited, 1998.

## Web Radio

Priestman, Chris. *Web Radio.* Sacramento, Calif.: Science & Technology Books, 2001.

## Writing

Addison-Wesley Educational Publishers. *Public Relations Writing Media Techniques.* Redding, Mass.: Addison-Wesley Educational Publishers, Inc., 2000.

Associated Press Staff. *AP Stylebook.* Old Tappan, N.J.: Addison-Wesley Longman, Incorporated, 1998.

Associated Press Staff. *The Associated Press Stylebook & Libel Manual.* Old Tappan, N.J.: Addison-Wesley Longman, Incorporated, 1996.

Bartram, Peter. *Writing a Press Release.* Northfield, Ill.: How to Books, 1999.

Borden, Kay. *Bulletproof News Releases.* Marietta, Ga.: Franklin-Sarrett Publishers, 1994.

Jacobi, Peter. *Writing With Style: The News Story and the Feature.* Chicago: Ragan Communications, 1982.

# B. PERIODICALS

Magazines, newspapers, membership bulletins, and newsletters may be helpful for finding information about a specific job category, finding a job in a specific field, or giving you insight into what certain jobs entail.

As with the books in the previous section, this list should serve as a starting point. There are many periodicals that are not listed here because of space limitations. The subject matter of some periodicals may overlap with others. Periodicals also tend to come and go. Look in your local library or in the newspaper/magazine shop for other periodicals that might interest you.

Addresses, phone numbers, websites, and e-mail addresses have been included when available.

## Advertising

*Advertisers Annual*
Hollis Publishing Ltd.
Harlequin House
7 High Street
Teddington TW 11 8EL, United Kingdom
**Phone:** 44 2089777711
**Fax:** 44 2089771133
**E-mail:** hollis@hollis-pr.co.uk,
   adannual@hollis-pr.co.uk
http://www.hollis-pr.com

*Media Market Guide*
Media Market Resources
P.O. Box 442
Littleton, NH 03561-0442
**Phone:** (603) 869-2418
**Fax:** (603) 869-3135
**E-mail:** mmresources@msn.com

*Radio Advertising Source*
SRDS
1700 E. Higgins Road, No. 500
Des Plaines, IL 60018-5610

**Phone:** (847) 375-5000 or
   (800) 851-7737 (toll-free)
**Fax:** (847) 375-5009
**E-mail:** contact@srds.com
http://www.srds.com

*Radio Co-op Directory*
Radio Advertising Bureau (RAB)
1320 Greenway Drive, 500
Irving, TX 75038
**Phone:** (972) 753-6786 or
   (800) 232-3131 (toll-free)

**Fax:** (972) 753-6727
http://www.rab.com

## Agricultural Radio

*Agri Marketing—Marketing Services
    Guide Issue*
Doane Agricultural Services
11701 Borman Drive
Suite 300
St. Louis, MO 63146-4199
**Phone:** (314) 569-2700 or
    (800) 535-2342 (toll-free)
**Fax:** (314) 569-1083
**E-mail:** doane@doane.com;
    info@agrimarketing.com

## Airplay and Music Reviews

*CMJ New Music Report*
CMJ Network
810 Seventh Avenue, 21st Floor
New York, NY 10019
**Phone:** (646) 485-6600 or
    (800) 265-9559 (toll-free)
**Fax:** (646) 557-0010
http://www.cmj.com

## Broadcasting

*Entertainment Law Reporter*
Entertainment Law Reporter
    Publishing Co.
2118 Wilshire Boulevard, No. 311
Santa Monica, CA 90403-5784
**Phone:** (310) 829-9335
**Fax:** (310) 829-9335
**E-mail:** editor@entertainmentlawreporter.
    com

*Feedback*
Broadcast Education Association
Fine Arts Building
East Stroudsburg University
East Stroudsburg, PA 18301
**Phone:** (570) 422-5051

*Journal of Broadcasting and
    Electronic Media*
Broadcast Education Association
1771 N Street, NW
Washington, DC 20036-2805

*Satellite Week*
Warren Communications News
2115 Ward Ct., NW
Washington, DC 20037
**Phone:** (202) 872-9200 or
    (800) 771-9202 (toll-free)

**Fax:** (202) 293-3435
**E-mail:** info@warren-news.com

*SPERDVAC Radiogram*
Society to Preserve and Encourage Radio
    Drama, Variety and Comedy
    (SPERDVAC)
P.O. Box 7177
Van Nuys, CA 91409

*Wireless Satellite and Broadcasting*
Information Gatekeepers Inc.
214 Harvard Avenue
Suite 200
Boston, MA 02134
**Phone:** (617) 232-3111 or
    (800) 323-1088 (toll-free)
**Fax:** (617) 734-8562
**E-mail:** info@igigroup.com
http://www.igigroup.com

## Broadcasting Education

*Journalism and Mass Communication
    Directory*
Association for Education in Journalism
    & Mass Communication
234 Outlet Pointe Boulevard
Suite A
Columbia, SC 29210-5667
**Phone:** (803) 798-0271
**Fax:** (803) 772-3509
**E-mail:** aejmchq@aol.com

*New Ears: The Audio Career and
    Education Handbook*
New Ear Productions
401 Benson Avenue
Milford, MI 48381-1802
**Phone:** (248) 684-0458

## Broadcasting Jobs

*BDAFAX*
BDA
2029 Century Park East
Suite 555
Los Angeles, CA 90067-2906
**Phone:** (310) 712-0040
**Fax:** (310) 712-0039
**E-mail:** anush@promax.org

## College Radio

*Journal of College Radio*
Intercollegiate Broadcasting System, Inc.
367 Windsor Highway
New Windsor, NY 12553-7900

**Phone:** (845) 565-0003
**Fax:** (845) 565-7446
**E-mail:** ibshq@aol.com
http://www.ibsradio.org

## Community Radio

*Community Radio News*
National Federation of Community
    Broadcasters
Fort Mason Center, Building D
San Francisco, CA 94123
**Phone:** (415) 771-1160
**Fax:** (415) 771-1160
**E-mail:** nfcb@aol.com

## Engineering

*BE Radio*
Primedia Business
29 N. Wacker Drive
Chicago, IL 60606
**Phone:** (312) 726-2802 or
    (800) 543-7771 (toll-free)
**Fax:** (312) 726-1905
**E-mail:** beradio@intertec.com
http://www.beradio.com

## Miscellaneous

*American Auto Racing Writers and
    Broadcasters Newsletter*
American Auto Racing Writers &
    Broadcasters Association
922 N. Pass Avenue
Burbank, CA 91505
**Phone:** (818) 842-7005
**Fax:** (818) 842-7020
http://www.aarwba.org

*Critical Studies in Media
    Communication*
National Communication Association
1765 N Street, NW
Washington, DC 20036-2801
**Phone:** (202) 464-4622
**Fax:** (202) 464-4600
**E-mail:** ajeffries@natcom.org,
    irouhani@natcom.org

*Listening In*
Ontario DX Association
P.O. Box 161, Sta. A
Willowdale, ON, Canada M2N 5S8
**E-mail:** odxa@compuserve.com;
    listeningin@home.com;
    dxontario@compuserve.com
http://www.odxa.on.ca

*QCWA News*
Quarter Century Wireless Association,
    Inc. (QCWA)
159 E. 16th Street
Eugene, OR 97401
**Phone:** (541) 683-0987
**Fax:** (541) 683-4181
**E-mail:** jwals@telport.com
http://www.teleport.com/qcwa

*Quarterly Journal of Speech*
National Communication Association
1765 N Street, NW
Washington, DC 20036-2801
**Phone:** (202) 464-4622
**Fax:** (202) 464-4600
**E-mail:** ajeffries@natcom.org;
    lrouhani@natcom.org

## Music Radio

*Impact!*
Vanguarde Media Inc.
315 Park Avenue S., 11th Floor
New York, NY 10010
**Phone:** (646) 654-4200
http://www.vanguardeneomedia.com/
    impact

## On-air Personalities

*One to One*
Cree Yadio Services
Box 9787
Fresno, CA 93794
**Phone:** (559) 448-0700
**Fax:** (559) 448-0761
**E-mail:** 121@att.net

*One to One II*
Cree Yadio Services
Box 9787
Fresno, CA 93794
**Phone:** (559) 448-0700
**Fax:** (559) 448-0761

## Programming

*Electronic Media*
Crain Communication Inc.
6500 Wilshire Boulevard
Suite 2300
Los Angeles, CA 90048
**Phone:** (323) 370-2432
**Fax:** (323) 653-4425
**E-mail:** emediachi@aol.com
http://www.emonline.com

*Programming Radio*
Mid-South Management, Inc.
P.O. Box 1051
Vicksburg, MS 39181-1051
**Phone:** (601) 922-8395
**Fax:** (601) 922-2856

*Radio Programming Profile*
BF/Communication Services, Inc.
311 Martling Avenue
Tarrytown, NY 10591-4709
**Phone:** (516) 364-2593

*Top 40 Airplay Monitor*
BPI Communications, Inc.
770 Broadway, 5th Floor
New York, NY 10036
**Phone:** (646) 654-5600
**Fax:** (646) 654-5514

## Public Radio

*Public Broadcasting Report*
Warren Communications News
2115 Ward Ct., NW
Washington, DC 20037
**Phone:** (202) 872-9200 or
    (800) 771-9202 (toll-free)
**Fax:** (202) 293-3435
**E-mail:** info@warren-news.com

*PTR*
Pacific Telecommunications Council
2454 S. Beretania Street
Honolulu, HI 96826-1596
**Phone:** (808) 941-3789
**Fax:** (808) 944-4874
**E-mail:** info@ptc.org
http://www.ptc.org

*WETA Magazine*
WETA Publishing
2775 S. Quincy Street
Arlington, VA 22206-2236

## Radio

*NAB RadioWeek*
National Association of Broadcasters
1771 N Street, NW
Washington, DC 20036-2891
**Phone:** (202) 429-5300 or
    (800) 368-5644 (toll-free)
**Fax:** (202) 429-5406
**E-mail:** nabpubs@nab.org;
    sbloomqu@nab.org

*NAB World*
National Association of Broadcasters
1771 N Street, NW
Washington, DC 20036-2891
**Phone:** (202) 429-5300 or
    (800) 368-5644 (toll-free)
**Fax:** (202) 429-5406
**E-mail:** nabpubs@nab.org
http://www.nab.org

*National Radio Guide*
Core Group Publishers Inc.
Box 48417
Bentall Centre
Vancouver, BC, Canada V7X 1A2
**Phone:** (902) 742-7111

*Radio World*
IMAS Publishing Inc.
5827 Columbia Pike
P.O. Box 1214
Falls Church, VA 22041
**Phone:** (703) 998-7600
**Fax:** (703) 998-2966
**E-mail:** radioworld@imaspub.com

*WBAI Folio*
Pacifica-WBAI Radio
120 Wall Street, 10th Floor
New York, NY 10005
**Phone:** (212) 209-2800
**Fax:** (212) 747-1698

## Radio News

*RTNDA Communicator*
Radio-Television News Directors
    Association
1000 Connecticut Avenue, NW
Suite 615
Washington, DC 20036
**Phone:** (202) 659-6510 or
    (800) 807-8632 (toll-free)
**Fax:** (202) 223-4007
**E-mail:** rtnda@rtnda.org
http://www.rtnda.org

*World News Connection*
National Technical Information Service
U.S. Department of Commerce
5285 Port Royal Road
Springfield, VA 22161-0001
**Phone:** (703) 605-6000 or
    (800) 553-6847 (toll-free)
**Fax:** (703) 605-6900
**E-mail:** orders@ntis.gov
http://wnc.Fedworld.gov

## Radio Operations and Management

*Radio Campaigns*
National Research Bureau
320 Valley Street
Burlington, IA 52601-5513
**Phone:** (319) 752-5415
**Fax:** (319) 752-3421

*Radio World*
IMAS Publishing Inc.
5827 Columbia Pike
P.O. Box 1214
Falls Church, VA 22041
**Phone:** (703) 998-7600
**Fax:** (703) 998-2966
**E-mail:** radioworld@imaspub.com

*US Radio Broadcasting Business
    Opportunities and Regulations
    Handbook*
International Business Publications,
P.O. Box 15343
Washington, DC 20003
**Phone:** (202) 546-2103
**Fax:** (202) 546-3275

## Radio Research

*Gavin*
CMP Media, Inc.
600 Community Drive
Manhasset, NY 11030
**Phone:** (516) 562-5000
**Fax:** (516) 562-5123
http://www.gavin.com/gavin

## Radio Stations

*Guide to the World's Radio Stations*
(Formerly *Radio Stations Guide*)
Bernard Babani (Publishing) Ltd.
The Grampians
Shepherds Bush Road
London W6 7NF, United Kingdom
**Phone:** 0171 6032581
**Fax:** 0171 6038203

## Religious Broadcasting

*Morality in Media Newsletter*
Morality in Media Inc.
475 Riverside Drive
Suite 239
New York, NY 10115

**Phone:** (212) 870-3222
**Fax:** (212) 870-2765
**E-mail:** mim@moralityinmedia.org
http://www.moralityinmedia.org

*NRB*
National Religious Broadcasters
7839 Ashton Avenue
Manassas, VA 20109
**Phone:** (703) 330-7000
**Fax:** (703) 330-6996
http://www.nrb.org

*SCRIBE*
Scribe Media
5606 Medical Circle
Madison, WI 53719
**Phone:** (608) 271-1025 or
    (800) 373-9692 (toll-free)
**Fax:** (608) 271-1150
**E-mail:** scribe@broadcast.net
http://www.fullfeed.com/lscribe/scribe1.
    htm

*Unda-USA Newsletter*
Unda-USA
901 Irving Avenue
Dayton, OH 45409-2316
**Phone:** (937) 229-2303
**Fax:** (937) 229-2300
**E-mail:** undausa1@aol.com

## Small Market Radio

*Small Market Radio Newsletter*
Jay Mitchell Associates
57 S. Court Street
Fairfield, IA 52556
**Phone:** (641) 472-4087 or
    (800) JAY-RADIO (toll-free)
**Fax:** (641) 472-2071
**E-mail:** jay@jaymitchell.com
http://www.smallmarketradio.com

## Talk Radio/Talk Shows

*Radio Talk Shows Need Guests*
Pacesetter Publications
P.O. Box 101975
Denver, CO 80250
**Phone:** (303) 722-7200 or
    (800) 945-2488 (toll-free)
**Fax:** (303) 733-2626
**E-mail:** talkshows@aol.com
http://www.joesabah.com

*Radio-TV Interview Report*
Bradley Communications
135 E. Plumstead Avenue
P.O. Box 1206
Lansdowne, PA 19050-8206
**Phone:** (800) 553-8002
**Fax:** (610) 259-5032
http://www.rtir.com

*Talk Radio/Talk TV*
Professional Press
P.O. Box 3581
Chapel Hill, NC 27515
**Phone:** (919) 942-8020 or
    (800) 277-8960 (toll-free)
**Fax:** (919) 942-3094

*Talk Shows and Hosts on Radio*
Whitefoord Press
23814 Michigan Avenue
Suite 314
Dearborn, MI 48124
**Phone:** (313) 274-1038
**Fax:** (313) 274-9263
**E-mail:** whitefoord@aol.com

## Trade Publications

*Billboard*
BPI Communications, Inc.
770 Broadway, 5th Floor
New York, NY 10036
**Phone:** (646) 654-5600
**Fax:** (646) 654-5514
**E-mail:** crosen@billboardgroup.com

*Radio and Records*
Radio and Records, Inc.
Los Angeles, CA 90067-4004
**Phone:** (310) 553-4330
**Fax:** (310) 203-9763
**E-mail:** mailroom@rronline.com,
    moreinfo@rronline.com
http://www.rronline.com

*Variety*
Cahners Business Newspapers
5700 Wilshire Boulevard
Suite 120
Los Angeles, CA 90036
**Phone:** (213) 965-4476
**Fax:** (213) 857-0742

## C. INDUSTRY AND MEDIA DIRECTORIES

The following are lists of industry and media directories that contain addresses, phone numbers, and websites of a variety of companies and media sources. Many directories are revised annually or even bi-annually. When checking for information, try to locate the latest edition of a directory. Most directories are quite expensive, but they can often be found in many public libraries.

### Industry Directories

*Broadcasting and Cable*
Cahners Publishing Co.
Entertainment Division
1705 DeSales Street, NW
Washington, DC 20036
**Phone:** (202) 659-2340
**Fax:** (202) 429-0651
http://www.broadcastingcable.com

*R and R Directory*
Radio and Records, Inc.
10100 Santa Monica Boulevard,
    5th Floor
Los Angeles, CA 90067-4004
**Phone:** (310) 553-4330
**Fax:** (310) 203-8727
**E-mail:** mailroom@rronline.com,
    moreinfo@rronline.com
http://www.rronline.com

*Radio and TV Broadcasting and
    Communications Equipment
    Manufacturers Directory*
infoUSA
5711 S. 86th Circle
P.O. Box 27347
Omaha, NE 68127
**Phone:** (402) 593-4600 or
    (800) 555-6124 (toll-free)
**Fax:** (402) 331-5481
**E-mail:** internet@infousa.com
http://www.abii.com

*Radio Co-op Directory*
Radio Advertising Bureau (RAB)
1320 Greenway Drive
Suite 500
Irving, TX 75038
**Phone:** (972) 753-6786 or
    (800) 232-3131 (toll-free)
**Fax:** (972) 753-6727
http://www.rab.com

*Radio Power Book*
Billboard Books
770 Broadway
New York, NY 10003
**Phone:** (646) 654-5000 or
    (800) 278-8477 (toll-free)
**Fax:** (646) 654-5487

*Radio Stations and Broadcasting
    Companies Directory*
infoUSA
5711 S. 86th Circle
P.O. Box 27347
Omaha, NE 68127
**Phone:** (402) 593-4600 or
    (800) 555-6124 (toll-free)
**Fax:** (402) 331-5481
**E-mail:** internet@infousa.com
http://www.abii.com

*Sports Market Place*
Sports Guide
13901 N. 73rd Street
Suite 219
Scottsdale, AZ 85260
**Phone:** (800) 776-7877
**E-mail:** training@franklincoveysports.
    com; smp@franklincoveysports.com;
    sportsmarketplace@
    franklincoveypsports.com
http://www.sportsmarketplace.com

*Who's Who in the Media and
    Communications*
Marquis Who's Who
Reed Elsevier
121 Chanlon Road
New Providence, NJ 07974
**Phone:** (908) 464-6800 or
    (800) 521-8110 (toll-free)
**Fax:** (908) 464-3553
**E-mail:** marquis@prod.lexis-nexis.com

### Media Directories

*Alaska Media Directory*
Sally Blackford & Harry Walker
6828 Cape Lisburne
Anchorage, AK 99504
**Phone:** (907) 338-7288
**Fax:** (907) 338-8339
**E-mail:** akmedia@ak.net

*Benn's Media Directory*
Data & Information Services Division
CMP Information Ltd.
Riverbank House
Angel Lane
Tonbridge, Kent TN9 6AT, United
    Kingdom

**Phone:** 01732 377 591
**Fax:** 01732 377 479
**E-mail:** orders@ubminternational.com
http://www.ubminfo.co.uk

*Boston University Media Guidebook*
Office of Public Relations
Boston University
25 Buick Street
Boston, MA 02215
**Phone:** (617) 353-2240
**Fax:** (617) 353-7630
**E-mail:** mgb@bu.edu
http://www.bu.edu/mediaguidebook

*Bowdens Media Directory*
Bowdens Information Services Ltd.
2206 Eglinton Avenue, E
Suite 190
Scarborough, ON, Canada M1L 4T5
**Phone:** (416) 750-2220 or
    (800) 269-8145 (toll-free)
**Fax:** (800) 247-5537
**E-mail:** tor123@flexnet.com

*College Media Advisers Directory*
College Media Advisers Inc.
University of Memphis
Department of Journalism
3711 Veterans Avenue
Memphis, TN 38152-6661
**Phone:** (901) 678-2403
**Fax:** (901) 678-4798

*Commonwealth Broadcaster Directory*
Commonwealth Broadcasting Association
    (CBA)
17 Fleet Street
London EC4Y 1AA, United Kingdom
**Phone:** 20 7583 5550
**Fax:** 20 7583 5549
**Telex:** 265781
**E-mail:** cba@cba.org.uk
http://www.oneworld.org/cba

*Communications Daily*
Warren Communications News
2115 Ward Ct., NW
Washington, DC 20037
**Phone:** (202) 872-9200 or
    (800) 771-9202 (toll-free)
**Fax:** (202) 293-3435

**E-mail:** info@warren-news.com
http://www.warren-news.com

*CPB Public Broadcasting Directory*
Corporation for Public Broadcasting
401 Ninth Street, NW
Washington, DC 20004-2037
**Phone:** (202) 879-9600
**Fax:** (202) 783-9700
http://www.cpb.org/directory/home.html

*Florida News Media Directory*
Brian Highberger Publisher
P.O. Box 316
Mount Dora, FL 32756
**Phone:** (352) 589-9020 or
    (800) 749-6399 (toll-free)
**Fax:** (352) 589-7020
**E-mail:** NewsMedia@comcast.net

*Gale Directory of Publications and
    Broadcast Media*
Gale Group Inc.
27500 Drake Road
Farmington Hills, MI 48331-3535
**Phone:** (248) 699-4253 or
    (800) 877-GALE (toll-free)
**Fax:** (248) 699-8065
**E-mail:** galeord@gale.com,
    businessproducts@gale.com
http://www.galegroup.com

*Georgia News Media Directory*
Brian Highberger Publisher
P.O. Box 316
Mount Dora, FL 32756
**Phone:** (352) 589-9020 or
    (800) 749-6399 (toll-free)
**Fax:** (352) 589-7020
**E-mail:** NewsMedia@comcast.net

*International Dictionary of
    Broadcasting and Film*
Focal Press
225 Wildwood Avenue
Woburn, MA 01801
**Phone:** (617) 928-2500 or
    (800) 366-2665 (toll-free)
**Fax:** (800) 446-6520
**E-mail:** christine.degon@bhusa.com

*Internet Buyer's Guide*
ADBG Publishing
P.O. Box 25929
Los Angeles, CA 90025
**Phone:** (310) 914-9000
**E-mail:** podell@iname.com

*Mississippi News Media Directory*
Brian Highberger Publisher
P.O. Box 316
Mount Dora, FL 32756
**Phone:** (352) 589-9020 or
    (800) 749-6399 (toll-free)
**Fax:** (352) 589-7020
**E-mail:** NewsMedia@comcast.net

*National Evangelical Directory*
National Association of Evangelicals
P.O. Box 1325
Azusa, CA 91702-1325
**Phone:** (626) 963-5966
**Fax:** (626) 963-5068
**E-mail:** nae@nae.net
http://www.NAE.net

*North Carolina News Media
    Directory*
Brian Highberger Publisher
P.O. Box 316
Mount Dora, FL 32756
**Phone:** (352) 589-9020 or
    (800) 749-6399 (toll-free)
**Fax:** (352) 589-7020
**E-mail:** NewsMedia@comcast.net

*Ohio News Media Directory*
Brian Highberger Publisher
P.O. Box 316
Mount Dora, FL 32756
**Phone:** (352) 589-9020 or
    (800) 749-6399 (toll-free)
**Fax:** (352) 589-7020
**E-mail:** NewsMedia@comcast.net

*Oklahoma Media Guide*
Oklahoma Press Service Inc.
3601 N. Lincoln Boulevard
Oklahoma City, OK 73105-5499
**Phone:** (405) 524-4421

**Fax:** (405) 524-2201
**E-mail:** sysop@okpress.com

*Publicity Club of Chicago—
    Media/Membership Directory*
Publicity Club of Chicago
875 N. Michigan Avenue
Suite 2250
Chicago, IL 60611
**Phone:** (312) 640-6725
**Fax:** (312) 266-2874

*Scott's Canadian Sourcebook*
Business Information Group
1450 Don Mills Road
Toronto, ON, Canada M3B 2X7
**Phone:** (416) 445-6641 or
    (800) 668-2374 (toll-free)
**Fax:** (416) 442-2213
**E-mail:** medical@corporte.southam.ca
http://www.scottinfo.com

*Southeast News Media Directory*
Brian Highberger Publisher
P.O. Box 316
Mount Dora, FL 32756
**Phone:** (352) 589-9020 or
    (800) 749-6399 (toll-free)
**Fax:** (352) 589-7020
**E-mail:** NewsMedia@comcast.net

*Working Press of the Nation*
R. R. Bowker
630 Central Avenue
New Providence, NJ 07974
**Phone:** (908) 464-6800 or
    (888) 269-5372 (toll-free)
**Fax:** (908) 771-8784
**E-mail:** info@bowker.com

*M Street Radio Directory*
M Street Corporation
P.O. Box 442
Littleton, NH 03561
**Phone:** (603) 444-5720 or
    (800) 248-4242 (toll-free)
**Fax:** (603) 444-2872

# INDEX

# ABOUT THE AUTHOR

Shelly Field is a nationally recognized motivational speaker, career expert, stress specialist, and author of more than 25 best-selling books in the business and career fields.

Her books instruct people on how to obtain jobs in a wide variety of areas, including the hospitality, music, sports, and communications industries; casinos and casino hotels; advertising and public relations; theater, the performing arts, and entertainment; animal rights; health care; writing; and art.

She is a frequent guest on local, regional, and national radio, cable, and television talk, information, and news shows and also does numerous print interviews and personal appearances.

Field is a featured speaker at conventions, expos, casinos, corporate functions, employee training and development sessions, career fairs, spouse programs, and events nationwide. She speaks on empowerment, motivation, careers, gaming, and human resources; attracting, retaining, and motivating employees; customer service; and stress management. Her popular seminars, "STRESS BUSTERS: Beating the Stress in Your Work and Your Life," "The De-Stress Express," and "Lighten Up, Loosen Up and Make Life More Fun," are favorites around the country.

Field is a career consultant as well as a personal life and career coach to celebrities, executives, businesses, educational institutions, employment agencies, women's groups, and individuals. President and CEO of The Shelly Field Organization, a public relations and management firm handling national clients, she also does corporate consulting and has represented celebrities in the sports, music, and entertainment industries, as well as authors, businesses, and corporations.

For information about personal appearances or seminars, contact The Shelly Field Organization at P.O. Box 711, Monticello, NY 12701, or log on to www.shellyfield.com.